Praise for

NATO's Balancing Act

"After having published a seminal book on the post-Cold War NATO in 1999, David Yost has given us another superb analysis of NATO adapting its original collective defense mission to the new challenges of the 21st century. Like Yost's previous publications, *NATO's Balancing Act* is a magisterial, well-documented yet lively analysis of the transatlantic security relationship. It will remain the definitive study of Alliance policies for many years to come."
—**Karl-Heinz Kamp**, academic director, German Federal Academy for Security Policy

"David Yost's comprehensive and objective examination of NATO's evolution since the Cold War, its contemporary accomplishments and shortfalls, and its long-term challenges will serve as an invaluable reference for government and military officials, academics, media, and the broader public interested in international relations. He makes a convincing case that if NATO did not exist, we would have to invent it."
—**Leo Michel**, distinguished research fellow, Institute for National Strategic Studies, National Defense University

"After the acclaimed *NATO Transformed*, David Yost's *NATO's Balancing Act* demonstrates once again why the author ranks among the leading experts in his field: Those who want to understand NATO's internal and external challenges will not find a more thorough analysis."
—**Michael Rühle**, head of Energy Security, Emerging Security Challenges Division, NATO

"As a decade of counterinsurgency and stabilization operations in Afghanistan comes to an end, NATO is at another turning point in its post-Cold War transformation. In *NATO's Balancing Act*—a sequel to his much acclaimed earlier book, *NATO Transformed*, on the Alliance's adaptation to a new world in the 1990s—David Yost masterfully knits together into a compelling narrative the internal impulses and external influences that have shaped Allied policies and foreign engagements since 9/11. Thoroughly researched and written with clarity, NATO's Balancing Act is destined to become a lasting work of reference on the enduring transatlantic relationship in a turbulent world for practitioners and students alike."
—**Diego Ruiz Palmer,** special advisor to the NATO secretary general for Economics and Security, NATO

NATO's Balancing Act

NATO's Balancing Act

David S. Yost

UNITED STATES INSTITUTE OF PEACE PRESS
Washington, D.C.

United States Institute of Peace
2301 Constitution Avenue, NW
Washington, DC 20037
www.usip.org

Printed in the United States of America

The paper used in this publication meets the minimum requirements of American National Standards for Information Science—Permanence of Paper for Printed Library Materials, ANSI Z39.48-1984.

Library of Congress Cataloging-in-Publication Data

Yost, David S. (David Scott), 1948-
   NATO's balancing act / David S. Yost.
      pages cm
   Includes bibliographical references and index.
   ISBN 978-1-60127-202-7 (alk. paper)
   1. North Atlantic Treaty Organization—Military policy.   2. Peacekeeping forces.
   3. Intervention (International law)   4. Security, International.   I. United States
   Institute of Peace, issuing body.   II. Title.
   UA646.3.Y675 2014
   355'.031091821—dc23

                                                                    2013047273

For Catherine

Contents

Preface

The NATO Allies have since the end of the Cold War taken on a complex array of important responsibilities that oblige them to constantly reassess and redefine the balance among their priorities. Compared with the Alliance's current ambitions, NATO's core tasks during the Cold War were simple. As expressed most famously in the 1967 Harmel Report, the Alliance's tasks were twofold: to ensure reliable deterrence and defense and, on that basis, to pursue dialogue and arms control with adversaries to the east.

Since the early 1990s the Allies have retained their original missions of collective defense and dialogue with potential adversaries. They have, moreover, taken on (1) new crisis management functions, including peacekeeping and intervention in foreign conflicts, and (2) the pursuit of a cooperative security vision for democracy and peace in the Euro-Atlantic region and beyond, with many partnerships with non-NATO countries.

Although the concrete results of their efforts have often been mixed, their aspirations have continued to provide orientation as to the way forward. The Allies have done a surprisingly effective job in tackling their priorities. Given the intractable nature of the challenges they have chosen to address, their achievements—for instance, in promoting peace and security in the Balkans and building partnerships with other nations and organizations—are noteworthy. The Allies have succeeded in carrying forward their agenda despite their cumbersome decision-making processes and the other dysfunctions and impediments inherent in collective action by a standing coalition of twenty-eight sovereign nations. It has become clear that the Allies differ in the emphasis that they place on each of their agreed-upon core tasks—collective defense, crisis management, and cooperative security—but they continue to invest in each of them and to reach workable compromises on how to strike the balance among them.

Owing to tensions among the core tasks and divergent priorities among the Allies, compromises are unavoidable if the Allies are to make headway in pursuing their aims. Some compromises have concerned the Alliance's democratic values—for example, accepting the behavior in certain circumstances of specific Allies, partners, and candidates for membership. On the whole, the Allies have strived to uphold their values, which are important to their political identity and long-term purposes, but they have at times made compromises in deference to perceived immediate security requirements or on other grounds. Such compromises will be less damaging if the Allies are clear-eyed and honest about them, and return to honoring their values as promptly and as comprehensively as possible.

In short, this book is an assessment of the Alliance's performance in its increasingly complicated balancing act. The assessment flows from an attempt to present an accurate account of NATO's many activities, including how the Allies themselves describe them. For this purpose, a quotation is usually more authentic, precise, and telling than a paraphrase. In NATO, the specific wording of a communiqué often reflects a compromise with a struggle behind it, and the agreed-upon language matters to the Allies—though they may disagree on how to interpret it and sometimes deliberately leave it vague.

In contrast with works presenting the Alliance as moribund or increasingly irrelevant, this book holds that NATO remains of vital importance for the security of the Allies. The Allies have the resources and experience necessary to sustain and enhance their collective enterprise. Despite recurrent shortcomings and the structural obstacles to effective action, they will be able to continue to employ the Alliance for positive ends if they muster vision and political will.

This book derives from the advice and assistance of many generous people. In a sense it began with a conference paper presented in The Hague in May 2009, and published as "NATO's Evolving Purposes and the Next Strategic Concept," in *NATO's New Strategic Concept: Moving Beyond the Status Quo?*, edited by Bram Boxhoorn and David den Dunnen (The Hague: Netherlands Atlantic Association, 2009). This paper was published in revised form, with the same title, in the journal of the Royal Institute of International Affairs, Chatham House, *International Affairs* 86, no. 2 (March 2010). I would like to thank Bram Boxhoorn, the director of the Netherlands Atlantic Association, and Caroline Soper, the editor of *International Affairs*, for their backing in this endeavor.

In another sense this book originated from an earlier book—*NATO Transformed: The Alliance's New Roles in International Security*—published by the United States Institute of Peace (USIP) in 1998. In 2010 Chantal de Jonge Oudraat, then part of the USIP management team, supported the idea of a sequel to the earlier book, and I am most grateful for her help in launching the project. Elizabeth Cole, Kay Hechler, and Valerie Norville of the USIP endorsed the proposal for a sequel. Valerie Norville in particular took the lead in guiding the new book through the review and production process, and I thank her warmly for her encouragement and support. I would also like to thank Kurt Volkan for his patience and dedication in copyediting.

I began work on this book in early 2011 when I was a guest scholar at the NATO Defense College in Rome. I was able to study and write in this privileged venue thanks to sabbatical-year support from the Naval Postgraduate School.

At the NATO Defense College (NDC), I benefited from the support of Lieutenant General Wolf-Dieter Löser and Lieutenant General Arne Bard Dalhaug, then the commandants; Richard Hooker, the dean; and Karl-Heinz Kamp, the director of the research division. In the research division, Mary Di Martino, Eugenio Mengarini, and Isabella Silvestri provided valuable support. Among the researchers and other staff members at the NDC, Samir Battiss, Gerd Bischof, Patrick Desjardins, Florence Gaub, Murray "Sandy" Guptill, Jakob Henius, Dilshod Ibrokhimov, Guillaume Lasconjarias, Andrew Monaghan, Pierre Razoux, Heidi Reisinger, Jean-Loup Samaan, Brooke Smith-Windsor, and Joseph Wiley gave me valuable comments on drafts and enlightening perspectives on the issues. I am also grateful for the assistance of the NDC library staff, notably Stefania Calabrese, Paola Pudis, and Giuseppe Vitiello.

At the Naval Postgraduate School, I am indebted to my department chairman at that time, Harold Trinkunas, for supporting my sabbatical application, and to my colleague, Mikhail Tsypkin, who commented on a draft of the book. Thanks are owed as well to the NPS library staff for their assistance, particularly Irma Fink, Zooey Lober, Greta Marlatt, and Jeff Rothal. I would also like to thank Diana Wueger for her research assistance, and one of my students, Major Daniel Lang, USAF, for insights into Operation Unified Protector.

In Ankara, I appreciate the assistance of Oktay Aksoy, Özgür Kivanç Altan, Mehmet Ari, Resat Arim, Hüseyin Bagci, Serdar Erdurmaz, Cagri Erhan, Kemal Kaya, Hasan Selim Özertem, Seyfi Tashan, Kübra Türk, Ömer Burhan Tüzel, Sebnem Udum, Ilhan Uzgel, Osman R. Yavuzalp, and Mehmet Yegin.

In Berlin, I appreciate the assistance of Hannes Adomeit, Michael Angerer, Susanne Baumann, Caterina Becker, Christian Forneck, Uwe Halbach, Peter Hansen, Patrick Keller, Helene Kortländer, Rolf Nikel, Michael Paul, Wolfgang Richter, Henning Riecke, Robert Rohde, Ilka Schantz, Oliver Schmidt, Peter Schmidt, Ruth Surkau, Erich Vad, Julian Voje, Klaus Wittmann, and Alexander Zoklits.

In Brussels, I appreciate the assistance of Marc Abensour, William Alberque, Alicia Ambos, Suleyman Anil, Damien Arnaud, Stefanie Babst, Mira Banacka, Alberto Bin, Juliette Bird, Laure Borgomano, Heinrich Brauss, Andrew Budd, Jacek Bylica, Lars Carlstein, Mihai Carp, Christophe Cornu, Robert Dalsjö, Bernard Dartaguiette, Ineke Deserno, François Devoto, Bos de Wit, Ruben-Erik Diaz-Plaja, Giampaolo di Paola, Jean-Dominique Dulière, Douglas Edson, Martin Erdmann, Philippe Errera, Rastislav Fides, Ilay Ferrier, Fred Frederickson, Richard Froh, Vesselin Garvalov, Hermann Hanke, Joshua D. Hanson, Christopher Harness, Randy Hoag, G. Cem Isik, Dave Johnson, Lucien Kleinjan, Timo Koster, James Lovell, Jüri Luik, Merle Maigre, Joseph Manso, Krisztian Meszaros, Lorenz Meyer-Minnemann, Joaquin Molina Martinez Lozano, Ali Kaan Orbay, Alexandros Papaioannou, Jonathan Parish, Kestutis Paulauskas, Jessica Pfefferkorn, Jeroen Poesen, Theo Rikken, Michael Rühle, Diego Ruiz Palmer, Fred Charles Parker IV, Fabrice Pothier, Erik Sandahl, Marc Scheers, Jamie Shea, Anne-Marie Smith, Jim Squelch, Jaroslav Skonieczka,

Ian Stallion, Radoslava Stefanova, Colin Stockman, Steve Sturm, Sarah Tarry, Theo von Keller, Veronika Wand-Danielsson, Bastian Volz, Nicholas Williams, Roger Wyatt, Michel Yakovleff, and Roberto Zadra.

In Istanbul, I appreciate the assistance of Mustafa Aydin, Mesut Hakki Casin, Mehmet Hakki Demirer, Nursin Atesoglu Güney, Serhat Güvenç, Mustafa Kibaroglu, Duygu Sezer, and Sinan Ülgen.

In London, I appreciate the assistance of Michael Baker, Gordon Barrass, Margaret Beckett, Nigel Basing, Desmond Bowen, Desmond Browne, Malcolm Chalmers, Sir Lawrence Freedman, Martin Gilmore, Peter Hennessy, David Jarvis, Richard Ladd-Jones, Lindsay MacDonald, Sir Richard Mottram, Sir David Omand, Nick Pickard, David Prodger, Paul Schulte, Mark Smith, Chloe Squires, Sir Kevin Tebbit, Tomas Valasek, and Martin White.

In Oslo, I appreciate the assistance of Morten Aasland, Malfrid Braut-Hegghammer, Svein Efjestad, Arild Eikeland, Paal Hilde, Havard Klevberg, Janne Haaland Matlary, Lars Nordrum, Inga M. W. Nyhamar, Hilde Janne Skorpen, Bjorn Tore Solberg, Silje Solheim, and Rolf Tamnes.

In Paris, I appreciate the assistance of Marie Audouard, Jean-Jacques Bart, Henri Bentégeat, Yves Boyer, Corentin Brustlein, Jean-François Bureau, Marie Buscail, Alain Crémieux, Benoît d'Aboville, Dominique David, Paola Debril-Loiseau, Tiphaine de Champchesnel, Philippe Denier, Étienne de Durand, Alexandra de Hoop Scheffer, Emmanuel Delorme, Marc-Antoine de St. Germain, Muriel Domenach, Jean Dufourcq, Svend-Erik Estellon, Pierre Forterre, Michel Foucher, Louis Gautier, François Géré, Camille Grand, Pierre Hassner, François Heisbourg, Jean Klein, Pauline Kusak, Fabien Kuzniak, Anne Lazar-Sury, Georges Maron, Michel Masson, Michel Miraillet, Jean-Christophe Noël, Elisabeth Quanquin, Bruno Racine, Robert Ranquet, François Revardeaux, Guillaume Schlumberger, Bruno Sciascia, Jean-Luc Taquet, and Bruno Tertrais.

In Rome, I appreciate the assistance of Alberto Biavati, Giovanni Brauzzi, Vincenzo Camporini, Gianni Candotti, Fabrizio Colaceci, Stefano Cont, Giuseppe Cornacchia, Sandro De Bernardin, Massimo Drei, Silvano Frigerio, Giorgio Lazio, Alessandro Marrone, Valerio Negro, Alberto Rosso, Stefano Silvestri, and Carlo Trezza.

In Warsaw, I appreciate the assistance of Adam Bugajski, Zbigniew Ciolek, Jacek Durkalec, Artur Hrynkiewicz-Zabicki, Dominik Jankowski, Andrzej Karkoszka, Lukasz Kulesa, Robert Kupiecki, Roman Kuzniar, Tomasz Lekarski, Jerzy Nowak, Olaf Osica, Janusz Onyszkiewicz, Piotr Pacholski, Adam Daniel Rotfeld, Kazimierz Sikorski, Andrzej Towpik, Maria Wagrowska, and Witold Waszczykowski.

In Washington, D.C., I appreciate the assistance of Paul Amato, Elaine Bunn, Peppi DeBiaso, Frank Dellermann, François Delmas, Rod Fabrycky, Jakub Grygiel, David Hamon, Lawrence S. Kaplan, Kerry Kartchner, Jesse Kelso, Leo Michel, Jeffrey Larsen, Frank Miller, François Rivasseau, Brad Roberts, Greg Schulte, David Stein, Kurt Volker, and Joseph Wolfsheimer.

In visits to NATO headquarters I benefited greatly from the assistance and courtesy of the U.S. Mission to NATO. For this I would like to thank sincerely Robert Bell, the defense adviser and secretary of defense representative, and his deputy, Joseph Stein. At the Supreme Headquarters Allied Powers Europe (SHAPE) Steve Covington was especially helpful with advice on and insights into the Alliance.

I would like to thank in particular the experts who generously read major portions or all of the manuscript and offered valuable comments: Jacek Bylica, Richard Froh, Sandy Guptill, Christopher Harness, Dave Johnson, Karl-Heinz Kamp, Alexander Mattelaer, Leo Michel, Jonathan Parish, Kestutis Paulauskas, Peter Pavilionis, Joseph Pilat, Guy Roberts, Michael Rühle, Diego Ruiz Palmer, Charly Salonius-Pasternak, and Brooke Smith-Windsor.

Those providing advice or assistance naturally bear no responsibility for the book's shortcomings or for the views expressed. Indeed, the views expressed are mine alone and do not represent those of the Naval Postgraduate School, the Department of the Navy, the United States Institute of Peace, or any other U.S. government agency.

Finally, I would like to thank my wife, Catherine, for her great patience and encouragement with this project, as well as for her practical assistance in making it all possible.

—David S. Yost
Monterey, October 2013

1

Introduction

NATO's Post–Cold War Transformation

The British historian Martin Wight wrote, "To understand the unstable and intractable nature of international politics, you need only study the relations between the motives and the consequences of a war, or between the purposes and history of an alliance. The more general the scope of the alliance, the less does it work as either party intended. New circumstances constantly arise which show each ally its obligations in an unexpected light."[1]

The North Atlantic Treaty Organization's scope has since September 2001 become far "more general" than its founders could have envisaged during the Cold War, or even during the 1990s. The Allies have made extensive adaptations in the Alliance's purposes and operations in response to "new circumstances" that have shown "each ally its obligations in an unexpected light."

These adaptations have included measures to meet collective defense challenges that could not have been imagined in 1949, when the Alliance was founded, plus ambitious crisis management operations and the pursuit of a vision of cooperative security.

Any assessment of how well the Allies have done in meeting their declared goals in recent years must begin by acknowledging the aspirational nature of NATO's key policy documents, such as its Strategic Concepts and summit declarations. Like the mission statements of many organizations, these documents are often portraits of what the Allies would like to achieve rather than descriptions of their actual accomplishments.

When the visible realities fall short of the handsome portraits in the official policy statements, it should be recalled that the idealized images have set standards that have contributed to the better qualities of the admittedly uneven results. For NATO, aspiration has been the compass providing direction in the face of recurrent setbacks and recalcitrant realities.[2]

Given the constraints, internal and external, on the Alliance, it is remarkable how much the Allies have accomplished and continue to achieve. The constraints internal to the Alliance include the normal structural dysfunctions of a large intergovernmental organization, shortcomings in collective and national efforts, and disagreements among the Allies about priorities among NATO's core tasks and how to perform them. The external constraints are even more intractable, because other countries and organizations have their own agendas and idiosyncrasies. These agendas often clash with the Alliance's concepts of pursuing a synergistic "comprehensive approach" in crisis management and building harmonious "cooperative security" structures in the Euro-Atlantic region and beyond.

The Alliance's detractors argue that NATO is doomed. For example, Ted Galen Carpenter states that "NATO has outlived whatever usefulness it had. Superficially, it remains an impressive institution, but it has become a hollow shell—far more a political honor society than a meaningful security organization."[3] Similarly, Richard Rupp has described it as "an alliance in continuing decline."[4] Nick Witney has written that "NATO is dying."[5] According to Andrew Bacevich, "As a serious military enterprise, the alliance has all but ceased to exist.... To think of NATO as a great alliance makes about as much sense as thinking of Pittsburgh as the Steel City or of Detroit as the car capital of the world. It's sheer nostalgia."[6]

For critics, one of the proofs of the Alliance's growing irrelevance resides in its expanded set of tasks and the discord among the Allies about how to pursue them. Since the end of the Cold War in 1989–1991, the NATO Allies have substantially expanded the Alliance's missions to include crisis management interventions and the promotion of international security cooperation. Major developments have included NATO's interventions in the Balkan conflicts in the 1990s, NATO's response to the terrorist attacks against the United States in September 2001, NATO's command of the International Security Assistance Force (ISAF) in Afghanistan since 2003, and NATO's intervention in the Libya conflict in 2011.

Despite the jibes of the critics, the fact remains, as noted in the 2002 U.S. National Security Strategy, "There is little of lasting consequence that the United States can accomplish in the world without the sustained cooperation of its allies and friends in Canada and Europe."[7] NATO secretary general Anders Fogh Rasmussen has pointed out that there are firm grounds for regarding the Alliance as an essential foundation of security for its members and an instrument for them to pursue positive political objectives:

> Europe and North America still have tremendous resources, resolve, and ideas. And when we work together, there is no greater force for positive change.... It means we can face today's challenges from a position of strength.... We are an Alliance of 28 democracies. A unique forum for transatlantic dialogue—and transatlantic action. We can launch and sustain complex joint operations in a way that no one else can.[8]

The Allies have defined their current core tasks as collective defense, crisis management, and cooperative security. This book analyzes tensions among these tasks, and reviews the efforts by the Allies to perform them and achieve the right balance. It also examines growing problems of fragmentation and divergence in the Alliance. These problems were evident, for example, in the Libya conflict, when several Allies chose not to participate in strike operations or could not do so, owing to a lack of suitable capabilities.

This book also assesses internal and external constraints affecting the Alliance's performance and the prospects for surmounting these challenges.[9] Owing to the demands of events, the Allies have had little choice but to take on a broadened set of complex tasks. The additional tasks—and redefined tasks, as in collective defense—have involved challenges of great significance for their national security and their ability to contribute to international peace and security.

This chapter reviews the Alliance's origins and Cold War policies before turning to the transformation process that began in the 1990s. It also considers how the NATO Allies manage to work together and accomplish their main tasks, despite their differences and the inherent challenges of collective action. The subsequent chapters examine the exertions associated with the Alliance's three core tasks.[10] The final chapter discusses constraints affecting the Alliance's efforts to perform these tasks and devise an appropriate balance among them. The book concludes that vision and political will are imperative for the Allies to succeed in their balancing act.

NATO's Origins and Cold War Policies

NATO's origins reside in Soviet behavior during and immediately after World War II.[11] The Soviet Union's leader, Joseph Stalin, made clear his intention to establish Communist regimes wherever the Soviet Armed Forces could reach. Stalin told a group of Yugoslav Communists in April 1945, "This war is not as in the past; whoever occupies a territory also imposes on it his own social system. Everyone imposes his own system as far as his army can reach."[12] Stalin's determination to act on this principle meant that he had no intention of honoring his commitment at the February 1945 Yalta conference to hold free elections in Poland and other Central and Eastern European countries liberated from Nazi rule. In July–August 1945, at the Potsdam conference, "Stalin made the Soviet position clear when he stated that 'any freely elected government would be anti-Soviet and that we cannot permit.'"[13] In 1948 Stalin expressed regret that the Soviet military had not liberated France and Italy and thereby assisted the French and Italian Communist parties to take power.[14]

Soviet territorial acquisitions alarmed Western European governments. The USSR was the only great power that acquired territory in Europe in World War II. The Soviet Union annexed three previously independent countries (Estonia, Latvia, and Lithuania) and took territory from Czechoslovakia, Finland, Germany, Poland, and Romania. Konrad Adenauer, the chancellor of West Germany in 1949–1963, noted in his memoirs that the territories annexed by the Soviet Union since 1939 added up to 492,600 km^2—over twice the area of West Germany.[15]

The brutal and dictatorial policies the USSR pursued in the countries that it had liberated from Fascist rule gave governments in Western Europe and North America further grounds for apprehension, as did several Soviet actions abroad. These included the Communist takeover in Czechoslovakia in February 1948 and the Soviet block-ade of road and rail access to the British, French, and U.S. sectors of Berlin. It was during the Berlin blockade, which lasted from June 1948 to May 1949, that twelve countries completed the negotiation of the North Atlantic Treaty: Belgium, Canada, Denmark, France, Iceland, Italy, Luxembourg, the Netherlands, Norway, Portugal, the United Kingdom, and the United States.

At the beginning the main purpose of the North Atlantic Treaty, signed on April 4, 1949, was to communicate a deterrent message to the Soviet Union. In the U.S. Senate hearings on the treaty in 1949, Secretary of State Dean Acheson was asked, "Are we going to be expected to send substantial numbers of troops over there as a more or less permanent contribution to these countries' capacity to resist?" Acheson replied: "The answer to that question, Senator, is a clear and absolute 'No.'"[16]

Some U.S. senators believed that transmitting a message to Moscow via the North Atlantic Treaty would be sufficient to deter aggression. Senator Arthur Vandenberg said, "Senator, so far as I am concerned, I think a man can vote for this treaty and not vote for a nickel to implement it, because so far as I am concerned, the opening sentence of the treaty is a notification to Mr. Stalin which puts him in exactly the contrary position to that which Mr. Hitler was in, because Mr. Hitler saw us with a Neutrality Act. Mr. Stalin now sees us with a pact of cooperative action."[17]

In order to send a deterrent message to the Kremlin, the Allies made a mutual defense pledge in Article 5 of the North Atlantic Treaty:

> The Parties agree that an armed attack against one or more of them in Europe or North Amer-ica shall be considered an attack against them all and consequently they agree that, if such an armed attack occurs, each of them, in exercise of the right of individual or collective self-defense recognized by Article 51 of the Charter of the United Nations, will assist the Party or Parties so attacked by taking forthwith, individually and in concert with the other Parties, such action as it deems necessary, including the use of armed force, to restore and maintain the security of the North Atlantic area.

Although the treaty provided for the establishment of the North Atlantic Council and a defense committee, it was not until the North Korean invasion of South Korea in June 1950 that the Allies saw the need for a standing military command structure. In December 1950, the Allies appointed Dwight D. Eisenhower the first Supreme Allied Commander Europe (SACEUR), and he took command in April 1951. In March 1952 the Allies named Hastings Ismay, a British diplomat and former gen-eral, the first secretary general of the Alliance. NATO became a standing political-military organization in peacetime without precedent.

After the admission of Greece and Turkey to the Alliance in 1952, followed by the Federal Republic of Germany (West Germany) in 1955, there was no change in NATO membership until 1982, when Spain joined as part of its post-Franco "return to Europe."

In retrospect, the period from the mid-1950s to the breakdown of the Soviet empire in 1989–1991 appears to have been one of political and strategic stalemate. Europe, Germany, and Berlin remained divided, and Communist rule in the Warsaw Pact (founded in 1955) states was sustained, for the most part, through Soviet military power and internal security organs. Yugoslavia maintained a unique status throughout this period. Ruled by a Communist party, yet not a member of the Warsaw Pact, Yugoslavia enjoyed privileged relations with the West. Formal political-military alignments changed little. Partly because of its geographic isolation, Albania succeeded in leaving the Warsaw Pact in 1968. Romania, like Albania, declined to participate in the Soviet-led suppression of democratic tendencies in Czechoslovakia by other Warsaw Pact states in 1968. Romania was reluctant to participate in the Warsaw Pact's integrative schemes and managed to achieve an exceptional degree of foreign policy autonomy, owing in part to its having persuaded Soviet leader Nikita Khrushchev to withdraw Soviet forces from its territory in the late 1950s.[18]

Despite intermittent phases of détente, in which East-West tensions relaxed, the Soviet Union was a remarkably reliable stimulus for political cohesion in NATO. Soviet interventions—for instance, in East Germany in 1953, in Hungary in 1956, in Czechoslovakia in 1968, and in Afghanistan in 1979—and Soviet-provoked crises (such as the Berlin and Cuban episodes) reinforced consensus in NATO on the necessity for collective defensive precautions. Soviet triumphs in military technology (the world's first intercontinental ballistic missiles, for example) and periodic Soviet declarations, reaffirming profound ideological hostility, bolstered Western resolve.[19]

From the outset, however, the Alliance defined its purposes as involving more than simply collective defense against external aggression. The Allies repeatedly declared their interest in pursuing positive political changes in Europe and beyond while avoiding war: "to live in peace with all governments and all peoples" (1949), "to seek solutions by peaceful means" (1953), and to promote "peaceful change" (1957).[20] In the 1967 Harmel Report, the two main purposes of the Atlantic Alliance were recalled in a classic formulation. The first purpose was (and remains) to maintain sufficient military strength to deter aggression and attempts at coercion, to defend the Allies in the event of aggression, and "to assure the balance of forces, thereby creating a climate of stability, security, and confidence." Fulfillment of the first purpose would create a basis for the second: "to pursue the search for progress towards a more stable relationship in which the underlying political issues can be solved."[21]

In practice during the Cold War the second function meant that the NATO Allies pursued dialogue and arms control negotiations with adversaries to the east. The Allies also articulated a longer-term vision: "The ultimate political purpose of the Alliance is to achieve a just and lasting peaceful order in Europe accompanied by appropriate security guarantees."[22]

The Allies professed these goals throughout the Cold War. However, during the late 1950s and early 1960s, their attitudes slowly changed with respect to two key issues: the relative importance of pursuing arms control and changes in the political order in Europe, and the likely processes of change in the East. The Alliance initially held that a settlement of the German question on Western terms ("reunification of Germany through free elections,"[23] according to a 1955 communiqué) would have to precede the negotiation of arms limitations, and that the Soviets would in any case have to honor their promises at the 1945 Yalta conference for free elections in Eastern Europe before a fundamental improvement in East-West relations could take place. For several years after Stalin's death in 1953 (despite the Soviet Union's brutal suppression of the Hungarian uprising in 1956), there was a certain sensation of fluidity, in the West at least, regarding the European political order and hope that Western policies of "negotiating from strength" might somehow bring about a palpable relaxation in Soviet control over Eastern Europe and even German reunification.

Starting in the late 1950s, and especially after the construction of the Berlin Wall in 1961 and the Cuban Missile Crisis in 1962, issues of political order in Europe began to be clearly subordinated to arms control and the pursuit of East-West détente. The Atlantic Alliance devoted increasingly less attention to issues of political order and legitimacy in the Eastern European countries. While NATO communiqués in the 1950s referred to "the totalitarian menace"[24] and asserted that the peoples of Eastern Europe "have the right to choose their own governments freely, unaffected by external pressure and the use or threat of force,"[25] by 1966 the Alliance was calling for "removing barriers to freer and more friendly reciprocal exchanges between countries of different social and economic systems."[26] In the 1950s, the division of Germany was regarded as a "continuing threat to world peace."[27] During the 1960s, however, the goal of eventual German reunification was gradually transformed into simply "an essential factor for a just and lasting peaceful order in Europe,"[28] and the Alliance in 1969 applauded West Germany's proposals for a "modus vivendi between the two parts of Germany."[29]

These changes in priorities and assumptions were linked to the adoption of new views about the likely processes of change in the East. The Alliance eventually adopted the view that détente, which became shorthand for policies intended to reduce East-West tensions, could only succeed in reassuring the Soviet leadership about the Alliance's peaceful intentions and bringing about a freer circulation of people and ideas (and movement toward democratization in Eastern Europe) if many years were invested in promoting greater East-West understanding. The sensation of the 1950s as to a certain fluidity gave way to a conviction during the 1960s that change could be brought about only on the basis of a stabilization and acceptance of the existing order, which might then be transformed in a liberal democratic direction through a long-term process. Internal changes in the Soviet Union and Eastern European societies would, it was hoped, lead to a gradual East-West rapprochement, thus eventually ending the military confrontation.[30]

It should, however, be noted that despite their declared interest in democratization in the Warsaw Pact states and a process of reconciliation ending the East-West strategic stalemate, many Westerners were reasonably satisfied with the European political order during the Cold War. Some expressed concern that an inadvertent "destabilization" of Eastern European societies through political liberalization could result in war or, at the least, setbacks for détente as a gradual and ultimately effective process. Some even appeared willing to support repression for the sake of stability if it appeared that liberalization trends might escape control.[31] West German chancellor Helmut Schmidt said in December 1981, with respect to the imposition of martial law in Poland, "[East German leader] Honecker is as dismayed as I am, that this was necessary."[32] Some Western European officials even ventured to say that the Alliance's declared political goal of ultimate German reunification should be abandoned. In September 1984, Italian foreign minister Giulio Andreotti provoked formal West German protests with the following comments: "Everybody agrees that the two Germanys should have good relations. It should be clear, however, that pan-Germanism is something that must be overcome. There are two German states and two German states must remain."[33]

Western governments also disagreed frequently during the Cold War about how to relate the two alliance functions indicated in the Harmel Report. For example, when would economic transactions (including technology transfers) promote favorable political change in the Warsaw Pact, and when would they serve to strengthen Soviet military power and make it harder and more costly for the West to maintain an adequate military posture? Agreements on broad principles often broke down with respect to specific cases. The U.S. approach often conflicted with the general Western European view (upheld by West Germany in particular) that economic sanctions could not accomplish anything of value, and that East-West trade must be encouraged and expanded because of its political significance. Such disagreements led to difficulties in coordinating Alliance policies for change in the East.

In retrospect, it appears that the assumptions behind the Alliance's policies for peaceful change in the European political order were flawed. The vision of the gradual liberalization and democratization of the East assumed that the Soviet Union would moderate its control structure and that allied Communist regimes would accept evolutionary movement toward civil rights, pluralism, and democracy when East-West tensions had subsided and the Warsaw Pact nations had been reassured about the peaceful and nonthreatening intentions of the Atlantic Alliance. These assumptions, however, threatened the monopoly of power maintained by the Communist regimes.

The Soviet bloc's Communist regimes were not established with the consent of the governed as the principle of legitimacy but on the basis of a party elite's interpretation of an ideology of historical determinism. Although some party members were presumably faithful believers in Marxism-Leninism, the ideology was generally a tool to justify rule by what Milovan Djilas called "the new class" and to conceal its determination to hold power.[34] In a pattern that prevailed over decades, whenever popular pressures for change reached unacceptable thresholds and seemed likely to endanger a Communist regime's rule, repression to maintain power would follow. If the regime was unable to handle the pressures, allied regimes in the Warsaw Pact would offer fraternal assistance under Soviet leadership to maintain the gains of "socialism." Definite limits to Western-style liberalization appeared to apply to the Soviet Union in particular, because of its power structure and the interrelationship between its economic, military, and internal nationality problems.

The extent to which Western policies favoring gradual liberalization in Eastern European countries contributed to the disintegration of the Soviet empire remains unclear, and Allies differ in their general interpretations. As Peter Rudolf, a German scholar with the Stiftung Wissenschaft und Politik, has noted, "In the United States, the end of the Cold War is widely perceived to be a success of containment and a hard line approach. In the prevailing view in Germany, the end of the conflict was rather a result of détente and *Ostpolitik*."[35]

The Communist regimes in Eastern Europe were in fact not gradually liberalized as much as they were overthrown by popular movements when it became evident that the Soviet Union would no longer uphold them with force. Forcible Soviet interventions to keep Communist parties in power might have been an infeasible proposition in the late 1980s, given that several of these regimes were disintegrating in close succession. Such a nonviolent end to the Soviet empire—and the East-West competition—was by no means a foregone conclusion during the Cold War. The Warsaw Pact was formally dissolved in July 1991, and the Soviet Union collapsed in December 1991.[36]

NATO's Transformation in the 1990s

One of the noteworthy changes in the Alliance since the end of the Cold War has been the public prominence of its Strategic Concepts. During the Cold War these were classified documents dealing with military strategy for deterrence and defense and corresponding force requirements.[37] Since 1991, however, Strategic Concepts have become public documents setting out the Alliance's political strategy as well as guidelines for its military posture.

The Allies have composed the Strategic Concepts since 1991 with many audiences in mind (above all, parliaments and publics in NATO nations, partner governments, and potential partners and adversaries), and they have designed these documents to serve multiple purposes (such as deterrence of potential adversaries, reassurance of Allied publics and partners, and guidance for NATO officials). The internal purposes of composing and promulgating the Strategic Concepts and other policy declarations are particularly significant. As Lawrence Freedman has observed, "The cumulative effect, which is intended, is to encourage a sense of continuity as well as shared purpose."[38]

In the 1991 Strategic Concept the Allies recognized that dramatic changes in the European and Eurasian political landscape were under way. However, they could not foresee the extent to which the Balkan conflicts would involve their security interests and lead to direct military involvement.

The 1991 Strategic Concept retained the Alliance's traditional focus on collective defense but called for smaller forces with "enhanced flexibility and mobility and an assured capability for augmentation when necessary" to counter aggression against any Ally.[39] In order to respond to threats and risks that are "multifaceted in nature and multi-directional, which makes them hard to predict and assess," the Strategic Concept recommended "immediate and rapid reaction" forces for deterrence and defense against limited attacks, and supplemental main defense forces and reinforcements for the "unlikely" contingency of a "major conflict."[40]

The language of the Alliance's 1991 Strategic Concept suggests that NATO did not then envisage participating in any crisis management operations as they came to be understood in subsequent years; the core mission remained collective defense against aggression affecting Alliance territory, not intervention beyond that territory. According to the 1991 Strategic Concept, "The Alliance is purely defensive in purpose: none of its weapons will ever be used except in self-defense."[41]

The Allies did not anticipate in 1991 that the following year they would begin to engage in a wide range of demanding non-Article 5 operations in the Balkans. (The "non-Article 5" formula was devised to refer to Alliance military operations other than self-defense.) These operations, which the Allies have also pursued in Afghanistan since 2003 (and in Libya in 2011), have been called various names, including crisis management, crisis response, stabilization operations, and peace operations. In most of these operations the Allies have pursued what they have since 2006 called a "comprehensive approach." This approach has sought improved marshaling of the full range of crisis management tools—civil and military—within NATO, plus extensive coordination with local authorities and other international organizations, particularly the United Nations and the European Union, as well as a large array of nongovernmental organizations and partner countries, including Australia, Japan, New Zealand, and South Korea.[42]

In contrast with their failure in the 1991 Strategic Concept to envisage the requirement that would soon emerge for "crisis response" or "crisis management" interventions in the Balkans, the Allies did show foresight and imagination with regard to outreach and partnership activities intended to shape the Euro-Atlantic security environment.

In the 1990 London Declaration the NATO Allies set out a vision in which NATO would be "an agent of change." The Allies asserted that NATO could "help build the structures of a more united continent, supporting security and stability with the strength of our shared faith in democracy, the rights of the individual, and the peaceful resolution of disputes."[43] In order to achieve this objective, the Allies held, "The Conference on Security and Co-operation in Europe (CSCE) should become more prominent in Europe's future, bringing together the countries of Europe and North America."[44]

The CSCE at that time included Canada and the United States, the Soviet Union and its Warsaw Pact allies, and all the other countries of Europe, except for Albania. At the 1990 London Summit the Allies called for a CSCE summit in Paris later in the year to establish new CSCE institutions. The Paris CSCE Summit accomplished these goals, thanks to the concurrence of the Soviet Union and its European allies. In November 1991, at the Rome Summit, the NATO Allies asserted that

> The CSCE has the outstanding advantage of being the only forum that brings together all countries of Europe and Canada and the United States under a common code of human rights, fundamental freedoms, democracy, rule of law, security, and economic liberty. The new CSCE institutions and structures . . . must be consolidated and further developed so as to provide CSCE with the means to help ensure full implementation of the Helsinki Final Act, the Charter of Paris, and other relevant CSCE documents and thus permit the CSCE to meet the new challenges which Europe will have to face.[45]

The Soviet Union broke apart the following month, in December 1991, and all fifteen of the successor states of the Soviet Union became members of the CSCE.

The initial statements in the early 1990s about NATO's vision for positive peaceful change employed the deceptively simple word "Europe"—the original term chosen to describe the focus of the CSCE, despite the participation of Canada, Turkey, the United States, and the Soviet Union.

According to the ambitious language of the 1991 Rome Declaration, "The peoples of North America and the whole of Europe can now join in a community of shared values based on freedom, democracy, human rights and the rule of law. As an agent of change, a source of stability and the indispensable guarantor of its members' security, our Alliance will continue to play a key role in building a new, lasting order of peace in Europe: a Europe of cooperation and prosperity."[46]

The assumption that the CSCE participating states would cooperate in pursuing shared political and security ideals led to a distinction between the territory of the CSCE and the rest of the world, and the introduction of a new term—the "Euro-Atlantic area." In NATO's January 1994 Partnership for Peace (PfP) Framework Document, for example, the objective of "the strengthening of security within the Euro-Atlantic area" concerns subscribing states that "reaffirm their commitment to the Helsinki Final Act and all subsequent CSCE documents."[47]

In short, in NATO parlance, the "Euro-Atlantic area" has come to mean the territory of the participating states of the Organization for Security and Co-operation in Europe (OSCE). (The CSCE was renamed the OSCE in December 1994, effective January 1, 1995.)

Since the 1991 Strategic Concept the Allies have referred repeatedly to the idea that a function of the Alliance is to serve as "one of the indispensable foundations for a stable Euro-Atlantic security environment, based on the growth of democratic institutions and commitment to the peaceful resolution of disputes."[48] This is the wording in the 1999 Strategic Concept, and the NATO Allies have related it to the Alliance's post–Cold War enlargement process.

Since the early 1990s, the Allies have sought dialogue and common action with their former adversaries and other non-NATO countries via PfP and other cooperative security frameworks. The Allies developed PfP primarily in order to consolidate democratic progress in post–Cold War Europe. More broadly, they have reached out to non-NATO countries in the Euro-Atlantic region and beyond via PfP, the Euro-Atlantic Partnership Council, the Mediterranean Dialogue, the Istanbul Cooperation Initiative, the NATO-Russia Council, and other cooperative frameworks in order to pursue shared political and security objectives.[49] Through outreach, partnership, and enlargement the Allies have pursued the goal of creating what the 1999 Strategic Concept called "a just and lasting peaceful order in Europe"[50]—a phrase borrowed from the 1967 Harmel Report. Moreover, partner countries have contributed substantially to the conduct of NATO-led non-Article 5 operations in the Balkans, Afghanistan, and Libya.

The most important elements in the Alliance's transformation in the 1990s were the new missions that have become known as crisis management and cooperative security. It was also in the 1990s that the Allies defined an ambitious enlargement policy—clearly a collective defense matter, though often considered by the Allies to fall under the heading of cooperative security. Moreover, the Allies began to consider other new security tasks and challenges. For example, the first reference in a NATO communiqué to what became the Alliance function of supporting European Union–led crisis management operations came in July 1990.[51] It was also in 1990 that the North Atlantic Council referred to the proliferation of weapons of mass destruction (WMD) as one of the "new security risks and challenges of a global nature" facing the Alliance.[52]

NATO's Main Contemporary Missions

The Allies have redefined NATO's purposes and core tasks in multiple ways since the end of the Cold War in 1989–1991. The 1991 Strategic Concept identified four "fundamental security tasks," while the 1999 Strategic Concept specified five such tasks, and the 2010 Strategic Concept recast them as "three essential core tasks."

According to the 1991 Strategic Concept,

> NATO's essential purpose, set out in the Washington Treaty and reiterated in the [1990] London Declaration, is to safeguard the freedom and security of all its members by political and military means in accordance with the principles of the United Nations Charter. Based on common values of democracy, human rights and the rule of law, the Alliance has worked since its inception for the establishment of a just and lasting peaceful order in Europe. This Alliance objective remains unchanged.[53]

> The means by which the Alliance pursues its security policy to preserve the peace will continue to include the maintenance of a military capability sufficient to prevent war and to provide for effective defence; an overall capability to manage successfully crises affecting the security of its members; and the pursuit of political efforts favouring dialogue with other nations and the active search for a co-operative approach to European security, including in the field of arms control and disarmament.[54]

> To achieve its essential purpose, the Alliance performs the following fundamental security tasks:

> 1. To provide one of the indispensable foundations for a stable security environment in Europe, based on the growth of democratic institutions and commitment to the peaceful resolution of disputes, in which no country would be able to intimidate or coerce any European nation or to impose hegemony through the threat or use of force.

2. To serve, as provided for in Article 4 of the North Atlantic Treaty, as a transatlantic forum for Allied consultations on any issues that affect their vital interests, including possible developments posing risks for members' security, and for appropriate co-ordination of their efforts in fields of common concern.

3. To deter and defend against any threat of aggression against the territory of any NATO member state.

4. To preserve the strategic balance within Europe.[55]

The Allies were explicit in naming the main external factor that would affect their performance of this fourth "fundamental security task": "Even in a non-adversarial and cooperative relationship, Soviet military capability and build-up potential, including its nuclear dimension, still constitute the most significant factor of which the Alliance has to take account in maintaining the strategic balance in Europe."[56]

Declared Alliance policy changed fundamentally during the course of the 1990s in that the 1999 Strategic Concept made no reference to "the strategic balance within Europe." Indeed, the only explicit references to Russia in the 1999 Strategic Concept concerned dialogue, cooperation, and partnership.

The Allies reworded their definition of the Alliance's essential purpose in the 1999 Strategic Concept to encompass their continuing efforts to shape the broader international security environment, and not only to ensure the safety of Allied territory:

> NATO's essential and enduring purpose, set out in the Washington Treaty, is to safeguard the freedom and security of all its members by political and military means. Based on common values of democracy, human rights and the rule of law, the Alliance has striven since its inception to secure a just and lasting peaceful order in Europe. It will continue to do so. The achievement of this aim can be put at risk by crisis and conflict affecting the security of the Euro-Atlantic area. The Alliance therefore not only ensures the defence of its members but contributes to peace and stability in this region.[57]

Expressing an Alliance interest in contributing to "peace and stability" in "the Euro-Atlantic area" represented an extension of the Alliance's purview and responsibility, in comparison with its practical goals during the Cold War. It was, however, foreshadowed in the 1967 Harmel Report and in the 1990 London Declaration's vision of NATO as "an agent of change." As noted, the Euro-Atlantic area is usually defined as encompassing the territory of the states participating in the OSCE—that is, all the states of Europe and all the former Soviet republics, plus Canada, Turkey, and the United States.

In the 1999 Strategic Concept the Allies listed five "fundamental security tasks":

> **Security**: To provide one of the indispensable foundations for a stable Euro-Atlantic security environment, based on the growth of democratic institutions and commitment to the peaceful resolution of disputes, in which no country would be able to intimidate or coerce any other through the threat or use of force.
>
> **Consultation**: To serve, as provided for in Article 4 of the Washington Treaty, as an essential transatlantic forum for Allied consultations on any issues that affect their vital interests, including possible developments posing risks for members' security, and for appropriate co-ordination of their efforts in fields of common concern.
>
> **Deterrence and Defence**: To deter and defend against any threat of aggression against any NATO member state as provided for in Articles 5 and 6 of the Washington Treaty.

And in order to enhance the security and stability of the Euro-Atlantic area:

Crisis Management: To stand ready, case-by-case and by consensus, in conformity with Article 7 of the Washington Treaty, to contribute to effective conflict prevention and to engage actively in crisis management, including crisis response operations.

Partnership: To promote wide-ranging partnership, cooperation, and dialogue with other countries in the Euro-Atlantic area, with the aim of increasing transparency, mutual confidence and the capacity for joint action with the Alliance.[58]

The ambitious "security" purpose, as defined above, was consistent with the Harmel Report vision of "a just and lasting peaceful order in Europe accompanied by appropriate security guarantees." The tasks of "consultation" and "deterrence and defense" also represented continuity with the Alliance purposes articulated during the Cold War. The "crisis management" and "partnership" purposes have constituted significant departures from Cold War assumptions as to NATO's role.[59] However, both can be seen as supportive of the long-term "security" vision. As noted, the Allies have developed extensive partnership policies to promote the pursuit of shared political and security objectives within and beyond the Euro-Atlantic area.

In the 2010 Strategic Concept the Allies set out NATO's purpose in even more general terms than in the past, without limiting it by referring to "Europe," as in the 1991 Strategic Concept, or "the Euro-Atlantic area," as in the 1999 Strategic Concept:

NATO's fundamental and enduring purpose is to safeguard the freedom and security of all its members by political and military means. Today, the Alliance remains an essential source of stability in an unpredictable world.[60]

The Allies listed "three essential core tasks, all of which contribute to safeguarding Alliance members," in the 2010 Strategic Concept:

a. **Collective defence**. NATO members will always assist each other against attack, in accordance with Article 5 of the Washington Treaty. That commitment remains firm and binding. NATO will deter and defend against any threat of aggression, and against emerging security challenges where they threaten the fundamental security of individual Allies or the Alliance as a whole.

b. **Crisis management**. NATO has a unique and robust set of political and military capabilities to address the full spectrum of crises—before, during and after conflicts. NATO will actively employ an appropriate mix of those political and military tools to help manage developing crises that have the potential to affect Alliance security, before they escalate into conflicts; to stop ongoing conflicts where they affect Alliance security; and to help consolidate stability in post-conflict situations where that contributes to Euro-Atlantic security.

c. **Cooperative security**. The Alliance is affected by, and can affect, political and security developments beyond its borders. The Alliance will engage actively to enhance international security, through partnership with relevant countries and other international organisations; by contributing actively to arms control, non-proliferation and disarmament; and by keeping the door to membership in the Alliance open to all European democracies that meet NATO's standards.[61]

These task categories overlap in many ways. In the 2010 Strategic Concept, for example, the Allies called for enhanced capacity-building efforts with non-NATO partner countries under the heading of collective defense as well as crisis management.[62] Several non-NATO partner countries—linked to the Alliance via cooperative security frameworks—are engaged in operations in Afghanistan under the NATO-led ISAF. These crisis management operations, authorized under UN Security Council mandates, originated, one might argue, in NATO's invocation of the Article 5 collective defense pledge in response to the terrorist attacks against the United States in September 2001.

While the first priority of the Allies necessarily remains the security of their national territories, followed by the security of the Euro-Atlantic region as a whole, the Allies recognized in the 2010 Strategic Concept that, as noted, "the Alliance remains an essential source of stability in an unpredictable world." In addition to the collective defense of their own national territories, the Allies are concerned with crisis management in Europe (notably in the Balkans) and beyond (above all, in Afghanistan). Some Alliance activities remain limited to Allied territory in Europe and North America, while others extend to the larger Euro-Atlantic region and beyond and involve partnerships with countries as distant as Australia, Japan, and Mongolia.

The increasingly broad geographic scope of certain Alliance activities reflects the fact that the Allies face global security challenges, including cyber attacks; international terrorism; the proliferation of WMD, delivery systems, and advanced technologies, including sophisticated means of guidance and communications; threats to the security of energy supplies; and risks of conflicts in the Middle East and the Asia-Pacific region that could affect NATO's security interests. The Alliance is a permanent coalition of states with shared values and security interests. While some security risks remain centered in the Euro-Atlantic region, other challenges to these interests are increasingly global in scope.

The Allies have shown some restraint in their ever more expansive definitions of NATO's purposes. In October 2009, at the first of the seminars convened by Madeleine Albright and her Group of Experts to advise the NATO secretary general about the content of the 2010 Strategic Concept, the participants agreed that the Alliance's future tasks "are likely to include" the "stabilization of weak and fragile states" and "the prevention of genocide."[63] In its May 2010 report the Group of Experts wrote that "NATO may well be called upon" to deal with "the humanitarian consequences of a failed state . . . or the dangers posed by genocide or other massive violations of human rights."[64] In the 2010 Strategic Concept, however, the Allies did not employ the words "humanitarian" and "genocide," nor did they make any reference to failed or failing states beyond alluding to threats that might arise from "instability or conflict beyond NATO's borders."[65] The Allies nonetheless relied on UN Security Council resolutions that referred to "humanitarian" considerations and "the protection of civilians" to justify their intervention in Libya in 2011.[66]

Of the three core tasks, cooperative security remains the most difficult to define. According to Dutch scholar Rob de Wijk, "The object of co-operative security is to anticipate potential conflicts and prevent them breaking out, or to actively strive to suppress conflicts once they have broken out by means of joint international action within the system. Co-operative security does not mean that member states are treaty-bound to offer assistance. If that were the case it would be a question of collective, not co-operative, security."[67]

As de Wijk's comment suggests, the Allies have since the 1990s usually taken care not to confuse cooperative security with collective security. Indeed, they have generally used the latter term with caution, because it has multiple meanings and because it implies a sense of mutual obligation greater than that involved in most cooperative security efforts.[68]

The Allies and Alliance officials appear to have taken four courses with their preferred term—cooperative security. First, they have used the term without making any effort to define it, as in the 1997 NATO-Russia Founding Act.[69] Second, they have given examples of activities that, in their judgment, epitomize cooperative security. For instance, in 1997 a NATO assistant secretary general, Admiral Norman Ray, said that "SFOR's successful deployment of NATO and non-NATO forces in Bosnia . . . is the essence of the new cooperative security order."[70] Third, as with the 2010 Strategic Concept, they have listed specific activities as elements of cooperative security. In 1997, for example, the NATO secretary general catalogued the elements as PfP, the Euro-Atlantic Partnership Council, the partnerships with Russia and Ukraine, the Mediterranean Dialogue, and the NATO enlargement process.[71]

Fourth and finally, they have set out vague visions of what cooperative security involves or could lead to. In 1997, Javier Solana, then the NATO secretary general, evoked "a new cooperative security order for the Euro-Atlantic region" and said that it was "about building security within societies, creating the conditions of stability in which respect for human rights, consolidation of democratic reforms and economic patterns of trade and investment can flourish."[72] In 2012, Anders Fogh Rasmussen, the current NATO secretary general, extended the cooperative security vision beyond the Euro-Atlantic region to the entire world:

> Our economy is globalised. Our security is globalised. And if we are to protect our populations effectively, our approach to security has to be globalised too. This is why cooperative security is fundamental to the Alliance's way of doing business. It means NATO must be able, and willing, to engage politically and militarily with other nations, wherever they may be, and with other international organisations, such as the United Nations and the European Union.[73]

Rasmussen's definition implies that cooperative security means any political-military cooperation by states and international organizations. Although the French scholar Vivien Pertusot and other experts have argued for a more precise definition of cooperative security as a form of interaction distinct from security cooperation,[74] the Allies and high-level Alliance officials have not propounded a clear-cut definition of cooperative security. Nor have they drawn a clear distinction between cooperative security and security cooperation.[75] The predominant tendency has been to equate cooperative security with all the forms of outreach, dialogue, partnership, and cooperation listed under that heading in the 2010 Strategic Concept.

As noted, the Allies have placed the NATO enlargement process under the "cooperative security" heading, even though it is oriented toward the acceptance of Article 5 collective defense commitments. Such commitments—legally binding pledges of mutual defense—imply the acceptance of obligations much more profound and existential than those in, for example, partnership frameworks such as the Alliance's Mediterranean Dialogue. The Allies have nonetheless lumped NATO enlargement together with dialogues and partnership activities with non-Allies involving no more than a vague willingness to cooperate temporarily. The Alliance's broad approach to cooperative security does not require shared political values, only a willingness to exchange views and participate in specific activities, based on a circumstantial coincidence of security interests or an assessment of net advantage in the interaction.

Interdependence and Balance among the Three Core Tasks

The Allies profess continuing commitment to the three core tasks. At the Chicago Summit meeting in May 2012, the Allies declared, "Our 2010 Strategic Concept continues to guide us in fulfilling effectively, and always in accordance with international law, our three essential core tasks—collective defence, crisis management, and cooperative security—all of which contribute to safeguarding Alliance members."[76]

As this statement suggests, the three core tasks defined in the 2010 Strategic Concept can be regarded as interdependent sources of security. In principle, the Allies strive via cooperative security measures to shape the security environment and thereby prevent crises. This may lessen the need for crisis management operations and diminish the risk of a collective defense contingency. Conversely, collective defense fulfills the bedrock requirement of security that first brought the Allies together—and keeps them together—and that provides the basis for crisis management interventions and cooperative security activities. Moreover, the tasks overlap in some ways. Partner nations and organizations (such as the European Union and the United Nations) have worked in coordination with NATO (and each other) in crisis management operations, as in Afghanistan; and crisis management operations could in some circumstances become collective defense contingencies.

Terrorist threats may also require collective defense action by the Allies. In both the 1991 and 1999 Strategic Concepts, the Allies stated that terrorism could affect their security interests.[77] Moreover, in the 1999 Washington Summit Communiqué, the Allies called terrorism "a serious threat to peace, security and stability that can threaten the territorial integrity of States."[78] In September 2001, the terrorist attacks against the United States led the Allies to invoke Article 5 of the North Atlantic Treaty for the first time in history. This shows that—in some cases, at least—countering terrorism could be regarded as a collective defense task rather than a new function for the Alliance.

What was new in September 2001 was the discovery that a nonstate group could mount such a destructive attack against a state. This was almost certainly not what the authors of the North Atlantic Treaty had in mind in 1949 when they referred in Article 5 to the possibility of an "armed attack." The Allies maintain that Operation Active Endeavour—the maritime surveillance effort in the Mediterranean undertaken in response to the September 2001 terrorist attacks—is a collective defense action under Article 5, and they have reported it as such to the UN Security Council.[79]

At the same time, the Allies have given new meaning to their collective defense commitments. Without in any way abandoning the traditional meaning of collective defense (protection of the national territory of Allies against "armed attack"), the Allies have in some circumstances blurred the distinction between Article 5 (collective defense) and non-Article 5 missions. They have, for example, extended security commitments to non-Allies,[80] welcomed the participation of non-Allies in an Article 5 mission (Operation Active Endeavour), and conducted a nominally non-Article 5 mission (leading the ISAF in Afghanistan under UN Security Council mandates) in order to prevent the reemergence of an Article 5 threat. Moreover, some observers have discerned—to use Diego Ruiz Palmer's term—a certain "deterritorialization" of the Alliance's collective defense mission in conjunction with the emergence of a more "proactive" and "anticipatory" concept of Article 5 requirements.[81]

This redefinition of collective defense is discussed in chapter 2, together with other issues that illustrate the changing dimensions of collective defense—missile defense, cyber security, space operations, energy security, terrorism, and WMD proliferation.

To what extent is there a conflict or tension between the Alliance's original and enduring purpose of collective defense and its post–Cold War crisis management functions? This study suggests in chapter 5 that the dichotomy between expeditionary and territorial defense capabilities has to some extent been overstated. The continued development of expeditionary capabilities is a priority for both collective defense and crisis response contingencies. Certain tensions among the three core tasks have nonetheless become manifest. For example, the fact that Russia has become the Alliance's partner in the NATO-Russia Council and other cooperative security endeavors has not eliminated concern about Russia as a potential aggressor toward some of the new NATO Allies in Central and Eastern Europe. Nor did partnerships with NATO prevent Russia and Georgia from going to war with each other in 2008. This tension and others are discussed in this study.

Signs of tension among the core tasks are often accompanied by calls for a more appropriate balance among them. In February 2012, for example, Norwegian defense minister Espen Barth Eide deplored the decreased attention to collective defense in relation to non-Article 5 crisis management operations and warned that trends could "lead to a further weakening of the core capability to defend ourselves both against traditional and asymmetrical threats." In his view,

> We must continue recognising the importance of the Alliance's operational engagements. We should continue to use the Alliance when the UN and the global community request it. But the pendulum has swung too far. We have to find a sustainable balance.[82]

In March 2012 the NATO secretary general used "balance" imagery in comparing NATO's conduct of its missions to riding a bicycle:

> the key to success on a bike is to keep it in a regular, forward movement . . . and the same goes for our transatlantic alliance. And another key to success on a bike is balance. . . . The right balance is also the key to the continued success of our NATO Alliance.[83]

While everyone can endorse the principle of balance, its concrete applications in specific circumstances remain contentious. Resources are finite, and choices must be made among multiple preferences and priorities. The Allies have assigned three core tasks to NATO, but they have not always agreed on how to perform them and strike a balance among them.

Since the end of the Cold War, NATO's most visible day-to-day activities have consisted of cooperative security and crisis management. The institutionalization of the Alliance's cooperative security vision began with the North Atlantic Cooperation Council in 1991. Non-Article 5 crisis management activities began the following year. In 1992 the Allies transported humanitarian assistance to Russia and other former Soviet republics, monitored the air approaches from Libya, and began enforcing the maritime arms embargo and monitoring the no-fly zone affecting the warring parties in the former Yugoslavia.[84] The Allies adopted in practice the argument of Senator Richard Lugar and others in the early 1990s that NATO had to go "out of area or out of business" by assuming new tasks beyond collective defense.[85]

The original function of collective defense nonetheless remains the bedrock of the Alliance's cohesion. The mutual commitments to honor the pledge in Article 5 of the North Atlantic Treaty constitute the foundation on which the Allies have undertaken a balancing act—to maintain the credibility and effectiveness of this foundation while pursuing the demanding tasks of crisis management and cooperative security.

NATO's Ability to Act Despite Internal Disputes

The Alliance is an intergovernmental enterprise, a standing and highly institutionalized coalition of independent sovereign states, and it cannot take action unless all the member states agree to act—or at least to let certain Allies act in NATO's name and make use of its shared assets, such as communications and headquarters facilities.

Because the Alliance is a permanent coalition of sovereign states, each with its own internal political dynamics, each member can define its own status in relation to NATO's institutions. France has historically provided the most distinctive example. For decades, some French politicians, civil servants, military officers, and analysts pointedly distinguished between the Alliance, referring to the collective defense coalition established by the North Atlantic Treaty in 1949, and NATO, meaning the many institutional mechanisms the Alliance has set up over the years, including the civilian International Staff, the integrated military command structure, the International Military Staff under the Military Committee, and various agencies, boards, organizations, schools, and research centers. France has since 1949 participated fully in the work of the Alliance's supreme decision-making body, the North Atlantic Council, which was established by Article 9 of the North Atlantic Treaty. In 1966, however, President de Gaulle withdrew France from NATO's "integrated military structure" and demanded the removal of most NATO facilities from French soil, including the political and military headquarters, which the Allies moved to Belgium.[86]

From 1966 to 2009, France pursued an à la carte and selective approach to participation in NATO institutions other than the North Atlantic Council, and France did so to a greater extent than other member states. France alone defined the meaning of its "nonintegrated" status during this period, and modified it at times of its own choosing—for example, deepening its participation in deliberations of the Military Committee from 1992 on, in conjunction with the Alliance's operations in the Balkans. France made further adjustments in its status in relation to shared institutions in 1995, when it decided to return to regular participation in the Military Committee. It was not until 2009, however, that France chose to abandon its "nonintegrated" status in relation to the military command structure; and France has continued to abstain from participation in NATO's Nuclear Planning Group.

In 1995, in the Alliance's official *Study on NATO Enlargement*, the Allies discussed three distinct approaches to participation in NATO institutions. "There are currently three forms under which Allies contribute to NATO collective defence: full participation in the integrated military structure and the collective defence planning process [a reference to all of the Allies except France and Spain]; non-membership of the integrated military structure but full participation in the collective defence planning process together with a series of coordination agreements providing for cooperation with the integrated military structure in certain defined areas [a reference to Spain]; and non-participation in the integrated military structure and collective defence planning but cooperation with the integrated military structure in more limited defined areas under agreements between the Chief of Defence and the Major NATO Commanders (MNCs) [a reference to France]."[87]

The Allies, including France and Spain, agreed in 1995 that new Allies should not devise further variations on participation: "As a general principle, we should avoid new forms of contribution to NATO collective defence which would complicate unnecessarily practical cooperation among Allies and the Alliance's decision-making process."[88] Spain maintained its special status with reference to NATO institutions from 1986 to 1997, and (as noted) France has since 2009 participated in most NATO institutions.

All Allies continue to demonstrate their sovereignty and autonomy, however, by their choices as to what capabilities and resources to contribute to NATO-led operations and activities and by the restrictions (or caveats) they place on the employment of their forces in operations. Moreover, while all twenty-eight Allies have negotiated precise cost shares for their contributions to NATO's three common budgets (called the civil, military, and NATO Security Investment Program budgets), there are many specific funding arrangements to which fewer than twenty-eight Allies contribute.[89]

In the eyes of some observers, one of the Alliance's dysfunctions is its consensual decision-making structure, which can involve lengthy and contentious deliberations in the North Atlantic Council, the Military Committee, and many subordinate committees. According to General James Jones, who served as SACEUR in 2003–2006,

> The 350 committees in NATO behave as if they see themselves as mini-NACs—little versions of the North Atlantic Council that must operate on the same consensus system as the NAC itself. This means that slow and painful lowest-common-denominator decision-making prevails. The principle of consensus has been stretched to its limit. Consensus should not be regarded as necessary at the committee level. The committee chairman should note dissenting views and move the business on to the next stage in the decision-making process. The NAC, over time, has surrendered its prerogatives as a decision maker to committees, especially to its financial committees. There are too many committees, and they are much too slow to act.[90]

As noted on the NATO website, "This principle [of consensus] is applied at every committee level, and demonstrates clearly that NATO decisions are collective decisions made by its member countries."[91] In June 2010 the Allies initiated a review of the NATO committee structure, with a view to "eliminating obsolete committees and creating new bodies." Although the Allies intend to substantially reduce the total number of committees, "The principle of consensus decision-making is applied at each and every level of the committee structure, from the top political decision-making body to the most obscure working group."[92] In other words, there is no "voting" in NATO deliberations in the sense of decision making via a majority rule principle.

Because it is sometimes difficult to reach consensus, the Allies have over the years come up with several methods to achieve at least the appearance of consensus. These methods have included avoiding certain sensitive topics in some communiqués,[93] dealing with them in vague terms satisfactory to all Allies,[94] repeating previously agreed-upon wording, employing formulas such as "the Allies concerned" to subtly separate some Allies from specific policies,[95] using the word "appropriate" to obscure disagreements,[96] and attaching footnotes in which some Allies have reserved their national positions regarding particular decisions.[97] The Allies have chosen to tacitly accept the fact that they sometimes have differing interpretations of consensus-agreed wording.

When action has not appeared urgent, Allies have on some occasions postponed decisions by calling for further study of contentious questions.[98] In some cases, in order to preserve a modicum of harmony and defer difficult choices, Allies have compromised and "kicked the can down the road" by establishing policy reviews and/or new committees.[99] In actual operations, as discussed in chapters 4 and 5, Allies have revealed their distinct views regarding agreed-upon Alliance policies by defining contributions of resources on a national basis and placing restrictions on the usability of their forces.[100]

The argument that future collective defense and crisis management contingencies may require greater agility and less "micromanagement" by committees comprised of representatives from each member state has to date failed to bring about substantive change. The consensus system has remained in place because the political foundation of the Alliance is respect for the sovereignty and autonomy of each member. From this perspective, decision making by consensus is a source of strength.[101] Moreover, it can be argued that the Allies identified the appropriate means to hedge against the risk of a rapidly evolving threat during the Cold War, when they agreed to transfer authority over certain capabilities, such as parts of the integrated air defenses in NATO Europe, to SACEUR in peacetime.[102]

In 1956, the Allies endorsed the famous "Three Wise Men" report that concluded that governments should make their national policies conform to the agreed-upon Alliance consensus.[103] Allies dissatisfied with a consensus decision that they have ostensibly—and grudgingly—approved tend, however, not to regard the Alliance consensus as settled. As with domestic disputes (and sometimes because of such disputes), politicians continue to pursue their own agendas. They readily find justifications (such as changed circumstances) to return to questions that had supposedly been answered authoritatively in a recent meeting of the North Atlantic Council. When the Allies reconsider issues, they often devise new compromises.

The history of the Alliance nonetheless offers empirical backing for the thesis advanced by Wallace Thies—that NATO as an alliance of liberal democracies has demonstrated "self-healing tendencies" and an ability to surmount its internal clashes and move forward constructively. As Thies has observed, "What sets NATO apart from so many previous alliances is *not* the absence of disagreements among its members but the ability to act in concert *despite* disagreements among its members."[104]

That the consensus system works as well as it does may be attributed in part to the urgency of making decisions in order to protect the shared interests and values of the Allies. Crises and other major international events force the Allies to define agreed-upon policies and take action. In the absence of such events, summit and ministerial meeting deadlines concentrate the minds of national leaders and subordinate officials. Whereas NATO summit meetings were rare during the first decades of the Cold War (the first two NATO summit meetings were in 1957 and 1974), they have been more frequent in recent decades. Summit meetings have become important occasions to give the Alliance political direction and move its agenda forward.

Informal consultations "in the corridors" at NATO headquarters are continuous, and national delegations are usually familiar with the views of their counterparts before formal meetings of the North Atlantic Council and subordinate bodies begin. Individual Allies and groups of member states often find it useful to circulate informally "food-for-thought papers" and "non-papers"—unofficial discussions of problems and possible solutions—in order to carry forward the search for consensus without the impediments of rigidly maintained official positions. Informal compromise building often leads to functional consensus through the "silence procedure."[105]

In short, the consensual decision-making system is cumbersome, but it performs with a surprising level of effectiveness. It is dysfunctional only in relation to an ideal of centralized efficiency and agility that is politically impractical.[106]

The same might be said of the Alliance's personnel system for the International Staff. As Lithuanian expert Kestutis Paulauskas has observed, the "selection of top officials is a political and sometimes highly politicized matter" and the "distribution of posts is to some extent a reflection of Allies' comparative political weight, as well as an instrument of indirect influence upon decision shaping within NATO's bureaucracy."[107] This pattern entails inefficiencies, in that some critical posts are filled on the basis of nationality rather than through a hypothetically preferable merit system. Similarly, assignments in the International Military Staff reflect "national quotas," and the Allies take multiple criteria into account in the "flags to posts" bargaining as to which nations' officers will fill specific billets in the command structure.[108]

A countervailing consideration is the fact that certain appointments are made in all governments on political rather than meritocratic grounds. The NATO personnel systems can be seen as advantageous precisely because they reflect the "political weight" of specific Allies. These personnel arrangements correlate to some extent with the common budget and other practical contributions of particular Allies and promote their satisfaction with the policy formation and implementation structure. A related aspect of the "political weight" element in NATO decision making is the informal but de facto influence of the four leading powers in the Alliance—Britain, France, Germany, and the United States, often called the "quad."[109]

A more serious dysfunction of the Alliance has become apparent since the end of the Cold War: the tendency of the Allies to make political decisions to take action without backing up these decisions with national commitments of capabilities and resources.[110] This dysfunctional behavior was evident in the uneven contributions to the Alliance's intervention in the Libya conflict in 2011, but it has been perhaps most visible and persistent in the NATO-led operations in Afghanistan since 2003. The example of the Combined Joint Statement of Requirements stands out. In 2009, shortly after he stepped down from serving as SACEUR, General John Craddock pointed out that "since mission inception, NATO nations have *never* completely filled the *agreed* requirements for forces needed in Afghanistan."[111]

The same pattern—national failures to meet collectively agreed-upon commitments—has recurred with Operation Active Endeavour in the Mediterranean and Operation Ocean Shield off the coast of Somalia. Commitments of forces and resources remain in national hands, and national contributions are not determined until after a political decision to act. On many occasions member states have watched and waited on the decisions of fellow Allies before deciding whether and how (and how much) to contribute to a specific operation—or to a particular subset of an ongoing activity.

While the Allies are clearly not prepared to surrender any of their national sovereignty and autonomy, they have recognized the dysfunctional quality of this behavior. As part of the 2010 reform of the Alliance's committees, the Allies established the Operations Policy Committee (OPC). The OPC is supposed "to provide coherent and timely advice to the North Atlantic Council, to which it reports directly," and "to enhance collaboration between the political and military sides of NATO headquarters." One of the OPC's virtues is the fact that it "meets regularly in so-called ISAF and KFOR format, i.e., with non-NATO member countries that contribute troops to the International Security Assistance Force (ISAF) in Afghanistan and the Kosovo Force (KFOR) in Kosovo."[112] A similar operation-focused "decision-shaping" format for meetings involving Allies and non-NATO contributors was established for the NATO-led Operation Unified Protector in Libya in 2011. Whether this committee reform can effectively address the dysfunction in question remains to be seen, however. National control over force and resource contributions will remain.[113]

Conclusion

Whether the Alliance can maintain its cohesion and perform its tasks effectively is a question of fundamental importance for U.S. and international security. NATO has been for over sixty years the principal mechanism by which certain key powers of Europe and North America have engaged in political-military cooperation to ensure their security.

Despite the rather motley and sometimes cumbersome character of the organization, it has been remarkably successful in aggregating power and achieving fundamental objectives. Its challenges are serious, but surmountable and manageable with political determination. Its assets—above all, the transatlantic convergence of values and security interests—are greater than its problems. While the Allies are unlikely to achieve all their aspirations, notably regarding the vague vision of "cooperative security," they may continue to meet fundamental goals and even devise greater ambitions—if they succeed in mustering the necessary vision and political will. As German scholar Rafael Biermann has observed, "NATO's institutional decline is reversible. NATO has mastered many ups and downs throughout history."[114]

NATO's internal disputes and divisions should be put in historical and comparative perspective. To assume that NATO was more united during the Cold War than it has been since would not be true to the historical record. Divisions and disputes (over spending, force deployments, nuclear strategy, relations with Moscow, etc.) led frequently to a crisis atmosphere and to declarations that the Alliance's end was near. The Cold War Allies were usually divided over various issues, and evidence of fragmentation was obvious.[115]

It would at any rate be impractical to measure quantitatively the degree of discord in NATO during a particular phase of the Cold War and then compare it with the Alliance's degree of internal disarray during a particular post–Cold War crisis. As

Martin Wight noted, "every generation is confronted by problems of the utmost subjective urgency, but . . . an objective grading is probably impossible."[116]

Notes

1. Martin Wight, *Power Politics*, ed. Hedley Bull and Carsten Holbraad (London: Leicester University Press for the Royal Institute of International Affairs, 1978), 128.

2. It might be argued that NATO's "cooperative security" vision derives from Kantian or Wilsonian sources, in that it involves (at least in some policy statements) a vision of peaceful cooperation among like-minded democratic states. The shortcomings in actual achievements may remind one of the fact that even Kant expressed doubts at times about the feasibility of his design for enduring peace and international order, notably in his famous statement, "Nothing straight can be constructed from such warped wood as that which man is made of." Immanuel Kant, "Idea for a Universal History with a Cosmopolitan Purpose," first published in 1784, in Kant, *Political Writings*, 2nd ed., ed. Hans Reiss and trans. H. B. Nisbet (Cambridge: Cambridge University Press, 1991), 46.

3. Ted Galen Carpenter, *NATO at 60: A Hollow Alliance*, Policy Analysis no. 635 (Washington, DC: Cato Institute, March 30, 2009), 1.

4. Richard E. Rupp, *NATO after 9/11: An Alliance in Continuing Decline* (New York: Palgrave Macmillan, 2006).

5. Nick Witney, "The Death of NATO," *Europe's World*, Autumn 2008, www.europesworld.org/NewEnglish/Home_old/Article/tabid/191/ArticleType/articleview/ArticleID/21272/language/en-US/Default.aspx.

6. Andrew J. Bacevich, "NATO at Twilight," *Los Angeles Times*, February 11, 2008, http://articles.latimes.com/2008/feb/11/opinion/oe-bacevich11.

7. *The National Security Strategy of the United States of America* (Washington, DC: The White House, September 2002), 25.

8. NATO Secretary General Anders Fogh Rasmussen, "NATO—Delivering Security in the 21st Century" (speech, Chatham House, London, July 4, 2012), www.nato.int/cps/en/natolive/opinions_88886.htm.

9. This book is a sequel to David S. Yost, *NATO Transformed: The Alliance's New Roles in International Security* (Washington, DC: United States Institute of Peace Press, 1998). In this chapter and elsewhere the author has drawn at times from passages in the earlier book.

10. This book focuses on the Alliance's external functions. Although NATO's internal functions in support of international security and the interests of the Allies may be categorized and defined in various ways, at least nine have been identified: maintaining U.S. engagement in European security, resolving intra-European security dilemmas, reassuring Germany's neighbors and allies, limiting the scope of nuclear proliferation in NATO Europe, promoting a certain "denationalization" of defense planning, providing a forum for the coordination of Western security policies, supplying economic benefits to all the Allies, encouraging and legitimizing democratic forms of government, and (from the perspective of the non-American allies) serving as a check on U.S. power. The salience of specific internal functions has changed over the years. In current circumstances, for example, the prospect of nuclear proliferation in NATO Europe is remote; and once-vivid concerns about Germany as a potential military threat have become increasingly peripheral with the passage of the decades since 1945. For background on the first eight of these internal functions, see Yost, *NATO Transformed*, 50–72. With regard to the ninth, serving as a check on U.S. power, see Sean M. Maloney, "Limiting American Nuclear Omnipotence in NATO: The Canadian Method, 1951–68," in *A History of NATO: The First Fifty Years*, vol. 3, ed. Gustav Schmidt (Basingstoke, UK, and New York: Palgrave, 2001), 155–172; and David S. Yost, "Dissuasion and Allies," *Strategic Insights* 4 (February 2005), www.ccc.nps.navy.mil/si/2005/feb/yostfeb05.pdf.

11. No reasonably comprehensive history of NATO exists. Among the various studies of the Alliance's origins, the most current and informative is that by the dean of NATO historians in the United States: Lawrence S. Kaplan, *NATO 1948: The Birth of the Transatlantic Alliance* (Lanham, MD: Rowman and Littlefield, 2007). An excellent source on the early period remains Robert E. Osgood, *NATO: The Entangling Alliance* (Chicago: University of Chicago Press, 1962). An illuminating survey for the period up through the 1970s is Alfred Grosser, *The Western Alliance: European-American Relations Since 1945*, trans. Michael Shaw (London: Macmillan, 1980). A valuable one-volume survey of the Alliance's history through the end of the Cold War is Richard L. Kugler, *Commitment to Purpose: How Alliance Partnership Won the Cold War* (Santa Monica, CA: RAND Corp., 1993). The rich literature on NATO during the Cold War includes Gustav Schmidt, ed., *A History of NATO: The First Fifty Years*, 3 vols. (Basingstoke, UK, and New York: Palgrave, 2001). An illuminating recent analysis of the Europe-centered East-West competition during the Cold War is Gordon S. Barrass, *The Great Cold War: A Journey through the Hall of Mirrors* (Stanford, CA: Stanford University Press, 2009).

12. Stalin quoted in Milovan Djilas, *Conversations with Stalin*, trans. Michael B. Petrovich (New York: Harcourt, Brace & World, 1962), 114.

13. Stalin quoted in Philip E. Mosely, *The Kremlin and World Politics: Studies in Soviet Policy and Action* (New York: Vintage Books, 1960), 214.

14. Letter from the Central Committee of the Communist Party of the Soviet Union to the Central Committee of the Communist Party of Yugoslavia, May 4, 1948, in *The Soviet-Yugoslav Dispute: Text of the Published Correspondence* (London and New York: Oxford University Press for the Royal Institute of International Affairs, 1948), 51. See also Gale Stokes, ed., *From Stalinism to Pluralism: A Documentary History of Eastern Europe Since 1945* (Oxford and New York: Oxford University Press, 1996), 62–63.

15. Konrad Adenauer, *Erinnerungen 1953–1955* (Frankfurt am Main: Fischer Bücherei, 1968), 19. See also Hans-Peter Schwarz, "Adenauer's *Ostpolitik*," in *West German Foreign Policy: 1949–1979*, ed. Wolfram F. Hanrieder (Boulder, CO: Westview Press, 1980), 128.

16. Dean Acheson, testimony in U.S. Senate, *North Atlantic Treaty: Hearings before the Committee on Foreign Relations* (Washington, DC: U.S. Government Printing Office, 1949), 47.

17. Senator Arthur Vandenberg, Republican of Michigan, statement on March 8, 1949, in *The Vandenberg Resolution and the North Atlantic Treaty: Hearings held in Executive Session before the Committee on Foreign Relations, United States Senate*, 80th Cong., 2nd sess., in 1948 and 1949, and made public in 1973 (Washington, DC: U.S. Government Printing Office, 1973), 159.

18. For a useful analysis of national differences in foreign policy within the Warsaw Pact, see Edwina Moreton, "Foreign Policy Goals," in *The Warsaw Pact: Alliance in Transition?*, ed. David Holloway and Jane M. O. Sharp (London: Macmillan, 1984), especially the discussion of Romania on pp. 149–151.

19. At times the Soviets claimed credit for being the first to develop ICBMs and certain other capabilities, and at other times portrayed the United States as the sole "engine of the arms race," with the USSR in a purely reactive mode. For a discussion of Soviet ideology and propaganda about military-technical innovation during the Cold War, see David S. Yost, *Soviet Ballistic Missile Defense and the Western Alliance* (Cambridge, MA: Harvard University Press, 1988), 71–80.

20. Phrases used in NATO communiqués of September 17, 1949; December 14–16, 1953; and December 16–19, 1957, in *Texts of Final Communiqués, 1949–1974* (Brussels: NATO Information Service, 1975), 39, 79, and 109.

21. The Harmel Report, named after Pierre Harmel, a Belgian foreign minister, is available under its formal title, "The Future Tasks of the Alliance," Report of the Council, Annex to the Final Communiqué of the Ministerial Meeting, December 13–14, 1967. The passages cited are found in par. 5. The document is available at www.nato.int/cps/en/natolive/official_texts_26700.htm.

22. Ibid., par. 9.

23. North Atlantic Council communiqué of December 15–16, 1955, in *Texts of Final Communiqués, 1949–1974*, 95.

24. North Atlantic Council declaration of December 16–19, 1957, in *Texts of Final Communiqués, 1949–1974*, 109.

25. North Atlantic Council declaration of December 11–14, 1956, in *Texts of Final Communiqués, 1949–1974*, 102.

26. North Atlantic Council communiqué of December 15–16, 1966, in *Texts of Final Communiqués, 1949–1974*, 178.

27. North Atlantic Council communiqué of May 2–3, 1957, in *Texts of Final Communiqués, 1949–1974*, 106.

28. North Atlantic Council communiqué of June 13–14, 1967, in *Texts of Final Communiqués, 1949–1974*, 189.

29. North Atlantic Council declaration of December 4–5, 1969, in *Texts of Final Communiqués, 1949–1974*, 231.

30. This brief discussion omits national differences within the Alliance during the Cold War regarding how to pursue peaceful changes in the European political order. Among other sources, see Charles R. Planck, *The Changing Status of German Reunification in Western Diplomacy, 1955–1966* (Baltimore, MD: Johns Hopkins University Press, 1967); Bennett Kovrig, *The Myth of Liberation: East-Central Europe in U.S. Diplomacy and Politics since 1941* (Baltimore, MD: Johns Hopkins University Press, 1973); Lincoln Gordon et al., *Eroding Empire: Western Relations with Eastern Europe* (Washington, DC: Brookings Institution Press, 1987); and David S. Yost, *Alternative Structures of European Security*, Working Paper no. 81 (Washington, DC: Woodrow Wilson International Center for Scholars, 1987).

31. For a discussion of this attitude, see Ronald Steel, "The West Has Its Own Stake in the Eastern Status Quo," *Los Angeles Times*, January 17, 1982.

32. Helmut Schmidt cited in Timothy Garton Ash, *The Polish Revolution: Solidarity* (New York: Charles Scribner's Sons, 1984), 317.

33. Giulio Andreotti cited in James M. Markham, "For Both East and West Two Germanys Is Better," *New York Times*, September 23, 1984.

34. Milovan Djilas, *The New Class: An Analysis of the Communist System* (New York: Frederick A. Praeger, 1957).

35. Peter Rudolf, "Managing Strategic Divergence: German-American Conflict over Policy Towards Iran," in *The Iranian Dilemma: Challenges for German and American Foreign Policy*, ed. Peter Rudolf and Geoffrey Kemp (Washington, DC: Johns Hopkins University Press, 1997), 3.

36. Recent studies include Mary Elise Sarotte, *1989: The Struggle to Create Post–Cold War Europe* (Princeton, NJ: Princeton University Press, 2009), and Frédéric Bozo, *Mitterrand, the End of the Cold War, and German Unification* (Oxford and New York: Berghahn Books, 1989).

37. Prior to 1991, the Allies had not prepared a strategic concept since 1967, when they approved MC 14/3, widely known as the military strategy of "flexible response." In 1967 they also endorsed the Harmel Report, which set out the Alliance's broad political strategy for relations with the Soviet Union and its Warsaw Pact allies. MC 14/3 and the Harmel Report together, covering political as well as military strategy, dealt with approximately the same areas encompassed by the 1991 Strategic Concept. MC 14/3, "Overall Strategic Concept for the Defense of the North Atlantic Treaty Organization Area," approved by the Defence Planning Committee in Ministerial Session on 12 December 1967, is available in Gregory W. Pedlow, ed., *NATO Strategy Documents 1949–1969* (Brussels: NATO Information Service, 1997), 345–370.

38. Lawrence Freedman, *The Primacy of Alliance: Deterrence and European Security*, Proliferation Paper no. 46 (Paris: Institut Français des Relations Internationales, March–April 2013), 7.

39. North Atlantic Council, "The Alliance's New Strategic Concept," November 7, 1991, par. 47, www.nato.int/cps/en/natolive/official_texts_23847.htm.

40. Ibid., par. 9 and 47.

41. Ibid., par. 36.

42. The Allies agreed in 2006 that "experience in Afghanistan and Kosovo demonstrates that today's challenges require a comprehensive approach by the international community involving a wide spectrum of civil and military instruments, while fully respecting mandates and autonomy of decisions of all actors, and provides precedents for this approach." North Atlantic Council, "Riga Summit Declaration," November 29, 2006, par. 10, www.nato.int/docu/pr/2006/p06-150e.htm. NATO Allies nonetheless have differing definitions of the requirements of a "comprehensive approach," including the extent to which the Allies should develop and employ civilian capabilities under Alliance auspices. For background on national and NATO policies concerning the "comprehensive approach," see David S. Yost, *NATO and International Organizations*, Forum Paper no. 3 (Rome: NATO Defense College, September 2007), 19–30, 155–158, 176–183, www.ndc.nato.int/download/publications/fp_03.pdf; and Brooke Smith-Windsor, *Hasten Slowly: NATO's Effects Based and Comprehensive Approach to Operations*, Research Paper no. 38 (Rome: NATO Defense College, July 2008), www.ndc.nato.int/download/downloads.php?icode=10.

43. North Atlantic Council, "The London Declaration," July 5–6, 1990, par. 2, www.nato.int/cps/en/natolive/official_texts_23693.htm.

44. Ibid., par. 21.

45. North Atlantic Council, "Rome Declaration on Peace and Cooperation," November 8, 1991, par. 13, www.nato.int/docu/comm/49-95/c911108a.htm.

46. Ibid., par. 2.

47. North Atlantic Council, "Partnership for Peace: Framework Document," January 11, 1994, par. 1 and 2, www.nato.int/cps/en/natolive/official_texts_24469.htm?mode=pressrelease.

48. North Atlantic Council, "The Alliance's Strategic Concept," April 24, 1999, par. 10, www.nato.int/cps/en/natolive/official_texts_27433.htm.

49. These cooperative frameworks and the Alliance's partnership policies are discussed in chapter 6.

50. North Atlantic Council, "The Alliance's Strategic Concept," April 24, 1999, par. 6.

51. North Atlantic Council, "London Declaration," par. 3.

52. North Atlantic Council, "Final Communiqué," December 17–18, 1990, par. 15, www.nato.int/cps/en/natolive/official_texts_23690.htm. NATO statements calling for nuclear nonproliferation date back to the 1960s.

53. North Atlantic Council, "Strategic Concept," November 7, 1991, par. 15.

54. Ibid., par. 19.

55. Ibid., par. 20.

56. Ibid., par. 13.

57. North Atlantic Council, "Strategic Concept," April 24, 1999, par. 6.

58. Ibid., par. 10; bold in the original.

59. The layout of the missions in the document visually separated these new tasks from the continuing original tasks as a compromise to satisfy some Allies. The layout implied, at least in the eyes of some Allies, a difference in standing of the tasks.

60. North Atlantic Council, "Active Engagement, Modern Defence: Strategic Concept for the Defence and Security of the Members of the North Atlantic Treaty Organisation," November 19, 2010, par. 1, www.nato.int/cps/en/natolive/official_texts_68580.htm.

61. Ibid., par. 4; bold added.

62. Ibid., par. 19 and 25, www.nato.int/cps/en/natolive/official_texts_68580.htm.

63. NATO, "Highlights from the First Strategic Concept Seminar in Luxembourg," October 16, 2009, www.nato.int/cps/en/SID-45306560-524A167A/natolive/news_58816.htm.

64. *NATO 2020: Assured Security; Dynamic Engagement, Analysis and Recommendations of the Group of Experts on a New Strategic Concept for NATO* (Brussels: NATO Public Diplomacy Division, May 17, 2010), 15, www.nato.int/cps/en/natolive/official_texts_63654.htm.

65. "Instability or conflict beyond NATO borders can directly threaten Alliance security, including by fostering extremism, terrorism, and trans-national illegal activities such as trafficking in arms, narcotics and people." North Atlantic Council, "Strategic Concept," November 19, 2010, par. 11. The words "genocide" and "humanitarian" are also absent from the November 2010 Lisbon Summit Declaration, which likewise makes no allusion to failed or failing states.

66. UN Security Council Resolution 1970, February 26, 2011, and UN Security Council Resolution 1973, March 17, 2011.

67. Rob de Wijk, *NATO on the Brink of the New Millennium: The Battle for Consensus* (London: Brassey's, 1997), 143.

68. The three most common meanings of collective security are as follows: (1) the model of an ideal international order championed most famously, though with some differences, by Immanuel Kant and Woodrow Wilson, a pact against war by the community of states; (2) an intervention against international aggression or internal conflict or disorder with the implicit or explicit approval of a major-power consensus, as with a UN Security Council resolution authorizing the use of force; and (3) an intervention against international aggression or internal conflict or disorder without the approval of a major-power consensus. For a more extensive discussion, see David S. Yost, "NATO's Contributions to Conflict Management," in *Turbulent Peace: The Challenges of Managing International Conflict*, ed. Chester A. Crocker, Fen Osler Hampson, and Pamela Aall (Washington, DC: United States Institute of Peace Press, 2001), 590–592.

69. "The North Atlantic Treaty Organization and its member States, on the one hand, and the Russian Federation, on the other hand, hereinafter referred to as NATO and Russia, based on an enduring political commitment undertaken at the highest political level, will build together a lasting and inclusive peace in the Euro-Atlantic area on the principles of democracy and cooperative security." "Founding Act on Mutual Relations, Cooperation and Security between NATO and the Russian Federation Signed in, Paris, France," May 27, 1997, www.nato.int/cps/en/natolive/official_texts_25468.htm.

70. Admiral Norman Ray, "Security through NATO in the 21st Century: Vision to Reality" (opening remarks, SACLANT/RUSI International Security Symposium, London, October 9, 1997), www.nato.int/docu/speech/1997/s971009a.htm. Admiral Ray was then serving as the assistant secretary general for defense support.

71. Javier Solana, "NATO's Role in Building Cooperative Security in Europe and Beyond" (remarks, NATO at the Yomiuri Symposium on International Economy, Tokyo, Japan, October 15, 1997), www.nato.int/docu/speech/1997/s971015a.htm.

72. Ibid. For an even more ambitious vision of the potential of cooperative security, see Ray, "Security through NATO in the 21st Century."

73. Rasmussen, "NATO—Delivering Security in the 21st Century."

74. To quote Pertusot, "Partnerships are based on cooperative security as outlined in the new Strategic Concept. This notion remains very poorly understood. We define it here as an institutionalized or non-institutionalized arrangement, involving a group of states who pursue dialogue and cooperation on a wide variety of issues, primarily concerning security. This definition assumes that they can all share the same interpretations of the security challenges, whether internal or foreign, and thus cooperate to increase the level of confidence and trust among them, and to mitigate hypothetical conflicts, divergences, and misunderstandings." Vivien Pertusot, *NATO Partnerships: Shaking Hands or Shaking the System?*, Focus Stratégique no. 31 (Paris: Institut Français des Relations Internationales et Stratégiques, May 2011), 23. For an even broader definition, see Gareth Evans, "Cooperative Security and Instrastate Conflict," *Foreign Policy* 96, no. 3 (Autumn 1994): 7.

75. Pertusot holds that security cooperation is a more comprehensive concept than cooperative security. In his view, the latter is "a much more narrowed-down concept." Cooperative security, Pertusot maintains, is driven principally by "common interests" and "a common understanding of the challenges and issues at stake." The states involved may, despite their differences, "find solutions to security problems by cooperating with potential enemies . . . in a win-win game scenario." However, Pertusot adds, "no solidarity binds the members" of a cooperative security arrangement, and they retain "flexibility" as to whether to participate in, for example, a specific NATO partnership activity. Vivien Pertusot, *Cooperative Security and NATO Partnerships: What Means for What Ends?*, Diplôme privé d'études supérieures (Paris: Institut de Relations Internationales et Stratégiques, October 2, 2009), 18, 19, 23.

76. North Atlantic Council, "Chicago Summit Declaration," May 20, 2012, par. 2, www.nato.int/cps/en/SID-140D258B-1322853B/natolive/official_texts_87593.htm.

77. North Atlantic Council, "Strategic Concept," November 7, 1991, par. 12; and North Atlantic Council, "Strategic Concept," April 24, 1999, par. 24.

78. North Atlantic Council, "Washington Summit Communiqué," April 24, 1999, par. 42, www.nato.int/cps/en/natolive/official_texts_27440.htm.

79. For background, see Yost, *NATO and International Organizations*, 55–57.

80. This refers, for example, to the security assurances extended in 1999 to countries neighboring the Federal Republic of Yugoslavia. This is discussed in chapter 5.

81. The author thanks Diego Ruiz Palmer for having first raised this point with reference to Article 5 and for having suggested the term "deterritorialization." The development of a more "anticipatory" and "proactive" concept of collective defense requirements is discussed in chapter 5.

82. Espen Barth Eide, "Transatlantic Ties in Times of Financial Austerity" (speech, Leangkollen Security Conference, February 6, 2012), www.regjeringen.no/en/dep/fd/whats-new/Speeches-and-articles/minister/speeches-and-articles-by-minister-of-d-2/2012/transatlantic-ties-in-times-of-financial.html?id=671826.

83. Anders Fogh Rasmussen, "NATO 2020—Shared Leadership for a Shared Future" (speech, Brussels Forum, March 23, 2012), www.nato.int/cps/en/SID-40AEB457-0F83E57E/natolive/opinions_85443.htm.

84. *NATO's Operations 1949–Present* (Mons, Belgium: Supreme Headquarters, Allied Powers Europe, 2009), www.aco.nato.int/resources/21/NATO%20Operations,%201949-Present.pdf.

85. Senator Richard Lugar cited in Stephen S. Rosenfeld, "NATO's Last Chance," *Washington Post*, July 2, 1993.

86. Scholarly studies include Michael Harrison, *The Reluctant Ally: France and Atlantic Security* (Baltimore, MD: Johns Hopkins University Press, 1981); Philip H. Gordon, *A Certain Idea of France: French Security Policy and the Gaullist Legacy* (Princeton, NJ: Princeton University Press, 1993); and Anand Menon, *France, NATO and the Limits of Independence* (Basingstoke, UK: Palgrave Macmillan, 2000).

87. NATO, *Study on NATO Enlargement*, September 3, 1995, par. 47, www.nato.int/cps/en/natolive/official_texts_24733.htm.

88. Ibid.

89. For background on NATO funding arrangements, see NATO, "Paying for NATO," last updated December 14, 2010, www.nato.int/cps/en/natolive/topics_67655.htm; and Carl Ek, *NATO Common Funds Burdensharing: Background and Current Issues*, RL30150 (Washington, DC: Congressional Research Service, March 10, 2011).

90. David S. Yost, *An Interview with General James L. Jones, USMC, Retired, Supreme Allied Commander Europe (SACEUR), 2003–2006*, Research Paper no. 34 (Rome: NATO Defense College, January 2008), 3–4, www.ndc.nato.int/download/publications/rp_34.pdf.

91. "Consensus Decision-Making at NATO," last updated October 26, 2010, www.nato.int/cps/en/natolive/topics_49178.htm.

92. NATO, "NATO Committees," last updated June 21, 2013, www.nato.int/cps/cn/natolive/topics_49174.htm. The principal exception to this generalization is the "consensus-minus-one" practice in the NATO Defense Planning Process (NDPP), discussed in chapter 3. Also, on some comparatively rare occasions Allies have employed the "chairman's report" or "chairman's memorandum" instrument, which might be seen as a step away from the formal requirement of consensus.

93. For example, according to a German expert, "The rifts are so deep that the 28 NATO defense ministers decided at their spring meeting in Brussels in June 2010 to delete the nuclear paragraph from the final communiqué as there was no agreement on the wording." Karl-Heinz Kamp, *NATO's Nuclear Weapons in Europe: Beyond 'Yes' or 'No,'* Research Paper no. 61 (Rome: NATO Defense College, September 2010), 2n4.

94. Vague wording is an old tradition in NATO. It began from the outset, with the Truman administration's interest in satisfying the Senate with a vaguely worded Article 5 in the North Atlantic Treaty instead of the more strongly worded mutual defense pledge in the 1948 Brussels Treaty. As Ryan Hendrickson notes, Manlio Brosio, NATO's secretary general from 1964 to 1971, was reputed to be "unusually skilled in finding semantical nuances that permitted the allies to find agreement in the NAC's written memoranda." Ryan C. Hendrickson, *Diplomacy and War at NATO: The Secretary General and Military Action after the Cold War* (Columbia and London: University of Missouri Press, 2006), 25.

95. The phrase "the Allies concerned" was featured six times in the 1991 Strategic Concept and twice in the 1999 Strategic Concept.

96. The word "appropriate" functions as a consensus-builder, at least in drafting communiqués, in that no member state is likely to argue for replacing the word with "inappropriate." Employing the word often signals that an issue remains less than fully resolved but the Allies wish to present a facade of consensus. The Allies used the word "appropriate" seven times in the November 2010 Lisbon Summit Declaration.

97. In the early and mid-1980s Denmark and Greece attached many footnotes to paragraphs in communiqués dealing with intermediate-range nuclear force (INF) issues.

98. For example, at the Riga Summit, the Allies announced, "At Prague we initiated a Missile Defence Feasibility Study in response to the increasing missile threat. We welcome its recent completion. It concludes that missile defence is technically feasible within the limitations and assumptions of the study. We tasked continued work on the political and military implications of missile defence for the Alliance including an update on missile threat developments." North Atlantic Council, "Riga Summit Declaration," November 29, 2006, par. 25.

99. Some observers have seen two of the 2010 Lisbon Summit decisions in this light: the launching of the Deterrence and Defense Posture Review (DDPR) and the establishment of the Weapons of Mass Destruction Control and Disarmament Committee (WCDC).

100. One of the most striking "red card" incidents in the history of the Alliance was the June 1999 decision by British General Sir Michael Jackson not to follow General Wesley Clark's orders regarding the Russian forces at the Pristina airfield, even though Clark was the SACEUR. For accounts of this incident, see Clark, *Waging Modern War: Bosnia, Kosovo, and the Future of Combat* (New York: PublicAffairs, 2001), 375–403; and Jackson, *Soldier: The Autobiography of General Sir Mike Jackson* (London and Toronto: Bantam Press, 2007), 255–275.

101. For a balanced and well-informed analysis, see Leo G. Michel, *NATO Decisionmaking: Au Revoir to the Consensus Rule?*, Strategic Forum no. 202 (Washington, DC: National Defense University, August 2003).

102. Yost, *NATO Transformed*, 59–60.

103. "Where a consensus has been reached, it should be reflected in the formation of national policies. When, for national reasons, the consensus is not followed, the government concerned should offer an explanation to the Council." "Report of the Committee of Three on Non-Military Cooperation in NATO," December 13, 1956, www.nato.int/cps/en/SID-7F397637-25F019C6/natolive/official_texts_17481.htm. The "Three Wise Men" were Halvard Lange, the foreign minister of Norway, Gaetano Martino, the foreign minister of Italy, and Lester B. Pearson, the foreign minister of Canada.

104. Wallace J. Thies, *Why NATO Endures* (New York: Cambridge University Press, 2009), 20, 296; italics in the original.

105. Under the "silence procedure" a draft text is distributed to all the Allies and regarded as agreed unless a member state "breaks silence" by objecting to its wording before a specified deadline. Maintaining silence signifies approval or at least acquiescence. "Breaking silence" obliges the Allies to engage in further consultations in pursuit of consensus.

106. If the Allies agreed to abandon the consensus principle (an unlikely circumstance), a "streamlined" nonconsensual approach might result in a few quick decisions at the outset, but it would run the risk of rapidly eroding Alliance solidarity.

107. Kestutis Paulauskas, "NATO at 60: Lost in Transformation," *Lithuanian Annual Strategic Review 2009–2010* (Vilnius: General Jonas Zemaitis Military Academy of Lithuania and the Institute of International Relations and Political Science of the University of Vilnius, 2010), 52.

108. Karel Kovanda, "Preparing for Membership," *NATO Review*, Special Issue, Interpreting Prague, Spring 2003, 27, www.nato.int/docu/review/pdf/i1_en_review2003.pdf.

109. For background, see Yost, *NATO Transformed*, 183–187; and Helga Haftendorn, "The 'Quad': Dynamics of Institutional Change," in Helga Haftendorn, Robert O. Keohane, and Celeste A. Wallander, eds., *Imperfect Unions: Security Institutions over Time and Space* (Oxford and New York: Oxford University Press, 1999), 162–194.

110. Allies often failed to meet their agreed force commitments during the Cold War as well, but this shortcoming was less visible when the Alliance was not engaged in actual operations. General Bernard Rogers, SACEUR in 1979–1987, pointed out frequently that "despite these repeated expressions of intent to bolster conventional capabilities, nations have fallen quite short of their fulfillment and cannot realize them at current levels of effort." General Bernard W. Rogers, "The Atlantic Alliance: Prescriptions for a Difficult Decade," *Foreign Affairs* 60, no. 5 (Summer 1982): 1151.

111. General John Craddock, interview with Arnaud de Borchgrave, "'Caveats' Neuter NATO Allies," *Washington Times*, July 15, 2009, italics in the original, www.washingtontimes.com/news/2009/jul/15/caveats-neuter-nato-allies/.

112. NATO, "Operations Policy Committee," last updated December 14, 2010, www.nato.int/cps/en/natolive/topics_69312.htm

113. The two paragraphs above are based on the author's interviews with British and French experts in Brussels, October 24–25, 2011.

114. Rafael Biermann, "NATO's Institutional Decline in Post–Cold War Security Governance," in *European Security Governance: The European Union in a Westphalian World*, ed. Charlotte Wagnsson, James A. Sperling, and Jan Hallenberg (London and New York: Routledge, 2009), 58.

115. Similarly, there were caveats during the Cold War, but they were less visible than those in, for example, the operations in the Balkans and Afghanistan. NATO during the Cold War was oriented mainly toward deterrence and defense preparedness, in contrast with the Alliance's conduct of multiple operations since 1990–1991. As examples of Cold War caveats, one might consider the refusals of Denmark and Norway to accept the presence in peacetime of foreign military bases or U.S. nuclear weapons on their soil, and France's insistence on a policy of "non-automaticity" with regard to participation in the defense of Central Europe against Warsaw Pact aggression and its decision not to accept a place in the "layer cake" array of Allied force deployments on the inter-German border.

116. Martin Wight, *International Theory: The Three Traditions*, ed. Gabriele Wight and Brian Porter (London: Leicester University Press for the Royal Institute of International Affairs, 1991), 6.

2

Collective Defense and the Evolving Security Environment

While non-Article 5 crisis management operations have taken up increasing proportions of the time and attention of the Alliance's military and civilian personnel in their day-to-day activities, the Allies have continued to uphold the primacy of collective defense. According to NATO's 2006 Comprehensive Political Guidance, "Collective defense will remain the core purpose of the Alliance."[1] Collective defense is the ultimate reason why the founding members formed the Alliance in 1949, and it remains NATO's cornerstone, even as the Alliance has taken on additional roles and responsibilities. It is therefore not surprising that the Allies listed collective defense as the first of the Alliance's "three essential core tasks" in the 2010 Strategic Concept.

The Allies declared in this document that "NATO will deter and defend against any threat of aggression, and against emerging security challenges where they threaten the fundamental security of individual Allies or the Alliance as a whole."[2] The Allies have made clear a distinction between the traditional threat of state aggression and risks that have become more prominent since the end of the Cold War in 1989–1991. In 2010 the Alliance established a new Emerging Security Challenges Division in the International Staff at NATO headquarters in Brussels. The NATO website indicates that the new division will address "non-traditional risks and challenges" such as cyber defense, energy security, terrorism, and WMD proliferation.[3]

This chapter discusses long-standing concerns, stronger in some Alliance countries than in others, about Russia as a potential security challenge before turning to what the Allies refer to as the "broader security environment"—that is, possible non-Russian collective defense risks. The chapter then examines the "emerging security challenges" of cyber security, space operations, energy security, terrorism, and WMD proliferation.

It should be noted at the outset that the NATO Allies have long differed regarding threat assessments. As several experts from NATO countries noted in May 2010, "The alliance is having trouble producing an objective threat assessment because governments disagree on what it should say, and they withhold or manipulate intelligence to advance their point of view."[4]

In the same month, the Group of Experts, appointed by NATO secretary general Anders Fogh Rasmussen and chaired by former U.S. secretary of state Madeleine Albright, submitted an analysis and recommendations in support of NATO's Strategic Concept review. It is noteworthy that while the Albright group's report provided a reasonably thorough and balanced discussion of the security environment that named potential state adversaries (including Iran, North Korea, and Russia),[5] the Alliance's November 2010 Strategic Concept did not specify any possible state adversaries. Instead, the Strategic Concept kept its discussion of threats at the generic and abstract level (for instance, cyber attacks, terrorism, and the proliferation of WMD). According to interview sources, the Strategic Concept was silent as to the identity of potential state adversaries because the Allies could not reach a consensus in this regard or even on the gravity of certain generic threats, such as terrorism.

Aside from the lack of consensus among the Allies, another obstacle to naming specific potential threats has been the Alliance's interest in promoting dialogue, cooperation, and partnership with former and possible adversaries. The Albright report stated, "Because Russia's future policies toward NATO remain difficult to predict, the Allies must pursue the goal of cooperation while also guarding against the possibility that Russia could decide to move in a more adversarial direction."[6]

The Strategic Concept included no reference to a need to hedge against such possible Russian behavior (or to potential threats from Iran and other countries), owing in part to a concern that public recognition of adverse possibilities involving particular countries could complicate the pursuit of the Alliance's cooperative security agenda. Furthermore, naming potential adversaries could degrade prospects for support from Russia and other countries in the Alliance's crisis management operations.

Russia as a Potential Security Challenge

Since the end of the Cold War, NATO has increasingly avoided explicit references to Moscow as a potential security challenge. In the 1991 Strategic Concept, approved the month before the collapse of the Soviet Union in December 1991, the Allies declared that one of their "fundamental security tasks" was "to preserve the strategic balance within Europe."[7] In this regard, as noted in chapter 1, the Allies added, "Even in a non-adversarial and cooperative relationship, Soviet military capability and build-up potential, including its nuclear dimension, still constitute the most significant factor of which the Alliance has to take account in maintaining the strategic balance in Europe."[8]

In December 1991 the Alliance invited the foreign ministers of all the former Warsaw Pact states to meet with their NATO counterparts, and the first meeting of the North Atlantic Cooperation Council (NACC) was held in December 1991. The disintegration of the Soviet Union later that month led to the expansion of the NACC to all former Soviet republics, including Russia. The Alliance also invited Russia to join NATO's Partnership for Peace, founded in 1994. In May 1997, at a summit meeting in Paris, Russia and the Allies concluded the NATO-Russia Founding Act, and the principles of dialogue and cooperation in that document were reaffirmed and developed in the 2002 Rome Declaration by Russia and the NATO Allies.

As noted in chapter 1, the 1999 Strategic Concept included no reference to "the strategic balance within Europe" and the only explicit allusions to Russia in this document involved cooperation, dialogue, and partnership.

The 1999 Strategic Concept noted, however, that "the existence of powerful nuclear forces outside the Alliance also constitutes a significant factor which the Alliance has to take into account if security and stability in the Euro-Atlantic area are to be maintained."[9] The most "powerful nuclear forces outside the Alliance" were and remain those of Russia.

The 2010 Strategic Concept alluded indirectly to Russia as a potential security concern by taking note of the extensive reductions in U.S. nuclear weapons in Europe since the end of the Cold War and stating that "in any future reductions, our aim should be to seek Russian agreement to increase transparency on its nuclear weapons in Europe and relocate these weapons away from the territory of NATO members. Any further steps must take into account the disparity with the greater Russian stockpiles of short-range nuclear weapons."[10]

The essential thrust of the 2010 Strategic Concept concerning Russia was nonetheless to champion partnership with the Alliance.

> NATO-Russia cooperation is of strategic importance as it contributes to creating a common space of peace, stability and security. NATO poses no threat to Russia. On the contrary: we want to see a true strategic partnership between NATO and Russia, and we will act accordingly, with the expectation of reciprocity from Russia.
>
> The NATO-Russia relationship is based upon the goals, principles and commitments of the NATO-Russia Founding Act and the Rome Declaration, especially regarding the respect of democratic principles and the sovereignty, independence and territorial integrity of all states in the Euro-Atlantic area. Notwithstanding differences on particular issues, we remain convinced that the security of NATO and Russia is intertwined and that a strong and constructive partnership based on mutual confidence, transparency and predictability can best serve our security. We are determined to:
>
> - enhance the political consultations and practical cooperation with Russia in areas of shared interests, including missile defence, counter-terrorism, counter-narcotics, counter-piracy and the promotion of wider international security;
> - use the full potential of the NATO-Russia Council for dialogue and joint action with Russia.[11]

The NATO-Russia Council, composed of Russia and the NATO member states, agreed in November 2010 to "work towards achieving a true strategic and modernised partnership based on the principles of reciprocal confidence, transparency, and predictability, with the aim of contributing to the creation of a common space of peace, security and stability in the Euro-Atlantic area."[12]

Since the end of the Cold War, the official Alliance position has been that Russia is a partner. Indeed, constructive relations with Russia remain of paramount importance for all the Allies. However, Moscow has become increasingly assertive since early 2007. The list of adverse actions attributed to Russia since that time includes its 2007 suspension of compliance with the 1990 Conventional Armed Forces in Europe (CFE) Treaty, its mixed record regarding Iran's nuclear activities, the 2007 cyber attacks on Estonia, its declarations that Poland and the Czech Republic have made themselves potential targets for nuclear attack by supporting U.S. missile defense plans,[13] its use of energy supplies as an instrument of coercion, its use of force against Georgia in August 2008, its military exercises in 2009 that simulated an incursion into the Baltic states and a nuclear attack on Poland,[14] and its support for the Bashar al-Assad regime in the Syrian civil war since March 2011.

Despite the shared aspiration of the NATO Allies for positive relations with Moscow, collective defense has been reconfirmed as the top priority of several new Allies in Central and Eastern Europe by recent Russian behavior. In particular, Moscow's use of force against Georgia in August 2008 has raised anxieties in some Allied nations.

The Allies stated in this regard in August 2008 that "Russian military action has been disproportionate and inconsistent with its peacekeeping role, as well as incompatible with the principles of peaceful conflict resolution set out in the Helsinki Final Act, the NATO-Russia Founding Act and the Rome Declaration."[15] Moreover, the Allies hold that Russia violated Georgia's territorial integrity when it sent its forces beyond the enclaves of Abkhazia and South Ossetia, and that Russia's recognition of these enclaves as independent states is unwarranted and inconsistent with Russia's previous avowed support for Georgia's territorial integrity in UN Security Council resolutions. Russia's recognition of these enclaves, the Allies have noted, contravenes the principles of the Organization for Security and Co-operation in Europe (OSCE).[16] It implies a willingness to modify international borders by force.

One of Russia's declared justifications for its forceful intervention in Georgia—to protect Russian citizens in Abkhazia and South Ossetia—alarmed the Baltic states, because their populations include large numbers of ethnic Russians. As Ronald Asmus and his coauthors pointed out in a 2010 study, "Large-scale military conflict is only one type, and arguably the least likely, of possible confrontation with Russia. A smaller regional conflict, which is much harder to plan against or deter, is a far more probable scenario. It could take several forms. Some of the Baltic states, in particular Estonia and Latvia, have sizeable Russian minorities on their territory. They are concerned that Moscow could use the presence of those minorities as a pretext for limited military incursion."[17] As Tomas Valasek has noted, "A new law proposed by the Kremlin in August 2009 authorises the president to use force to defend the lives of Russian 'citizens' abroad. Thousands of people in Estonia, Latvia and elsewhere in Eastern Europe could technically be considered Russian citizens because Moscow has distributed Russian passports to its ethnic kin all across the region."[18]

Allies such as the Baltic states, the Czech Republic, and Poland have been less concerned about the military capability of the Alliance to employ forces for collective defense than about the political will of some Allies to honor their Article 5 commitments in a serious crisis. A poll conducted in five Western European states soon after the August 2008 Russia-Georgia conflict found that in three of the states—Germany, Italy, and Spain—more people would oppose the idea of troops from their respective countries defending the Baltic states than would support it. Only in two states—Britain and France—did more people support the prospect of their national troops defending fellow NATO members Estonia, Latvia, and Lithuania than oppose it.[19]

The Alliance has nonetheless clearly not abandoned the traditional meaning of collective defense. NATO's new Allies—above all, the Baltic states, the Czech Republic, and Poland—have placed particular emphasis on maintaining the priority of collective defense in the sense of protecting national territory from external aggression. In December 2006, well before the Georgia-Russia conflict of August 2008, Vaira Vike-Freiberga, then president of Latvia, said, "If we were invaded . . . I would expect the NATO alliance to immediately react and to take all measures to defend us. This is absolutely the fundamental principle of the alliance and if ever the alliance falls down on it, the alliance collapses."[20]

Expressions of anxiety about Russia have multiplied since August 2008, especially in Eastern and Central Europe. In December 2008, Toomas Hendrik Ilves, the president of Estonia, said, "The fact that NATO is serious about its security has proved to be a powerful deterrent. Indeed, only an actor as irrational as Al Qaeda has dared to gamble with an attack against the world's strongest conventional, nuclear, economic, and political organization. . . . As this summer showed us, the reasons for NATO have not disappeared, but have in fact returned, if not with a vengeance, then certainly with a strong taste of revanche."[21]

The various "open letters" to U.S. president Barack Obama calling for greater U.S. caution concerning Russia reflect the fact that Central and Eastern European NATO Allies generally hold that only the United States can provide a credible Article 5 guarantee, including nuclear protection. Indeed, these countries would generally appreciate a U.S. guarantee "above and beyond" Article 5 of the North Atlantic Treaty.

Some officials in these countries speak of the United States as a source of security distinct from NATO. For example, Bogdan Klich, then the defense minister of Poland, said in April 2008, "It is necessary to host on our territory institutions either from the alliance, the EU or the United States. These are the three pillars of our security."[22] According to a Slovak expert, among the countries of Central and Eastern Europe, Poland and Romania are regarded as having been "upgraded to business class" owing to the U.S. military presence in these countries.[23] In August 2008, in the wake of the Russia-Georgia war, Warsaw "insisted on the inclusion of a bilateral defence commitment with the US as part of the missile defence basing agreement" it concluded with Washington.[24] Donald Tusk, the prime minister of Poland, said that his country and the United States had concluded "a 'mutual commitment'... to come to each other's assistance 'in case of trouble.'" Tusk added that NATO "would be too slow in coming to Poland's defense if threatened and that the bloc would take 'days, weeks to start that machinery.'" In Tusk's words, "Poland and the Poles do not want to be in alliances in which assistance comes at some point later— it is no good when assistance comes to dead people. Poland wants to be in alliances where assistance comes in the very first hours of—knock on wood—any possible conflict."[25]

Ragnheidur Arnadottir, an Icelandic parliamentarian, has pointed out that Tusk's statement illustrates the need for the Alliance to sustain confidence in its collective defense capabilities and commitments, lest Europe face a return to national defense postures. In her words, "if such statements indicate the disconcerting possibility of a broader lack of confidence in NATO's ability to effectively provide its fundamental benefit of collective defence, another key element of NATO's purpose will be undermined, namely preventing the re-emergence of conflicting security guarantees and purely nationally-based defence in Europe that proved disastrous in the 20th century."[26]

A July 2009 "open letter" to President Obama, signed by former presidents of the Czech Republic, Latvia, Lithuania, Poland, and Romania, and by former foreign and defense ministers and ambassadors of countries in Central and Eastern Europe, noted that NATO is

> the only credible hard power security guarantee we have.... It was a mistake not to commence with proper Article 5 defense planning for new members after NATO was enlarged. NATO needs to make the Alliance's commitments credible and provide strategic reassurance to all members. This should include contingency planning, prepositioning of forces, equipment, and supplies for reinforcement in our region in case of crisis as originally envisioned in the NATO-Russia Founding Act.[27]

In the 1997 Founding Act, the Allies endorsed the following statement: "NATO reiterates that in the current and foreseeable security environment, the Alliance will carry out its collective defence and other missions by ensuring the necessary interoperability, integration, and capability for reinforcement rather than by additional permanent stationing of substantial combat forces. Accordingly, it will have to rely on adequate infrastructure commensurate with the above tasks."[28]

Critics charge, however, that the Allies subsequently failed to develop the necessary infrastructure or the "capability for reinforcement" suitable for defending the newest members of the Alliance in Central and Eastern Europe.

Ronald Asmus, who was the U.S. deputy assistant secretary of state for European Affairs in 1997–2000, during NATO's first round of post–Cold War enlargement, deplored in 2009 the Alliance's

> poor handling of our commitment to defend Central and Eastern Europe countries under Article 5 of the NATO Treaty. Given the low-threat environment, we decided NATO did not need to station troops in those countries' territory and pledged instead to create a reinforcement capability that could be used in times of crisis. I sat at the table in the mid-1990s as Washington promised Polish leaders that NATO would have a corps-size reinforcement capability to provide for their security. But that NATO corps-size reinforcement capability never material-

ized. There are not even official defense plans for these countries. The power of Article 5 was always the fact that these commitments were backed up by planning, exercises and boots on the ground. Yet a lack of leadership and divisions within NATO prevented the alliance from fulfilling such pledges.[29]

According to Asmus and several European coauthors,

> The US pledged—with NATO's highest military commander, SACEUR, at the table—to dedicate two to three divisions (20,000–40,000 soldiers) to the task, and to upgrade or build airfields, bridges, gas depots and other military infrastructure needed to receive and host such forces in the acceding countries.... But the alliance has failed to follow through on its pledges and no such dedicated forces were built or exist today.[30]

Some important steps have, however, been taken. The Allies have in recent years—particularly since the Russia-Georgia conflict in August 2008—recognized the need for contingency planning and collective defense preparations for all members of the Alliance. In late 2008 the *Economist* reported that General John Craddock, then serving as SACEUR, was engaged on his own authority in "prudent planning" about the security of the newer NATO Allies.[31] In February 2009 Poland publicly called for the updating or composition of contingency plans for the defense of all Allies.[32] In April 2009 President Obama stated that "we must work together as NATO members so that we have contingency plans in place to deal with new threats, wherever they may come from."[33] The Baltic states took the lead in arguing for the commitment in the April 2009 Strasbourg/Kehl Summit Declaration to "adequate planning, exercises and training" in support of collective defense.[34]

It was not until December 2009, however, that the NATO Allies reportedly agreed to prepare contingency plans for the defense of the Baltic states.[35] According to Mark Kramer of Harvard University, it was at that time that the Allies endorsed a proposal to revise a long-standing contingency plan for the defense of Poland to encompass the three Baltic states—Estonia, Latvia, and Lithuania.[36] These Baltic Allies had sought such contingency planning for their defense since they joined the Alliance in 2004, but such planning had reportedly been resisted by some Western European allies, notably Germany.[37] According to some published sources, however, in late 2009 the German government suggested that the contingency plan for the defense of Poland be revised to encompass the defense of the Baltic states. Berlin's motive was reportedly to provide assurance to the Baltic states, so that they would accept efforts to promote closer NATO-Russia cooperation.[38]

When news of this contingency planning was made public in December 2010, Jaak Aaviksoo, then the Estonian minister of defense, said that "neither NATO nor Estonia consider Russia to be an enemy. However, we must have plans in order to combat the risks, and NATO is working on such plans."[39] Anders Fogh Rasmussen, NATO's secretary general, had said, "We have all necessary plans in place to defend and protect all allies. I think the Russians would be surprised if we didn't. That's the core purpose of the alliance."[40]

Indeed, in December 2010, the Russians indicated that they were not surprised. Dmitriy Rogozin, then Russia's permanent representative to NATO, said, "We have known about this plan for quite a long time."[41] Colonel-General Leonid Ivashov, the head of the Russian Academy for Geopolitical Problems, put the press reports of NATO contingency planning in perspective. "'What else have you expected? . . . Had NATO had no such plans, it would have been disbanded long ago,' said Ivashov, stressing that Russia had its own defensive concepts and contingency action plans."[42]

The Alliance's decisions about how to conduct exercises, planning, force development, and infrastructure upgrading in support of collective defense and assurance to specific Allies will be influenced by judgments about Russia's policies and prospects, among other factors. In the Deterrence and Defense Posture Review (DDPR) made public in May 2012, the Allies pointed out that "while the threat of conventional attack against NATO is low, the conventional threat cannot be ignored."[43]

Some Allied observers saw articulating this judgment as a recognition of the concerns of NATO's Central and Eastern European Allies. An Estonian expert said, "We fought for the half sentence in the DDPR that reads that 'the conventional threat cannot be ignored.'"[44]

As the Allies noted in the DDPR, conventional forces "contribute to providing visible assurance of NATO's cohesion as well as the Alliance's ability and commitment to respond to the security concerns of each and every Ally."[45] The Central and Eastern European Allies have shown considerable interest in "visible assurances" from the Alliance as a whole. Visible assurances include NATO sustaining its Baltic air policing mission, maintaining and enhancing its institutions on the soil of Central and Eastern European Allies, conducting reinforcement exercises, and improving the military infrastructure to support reinforcements in the event of aggression.[46] In April 2012 the ministers of defense and foreign affairs of the Czech Republic, Hungary, Poland, and Slovakia issued a declaration:

> We strongly support conducting exercises based on Article 5 scenarios, including live exercises of the NATO Response Force on our territories. In this respect, we urge Exercise Steadfast Jazz 2013 to be conducted as a live exercise. We encourage Allies to actively engage in this exercise. On our part, we reaffirm our determination to provide robust force contributions to this exercise, as well as to other multinational military exercises in the region, covering, among other things, military police activities, logistics and engineering.[47]

It is noteworthy that these NATO nations urged their fellow Allies to agree that this projected exercise be held as "a live exercise"—as opposed to a "command post" or "tabletop" exercise not involving actual force movements—and to "actively engage" in the exercise. However, few Allies outside Central and Eastern Europe are expected to make substantial contributions to Steadfast Jazz 2013. According to the *Economist*, "as many as 70% of the forces taking part will be provided by Poland, its partners from the Visegrad group (the Czech Republic, Slovakia and Hungary) and the Baltics."[48] Edward Lucas has referred to "significant contributions from some countries elsewhere in NATO (such as France) . . . [and] lamentably small ones from others (e.g. Germany)."[49] According to a Polish commentator, "not all the NATO countries are eager to take part," to some extent owing to "financial reasons," and to some extent "out of a fear of Russia's reaction."[50] A NATO spokesperson pointed out that the starting point for such exercises "is always a fictional scenario involving a fictional opposing force from a fictional country.... Steadfast Jazz 2013 is not directed against any particular country, any more than its 17 predecessors were."[51]

The differing reactions to Steadfast Jazz 2013 illustrate divisions among the Allies about collective defense that have emerged in recent years. In 2010 Pal Jonson, a Swedish scholar, identified three groups. The first consists of the "collective defenders," who champion efforts to reinforce the credibility of the Article 5 commitment—the Baltic states, the Czech Republic, Iceland, Norway,[52] Poland, and Slovakia. The second comprises the "expeditionaries," who emphasize force transformation, power projection, and crisis management operations—Canada, Denmark, the Netherlands, the United Kingdom, and the United States. The third is composed of "Russia firsters," who prize the cultivation of better relations with Moscow and are exceptionally sensitive to Russian perceptions of NATO's behavior—Belgium, France, Germany, Italy, Portugal and Spain.[53]

As Jonson pointed out, this categorization is "an issue of degrees rather than any major principled disagreement about the fact that Article 5 is the bedrock of the Alliance." For example, Germany, widely regarded as the Ally "most receptive within NATO to Russian reactions," has contributed substantially to the Alliance's air policing operation for the Baltic states and has participated in naval exercises with them.[54] The United Kingdom, which has been among the Allies "most reluctant to support the continuation of NATO's air policing mission over the Baltic states,"[55] proposed in February 2009 that the Allies establish a small high-readiness Allied Solidarity Force dedicated to collective defense. John Hutton, then the British secretary of state for defense, said that the purpose of the force would be to reassure the Eastern European Allies, especially the Baltic states, about the credibility of the Article 5 commitment and thus encourage them to make greater contributions to the NATO-led operations in Afghanistan.[56]

The fact that Hutton offered this rationale demonstrates that, even with regard to collective defense, tensions are visible among the priorities pursued by the Allies. For some Allies, crisis management operations are the top objective, and for others, cooperative security and partnership with non-NATO countries, particularly Russia. Jonson summed up the competition among priorities as follows: "The quest for strengthening Article 5 is carefully weighed by the reluctant Allies against any possible opportunity costs that it could generate for ongoing or future crisis response operations, and what unintended consequences it could have for NATO's relations with Russia."[57]

NATO's Broader Security Environment

During the Cold War, the Soviet Union and its Warsaw Pact allies stood out as the Alliance's main collective defense preoccupation. The final years of the Soviet Union—1990–1991—coincided with events that reminded the NATO Allies that the Alliance's founders were prudent in not specifying any particular adversary in the North Atlantic Treaty.

Iraq's invasion and occupation of Kuwait in August 1990 triggered the formation of a UN Security Council–authorized coalition to liberate the country. The NATO Allies prepared in 1990–1991 for a potential collective defense contingency—the possibility of an Iraqi attack on Turkey—by deploying NATO Airborne Early Warning (NAEW) aircraft to Turkey to monitor events as well as Allied Command Europe Mobile Force (Air) and air defense capabilities. In the event, there was no Iraqi attack against Turkey, but these precautionary measures constituted the Alliance's first operations in history.[58] The Allies undertook similar precautionary operations in February–April 2003, deploying NAEW aircraft and air defense batteries to Turkey as a hedge against possible Iraqi aggression, which once again did not occur.[59]

Both of the above crises involved discord among the Allies. In the first case, Germany in particular showed hesitancy about taking action to honor its Article 5 obligation to Turkey. Some prominent German politicians questioned whether Germany's NATO commitment would apply in the event of Iraqi aggression against Turkey, because the possible Iraqi attack would be provoked by U.S. operations against Iraq from bases in Turkey. In retrospect, German scholars Karl Kaiser and Klaus Becher concluded, the debate and delay in deploying capabilities to Turkey affected "Germany's credibility as a NATO ally."[60] This appears to have been the case in Ankara in particular.

In the second case, Belgium, France, and Germany resisted the plans of a U.S.-led coalition to intervene in Iraq by opposing proposed precautionary measures, including some in defense of Turkey, under NATO auspices. In their view, these measures were unnecessary and would politically facilitate the intervention by endorsing what the Belgian foreign minister, Louis Michel, called "the logic of war."[61] The stalemate was resolved when Belgium and Germany decided in February 2003 to accept a scaled-back package of precautionary measures in NATO's Defense Planning Committee, a group from which France had withdrawn in 1966. As Philip Gordon and Jeremy Shapiro observed, "No matter how much the French, Germans, and Belgians insisted that their solidarity with Turkey was complete, the way events transpired left an impression of allies unwilling to stand together in a time of need."[62] In the event, the precautionary measures were taken, but with some damage to the credibility of the Alliance and specific Allies, not least in Ankara.

The Syrian crisis since 2011 has led the Allies to again take precautionary measures in defense of Turkey. At Ankara's request, the Allies held security consultations under Article 4 of the North Atlantic Treaty after Syria shot down a Turkish jet, killing the two crew members, in June 2012, and after Syria killed five Turkish civilians in Akçakale, Turkey, with artillery shells in October 2012. In November–December 2012, Alliance deliberations led to decisions to reinforce Turkish air defenses. The United States sent two Patriot missile batteries and four hundred military personnel to operate and support them. Germany and the Netherlands each sent two Patriot missile batteries and approximately the same number of personnel. The six Patriot units have been operational and under the command of SACEUR since February 2013.[63]

The Alliance's objectives include reassuring Turkey by being prepared to counter Syrian air or missile attacks and deterring Syria from undertaking any such attacks against Turkey. In the words of NATO secretary general Rasmussen, "To the Turkish people we say, 'We are determined to defend you and your territory.' To anyone who would want to attack Turkey we say, 'Don't even think about it.'"[64] As the Dutch defense minister said, "NATO does not exist for nothing."[65]

In December 2012 the foreign ministers of the NATO Allies referred to a third objective: to "contribute to the de-escalation of the crisis along the Alliance's border." In welcoming the commitment of Patriot missile batteries by Germany, the Netherlands, and the United States, the foreign ministers stipulated that "any deployment will be defensive only. It will in no way support a no-fly zone or any offensive operation."[66]

These stipulations reflect the caution of the Allies about deeper military involvement in the Syrian civil war. As experts have pointed out, however, the Allies could, with a change in policy, choose to employ the Patriot missile batteries to help establish a no-fly zone and/or to provide cover for other operations.[67]

As with the 1990–1991 Gulf War, it was also in the early 1990s, in conjunction with the end of the Cold War, that the Allies began to draw a distinction between the territory of the former Cold War antagonists in Europe (plus the neutral and nonaligned states of Europe) and the rest of the world. As discussed in chapter 1, the Allies have since the mid-1990s defined the "Euro-Atlantic area" as the territory of the participating states of the OSCE, including Russia and all the other Soviet successor states.

The Allies referred to the political and territorial delimitation specified by the term "Euro-Atlantic area" at various points in the 2010 Strategic Concept—for instance, in their assertion that "today, the Euro-Atlantic area is at peace and the threat of a conventional attack against NATO territory is low."[68] The statement that "the proliferation of ballistic missiles . . . poses a real and growing threat to the Euro-Atlantic area" implicitly suggested that Russia should cooperate with NATO's missile defense efforts.[69]

The Allies also employed the "Euro-Atlantic area" formula in the May 2012 DDPR, notably with regard to missile threats arising "from outside the Euro-Atlantic area" and with respect to "Russian stockpiles of non-strategic nuclear weapons stationed in the Euro-Atlantic area."[70]

The NATO Allies have differed as to whether it is advisable to refer specifically to potential threats outside the Euro-Atlantic area. In March 2008 Nicolas Sarkozy, then the president of France, said,

> Today we must all be mindful of the fact that the nuclear missiles of even distant powers can reach Europe in less than half an hour. Currently only the great powers have such means. But

other countries, in Asia and the Middle East, are vigorously developing ballistic capabilities. I am thinking in particular of Iran. Iran is increasing the range of its missiles, while grave suspicions surround its nuclear program. It is indeed Europe's security that is at stake.[71]

In November 2010, at NATO's Lisbon Summit, President Sarkozy said, "No name appears in NATO's public documents, but France calls a cat a cat, and today's missile threat is Iran."[72]

At an international conference at the NATO Defense College in June 2012, a Turkish participant expressed reservations about the insistence of "some Allies . . . to call a cat a cat." In his view, there was no need "to give the cat a name." He said,

> to put it bluntly, being the only Ally that shares a border with Iran—and this border was delineated in 1639 and hasn't changed since then—Turkey does not see Iran as a threat. . . . Iran hasn't threatened NATO. It is not realistic to expect Iran to initiate hostilities with NATO either. . . . This does not mean we are imprudent or oblivious to developments. We continue to closely follow the developments regarding the Iranian nuclear program. We have undersigned the Chicago Summit Declaration, which devotes a paragraph to the shared concerns of the international community on Iran. But, we don't think that the right way to address these concerns is to label Iran as a threat and turn it into . . . a self-fulfilling prophecy.

From a Turkish viewpoint, he added, there was no need for the Alliance to name the objects of its deterrence policies, which were addressed "to whom it may concern." The Alliance should develop core capabilities suitable for certain types of contingencies. The Allies should seek missile defenses, for example, against the threat of the proliferation of ballistic missiles, not against Iran. A French participant replied that Allies can "pretend that a cat is not a cat or pretend not to see the cat—or that it is a dog—but it may be like a Cheshire cat." In not naming potential adversaries, he added, the Alliance ran "a risk of miscalculation" and vulnerability to "a bear, a snake, a scorpion," or some other threat. "If NATO cannot use the words used by the IAEA and the UN Security Council in public documents, what does this say about NATO as a security organization?" A Turkish participant replied that "NATO has a security role distinct from the roles of the IAEA and the UN Security Council. There is no need for NATO to mention names in order to be watchful and prudent."[73]

As the above exchange suggests, sharp disagreements persist among the Allies about whether and how to refer to potential collective defense threats outside the Euro-Atlantic area. Some Allies that are reluctant to discuss Iranian issues, even behind closed doors in the North Atlantic Council, argue that doing so might "prejudge action" and create a presumption of possible military engagement, and that it would be wiser for the Alliance to defer to the P-5 + 1—that is, the group of states consisting of the five permanent members of the UN Security Council plus Germany—regarding Iran's nuclear program and related activities.[74]

In their collective agreed-on statements, the Allies have been able to reach a consensus by making reference to "generic" threats instead of specifying potential adversaries by name—referring, for example, to the proliferation of missiles and WMD rather than to Iran or other specific proliferants. In the 2010 Strategic Concept, owing to the reservations of some Allies about specificity, the Allies even avoided phrases such as "the Middle East" and preferred more general formulas—for instance, "During the next decade, proliferation will be most acute in some of the world's most volatile regions."[75]

The references in NATO's May 2012 DDPR to the "broader security environment" are nonetheless meant to encompass potential adversaries outside the Euro-Atlantic area—e.g., non-Russian threats that might arise in the Middle East or Asia.[76] Since the end of the Cold War, the NATO Allies have taken an increasingly global view of security challenges, and they should not—indeed, cannot—be confined to a regional box. NATO's operations, partnership activities, and threat assessments have increasingly extended beyond Europe to Africa, the Middle East, and Asia, notably with reference to Afghanistan and the Persian Gulf.

Nontraditional Security Challenges

The Allies showed foresight in the 1991 Strategic Concept's discussion of collective defense by looking beyond the traditional threat of state aggression, a military attack on a NATO member by a foreign government.

> Any armed attack on the territory of the Allies, from whatever direction, would be covered by Articles 5 and 6 of the Washington Treaty. However, Alliance security must also take account of the global context. Alliance security interests can be affected by other risks of a wider nature, including proliferation of weapons of mass destruction, disruption of the flow of vital resources and actions of terrorism and sabotage. Arrangements exist within the Alliance for consultation among the Allies under Article 4 of the Washington Treaty and, where appropriate, coordination of their efforts including their responses to such risks.[77]

The discussion of such nontraditional security challenges in the 1999 Strategic Concept was similar, except that its reference to "other risks of a wider nature" encompassed "acts of terrorism, sabotage and organised crime, and . . . the disruption of the flow of vital resources."[78] The term "vital resources" has usually been construed to mean energy supplies—oil and natural gas. The 1999 Strategic Concept discussed WMD proliferation much more extensively than did the 1991 Strategic Concept. The increased attention to this source of danger was consistent with the rising prominence of this threat and other nontraditional security challenges.

In the 2010 Strategic Concept the Allies listed an even wider array of nontraditional risks and threats, including cyber attacks; WMD and missile proliferation; the vulnerability of energy supplies and transit routes; new technologies affecting military operations; "extremism, terrorism, and trans-national illegal activities such as trafficking in arms, narcotics and people"; and "environmental and resource constraints, including health risks, climate change, water scarcity and increasing energy needs."[79] In all of these areas the Allies are still refining and adapting their policies; and some of these policies may have implications for traditional concepts of collective defense in the sense of an "armed attack" against a member state. Climate change and environmental security may become increasingly significant challenges for the Alliance.[80]

Cyber Security

The vulnerability of communications and information systems raises the threat that an adversary could achieve strategic effects without undertaking overt military aggression. In October 2008, Robert Gates, then the U.S. secretary of defense, stated,

> As we know from recent experience, attacks on our communications systems and infrastructure will be a part of future war. Our policy goal is obviously to prevent anyone from being able to take down our systems. Deterrence here might entail figuring out how to make our systems redundant, as with the old Nuclear Triad. Imagine easily deployable, replacement satellites that could be launched from high-altitude planes—or high-altitude UAVs [unmanned aerial vehicles] that could operate as mobile data links. The point is to make the effort to attack us seem pointless in the first place. Similarly, future administrations will have to consider new declaratory policies about what level of cyber-attack might be considered an act of war—and what type of military response is appropriate.[81]

The difficulty identified by Secretary Gates has remained, notably with regard to defining suitable responses to cyber attacks, but the United States has in recent years clarified "what level of cyber-attack might be considered an act of war" or "use of force" that would justify an armed response. In September 2012, Harold Koh, then the legal adviser at the State Department, said,

> *Cyber activities that proximately result in death, injury, or significant destruction would likely be viewed as a use of force.* . . . Commonly cited examples of cyber activity that would constitute a use of force include, for example: (1) operations that trigger a nuclear plant meltdown; (2) operations that open a dam above a populated area causing destruction; or (3) operations that disable air traffic control resulting in airplane crashes. . . . If the physical consequences of a cyber attack work the kind of physical damage that dropping a bomb or firing a missile would, that cyber attack should equally be considered a use of force.[82]

It has become clear since the late 1990s that most civilian critical infrastructures—for transport, energy, water, financial transactions, and so forth—are vulnerable to many types of cyber attacks. The attackers could be foreign governments or nonstate adversaries, such as terrorists or other extremists.

The Allies noted in the 1999 Strategic Concept that "state and non-state adversaries may try to exploit the Alliance's growing reliance on information systems through information operations designed to disrupt such systems."[83] The Alliance in fact "faced its first serious incidents of cyber-attacks" during the 1999 Kosovo conflict. The effects of these attacks included "the Alliance's e-mail account being blocked for several days for external visitors, and repeated disruption of NATO's website."[84]

The Allies expressed an intention to "strengthen . . . capabilities to defend against cyber attacks" in the 2002 Prague Summit Declaration, and articulated more detailed policies in this regard at the summits in Bucharest in 2008 and Strasbourg/Kehl in 2009.[85] The Alliance has, moreover, established institutions to deal with the cyber defense challenge.[86] The challenge is grave because, as the U.S. Department of Defense noted in February 2010, "In the 21st century, modern armed forces simply cannot conduct high-tempo, effective operations without resilient, reliable information and communication networks and assured access to cyberspace. . . . Moreover, the speed of cyber attacks and the anonymity of cyberspace greatly favor the offense.

This advantage is growing as hacker tools become cheaper and easier to employ by adversaries whose skills are growing in sophistication."[87]

Greg Rattray, Chris Evans, and Jason Healey, all with Delta Risk Consulting, have argued that responsibility for cyber attacks can in some cases be reliably assigned to states: "Determining responsibility re-establishes some state-to-state symmetry and enables deterrence, as well as a wider range of options open to sovereign nations: diplomatic, intelligence, military and/or economic responses."[88] In their view, in the case of the attacks against Estonia in 2007, "All signs pointed to Russian involvement."[89]

In this very case, however, the Estonian government concluded that it could not prove the Russian government's participation in the cyber assault, and Tallinn therefore never accused the Russian state. As an Estonian expert said at a NATO conference in Tallinn in 2011, "When Estonia was attacked in 2007, national leaders asked, 'Who is attacking?' The honest answer was, 'We don't know. We don't have a proof, and we can't identify any single party.' Estonia is still analyzing the data from the 2007 attacks."[90] Relying on proxies enables attackers to enjoy "deniability."[91]

The Allies highlighted the importance of cyber capabilities in the 2010 Strategic Concept and the Lisbon Summit Declaration. According to the latter document,

> Cyber threats are rapidly increasing and evolving in sophistication. In order to ensure NATO's permanent and unfettered access to cyberspace and integrity of its critical systems, we will take into account the cyber dimension of modern conflicts in NATO's doctrine and improve its capabilities to detect, assess, prevent, defend and recover in case of a cyber attack against systems of critical importance to the Alliance.[92]

It is clear in the abstract that resiliency and robustness in cyber assets could help to convince an adversary that an attack would probably be defeated (thereby contributing to deterrence by denial) and could protect the Alliance's means of retaliation (thereby reinforcing deterrence by threat of punishment). The Allies have yet, however, to determine whether much should be said publicly about these capabilities with a view to enhancing deterrence. Nor have the Allies yet solved the most difficult challenge in cyber defense and deterrence: identifying attackers in a timely and precise manner. In the cyber domain, experts hold, deterrence hinges not only on attribution capabilities but also on "opponent perception" of those capabilities and "probable punitive consequences."[93]

The Allies have evidently agreed to deliberately not specify the type or level of damage from a cyber assault that would provoke a forceful reply. In the 2010 Strategic Concept they noted that cyber attacks "can reach a threshold that threatens national and Euro-Atlantic prosperity, security and stability," notably by disabling "critical infrastructure,"[94] but the Allies have chosen not to publicly inform adversaries how NATO defines that threshold. Providing such a definition might undermine deterrence and invite attacks below the threshold.

In the 2010 Strategic Concept the Allies also stated that "NATO will deter and defend against any threat of aggression, and against emerging security challenges where they threaten the fundamental security of individual Allies or the Alliance as a whole."[95] Cyber attacks could today cause a "fundamental security" level of damage, owing to the high levels of reliance on vulnerable information networks in NATO nations.[96]

Cyber attacks against critical infrastructure could do more than disrupt economic, financial, and social activities. Compromising air traffic control could, for example, quickly result in hundreds of deaths. The cumulative effect of cyber attacks on other vulnerable assets—such as power grids, financial systems, and communications networks—could be enormous, effectively paralyzing governments, economies, and societies. As U.S. secretary of defense Leon Panetta observed in October 2012, "foreign cyber actors are probing America's critical infrastructure networks. They are targeting the computer control systems that operate chemical, electricity and water plants and those that guide transportation throughout this country."[97]

Panetta's use of the term "foreign cyber actors" made clear that nonstate organizations as well as governments could pose cyber threats. Panetta referred to "violent extremist groups," and said that "a destructive cyber-terrorist attack could virtually paralyze the nation." With regard to states, Panetta said, "It's no secret that Russia and China have advanced cyber capabilities. Iran has also undertaken a concerted effort to use cyberspace to its advantage."[98]

The Allied response to cyber attacks might well be proportional, but it would almost certainly not be confined to the cyber domain. In a sign of the growing importance of cyber-security issues, the Allies in November 2012 conducted a cyber-defense exercise called Cyber Coalition 12 concurrently with NATO's annual Crisis Management Exercise (CMX 12). The exercise scenario was modeled in part on the cyber attacks against Estonia in 2007 but involved a broader context. It posited large cyber attacks against national and Alliance critical infrastructures, including cyber assaults causing the collapse of banking and air traffic control systems. The enemy also employed biological, chemical, and radiological weapons. This was the first exercise in which the Allies discussed the possible invocation of Article 5 in the framework of a cyber attack.[99]

The Allies have yet to determine how they could collectively deter, prevent, or respond to cyber attacks. Effectiveness in such an endeavor might be hindered by the broad spectrum of cyber capabilities among the Allies. Their capacity to contribute differs substantially. The larger Allies, the United States in particular, would probably not seek technical or physical assistance from NATO in response to a major cyber attack but from their closest partners in the cyber domain. The same principle would probably apply to intelligence sharing and help with attribution. In some cases, NATO's role in the face of "strategic" cyber attacks on a member state might be less about specifically cyber assistance than broader political-military solidarity.

The Allies have yet to agree on what types and levels of damage from cyber attacks would provoke a collective response. A related issue is whether the Allies would regard a crisis precipitated by a member state's lack of fundamental cyber defense capabilities as an Article 5 case. In June 2013, the NATO secretary general pointed out that the Alliance in 2012 had to deal with "over 2,500 'significant cases' of cyber attacks on its systems,"[100] but evidently none of these "significant cases" provoked a crisis or justified a forceful response.

Some Allies, such as Britain, France, Germany, and the United States, regard cyber security as essentially a national responsibility, and have reportedly been "reluctant to divert money to NATO activities" in the cyber domain.[101] Philippe Errera, France's permanent representative to NATO, said in January 2013 that in France's view it is not NATO's role to take over national responsibilities in acquiring and maintaining capabilities, and this is "particularly true in certain domains such as cyber defense, in which we consider that NATO has no role to play in the protection of national networks."[102] The Allies have nonetheless agreed to protect the Alliance's own cyber networks. NATO defense ministers agreed in June 2013, at "their first-ever meeting dedicated to cyber defence," that "the Alliance's cyber-defence capability should be fully operational by the autumn, extending protection to all the networks owned and operated by the Alliance."[103]

According to a policy adopted in 2011, NATO is committed to aid member states requesting assistance in responding to a cyber attack,[104] but the scope and level of that assistance have not yet been defined by the Allies. With a view to deterrence as well as flexibility, the Allies have not committed themselves to a particular type of response to cyber attacks. "NATO will maintain strategic ambiguity as well as flexibility on how to respond to different types of crises that include a cyber component."[105] As Harold Koh noted in 2012, "There is no legal requirement that the response to a cyber armed attack take the form of a cyber action, as long as the response meets the requirements of necessity and proportionality."[106]

The NATO Allies have initiated cooperation with partner nations and the European Union about cyber defense, and they will probably need to deepen their interactions with industry in order to meet the cyber challenge successfully.

Space Operations

Robert Gates's reference in 2008 to developing redundant communications systems—including the option of launching "easily deployable, replacement satellites"—as a hedge against cyber attacks underscores the close linkages between cyber defense and space operations. As Michèle Flournoy and Shawn Brimley have noted, cyberspace and outer space, together with the sea and the atmosphere, constitute "the global commons, those areas of the world beyond the control of any one state." From a U.S. national security perspective, they added, "stability and security in space and cyberspace will depend on working with our allies and partners to develop a common framework and advance international norms that can shape the choices and behavior of others."[107]

The armed forces of the NATO Allies depend heavily on national space capabilities in expeditionary and other operations for command, control, communications, and intelligence (C3I), as well as for navigation, guidance, surveillance, and other functions. Owing to the increasing reliance of the Allies on such capabilities, Thomas Single argued in 2009, "it is time to break the paradigm that Space capabilities are veiled in secrecy, are strategic in nature only or are too politically sensitive to discuss in an Alliance forum."[108] If the NATO Allies do not determine their requirements collectively, Single wrote, they "will continue to duplicate efforts, field systems that are not interoperable, and retain stove-piped intelligence networks. . . . There is an urgent need for NATO to state the intended Alliance use of Space capabilities."[109]

In the 2010 Strategic Concept the Allies noted that "a number of significant technology-related trends—including the development of laser weapons, electronic warfare and technologies that impede access to space—appear poised to have major global effects that will impact on NATO military planning and operations."[110] How the Allies might deter—and defend against—an adversary's use of such capabilities raises fundamental questions. The Allies evidently agree on the importance of assured "access to space," but they have yet to reach a consensus on the means, diplomatic and/or military, to achieve that goal.

The United States took an important step forward in this respect in 2011 with the first National Security Space Strategy.[111] As Gregory Schulte, then the U.S. deputy assistant secretary of defense for space policy, pointed out in May 2012, "In the past, space was a domain in which the United States operated largely alone or with only a few Allies. Under the new strategy, we plan to operate increasingly in coalitions, as we do routinely in other domains."[112] U.S. experts have argued that the NATO Allies should work together to help establish standards of responsible behavior in space and improve their collective ability to conduct operations even if their space capabilities for navigation, communications, and other purposes are degraded or destroyed. Because space has become an increasingly important domain of operations for deterrence, collective defense, and other missions, the NATO Allies will have to update their doctrine, planning, training, command structure, and so forth to take space into account.[113] The U.S. Air Force Space Command asked the Alliance to participate in the 2012 Schriever Wargame concerning the spacecyber continuum, and nine NATO nations (Canada, Denmark, France, Germany, Italy, the Netherlands, Turkey, the United Kingdom, and the United States) did so, together with Australia.[114]

Differences persist among the Allies in their space policies and interpretations of international law affecting space. Except for consensus on some general principles, such as the value of assured "access to space," the NATO Allies do not have an agreed-on space policy, nor do they conduct space operations collectively. Only the larger and/or wealthier Allies participate in space operations, and this fact has hampered the development of an agreed-on Alliance policy.

Gregory Schulte observed, "With the Alliance increasingly reliant on space for its collective defense and economic prosperity, an attack on the space assets of any one Ally impacts the security of all Allies."[115] An attack that "impacts the security of all Allies" may not, however, be one that all Allies regard as an Article 5 case. As with cyber attacks, the level of damage or disruption to a member state's space capabilities through an enemy's attack that might be regarded by the Allies as "an armed attack" or "an act of war"—or, in NATO terms, an Article 5 collective defense contingency—is not self-evident, particularly if the attack causes no direct fatalities.[116]

An obstacle to achieving Allied consensus on devoting more attention to space security issues in NATO is the widespread judgment that no ally's space assets have yet come under "armed attack." Nor is it clear how such an attack should be defined in the case of space assets. Would jamming Global Positioning System (GPS) signals constitute such an attack? Would "blinding" a satellite with a laser amount to such an attack? The same lack of agreed-on definitions applies to cyber attacks. To what extent, for example, could hacking a website, destroying data, denying service, or inserting a virus constitute "an armed attack"? In contrast with space, however, a NATO ally has experienced large-scale cyber attacks—Estonia in 2007.[117]

Various actions have affected satellite functions without being widely characterized as attacks. For example, in 2003 Iraq reportedly used Russian-supplied GPS jammers against the United States; in 2006 U.S. officials revealed that China had directed a laser at a U.S. satellite and "painted" it; and since 2003 Iran has repeatedly jammed satellite communications signals from foreign broadcasters and network services. Moreover, hackers have targeted the functions of some satellites via cyberspace. According to Eric Sterner of the George C. Marshall Institute, "If threats are interpreted as a function of both intent and capability, multiple state and non-state actors have demonstrated ample intentions and capabilities to attack space systems."[118]

Because of Estonia's experience in 2007, it may be easier to gain consensus in NATO about the significance of cyber attacks than about that of assaults on space capabilities. In other words, it is harder to gain consensus when the gravity of a threat has not yet been dramatically demonstrated. NATO agreement on an enhanced cyber policy might, however, be a step toward greater consensus on space policy.

As in cyberspace, a fundamental question is whether the Alliance should specify a threshold of damage or disruption that would provoke retaliation. Some observers have argued that "greater public clarity" about the threshold of unacceptable damage or interference would be desirable because it would "reduce the opponent's uncertainty on the likelihood of a response." For deterrence purposes, an American expert argued in June 2012, it would be useful to reach an agreement on criteria for attacks that would justify forceful retaliation. Allies and adversaries would then know what sort of attack would trigger Article 5, the mutual defense commitment in the North Atlantic Treaty. It would then be more practical to pursue cross-domain deterrence.[119] The message could then be, "If you launch a cyber attack against me, I may respond with a cruise missile."[120] The same principle of cross-domain retaliation could apply to attacks against space assets.

Another American at the same NATO workshop said that, mindful of Dean Acheson's experience in 1950,[121] the U.S. government has decided not to draw red lines. Specifying such boundaries could present the risk of opening the door to certain targets or types of targets. The U.S. decision has been not to draw lines publicly and thereby to promote uncertainty in the assessments of adversary leaders. Ellen Nakashima of the *Washington Post* summed up the U.S. decision as follows: "Why tell other nations what the United States is willing to tolerate before it will respond forcefully?"[122]

At the same time, the United States has made clear its capacity to respond and to escalate in ways that adversaries cannot anticipate and discount. In May 2012, the U.S. deputy assistant secretary of defense for space policy said that "interference with U.S. space capabilities ... could prompt an asymmetric response, imposing strategic or operational costs that outweigh any tactical benefits," and "create a real risk of miscalculation and rapid escalation." As a result, an adversary's national leadership should "understand the escalation risks, the strategic consequences ... and the wisdom of restraint."[123] In other words, without specifying a threshold of unacceptable interference with U.S. space assets and operations, the United States has accepted the logic of cross-domain deterrence. The United States has "a readiness and capability to respond in self-defense, and not necessarily in space. This further complicates the calculus of a potential adversary contemplating an attack on our space assets."[124]

Energy Security

NATO's potential contributions in energy security remain largely undeveloped. As mentioned, both the 1991 and 1999 Strategic Concepts referred to a possible "disruption of the flow of vital resources" as one of the "risks of a wider nature" that could affect "Alliance security interests." The "vital resources" in question were assumed to consist largely of energy supplies, although the words "energy," "oil," and "gas" did not appear in either of these documents. Neither "energy security" nor the undefined "flow of vital resources" was mentioned in the 2002 Prague Summit Declaration, the 2004 Istanbul Summit Communiqué, or the 2005 Brussels Summit Statement.

It was not until the 2006 Riga Summit, convened after a Russian-Ukrainian gas dispute had left much of Central and Eastern Europe without normal supplies of gas for heating and other purposes, that the Allies discussed "energy security" in more detail. In doing so, they established a tradition of carefully circumscribing their intentions and calling for clarification as to "where NATO may add value," in light of efforts already undertaken under other auspices, national and international.[125]

At the 2008 Bucharest Summit, the Allies agreed on a confidential report on NATO's role in energy security and announced with respect to energy security that "NATO will engage in the following fields: information and intelligence fusion and sharing; projecting stability; advancing international and regional cooperation; supporting consequence management; and supporting the protection of critical energy infrastructure."[126] The vague goal of "projecting stability" has been linked to NATO's partnerships with non-NATO countries. Michael Rühle, the head of the Energy Security Section in NATO's Emerging Security Challenges Division, has written that "projecting stability . . . means first and foremost shaping the reform processes in NATO's broader strategic environment. The emphasis is on political dialogue and military cooperation with partner countries in Europe, the Caucasus, Central Asia, the Middle East and the Gulf region. This group comprises energy producers, transit countries and consumers."[127]

In their summit declarations in 2008, 2009, 2010, and 2012, the Allies repeated the stipulation that NATO's activities in energy security must "add value" in relation to the efforts of other international organizations.[128] Other consistent themes have included the commitment of the Allies to consultations and information sharing and the Alliance's preparedness to supplement national energy infrastructure protection efforts. In the 2010 Strategic Concept the Allies expressed an intention to "develop the capacity to contribute to energy security, including protection of critical energy infrastructure and transit areas and lines, cooperation with partners, and consultations among Allies on the basis of strategic assessments and contingency planning."[129]

The Allies have authoritatively underscored the significance of energy security. In 2009, at the Strasbourg/Kehl Summit, they noted (diplomatically avoiding any explicit reference to Russia or Ukraine) that "the disruption of the flow of natural gas in January 2009 seriously affected a number of Allies and Partner countries."[130] In the 2010 Strategic Concept the Allies observed that "some NATO countries will become more dependent on foreign energy suppliers and in some cases, on foreign energy supply and distribution networks for their energy needs. As a larger share of world consumption is transported across the globe, energy supplies are increasingly exposed to disruption."[131]

Despite their recognition of the importance of energy security,[132] the Allies have in practice approached the topic with great caution. In December 2008, Jaap de Hoop Scheffer, then the NATO secretary general, declared that "NATO Allies should regularly consult on energy trends, try to reach a common analysis of our strategic vulnerabilities, and make sure that the Alliance is prepared to play its part both in addressing those vulnerabilities and responding to more immediate crisis situations.... NATO can, and should, act as a catalyst in persuading our member countries to take a more strategic look at energy security and to develop a more collective approach."[133] In other words, despite their declared commitment to dialogue, the Allies had not yet agreed on "a common analysis of our strategic vulnerabilities" or worked out "a more collective approach."

In 2011, Michael Rühle called for making energy security "a regular discussion item in NATO's internal consultations." As Rühle pointed out, "Such an institutionalized dialogue among Allies is the precondition for considering further steps, such as, for example, discussions between the North Atlantic Council with individual partner countries or groups of partners (the so-called '28+n' formula) on energy security, or the setting up of training and defence reform teams for the protection of critical infrastructure."[134]

The European Union has not achieved much more than NATO regarding the definition of a coherent energy security policy, and for similar reasons. Member gov-

ernments in both organizations have long histories of satisfying their energy requirements on a national basis, and they regard energy security as a matter of paramount
importance for their economic well-being as well as their national security. Their national interests diverge substantially because they have differing levels of dependence
on specific external energy suppliers, including Russia, the owner of the largest coal
and gas reserves in the world. Ovidiu Dranga, the Romanian ambassador to Belgium,
pointed out in 2010 that "the EU lacks genuine political will to reach a decision
together and take common actions. . . . Unfortunately, national interests take precedence over common actions in the EU, a fact that is rooted in the fear that common
action would not provide the same benefits as individual actions."[135]

The NATO Allies have insisted on the "where NATO may add value" principle
partly because other international institutions—including the European Union, the
International Energy Agency, and the Organisation for Economic Co-operation
and Development—have significant responsibilities in this domain. Perceptions of
the Alliance as an organization for military action also hamper the development of
NATO's potential as an instrument of energy security. In Rühle's words, "While it is
obvious that energy security can have a military dimension—as is demonstrated by
NATO's current anti-piracy operations off the coast of Somalia, which also help protect oil tankers—many Allies remain concerned that too visible a NATO role might
unduly 'militarise' what was essentially an economic subject."[136]

According to Loïc Simonet, a French expert, since the 2006 Riga Summit, when
the Allies first explicitly evoked the issue of energy security, some NATO states—including France and Germany—have favored a "minimalist" approach, while others—
including the Baltic countries, Hungary, Poland, and the United States—have argued
for a more ambitious agenda.[137] The French have held that energy security is not an
appropriate task or "core business" for the Alliance, and the Germans that it could
create irritants in relations with Russia. Energy-producing Allies such as Canada and
Norway see little need for NATO involvement in energy security.[138]

Despite disagreements among the Allies, maritime security stands out as one of
the most promising areas for cooperation related to energy security and collective
defense, among other tasks.[139] It plays to NATO's strength as a political-military
organization, and it builds on decades of experience in naval affairs, including ongoing operations, such as Active Endeavour in the Mediterranean and Ocean Shield in
the Gulf of Aden. In 2008 the Allies initiated a program called Maritime Situational
Awareness that is intended, in cooperation with the Allied Maritime Command at
Northwood, England, to enhance the ability of the Allies to monitor maritime activities and counter piracy, terrorism, and various types of trafficking. Events may oblige
the Allies to take a greater interest in helping to protect the Strait of Hormuz and
other critical sea-lanes.[140]

The NATO Allies have at times linked energy security to broader ecological and
resource issues. In the 2010 Strategic Concept the Allies noted that "key environmental and resource constraints, including health risks, climate change, water scarcity

and increasing energy needs, will further shape the future security environment in areas of concern to NATO and have the potential to significantly affect NATO planning and operations."[141] The Allies repeated this statement verbatim in their 2012 Chicago Summit Declaration.[142] How the Allies will choose to address these issues remains to be seen.[143] In some cases, they may choose to work through other international organizations, such as the United Nations, or specialized bodies such as the World Health Organization or the International Energy Agency.

Terrorism

Despite the widespread impression that the Alliance only recognized the relevance of terrorist threats to Allied security in the face of the attacks against the United States in September 2001, NATO was concerned about terrorism during the Cold War. For example, in 1986, Merrill Walters, who was then NATO's director for nuclear planning, wrote that "an attack [by terrorists] on our nuclear forces could indeed have a very high public and political impact, even if unsuccessful. The nuclear sites are well known, and any event that is connected with nuclear weapons, even with the delivery system in which nuclear weapons are not involved, still raises a great deal of hysteria and concern all over the world, and in particular in NATO."[144]

In their 1991 Strategic Concept the NATO Allies described terrorism as one of several "risks of a wider nature" that they might consult about under Article 4 of the North Atlantic Treaty with a view to possible "coordination of their efforts."[145] The Allies included a similar statement in their 1999 Strategic Concept, and again implied that this was an Article 4 matter.[146] Up to that point, most terrorist threats had been regarded as tasks for the domestic law enforcement agencies of specific NATO Allies to handle. As with the statement by Merrill Walters in 1986, the Allies in 1999 expressed particular concern about terrorist threats to Alliance forces and infrastructure.[147] However, as noted in chapter 1, in the 1999 Washington Summit Communiqué the Allies stated that "terrorism constitutes a serious threat to peace, security and stability that can threaten the territorial integrity of States."[148]

The Allies had nonetheless evidently not imagined that a terrorist attack against a member state could constitute a collective defense contingency falling under Article 5 of the North Atlantic Treaty. However, the Allies invoked Article 5 the day after the terrorist attacks against the United States on September 11, 2001. It was not until October 4, 2001, that the NATO secretary general announced that

> the NATO Allies agreed today—at the request of the United States—to take eight measures, individually and collectively, to expand the options available in the campaign against terrorism. Specifically, they agreed to:
>
> - enhance intelligence sharing and co-operation, both bilaterally and in the appropriate NATO bodies, relating to the threats posed by terrorism and the actions to be taken against it;
>
> - provide, individually or collectively, as appropriate and according to their capabilities, assistance to Allies and other states which are or may be subject to increased terrorist threats as a result of their support for the campaign against terrorism;

- take necessary measures to provide increased security for facilities of the United States and other Allies on their territory;

- backfill selected Allied assets in NATO's area of responsibility that are required to directly support operations against terrorism;

- provide blanket overflight clearances for the United States and other Allies' aircraft, in accordance with the necessary air traffic arrangements and national procedures, for military flights related to operations against terrorism;

- provide access for the United States and other Allies to ports and airfields on the territory of NATO nations for operations against terrorism, including for refuelling, in accordance with national procedures.

The North Atlantic Council also agreed:

- that the Alliance is ready to deploy elements of its Standing Naval Forces to the Eastern Mediterranean in order to provide a NATO presence and demonstrate resolve; and

- that the Alliance is similarly ready to deploy elements of its NATO Airborne Early Warning force to support operations against terrorism.

Today's collective actions operationalise Article 5 of the Washington Treaty. These measures were requested by the United States following the determination that the 11 September attack was directed from abroad.[149]

The other NATO Allies were disappointed that the United States had asked for so little assistance. The first six of the eight requested measures were rather general, while the last two measures were comparatively limited.

In Operation Eagle Assist the Allies employed NATO Airborne Warning and Control System (AWACS) aircraft to patrol U.S. skies from October 2001 to May 2002. This enabled the United States to use its own AWACS aircraft in Operation Enduring Freedom in Afghanistan. The Allies decided to end Operation Eagle Assist in view of "material upgrades to the US air defence posture and enhanced cooperation between civil and military authorities, and following a recent US evaluation of homeland security requirements."[150]

While the deployment of naval forces to the eastern Mediterranean was originally intended, in October 2001, "to provide a NATO presence and demonstrate resolve," Operation Active Endeavour has become a more significant effort in multiple ways. In March 2004 the NATO Allies extended the operation's area of responsibility to the entire Mediterranean.[151] Its functions now include maritime surveillance, deterrence of terrorist activities at sea, the protection of shipping, and ad hoc support for specific events, such as security for the 2004 Olympic Games in Greece. It has also provided a vehicle for cooperation with Alliance partners, particularly countries in NATO's Mediterranean Dialogue. According to the NATO website, the Allies that have contributed naval assets have been "mainly Greece, Italy, Spain and Turkey." In accordance with an operational plan approved in January 2010, however, Operation Active Endeavour is changing "from a platform-based to a network-based operation, using a combination of on-call units and surge operations instead of deployed forces; it is also seeking to enhance cooperation with non-NATO countries and international organizations in order to improve Maritime Situational Awareness."[152] Given the short duration of Operation Eagle Assist, Operation Active Endeavour stands out as the Alliance's only continuing Article 5 operation.

Despite NATO's invocation of Article 5 in response to the terrorist attacks of September 2001, the United States did not seek any formal role for the Alliance when it organized and led a coalition against al-Qaeda and the Taliban in Afghanistan.

According to the *Economist* in October 2001, "Some Europeans are hurt. As one recent headline put it, NATO is 'all dressed up with nowhere to go.'"[153] Ambrose Evans-Pritchard, a British journalist, reported that "the chief complaint from this 'coalition of the willing' is that Washington has not yet taken up their offers of military support and has kept them in the dark about the overall plan of attack. At NATO headquarters, officials say they do not know any more about the US military operations than newspaper readers."[154] Jim Hoagland of the *Washington Post* wrote that "leaving European allies feeling underutilized, underconsulted and perhaps even underappreciated in this global struggle is an outcome that should be avoided, even in history's gallop."[155]

Two prominent U.S. senators, Richard Lugar and Joseph Biden, pointed out that "for 50 years Article 5 meant collective military action. Invoking it, but failing to back it up by collective action, especially when the allies are prepared to help, runs the risk of eviscerating this common defense pledge. It is not something the American people or our European allies will understand."[156]

Lord Robertson, then the NATO secretary general, in a February 2002 article rather defensively titled "NATO Still Matters," suggested that the explanation for the limited role of the Alliance in the operations in Afghanistan resided in the need for a broad coalition like that assembled against Iraq in 1991. "NATO did not lead the campaign against the Taliban in Afghanistan because, as in Desert Storm, a larger, more diverse coalition was needed."[157]

Robertson's argument had merit, but it disregarded three factors that appear to have contributed to the U.S. government's reluctance to give NATO a leading role in Afghanistan in the weeks and months immediately following the September 2001 terrorist attacks. The first was the widespread impression in U.S. defense leadership circles that the air campaign in the 1999 Kosovo conflict had been distorted by a NATO "war by committee" dynamic that hampered U.S. freedom of action. The second was the judgment that the power-projection capabilities of some NATO Allies were so limited that they would have little to contribute to the expeditionary operations in Afghanistan. A third factor was the widening gap between the United States and its NATO allies in the technological sophistication of their equipment, notably information systems.[158] These three factors were linked in that many U.S. political and military leaders opposed subjecting decisions to NATO consensus procedures when the United States was providing the bulk of the military effort.[159]

In January 2002, Donald Rumsfeld, then the U.S. secretary of defense, declared that "wars can benefit from coalitions of the willing, to be sure. But they should not be fought by committee. The mission must determine the coalition, and the coalition must not determine the mission. If it does, the mission will be dumbed down to the lowest common denominator, and we can't afford that."[160]

Allied observers construed Rumsfeld's statement as implying that consensus decision making in NATO would "dumb down" the strategy and conduct of operations. His statement typified the views of some influential U.S. policymakers in the wake of the 1999 Kosovo air campaign.

From the start of Operation Enduring Freedom in Afghanistan in October 2001, however, NATO Allies—though not operating under Alliance auspices—made significant contributions. Moreover, the International Security Assistance Force (ISAF) in Afghanistan was led by a series of NATO Allies—the United Kingdom, Turkey, and Germany and the Netherlands—from December 2001 to August 2003, when NATO took over leadership of the operation.

Since 2001–2003 the United States has increasingly recognized the value of NATO contributions in Afghanistan (see chapter 4). Afghanistan has become the Alliance's largest and costliest crisis management operation.

The Allies have taken several other steps since the September 2001 attacks compelled them to recognize that terrorist movements could constitute a collective defense threat.[161] At the November 2002 Prague Summit, the first after the September 2001 terrorist attacks, the Allies approved a package of innovative measures designed to enable NATO to contribute to the struggle against terrorism. The Allies declared, "In order to carry out the full range of its missions, NATO must be able to field forces that can move quickly to wherever they are needed, upon decision by the North Atlantic Council, to sustain operations over distance and time, including in an environment where they might be faced with nuclear, biological and chemical threats, and to achieve their objectives."[162]

The Prague Summit decisions included the establishment of "a NATO Response Force (NRF) consisting of a technologically advanced, flexible, deployable, interoperable and sustainable force including land, sea, and air elements ready to move quickly to wherever needed"; the streamlining of the Alliance's military command structure; the endorsement of the Prague Capabilities Commitment, a large set of force improvements to be undertaken by individual Allies; the approval of NATO's Military Concept for Defence against Terrorism; the implementation of "the Civil Emergency Planning (CEP) Action Plan for the improvement of civil preparedness against possible attacks against the civilian population with chemical, biological or radiological (CBR) agents"; the pursuit of "five nuclear, biological and chemical weapons defence initiatives, which will enhance the Alliance's defence capabilities against weapons of mass destruction"; and the launching of "a new NATO Missile Defence feasibility study to examine options for protecting Alliance territory, forces and population centres against the full range of missile threats."[163]

The NATO Allies have also undertaken several institutional adaptations since the September 2001 terrorist attacks. At the 2002 Prague Summit the Allies and their partners in the Euro-Atlantic Partnership Council launched the Partnership

Action Plan against Terrorism (PAP-T) as a framework for cooperation.[164] Since 2004 NATO's armaments community, including the two Strategic Commands (Allied Command Operations and Allied Command Transformation) and the Conference of National Armaments Directors (CNAD), has pursued a Defence Against Terrorism (DAT) Program of Work. The DAT program includes projects such as protecting helicopters from rocket-propelled grenades (RPGs); defeating improvised explosive devices (IEDs); and detecting and countering chemical, biological, radiological, and nuclear (CBRN) threats. In addition to the CNAD work against CBRN threats, the Allies have certified centers of excellence on CBRN defense (founded in Vyskov, the Czech Republic, in 2007) and defense against terrorism (inaugurated in Ankara, Turkey, in 2005). Since 2001, NATO's Euro-Atlantic Disaster Response Coordination Centre, originally established in 1998 to help coordinate relief measures for man-made as well as natural disasters, has had the additional responsibility of preparedness for terrorist attacks, including those involving CBRN weapons.[165]

The Allies established the Terrorism Threat Intelligence Unit (TTIU) in 2003. The TTIU staff (six to eight civilian and military experts) focused on the analysis of intelligence data provided by Allies and liaison with national and Allied agencies. In 2011 the Allies transformed the TTIU into an intelligence unit with about twenty staff members. Terrorism is reportedly a small facet of this body's overall intelligence assessment.[166]

Four factors have bound the extent of NATO's contribution to the struggle against international terrorism. First, prior to September 2001, despite the 1999 Washington Summit Communiqué and other declarations, the Allies did not see terrorism as a collective defense concern but as a challenge for domestic law enforcement agencies to handle. This has remained the case for most Allies in relation to subsequent terrorist attacks, including those in Madrid in 2004 and in London in 2005. From the viewpoint of most Allies, the Alliance's involvement is most pertinent in the event of a terrorist threat to NATO forces and facilities, and terrorist threats will remain a matter for possible Article 4 consultation and policy coordination unless a threat arises comparable to that in September 2001. In short, despite the fact that the Allies recognized the terrorist attacks against the United States in September 2001 as a collective defense contingency, with the invocation of Article 5, the Allies generally do not see terrorism as a major collective defense matter.

Second, significant differences have persisted among the Allies regarding terrorism. To the dismay of many European Allied observers, the United States in September 2001 took the view that the struggle against terrorism should be regarded as a war. One of the central themes of U.S. foreign and security policy during the George W. Bush administration (2001–2009) was the global war on terror, also called the global war on terrorism or the long war. The European Allies have generally avoided the U.S. "war on terror" phrase and have continued to regard terrorism as essentially a criminal matter to be addressed by the police and the judiciary. France in particular has minimized the Alliance's role in relation to national law enforcement

These factors help to explain why NATO's approach to countering terrorism has at times appeared fragmented and even incoherent. Some expert observers hold that there has been little coherence between national counterterrorism activities and those that the Alliance has promoted in technical and partnership programs.[174]

In comparison with the years immediately after the September 2001 terrorist attacks, the Allies seem to have lowered the priority of countering terrorism as a role for NATO. Their long-standing preference to rely on national capabilities has come to the fore. The Alliance can perform useful functions in countering terrorism, Allies generally agree, but these will be in support of national efforts, which most Allies will pursue with nonmilitary means. NATO's distinctive "value-added" contributions will therefore probably reside in conducting military operations, as in Afghanistan, thereby denying havens to terrorist groups; helping Allies strengthen their national defense capabilities via NATO education, training, and exercises; facilitating consultations and cooperation among the Allies; and developing collective capabilities and assessments via focused activities such as the Defense against Terrorism Program of Work and the Science for Peace and Security Program.

The counterterrorism policy guidelines published by the Allies at the May 2012 Chicago Summit show that the Allies have concluded that they could benefit from other organizational frameworks for the coordination of national activities. According to these guidelines,

> In defining NATO's overarching approach to terrorism, Allies recognise that most counter terrorism tools remain primarily with national civilian and judicial authorities. Allies acknowledge that other International Organisations have mandates and capabilities that could enhance Allies' efforts to counter terrorism. NATO will place particular emphasis on preventing terrorist attacks and enhancing resilience through contributing to national and international efforts while avoiding unnecessary duplication and respecting the principles of complementarity.[175]

The document emphasizes that "individual NATO members have primary responsibility for the protection of their populations and territories against terrorism. . . . NATO, upon request, may support these efforts."[176]

Without the Action Plan for Implementation process for these guidelines endorsed at the Chicago Summit,[177] some Brussels observers hold, NATO's residual roles regarding terrorism "would be allowed to just shrivel."[178]

WMD Proliferation

It was not until after the outbreak of the August 1990–February 1991 Gulf War—the Iraqi occupation of Kuwait and the operations under the authority of the UN Security Council to expel the Iraqi forces—that the Alliance began to identify countering the spread of WMD as one of the main challenges in the post–Cold War world. The subject was not even mentioned in the Alliance's July 1990 London Declaration. In December 1990, however, the North Atlantic Council noted that "the proliferation of weapons of mass destruction and the spread of destabilizing military technology have implications for Allies' security and illustrate that in an ever more interdependent world, we face new security risks and challenges of a global nature. . . . Where they pose a threat to our common interests we will consider what individual or joint action may be most appropriate under the circumstances."[179]

By June 1991, the UN Special Commission and the International Atomic Energy Agency and other organizations had made a number of unanticipated discoveries about the magnitude and progress of Iraqi programs to build chemical, biological, and nuclear weapons. The Allies noted the dangers of WMD proliferation identified in the wake of the Gulf War, but saw no need at that time for Alliance action. Instead, the Allies restated their "commitment to the earliest possible achievement of advances in the international forums dealing with specific proliferation issues," such as efforts to conclude a Chemical Weapons Convention and strengthen the Biological and Toxin Weapons Convention.[180] Similarly, the November 1991 Rome Declaration did not call for any specific Alliance initiative and repeated support for international arms control regimes.[181] In contrast, the November 1991 Strategic Concept referred to WMD proliferation as a risk for "Alliance security interests" and drew attention to the need for "missile defenses" in light of "the proliferation of ballistic missiles and weapons of mass destruction" and for "precautions of a purely defensive nature" against chemical weapons, "even after implementation of a global ban."[182]

It was not until the January 1994 summit that the Alliance "decided to intensify and expand NATO's political and defence efforts against proliferation, taking into account the work already underway in other international fora and institutions." The Allies directed "that work begin immediately . . . to develop an overall policy framework to consider how to reinforce ongoing prevention efforts and how to reduce the proliferation threat and protect against it."[183] The Alliance established a Joint Committee on Proliferation, composed of a Senior Political-Military Group on Proliferation and a Senior Defense Group on Proliferation (DGP). The Joint Committee on Proliferation was noteworthy, among other reasons, because France participated fully. The DGP was cochaired by the United States and, on a rotating basis, a European ally; France served as the first European cochair. In June 1996 the North Atlantic Council endorsed recommendations by the DGP "to improve Alliance military capabilities to address the risks posed by NBC [nuclear, biological, and chemical weapons] proliferation."[184] The Allies replaced these committees in 2010 with a single Committee on Proliferation, which works in two formats: a politico-military format for foreign ministry representatives and a defense format for defense ministry officials.[185]

The Allies pointed out in the 1999 Strategic Concept that WMD proliferation "can pose a direct military threat to the Allies' populations, territory, and forces."[186] In the same document the Allies stated that "the Alliance will enhance its political efforts to reduce dangers arising from the proliferation of weapons of mass destruction and their means of delivery." The Allies added, "By deterring the use of NBC weapons," NATO's forces "contribute to Alliance efforts aimed at preventing the proliferation of these weapons and their delivery means."[187]

The main institutional consequence of the Alliance's 1999 WMD Initiative was the establishment the following year of the WMD Centre at NATO headquarters. Ted Whiteside, the first head of the WMD Centre, described it in 2003 as "a small group of 10 people" striving to meet three objectives: "To improve intelligence and information-sharing about proliferation issues. Second, to assist Allies in enhancing the military capabilities to work in a WMD environment and third, to discuss and bring the Alliance's support to non-proliferation efforts in the world, generally."[188] To clarify the WMD Centre's function, the Allies renamed it the WMD Non-Proliferation Centre in 2010.

The Allies stated in the 2010 Strategic Concept that "the proliferation of nuclear weapons and other weapons of mass destruction, and their means of delivery, threatens incalculable consequences for global stability and prosperity. During the next decade, proliferation will be most acute in some of the world's most volatile regions."[189]

The Allies also drew attention to the potential nexus between terrorism and WMD proliferation: "Extremist groups continue to spread to, and in, areas of strategic importance to the Alliance, and modern technology increases the threat and potential impact of terrorist attacks, in particular if terrorists were to acquire nuclear, chemical, biological or radiological capabilities."[190] In the 2010 Lisbon Summit Declaration, the Allies called for "full implementation of UNSCR 1540,"[191] the April 2004 resolution establishing obligations for states to strengthen their legislation against WMD proliferation, with a view to preventing the spread of WMD to nonstate actors. Michael Rühle has pointed out, "While NATO is only indirectly supporting some of these developments, such as the implementation of UNSC Resolution 1540, the discussion about a potential role of the Alliance in the PSI [Proliferation Security Initiative] indicates the possibility of its becoming more actively involved in non-traditional non-proliferation schemes."[192]

The Allies had noted in the 1999 Strategic Concept that "non-state actors have shown the potential to create and use some of these weapons"—that is, nuclear, biological, and chemical weapons—but they did not discuss the possible risk of state-sponsored WMD terrorism.[193] In the 2006 Comprehensive Political Guidance, the Allies came close to referring to such a contingency: "As shown by the terrorist attacks on the United States in 2001 following which NATO invoked Article 5 for the first time, future attacks may originate from outside the Euro-Atlantic area and involve unconventional forms of armed assault. Future attacks could also entail an increased risk of the use of asymmetric means, and could involve the use of weapons of mass destruction."[194]

In recent years, Britain, France, and the United States have recognized the threat of state-sponsored terrorist attacks employing nuclear weapons, and they have made clear their determination to identify any anonymous attacker and retaliate.

In January 2006, Jacques Chirac, then the president of France, said that "the leaders of states who would have recourse to terrorist means against us, as well as those who would envisage using, in one way or another, weapons of mass destruction, must understand that they expose themselves to a firm and appropriate response on our part."[195] In December 2006 the British government articulated a similar policy:

> We know that international terrorists are trying to acquire radiological weapons. In future, there are risks that they may try to acquire nuclear weapons. While our nuclear deterrent is not designed to deter non-state actors, it should influence the decision-making of any state that might consider transferring nuclear weapons or nuclear technology to terrorists. We make no distinction between the means by which a state might choose to deliver a nuclear warhead, whether, for example, by missile or sponsored terrorists. Any state that we can hold responsible for assisting a nuclear attack on our vital interests can expect that this would lead to a proportionate response.[196]

London and Paris made clear their determination to trace the origins of any nuclear attack via forensic analysis, and this resolve also featured in the policy articulated by Robert Gates, then the U.S. secretary of defense, in October 2008:

> The United States has made it clear for many years that it reserves the right to respond with overwhelming force to the use of weapons of mass destruction against the United States, our people, our forces, and our friends and allies. Today we also make clear that the United States will hold any state, terrorist group, or other non-state actor or individual fully accountable for supporting or enabling terrorist efforts to obtain or use weapons of mass destruction—whether by facilitating, financing, or providing expertise or safe haven for such efforts. To add teeth to the deterrent goal of this policy, we are pursuing new technologies to identify the forensic signatures of any nuclear material used in an attack—to trace it back to the source.[197]

The reference by Secretary Gates to responding "with overwhelming force to the use" of WMD against "our friends and allies" may serve as a sufficiently explicit link to the mutual defense pledge in Article 5 of the North Atlantic Treaty.

The credibility of the deterrence strategy of holding state sponsors of terrorism accountable for anonymous attacks with WMD clearly hinges on solving the problem of timely and accurate attribution of responsibility for a state-sponsored terrorist attack, given the difficulties of nuclear forensics. Since at least 2006, the U.S. government has made public its intention to meet the challenges of post-attack attribution.[198] Communicating the message that the United States and its allies have the means to identify the origins of the attack and retaliate is essential for deterrence.[199] In September 2009 the Allies stated, "In order to discourage any State from transferring nuclear weapons or technology to non-State actors, Allies need to continue working to develop a proven ability to identify State responsibility through intelligence and forensic attribution."[200] In February 2011 the Allies convened a conference on WMD forensic attribution challenges.[201]

Since 1990, when the NATO Allies first recognized that WMD proliferation had implications for the Alliance's security, they have pursued three policies: promoting arms control, disarmament, and nonproliferation with a view to preventing or limiting WMD proliferation; developing military capabilities for deterrence and defense; and preparing recovery capabilities (also known as consequence management assets) to deal with the effects of WMD attacks. The Alliance's recovery capabilities consist principally of CBRN defense units and the Euro-Atlantic Disaster Response Coordination Centre, which could assist in bringing together national assets, including those of partner nations.[202]

Conclusion

Owing perhaps to the stature of collective defense as the Alliance's original and most fundamental core task, combined with the gravity of collective defense operations, the Allies have at times had heated disagreements about it. An example is the ongoing debate about the appropriate "level of ambition" for contingency planning.

According to a standard formulation of NATO's current level of ambition since 2006, "Next to Article 5 Operations ('Collective Defence'), NATO should be able to concurrently conduct up to two Major Joint Operations and six Smaller Joint Operations."[203] Even setting aside collective defense, this declared level of ambition strikes some observers as implausibly demanding in relation to NATO's capabilities. In 2011 Kurt Volker and Kevin Green wrote, "The gap between the assertion of NATO's level of ambition and declared force posture—and the reality of what NATO nations provide and the Alliance as a whole can project—has grown to such a point that it strains credulity."[204] In 2012, Claudia Major, Christian Mölling, and Tomas Valasek reached a similar verdict: "NATO countries say that they want the alliance to be able to fight two big wars and six minor ones simultaneously, but they would have trouble doing half that."[205]

Other observers, however, find NATO's declared level of ambition consistent with recent Alliance missions. From March to October 2011 (the duration of Operation Unified Protector—OUP—in Libya), they hold, NATO was engaged in two major operations (ISAF in Afghanistan and OUP in Libya) and six smaller operations (KFOR in Kosovo, Active Endeavour in the Mediterranean, Ocean Shield off the Horn of Africa and in the Gulf of Aden, and air policing operations over the Adriatic, the Baltic, and Iceland). Whether these smaller operations—particularly the air policing missions—are sufficiently large and complex to qualify as Smaller Joint Operations is open to debate. Some observers maintain that the air policing operations should not be considered stand-alone operations but standing operations within the NATO Integrated Air Defense System. Moreover, some question whether OUP in Libya should be deemed a major joint operation, given the comparatively small number of daily flight sorties during most of the air campaign.[206] The Allies have not publicly defined with any precision their level of ambition and the requirements for major and smaller joint operations.[207]

The collective defense contingency is often called a "Major Joint Operation Plus." Decision makers in various capitals differ sharply as to how much emphasis should be placed on "the most demanding" contingency (Article 5) as opposed to "the most likely" cases (non-Article 5 interventions). According to Polish observers, Poland has taken a leading role in arguing for "the most demanding" contingency as the appropriate level of ambition, with support from the Baltic states, Norway, Romania, and Turkey. As one Pole put it, the Allies favoring "the most likely" principle, such as the Netherlands and the United Kingdom, "feel safe" and "are not affected by the threats we see as still important."[208] Allies arguing for preparedness for "the most demanding" contingencies can cite the Alliance's 2006 Comprehensive Political Guidance in support of their position.[209]

For Poland and some other NATO Allies in Central and Eastern Europe, as well as Norway and Turkey, concerns persist about Russia as a potential security challenge. Authoritarian trends in Russian domestic politics have reinforced concerns arising from certain steps taken by Moscow—above all, its forceful intervention in Georgia in 2008 and its occupation of two Georgian territories that it has recognized as independent states. The Allies geographically closest to Russia have generally been those most anxious about possible confrontations or conflicts with Moscow.

Even more than with respect to Russia, the NATO Allies have generally favored "generic" terminology in order to avoid referring explicitly to potential adversaries in Asia and the Middle East, including Iran. The semantic construction "outside the Euro-Atlantic area" excludes Russia and other former Soviet republics but offers the great advantage of covering most of the world without alluding to any specific states.

The "emerging" or "nontraditional" security challenges identified by the Alliance include cyber security, space operations, energy security, climate change, terrorism, and WMD proliferation. Despite the impression conveyed by the adjectives "emerging" and "nontraditional," all of these security challenges have lengthy and complex histories, and all of them could be significant factors in countering "traditional" military threats.

Cyber security and space operations are, for example, likely to figure in future NATO collective defense missions. The dependence of the NATO Allies on computer-based information systems and space-based capabilities for communications, navigation, guidance, and other functions has become so great that it is difficult to imagine future adversaries failing to try to destroy, disrupt, or disable them. Daily cyber attacks of various kinds ensure that the NATO Allies have this threat constantly in mind.

As noted, Allied cooperation regarding energy security issues remains touchy and incomplete, owing in part to substantial differences among the Allies—including whether they are exporters of energy resources and, if they are importers, their level of dependence on specific foreign suppliers. Experiences in NATO-led operations, notably in Afghanistan, have nonetheless demonstrated the profound importance of reliable sources of energy in missions challenged by difficult terrain.[210] Demanding collective defense operations would in all likelihood, more than non-Article 5 crisis management operations, underscore the need for the Allies to look beyond their "value-added" and other energy security caveats and define more comprehensive Alliance policies.

While the NATO Allies have generally reverted to their pre–September 11, 2001, view that terrorism is above all a matter for national intelligence and law enforcement agencies, they continue to acknowledge possible NATO contributions to the fight against terrorism. Moreover, they have seen that the threat of large-scale terrorist attacks could require combined action, from prevention to consequence management.

Terrorism and WMD proliferation may be linked, particularly in the case of state-sponsored terrorism. The NATO Allies have recognized that a state might attempt to employ a terrorist group to conduct an attack with WMD and make it appear that the terrorist group—or another state—was responsible. This consideration—and the interest in deterring such attacks—help to account for the considerable interest in improved forensic capabilities in Britain, France, the United States, and the Alliance as a whole.

To be sure, WMD proliferation—for instance, nuclear-armed ballistic missiles deployed by state adversaries—does not truly represent an "emerging" or "nontraditional" threat. The Soviet Union threatened targets in NATO nations with nuclear-armed ballistic missiles from the late 1950s on. At first glance, the only aspect of this threat that is "emerging" or "nontraditional" is the identity of the prospective state possessors. The NATO Allies have named Iran and North Korea in this regard publicly and consistently, usually in the context of arms control and nonproliferation commitments.[211] The declarations calling upon these countries to honor their international treaty commitments show that NATO's "broader security environment" might in some circumstances encompass state adversaries other than Russia.

A single state adversary could, moreover, hypothetically combine multiple types of threats, both traditional and nontraditional. For example, Iran has undertaken cyber attacks against foreign governments and businesses. It has also pursued ballistic missiles and improved its capacity to produce nuclear weapons. With regard to space, Iran has jammed satellite communications signals since 2003 and has launched satellites since 2008. Iran has sponsored terrorist movements, including Hezbollah. Finally, Iran has for decades been a leading energy supplier and a country of critical importance for the security of energy-resource shipping routes. The Iranian example shows the variety and complexity of potential challenges to Alliance security.

NATO's response has consisted not only of its deterrence and defense posture (discussed in chapter 3) and its engagement in crisis management operations (considered in chapters 4 and 5) but also its pursuit of cooperative security with partner nations and international organizations (examined in chapters 6 and 7). Furthermore, the Allies intend via NATO's "open door" to new members (reviewed in chapter 8) and its commitment to arms control, nonproliferation, and disarmament (surveyed in chapter 9) to hedge against and, if possible, prevent the emergence of security threats. The relevance of a collective defense strategy is not limited to immediate security challenges. The Alliance's deterrence and defense posture, and its overall preparedness for unpredictable future contingencies, may serve to avert the development of some threats.

Notes

1. North Atlantic Council, "Comprehensive Political Guidance," November 29, 2006, par. 5, www.nato.int/cps/en/SID-53EB9F5E-EC448DBF/natolive/official_texts_56425.htm?.
2. North Atlantic Council, "Strategic Concept," November 19, 2010, par. 4a.

3. NATO, "New NATO Division to Deal with Emerging Security Challenges," August 4, 2010, www.nato.int/cps/en/SID-6E509263-1BF11962/natolive/news_65107.htm?selectedLocale=en.

4. Ronald Asmus, Stefan Czmur, Chris Donnelly, Aivis Ronis, Tomas Valasek, and Klaus Wittmann, *NATO, New Allies, and Reassurance* (London: Centre for European Reform, May 2010), 2, www.cer.org.uk/pdf/pb_nato_12may10.pdf.

5. *NATO 2020: Assured Security; Dynamic Engagement, Analysis and Recommendations of the Group of Experts on a New Strategic Concept for NATO* (Brussels: NATO Public Diplomacy Division, May 17, 2010), 13–17, www.nato.int/cps/en/natolive/official_texts_63654.htm.

6. Ibid., 16.

7. North Atlantic Council, "Strategic Concept," November 7, 1991, par. 20.

8. Ibid., par. 13.

9. North Atlantic Council, "Strategic Concept," April 24, 1999, par. 21.

10. North Atlantic Council, "Strategic Concept," November 19, 2010, par. 26.

11. Ibid., par. 33–34.

12. "NATO-Russia Council Joint Statement at the Meeting of the NATO-Russia Council Held in Lisbon on 20 November 2010," November 20, 2010, www.nato.int/cps/en/natolive/news_68871.htm.

13. See, among other examples, the statement by Colonel General Anatoly Nogovitsyn, the deputy chief of Russia's General Staff, quoted in Damien McElroy, "Russian General Says Poland a Nuclear 'Target,'" *Daily Telegraph*, August 15, 2008, www.telegraph.co.uk/news/worldnews/europe/georgia/2564639/. Russian-general-says-Poland-a-nuclear-target-as-Condoleezza-Rice-arrives-in-Georgia.htm. Russian statements regarding possible deployment of the dual capable Iskander missile in Kaliningrad have also been significant in this respect.

14. Matthew Day, "Russia 'Simulates' Nuclear Attack on Poland," *Daily Telegraph*, November 1, 2009, www.telegraph.co.uk/news/worldnews/europe/poland/6480227/Russia-simulates-nuclear-attack-on-Poland.html; Andres Reimer, "Expert: Russia Exercising Attacks against Baltic States," *Eesti Paevaleht Online* (in Estonian), December 9, 2010, available at OpenSource.gov, EUP20101209235001.

15. NATO, "Statement: Meeting of the North Atlantic Council at the level of Foreign Ministers Held at NATO Headquarters, Brussels," August 19, 2008, press release (2008) 104, www.nato.int/docu/pr/2008/p08-104e.html.

16. North Atlantic Council, "Strasbourg/Kehl Summit Declaration," April 4, 2009, par. 34, www.nato.int/cps/en/natolive/news_52837.htm.

17. Asmus et al., *NATO, New Allies, and Reassurance*, 2.

18. Tomas Valasek, *NATO, Russia and European Security* (London: Centre for European Reform, November 2009), 7.

19. James Blitz, "Europeans See Moscow as Security Threat," *Financial Times*, September 22, 2008.

20. Vaira Vike-Freiberga quoted in Stefan Wagstyl, "Vaira Vike-Freiberga, Latvia's President," *Financial Times*, December 15, 2006, 6.

21. Toomas Hendrik Ilves, "NATO in Estonia, Estonia in NATO: Our Common Security in the 21st Century," Helsinki, December 1, 2008, www.president.ee/en/duties/speeches.php.

22. Bogdan Klich quoted in Judy Dempsey, "Poland Wants U.S. to Be 3rd Leg of Its Security Plan," *New York Times*, April 21, 2008.

23. This judgment was expressed by a Slovak scholar at an off-the-record workshop in Paris, May 26, 2011.

24. Ragnheidur Arnadottir (Iceland), Rapporteur, *Protecting to Project: NATO's Territorial Defence and Deterrence Needs*, 174 DSCTC 09 E BIS (Brussels: NATO Parliamentary Assembly, 2009), par. 9, www.nato-pa.int/Default.asp?SHORTCUT=1781.

25. Donald Tusk quoted in Vanessa Gera and Monika Scislowska, "U.S., Poland Agree to Anti-missile Defense Deal," Associated Press, August 14, 2008, http://legacy.utsandiego.com/news/world/20080814-1513-poland-us-missiledefense.html.

26. Arnadottir, *Protecting to Project*, par. 10.

27. "An Open Letter to the Obama Administration from Central and Eastern Europe," July 16, 2009, www.wyborcza.pl. See also *Why the Obama Administration Should Not Take Central and Eastern Europe for Granted*, Policy Brief (Washington, DC: German Marshall Fund of the United States, July 13, 2009), www.gmfus.org/publications/article.cfm?id=621&parent_type=P.

28. "Founding Act on Mutual Relations, Cooperation and Security," May 27, 1997.

29. Ronald D. Asmus, "Shattered Confidence in Europe," *Washington Post*, September 19, 2009. It should be noted that some observers hold that Asmus may have overstated or dramatized the situation in that the Alliance had general contingency plans that might have been applied, if necessary, to specific situations. Authoritative and precise unclassi-

fied sources on the Alliance's contingency planning for collective defense since post–Cold War NATO enlargement began in the 1990s may not be available for decades.

30. Asmus et al., *NATO, New Allies, and Reassurance*, 1–2. See also Ronald D. Asmus, "NATO's Hour," *Wall Street Journal Europe*, August 18, 2008.

31. "What about NATO?: How the Alliance Should Move Forward," *Economist*, December 11, 2008, www.economist.com/node/12758375.

32. Arnadottir, *Protecting to Project*, par. 29.

33. President Barack Obama, remarks in Prague, Czech Republic, April 5, 2009, www.whitehouse.gov/the_press_office/Remarks-By-President-Barack-Obama-In-Prague-As-Delivered/.

34. "We will continue to improve and demonstrate more clearly our ability to meet emerging challenges on and beyond Alliance territory, including on its periphery, inter alia by ensuring adequate planning, exercises and training." North Atlantic Council, "Strasbourg/Kehl Summit Declaration," par. 48. With regard to the role of the Baltic states in introducing this paragraph in the declaration, see Pal Jonson, *The Debate about Article 5 and Its Credibility: What Is It All About?*, NATO Defense College Research Paper no. 58 (Rome, May 2010), 4n5.

35. Mark Kramer, *Russia, the Baltic Region, and the Challenge for NATO*, PONARS Eurasia Policy Memo no. 267 (Washington, DC: PONARS Eurasia, Elliott School of International Affairs, George Washington University, July 2013), 5. See also "Border Controls: Thanks to Poland, the Alliance Will Defend the Baltics," *Economist.com*, 14 January 2010, www.economist.com/world/europe/displaystory.cfm?story_id=15268095.

36. Kramer, *Russia, the Baltic Region, and the Challenge for NATO*.

37. Ulrike Demmer and Ralf Neukirch, "Fear of Russia: NATO Developed Secret Contingency Plans for Baltic States," *Spiegel Online*, December 7, 2010, www.spiegel.de/international/europe/0,1518,733361,00.html. See also Jonson, *The Debate about Article 5 and Its Credibility*, 9.

38. Demmer and Neukirch, "Fear of Russia." See also "Nato-Verteidigungsplan für das Baltikum und Polen, Wikileaks: Deutschland war treibende Kraft bei Ausarbeitung/Russland 'befremdet,' aber informiert," *Frankfurter Allgemeine Zeitung*, December 8, 2010.

39. Inga-Gretel Linkgreim, "Aaviksoo: Estonia Has No Reason to Consider Russia Enemy," *ERR Uudised Online* (in Estonian), December 7, 2010, available at OpenSource.gov, EUP20101208235001.

40. Rasmussen quoted in "NATO and Russia: Trust, but Make Military Plans," *Economist*, July 29, 2010.

41. Interview with Dmitriy Rogozin by Nadezhda Yermolayeva, *Rossiyskaya Gazeta Online* (in Russian), December 9, 2010, available at OpenSource.gov, CEP20101209009004.

42. Ivashov quoted in "Wikileaks Row Unlikely to Harm Russia-NATO Relations—Analysts," *ITAR-TASS* (in English), December 8, 2010, available at OpenSource.gov, CEP20101208950138.

43. North Atlantic Council, "Deterrence and Defence Posture Review," May 20, 2012, par. 4.

44. Author's interview with an Estonian expert in Brussels, July 5, 2012.

45. North Atlantic Council, "Deterrence and Defence Posture Review," May 20, 2012, par. 13.

46. See, for example, Jacek Durkalec, *New Strategic Concept and NATO's "Visible Assurances" towards Central and Eastern Europe*, Bulletin no. 140 (Warsaw: Polish Institute of International Affairs, December 15, 2010).

47. Declaration of the Visegrad Group, "Responsibility for a Strong NATO," April 18, 2012, www.mzv.cz/file/804857/Deklarace_V4_k_NATO_text_18._4._2012.pdf.

48. "Flexing Its Muscles," *Economist*, August 17, 2013.

49. Edward Lucas, "Time to Bang the Drums for Steadfast Jazz," Center for European Policy Analysis, March 1, 2013, www.cepa.org/content/time-bang-drums-steadfast-jazz.

50. Pawel Wronski, "Before the Chicago Summit—NATO Has Been Through a Lot," *Gazeta Wyborcza Online* (in Polish), Warsaw, May 19, 2012, available at OpenSource.gov, EUP20120521232003.

51. Oana Longescu, NATO spokesperson, letter in the *Economist*, November 17, 2012, 18.

52. In April 2008 the Norwegian government circulated a nonpaper titled "Strengthening NATO—Raising Its Profile and Ensuring Its Relevance." Jonson, *The Debate about Article 5 and Its Credibility*, 4n5. See also the study by Norwegian scholar Paal Sigurd Hilde, "The Strategic Concept and NATO's Command Structure: Shifting Gears?," in *NATO's New Strategic Concept: A Comprehensive Assessment*, DIIS Report 2011:02, ed. Jens Ringsmose and Sten Rynning (Copenhagen: Danish Institute for International Studies, 2011), 128.

53. Jonson, *The Debate about Article 5 and Its Credibility*.

54. Ibid., 8.

55. Ibid., 7n16.

56. "I hope it might make it easier for Nato to do more in Afghanistan, certain in the knowledge that there is a dedicated homeland security force that will have no other call on its priorities [other] than European homeland security." John

Hutton quoted in James Blitz and Alex Barker, "UK Calls for Unit to Defend NATO Territory," *Financial Times*, February 19, 2009. See also "Britain Proposes Standing NATO Force for Europe," Reuters, February 19, 2009, www. reuters.com/article/2009/02/19/idUSLJ89251.

57. Jonson, *The Debate about Article 5 and Its Credibility*, 3.

58. *NATO's Operations 1949–Present*, 1, www.aco.nato.int.

59. Ibid., 5.

60. Karl Kaiser and Klaus Becher, "Germany and the Iraq Conflict," in *Western Europe and the Gulf*, ed. Nicole Gnesotto and John Roper (Paris: Institute for Security Studies, Western European Union, 1992), 49–50.

61. Louis Michel quoted in Philip H. Gordon and Jeremy Shapiro, *Allies at War: America, Europe, and the Crisis Over Iraq* (New York: McGraw-Hill, 2004), 138.

62. Gordon and Shapiro, *Allies at War*, 141.

63. Eric Schmitt and Michael R. Gordon, "U.S. to Send 2 Missile Units to Turkey to Deter Syrians," *New York Times*, December 14, 2012; and "NATO Support to Turkey : Background and Timeline," last updated February 19, 2013, www.nato.int/cps/en/SID-F62FAE77-42F9F246/natolive/topics_92555.htm?.

64. Anders Fogh Rasmussen quoted in Anne Gearan, "Turkey Will Get NATO Missiles," *Washington Post*, December 5, 2012.

65. Dutch defense minister Jeanine Hennis Plasschaert quoted in "Netherlands, Germany May Send Missiles to Turkey: Report," *Reuters.com*, November 18, 2012.

66. NATO, "NATO Foreign Ministers' Statement on Patriot Deployment to Turkey," December 4, 2012, www.nato.int/cps/en/natolive/news_92476.htm.

67. Gearan, "Turkey Will Get NATO Missiles"; and Ernesto Londono, "Patriots Likely to Serve as Symbol, Not Tactical Asset," *Washington Post*, December 5, 2012.

68. North Atlantic Council, "Strategic Concept," November 19, 2010, par. 7.

69. Ibid., par. 8.

70. North Atlantic Council, "Deterrence and Defence Posture Review," May 20, 2012, par. 20 and 26.

71. Nicolas Sarkozy, speech at Cherbourg, March 21, 2008.

72. Agence France-Presse, "Selon Sarkozy, la menace des missiles vient d'Iran," *Le Point*, November 20, 2010, www.lepoint.fr/monde/selon-sarkozy-la-menace-des-missiles-vient-d-iran-20-11-2010-1264946_24.php.

73. The quotations in this paragraph and the preceding paragraph are drawn from David S. Yost, *NATO's Deterrence and Defense Posture after the Chicago Summit: A Report on a Workshop in Rome, 25–27 June 2012* (Rome: NATO Defense College, October 2012), 12–13, www.ndc.nato.int/download/downloads.php?icode=356.

74. Author's interview with a German observer in Brussels, May 30, 2013.

75. North Atlantic Council, "Strategic Concept," November 19, 2010, par. 9.

76. North Atlantic Council, "Deterrence and Defence Posture Review," May 20, 2012, par. 26 and 27.

77. North Atlantic Council, "Strategic Concept," November 7, 1991, par. 12.

78. North Atlantic Council, "Strategic Concept," April 24, 1999, par. 24.

79. North Atlantic Council, "Strategic Concept," November 19, 2010, par. 8–15.

80. Anders Fogh Rasmussen, "NATO and Climate Change," *Huffington Post*, December 15, 2009, www.huffingtonpost.com/anders-fogh-rasmussen/nato-and-climate-change_b_392409.html; and NATO, "Environmental Security," last updated October 24, 2011, www.nato.int/cps/en/natolive/topics_49216.htm. NATO has been sponsoring research on the security implications of climate change (including with regard to water scarcity and food insecurity) as part of its Science for Peace and Security Program, which is discussed at www.nato.int/cps/en/natolive/78209.htm. See also the collection of *NATO Review* articles on climate change available at www.nato.int/docu/review/topics/EN/climate-change.htm.

81. Robert M. Gates, speech delivered at the Carnegie Endowment for International Peace, Washington, DC, October 28, 2008, www.defenselink.mil/speeches/speech.aspx?speechid=1305.

82. Harold Hongju Koh, "International Law in Cyberspace" (remarks, USCYBERCOM Inter-Agency Legal Conference, Ft. Meade, MD, September 18, 2012), italics in the original, www.state.gov/s/l/releases/remarks/197924.htm.

83. North Atlantic Council, "Strategic Concept," April 24, 1999, par. 23.

84. Olaf Theiler, "New Threats: The Cyber-dimension," *NATO Review*, September 2011, www.nato.int/docu/review/2011/11-september/Cyber-Threats/EN/index.htm.

85. North Atlantic Council, "Prague Summit Declaration," November 21, 2002, par. 4f, www.nato.int/docu/pr/2002/p02-127e.htm; North Atlantic Council, "Bucharest Summit Declaration," April 3, 2008, www.nato.int/docu/pr/2008/p08-049e.html; and North Atlantic Council, "Strasbourg/Kehl Summit Declaration," par. 49.

86. These institutions include the NATO Computer Incident Response Capability (NCIRC) approved at the Prague Summit in 2002 and two organizations established in 2008: the NATO Cyber Defence Management Board (NCDMB) and the NATO Cooperative Cyber Defence Centre of Excellence (CCDCOE), the latter based in Tallinn, Estonia. The Allies also created the Cyber Defence Management Authority (NCDMA) in 2008 as an umbrella organization, but it was dissolved in June 2011, to avoid confusion with the NCDMB. Author interview in Brussels, July 5, 2012.

87. U.S. Department of Defense, *Quadrennial Defense Review Report* (Washington, DC: U.S. Department of Defense, February 2010), 37.

88. Greg Rattray, Chris Evans, and Jason Healey, "American Security in the Cyber Commons," in *Contested Commons: The Future of American Power in a Multipolar World*, ed. Abraham M. Denmark and James Mulvenon (Washington, DC: Center for a New American Security, January 2010), 171, www.cnas.org/node/4012.

89. "Many of the cyber attacks themselves were traced to Russia; many of the attack tools were written in Russian; many of the corrupted Estonian websites were polluted with strong nationalist Russian reactions; numerous Russian politicians openly supported the attacks; and the Russian government refused to stop or even investigate the attacks." Rattray et al., "American Security," 170.

90. Estonian expert quoted in David S. Yost, *Adapting NATO's Deterrence Posture: The Alliance's New Strategic Concept and Implications for Nuclear Policy, Non-Proliferation, Arms Control, and Disarmament: A Report on a Workshop in Tallinn, 4–6 May 2011* (Rome: NATO Defense College, June 2011), 4, www.ndc.nato.int/download/downloads.php?icode=294.

91. According to an American expert, "Russian proxies conducted the cyber attacks against Estonia in 2007 and Georgia in 2008, and these attacks were coordinated with Russian military activities." American expert cited in Yost, *NATO's Deterrence and Defense Posture*, 6.

92. North Atlantic Council, "Lisbon Summit Declaration," November 20, 2010, par. 40, www.nato.int/cps/en/natolive/official_texts_68828.htm?mode=pressrelease.

93. American expert cited in Yost, *NATO's Deterrence and Defense*, 6.

94. North Atlantic Council, "Strategic Concept," November 19, 2010, par. 12.

95. Ibid., par. 4a.

96. Some experts have termed this a problem of "asymmetric vulnerabilities." As an American professional put it at a NATO workshop, "The United States and its allies present such a rich array of targets for Russia and China that 'we'll run out of targets before they do.'" American expert cited in Yost, *NATO's Deterrence and Defense Posture*, 6.

97. Secretary of Defense Leon E. Panetta, remarks on cybersecurity to the Business Executives for National Security, New York, October 11, 2012, www.defense.gov/transcripts/transcript.aspx?transcriptid=5136.

98. Ibid.

99. For further details on the concurrent exercises, see NATO, "NATO Conducts Annual Crisis Management Exercise (CMX) and Cyber Coalition Exercise," press release (2012) 131, www.nato.int/cps/en/natolive/news_91115.htm?mode=pressrelease; and Government of Hungary, Ministry of Defense, "Hungary Has Performed Excellently on Two NATO Exercises," November 21, 2012, www.kormany.hu/en/ministry-of-defence/news/hungary-has-performed-excellently-on-two-nato-exercises.

100. Adrian Croft, "NATO Boosts Cyber Defences but Members Differ on Its Role," *Reuters.com*, June 4, 2013.

101. Ibid.

102. Audition au Sénat de M. Philippe Errera, Ambassadeur, Représentant Permanent de la France à l'OTAN, January 22, 2013.

103. NATO, "Defence Ministers Make Progress on Cyber Protection," last updated June 4, 2013, www.nato.int/cps/en/SID-3C648492-46C41C9C/natolive/news_101143.htm.

104. "NATO Will Provide Coordinated Assistance if an Ally or Allies Are Victims of a Cyber Attack." NATO, "Defending the Networks: The NATO Policy on Cyber Defence," 2011, www.nato.int/nato_static/assets/pdf/pdf_2011_09/20111004_110914-policy-cyberdefence.pdf.

105. Ibid. "Cyber defense" is the term preferred in NATO (instead of, for example, "cyber war") in order to underline the Alliance's defensive orientation.

106. Koh, "International Law in Cyberspace."

107. Michèle Flournoy and Shawn Brimley, "The Contested Commons," *Proceedings* 135, no. 7 (July 2009), www.usni.org/magazines/proceedings/story.asp?STORY_ID=1950. Michèle Flournoy served as the U.S. under secretary of defense for policy in 2009–2012. Shawn Brimley is a strategist in the Office of the Secretary of Defense.

108. Thomas Single, *NATO Space Operations Assessment* (Kalkar, Germany: Joint Air Power Competence Centre, January 2009), 51, www.japcc.org.

109. Ibid., 7, 9.

110. North Atlantic Council, "Strategic Concept," November 19, 2010, par. 14.

111. For an official discussion, see "National Security Space Strategy: Unclassified Summary," published by the U.S. Secretary of Defense and the U.S. Director of National Intelligence, January 2011, www.defense.gov/home/features/2011/0111_nsss/docs/NationalSecuritySpaceStrategyUnclassifiedSummary_Jan2011.pdf.

112. Gregory L. Schulte, *Protecting NATO's Advantage in Space*, Transatlantic Current no. 5 (Washington, DC: National Defense University, May 2012), 2.

113. This discussion is based on Schulte, *Protecting NATO's Advantage in Space*, as well as on the comments of an American participant at a recent NATO workshop, in Yost, *NATO's Deterrence and Defense Posture*, 6–7.

114. For details, see NATO, "Schriever Wargame 2012 International," www.act.nato.int/mainpages/schriever-wargame-2012-international.

115. Schulte, *Protecting NATO's Advantage in Space*, 4.

116. Some observers have pointed out that Article 6 of the North Atlantic Treaty stipulates that Article 5 would apply in the event of "an armed attack . . . on the forces, vessels or aircraft of any of the Parties, when in or over these territories." Of course, no NATO Ally had any "forces, vessels or aircraft" in space in 1949, and in the late 1950s the policies adopted regarding the first satellites established the international legal principle that national sovereignty does not extend beyond a country's airspace into space. This suggests that a member state's military assets in space are implicitly excluded from the geographic coverage specified in Article 6. The effects of attacks damaging or disrupting a member-state's military assets in space could, however, extend with decisive impact to the territories and/or "the forces, vessels or aircraft" of NATO Allies.

117. Comparatively "small-scale" cyber attacks are virtually continuous. According to a July 2011 U.S. Department of Defense (DoD) report, "DoD networks are probed millions of times every day, and successful penetrations have led to the loss of thousands of files from U.S. networks and those of U.S. allies and industry partners." *Department of Defense Strategy for Operating in Cyberspace* (Washington, DC: U.S. Department of Defense, July 2011), 3.

118. Eric Sterner, "Beyond the Stalemate in the Space Commons," in *Contested Commons: The Future of American Power in a Multipolar World*, ed. Abraham M. Denmark and James Mulvenon (Washington, DC: Center for a New American Security, January 2010), 117-118, www.cnas.org/node/4012.

119. For background on cross-domain deterrence, see Vincent Manzo, *Deterrence and Escalation in Cross-Domain Operations: Where Do Space and Cyberspace Fit?*, Strategic Forum no. 272 (Washington, DC: National Defense University, December 2011).

120. This paragraph and the next two paragraphs are based on Yost, *NATO's Deterrence and Defense*, 7.

121. This was a reference to Secretary of State Dean Acheson's controversial speech at the National Press Club on January 12, 1950. In this speech Acheson defined the U.S. "defensive perimeter" in the Asia-Pacific region in a way that seemed to deny protection to the Republic of Korea. Among many studies, see James I. Matray, "Dean Acheson's Press Club Speech Reexamined," *Journal of Conflict Studies* 22, no. 1 (Spring 2002), http://journals.hil.unb.ca/index.php/jcs/article/view/366/578

122. Ellen Nakashima, "We Know What War Looks Like Here, but What Does It Look Like Here?," *Washington Post*, October 28, 2012. This question followed comments by a U.S. "senior defense official" whom Ellen Nakashima interviewed on background.

123. Ambassador Gregory L. Schulte, "Protecting Global Security in Space" (presentation, S. Rajaratnam School of International Studies, Nanyang Technological University, Singapore, May 9, 2012), 6, http://singapore.usembassy.gov/events.html.

124. Schulte, *Protecting NATO's Advantage in Space*, 3.

125. "We support a coordinated, international effort to assess risks to energy infrastructures and to promote energy infrastructure security. With this in mind, we direct the Council in Permanent Session to consult on the most immediate risks in the field of energy security, in order to define those areas where NATO may add value to safeguard the security interests of the Allies and, upon request, assist national and international efforts." North Atlantic Council, "Riga Summit Declaration," par. 45.

126. North Atlantic Council, "Bucharest Summit Declaration," par. 48.

127. Michael Rühle, "NATO and Energy Security," *NATO Review*, 2011, www.nato.int/docu/review/2011/Climate-Action/Energy_Security/EN/index.htm. See also Jaap de Hoop Scheffer, "NATO and the Challenge of Energy Security," *RUSI Journal* 153, no. 6 (December 2008): 58.

128. North Atlantic Council, "Bucharest Summit Declaration," par. 48; North Atlantic Council, "Strasbourg/Kehl Summit Declaration," par. 59; North Atlantic Council, "Lisbon Summit Declaration," par. 41; North Atlantic Council, "Chicago Summit Declaration," par. 52.

129. North Atlantic Council, "Strategic Concept," November 19, 2010, par. 19.

130. North Atlantic Council, "Strasbourg/Kehl Summit Declaration," par. 59.

131. North Atlantic Council, "Strategic Concept," November 19, 2010, par. 13.

132. At the 2012 Chicago Summit the Allies declared, "While these issues are primarily the responsibility of national governments and other international organisations concerned, NATO closely follows relevant developments in energy security." North Atlantic Council, "Chicago Summit Declaration," par. 52.

133. De Hoop Scheffer, "NATO and the Challenge of Energy Security," 59.

134. Rühle, "NATO and Energy Security."

135. Dranga quoted in *Is Europe's Energy Security Policy a Reality or an Ambition?* (Brussels: Security and Defence Agenda, June 2010), 7.

136. Rühle, "NATO and Energy Security." See also Michael Rühle, "NATO and Energy Security: From Philosophy to Implementation," *Journal of Transatlantic Studies* 10, no. 4 (December 2012).

137. Loïc Simonet, "L'OTAN et la protection des infrastructures énergétiques: jusqu'où engager l'Alliance?," *La Revue Internationale et Stratégique*, no. 72 (Winter 20082009): 80.

138. Author interviews with experts in Brussels, July 2012.

139. In addition to NATO, "Alliance Maritime Strategy," March 18, 2011, www.nato.int/cps/en/natolive/official_texts_75615.htm, see Diego Ruiz Palmer, "Analysis—New Operational Horizons: NATO and Maritime Security," *NATO Review* (2007), www.nato.int/docu/review/2007/Growing_Dangers/Maritime_security_operational/EN/; Diego Ruiz Palmer, "The End of the Naval Era?," *NATO Review* (2010), www.nato.int/docu/review/2010/Maritime_Security/end_of_naval_era/EN/index.htm; Brooke Smith-Windsor, *Securing the Commons: Towards NATO's New Maritime Strategy*, Research Paper no. 49 (Rome: NATO Defense College, September 2009), www.ndc.nato.int/download/downloads.php?icode=110; and Brooke Smith-Windsor, *NATO's Maritime Strategy and the Libya Crisis as Seen from the Sea*, Research Paper no. 90 (Rome: NATO Defense College, March 2013), www.ndc.nato.int/download/downloads.php?icode=369.

140. De Hoop Scheffer, "NATO and the Challenge of Energy Security," 58.

141. North Atlantic Council, "Strategic Concept," November 19, 2010, par. 15.

142. North Atlantic Council, "Chicago Summit Declaration," par. 53.

143. For some reflections in this regard, see the article by Anders Fogh Rasmussen, "NATO and Climate Change," *Huffington Post*, December 15, 2009, www.huffingtonpost.com/anders-fogh-rasmussen/nato-and-climate-change_b_392409.html.

144. Merrill Walters, "Responses," in *Nuclear Terrorism: Defining the Threat*, ed. Paul Leventhal and Yonah Alexander (Washington, DC: Pergamon-Brassey's, 1986), 68.

145. North Atlantic Council, "Strategic Concept," November 7, 1991, par. 12.

146. North Atlantic Council, "Strategic Concept," April 24, 1999, par. 24.

147. "The terrorist threat against deployed NATO forces and NATO installations requires the consideration and development of appropriate measures for their continued protection, taking full account of host nation responsibilities." North Atlantic Council, "Washington Summit Communiqué," par. 42. See also North Atlantic Council, "Strategic Concept," April 24, 1999, par. 53i.

148. North Atlantic Council, "Washington Summit Communiqué," par. 42.

149. Lord Robertson, statement to the press on the North Atlantic Council decision on Implementation of Article 5 of the Washington Treaty following the September 11 attacks against the United States, NATO headquarters, Brussels, October 4, 2001, www.nato.int/docu/speech/2001/s011004b.htm. It was not until October 2, 2001, that Francis X. Taylor, then the U.S. coordinator for counterterrorism, presented to the North Atlantic Council the results of the U.S. investigations regarding the origins of the September 11, 2001 attacks. On the basis of this information, the North Atlantic Council concluded that the attacks were "directed from abroad" and thus constituted "an armed attack" falling under Article 5 of the North Atlantic Treaty. NATO, "NATO and the Fight against Terrorism," last updated March 9, 2011, www.nato.int/cps/en/natolive/topics_48801.htm.

150. Anders Fogh Rasmussen, statement on the conclusion of Operation Eagle Assist, April 30, 2002, www.nato.int/docu/update/2002/04-april/e0430a.htm.

151. Russia and Turkey opposed a U.S. proposal to extend Operation Active Endeavour's sphere of activity to the Black Sea. Igor Torbakov, "Turkey Sides with Moscow against Washington on Black Sea Force," *Eurasia Daily Monitor* 3, no. 43 (March 3, 2006).

152. NATO, "Operation Active Endeavour," last updated February 22, 2011, www.nato.int/cps/en/natolive/topics_7932.htm. See also Brian Finman, "Keeping the Med Safe—How It's Done," *NATO Review*, 2010, www.nato.int/docu/review/2010/Maritime_Security/Safe_Mediterranean/EN/index.htm; and the Web site for Operative Active Endeavour at the Allied Maritime Command Naples, www.manp.nato.int/operations/ActiveEndeavour/Endeavour.htm.

153. "George Robertson, NATO's Super-Policeman," *Economist*, October 6–12, 2001.

154. Ambrose Evans-Pritchard, "EU Leaders Demand a Place in Front Line," *Daily Telegraph* (London), November 7, 2001.

155. Jim Hoagland, "Our Underutilized Allies," *Washington Post National Weekly Edition*, October 29–November 4, 2001, 5.

156. Richard Lugar and Joseph R. Biden, Jr., "How to Revitalize NATO," *Wall Street Journal Europe*, November 9, 2001.

157. George Robertson, "NATO Still Matters: The Terrorist Threat Puts New Demands on Security Forces, and the Alliance Is Leading the Effort to Adapt," *Financial Times*, February 1, 2002.

158. The U.S. military services retained old-fashioned communications capabilities, euphemistically called "legacy" systems, to sustain their ability to communicate with Allies and coalition partners in the conduct of operations. Some Americans regarded such measures, which were necessary to enable the Allies to contribute effectively to operations, as burdensome. For background, see David S. Yost, "The NATO Capabilities Gap and the European Union," *Survival* 42, no. 4 (Winter 2000–2001), 97–128, esp. pp. 105–106.

159. The irritations in some U.S. political-military circles about Operation Allied Force, the air campaign in the 1999 Kosovo conflict, were summed up in General Michael Short's declarations: "It's my evaluation that NATO cannot go to war in the air against a competent enemy without the United States. If that's the case, and we're going to provide 70 percent of the effort . . . then we need to have more than one of 19 votes." In General Short's view, the United States should have told its allies: "We will take the alliance to war and we will win this thing for you, but the price to be paid is we call the tune." General Michael Short quoted in Michael Evans, "General Wanted US to Call the Shots in Kosovo," *Times*, January 27, 2000.

160. Secretary of Defense Donald Rumsfeld, remarks at National Defense University, Washington, DC, January 31, 2002, www.defenselink.mil/speeches/2002/s20020131-secdef.html.

161. It should nonetheless be noted that European Allies generally rejected the George W. Bush administration's phrases "the war on terror" and "the global war on terror," and preferred to call it a "fight" or "struggle" against terrorism—terms often found in NATO communiqués and other Alliance documents. Aside from politics, motives for rejecting the Bush administration's terms included the substantive arguments that terrorism is simply a tactic of political struggle, not a proper noun; that it is impractical to undertake combat against an abstraction; and that it would be more useful to focus on countering specific terrorist movements.

162. North Atlantic Council, "Prague Summit Declaration," par. 4.

163. Ibid.

164. Euro-Atlantic Partnership Council, "Partnership Action Plan against Terrorism," November 22, 2002, www.nato.int/cps/en/natolive/official_texts_19549.htm.

165. The information in this paragraph and the next is derived mainly from NATO, "NATO and the Fight against Terrorism."

166. Author interviews in Brussels, July 4, 2012.

167. Claudia Bernasconi, *NATO's Fight against Terrorism: Where Do We Stand?*, Research Paper no. 66 (Rome: NATO Defense College, April 2011), 4-5.

168. North Atlantic Council, "Lisbon Summit Declaration," par. 39.

169. Renée de Nevers, "NATO's International Security Role in the Terrorist Era," *International Security* 31, no. 4 (Spring 2007): 44.

170. Bernasconi, *NATO's Fight against Terrorism*, 7.

171. *Report on the Implementation of the European Security Strategy—Providing Security in a Changing World*, S407/08 (Brussels: European Council, December 11, 2008), 4.

172. Article 122, the "solidarity clause," in the Treaty on European Union, in *Consolidated Versions of the Treaty on European Union and the Treaty on the Functioning of the European Union* (Luxembourg: Publications Office of the European Union, 2010), 148.

173. NATO, "NATO and the Fight against Terrorism."

174. Author interviews in Brussels, July 2012.

175. North Atlantic Council, "NATO's Policy Guidelines on Counter-Terrorism: Aware, Capable and Engaged for a Safer Future," May 21, 2012, par. 4, www.nato.int/cps/en/natolive/official_texts_87905.htm?.

176. Ibid., par. 7.

177. Ibid., par. 5.

178. Author interviews in Brussels, July 2012.

179. North Atlantic Council, communiqué, December 18, 1990, par. 15.

180. North Atlantic Council, communiqué, June 7, 1991, par. 7.

181. North Atlantic Council, "Rome Declaration," par. 18.

182. North Atlantic Council, "Strategic Concept," November 7, 1991, par. 12, 49-50.

183. North Atlantic Council, declaration, January 11, 1994, par. 17.

184. North Atlantic Council, "Final Communiqué," June 13, 1996, par. 21.

185. As with the former DGP, the United States serves as the permanent cochair of the committee in the defense format and the other cochair is held by a European member-state on a rotating basis. When the foreign and defense ministry representatives meet together to constitute the Committee on Proliferation, it has three cochairs: the United States, a rotating European cochair, and the assistant secretary general for emerging security challenges.

186. North Atlantic Council, "Strategic Concept," April 24, 1999, par. 22.

187. Ibid., par. 40 and 41.

188. Ted Whiteside, head of NATO's Weapons of Mass Destruction (WMD) Centre, video interview, NATO headquarters, May 22, 2003, www.nato.int/docu/speech/2003/s030522b.htm.

189. North Atlantic Council, "Strategic Concept," November 19, 2010, par. 9. Some observers hold that the Allies agreed to refer vaguely to "some of the world's most volatile regions" out of deference to Turkish sensitivities about alluding specifically to the Middle East or Iran in particular.

190. Ibid., par. 10.

191. North Atlantic Council, "Lisbon Summit Declaration," par. 34.

192. Michael Rühle, *The Broader Context of NATO's Nuclear Policy and Posture*, Research Paper no. 89 (Rome: NATO Defense College, January 2013), 5.

193. North Atlantic Council, "Strategic Concept," April 24, 1999, par. 22.

194. North Atlantic Council, "Comprehensive Political Guidance," November 29, 2006, par. 5.

195. Jacques Chirac at Landivisiau-l'Ile Longue, speech on January 19, 2006, www.elysee.fr/elysee/elysee.fr/francais_archives/interventions/discours_et_declarations/2006/janvier/allocution_du_president_de_la_republique_lors_de_sa_visite_aux_forces_aeriennes_et_oceanique_strategiques-landivisiau-l_ile_longue-finistere.38406.html. For background on this and other policy innovations articulated by President Chirac in January 2006, see David S. Yost, "France's New Nuclear Doctrine," *International Affairs* 82, no. 4 (July 2006): 701–721.

196. *The Future of the United Kingdom's Nuclear Deterrent*, presented to Parliament by the Secretary of State for Defence and the Secretary of State for Foreign and Commonwealth Affairs by Command of Her Majesty, Cm 6994 (London: Her Majesty's Stationery Office, December 2006), 19, par. 3-11, www.mod.uk/NR/rdonlyres/AC00DD79-76D6-4FE3-91A1-6A56B03C092F/0/DefenceWhitePaper2006_Cm6994.pdf.

197. Gates, speech, October 28, 2008, www.defenselink.mil/speeches/speech.aspx?speechid=1305. While U.S. and French statements have referred to states employing terrorist groups to deliver "weapons of mass destruction," the December 2006 British white paper focused on the narrower category of state sponsors "transferring nuclear weapons or nuclear technology to terrorists."

198. William J. Broad, "New Team Plans to Identify Nuclear Attackers," *New York Times*, February 2, 2006.

199. Steven Aoki, deputy under secretary of energy for counterterrorism, statement before the House Committee on Homeland Security, Subcommittee on Emerging Threats, Cybersecurity, and Science and Technology, October 10, 2007.

200. NATO, "NATO's Comprehensive, Strategic-Level Policy for Preventing the Proliferation of Weapons of Mass Destruction (WMD) and Defending against Chemical, Biological, Radiological and Nuclear (CBRN) Threats," September 1, 2009, par. 12, www.nato.int/cps/en/natolive/official_texts_57218.htm.

201. See the report by Arne Thomas and Wing Commander Jonathan Archer on the conference held in Prague on February 2-4, 2011, "NATO's Weapons of Mass Destruction Forensic Conference," www.nato.int/nato_static/assets/pdf/pdf_2011_02/20110615_WMD-Forensics-Conference-Report.pdf.

202. See NATO, "The Euro-Atlantic Disaster Response Coordination Centre," last updated 20 July 2012, www.nato.int/cps/en/natolive/topics_52057.htm, as well as NATO, "NATO's Comprehensive, Strategic-Level Policy for Preventing the Proliferation of Weapons of Mass Destruction (WMD) and Defending against Chemical, Biological, Radiological and Nuclear (CBRN) Threats," September 1, 2009, www.nato.int/cps/en/natolive/official_texts_57218.htm.

203. Allied Force Command Headquarters Heidelberg, "The DJSE [Deployable Joint Staff Element] Concept," www.nato.int/fchd/FCHD/djse-concept.html.

204. Kurt Volker and Kevin Green, *NATO Reform: Key Principles* (Washington, DC: Atlantic Council of the United States, 2011), 3. Kurt Volker is a former U.S. ambassador to NATO, and Kevin Green is a retired U.S. Navy vice admiral.

205. Claudia Major, Christian Mölling, and Tomas Valasek, *Smart But Too Cautious: How NATO Can Improve Its Fight Against Austerity* (London: Centre for European Reform, May 2012), 2. Claudia Major and Christian Mölling are with the Stiftung Wissenschaft und Politik in Berlin. Tomas Valasek was then with the Centre for European Reform and is now the permanent representative of Slovakia to NATO.

206. Author interviews in Brussels, May 2013, and correspondence with experts in Brussels, September 2013.

207. The operations listed in this paragraph are discussed in chapters 4 and 5.

208. Author interviews in Warsaw, July 2012.

209. "NATO must retain the ability to conduct the full range of its missions, from high to low intensity, placing special focus on the most likely operations, being responsive to current and future operational requirements, and still able to conduct the most demanding operations." North Atlantic Council, "Comprehensive Political Guidance," November 29, 2006, par. 7.

210. NATO forces in Afghanistan consumed per day an average of 1.8 million gallons of fuel in November 2011, and 99 percent of that fuel was provided by trucks via Pakistan. When Pakistan shut the border crossings that month, NATO had to abruptly increase its reliance on the Northern Distribution Network via Latvia, Russia, Kazakhstan, and Uzbekistan, at a price almost three times more costly than via Pakistan. For background, see Mehmet Kinaci, "Energy Security: Tough Lessons of Afghanistan," *The Transformer* 8, no. 1 (Spring 2012); "Allied Command Transformation," www.act.nato.int/transformer-2012-01/article-7; and John C.K. Daly, "Energy: NATO's 'Achilles' Heel'?," July 26, 2012, www.isn.ethz.ch/Digital-Library/Articles/Detail/?id=150662.

211. North Atlantic Council, "Strasbourg/Kehl Summit Declaration," par. 56; North Atlantic Council, "Lisbon Summit Declaration," par. 33; and North Atlantic Council, "Chicago Summit Declaration," par. 50.

3

Deterrence and Defense Posture

NATO's capabilities for deterrence and defense have historically pertained mainly to the risk of state aggression or coercion. During the Cold War, the NATO Allies were concerned about the risk of aggression by the Soviet Union and its allies, particularly during key crises after the formation of the Warsaw Pact in 1955.

Since the end of the Cold War in 1989–1991, the NATO Allies have seen their deterrence and defense capabilities as relevant not only to the risk of state aggression or coercion but also as potentially useful in countering terrorism and WMD proliferation as well as certain nontraditional security challenges such as cyber attacks.

The Alliance's deterrence and defense capabilities may be especially pertinent to deterring or combating state-sponsored terrorism and the acquisition and use by regional powers of WMD and delivery means, such as cruise and ballistic missiles.

The relevance of conventional military forces and other capabilities to new challenges such as energy and cyber security appears at first glance to be marginal, even questionable, but such capabilities may make an indirect contribution to security against cyber attacks or the exploitation of energy vulnerabilities by deterring aggression and promoting strategic stability. In an actual conflict, moreover, certain nontraditional instruments—including cyber and space capabilities—would in all likelihood be employed.

As noted in chapter 2, the NATO Allies may face cross-domain deterrence and operational challenges. One might consider as an example certain aspects of energy security. Energy supplies have been a key factor in international rivalry and conflict since the late nineteenth century, as with the British-German competition for oil resources for naval power in the years leading up to World War I. Experts have noted that in a conflict, Iran might try to shut the Persian Gulf and the Strait of Hormuz, immediately affecting 40 percent of the world's energy commerce.[1] Keeping these lines of communication open might well require conventional military forces and other capabilities, including cyber assets and missile defenses, to protect command and control capabilities, deployed forces, and national territories and populations. At the same time, protecting critical infrastructure could deter—or counter—attacks on essential energy assets.

The NATO Allies have been dealing with cyber attacks since the 1999 Kosovo conflict, as discussed in chapter 2. It has become widely recognized that conflicts will increasingly include a cyber dimension. As Olaf Theiler of NATO's International Staff recently noted, "Massive attacks on government websites and servers in Georgia took place during the [2008] Georgia-Russia conflict, giving the term of cyber-war a more concrete form. These actions did no actual physical damage. They did, however, weaken the Georgian government during a critical phase of the conflict."[2]

Cyber attacks are, it should be added, more and more capable of causing "actual physical damage," notably by disrupting utilities such as water and electricity supplies and communications networks. Deterring cyber attacks and responding to them may well depend in part on conventional military forces and other assets, in addition to capabilities to block cyber attacks and to respond in kind—and to identify attackers promptly. Because the Allies face multiple threats, they need a full range of deterrence and defense capabilities.

The Allies have in recent years given increased attention to missile defenses, but they have yet to fully acknowledge the importance of the cyber dimension, at least in their declaratory policy.

In the 1991 Strategic Concept, the first such document after the end of the Cold War, the Allies discussed two main categories of capabilities for deterrence and defense: conventional and nuclear forces. The Allies mentioned missile defenses only once—as a possible response, along with export controls, to ballistic missile and WMD proliferation.[3] The Allies took the same approach in the 1999 Strategic Concept. They examined conventional and nuclear forces at length as instruments of defense and deterrence, and made only one reference to missile defenses, again as a possible response to missile and WMD proliferation.[4] As recently as 2009, at the Strasbourg/Kehl Summit, the Allies held that deterrence was "based on an appropriate mix of nuclear and conventional capabilities."[5]

In contrast, at the 2010 Lisbon Summit, the Allies featured missile defenses much more prominently than in the past. They declared that they had decided to "develop the capability to defend our populations and territories against ballistic missile attack as a core element of our collective defence."[6]

At least three contextual factors contributed to the change in policy. First, as the Allies indicated in the 2010 Strategic Concept, "the proliferation of ballistic missiles . . . poses a real and growing threat to the Euro-Atlantic area."[7] Second, another major factor that had changed between 1999 and 2010 was the termination of the ABM Treaty regime, which took effect in 2002. The termination of that regime meant that there were no longer any legal obstacles to U.S. missile defense deployments or technology transfers to allies. It was after the end of the ABM Treaty that the Allies commissioned a multiyear feasibility study on missile defense, and the decision-making process in this regard came to a head at the

2010 summit. Third, missile defense technology had matured considerably over the previous decade.

While the Allies have mentioned the growing significance of cyber capabilities in recent high-level declarations, they have highlighted conventional, nuclear, and missile defense capabilities. In the 2010 Lisbon Summit Declaration the Allies prescribed "an appropriate mix of conventional, nuclear, and missile defence forces."[8] A formula repeating these three elements—"an appropriate mix of nuclear, conventional and missile defence capabilities"—gained approval in the Chicago Summit Declaration and the Deterrence and Defense Posture Review (DDPR) published in May 2012.[9]

Conventional Military Forces

Although the Allies have a number of significant commonly procured and maintained capabilities, such as radars and communications systems and the NATO AWACS aircraft, most of their conventional military forces derive from national acquisition programs and are maintained under national command. As during the Cold War, decision-making authority remains in the hands of Allied national governments. The Allies share information about their actual and projected capabilities in collective Alliance institutions and take this information into account in making their national decisions, but Alliance institutions have no legal authority over national governments and no ability to compel them to acquire capabilities. An exchange in 1981 between a U.S. congressman, Representative Norman Dicks (D-Washington), and General Bernard Rogers, then SACEUR, illustrated this fact.

> Mr. DICKS. One of the factors involved in the ammunition equation is the fact that many of our allies have even fewer stocks than we do.
>
> General ROGERS. That is correct.
>
> Mr. DICKS. What efforts are you making to improve the overall alliance posture in this respect?
>
> General ROGERS. Cajole, plead, prod. That is just about the extent of it.[10]

A post–Cold War counterpart of this exchange would be the efforts by a subsequent SACEUR, General James Jones. In 2006 General Jones urged NATO nations to adopt a common funding mechanism to support NATO Response Force deployments.[11] He formulated eloquent arguments, but Allied governments chose to disregard them. Throughout the Alliance's history, Allied governments have been more susceptible to persuasion and "peer pressure" from fellow Allies than to pleas advanced by NATO institutions such as the International Staff and the NATO Military Authorities.

The "peer pressure" mechanism on force procurement has nonetheless become more comprehensive and systematic since the introduction in 2009 of the new NATO Defense Planning Process (NDPP). The NDPP is intended to enable the Allies to acquire all the capabilities necessary to reach the Alliance's level of ambition—"two major joint operations and six small joint operations, if required."[12] In view of the level of ambition, the Defense Planning Staff Team, under the leadership of the Strategic Commands (particularly Allied Command Transformation), defines "one single consolidated list of Minimum Capability Requirements [MCRs], including eventual shortfalls."[13] The Defense Planning Staff Team then apportions the MCRs to specific NATO countries and NATO entities, "respecting the principles of fair burden-sharing and reasonable challenge." Each Ally can "present its national views" in the NDPP, but each Ally is subject to "a series of multilateral examinations" involving all the Allies. As noted on the NATO website, "During these examinations, the working practice of consensus-minus-one will be continued."[14]

Some experts hold that the NDPP procedure is "the only time in NATO that the consensus rule does not apply."[15] This procedure can place an Ally's defense minister in a position to tell his national authorities that the other NATO Allies expect the country to take specific capability development and procurement action. This circumstance may make a difference with some Allies but not with others. To the extent that Allies "plead austerity" or set out other reasons as an excuse for not satisfying the assigned MCRs, the Alliance will fall short of meeting its level of ambition. The NDPP process has exerted some influence on national plans and decisions. According to informed observers, however, vigilance in meeting capability targets has been uneven.

The NDPP mechanism has two merits. First, it specifies with clarity and precision (on a classified basis, to be sure) what the Allies require to meet their agreed-upon level of ambition. Second, it functions as a disciplining tool that comes close to being compulsory in the eyes of some Allies—a hallmark of national honor and credibility. Its shortcoming is that, even with the isolating and "shaming" power of the "consensus-minus-one" method, Allies are still free not to accept the capability responsibilities assigned to them. As NATO secretary general Rasmussen has observed, "it is more or less a voluntary process. Nations have not handed over sovereignty to NATO, as they have done to the European Commission, and realistically I don't think they will."[16] Moreover, even if Allies do meet their assigned capability goals, their contributions to a specific NATO operation remain subject to national decisions in a force generation conference.[17]

In recent years, one of the chief elements in the NDPP effort to implement the "fair burden-sharing and reasonable challenge" principles has been the 50 percent guideline. According to this guideline, it is fair and reasonable not to expect any single Ally to provide more than 50 percent of any capability. In practice, this means that the other Allies should be doing more to diminish the current capability responsibilities on U.S. shoulders.[18] In certain conventional capability areas (such as suppression of enemy air defenses, electronic warfare, unmanned aerial vehicles for surveillance and reconnaissance, and aerial refueling tankers), the U.S. contribution is well over 50 percent.

According to informed observers, Allied capabilities are currently and prospectively below the Alliance's level of ambition, owing to national spending shortfalls—setting aside the continuing debate about preparedness for a "Major Joint Operation Plus" (collective defense). The 50 percent capability guideline appears unlikely to be more successful than the agreement calling upon all Allies to spend at least 2 percent of GDP on defense. The Allies appear to be wagering that the United States will continue to provide capabilities to make up for their shortfalls, despite warnings such as those sounded by Robert Gates, then the U.S. secretary of defense, in June 2011.

As a result, another continuity from the Cold War has been the tendency of a number of non-U.S. Allies to spend little more on conventional forces than they deem necessary to ensure the ongoing engagement of the United States as their security guarantor, notably in the nuclear domain.

In 1981, in order to explain Britain's "steadfastness" in maintaining the British Army of the Rhine and other conventional military forces in Germany, British scholar Laurence Martin wrote, "It is in large part a subscription to retain the American nuclear guarantee; a contribution to the military arrangements that, by justifying a substantial American military presence in Europe, lends the guarantee much of its credibility."[19] Similarly, as Josef Joffe pointed out, once West Germany had gained membership in NATO, the key question was, "How much do we have to contribute in order to maintain the American guarantee?"[20]

The burden-sharing debate regarding conventional military forces has since the 1950s and over the decades usually taken the form of U.S. complaints and pressures on the other Allies to do more. The other Allies have made investments in conventional military forces calculated in part to assuage the concerns of American officials and legislators, and the United States has introduced a series of initiatives intended to get the Allies to invest more in conventional forces, but with limited success. The results of these initiatives have frequently fallen short of U.S. ambitions and expectations.

The key difference from the Cold War pattern has been that the post–Cold War NATO has been undertaking actual operations since 1990. As a result, the mainly U.S.-inspired initiatives for conventional force improvements in the Alliance since the early 1990s have been increasingly oriented toward the conduct of crisis management operations in addition to deterrence and force readiness in support of collective defense. Continuity with the Cold War pattern persists in that, as a number of European Allied observers have made clear, national engagements in Afghanistan have been undertaken largely to show good will to the United States and thereby sustain U.S. commitment to the Alliance for broader purposes, including collective defense and cooperative security.[21]

Conventional Force Transformation Efforts

Since the end of the Cold War, and beginning with the 1991 Rome Summit, the Allies have engaged in a series of conventional force transformation efforts to adapt to new and evolving operational requirements.

Diego Ruiz Palmer has rightly emphasized the "transformational impact" of crisis management operations on NATO's conventional military forces. In the 1990s, for example, operations in the Balkans led the Allies to establish "Multinational Specialised Units, composed of French *gendarmes* and Italian *carabinieri*, to assist SFOR and KFOR with riot control." In his judgment, "From a military transformation standpoint, perhaps the most remarkable achievement of NATO's engagement in Afghanistan has been the unprecedented commitment and capacity by European Allies and Canada to deploy in support of ISAF, on six-month or longer rotations, a multinational HRF [high readiness force] corps headquarters together with battalion or brigade-size combat groups."[22]

The operations in Afghanistan have strengthened the expeditionary capabilities of the Allies, and some observers contend that these operations have led the European Allies to adopt a more combat-oriented approach to security matters. According to Alexander Mattelaer, "Today, the notion that any military ultimately has a war-fighting role is unmistakeably gaining political acceptance in a supposedly postmodern Europe. . . . The old continent is close to bottoming out in terms of taking its security ever less seriously."[23]

While Mattelaer and like-minded observers see grounds for hope regarding conventional force transformation in NATO Europe, others see clear limits to such progress. The United States has since the early 1990s been pressing its NATO Allies to adopt the U.S. model of high-technology expeditionary forces. Although the Allies have accepted this model as an objective on the declaratory level, actual achievements have fallen short of the announced goals. What Anthony Cordesman wrote in 2005 remains true: "NATO has made some progress along these lines, but much of it is more cosmetic than real. . . . Most country defence plans and budgets reflect slow progress, a continuing lack of interoperability, and the inability to move and sustain more than a small fraction of national forces much beyond national boundaries."[24]

In Cordesman's view, the explanation resides in a lack of motivation on the part of the European Allies to prepare for additional expeditionary operations on the model of Afghanistan. "Alliance-wide force transformation of any kind will never happen at more than token levels because many—if not most—European states have no clear motive to become involved and pay the cost."[25]

Owing in large part to the demands of ongoing operations, the Allies have since the 1990s launched a series of initiatives designed to improve their conventional military forces and enhance their force-generation processes. For example, the Prague Capabilities Commitment (PCC) was intended to enhance Alliance conventional forces across a wide range of capabilities spelled out in the 2002 Prague Summit Declaration.[26] In practice, as Robert Bell, a former NATO assistant secretary general for defense investment,[27] pointed out in 2006, the actions of the Allies have not matched their pledges to achieve specific force enhancement objectives.

> Disconnects have bedeviled progress in realising the Prague goals for the PCC, particularly in the areas of air-to-ground surveillance, strategic airlift, aerial refueling, suppression of enemy air defences, and combat support and combat service support. In large measure, these failures to

follow through are directly linked with the declining defence budgets of most NATO member states and the growing necessity within these nations to earmark increasing percentages of what *is* spent on defence on the operations and maintenance costs of NATO's many ongoing crisis response operations, including its expanding operations in Afghanistan.[28]

Since the economic crisis began in 2008, defense spending in most NATO countries has again contracted. This has led to further decreases in investment in conventional military forces. In September 2012, General Hakan Syren, a Swedish officer serving as chairman of the European Union's Military Committee, said, "The military capabilities of the EU member states are on a steady downward slope. . . . Looking a few years into the future, it is simple mathematics to predict that many member states will be unable to sustain essential parts of their national forces, air forces being the prime example."[29] (It should be recalled that twenty-two of the European Union's member states are NATO Allies.)

In May 2012 Nick Witney, the former chief executive of the European Union's European Defense Agency, deplored the fact that "every member state is cutting armed forces without transparency and consultation, without an architectural idea for what will be left."[30] This implies that the Allies have generally not succeeded in making optimal use of their consultative arrangements in the European Union and NATO.

In order to maximize the value of their increasingly scarce budgetary resources, the Allies have in recent years endorsed "smart defense" as an economical approach to acquiring, maintaining, and operating capabilities.[31] In one of their May 2012 Chicago Summit documents, the Allies described "smart defense" as an "opportunity for a renewed culture of cooperation in which multinational collaboration is given new prominence as an effective and efficient option for developing critical capabilities."[32] The Allies intend to "work closely with the EU, as agreed, to ensure that our Smart Defence and the EU's Pooling and Sharing initiatives are complementary and mutually reinforcing."[33] The smart defense initiative is also intended to promote coordination in defense spending cuts so that Allies engage in specialization by purposeful design rather than by random default.

Smart defense falls short of serving as a remedy for the defense budget cutbacks by NATO governments. As critics note, the term implies that the Alliance's previous approach was "dumb defense," and that "smart defense" involves something new in multinational capability arrangements in NATO. In fact, although the results of multinational efforts have often been disappointing, the Allies have a long history of obtaining and maintaining capabilities on a multinational basis, going back to the foundation of the Supreme Headquarters Allied Powers Europe (SHAPE) in 1951.[34] In February 2012 the Norwegian minister of defense, Espen Barth Eide, said that smart defense is "something Norway has been working on for many years. . . . Together with Belgium, Denmark and the Netherlands, we were founders of the European Participating Air Forces (EPAF) in the late 1970s."[35] Eide also pointed out that it may take several years to achieve financial benefits from new multinational "smart defense" arrangements.[36]

As Tomas Valasek, a Slovak expert,[37] has noted, it may be difficult to organize new "smart defense" arrangements if they require national role specialization and a higher degree of mutual reliance among Allies. The problem of inefficiencies in spending owing to the fragmentation of efforts by the European Allies has been recognized for decades. Surmounting this problem would require consolidating or otherwise rationalizing national acquisition, production, training, and maintenance activities. Long-established national bureaucracies have historically resisted such efforts. Valasek has suggested that solutions might include (1) assurances to convince Allies to give up national capabilities and rely to a greater extent on multinational arrangements and (2) common funding arrangements to cover the "start-up" costs of new collaborative arrangements.[38] Even with such measures, the savings from new "smart defense" arrangements will probably not compensate for the defense budget reductions of NATO Allies in recent years. As a result, "The danger is that the European allies will not do 'more with less,' . . . but less with less."[39]

Another aspect to the resources problem is that growing proportions of increasingly smaller defense budgets are dedicated to personnel costs, including salaries, health care, and pensions, as well as to ongoing operations. As a result, the amounts available for the procurement of equipment have been shrinking in many NATO nations.

NATO secretary general Rasmussen has argued that NATO nonetheless "will succeed in more multinational cooperation now" because of economic factors: "It is first and foremost because of declining defence budgets and the economic austerity. . . [and] because the long-term trend is that . . . the cost of advanced military equipment rises more rapidly than inflation and GDP."[40]

Some positive examples lend support to Rasmussen's thesis. A case of successful multinational cooperation is the 2006 Strategic Airlift Capability (SAC) initiative to procure, maintain, and employ three Boeing C-17 strategic transport aircraft. Operating since 2009 from Pápa Air Base in Hungary, the SAC initiative is manifest in the Heavy Airlift Wing with staff from NATO and Partnership for Peace participating nations.[41] More recently, in November 2012 ten European Allies (Belgium, France, Greece, Spain, Hungary, Luxembourg, the Netherlands, Norway, Poland, and Portugal) signed a "letter of intent" to work together on buying or leasing tanker aircraft for aerial refueling. While they have not yet identified a specific type of tanker to buy or rent, their letter expresses a constructive intention to cooperate.[42]

While many analysts have underscored the limitations of "smart defense" and "pooling and sharing" as means to compensate for diminished defense spending, the political dimension of these cooperative arrangements has gained increasing recognition. As Michael Rühle has observed, such efforts have become "indispensable," because they serve as "symbols of both fiscal responsibility and political aspiration."[43]

NATO Response Force

The NATO Response Force (NRF) stands out as perhaps the most revealing example of the challenges facing the Alliance in conventional force improvement. The NATO

Allies first approved the constitution of an NRF at the Prague Summit in 2002. The NATO secretary general and SACEUR announced in October 2004 that the NRF had attained "its initial operational capability of approximately 17,000 troops and was ready to take on the full range of missions."[44] At the Riga Summit in November 2006, the Allies declared that the NRF was "at full operational capability,"[45] with (according to the NATO website) "up to 25,000 troops."[46]

In addition to the command structure, the NRF is composed of an Immediate Response Force (IRF) with "approximately 14,000 personnel" maintained at high readiness and a Response Forces Pool (RFP) consisting of the remaining forces pledged by Allies for the NRF.[47] The IRF includes "a brigade-sized land component based on three Battle Groups and their supporting elements; a maritime component based on NATO's Standing Naval Maritime Groups and Standing Naval Mine Counter Measures Groups; a combat air and air support component; special forces; and a CBRN (chemical, biological, radiological and nuclear) defence task force."[48]

NRF elements have to date helped to provide security for the 2004 summer Olympics in Athens and the September 2004 presidential elections in Afghanistan. NRF elements have also assisted in providing disaster relief to the United States (transporting relief supplies in the wake of Hurricane Katrina in September–October 2005) and Pakistan (deploying engineers and medical staff and delivering supplies from October 2005 to February 2006).

The Allies have agreed to general principles relating to the NRF. At the Riga Summit in 2006 they declared that "continuing defence transformation is essential to ensure that the Alliance remains able to perform its full range of missions, including collective defence and crisis response operations." They added that the NRF "plays a vital part in the Alliance's response to a rapidly emerging crisis."[49] Despite the references to NATO's "full range of missions," the Allies have disagreed about employing the NRF in particular cases. As Robert Bell has noted,

> Not everyone agreed that it was an appropriate use of the NRF to deploy it to Afghanistan to bolster security during local elections there. Some nations have argued that the NRF should be restricted to "defence and security" deployments, and not be employed in the disaster relief or humanitarian operations mode.... The lack of a clear consensus as to where the NRF should be dispatched has undoubtedly affected at least some nations' inclination to fully embrace the initiative.[50]

Some Allies have seen the NRF as most useful as an expeditionary force for non-Article 5 crisis response operations, while most of the new Allies in Central and Eastern Europe "favor assigning the NRF for the defense of the alliance's territory and keeping this force at permanent readiness, to deter or defend against possible Russian military provocations."[51]

The United Kingdom's February 2009 proposal for a dedicated standing Allied Solidarity Force as a means to demonstrate NATO's commitment to Article 5 missions was soon abandoned, owing to "cost and force generation issues."[52] The Allies decided, on the basis of a Norwegian initiative, to assign the functions of the proposed Allied Solidarity Force to the NRF.[53] Despite continuing disagreements among the Allies about the NRF's operational missions, this decision was seen as "an important sign of movement in the 'right' direction by those Allies concerned about their strategic exposure."[54] The June 2009 agreed-upon concept for the NRF included "a more explicit focus on Article 5 missions."[55]

Aside from its operational missions, the NRF was intended to serve as "a driving engine of NATO's military transformation."[56] According to the 2002 Prague Summit Declaration, "The NRF will also be a catalyst for focusing and promoting improvements in the Alliance's military capabilities."[57] The 2006 Riga Summit Declaration stated that the NRF "serves as a catalyst for transformation and interoperability and will enhance the overall quality of our armed forces."[58]

Some analysts judge, however, that the NRF's utility in this regard is limited. According to Jeffrey Bialos and Stuart Koehl, "SHAPE's planning, by necessity, reflects the notion that the NRF will be comprised of what forces actually exist rather than those SHAPE would like to see for the future." As a result, "the NRF certification process is likely to follow armaments capability development and innovation rather than catalyze it."[59]

The NRF has nonetheless had a positive transformational effect on Alliance forces, notably in enhancing their "operational readiness and effectiveness."[60] As Guillaume Lasconjarias has observed, the NRF may serve as an important instrument in the Alliance's Connected Forces Initiative.[61]

The most serious problem with the NRF initiative has been getting the Allies to provide capabilities for it. Robert Bell has compared the NRF capability-pledging process to the endless labors of Sisyphus.

> Like the mythological figure Sisyphus, forever condemned by the Greek gods to push a rock up a hill only to have it roll back down each time before he could reach the summit, NATO seems, under current NRF planning and funding arrangements, destined to a continuing series of high-drama trials twice each year. For each six-month NRF rotation, the CJSOR [Combined Joint Statement of Requirements] again threatens to come up short unless the NATO leadership makes heroic efforts to cajole last-minute commitments from reluctant member states. As former Secretary General Lord Robertson was fond of saying, constantly having to go around with a "begging bowl" is no way to run a railroad—or an Alliance.[62]

The Allies have agreed to extend the duration of NRF rotation periods from six to twelve months, beginning in 2012.[63] It remains to be seen whether the capability-pledging shortfalls will be addressed more readily at twelve-month intervals instead of six-month ones.

Funding NRF deployments remains a closely related challenge. The current arrangement calls for the nations pledging capabilities to the NRF to pay the force deployment costs in the event of a crisis during their rotation period. This arrangement functions, critics say, as a "reverse lottery," in that the nations pledging capabilities are responsible for most of the costs of any operations, and this explains the reluctance of Allies to make capability pledges for NRF rotations. Allies opposed to common funding of NRF deployments prefer the traditional Alliance principle holding that "costs lie where they fall"—that is, nations are responsible for costs of their own force deployments. Some of these Allies hold that they are already paying for their "fair share" of the Alliance's conventional force posture and that contributing to common funding for the NRF would amount to "paying twice," subsidizing Allies that are not paying their fair share, and creating a "disincentive" for lagging Allies to improve their national military capabilities.[64]

Disagreements among the Allies on funding the NRF and on its missions reflect deeper differences as to NATO's core tasks—above all, the relative urgency of collective defense and crisis management priorities. These differences stand out when the Allies deliberate about how to equip, train, and exercise their military forces, and they come even more sharply to the fore when the Allies have to decide whether, when, where, and how to commit their forces to operations.

Conventional Military Forces and Deterrence

The contributions of conventional forces to the Alliance's defense and deterrence posture—and their relationship to nuclear and missile defense capabilities—deserve particular attention, notably in an era of tightened constraints on defense spending.

One of the key unanswered questions facing the Alliance remains how reliable conventional military forces can be as a means of deterrence. Some Allied observers hold that the entire history of international politics demonstrates the unreliability of conventional deterrence, and that only nuclear threats have shown the degree of reliability necessary for effective deterrence. This view is particularly widespread in France.[65]

The Allies have avoided an "either/or" perspective in each of their three post–Cold War Strategic Concepts. In the 1991 Strategic Concept, the Allies stated that both conventional and nuclear forces are required for deterrence.

> Conventional forces contribute to war prevention by ensuring that no potential aggressor could contemplate a quick or easy victory, or territorial gains, by conventional means. . . . But the Alliance's conventional forces alone cannot ensure the prevention of war. Nuclear weapons make a unique contribution in rendering the risks of any aggression incalculable and unacceptable. Thus, they remain essential to preserve peace.[66]

The Allies offered a similar judgment in the 1999 Strategic Concept, stating that "the Alliance's conventional forces alone cannot ensure credible deterrence." As a result, "To protect peace and to prevent war or any kind of coercion, the Alliance will maintain for the foreseeable future an appropriate mix of nuclear and conventional forces based in Europe and kept up to date where necessary, although at a minimum sufficient level."[67] In the 2010 Strategic Concept the Allies repeated their call for deterrence "based on an appropriate mix of nuclear and conventional capabilities."[68] At the 2012 Chicago Summit the Allies stated, "Missile defence can complement the role of nuclear weapons in deterrence; it cannot substitute for them."[69]

From the perspective of many Allied observers, notably in Turkey and in Central and Eastern Europe, the same principle applies to conventional military forces. In their view, missile defenses and contingency plans and exercises involving conventional military forces are no substitute for retaining U.S. nuclear weapons in Europe as a key element of the Alliance's deterrence posture.[70] As Jacek Durkalec, a Polish scholar, wrote in a valuable analysis of views in Central and Eastern Europe, "Especially in times of a shrinking conventional presence in Europe, the U.S. nuclear presence in Europe is the ultimate demonstration of the United States' commitment to the defence of Europe."[71] Similarly, Nursin Atesoglu Güney, a Turkish professor, has written that "the current proposals regarding missile defence systems and conventional precision guided weapons as the optimum tools of deterrence continue to fall short as valid alternatives when compared with a credible reliable nuclear deterrence."[72]

The Allies have repeatedly revised their threat assessments and corresponding conventional force capability requirements since 1991. In the 1991 Strategic Concept, published just weeks before the Soviet collapse, the main threat for the NATO Allies to deter and hedge against was the Soviet Union, whose conventional forces were "significantly larger than those of any other European State."[73] The Allies concluded in 1991 that "with the radical changes in the security situation, including conventional force levels in Europe maintained in relative balance and increased reaction times, NATO's ability to defuse a crisis through diplomatic and other means or, should it be necessary, to mount a successful conventional defence will significantly improve. The circumstances in which any use of nuclear weapons might have to be contemplated by them are therefore even more remote."[74] As noted in chapter 1, in the 1991 Strategic Concept, the only function envisaged for NATO's conventional forces was to contribute to collective defense.[75]

In the 1999 Strategic Concept the Allies stated that "NATO's ability to defuse a crisis through diplomatic and other means or, should it be necessary, to mount a successful conventional defence has significantly improved. The circumstances in which any use of nuclear weapons might have to be contemplated by them are therefore extremely remote."[76] The Allies did not rule out conventional military threats. "Notwithstanding positive developments in the strategic environment and the fact that large-scale conventional aggression against the Alliance is highly unlikely, the possibility of such a threat emerging over the longer term exists."[77] In practice, however, the Allies were much more concerned about "regional crises at the periphery of the Alliance, which could evolve rapidly," and lead "to armed conflicts. Such conflicts could affect the security of the Alliance by spilling over into neighbouring countries, including NATO countries, or in other ways, and could also affect the security of other states."[78]

This concern with regional crises and conflicts stood out because it reflected the experience of the Allies in the Balkans in the 1990s, particularly the major interventions in the Bosnia and Kosovo conflicts. The requirements for conventional forces therefore encompassed "high readiness forces capable of beginning rapidly, and immediately as necessary, collective defence or non-Article 5 crisis response operations; forces at different levels of lower readiness to provide the bulk of those required for collective defence, for rotation of forces to sustain crisis response operations, or for further reinforcement of a particular region; and a longer-term build-up and augmentation capability for the worst case—but very remote—scenario of large scale operations for collective defence."[79]

In the 2010 Strategic Concept the Allies declared that "the threat of a conventional attack against NATO territory is low," but that "the conventional threat cannot be ignored."[80]

In view of the Alliance's continuing responsibilities in the Balkans and Afghanistan, the 2010 Strategic Concept called for "the ability to sustain concurrent major joint operations and several smaller operations for collective defence and crisis response, including at strategic distance."[81] The Allies do not appear to have publicly defined the term "strategic distance," but Jens Ringsmose and Sten Rynning have reported that it is 15,000 kilometers from Brussels.[82]

The NATO-led intervention in Libya in 2011 suggested that the conventional military capabilities of the Allies fall short of this level of ambition. Robert Gates, then the U.S. secretary of defense, said in June 2011,

> Libya has just hammered home the consequences of many years of underinvestment: if even our biggest allies are beginning to feel the stress and strain, where the hell would we have been if we'd actually had to deal with the Soviets? . . . For God's sake, this is Gaddafi, this isn't some big power. The fact that there are challenges in sustaining just an air campaign even for 90 days is, I think, revealing.[83]

According to the 2010 Strategic Concept, the Allies need "robust, mobile and deployable conventional forces to carry out both our Article 5 responsibilities and the Alliance's expeditionary operations." Moreover, they require missile defenses and forces adapted to defending against cyber, terrorist, and CBRN attacks.[84] As discussed in chapter 2, the Allies have nonetheless disagreed about defining their "level of ambition" in terms of precise force-generation objectives, particularly in reference to Article 5 contingencies.

Moreover, since the Alliance's interventions in the Balkan conflicts began in 1992, the Allies have been discussing the relationship between forces equipped and prepared for crisis management operations and those designed for collective defense. This question is examined in chapter 5, but the key point here is that some Allied observers are concerned about an erosion of the conventional military force contribution to NATO's deterrence and defense posture. In February 2012 the Norwegian minister of defense, Espen Barth Eide, said that

> Article five is not in such good shape as people might think. This is due to the confluence of two different trends: reduced military capability for deterrence, particularly on the conventional side, and the high operational tempo emphasizing non-article V and out of area operations over preparedness at the core. This was starkly illustrated by this fall's NATO CMX [crisis management] exercise, conducted in Norway [in October 2011]. . . . The institutional memory of Article V response mechanisms isn't what it once was in NATO's command structure. . . . Particularly our collective conventional capabilities . . . [have] been withering away faster than both our ability to deploy to distant theatres and our nuclear capabilities.[85]

Another aspect of the conventional deterrence debate concerns the continuing—and deepening—capabilities gap between the United States and the rest of the NATO Allies. As the NATO secretary general pointed out in February 2011,

> Over the past two years, defence spending by NATO's European member nations has shrunk by some 45 billion dollars—that is the equivalent of Germany's entire annual defence budget. Indeed, NATO Allies are starting the new decade further apart than ever before in terms of defence investment. Ten years ago, the United States accounted for just under half of NATO members' total defence spending. Today the American share is closer to 75 percent—and it will continue to grow, even with the new cuts in the Pentagon's spending.[86]

In these circumstances it is not clear how great a contribution to NATO's deterrence and defense posture the European Allies will be able to make with their conventional military forces.[87]

The consequences of the further reductions in the U.S. conventional military presence in Europe announced in early 2012 could be significant. If the U.S. military presence has in some cases allowed European governments to engage in what economists call "free-riding," it has in other cases probably encouraged European Allies to make an effort that would otherwise seem beyond their grasp and therefore futile. The decisions flowing from the January 2012 U.S. strategic guidance, including the rebalancing of U.S. priorities to the Asia-Pacific,[88] may not function as a "wake-up call" for the European Allies to spend more—and more wisely—under the "smart defense" banner. The U.S. force reductions in Europe may instead tempt many of them to indulge in more illusions about the sufficiency of "soft power" and economic sanctions as security instruments in isolation from military capabilities. Reassessments of security challenges may in some cases serve as rationales to justify further defense budget cuts and to do less to acquire and improve conventional military forces.

It should be understood that well before the financial crisis struck in 2008, the ISAF operation in Afghanistan had strained NATO European defense budgets. To meet their commitments in Afghanistan, Allies diverted resources from capability development to operations and maintenance, and thus postponed procurement and equipment modernization. The defense spending cuts driven by the financial crisis have compounded these investment shortcomings.

Despite the adverse financial context, smart defense and the Connected Forces Initiative (CFI) are designed to keep up the readiness, effectiveness, and usability of Allied forces. With the CFI, once the ISAF mission has been completed in 2014, the Allies intend to move "from operational engagement to operational preparedness." The Allies plan to build on their experiences in Afghanistan with a combination of education, training, and exercise activities as well as better use of modern technologies, such as simulators.[89] The Allies set out their objectives in this regard in the "NATO Forces 2020" declaration at the NATO Summit in Chicago in May 2012.[90]

NATO's Nuclear Posture and U.S. Extended Deterrence

NATO's collective defense preoccupations during the Cold War focused on how to deter the Soviet Union from undertaking aggression or coercion. Because the protection afforded to NATO Europe by U.S. strategic nuclear commitments was seen as a decisively important element of deterrence from the earliest days of the Alliance,[91] a primary issue throughout the Cold War was the credibility of what came to be known as U.S. "extended deterrence"—that is, the prevention of aggression or coercion against U.S. allies or security partners through threats of U.S. retaliation. While the United States has relied on its full range of capabilities to honor its extended deterrence commitments, U.S. nuclear forces have been central to this role and have received the greatest amount of attention from governments and publics.[92]

Extended deterrence involves issues of credibility, command and control, and decision making that have been intrinsically more contentious and more difficult to resolve than those associated with "central deterrence"—the prevention of aggression or coercion against the United States itself. Associated issues during the Cold War concerned Allied involvement in U.S. decision making on the potential operational use of nuclear weapons, the types and roles of U.S. nuclear forces in Europe, and the utility and functions of the British and French independent nuclear forces.[93] Nuclear controversies were closely tied to European-American debates about the proper level of investment in conventional forces and burden sharing, about how to assess the NATO–Warsaw Pact conventional force balance, and about what approaches to arms control to pursue in negotiations with the Soviet Union and its Warsaw Pact allies.

In a concerted dialogue spanning decades, the NATO Allies concluded that U.S. extended deterrence requires, among other things, U.S. nuclear forces based in Europe. A substantial consensus of officials and experts on both sides of the Atlantic has held that U.S. nuclear commitments would be less credible if they depended solely on forces at sea and in North America. Nonetheless, large-scale reductions in U.S. nuclear forces in Europe began in the late 1970s, and continued with the 1987 Intermediate-range Nuclear Force (INF) Treaty eliminating U.S. and Soviet land-based missiles with ranges between 500 and 5,500 kilometers.

The INF Treaty created an impetus for deliberations about constraints on short-range systems, defined as those with ranges less than 500 kilometers. When negotiations on such forces appeared impractical, notably in the turbulent circumstances in the final years of the Soviet Union, the U.S. administration under President George H. W. Bush took decisions in 1991 in coordination with Moscow to define reciprocal presidential initiatives concerning nuclear forces. U.S. and NATO decisions in September–October 1991 eliminated all U.S. ground-launched nuclear systems (including artillery, surface-to-air missiles, and surface-to-surface missiles). The only U.S. nuclear weapons remaining in Europe are a reduced number of gravity bombs for U.S. and Allied dual-capable aircraft.

In other words, these cutbacks spared some of the most politically visible elements of the U.S. nuclear posture then remaining in Europe—the gravity bombs for dual-capable aircraft, which give several of the Allies a direct role in nuclear risk and responsibility sharing. According to an unclassified NATO report in 1988, seven allies (Belgium, Germany, Greece, Italy, the Netherlands, Turkey, and the United Kingdom) have provided dual-capable aircraft and warhead storage sites for U.S. nuclear forces.[94]

While the 1991 decisions mean that only nuclear gravity bombs associated with dual-capable aircraft remain, the central importance of their continuing presence in Europe was reaffirmed in the Alliance's 1991 Strategic Concept:

> A credible Alliance nuclear posture and the demonstration of Alliance solidarity and common commitment to war prevention continue to require widespread participation by European Allies involved in collective defence planning in nuclear roles, in peacetime basing of nuclear forces on their territory and in command, control and consultation arrangements. Nuclear forces based in Europe and committed to NATO provide an essential political and military link between the European and the North American members of the Alliance. . . . These forces need to have the necessary characteristics and appropriate flexibility and survivability, to be perceived as a credible and effective element of the Allies' strategy in preventing war. They will be maintained at the minimum level sufficient to preserve peace and stability.[95]

The document noted, moreover, that the "supreme guarantee of the security of the Allies is provided by the strategic nuclear forces of the Alliance, particularly those of the United States," and that "adequate sub-strategic forces based in Europe . . . will provide an essential link with strategic nuclear forces, reinforcing the trans-Atlantic link."[96] The wording in the 1999 Strategic Concept was almost identical concerning all of these points.[97]

Under the auspices of the Nuclear Planning Group (NPG), founded in 1966–1967, the Allies (except for France) have been able to resolve many of the consultation and decision-making issues that were so contentious during the 1950s and early 1960s. The Alliance's nuclear arrangements include multinational risk and responsibility sharing and multinational decision making and policy implementation. These arrangements have promoted Alliance cohesion, increased the influence of the non-nuclear European Allies regarding U.S. nuclear policy, and reassured the Allies as to the genuineness and effectiveness of U.S. nuclear commitments.

While the United States is the ultimate nuclear guarantor of NATO European security, Britain and France contribute to the Alliance's overall deterrent posture.[98] Although the French have never participated in NATO's NPG, France has provided an additional independent locus of nuclear decision making, which has complicated the risk calculations of any nation contemplating aggression or coercion against the Alliance. Since the early 1960s, France has insisted on the distinctness and autonomy of the French approach to nuclear strategy in relation to U.S. and NPG concepts. The British have committed their nuclear forces to NATO planning since 1962, though they have retained national command and control at all times. Moreover, London has reserved the possibility of national use independent of coordinated action in defense of the Alliance in cases involving "supreme national interests."[99] None of the Alliance arrangements changes the fact that any actual nuclear use decisions would depend on national choices and would therefore ultimately reside with the U.S. president, the British prime minister, and the French president.[100]

The 2010 Strategic Concept featured continuity in several elements of the Alliance's nuclear deterrence posture and policy but also left open the possibility of change. Reaffirming the importance of British, French, and U.S. strategic nuclear forces for the overall deterrence posture of the Alliance represented an element of continuity: "The supreme guarantee of the security of the Allies is provided by the strategic nuclear forces of the Alliance, particularly those of the United States; the independent strategic nuclear forces of the United Kingdom and France, which have a deterrent role of their own, contribute to the overall deterrence and security of the Allies."[101]

A related element of continuity was the stipulation that the Alliance's review of its deterrence and defense posture in 2011–2012 would exclude France's nuclear forces, on the grounds that the review "only applies to nuclear weapons assigned to NATO."[102] French nuclear forces were excluded from the 1991 and 1999 Strategic Concepts by the "allies concerned" formula and by the references to "European Allies involved in collective defence planning in nuclear roles, in peacetime basing of nuclear forces on their territory and in command, control and consultation arrangements."[103] As has been the case since the NPG was founded, France does not intend to participate in NPG deliberations. Paris has upheld this position despite France's return to the Alliance's integrated military structure in 2009.

The 2010 Strategic Concept's statement that "deterrence, based on an appropriate mix of nuclear and conventional capabilities, remains a core element of our overall strategy"[104] amounts to a summary version of what was said in the two previous Strategic Concepts.[105] The 2010 Strategic Concept's judgment that "the circumstances in which any use of nuclear weapons might have to be contemplated are extremely remote"[106] repeated the "extremely remote" phrase employed in the 1999 Strategic Concept.[107]

The 2010 Strategic Concept included, however, a statement with no precedent in the 1991 and 1999 Strategic Concepts: "As long as nuclear weapons exist, NATO will remain a nuclear alliance."[108] This same statement was made by U.S. secretary of state Hillary Clinton at the meeting of NATO foreign ministers in Tallinn in April 2010. On that occasion, Secretary Clinton also said, "As a nuclear alliance, sharing nuclear risks and responsibilities widely is fundamental."[109]

The only statement about sharing nuclear risks and responsibilities in the 2010 Strategic Concept was the commitment by the Allies to "ensure the broadest possible participation of Allies in collective defence planning on nuclear roles, in peacetime basing of nuclear forces, and in command, control and consultation arrangements."[110]

This statement was consistent with the policy formulations in the 1991 and 1999 Strategic Concepts, but much briefer than the discussions in the earlier documents. It is noteworthy that the 2010 Strategic Concept omitted the explicit references in the earlier documents to basing U.S. nuclear forces "in Europe." For example, the 1999 Strategic Concept had stated that "NATO will maintain, at the minimum level consistent with the prevailing security environment, adequate sub-strategic forces based in Europe which will provide an essential link with strategic nuclear forces, reinforcing the transatlantic link."[111] The less precise language in the 2010 Strategic Concept may be attributed, at least in part, to a desire on the part of some Allies not to influence or prejudge the outcome of the DDPR, while others wanted to keep open options for change.

As noted, since the late 1950s NATO's nuclear deterrence posture has involved "nuclear sharing"—that is, risk and responsibility sharing, with some European Allies hosting U.S. nuclear weapons and delivery systems and/or providing delivery systems of their own. The reference in the 2010 Strategic Concept to "the broadest possible participation of Allies in collective defence planning on nuclear roles, in peacetime basing of nuclear forces, and in command, control and consultation arrangements" could be seen as a strong endorsement of continuity in risk and responsibility sharing.

Whether the Allies will choose to maintain the risk and responsibility sharing arrangements in NATO's long-standing nuclear deterrence posture remains to be seen, however. In the current political climate strong constituencies support proposals for nuclear force reductions, and some political movements have advocated the removal of all the remaining U.S. nuclear weapons in Europe.

Perhaps the most significant recent development in this regard was the October 2009 coalition agreement of the CDU/CSU-FDP government in Berlin. The key sentence might be translated as follows: "In this context, and in the drafting of a new NATO Strategic Concept, we will engage within the Alliance, as well as across the table with the American Allies, such that the remaining nuclear weapons in Germany are removed."[112]

With the German coalition agreement still in effect, Germany's ambassador to NATO cosigned in April 2011 the "Letter of 10" (released at the NATO Foreign Ministerial meeting in Berlin) that made clear in the accompanying cover note that any reductions in NATO nonstrategic nuclear weapons would have to come on the basis of reciprocity with Russia and that the focus for now should be on transparency and confidence-building measures. In short, Germany accepted this policy as an Alliance compromise,[113] and there now appears to be a consensus among the twenty-eight Allies that there should be no further unilateral reductions by NATO.[114]

With reference to possible further reductions in U.S. nuclear weapons in Europe, the 2010 Strategic Concept stated, "In any future reductions, our aim should be to seek Russian agreement to increase transparency on its nuclear weapons in Europe and relocate these weapons away from the territory of NATO members. Any further steps must take into account the disparity with the greater Russian stockpiles of short-range nuclear weapons."[115]

Most proponents of withdrawing the remaining U.S. nuclear weapons in Europe hold (1) that these weapons are less important than in the past because the scenarios in which they might be useful are improbable and remote; (2) that they entail "opportunity costs" and expenses in maintaining nuclear certification for dual-capable aircraft and crews, as well as in providing security at weapons storage sites; and (3) that in a crisis their operational role in striking targets could be performed by U.S. strategic systems.[116]

These arguments rule out entirely what cannot be fully excluded: the possibility that a contingency could arise in which the Alliance's possession of a multinational nuclear deterrent posture could be relevant for successful crisis management and deterrence. These arguments also overstate the "opportunity costs" and financial investments required to maintain the Alliance's nuclear deterrence posture. According to the *Report of the Secretary of Defense Task Force on DoD Nuclear Weapons Management*, the cost of maintaining U.S. nuclear weapons in Europe is "low and worth paying" as the price of an Alliance deterrent with transatlantic risk and responsibility sharing.[117] Relying solely on U.S. strategic systems would tend to politically isolate the United States and, as some Allied observers have noted, empty the Alliance consultation mechanisms of much of their content.

The United States and its NATO Allies have for decades supported concepts of deterrence, signaling, and crisis management, not of war fighting, for their nuclear forces. From this perspective the "target coverage" or "military utility" approach fails to grasp the political and strategic concepts behind U.S. and Alliance policy. Presenting the fact that nonnuclear air operations are much more probable than nuclear missions as a justification for abandoning nuclear capabilities confuses deterrence and crisis management with war fighting and overlooks the fact that low-probability events may be of profound importance. Furthermore, maintaining the Alliance's unique capability to mount a combined air operation for nuclear crisis management involving contributions from multiple Allies would seem to be consistent with the U.S. interest in recent years in cultivating "tailored deterrence" options suitable for diverse contingencies.[118] The Alliance's "nuclear-sharing" arrangements with dual-capable aircraft allow "many Allies who do not host such aircraft to play a part in the nuclear mission (e.g. through the suppression of enemy air defences)."[119] Improvements in capabilities to suppress enemy air defenses may therefore have value for the Alliance's nuclear deterrence posture as well as for its conventional military strength.

The long-standing judgment of many officials and experts in NATO countries remains pertinent: U.S. nuclear weapons based in Europe send a more potent deterrent message about U.S. commitments than reliance solely on U.S. nuclear weapons deployed at sea or based in North America. With the U.S. nuclear weapons presence in Europe, extensive nuclear risk and responsibility sharing, and consultative arrangements for decision making, the Alliance has greater confidence in its strength and cohesion than it would have without these interrelated attributes—and greater confidence that adversaries will recognize NATO's resolve and capabilities.

It was in view of these considerations that the U.S. Congressional Commission, after undertaking an extensive effort to elicit the views of NATO allies, concluded in 2009 that the nuclear-sharing arrangements involving U.S. and Allied dual-capable aircraft and U.S. nuclear weapons in Europe should be continued: "In Europe, the current fleet of dual-capable aircraft is slated for retirement within the next decade. A future variant of the advanced fighter, the F-35 or Joint Strike Fighter, is intended to be a replacement for the current dual-capable aircraft beginning in 2016. NATO allies are committed to the modernization of dual-capable aircraft and the United States should proceed in partnership with them."[120]

While the United States made clear in the April 2010 Nuclear Posture Review (NPR) its intention to acquire the F-35 as a dual-capable aircraft and to pursue full-scope life extension of the B-61 bomb, at this writing it is unclear whether other NATO Allies will take comparable decisions regarding dual-capable aircraft modernization. A distinctive feature of the current nuclear-sharing discussions in the Alliance is that experts and political leaders in Allied nations in Western Europe with long-standing host and delivery responsibilities appear to place less emphasis on the imperative of maintaining NATO's established nuclear deterrence posture, including U.S. nuclear weapons in Europe, than experts and political leaders in some of the new Allied nations in Central and Eastern Europe.[121]

The Alliance's 2011–2012 DDPR reaffirmed the commitment of the NATO Allies to the long-standing arrangements for risk and responsibility sharing in nuclear deterrence. In May 2012 the Allies released the DDPR, which stated that "the review has shown that the Alliance's nuclear force posture currently meets the criteria for an effective deterrence and defence posture."[122]

With regard to the future of risk and responsibility sharing in the Alliance's nuclear deterrence posture, the Allies included the following announcement in the DDPR: "Consistent with our commitment to remain a nuclear alliance for as long as nuclear weapons exist, Allies agree that the NAC will task the appropriate committees to develop concepts for how to ensure the broadest possible participation of Allies concerned in their nuclear sharing arrangements, including in case NATO were to decide to reduce its reliance on non-strategic nuclear weapons based in Europe."[123]

Nuclear Deterrence Policy

The Allies noted in the November 2010 Lisbon Summit Declaration, "With the changes in the security environment since the end of the Cold War, we have dramatically reduced the number of nuclear weapons stationed in Europe and our reliance on nuclear weapons in NATO strategy. We will seek to create the conditions for further reductions in the future."[124]

Owing in part to the reduced salience of nuclear weapons in NATO's posture and policy since the end of the Cold War, two declaratory nuclear policy issues deserve attention: the negative security assurances articulated by Britain, France, and the United States, and the responses by these three Allies to "sole purpose" advocacy.

With regard to negative security assurances, it should be recalled that the 1999 Strategic Concept stated that "the fundamental purpose of the nuclear forces of the Allies is political: to preserve peace and prevent coercion and any kind of war. They will continue to fulfil an essential role by ensuring uncertainty in the mind of any aggressor about the nature of the Allies' response to military aggression. They demonstrate that aggression of any kind is not a rational option."[125]

The principle of "ensuring uncertainty in the mind of any aggressor about the nature of the Allies' response to military aggression" has historically been interpreted as a rejection of a "no-first-use" pledge. NATO does not have a "first-use" policy, but it has historically refused to make a "no-first-use" pledge because it could undermine the key objective of deterrence, the prevention of war. It was widely reported in 1998 that Germany had advocated that the Alliance make a "no-first-use" pledge but that this was opposed by other Allies, notably Britain, France, and the United States.[126]

The 2010 Strategic Concept was silent on the "no-first-use" question, perhaps because the Allies could not reach a consensus on this aspect of declaratory doctrine—or perhaps did not even try to do so. The doctrinal differences among the Alliance's three nuclear weapon states may have deterred the Allies from attempting to formulate a statement on the question.

Alternatively, the Allies may have decided that a statement repeating the imperative of "ensuring uncertainty in the mind of any aggressor about the nature of the Allies' response to military aggression" was unnecessary, since they had just made such a statement in 2009 in NATO's Comprehensive, Strategic-Level Policy for Preventing the Proliferation of Weapons of Mass Destruction (WMD) and Defending against Chemical, Biological, Radiological and Nuclear (CBRN) Threats.[127] Moreover, they called attention to this document in the 2010 Lisbon Summit Declaration, confirming its current validity.[128]

Britain, France, and the United States continue to concur in rejecting a "no-first-use" pledge, but the United States in its April 2010 NPR report announced a new formulation of its negative security assurance (NSA) that appears to be inconsistent with the principle of "ensuring uncertainty in the mind of any aggressor about the nature of the Allies' response to military aggression." According to the new formulation of the U.S. NSA,

> The United States will continue to reduce the role of nuclear weapons in deterring non-nuclear attack. To that end, the United States is now prepared to strengthen its long-standing "negative security assurance" by declaring that the United States will not use or threaten to use nuclear weapons against non-nuclear weapons states that are party to the Nuclear Non-Proliferation Treaty (NPT) and in compliance with their nuclear non-proliferation obligations.[129]

The United States qualified this NSA in three ways. First, any use of chemical or biological weapons (CBW) could result in "a devastating conventional military response." Second, those responsible for CBW use, "whether national leaders or military commanders, would be held fully accountable." Third, "Given the catastrophic potential of biological weapons and the rapid pace of bio-technology development, the United States reserves the right to make any adjustment in the assurance that may be warranted by the evolution and proliferation of the biological weapons threat and U.S. capacities to counter that threat."[130]

France's current NSA, first articulated in 1995, differs from that of the United States, notably by keeping open the option of nuclear retaliation in the event of an attack:

> France reaffirms that it will not use nuclear weapons against non-nuclear-weapon States Parties to the Treaty on the Non-Proliferation of Nuclear Weapons, except in the case of an invasion or any other attack on France, its territory, its armed forces or other troops, or against its

allies or a State towards which it has a security commitment, carried out or sustained by such a
State in alliance or association with a nuclear-weapon State.[131]

Britain's current NSA, announced in October 2010, is closer to the current U.S.
NSA than is the French NSA in its conditions and reservations:

> We are now able to give an assurance that the UK will not use or threaten to use nuclear
> weapons against non-nuclear weapon states parties to the NPT. In giving this assurance, we
> emphasise the need for universal adherence to and compliance with the NPT, and note that
> this assurance would not apply to any state in material breach of those non-proliferation obliga-
> tions. We also note that while there is currently no direct threat to the UK or its vital interests
> from states developing capabilities in other weapons of mass destruction, for example chemical
> and biological, we reserve the right to review this assurance if the future threat, development
> and proliferation of these weapons make it necessary.[132]

Proponents of nonproliferation and disarmament have viewed the new formulation of the U.S. NSA as a positive step. Some expert observers have nonetheless been
concerned that it seems to be inconsistent with the long-standing Alliance policy, as
it was put in the 1999 Strategic Concept, of "ensuring uncertainty in the mind of any
aggressor about the nature of the Allies' response to military aggression."

It can be argued, however, that the principle of "ensuring uncertainty in the mind
of any aggressor about the nature of the Allies' response to military aggression" remains present, at least to some extent, with the new British and U.S. NSAs, for two
reasons. First, London and Washington would each decide whether an adversary is
in compliance with the NPT and other nuclear nonproliferation obligations. Second,
the United States explicitly reserves the right to modify the assurance with regard
to biological weapons threats, and the United Kingdom's reservation of a right to
review includes chemical as well as biological weapons threats. The new British and
U.S. NSAs would obviously not apply to Iran (which has violated its International
Atomic Energy Agency safeguards agreement) or to North Korea or any nuclear-
armed state.[133]

It is not clear whether the Allies made any effort to integrate the redefined British
and U.S. NSAs in a new formulation of Alliance policy in drafting the 2010 Strategic
Concept. Britain, France, and the United States have in the past resisted the formulation of an Alliance policy on NSAs on the grounds that such unilateral national
undertakings are matters for the countries making them, not their allies. Some Allied
observers hold that NATO itself could not offer an NSA anyway, since such pledges
can only be offered by state possessors of nuclear weapons.[134] The differences in the
British, French, and U.S. NSAs may contribute to deterrence, some experts have
argued, because they illustrate the autonomy of the decision making of the Alliance's
three nuclear-weapon states.

In May 2012 the Allies included the following statement about NSAs in their
DDPR:

> Allies acknowledge the importance of the independent and unilateral negative security assur-
> ances offered by the United States, the United Kingdom and France. Those assurances guaran-
> tee, without prejudice to the separate conditions each State has attached to those assurances, in-
> cluding the inherent right to self-defence as recognised under Article 51 of the United Nations

Charter, that nuclear weapons will not be used or threatened to be used against Non-Nuclear Weapon States that are party to the Non-Proliferation Treaty and in compliance with their nuclear non-proliferation obligations. Allies further recognise the value that these statements can have in seeking to discourage nuclear proliferation. Allies note that the states that have assigned nuclear weapons to NATO apply to these weapons the assurances they have each offered on a national basis, including the separate conditions each state has attached to these assurances.[135]

This statement highlights the fact that these negative security assurances are "independent and unilateral" commitments by the three NATO nuclear-weapon states. Furthermore, the final sentence in the paragraph uses the formula "states that have assigned nuclear weapons to NATO" in order to make clear that the final sentence concerns Britain and the United States, not France. Finally, in this single paragraph the Allies twice refer to "the separate conditions each state has attached to these assurances." It points out that these "separate conditions" include "the inherent right to self-defence as recognised under Article 51 of the United Nations Charter." These qualifications suggest that the Allies are striving to sustain deterrence while sending a message of reassurance for nonproliferation purposes.

Some nongovernmental organizations have championed the idea of a "sole purpose" approach to nuclear weapons—that is, a policy that the sole purpose of nuclear weapons ought to be to deter the use of nuclear weapons by others. For example, the International Commission on Nuclear Non-Proliferation and Disarmament argued in 2009 that all nuclear-armed states should express commitment to a "sole purpose" principle:

This Commission believes it is crucial that, at the very least, every nuclear-armed state be unequivocally committed to the principle that the sole purpose of possessing nuclear weapons—until such time as they can be eliminated completely—is to deter others from using such weapons against that state or its allies. We would prefer that sooner rather than later, such declaratory "sole purpose" statements be hardened into unequivocal "no first use" commitments, but acknowledge that there has been an issue in the past as to whether such commitments have been seriously attended.[136]

The United States announced in the NPR report that it is not ready to make such a commitment but "will work to establish conditions under which such a policy could be safely adopted." To quote the NPR report,

In the case of countries not covered by this [negative security] assurance—states that possess nuclear weapons and states not in compliance with their nuclear non-proliferation obligations—there remains a narrow range of contingencies in which U.S. nuclear weapons may still play a role in deterring a conventional or CBW attack against the United States or its allies and partners. The United States is therefore not prepared at the present time to adopt a universal policy that the "sole purpose" of U.S. nuclear weapons is to deter nuclear attack on the United States and our allies and partners, but will work to establish conditions under which such a policy could be safely adopted.[137]

NATO's other nuclear weapon states, France and the United Kingdom, have also declined to adopt a "sole purpose" policy. In 2009 the United Kingdom's Foreign and Commonwealth Office stated that "there are some powerful arguments for reducing the role of nuclear weapons solely to deterring the use of nuclear weapons by others," but noted that some nuclear-weapon states continue to find such weapons useful to deter the use of conventional, chemical, and biological weapons.[138]

The French government does not appear to have specifically rejected "sole purpose." French experts hold, however, that it has been implicitly rejected in various official statements.[139] For example, in March 2008 President Nicolas Sarkozy said, "Our nuclear deterrence protects us from any aggression against our vital interests emanating from a state—wherever it may come from and whatever form it may take."[140] The "whatever form it may take" clause implies that the French would not rule out nuclear retaliation against a nonnuclear threat to their vital interests.

In short, Britain, France, and the United States have not embraced "sole purpose" proposals. In their view, adopting a "sole purpose" doctrine could have a negative impact on the credibility and effectiveness of their nuclear deterrence postures.

A distinct but comparable formulation—that the "fundamental purpose" of nuclear weapons is to deter the use of nuclear weapons—reportedly drew attention during the DDPR. Lord Robertson, Franklin Miller, and Kori Schake have written that, to the new Allies that remain concerned about possible conventional aggression, the "fundamental purpose" formula "seemed to de-link the nuclear deterrent from the Strategic Concept's pledge to 'deter and defend against any threat of aggression, and against emerging security challenges where they threaten the fundamental security of individual allies or the Alliance as a whole.' This concern, hearkening back to the issue raised during the winter of 2010 and seemingly put to rest in the Strategic Concept, caused a backlash against the proposal."[141]

The Allies did not include a "fundamental purpose" statement in the final May 2012 text of the DDPR. The United States, however, had stated in its 2010 NPR that "the fundamental role of U.S. nuclear weapons, which will continue as long as nuclear weapons exist, is to deter nuclear attack on the United States, our allies, and partners."[142] The U.S. Department of Defense included a similar statement in its 2013 report to Congress on U.S. nuclear employment strategy.[143]

Missile Defense

As noted, NATO's 1991 Strategic Concept mentioned missile defense as a possible response to the proliferation of WMD and ballistic missiles.[144] The 1999 Strategic Concept made a similar reference to missile defense: "The Alliance's defence posture against the risks and potential threats of the proliferation of NBC [nuclear, biological, and chemical] weapons and their means of delivery must continue to be improved, including through work on missile defences."[145]Until 2002, however, work on missile defense under Alliance auspices concentrated on "theater missile defense" (TMD)—that is, systems configured to protect forces deployed on operations from shorter-range ballistic and cruise missiles, not systems designed to shield national territory and population centers. The focus on TMD reflected operational requirements as well as the political and legal obstacles to pursuing defenses against "strategic ballistic missiles" in the 1972 U.S.-Soviet Anti-Ballistic Missile Treaty. This treaty prohibited the construction of such defenses by the United States beyond the single site in North Dakota permitted after the treaty's amendment in 1974, so there was no question of building such defenses in NATO Europe. Moreover, the treaty prohibited transfers of technology for such defenses to third parties, including the NATO Allies.

The U.S. withdrawal from the ABM Treaty took effect in June 2002, ending the treaty obstacles to the construction of missile defenses for the protection of NATO European cities and territories. In November 2002, at the Prague summit, the Allies agreed to "examine options for addressing the increasing missile threat to Alliance territory, forces and population centres in an effective and efficient way through an appropriate mix of political and defence efforts, along with deterrence. Today we initiated a new NATO Missile Defence feasibility study to examine options for protecting Alliance territory, forces and population centres against the full range of missile threats, which we will continue to assess. Our efforts in this regard will be consistent with the indivisibility of Allied security."[146]

The reference to "along with deterrence" in the decision to launch the feasibility study was significant because it reflected the conviction of some Allies (France in particular) that the threat of retaliation, potentially with nuclear weapons, could serve as a sufficient means of protection against missile attack. The NATO Allies had a history of discord regarding the implications of U.S. strategic missile defenses extending back to the late 1960s, when the United States under President Lyndon Johnson first proposed the acquisition of such capabilities. It was at that time that a number of themes first appeared that were to recur in subsequent Alliance missile defense debates, notably in the early 1980s, when President Ronald Reagan's Strategic Defense Initiative was dubbed "Star Wars" by its critics in the United States and abroad. These themes included the implications of U.S. strategic missile defenses for constructive relations with Moscow, strategic stability, arms control and disarmament, deterrence, the transatlantic link, and the long-term credibility of the British and French nuclear forces—to say nothing of the cost and technical feasibility issues.[147]

In November 2006, the Allies announced the completion of the feasibility study commissioned in 2002: "It concludes that missile defence is technically feasible within the limitations and assumptions of the study. We tasked continued work on the political and military implications of missile defence for the Alliance including an update on missile threat developments."[148]

In December 2009 the Allies endorsed the Obama administration's decision in September of that year to refine the plans for missile defense system element deployments in Poland and the Czech Republic that it had inherited from the George W. Bush administration: "We welcome the new phased adaptive approach of the United States to missile defence, which further reinforces NATO's central role in missile defence in Europe. This approach would further anchor European missile defence work in NATO, which continues to bear in mind the principle of the indivisibility of Alliance security as well as NATO solidarity."[149] The Allies in December 2009 also approved studies concerning possible expanded work on the Alliance's TMD program "beyond the protection of NATO deployed forces to include territorial missile defence."[150]

The Allies did not, however, make a decision to pursue missile defenses designed to protect their people and territories until the November 2010 summit in Lisbon:

> The threat to NATO European populations, territory and forces posed by the proliferation of ballistic missiles is increasing. As missile defence forms part of a broader response to counter this threat, we have decided that the Alliance will develop a missile defence capability to pursue its core task of collective defence. The aim of a NATO missile defence capability is to provide full coverage and protection for all NATO European populations, territory and forces against the increasing threats posed by the proliferation of ballistic missiles, based on the principles of the indivisibility of Allied security and NATO solidarity, equitable sharing of risks and burdens, as well as reasonable challenge, taking into account the level of threat, affordability and technical feasibility, and in accordance with the latest common threat assessments agreed by the Alliance.
>
> To this end, we have decided that the scope of NATO's current Active Layered Theatre Ballistic Missile Defence (ALTBMD) programme's command, control and communications capabilities will be expanded beyond the protection of NATO deployed forces to also protect NATO European populations, territory and forces. In this context, the United States European Phased Adaptive Approach is welcomed as a valuable national contribution to the NATO missile defence architecture, as are other possible voluntary contributions by Allies.151

The Allies emphasized in the Lisbon Summit Declaration that they expected missile defense to become a central capability for deterrence and defense, along with nuclear and conventional forces: "NATO will maintain an appropriate mix of conventional, nuclear, and missile defence forces. Missile defence will become an integral part of our overall defence posture."[152]

As in the past, despite such declarations, disagreements persist among the NATO Allies with regard to U.S.-led strategic missile defense efforts. The reservations of some Allies—and some Allied experts and officials—are apparent in the wording of the November 2010 decision just cited, notably the references to "reasonable challenge, taking into account the level of threat, affordability and technical feasibility, and in accordance with the latest common threat assessments agreed by the Alliance." The reluctance of some Allies derived from long-standing concerns about the implications of strategic missile defenses for relations with Moscow and the future of nuclear arms control and disarmament, among other issues.

However, contextual factors such as continuing ballistic missile proliferation and progress in missile defense technology appear to have contributed to the Alliance decision to pursue strategic missile defense efforts. Among the additional factors that may have also led to this decision, two stand out: first, the willingness of the United States to pay for the largest share of the effort with its European Phased Adaptive Approach, and second, the emphasis on "full coverage and protection for all NATO European populations, territory and forces." Previous U.S. strategic missile defense efforts were widely perceived in Europe as oriented mainly toward shielding the United States itself rather than the Alliance as a whole.

Four questions stand out with regard to the Alliance's strategic missile defense program. To what extent will Allies other than the United States contribute radars, interceptor missiles, and other missile defense assets? How substantial a contribution to the Alliance's overall posture for deterrence and defense will missile defense make over the next decade and beyond, given the probable numerical and other constraints? How will the Allies integrate missile defense with offensive strike capabilities for deterrence? To what extent will NATO-Russian cooperation on missile defense be possible, and what might be the implications of such cooperation for the Alliance's deterrence and defense posture?

The Allies have agreed to fund on a common basis enhancements to NATO's ALTBMD command, control, and communications program in order to "protect NATO European populations, territory and forces." At the outset the only definite "national contribution to the NATO missile defence architecture" was the U.S. European Phased Adaptive Approach (EPAA). The Lisbon Summit Declaration anticipated "other possible voluntary contributions by Allies," and several have now come into focus. Since late 2011, for example, Turkey has hosted an AN/TPY-2 missile defense radar at Kürecik. Romania and Poland have agreed to host U.S. SM-3 interceptors, and Spain will host four U.S. Aegis destroyers at Rota. The Netherlands has decided to upgrade four air defense frigates with extended long-range missile defense early-warning radars.[153] The United Kingdom and the United States have for decades cooperated regarding the Ballistic Missile Early Warning System (BMEWS) radar at Fylingdales, England. France and Italy might contribute SAMP surface-to-air missile batteries.[154]

The reference in the November 2010 Lisbon Summit Declaration to "affordability" as a key factor to take into account may prove to be significant. The European Allies agreed to the pursuit of missile defenses for the protection of national territories and population centers largely because the U.S. government offered to assume the largest part of the costs—the "upper tier" defense. The EPAA outlined by the United States in September 2009 was presented as the U.S. contribution to NATO's strategic missile defense architecture.

The European Allies generally hold that they cannot afford to spend much on strategic missile defense. It is assumed that the United States will pay for the upper tier, that all the Allies will collectively pay for the ALTBMD command and control system, and that national contributions will make up the rest of the Alliance's strategic missile defense architecture. It is not clear, however, that national or collective contributions will be sufficient to pay for a comprehensive strategic missile defense posture. Some Allied observers have rejected informal proposals that their nations consider NATO common funding beyond the ALTBMD command and control system (for instance, for sensors or interceptors), on the grounds that such funding would be unaffordable and inconsistent with agreed-upon principles.

Allied support for missile defense would probably decline if the United States asked the European member states to pay for a larger share of the costs than was agreed to at Lisbon in 2010. Some European Allied observers see other capabilities as higher priorities for scarce defense resources.[155] Pressures to reduce defense spending in the United States may put the "affordability" issue on the Alliance agenda, because some U.S. members of Congress favor legislation that would direct the executive to seek NATO common funding for at least half of the costs of the EPAA.[156]

The U.S. EPAA is by definition "adaptive" in relation to technology or threat developments, but the United States envisages a capability by 2020 that could protect U.S. forces and allies in Europe from attacks involving "dozens or scores of missiles."[157] In December 2010 James N. Miller of the U.S. Department of Defense described the plan as follows:

> As the United States deploys SM-3 interceptors in Romania by 2015 and in Poland by 2018, a number of missiles will be deployed in their launchers on a day-to-day basis. Plans call for deploying 24 interceptors per site . . . plus additional re-loads, plus additional ship-based interceptors. . . . The SM-3 Block IB will be utilized at the Romanian site and will also be phased in at sea for use by our Aegis BMD ships. . . . The key additional capability in Phase 4 in the 2020 timeframe will be the deployment of the next generation SM-3 interceptor, the Block IIB, which will provide the ability to perform early intercept against medium- and intermediate-range ballistic missiles, and potential ICBM threats from the Middle East.[158]

The United States has highlighted the numerical constraints of this missile defense capability in relation to the threat. As Rear Admiral Archer Macy observed in congressional testimony, "As the number of threats grow, we increase the number of our defensive interceptors. This is workable to a point, but . . . it rapidly becomes unaffordable as the threats continue to grow in numbers over time."[159] It is partly for this reason that the U.S. defense and deterrence posture requires offensive response forces in addition to air and missile defenses. Offensive strike capabilities could be employed to diminish the adversary's missile forces, and thereby make the missile defense challenge more manageable. In Rear Admiral Macy's words,

> While missile defenses, of themselves, do enhance our deterrent against potential adversaries, should an attack occur they are not meant to be the sole means of response. Rather, missile defenses prevent an adversary from winning the fight with the first wave of their attack, and provide time for our offensive response capabilities to be brought to bear. . . . We are not shooting for perfect defense. . . . Each Combatant Command will have some capability to degrade an adversary's ballistic missile launch capability, lessening the load on missile defense assets.[160]

The NATO Allies did not provide any public statement about possible plans to integrate offensive response forces with air and missile defenses in their May 2012 DDPR. They did, however, offer the following discussion of the potential utility of missile defenses for NATO:

> It is expected that NATO's missile defence capabilities would complicate an adversary's planning, and provide damage mitigation. Effective missile defence could also provide valuable decision space in times of crisis. Like other weapons systems, missile defence capabilities cannot promise complete and enduring effectiveness. NATO missile defence capability, along with effective nuclear and conventional forces, will signal our determination to deter and defend against any threat from outside the Euro-Atlantic area to the safety and security of our populations.[161]

The emphasis on the fact that NATO is pursuing missile defense in order to counter potential missile threats from "outside the Euro-Atlantic area" enables the Allies to avoid referring explicitly to Iran or any other power in the Middle East or Asia that might in some future circumstances pose a threat to NATO's security interests. Moreover, the phrase "outside the Euro-Atlantic area" is consistent with the point made in the next paragraph of the DDPR: "NATO missile defence is not oriented against Russia nor does it have the capability to undermine Russia's strategic deterrent."[162]

It is important to note in this regard that the United States scaled back its plans for the EPAA in March 2013. U.S. secretary of defense Chuck Hagel announced that the United States was "restructuring" its missile defense program, acquiring fourteen additional ground-based interceptors in Alaska as a hedge against North Korean missiles, and cancelling phase 4 of the EPAA. He underscored, "The missile deployments the United States is making in phases one through three of the European Phased Adaptive Approach, including sites in Poland and Romania, will be able to provide coverage of all European NATO territory as planned by 2018."[163] Some European observers nonetheless expressed concern, because phase 4 was intended to be capable of defending the United States from ICBMs launched from the Middle East. In contrast, as indicated by Secretary Hagel, the initial three phases are for the defense of NATO Europe.

A French observer wrote that cancelling phase 4 signified "a weakening of the transatlantic link by decoupling the European and American systems of missile defense."[164] U.S. officials have, however, rejected the view that not developing and deploying the projected fourth phase of the EPAA could weaken NATO Europe's coupling with the United States. Frank Rose of the State Department pointed out that the U.S. radar in Turkey "can provide important early tracking data on any Iranian missile launches against the United States," and that the remaining phases of the EPAA will "contribute to protecting the U.S. radar at Fylingdales, which is important to the defense of the U.S. homeland."[165]

Some European experts and officials have argued that the cancellation of phase 4 has made phase 3 more vulnerable in U.S. budget planning and politics, because phase 3 is configured essentially for the defense of Europe. In their view, the abandonment of the fourth phase has raised uncertainty about future U.S. missile defense investments, since this phase was the part of the EPAA most pertinent to U.S. national defense. In these circumstances, they hold, the cancellation of phase 4 has reinforced the likelihood that U.S. legislators may ask the European Allies to make greater financial contributions to strategic missile defense in NATO. To quote a French observer, "The American taxpayer has henceforth every reason to ask that the Europeans pay much more for systems that are intended for them and that are no longer designed to contribute directly to American security."[166]

When the United States announced the cancellation, the first Russian reactions were negative, with more nuanced subsequent judgments. The cancellation of phase 4 of the EPAA nonetheless appears to have had no effect on Russian policy, despite the fact that Russian commentators had singled out its projected counter-ICBM capability for special criticism. Russia has continued to insist on guarantees that the EPAA will not affect its strategic forces, and to make its cooperation on strategic missile defense contingent on terms unacceptable to the United States and its NATO allies.

The prospects for Russian cooperation with NATO regarding missile defense therefore remain uncertain, owing to the conditions established by Moscow. In November 2010, Dmitry Medvedev, then the president of Russia, said, "The choice for us for the coming decade is as follows: we will either come to terms on missile defense and form a full-fledged joint mechanism of cooperation, or, if we fail to forge a constructive agreement, we will plunge into a new arms race and have to think of deploying new strike means."[167] Moscow has reportedly insisted that it will cooperate with NATO and the United States on missile defense only if the command and control system is shared with Russia. In February 2011, Deputy Foreign Minister Sergei Ryabkov said, "This must be a joint system with shared responsibilities, information exchange and decision-making in order to make us an equal and responsible member. ... If two separate networks are built, things won't change for us and we will see a situation when the NATO system could potentially be used against Russia's security interests. Cooperating on such a system would mean hurting ourselves."[168]

It is unclear whether the Russian condition can be satisfied, since the United States does not intend to grant a command and control "veto" even to its NATO Allies. In the words of James Miller, "Our commitment to ensure protection of NATO Allies does not mean NATO will have a 'veto' over the protection of the United States and our deployed forces. Interoperability with NATO command and control systems will not diminish our ability to defend U.S. deployed forces, our partners, and, of course, the U.S. homeland."[169]

Moreover, President Barack Obama wrote to the U.S. Senate in December 2010 that "the system we intend to pursue with Russia will not be a joint system, and it will not in any way limit United States' or NATO's missile defense capabilities."[170] As James Miller noted, "NATO must be responsible for defense of NATO territory and Russia should be responsible for defense of Russian territory. We would operate our respective systems independently but cooperatively, including sharing of sensor data that may improve the ability of both systems to defeat missile attacks by regional actors such as Iran."[171]

One of the obstacles to creating a "joint mechanism" such as the Russians have advocated is the fact that ballistic missile attacks offer little warning time for consultations. In May 2012, at the Chicago Summit, the Allies announced that they had achieved "an Interim NATO BMD Capability" and had approved a command and control mechanism for it, taking into account the speed of ballistic missiles:

> As with all of NATO's operations, full political control by Allies over military actions undertaken pursuant to this Interim Capability will be ensured. Given the short flight times of ballistic missiles, the Council agrees the pre-arranged command and control rules and procedures including to take into account the consequences of intercept compatible with coverage and protection requirements.[172]

If the Russian demand for a "joint mechanism" could be somehow satisfied or redefined, the implications for the Alliance would hinge on whether Russia could somehow exercise a veto over U.S. or Alliance decisions on missile defense. In February 2012, Vladimir Putin, then Russia's prime minister, declared,

> We are worried that although the outlines of our "new" relations with NATO are not yet final, the alliance is already providing us with "facts on the ground" that are counterproductive to confidence building.... Why does that [missile defense] system worry us more than others? Because it affects the strategic nuclear deterrence forces that only Russia possesses in that theatre, and upsets the military-political balance established over decades.[173]

The Russians have continued to reject U.S. and NATO assurances that the projected missile defenses will be incapable of intercepting Russian strategic missiles. In February 2012, Putin warned that "Russia's military-technical response to a global American missile defense system and its segment in Europe will be effective and asymmetric."[174] In May 2012, General Nikolai Makarov, then the chief of the general staff of the Russian Armed Forces, presented a more specific warning: "Taking into account a missile-defense system's destabilizing nature, that is, the creation of an illusion that a disarming strike can be launched with impunity, a decision on pre-emptive use of the attack weapons available will be made when the situation worsens."[175]

In his reply to General Makarov's remarks, Alexander Vershbow, NATO's deputy secretary general, said, "We think the system we are developing poses no threat to Russia, so the whole notion of retaliation or countermeasures has no foundation."[176] At the Chicago Summit in May 2012, the Allies declared,

> Through ongoing efforts in the NATO-Russia Council, we seek to determine how independent NATO and Russian missile defence systems can work together to enhance European security. We look forward to establishing the proposed joint NATO-Russia Missile Data Fusion Centre and the joint Planning Operations Centre to cooperate on missile defence.[177]

This wording might be construed to imply that Russia has agreed to establish these two centers, but in fact these are simply NATO proposals. Russia has to date shown no interest in NATO-proposed arrangements that would politically facilitate the pursuit of strategic missile defense by NATO. Russia has continued to call for "legally binding" guarantees regarding the technical parameters and capabilities of U.S. and NATO missile defenses.[178]

The NATO Allies and Alliance officials, notably Secretary General Rasmussen, have continued to hold that the projected missile defenses would not threaten Russia's nuclear deterrent and that NATO would welcome cooperation with Russia in missile defense. In September 2012, Vershbow said,

> Russia's continuing objections to NATO's missile defence plans are simply not grounded on facts. For geographical, scientific and numerical reasons, NATO's missile defence cannot and will not change the strategic balance nor pose any threat to Russia's assured second-strike capability. The system's infrastructure is specifically configured and optimised to protect against missile threats from outside the Euro-Atlantic area—not from Russia. That's true today and it will remain the case when NATO deploys the later phases of the system at the end of this decade. And if the Russians were to work with us on missile defence, they wouldn't have to take my word for it; they would see it with their own eyes.... If NATO and Russian officers worked together 24/7 to plan and conduct combined missile defence operations, it would also create greater confidence and trust between us and show the world that NATO's and Russia's interests coincide.[179]

Long-standing disagreements remain manifest among the Allies about missile defense for the protection of national territories and populations. (Limited missile defenses, especially those for the protection of deployed forces, often called theater missile defenses, or TMD, have remained comparatively uncontroversial.) As in the past, the French express with great firmness the judgment that missile defense can complement nuclear deterrence but cannot replace it.[180] Indeed, it was partly owing to France's strong position in this regard that the Allies declared at the 2012 Chicago Summit that "missile defence can complement the role of nuclear weapons in deterrence; it cannot substitute for them."[181]

Expansive Approaches to Collective Defense

The NATO Allies have chosen in recent years to open their principal ongoing Article 5 mission, Operation Active Endeavour in the Mediterranean, to contributions by non-Allies. At the June 2004 Istanbul Summit, the Allies decided to welcome "the contributory support of partner countries, including the Mediterranean Dialogue countries."[182] To date two Mediterranean Dialogue countries, Morocco and Israel, have corresponded with NATO regarding participation in Operation Active Endeavour.

Morocco and NATO have exchanged letters and agreed on a technical memorandum of understanding for Morocco to contribute a ship to Operation Active Endeavor, but a mutually acceptable understanding on supplying Morocco with communications and identification-friend-or-foe equipment has not yet been reached.

Israel and the Alliance exchanged letters in 2006 concerning information-sharing and the establishment of an Israeli liaison officer at the NATO command in Naples, but the process of preparing an exchange of letters covering the deployment of an Israeli ship has been stopped since the May 2010 Gaza flotilla incident. Because of this incident, in which eight Turkish citizens were killed in combat with Israeli naval commandos, Ankara has blocked further steps regarding possible Israeli participation in Operation Active Endeavor. Although the Israeli prime minister apologized to the Turkish prime minister in March 2013, Israeli participation in Active Endeavour remains blocked by Turkey.

Russia participated briefly in Active Endeavour in 2006 and 2007, and Ukraine did so in 2007, 2008, 2009, and 2010.[183] Georgia and NATO completed an Exchange of Letters about participation in the operation in 2008, and signed a Tactical Memorandum of Understanding in 2010.[184]

It is noteworthy that the Allies, having initiated Operation Active Endeavour as a collective defense mission under Article 5 of the North Atlantic Treaty and Article 51 of the UN Charter, have subsequently reached beyond the Alliance to "work very closely with the relevant law enforcement and intelligence agencies of . . . partner nations."[185] Moreover, the Alliance has placed Operation Active Endeavour within the context of "NATO's determination to consult and cooperate closely with the United

Nations in the fight against terrorism," including "full implementation of United Nations Security Council Resolution 1373 and support to the UN Global Strategy in the fight against terrorism."[186]

NATO collective defense (Article 5) obligations have historically been bounded by Article 6 of the North Atlantic Treaty, which defines the geographic area in which an "armed attack" would oblige the Allies to honor their Article 5 commitments as consisting essentially of the territory of the Allies in Europe and North America.[187]

Some experts have nonetheless observed that since the terrorist attacks against the United States in September 2001, the Allies have adopted policies that imply a geographic expansion of collective defense obligations under Article 5. Diego Ruiz Palmer has called this a "deterritorialization" of collective defense, while Gülnur Aybet has referred to "borderless collective defense."[188]

This tendency may be discerned in key definitions of the Alliance's security requirements since September 2001. In May 2002, the North Atlantic Council declared, "To carry out the full range of its missions, NATO must be able to field forces that can move quickly to wherever they are needed, sustain operations over distance and time, and achieve their objectives. This will require the development of new and balanced capabilities within the Alliance, including strategic lift and modern strike capabilities, so that NATO can more effectively respond collectively to any threat of aggression against a member state."[189]

The geographic limitations on the contingencies that could lead the Allies to take action regarding their collective defense obligations specified in Article 6 still apply juridically, and the Allies have not assumed legal obligations to adopt a new approach to collective defense beyond Articles 5 and 6 of the North Atlantic Treaty. However, some experts maintain that the phrase "wherever they are needed," in conjunction with the decision to prepare to "more effectively respond collectively to any threat of aggression against a member state," represented a politically significant departure from the comparatively passive attitude to collective defense expressed by the Allies in the decades before September 2001.[190] It implied a shift away from a static, reactive, and territorial concept of collective defense in which the Allies would act to protect their security interests only in response to "an armed attack" in Europe or North America.

Henceforth, rather than waiting for "an armed attack," the Allies—to repeat the terms of their communiqué—expressed a determination to "respond collectively to any threat of aggression against a member state." The concept of moving forces "quickly to wherever they are needed" also suggested an interest in taking action against emerging threats at their point of origin. This shift was confirmed at the Prague Summit in November 2002, when the NATO Allies "approved a comprehensive package of measures . . . to strengthen our ability to meet the challenges to the security of our forces, populations and territory, from wherever they may come."[191]

The Alliance's move toward a more "proactive" and "anticipatory" concept of Article 5 requirements became even more explicit when it published a summary of its Military Concept for Defence Against Terrorism in October 2003:

> The Political Guidance provided by [the North Atlantic] Council . . . stipulated that NATO's actions should: . . . Help deter, defend, disrupt and protect against terrorist attacks or threat of attacks, directed from abroad against populations, territory, infrastructure and forces of any NATO member state, including by acting against these terrorists and those who harbour them . . . [and] work on the assumption that it is preferable to deter terrorist attacks or to prevent their occurrence rather than deal with their consequences and be prepared to deploy as and where required to deal with particular circumstances as they arise. . . . Therefore the following planning aspects need special attention: Procedures and capabilities that support accelerated decision cycles, in order to be successful in detecting and attacking time sensitive targets in the Counter Terrorist environment. . . . Once it is known where the terrorists are or what they are about to do, military forces need the capability to deploy there. Due to the likelihood that warnings will be received only at very short notice, forces need to be at a high state of readiness. . . . In addition to the capabilities described above, the Concept identifies certain procedures that need to be developed or enhanced. These include: . . . Making Alliance decision making as effective and timely as possible in order that, given the very short warnings that are likely for terrorist activity and intentions, Alliance forces can be deployed and employed appropriately.[192]

One of the key points about this Military Concept is that it may be impossible to "disrupt" the "threat of attacks" or "prevent their occurrence" or take action "once it is known where the terrorists are or what they are about to do" without engaging in anticipatory action. It therefore appears that the Allies are in fact willing (at least as a matter of abstract principle) to make effective use of what they have referred to in this Military Concept as "the very short warnings that are likely for terrorist activity and intentions."[193] Questions nonetheless persist about the collective ability of the Allies to take effective counterterrorist action, as well as their will to do so in the wake of Afghanistan.

At the same time, some Allies have invested in measures designed to deter terrorist attacks, particularly enhanced protection for specific sites and resilience and consequence mitigation capabilities. Such capabilities may promote "deterrence by denial" by communicating the message that "hard targets" involve a high risk of operational failure for terrorists.[194] Moreover, the Allies collectively have developed policies and capabilities designed to manage the effects of terrorist attacks.[195]

In an intriguing parallel with NATO's Military Concept for Defence Against Terrorism, Leon Panetta, then the U.S. secretary of defense, made clear in October 2012 the U.S. willingness to undertake anticipatory action against cyber threats. "If we detect an imminent threat of [cyber] attack that will cause significant, physical destruction in the United States or kill American citizens, we need to have the option to take action against those who would attack us to defend this nation when directed by the president." He also confirmed that the United States is "deepening cooperation with our closest allies with the goal of sharing threat information, maximizing shared capabilities and determining [the origin of] malicious activities."[196]

U.S. policy on countering cyber threats has shown a determination to overcome the absence of "traceable sponsorship."[197] In October 2012 Secretary Panetta revealed that the Department of Defense had in the previous two years "made significant investments in forensics to address this problem of attribution and we're seeing the returns on that investment. Potential aggressors should be aware that the United States has the capacity to locate them and to hold them accountable for their actions that may try to harm America."[198] Some experts nonetheless hold that attribution means remain "not very robust."[199]

It was mainly owing to the increased prominence of cyber challenges that a Hungarian expert said in June 2012 that the focus in the Alliance's DDPR on "an appropriate mix of nuclear, conventional, and missile defence capabilities" was "necessary," but "too narrow" and simply "not sufficient" for future requirements.[200] NATO's deterrence and defense posture must, he said, be "far more comprehensive." The DDPR mentioned "cyber threats," but cyber defense must be accorded "higher priority" in NATO. "It is inconceivable that any major future conflict would unfold without a cyber dimension."[201]

In short, the political meaning given to collective defense by the Allies appears to be in transition. It seems to be no longer limited to the reactive defense of the national territories of the Allies. Mainly in response to the new threats apparent since September 2001, the Allies have taken a more "proactive" approach and have articulated a willingness to act against emerging and imminent threats. While the treaty obligations for collective defense remain as defined by Articles 5 and 6, the Allies have suggested a broader scope for collective defense in some of their statements and actions, notably with respect to challenges such as cyber attacks, terrorism, and WMD proliferation.

Moreover, some eminent observers have recently pointed to a broader conception of collective defense. In July 2009, at a seminar launching NATO's Strategic Concept review, Madeleine Albright said that collective defense and Article 5 "remain, properly, the cornerstone of our alliance. However, we must also be prepared to respond to threats that arise beyond our territory, taking into account the urgency of those threats, the availability of other security options, and the likely consequences of acting or of failing to act."[202] As noted in chapter 2, the Allies declared in the 2010 Strategic Concept that "NATO will deter and defend against any threat of aggression, and against emerging security challenges where they threaten the fundamental security of individual Allies or the Alliance as a whole."[203]

The distinction between Article 5 and non-Article 5 operations thus appears less clear-cut than it was during the Balkan conflicts of the 1990s. Nominally Article 5 operations, such as Operation Active Endeavour in the Mediterranean, have been supported by non-Allies, including states in the Alliance's Partnership for Peace and Mediterranean Dialogue. Operation Active Endeavour has been placed in the context of UN Security Council resolutions and UN-led counterterrorism efforts. Similarly, nominally non-Article 5 operations, notably in Afghanistan, can be seen as serving a purpose consistent with Article 5—that is, preventing the emergence of a new Article 5 threat. Afghanistan in particular marks the Alliance's shift from a geographic view of security to a functional approach. This means a focus on countering threats, whatever their geographic origin, in addition to being prepared to defend the territorial integrity of the Allies against military attack.

As Michael Rühle has pointed out, several of the challenges facing the Alliance, such as cyber attacks, terrorism, "failing states," WMD proliferation, and threats to energy supplies, are not most effectively countered by NATO's traditional policy tools of deterrence and, if necessary, retaliation. It may, for example, be difficult to accurately identify the source of a terrorist, cyber, or WMD attack in a timely fashion. The NATO Allies will therefore be obliged to rely increasingly on measures of farsighted prevention and resilience.

> Hence, while the preparedness to intervene militarily without geographical restrictions is indispensable for any meaningful security policy in the globalization age, it is not sufficient for addressing the full spectrum of risks and threats. . . . Whether it is terrorist attacks against pipelines or cyberattacks on power networks: deterrence by the threat of military retaliation is as irrelevant as is a military operation against the (mostly anonymous) perpetrators. As with cyberdefense, the key to security lies in the resilience of the infrastructure itself: redundancies make it possible to ensure the uninterrupted flow of oil and gas, the rapid repair of the damaged pipelines can keep the losses within acceptable limits, and the electronic systems in control centers must be designed in such a way as to "ride out" even a sophisticated cyberattack.[204]

Resilience measures encompass a full range of active and passive defenses, including air and missile defenses as well as consequence management capabilities to counter or mitigate the effects of attacks. Preventive measures adopted by the Allies in recent years include more extensive intelligence and law enforcement cooperation against terrorists, export controls, sanctions to hinder WMD proliferation, and the "hardening" of electronic communications and information systems against cyber aggression.

Conclusion

During NATO's Cold War period, from 1949 to 1989, the Alliance's deterrence and defense posture relied heavily on nuclear forces because the Alliance was in a position of conventional military inferiority in relation to the Soviet Union and its allies. Furthermore, in the event of war, the NATO Allies expected that they would have to employ nuclear weapons within days in an attempt to convince the Soviets to stop the war.

In the post–Cold War period, since the collapse of the Soviet-led Warsaw Pact and the Soviet Union itself in 1991, NATO has increasingly relied on conventional and missile defense capabilities to supplement its nuclear deterrence posture. The Alliance's DDPR, published at the Chicago Summit in May 2012, focused on these three categories of capabilities. Since the Chicago Summit, however, it has become increasingly apparent that cyber capabilities deserve much more attention and effort from the Allies. State and nonstate adversaries have employed cyber capabilities and could do so in the future with highly destructive effects. The Allies have yet to master the challenge, nationally or collectively.

Secretary Panetta's use of the term "cyber-terrorist" has underscored the potential linkage between terrorist and cyber threats.[205] With regard to terrorist threats and the danger of a transfer of WMD to terrorist groups, the NATO Allies have been obliged to consider and prepare for the anticipatory use of force.[206]

The Allies are, however, becoming increasingly less capable of effective military action. With the exception of certain niche capabilities, such as special operations forces,[207] Allied governments are spending less on military forces and cutting back existing military assets. In these circumstances, despite U.S. defense budget cuts, the long-standing gap between U.S. capabilities and those of the other Allies is widening.[208]

European Allied dependence on U.S. military capabilities has always been at a high level in certain domains, such as nuclear forces during the Cold War and power projection and intelligence, surveillance, and reconnaissance assets subsequently. However, the growing imbalance in capabilities could become politically debilitating and undermine NATO's capacity for decisive collective action.

Disputes within the Alliance about burden sharing began with NATO's foundation, but an excessive level of European dependence on the United States could weaken Alliance cohesion. European Allies could more sharply resent their dependence on U.S. capabilities—and the political leadership that inevitably accompanies superior capabilities. U.S. officials and legislators could more disdainfully deplore European Allied "burden shedding" and "free riding."

Part of the Alliance's balancing act must be to restore a more healthy equilibrium between the military capabilities of the United States and the rest of the NATO Allies. The capabilities gap has widened for multiple reasons, including more substantial U.S. investments in defense capabilities and the much greater efficiency of U.S. defense spending, in contrast with the fragmentation of European military training and procurement.

One of the essential causes of the gap remains, however: the comparatively low level of European spending on military capabilities—cut back even further by the financial crisis since 2008. In the context of the financial crisis, the urgency that governments attach to other social priorities is especially high. It is accordingly difficult to sustain, much less increase, defense spending.[209] Capability shortcomings and perceived lessons from Afghanistan and other operations may affect the Alliance's transition to a more "proactive" approach to collective defense and other security tasks.

The United States has recognized that it will be impractical for the European Allies to increase defense spending during the economic crisis. However, according to Liz Sherwood-Randall, the U.S. National Security Council's senior director for Europe, "We can anticipate growth in European defense spending when Europe has recovered from its economic crisis."[210]

Given the trends in recent years, what Lord Robertson, then the NATO secretary general, said in 2002 is more pertinent than ever:

If Europe is to play its proper part in NATO and more widely, and if we are to ensure that the US moves neither towards unilateralism nor isolationism, all European countries must show a new willingness to develop effective crisis management capabilities. . . . Unless the Europeans do better militarily in NATO and the EU, their influence in the Euro-Atlantic area and more widely will remain limited.[211]

Another part of NATO's balancing act must be to invest more in prevention and resilience measures while continuing preparedness for collective defense and deterrence in the more traditional sense, conducting crisis management operations, and cultivating relations with partners ready to take action against common threats. The Allies recognize that meeting the new prevention and resilience requirements is a form of collective defense and indeed essential in order to be able to deal effectively with multiple types of security contingencies. If the Allies reconfigure and adapt their collective defense posture effectively, this will provide a foundation for them to pursue the other two core tasks they have assumed: crisis management and cooperative security.

Notes

1. Rowan Scarborough, "Attack on Iran Could Risk Gulf Oil Supplies," *Washington Times*, November 15, 2011.
2. Olaf Theiler, "New Threats: The Cyber-dimension," *NATO Review*, September 2011, www.nato.int/docu/review/2011/11-september/Cyber-Threads/EN/index.htm.
3. North Atlantic Council, "Strategic Concept," November 7, 1991, par. 49.
4. North Atlantic Council, "Strategic Concept," April 24, 1999, par. 56.
5. "Deterrence, based on an appropriate mix of nuclear and conventional capabilities, remains a core element of our overall strategy." North Atlantic Council, "Declaration on Alliance Security," April 4, 2009, www.nato.int/cps/en/natolive/news_52838.htm?mode=pressrelease.
6. North Atlantic Council, "Strategic Concept," November 19, 2010, par. 19.
7. Ibid., par. 8.
8. North Atlantic Council, "Lisbon Summit Declaration," par. 30. The Allies were, however, not entirely consistent about the components of "an appropriate mix" in 2010. In the 2010 Strategic Concept, released simultaneously with the Lisbon Summit Declaration, the Allies called for "an appropriate mix of nuclear and conventional capabilities." North Atlantic Council, "Strategic Concept," November 19, 2010, par. 17.
9. North Atlantic Council, "Chicago Summit Declaration," par. 54. According to the DDPR, "NATO has determined that, in the current circumstances, the existing mix of capabilities and the plans for their development are sound. . . . NATO is committed to maintaining an appropriate mix of nuclear, conventional, and missile defence capabilities for deterrence and defence to fulfil its commitments as set out in the Strategic Concept." North Atlantic Council, "Deterrence and Defence Posture Review," May 20, 2012, par. 31–32.
10. Testimony in *Department of Defense Appropriations for 1981: Hearings before the Defense Subcommittee of the Appropriations Committee, House of Representatives* (Washington, DC: U.S. Government Printing Office, 1980), Part 4, 55, quoted in Thomas A. Callaghan, Jr., "Nuclear Parity Requires Conventional Parity," in *NATO's Strategic Options: Arms Control and Defense* , ed. David S. Yost (New York: Pergamon Press, 1981), 187.
11. General James L. Jones, statement before the Senate Armed Services Committee, March 7, 2006, 43, http://armed-services.senate.gov/statemnt/2006/March/Jones%2003-07-06.pdf.
12. NATO, "Allied Command Operations (ACO)," last updated May 10, 2013, www.nato.int/cps/en/natolive/topics_52091.htm.
13. NATO, "The NATO Defence Planning Process," last updated May 18, 2012, www.nato.int/cps/en/natolive/topics_49202.htm.
14. Ibid.
15. Author's interview with an American observer in Brussels, May 31, 2013.
16. Rasmussen, "NATO 2020—Shared Leadership for a Shared Future." One might add that the member states of the European Union have retained national sovereignty in the domain of security and defense. The European Union's

CSDP has been pursued on an intergovernmental basis. Rasmussen was evidently referring to trade and other policy domains in which EU member states have transferred sovereignty to common institutions.

17. Despite the fact that Allies have exercised their sovereign right not to fulfill assignments arising from the NDPP, some have reportedly found the process of identifying national shortfalls in meeting requirements so unpleasant that they wish to "reform" this new defense planning process and its rigorous specification of "level of ambition" capability requirements and reasonable national responsibilities.

18. In a reference to the United States, Vice Admiral Charles A. Johnstone-Burt, Royal Navy, Chief of Staff, Allied Command Transformation, said, "There's one nation that traditionally delivers far more than the others. . . . The European NATO nations accepted that fully . . . and came up with a tacit understanding that no nation should . . . contribute more than 50 percent to any one capability, if at all possible." Johnstone-Burt quoted in Amaani Lyle, "Training, Resource Sharing Boost NATO Transformation Initiatives," American Forces Press Service, December 13, 2012, www.defense.gov/News/NewsArticle.aspx?ID=118784.

19. Laurence Martin, "The Domestic Context of British Defense Policy," in *The Internal Fabric of Western Security*, ed. Gregory Flynn et al. (London: Croom Helm, 1981), 154.

20. Josef Joffe, "German Defense Policy: Novel Solutions and Enduring Dilemmas," in *The Internal Fabric of Western Security*, ed. Gregory Flynn et al. (London: Croom Helm, 1981), 68.

21. See the statements cited in chapter 4 by General Harald Kujat, Brigadier General Jo Coelmont, and Alexander Mattelaer.

22. Diego Ruiz Palmer, "The Enduring Influence of Operations on NATO's Transformation," *NATO Review*, Winter 2006, www.nato.int/docu/review/2006/issue4/english/analysis1.html.

23. Alexander Mattelaer, "How Afghanistan Has Strengthened NATO," *Survival* 53, no. 6 (December 2011–January 2012): 134–135.

24. Anthony H. Cordesman, "Rethinking NATO's Force Transformation," *NATO Review*, Spring 2005, www.nato.int/docu/review/2005/issue1/english/art4.html.

25. Ibid.

26. North Atlantic Council, "Prague Summit Declaration," par. 4.

27. Robert Bell is currently the senior civilian representative of the U.S. Secretary of Defense in Europe and defense adviser, U.S. Mission to NATO.

28. Robert Bell, "Sisyphus and the NRF," *NATO Review*, Autumn 2006, www.nato.int/docu/review/2006/issue3/english/art4.html; italics in the original.

29. Adrian Croft, "Some EU States May No Longer Afford Air Forces: General," Reuters.com, September 19, 2012.

30. Witney quoted in Isabelle de Pommereau, "France's Afghanistan Pull-Out Signals War Fatigue Driving European Defense Cuts," *Christian Science Monitor* (csmonitor.com), May 25, 2012. See also Nick Witney, *How to Stop the Demilitarisation of Europe* (London: European Council on Foreign Relations, November 2011).

31. Anders Fogh Rasmussen has promoted the term "smart defense." One of his predecessors, Lord Robertson, prescribed what he called "smart investment." Lord Robertson, speech at the First Magazine Dinner, Claridge's Hotel, London, January 24 2002, www.nato.int/docu/speech/2002/s020124a.htm.

32. North Atlantic Council, "Summit Declaration on Defence Capabilities: Toward NATO Forces 2020," May 20, 2012, par. 8.

33. North Atlantic Council, "Chicago Summit Declaration," par. 20.

34. In 1949, the Allies agreed to pursue "cooperation, within the legal limitations and administrative restrictions of each country, in research and development of new weapons and in the development of new methods of warfare." DC 6/1, "Strategic Concept for the Defense of the North Atlantic Area," December 1, 1949, 7, par. 8h, in *NATO Strategy Documents 1949–1969*, ed. Gregory W. Pedlow (Brussels: NATO Information Service, 1997), 57–64.

35. The EPAF nations all operate F-16 fighter aircraft. Originally intended to assist in the modernization of the F-16 to the Mid-Life Update (MLU) standard, the EPAF arrangement has been extended to support combined operations by EPAF nations in an EPAF Expeditionary Air Wing. EPAF cooperation facilitated F-16 deployments to Italy in support of Operation Allied Force in 1999 and to Afghanistan in support of ISAF.

36. Espen Barth Eide, "Transatlantic Ties in Times of Financial Austerity" (speech, Leangkollen Security Conference, February 6, 2012), www.regjeringen.no/en/dep/fd/whats-new/Speeches-and-articles/minister/speeches-and-articles-by-minister-of-d-2/2012/transatlantic-ties-in-times-of-financial.html?id=671826.

37. Tomas Valasek has been Slovakia's permanent representative to NATO since April 15, 2013.

38. Tomas Valasek, *How to Make "Smart Defence" a Success* (Bratislava: Slovak Atlantic Commission, 2012), www.ata-sac.org/globsec2012/uploads/documents/GPB/GPB%20Valášek.pdf.

39. F. Stephen Larrabee and Peter A. Wilson, "NATO's Shrinking Resources," *International Herald Tribune*, May 16, 2012.

40. Rasmussen, "NATO 2020—Shared Leadership for a Shared Future."

41. The twelve nations participating in the SAC initiative's Heavy Airlift Wing comprise two PfP countries (Finland and Sweden) and ten NATO countries (Bulgaria, Estonia, Hungary, Lithuania, the Netherlands, Norway, Poland, Romania, Slovenia and the United States). "Strategic Airlift Capability (SAC)," last updated August 7, 2012, www.nato.int/cps/en/natolive/topics_50105.htm.

42. Adrian Croft, "Ten European States Agree Military Air Tanker Cooperation," Reuters.com, November 19, 2012.

43. Michael Rühle, "The Future of the Transatlantic Security Relationship," *American Foreign Policy Interests* 35, no. 5 (2013): 286. In Rühle's judgment, "pooling and sharing cannot compensate for the massive decline in defense spending: current efforts to reduce redundancies could potentially save European nations a few hundred million euros, yet the budget cuts since the beginning of the financial crisis in 2008 amount to more than 30 billion euros." (Ibid., 285.)

44. NATO, "The NATO Response Force: At the Centre of NATO Transformation," www.nato.int/cps/en/natolive/topics_49755.htm, last updated March 5, 2012.

45. North Atlantic Council, "Riga Summit Declaration," par. 23.

46. NATO, "The NATO Response Force."

47. Allied Command Operations, "The NATO Response Force," www.aco.nato.int/page349011837.aspx.

48. NATO, "The NATO Response Force."

49. North Atlantic Council, "Riga Summit Declaration," par. 22, 23.

50. Bell, "Sisyphus and the NRF."

51. Vladimir Socor, "NATO's Response Force, Other Planned Capabilities Stillborn," *Eurasia Daily Monitor* 6, no. 38 (February 26, 2009).

52. Arnadottir, *Protecting to Project*, par. 49.

53. Jonson, *The Debate about Article 5 and Its Credibility*, 7.

54. Arnadottir, *Protecting to Project*, par. 49.

55. Jonson, *The Debate about Article 5 and Its Credibility*, 4n5.

56. NATO, "The NATO Response Force."

57. North Atlantic Council, "Prague Summit Declaration," par. 4a.

58. North Atlantic Council, "Riga Summit Declaration," par. 23.

59. Jeffrey P. Bialos and Stuart L. Koehl, *The NATO Response Force: Facilitating Coalition Warfare through Technology Transfer and Information Sharing* (Washington, DC: National Defense University, September 2005), 17.

60. Diego Ruiz Palmer, "Afghanistan's Transformational Challenge," *NATO Review*, Summer 2005, www.nato.int/docu/review/2005/issue2/english/art2.html.

61. Guillaume Lasconjarias, *The NRF: From a Key Driver of Transformation to a Laboratory of the Connected Forces Initiative*, Research Paper no. 88 (Rome: NATO Defense College, January 2013).

62. Bell, "Sisyphus and the NRF."

63. NATO, "The NATO Response Force."

64. See the incisive discussion in Jens Ringsmose, "NATO's Response Force: Finally Getting It Right?," *European Security* 18, no. 3 (September 2009): 300–302.

65. For a classic statement of this position, see the 1994 French Ministry of Defense white paper: "It is illusory and dangerous to claim that such [conventional] technologies could have the effect of preventing war as nuclear weapons do. All the lessons of history argue against it. These conceptions emphasize conventional force balances, which are by nature unstable and based on operational strategies, for preparing and conducting war. They suggest the possibility of resolving international problems through the use of force and imply an arms race. They are not compatible with our strategy. Far from substituting for nuclear deterrence, a so-called conventional deterrent could only complement it. . . . Moreover, nuclear weapons remain the means to compensate, if necessary, for possible insufficiencies in other areas, and allow for an avoidance of a 'conventional arms race' that would be contrary to our defense policy and unacceptable from a financial viewpoint." Ministère de la Défense, *Livre Blanc sur la Défense* (Paris: Service d'Information et de Relations Publiques des Armées, February 1994), 56–57.

66. North Atlantic Council, "Strategic Concept," November 7, 1991, par. 38.

67. North Atlantic Council, "Strategic Concept," April 24, 1999, par. 46.

68. North Atlantic Council, "Strategic Concept," November 19, 2010, par. 17.

69. North Atlantic Council, "Chicago Summit Declaration," par. 59.

70. See, for example, the August 2011 statement by Mart Laar, then the Estonian minister of defense, cited in chapter 9.

71. Jacek Durkalec, *NATO Defence and Deterrence Posture: Central and Eastern European Perspectives*, Policy Paper no. 29 (Warsaw: Polish Institute of International Affairs, May 2012), 3.

72. Nursin Atesoglu Güney, "Turkish Nuclear Security after Iranian Nuclearization," *Contemporary Security Policy* 33, no. 3 (December 2012): 526.

73. North Atlantic Council, "Strategic Concept," November 7, 1991, par. 10.

74. Ibid., par. 56.

75. Ibid., par. 47–48.

76. North Atlantic Council, "Strategic Concept," April 24, 1999, par. 64.

77. Ibid., par. 20.

78. Ibid., par. 20.

79. Ibid., par. 54.

80. North Atlantic Council, "Strategic Concept," November 19, 2010, par. 7 and 8.

81. Ibid., par. 19.

82. Jens Ringsmose and Sten Rynning, *Come Home, NATO? The Atlantic Alliance's New Strategic Concept*, DIIS Report 2009:04 (Copenhagen: Danish Institute for International Studies, 2009), 22.

83. Gates quoted in Peter Spiegel, "Last of The Cold Warriors: Robert Gates' Parting Shots at Europe," *Financial Times*, June 28, 2011.

84. North Atlantic Council, "Strategic Concept," November 19, 2010, par. 19.

85. Eide, "Transatlantic Ties in Times of Financial Austerity."

86. Anders Fogh Rasmussen, "Building Security in an Age of Austerity" (keynote speech, Munich Security Conference, February 4, 2011), www.nato.int/cps/en/natolive/opinions_70400.htm.

87. See the annual *Military Balance* of the International Institute for Strategic Studies and the Alliance's own yearly compendium of national statistics on defense expenditures, www.nato.int/cps/en/natolive/topics_49198.htm.

88. According to the strategic guidance, "while the U.S. military will continue to contribute to security globally, *we will of necessity rebalance toward the Asia-Pacific region.*" *Sustaining U.S. Global Leadership: Priorities for 21st Century Defense* (Washington, DC: U.S. Department of Defense, January 2012), 2; italics in the original.

89. "The Connected Forces Initiative," last updated February 21, 2013, www.nato.int/cps/en/SID-107090C3-88095132/natolive/topics_98527.htm.

90. North Atlantic Council, "Summit Declaration on Defence Capabilities: Toward NATO Forces 2020," May 20, 2012, www.nato.int/cps/en/SID-140D258B-1322853B/natolive/official_texts_87594.htm.

91. The first Strategic Concept, approved by the Allies in December 1949, included a U.S. commitment to employ nuclear weapons in defense of the Allies. "Strategic Concept for the Defense of the North Atlantic Area," DC 6/1, approved by the North Atlantic Defense Committee on December 1, 1949, in *NATO Strategy Documents 1949–1969*, ed. Gregory W. Pedlow (Brussels: NATO Information Service, 1997), 5, par. 7a. See also Pedlow, "The Evolution of NATO Strategy, 1949–1969," in ibid., xii–xiii. A few days before the Allies concluded the North Atlantic Treaty on April 4, 1949, Winston Churchill said, "It is certain that Europe would have been Communized, like Czechoslovakia, and London under bombardment some time ago but for the deterrent of the atomic bomb in the hands of the United States." Winston Churchill, speech on March 31, 1949, in Winston S. Churchill, *His Complete Speeches, 1897–1963*, vol. VII, ed. Robert Rhodes James (New York and London: Chelsea House Publishers in association with R. R. Bowker Company, 1974), 7809.

92. This discussion is based in part on other works by the author, especially "Assurance and US Extended Deterrence in NATO," *International Affairs* 85, no. 4 (July 2009): 755–780; and "The US Debate on NATO Nuclear Deterrence," *International Affairs* 87, no. 6 (November 2011): 1401–1438.

93. Of the vast literature on this subject, two books deserve particular mention: David N. Schwartz, *NATO's Nuclear Dilemmas* (Washington, DC: Brookings Institution Press, 1983), and Jane E. Stromseth, *The Origins of Flexible Response: NATO's Debate over Strategy in the 1960s* (London: Macmillan, 1988). For further background, including a discussion of key questions about extended deterrence and limited nuclear operations that were never fully answered during the Cold War, see David S. Yost, "The History of NATO Theater Nuclear Force Policy: Key Findings from the Sandia Conference," *Journal of Strategic Studies* 15, no. 2 (June 1992): 228–261.

94. Defense Planning Committee, *Enhancing Alliance Collective Security: Shared Roles, Risks and Responsibilities in the Alliance* (NATO, December 1988), par. 36. It should be noted that the United Kingdom provided its own nuclear gravity bombs for its dual-capable aircraft, and that all British air-delivered nuclear weapons were phased out in early 1998.

95. North Atlantic Council, "Strategic Concept," November 7, 1991, par. 56.

96. Ibid., par. 55 and 57.

97. North Atlantic Council, "Strategic Concept," April 24, 1999, par. 62–64.

98. The U.S. nuclear arsenal available to uphold U.S. security commitments includes forces in addition to those actually based in Europe. The U.S. nuclear posture includes Trident submarines equipped with ballistic missiles, Minuteman III intercontinental ballistic missiles, B-52 and B-2 bombers, and bombs for fighter aircraft in addition to those in Europe. Since the withdrawal of its last air-delivered bombs in early 1998, the United Kingdom's nuclear forces have consisted solely of submarines equipped with ballistic missiles. Since the deactivation of its intermediate-range missile force on the Plateau d'Albion in 1996, France's nuclear forces have consisted solely of submarines equipped with ballistic missiles and aircraft armed with air-launched missiles.

99. Paragraph 8 of the communiqué regarding the December 1962 U.S.-British summit at Nassau. This communiqué is reproduced in Andrew J. Pierre, *Nuclear Politics: The British Experience with an Independent Strategic Force, 1939–70* (London: Oxford University Press, 1972), 346–347.

100. See, among other sources, Shaun R. Gregory, *Nuclear Command and Control in NATO: Nuclear Weapons Operations and the Strategy of Flexible Response* (London: Macmillan, 1996).

101. North Atlantic Council, "Strategic Concept," November 19, 2010, par. 18. This statement repeated an almost identical statement in the Alliance's Strategic Concepts of November 7, 1991 (par. 54) and April 24, 1999 (par. 62). The 1991 and 1999 statements paraphrased the judgment in the 1974 Ottawa Declaration on Alliance Relations, which noted that two of the European Allies "possess nuclear forces capable of playing a deterrent role of their own contributing to the overall strengthening of the deterrence of the Alliance." North Atlantic Council, "Declaration on Atlantic Relations," Ottawa, June 19, 1974, in *Texts of Final Communiqués, 1949–1974* (Brussels: NATO Information Service, 1975), 319, par. 6.

102. "Essential elements of the review would include the range of NATO's strategic capabilities required, including NATO's nuclear posture, and missile defence and other means of strategic deterrence and defence. This only applies to nuclear weapons assigned to NATO." North Atlantic Council, "Lisbon Summit Declaration," par. 30.

103. North Atlantic Council, "Strategic Concept," November 7, 1991, par. 39, 55, 56, and 59; and North Atlantic Council, "Strategic Concept," April 24, 1999, par. 63 and 64.

104. North Atlantic Council, "Strategic Concept," November 19, 2010, par. 17.

105. In the 1991 Strategic Concept, the Allies said, "To protect peace and to prevent war or any kind of coercion, the Alliance will maintain for the foreseeable future an appropriate mix of nuclear and conventional forces based in Europe and kept up to date where necessary, although at a significantly reduced level." North Atlantic Council, "Strategic Concept," November 7, 1991, par. 38. In the 1999 Strategic Concept, the final clause was reworded to read "although at a minimum sufficient level." North Atlantic Council, "Strategic Concept," April 24, 1999, par. 46.

106. North Atlantic Council, "Strategic Concept," November 19, 2010, par. 17.

107. North Atlantic Council, "Strategic Concept," April 24, 1999, par. 64. In the 1991 Strategic Concept, the "Allies concerned" held that "[t]he circumstances in which any use of nuclear weapons might have to be contemplated . . . are . . . even more remote" than during the Cold War, owing to the new strategic situation. North Atlantic Council, "Strategic Concept," November 7, 1991, par. 56.

108. North Atlantic Council, "Strategic Concept," November 19, 2010, par. 17.

109. Secretary of State Hillary Clinton quoted in Mark Landler, "U.S. Resists Push by Allies for Tactical Nuclear Cuts," *New York Times*, April 23, 2010.

110. North Atlantic Council, "Strategic Concept," November 19, 2010, par. 19.

111. North Atlantic Council, "Strategic Concept," April 24, 1999, par. 64.

112. "In diesem Zusammenhang sowie im Zuge der Ausarbeitung eines strategischen Konzeptes der NATO werden wir uns im Bündnis sowie gegenüber den amerikanischen Verbündeten dafür einsetzen, dass die in Deutschland verbliebenen Atomwaffen abgezogen werden." *Wachstum. Bildung. Zusammenhalt: Koalitionsvertrag zwischen CDU, CSU und FDP*, 17 Legislaturperiode, Oktober 26, 2009, 120.

113. Individual German government advocates of removing the remaining U.S. nuclear weapons in Europe have made clear that this was a compromise. For example, according to Ambassador Rolf Nikel, federal government commissioner for disarmament and arms control, "Substrategic nuclear weapons in Europe are of a questionable military value. If it had only been for us, we could live without them. As a member of the Alliance, however, we cannot and do not want to act unilaterally. We have to take the more reluctant viewpoints of our allies into consideration." Speech at the opening of the "Berlin Framework Forums: Creating the Conditions and Building the Framework for a Nuclear Weapons-Free World," February 21, 2013, in the Federal Foreign Office, Berlin.

114. Nonpaper submitted by Poland, Norway, Germany, and the Netherlands on increasing transparency and confidence with regard to tactical nuclear weapons in Europe, April 14, 2011. The ambassadors to NATO of Belgium, the Czech Republic, Germany, Hungary, Iceland, Luxembourg, the Netherlands, Norway, Poland, and Slovenia signed the April 15, 2011, cover letter to Anders Fogh Rasmussen. This document is available at www.fas.org/blog/ssp/2011/04/nato-proposal.php.

115. North Atlantic Council, "Strategic Concept," November 19, 2010, par. 26. The possible implications of relocating Russian nuclear weapons "away from the territory of NATO members" are discussed in chapter 9.

116. Some proponents of withdrawing the remaining U.S. nuclear weapons in Europe make a strikingly different argument, stating that the B-61 life extension program and the introduction of the F-35 Joint Strike Fighter would radically enhance the Alliance's military capabilities and provoke competition with Russia. See, for example, Edmond Seay, "Escalation by Default: The Future of NATO Nuclear Weapons in Europe," May 10, 2012, www.europeanleadershipnetwork.org/escalation-by-default-the-future-of-nato-nuclear-weapons-in-europe_380.html; and Hans M. Kristensen, *Non-Strategic Nuclear Weapons*, Special Report no. 3 (Washington, DC: Federation of American Scientists, May 2012), 24–27. This view stands in contrast to declared U.S. policy: "The United States will not develop new nuclear warheads. Life Extension Programs will use only nuclear components based on previously tested designs, and will not support new military missions or provide for new military capabilities." *Nuclear Posture Review Report* (Washington, DC: U.S. Department of Defense, April 2010), 39.

117. James R. Schlesinger, chairman, *Report of the Secretary of Defense Task Force on DoD Nuclear Weapons Management, Phase II: Review of the DoD Nuclear Mission* (Arlington, VA: Secretary of Defense Task Force on DoD Nuclear Weapons Management, December 2008), 60, www.defenselink.mil/pubs/pdfs/PhaseIIReportFinal.pdf.

118. For background, see David S. Yost, "NATO and Tailored Deterrence: Surveying the Challenges," in *NATO and 21st Century Deterrence*, Forum Paper no. 8, ed. Karl-Heinz Kamp and David S. Yost (Rome: NATO Defense College, May 2009), 11–31, www.ndc.nato.int/download/publications/fp_08.pdf.

119. Rühle, *The Broader Context of NATO's Nuclear Policy and Posture*, 6.

120. Congressional Commission on the Strategic Posture of the United States, *America's Strategic Posture: The Final Report of the Congressional Commission on the Strategic Posture of the United States* (Washington, DC: United States Institute of Peace Press, 2009), 26, www.usip.org/programs/initiatives/congressional-commission-the-strategic-posture-the-united-states.

121. A Lithuanian expert said in June 2012 that for NATO as a coalition "there is no better way to communicate deterrence than the DCA arrangement." He said that "the much advertised smart defence rests upon the idea that several nations should pool and share certain capabilities that they cannot sustain individually. This, to me, sounds very much like NATO's nuclear sharing arrangements. We already have a smart deterrent; and it would be smart to keep it." Yost, *NATO's Deterrence and Defense Posture*, 5.

122. North Atlantic Council, "Deterrence and Defence Posture Review," May 20, 2012, par. 8.

123. Ibid., par. 12. The DDPR included a footnote specifying that the "Allies concerned" are all the members of the Nuclear Planning Group—in other words, all the Allies except France.

124. North Atlantic Council, "Lisbon Summit Declaration," par. 31.

125. North Atlantic Council, "Strategic Concept," April 24, 1999, par. 62.

126. See, among other sources, Wade Boese, "Germany Raises No-First-Use Issue at NATO Meeting," *Arms Control Today* 28, no. 8 (November/December 1998): 24; François Géré, "Divergences sur l'arme nucléaire," *Le Figaro*, December 3, 1998; and "NATO's Mid-Life Crisis," *Economist*, December 12, 1998, 17. According to Boese's account, "No other NATO capitals have publicly endorsed the German position, although the idea of no-first-use is widely supported throughout the Canadian government, including by Foreign Affairs Minister [Lloyd] Axworthy."

127. "NATO's nuclear forces . . . fulfil an essential role by ensuring uncertainty in the mind of any aggressor about the nature of the Allies' response to military aggression." NATO, "NATO's Comprehensive, Strategic-Level Policy for Preventing the Proliferation of Weapons of Mass Destruction (WMD) and Defending against Chemical, Biological, Radiological and Nuclear (CBRN) Threats," par. 14.

128. "We will continue to implement NATO's Strategic-Level Policy for Preventing the Proliferation of WMD and Defending Against Chemical, Biological, Radiological and Nuclear Threats." North Atlantic Council, "Lisbon Summit Declaration," par. 34.

129. *Nuclear Posture Review Report* (Washington, DC: U.S. Department of Defense, April 2010), 15.

130. Ibid., 16.

131. Letter dated April 6, 1995, from Jean-Bernard Mérimée, the permanent representative of France to the United Nations, addressed to the secretary-general, A/50/154, S/1995/264.

132. *Securing Britain in an Age of Uncertainty: The Strategic Defence and Security Review*, Cm 7948 (London: The Stationery Office, October 2010), par. 3.7, 37–38.

133. With regard to Iran's violations of its IAEA safeguards agreement, see Paul K. Kerr, *Iran's Nuclear Program: Tehran's Compliance with International Obligations*, CRS R40094 (Washington, DC: Congressional Research Service, September 18, 2012), 10–12.

134. Paul Zajac, a French diplomat, recently wrote that "it is the sole responsibility of the nuclear-weapon states to decide, at the last instance, on the conditions for the use of nuclear weapons. In particular, there can be no question of NATO committing itself on the issue of negative security assurances, which are unilateral legal acts adopted by nuclear-weapon states." Paul Zajac, *NATO's Defense and Deterrence Posture Review: A French Perspective on Nuclear Issues*, Nuclear Policy Paper no. 7 (Arms Control Association, the British American Security Information Council, and the Institute for Peace Research and Security Policy at the University of Hamburg, April 2011), 4.

135. North Atlantic Council, "Deterrence and Defence Posture Review," May 20, 2012, par. 10.

136. Gareth Evans and Yoriko Kawaguchi, co-chairs, *Eliminating Nuclear Threats: A Practical Agenda for Global Policymakers, Report of the International Commission on Nuclear Non-Proliferation and Disarmament* (Barton, Australia: ICNND Secretariat, December 2009), 75, par. 7.11.

137. *Nuclear Posture Review Report* (Washington, DC: U.S. Department of Defense, April 2010), 16.

138. *Lifting the Nuclear Shadow: Creating the Conditions for Abolishing Nuclear Weapons* (London: Foreign and Commonwealth Office, February 4, 2009), 39–40.

139. Author interviews in Paris, May 2011.

140. Nicolas Sarkozy, president of the French Republic, speech at the presentation of *Le Terrible*, Cherbourg, March 21, 2008.

141. Lord Robertson, Franklin C. Miller, and Kori Schake, *It's Time to Put the Nuclear Issue Behind Us: The Chicago Summit Has More Urgent Priorities Than Nuclear Theology*, Atlantic Council Issue Brief (Washington, DC: Atlantic Council of the United States, May 2012), 3.

142. *Nuclear Posture Review Report* (Washington, DC: U.S. Department of Defense, April 2010), 15.

143. "The fundamental role of U.S. nuclear weapons remains to deter nuclear attack on the United States and its Allies and partners." *Report on Nuclear Employment Strategy of the United States Specified in Section 491 of 10 U.S.C.* (Washington, DC: U.S. Department of Defense, June 12, 2013), 4.

144. North Atlantic Council, "Strategic Concept," November 7, 1991, par. 49.

145. North Atlantic Council, "Strategic Concept," April 24, 1999, par. 56.

146. North Atlantic Council, "Prague Summit Declaration," par. 4g.

147. For background on the Reagan-era NATO debate on U.S. strategic missile defenses, see David S. Yost, "Western Europe and the U.S. Strategic Defense Initiative," *Journal of International Affairs* 41 (Summer 1988): 269–323.

148. North Atlantic Council, "Riga Summit Declaration," par. 25.

149. North Atlantic Council, "Final Statement," December 4, 2009, par. 14. The Obama administration's September 2009 redefinition of U.S. missile defense plans in Europe initially provoked strong reservations, particularly in the Czech Republic, Poland, and elsewhere in Central and Eastern Europe. However, these Allies soon endorsed the redefined U.S. missile defense plans. For example, in October 2009, Rasa Jukneviciene, then the Lithuanian minister of defense, said, "The recently announced changes to the original US plan for missile defence in Europe were originally mistaken in some capitals for a sign of the US losing interest in the security of Europe and making concessions to Russia. As the US has shared more details about the new design of the system, we are satisfied to see that, if anything, the system will become more robust, technically advanced, mobile and adaptive to threats. The US is committed to building the system and to place some of its elements in Europe. To me, it means that the US is as committed to our security as ever and, rather than making concessions to Russia's unreasonable demands, it opens new opportunities for cooperation with Russia in credibly addressing a serious growing threat." Rasa Jukneviciene, *Latest Developments in European Security: A Baltic Perspective* (London: Chatham House, October 20, 2009), 3.

150. North Atlantic Council, "Final Statement," December 4, 2009, par. 15.

151. North Atlantic Council, "Lisbon Summit Declaration," par. 36 and 37.

152. Ibid., par. 30.

153. For background on additional current and potential Allied contributions to NATO's missile defense posture, see Brad Roberts, then deputy assistant secretary of defense for nuclear and missile defense policy, statement before the Senate Armed Services Committee, April 25, 2012.

154. In March 2013, a French-Italian team tested the integration of the SAMP/T (*Sol-Air-Moyenne Portée-Terre*) missile in a NATO missile defense architecture at the Biscarrosse firing range on France's Atlantic coast. The Eurosam SAMP successfully intercepted a ballistic missile in coordination with the NATO BMD Operations Cell at Ramstein, Germany. According to Eurosam, the test firing was "close to what would be an operational use for an anti-theater ballistic missile mission under the aegis of the alliance Active Layered Theater Ballistic Missile Defense program." Tony Osborne, "European SAMP/T Destroys Ballistic Missile in Test," *Aerospace Daily & Defense Report*, March 11, 2013, 3, quoted in Ronald O'Rourke, *Navy Aegis Ballistic Missile Defense (BMD) Program: Background and Issues for Congress*, RL33745 (Washington, DC: Congressional Research Service, March 27, 2013), 87–88.

155. In the words of a French expert, "The French have always been doubtful about the cost-benefit payoff of missile defense. It is all right with France if the U.S. pays for it, but it is still a poor use of scarce defense resources. Airlift, refueling aircraft, surveillance and reconnaissance, and other operational assets should be higher priorities." Author interview with a French observer in Brussels, May 28, 2013.

156. Rachel Oswald, "U.S. Official Defends Spending on NATO Missile Shield, under GOP Attack," *Global Security News-wire*, June 25, 2013, www.nti.org/gsn/article/us-official-defends-spending-nato-missile-shield-under-gop-attack/.

157. James N. Miller, principal deputy under secretary of defense for policy, statement before the House Armed Services Committee, Subcommittee on Strategic Forces, December 1, 2010, 3.

158. Ibid., 4, 5, and 6.

159. Rear Admiral Archer M. Macy, USN, statement before the House Armed Services Committee, Subcommittee on Strategic Forces, December 1, 2010, 4. According to the BMD review report, "Perhaps the most important [challenge] derives from the fact that regional demand for U.S. BMD assets is likely to exceed supply for some years to come. Although the missile threat is developing at different rates in different regions, overall it is developing rapidly. Today there are thousands of ballistic missiles and hundreds of launchers in countries other than Russia, China, the United States, and NATO members; roughly 90 percent of those missiles have ranges less than 1,000 kilometers. Against this threat, the United States currently has only a few hundred defensive short-range interceptors deployed in multiple regions." *Ballistic Missile Defense Review Report* (Washington, DC: U.S. Department of Defense, February 2010), 26.

160. Rear Admiral Macy, USN, statement before the House Armed Services Committee, December 1, 2010, 8, 10.

161. North Atlantic Council, "Deterrence and Defence Posture Review," May 20, 2012, par. 20.

162. Ibid., par. 21.

163. Secretary of Defense Chuck Hagel, news briefing on missile defense, Department of Defense, March 15, 2013, www.defense.gov/Transcripts/Transcript.aspx?TranscriptID=5205.

164. "DAMB: Les Américains sont-ils des alliés?," *TTU: Lettre Hebdomadaire d'Informations Stratégiques*, no. 884 (March 27, 2013): 4.

165. Frank A. Rose, remarks at the 3AF 9th Annual International Conference on Missile Defense, Bucharest, Romania, May 1, 2013, www.state.gov/t/avc/rls/2013/208667.htm.

166. "DAMB: Les Américains sont-ils des alliés?" 4.

167. Dmitry Medvedev, State of the Nation address to the Federal Assembly, November 30, 2010, Interfax (in English), November 30, 2010, available at OpenSource.gov, CEP20101130964185.

168. Ryabkov quoted in Vladimir Isachenkov, "Russia Warns U.S. over Missile Defense Plans," Associated Press, February 7, 2011, www.airforcetimes.com/news/2011/02/ap-russia-warns-us-over-missile-defense-plans-020711/.

169. Miller, statement before the House Armed Services Committee, December 1, 2010, 7.

170. President Obama's letter to Senator Harry M. Reid on missile defense and New START, December 18, 2010, www.america.gov/st/texttrans-english/2010/December/20101220112111su0.6327565.html.

171. Miller, statement before the House Committee on Armed Services, March 2, 2011, 13.

172. North Atlantic Council, "Chicago Summit Declaration," par. 61.

173. Vladimir Putin, "Russia and the Changing World" (in English), on the Russian prime minister's official website, February 26, 2012, available at OpenSource.gov, CEP20120227950106.

174. Vladimir Putin, "We Must Be Strong: Guarantees of National Security for Russia," *Rossiyskaya Gazeta Online* (in Russian), February 20, 2012, 1–3, available at OpenSource.gov, CEP20120220046001.

175. Makarov quoted in Andrew E. Kramer, "Russian General Makes Threat on Missile-Defense Sites," *New York Times*, May 4, 2012.

176. Vershbow quoted in Kramer, "Russian General Makes Threat."

177. North Atlantic Council, "Chicago Summit Declaration," par. 62.

178. Aleksandr Grushko, Russia's permanent representative to NATO, quoted in "Russia Wants 'Clear' Guarantees on ABM from NATO—Envoy," Interfax (in Russian), November 30, 2012, available at OpenSource.gov, CEP20121130950112.

179. General Alexander Vershbow, remarks at the security and defence agenda roundtable "Next Steps in Missile Defence," September 27, 2012, www.nato.int/cps/en/natolive/opinions_90261.htm.

180. A French participant at a recent NATO workshop argued that "deterrence by denial capabilities are intrinsically less threatening, for psychological as well as technical reasons, than the deterrence by punishment potential of nuclear weapons." Yost, *NATO's Deterrence and Defense*, 3.

181. North Atlantic Council, "Chicago Summit Declaration," par. 59.

182. North Atlantic Council, "Istanbul Summit Communiqué," par. 10.

183. A Russian frigate participated in Active Endeavour from September 9 to 25, 2006, and from September 3 to 25, 2007. The planned deployment of a Russian frigate from August 11 to September 30, 2008, was cancelled, owing to the Georgia crisis. Ukraine has to date contributed a ship on six occasions: May 25–July 2, 2007, November 24–December 11, 2007, May 30–August 2, 2008, November 18–December 3, 2008, October 22–November 23, 2009, and November 10–December 17, 2010. Information in these paragraphs regarding historical and prospective Active Endeavour participation was furnished by NATO HQ, October 25, 2011, and June 13, 2013.

184. NATO, "Operation Active Endeavour," www.nato.int/cps/en/natolive/topics_7932.htm (accessed July 16, 2011); and Allied Command Operations, "NATO and Georgia Sign Agreement on Operation Active Endeavour," www.aco.nato.int/page272201213.aspx.

185. Letter from NATO secretary general Jaap de Hoop Scheffer to UN secretary-general Kofi A. Annan, SG (2006) 0013, January 10, 2006.

186. Letter from NATO secretary general Jaap de Hoop Scheffer to UN secretary-general Ban Ki-moon, SG (2007) 0260, April 18, 2007.

187. Article 6 of the North Atlantic Treaty reads as follows: "For the purpose of Article 5, an armed attack on one or more of the Parties is deemed to include an armed attack: on the territory of any of the Parties in Europe or North America, on the Algerian Departments of France, on the territory of or on the Islands under the jurisdiction of any of the Parties in the North Atlantic area north of the Tropic of Cancer; on the forces, vessels, or aircraft of any of the Parties, when in or over these territories or any other area in Europe in which occupation forces of any of the Parties were stationed on the date when the Treaty entered into force or the Mediterranean Sea or the North Atlantic area north of the Tropic of Cancer." The geographic area of application of Article 6 is clarified by two notes. The first note makes clear that Turkish territory outside Europe is covered by Article 5: "The definition of the territories to which Article 5 applies was revised by Article 2 of the Protocol to the North Atlantic Treaty on the accession of Greece and Turkey signed on 22 October 1951." The second note excludes France's former possessions in Algeria: "On January 16, 1963, the North Atlantic Council noted that insofar as the former Algerian Departments of France were concerned, the relevant clauses of this Treaty had become inapplicable as from July 3, 1962."

188. Gülnur Aybet, "The Evolution of NATO's Three Phases and Turkey's Transatlantic Relationship," *Perceptions: Journal of International Affairs* 17, no. 1 (Spring 2012): 20, 25.

189. North Atlantic Council, "Final Communiqué," May 14, 2002, par. 5.

190. The Allies employed the word "wherever" with an expansive connotation on some occasions during the Cold War. For example, according to the 1957 summit communiqué, "The aim of the Soviet bloc is to weaken and disrupt the free world. Its instruments are military, political and economic: and its activities are world wide. To meet this challenge the free world must organize its resources--moral, military, political and economic—and be ready to deploy them wherever the situation demands. Our Alliance cannot therefore be concerned only with the North Atlantic area or only with military defence." North Atlantic Council, "Final Communiqué," December 16–19, 1957, par. 1, www.nato.int/docu/comm/49-95/c571219a.htm. This appears to have been a statement of principle without concrete operational steps such as the NATO Allies have taken since 2001 to be able to conduct expeditionary crisis management interventions within and outside the Euro-Atlantic area.

191. North Atlantic Council, "Prague Summit Declaration," par. 3.

192. NATO, "NATO's Military Concept for Defence against Terrorism," October 2003, www.nato.int/ims/docu/terror-ism.htm. This document is an authoritative description of the concept endorsed at the NATO summit in Prague on November 21, 2002.

193. For background, see David S. Yost, "NATO and the Anticipatory Use of Force," *International Affairs* 83 (January 2007): 39-68.

194. David S. Yost, "New Approaches to Deterrence in Britain, France, and the United States," *International Affairs* 81 (January 2005): 86, 91, 100-102, 109.

195. Allied Command Operations, "Managing the Consequences of Terrorist Attacks," www.aco.nato.int/page142154053.aspx.

196. Secretary of Defense Leon E. Panetta, remarks on cybersecurity, October 11, 2012.

197. Michael J. Glennon of Tufts University quoted in Ellen Nakashima, "We Know What War Looks Like Here, but What Does It Look Like Here?," *Washington Post*, October 28, 2012.

198. Panetta, remarks on cybersecurity, October 11, 2012.

199. William Robertson of Northeastern University, quoted in David Alexander, "Defense Chief Calls Cyberspace Battlefront of the Future," Reuters.com, October 20, 2012.

200. North Atlantic Council, "Deterrence and Defence Posture Review," May 20, 2012, par. 32.

201. Hungarian expert quoted in Yost, *NATO's Deterrence and Defense Posture*, 5.

202. Madeleine Albright, "NATO 2009: Past Lessons, Future Prospects" (speech at the Strategic Concept seminar, Brussels, July 7, 2009), www.nato.int/cps/en/natolive/opinions_56158.htm. Albright served as the chair of the group of twelve experts appointed by the NATO secretary general to serve as advisers on the new Strategic Concept. For background on the Strategic Concept review process, see "Group of Experts," www.nato.int/strategic-concept/experts-strategic-concept.html, and "A Three-Phased Approach," www.nato.int/strategic-concept/roadmap-strategic-concept.html#approach (accessed January 21, 2010).

203. North Atlantic Council, "Strategic Concept," November 19, 2010, par. 4a.

204. Michael Rühle, "NATO and Emerging Security Challenges: Beyond the Deterrence Paradigm," *American Foreign Policy Interests* 33 (2011): 279–280.

205. Panetta, remarks on cybersecurity, October 11, 2012.

206. The extent to which nonstate actors might seek and effectively employ "cyber-terrorist" capabilities remains open to debate. For a thoughtful analysis, see William McCants, William Rosenau, and Eric Thompson, *Cyberspace and Violent Non-State Groups: Uses, Capabilities, and Threats* (Alexandria, VA: CNA, September 2011).

207. Arthur D. Davis, "The Regional Special Operations Headquarters: Franchising the NATO Model as a Hedge in Lean Times," *Joint Force Quarterly*, no. 67 (Fourth Quarter 2012): 71–76.

208. For background, see David S. Yost, "The NATO Capabilities Gap and the European Union," *Survival* 42, no. 4 (Winter 2000–2001): 97–128.

209. For an incisive analysis of the dilemma facing French decision makers, see Martial Foucault, *Les budgets de défense en France, entre déni et déclin*, Focus Stratégique 36 (Paris: Institut Français des Relations Internationales et Stratégiques, April 2012).

210. Sherwood-Randall quoted in Josh Rogin, "Obama Official: No NATO Planning Underway For Syria," *Cable*, April 30, 2012, http://thecable.foreignpolicy.com/posts/2012/04/30/obama_official_no_nato_planning_underway_for_syria.

211. Robertson, speech at the First Magazine Dinner, January 24, 2002.

4

Crisis Management in the Balkans and Afghanistan

During the Cold War, the phrase "crisis management" was, in NATO circles, applied above all to the Alliance's Article 5 mission of collective defense. It signified NATO's intention to bring any eventual violent confrontation with the Warsaw Pact to a conclusion as rapidly as possible, with a minimum of armed combat and destructive use of force. Moreover, during the Cold War, Article 6 of the North Atlantic Treaty was generally interpreted restrictively to exclude military operations "out of area"—in practice, ruling out operations other than those in defense of Allied territory and forces (including naval forces at sea) in the European and North Atlantic area. This served, among other things, to keep the Alliance focused on security in the NATO area and to avoid intra-Alliance disputes regarding the decolonization conflicts of some Allies (particularly Belgium, Britain, France, the Netherlands, and Portugal) and the non-European engagements of the United States (especially in East Asia and the Middle East).[1]

The Alliance's main preoccupation during the Cold War was defense of NATO territory against the threat of Soviet aggression or coercion; NATO operations beyond the territory of the Alliance were unthinkable. In 1983, Manfred Wörner, then the West German minister of defense, wrote, "For the Federal Republic of Germany, deployment of forces outside the NATO area is out of the question. Moreover, such operations would have no strategic meaning. Any withdrawal of forces earmarked for the defense of Europe would increase the present disadvantage of NATO in the East-West force ratio."[2]

There were no armed conflicts in Europe during the Cold War comparable to those that have emerged since the disintegration of the Soviet empire and the former Yugoslavia. The political and strategic stalemate in Europe from the mid-1950s to 1989–1991 meant that, in many ways, the situation was frozen. The Soviet interventions in East Germany, Hungary, and Czechoslovakia and the actions of Communist regimes in Eastern Europe against domestic adversaries (such as the imposition of martial law in Poland in 1981) were in no way occasions for the Alliance to intervene. Indeed, the Alliance went out of its way to signal its restraint and its desire to avoid an East-West war during such events.

Since the end of the Cold War, crisis management has increasingly come to mean non-Article 5 operations beyond the territory of NATO Allies—not the direct defense of NATO territory. The response to Iraqi aggression against Kuwait in August 1990 was organized under the aegis of the United Nations; the only military activities that were officially NATO operations were the preparations made to monitor events and defend Turkey and other Allies against Iraqi aggression, if necessary.[3] According to the list of NATO operations since 1949 published by SHAPE, the Alliance's first two operations in history consisted of the deployment to Turkey of NATO Airborne Early Warning aircraft (August 1990–March 1991) and the Allied Command Europe Mobile Force (Air) and air defense packages (January–March 1991).[4] These operations were undertaken in support of collective defense and deterrence, but they may have also contributed to containing the scope of the crisis provoked by Iraq's aggression against Kuwait.[5]

The 1991 Strategic Concept showed the interest of the Allies in risk management after the collapse of the historic Soviet threat. The NATO Allies recognized that the new context would demand new means of outreach and preparedness to contain and cope with unforeseeable challenges. As the Allies put it in the 1991 Strategic Concept, "The monolithic, massive and potentially immediate threat which was the principal concern of the Alliance in its first forty years has disappeared. On the other hand, a great deal of uncertainty about the future and risks to the security of the Alliance remain."[6] As early as December 1991, the Allies announced that they were "reviewing our crisis management arrangements to ensure the Alliance is capable of responding appropriately to the future risks and challenges which we may face."[7]

NATO's new role in non-Article 5 crisis management operations emerged under the pressure of necessity, with the agenda driven by events. After the Gulf War–related collective defense operations in 1990–1991, the Alliance's next operations consisted of employing cargo aircraft to take humanitarian aid and medical experts to Russia and other former Soviet republics in February–March 1992.[8] This was followed in May 1992 by the use of NATO AWACS aircraft to monitor the air approaches from Libya in the central Mediterranean after the imposition of UN Security Council sanctions on Tripoli.[9]

Subsequent operations—often of greater magnitude and/or duration than the initial missions noted above—began in July 1992 with the maritime enforcement of a UN Security Council arms embargo on the former Yugoslavia.

The new crisis management mission—often called the conduct of non-Article 5 operations—has involved the definition of new policies and institutions, with particular provisions being made for coalitions of the willing with non-NATO countries. The Allies have sought to reconcile requirements for close political control over the conduct of operations with the need to create structures flexible enough to accommodate the participation of non-NATO states, including countries in the Alliance's multinational partnership frameworks as well as partners outside such frameworks.

NATO's post–Cold War crisis management role developed during the 1990s mainly in response to conflicts in the former Yugoslavia. NATO retains a residual role in Kosovo through the Kosovo Force (KFOR), and conducts partnership activities with Bosnia and Herzegovina, the former Yugoslav Republic of Macedonia, Montenegro, and Serbia. The International Security Assistance Force (ISAF) in Afghanistan has been under NATO leadership since 2003, and this has become NATO's largest and most challenging operation. This chapter examines NATO's lengthiest ongoing crisis management operations, those in the Balkans and Afghanistan.

From 1949, when the Alliance was founded, to 1992, when the Allies undertook humanitarian relief operations to assist former Soviet republics, NATO's geographic mandate was limited to the area described in Article 6 of the North Atlantic Treaty—the zone in which the Article 5 mutual defense commitment applied.[10]

The protracted conduct of non-Article 5 operations in the Balkans raised the question whether there was any geographic boundary to such operations. The "global NATO" discussion began in the 1990s and was inconclusive until the terrorist attacks against the United States in September 2001. Dutch scholar Rob de Wijk said that the invocation of Article 5 in response to these attacks "crossed a threshold and turned NATO into a global organization."[11] It meant that NATO's collective defense mission could encompass combating terrorist or other threats to Allied security. In practice, this also meant that there were no geographic limits to NATO's crisis management and cooperative security tasks. The North Atlantic Council drew the logical inference in May 2002: "To carry out the full range of its missions, NATO must be able to field forces that can move quickly to wherever they are needed, sustain operations over distance and time, and achieve their objectives."[12]

NATO's Engagement in the Balkans

The conflicts regarding Bosnia and Kosovo were the two main areas of NATO's crisis management activity until Afghanistan attracted official NATO attention in 2001–2002. Moreover, NATO played a significant role in conflict management and resolution in the former Yugoslav Republic of Macedonia in 2001–2003.

In other words, the western Balkans were the main operational focus of NATO's attention during the first decade after the end of the Cold War. Since December 2004, when the lead responsibility for peacekeeping in Bosnia was handed over to the European Union, KFOR has been the principal ongoing NATO-led operation in the Balkans.

NATO did not intend to become involved in the wars of the Yugoslav succession. These wars began in 1991, when the breakup of the Socialist Federal Republic of Yugoslavia (SFRY) became violent. Various component republics of the SFRY declared their independence from Belgrade and sought recognition from the United

States, the member states of what was then the European Community (EC), and other powers.

The Yugoslav breakup raised questions for outside governments. What should be the criteria for recognizing Yugoslav successor states? Should any action be taken to stop the violence? If so, what action should be taken, and who should take it? Which belligerents should be favored over others via intervention or nonintervention? Arms embargos, for example, would by definition favor the parties that were already well armed, while no-fly zones would disproportionately hamper the parties with aircraft. Nonintervention by certain outside powers would simplify matters for those willing to intervene, and for those on the ground with superior assets. As the French diplomat Talleyrand said, "non-intervention is a term of political metaphysics signifying almost the same thing as intervention."[13] The NATO Allies sometimes disagreed fundamentally about which course to pursue, notably with regard to Bosnia in 1992–1995.

The conflict in what rapidly became the former Yugoslavia was not initially seen as NATO's responsibility in any way. Officials of the EC asserted at the outset that it was a challenge for the EC to settle, and the U.S. administration agreed. Luxembourg foreign minister Jacques Poos, speaking as chairman of the EC Council of Ministers (composed of the foreign ministers of all the EC countries), said that it was "the hour of Europe," and "if one problem can be solved by the Europeans, it's the Yugoslav problem. This is a European country and it's not up to the Americans and not up to anybody else."[14]

That NATO had no intention of intervening militarily in the wars of the Yugoslav succession was apparent in the 1991 Strategic Concept. As noted in chapter 1, the Allies declared in the 1991 Strategic Concept that "the Alliance is purely defensive in purpose: none of its weapons will ever be used except in self-defense."[15] In the same document, the Allies stated, "In the new political and strategic environment in Europe, the success of the Alliance's policy of preserving peace and preventing war depends even more than in the past on the effectiveness of preventive diplomacy and successful management of crises affecting the security of its members."[16] Their objective was therefore crisis prevention, or at least "the successful resolution of crises at an early stage."[17] This aspiration was not, however, uniformly fulfilled in practice. The Alliance's avowed preference—avoiding the use of force while pursuing preventive diplomacy and resolving crises at an early stage—proved impractical in the Balkans.

Bosnia

UN Security Council resolutions led the Allies into the Yugoslav succession conflicts, which became intense after Bosnia won international recognition in April 1992. By the end of 1992, the Alliance, in cooperation with the Western European Union (WEU), was enforcing the UN economic sanctions against Serbia and Montenegro and the arms embargo against the former Yugoslavia as a whole. The

United Nations Protection Force (UNPROFOR), composed to a large extent of European troops (particularly from Britain and France), was employing "elements" from NATO's Northern Army Group command for its operational headquarters, and NATO airborne early-warning aircraft were monitoring the no-fly zone over Bosnia.[18] NATO air operations subsequently included the enforcement of the no-fly zone, close air support to UNPROFOR in Bosnia, and air strikes to break the siege of Sarajevo and other areas.

NATO was engaged in embargo and no-fly-zone enforcement relating to the former Yugoslavia and Bosnia in particular from July 1992 on, but it was not until February 28, 1994, that NATO aircraft—in fact, U.S. aircraft operating under NATO auspices—shot down four Bosnian Serb aircraft. This was significant in NATO's history as the Alliance's first use of deadly force. With that act, in the words of one analyst, "NATO redeemed its credibility"—at least temporarily.[19] This phase of the Bosnia conflict was nonetheless one of acrimony in European-American relations.

The Americans and their European Allies differed fundamentally about whether and how to take action. The United States declined to place any of its forces on the ground in Bosnia. The Americans who favored taking any action supported a "lift and strike" policy—that is, to lift the arms embargo, which objectively favored the belligerents already well armed (notably the Bosnian Serbs), and to conduct air strikes against the Bosnian Serbs. The Europeans who favored action—above all, the British and the French—were in Bosnia on the ground under the auspices of UN-PROFOR. Nicole Gnesotto, a prominent French analyst, summed up the situation in early 1994 from a perspective widely shared in NATO Europe:

> The Yugoslav war . . . remains . . . the symbol of a slow, progressive dissociation of the security interests of the Europeans and the United States, in the absence of any major, collective threat to their survival. . . . Indeed, until summer 1992, the Bush presidency refused to consider Yugoslavia as one of the United States's security interests. . . . The Yugoslav war is . . . the first example since 1945 of a conflict in continental Europe in which the risk that European soldiers may suffer fatalities is not matched by a similar risk for American troops. . . . Can the United States maintain and exercise a certain degree of leadership in Europe even though it does not take the risk of physical involvement in the management of real crises alongside the Europeans?[20]

As a Dutch expert noted in retrospect, the "transatlantic relationship reached an all-time low" in November 1994, with European-American disagreements about intelligence sharing and the enforcement of the arms embargo on the Bosnian government.[21] General Sir Michael Rose, the commander of UNPROFOR in 1994–1995, wrote as follows with regard to a Clinton administration policy that would have required UNPROFOR troops "to punish the Serbs" while continuing to conduct their peacekeeping mission: "The peacekeepers referred to this new policy as 'stay and pray,' observing that it was, after all, *their* lives, not American lives, that were put at risk by this policy."[22]

The Srebrenica massacre in July 1995 was one of several factors, including the taking of UNPROFOR troops as hostages by the Bosnian Serbs, that ultimately led the NATO Allies to take action.[23] In August–September 1995, in Operation Deliberate Force, NATO attacked Bosnian Serb forces under a UN Security Council mandate.[24] The Alliance's objectives were to impose an end to combat and to create the conditions for a lasting peace in Bosnia.

In the fall of 1995 Richard Holbrooke led the negotiation of the Dayton settlement for Bosnia.[25] In December 1995 the Dayton Implementation Force (IFOR) in Bosnia began its work, and it was replaced in December 1996 by a Stabilization Force (SFOR). The NATO-led SFOR came to an end in December 2004, when it was replaced by the European Union–led EUFOR in Operation Althea. Many of the European troops serving in Bosnia just changed the patches on their sleeves from SFOR to EUFOR.

NATO continues to provide support to the EU operation in Bosnia under the auspices of the NATO-EU "Berlin Plus" agreement. NATO maintains a presence in Sarajevo, and not only for Partnership for Peace, defense reform, and membership-candidacy purposes. NATO is the on-call over-the-horizon rescue force in case the European Union's EUFOR needs help urgently.

The succession of peacekeeping forces in Bosnia—IFOR, SFOR, and EUFOR—has to date prevented a return to combat among the formerly warring parties. However, a key question remains unanswered: would it be possible to maintain peace and public order in Bosnia without the presence of an external power imposing political stability?

The declared goals for Bosnia include the return of refugees and building a democratic, multiethnic society. Progress in meeting these goals has been slow, and some observers expect the European Union and NATO to have some sort of guarantor role for at least a generation. During this generation-long period, if Bosnia can be held together and can meet the membership criteria, it may join both organizations. The Allies have repeatedly used the phrases "Euro-Atlantic aspirations," "Euro-Atlantic institutions," and "Euro-Atlantic structures" to refer, above all, to NATO and the European Union.

In 2008 the Peace Implementation Council (PIC) for Bosnia agreed on a "transition strategy" for the country that could lead to the closure of the Office of the High Representative (established in conjunction with the Dayton Peace Agreement) and the withdrawal of external peacekeeping forces.[26] This transition strategy is based on objectives such as "Fiscal Sustainability of the State" and "Entrenchment of the Rule of Law" and on conditions, including the conclusion of a Stabilisation and Association Agreement with the European Union.[27]

Dissatisfaction with the status quo appears to be higher in Republika Srpska than in the Federation of Bosnia and Herzegovina, the other semiautonomous entity within Bosnia and Herzegovina. In late 2010 Milorad Dodik, then the prime minister of Republika Srpska (and now the president), asserted that "Only in Republika Srpska are we free people. Only here are we on our own land. Republika Srpska forever. The country of Bosnia as long as we have to."[28] In May 2011 the European

Union persuaded Dodik not to hold a referendum in Republika Srpska that could have challenged the legitimacy of the state-level courts.[29]

In April 2009, the NATO Allies applauded Bosnia's cooperation with NATO, but said that they remained "deeply concerned that irresponsible political rhetoric and actions continue to hinder substantive progress in reform. We urge Bosnia and Herzegovina's political leaders to take further genuine steps to strengthen state-level institutions and reinvigorate the reform process to advance the country's Euro-Atlantic aspirations."[30]

In a speech the following month in Sarajevo, U.S. vice president Joseph Biden transmitted the message more bluntly:

> Let me be clear: Your only real path to a secure and prosperous future is to join Europe as Bosnia and Herzegovina. Right now, you're off that path. To get back on track, you need to work together across ethnic and party lines so that your country functions like a country—and so that you interact with the rest of the world as a single, sovereign state. . . . Among the most urgent challenges is completing the objectives and conditions established by the Peace Implementation Council for the closure of the Office of the High Representative. . . . The international community must be satisfied that all levels of government are prepared to fully comply with the Dayton Peace Agreement—and that their leaders are prepared to abandon rhetoric and actions that would threaten or violate the Peace Agreement—before the international community presence and role here can change. In my view, the children of this country deserve a democratic Bosnia in which all live in peace and cooperation inside Euro-Atlantic institutions.[31]

In October 2010, Philip Gordon of the U.S. State Department said that U.S. policy, like that of the European Union, expresses "strong support for Bosnia and its sovereignty and territorial integrity and encouragement of leaders to move forward to help build a functioning state."[32] As this statement implies, Bosnia does not yet have "a functioning state" in the full sense of the term.

In November 2010, at the Lisbon Summit, the NATO Allies nonetheless encouraged Bosnia to pursue membership in the Alliance, on the basis of certain conditions:

> We reaffirm the decision taken by NATO Foreign Ministers in Tallinn in April 2010 to invite Bosnia and Herzegovina to join the Membership Action Plan [MAP], authorizing the Council to accept Bosnia and Herzegovina's first Annual National Programme under the MAP only when all immovable defence properties identified as necessary for future defence purposes have been officially registered as the state property of Bosnia and Herzegovina, for use by the country's Ministry of Defence.[33]

In May 2012, at the Chicago Summit, the NATO Allies took note of a political agreement to this effect in Bosnia and Herzegovina in March 2012, and urged the country's political leaders "to implement the agreement without delay in order to start its first MAP cycle as soon as possible."[34] To date, they have not done so.

Kosovo

As with Bosnia, the involvement of NATO nations in the Kosovo conflict began soon after the breakup of the former Yugoslavia in 1991. In December 1992, U.S. president George H. W. Bush wrote to Serbian president Slobodan Milošević as follows: "In the event of conflict in Kosovo caused by Serbian action, the United States will be prepared to employ military force against the Serbians in Kosovo and in Serbia proper."[35] This warning was repeated by Bush's successor, President Bill Clinton, in March 1993.[36]

The United States and other NATO countries were concerned about the increasingly violent persecution of ethnic Albanians in Serbia, particularly in Kosovo. U.S. secretary of state Madeleine Albright said in March 1998, "We are not going to stand by and watch the Serbian authorities do in Kosovo what they can no longer get away with doing in Bosnia."[37]

The NATO Allies pursued negotiations at Rambouillet with the Belgrade authorities regarding measures to provide for autonomous self-administration by ethnic Albanian Kosovars within Serbia, but these negotiations failed. In October 1998 the Allies approved activation orders for air strikes against Serbia. From March 24 to June 10, 1999, NATO conducted air strikes against the Federal Republic of Yugoslavia, mainly in Serbia.[38] The Alliance called this air campaign Operation Allied Force.

Allied leaders clearly miscalculated what would be required to make Milošević yield control of Kosovo. In March 1999, soon after the bombing began, Javier Solana, then the NATO secretary general, said that "he was sure the bombing would be over before April 23, the planned start of a summit meeting in Washington to celebrate NATO's 50th anniversary."[39] General Wesley K. Clark, then SACEUR, said, "We thought the Serbs were preparing for a spring offensive that would target KLA [Kosovo Liberation Army] strongholds. . . . But we never expected the Serbs would push ahead with the wholesale deportation of the ethnic Albanian population."[40]

The NATO Allies mistakenly assumed that Milošević would accept the Rambouillet package after a few air strikes demonstrated the Alliance's resolve. As Clark's statement suggests, the Allies thought that the Serb military preparations were intended for an offensive against the KLA, and thus failed to anticipate a massive "ethnic cleansing" operation to expel hundreds of thousands of ethnic Albanians from Kosovo. Tony Blair, the British prime minister, said at the outset of Operation Allied Force that NATO intended "to avert a humanitarian disaster."[41] The Allies did not anticipate that such a disaster would occur during the NATO air strikes, owing mainly to Serb efforts to force out ethnic Albanians. Above all, the magnitude and duration of the air campaign—over 38,000 sorties, including 10,484 strike sorties, over 78 days—suggest that the Allies underestimated the political and military resilience of the Serbs.[42] The Serb military authorities astutely husbanded and concealed a large part of their arms and equipment, including their air defenses, and they employed tactics that enabled them to prolong their resistance.[43]

Various factors help to explain the apparent miscalculations. In October 1998 the threat to use force seemed to have been effective, when NATO activation orders apparently persuaded Milošević to accept OSCE monitors in Kosovo. Moreover, in Operation Deliberate Force in 1995 (a twenty-one-day air campaign) the Allies had successfully convinced Milošević to participate in the negotiations that produced the Dayton Peace Agreement. In Operation Allied Force, however, the Allies were trying to compel Milošević to accept the end of Serb control over Kosovo—a significantly greater loss in his eyes than accepting that Republika Srpska would become part of Bosnia and Herzegovina.

The Alliance's open-ended air campaign, its buildup of ground forces in the region, and its political and economic measures probably contributed to Milošević's decision to capitulate, along with the resistance of the ethnic Albanian Kosovars to Belgrade's rule. Another important factor may have been Milošević's sense of isolation. According to a U.S. Department of Defense report, "When Finnish President Martti Ahtisaari and Russian Special Envoy Viktor Chernomyrdin met with Milošević in Belgrade [on June 3, 1999] and spoke with one voice, Milošević realized that he had become politically isolated and could expect no help from Russia."[44]

Despite Moscow's strong disapproval of the Alliance's armed intervention in the Kosovo conflict, Russia supported UN Security Council Resolution 1244. This UNSCR provided for the withdrawal from Kosovo of Serb military, paramilitary, and police forces, and it furnished the basis for a NATO-led peacekeeping mission, KFOR, and for the United Nations Interim Administration Mission in Kosovo (UNMIK).

Kosovo had historically been considered part of Serbia, and this view was reflected in UNSCR 1244. This UNSCR referred repeatedly to the "sovereignty and territorial integrity of the Federal Republic of Yugoslavia" and authorized the UN secretary-general, "with the assistance of relevant international organizations, to establish an international civil presence in Kosovo in order to provide an interim administration for Kosovo under which the people of Kosovo can enjoy substantial autonomy within the Federal Republic of Yugoslavia."[45]

Although Kosovo's independence was not envisaged in UNSCR 1244, that was the objective of the overwhelming majority of ethnic Albanian Kosovars, who gained support from the United States, among other countries. When Kosovo declared its independence in February 2008, it won recognition from a majority of NATO and EU members. However, five EU countries did not promptly recognize Kosovo's independence—Cyprus, Greece, Romania, Slovakia, and Spain. It was reported in October 2013 that Cyprus, Greece, and Slovakia were "reconsidering their positions," but that Romania and Spain remained opposed to recognition.[46] (Of these five countries, only Cyprus is not a member of NATO.) Other countries opposing Kosovo's independence have included, in addition to Serbia, Brazil, China, Cuba, Egypt, India, Indonesia, Russia, and South Africa.

Marc Weller of Cambridge University has hypothesized that at least three factors contributed to decisions to recognize Kosovo's independence. First, there has been an "increasing emphasis . . . on the rights of peoples and populations, at the expense of the claim to sovereignty inherent in the abstraction of the state." Second, the "suffering of the population in Kosovo under the Milošević regime had been well documented," so "it would simply not be realistic to place Kosovo under Serb sovereignty once again." Third, there was "a strong fear that any settlement short of independence would lead to an uncontrollable situation in Kosovo."[47] The *Economist* has speculated that the opponents of Kosovo's independence have mixed motives, including "solidarity with the Orthodox Serbs," "nostalgia" for Cold War nonalignment policies, "geopolitical concerns," and commitment to upholding the principle of "territorial integrity," the last owing in part to "domestic secessionist issues."[48]

The problems of international legitimacy and legal authority associated with Kosovo's international status remain less than fully resolved. In November 2008, however, UN secretary-general Ban Ki-moon worked out an agreement endorsed by the UN Security Council whereby UNMIK's role and presence would be substantially reduced and the European Union's Rule of Law Mission in Kosovo (EULEX) would essentially take over UNMIK's governance functions "under the overall authority of and within the status neutral framework of the United Nations."[49] As David Harland has pointed out, this agreement satisfied multiple parties:

> The UN needed to draw down an interim administration that had served its purpose, was no longer realistically able to perform its mandated tasks, and which was now deeply unwanted by the majority population. The EU needed to find a way to deploy, and to bring Kosovo closer to its European future. Belgrade and Pristina also wanted the transition: Belgrade to bring it closer to the EU, Pristina to help it consolidate its declaration of independence.[50]

This arrangement has left the NATO-led KFOR mission in place. While KFOR began in 1999 with some 50,000 troops from NATO and non-NATO countries, by May 2011 this had been reduced to around 6,300 troops. The Allies agreed in June 2009 to reduce their forces in Kosovo to "a deterrent presence," "with the remaining forces in theatre progressively relying more on intelligence and flexibility." One of the functions of NATO's voluntary trust funds is to support the development of the locally staffed Kosovo Security Force.[51]

In October 2010 U.S. assistant secretary of state Philip Gordon indicated that the United States expected KFOR's role to continue for the "foreseeable future." He added, "One day, we would like to get to the point where KFOR is no longer necessary and an independent and sovereign and safe and secure Kosovo . . . has good relations with its neighbors. We're not there yet."[52]

Some analysts have offered a grim prognosis for Kosovo's future. R. Craig Nation of the U.S. Army War College has described it as "a dysfunctional mini-state absolutely dependent upon international largesse to keep its head above water, a source of permanent instability for all of the Western Balkans."[53] Jean-Christian Cady, a French expert, has noted that "Kosovo's independence solved few problems. . . . The former UN protectorate has become an EU protectorate."[54] Security for this EU protectorate will probably remain NATO's responsibility for the indefinite future.

Despite the fact that four NATO Allies do not recognize Kosovo, the Allies at the November 2010 Lisbon Summit confirmed that

> KFOR remains in Kosovo on the basis of United Nations Security Council Resolution 1244 to support a stable, peaceful and multi-ethnic environment, cooperating with all relevant actors, in particular the European Union Rule of Law Mission in Kosovo (EULEX), and the Kosovo Police, in accordance with NATO agreed decisions and procedures. We welcome the progress made by the Kosovo Security Force, under NATO's close supervision, and the Kosovo Police, and commend them for their readiness and growing capability to implement their security tasks and responsibilities.[55]

At the Chicago Summit in May 2012, the Allies exhorted Kosovo and Serbia to respect and cooperate with EULEX and KFOR and "to take full advantage of the opportunities offered to promote peace, security, and stability in the region, in particular by the European Union-facilitated dialogue."[56]

Former Yugoslav Republic of Macedonia

At the request of the government of the former Yugoslav Republic of Macedonia (FYROM),[57] NATO conducted three peace support operations in the country in 2001–2003. The purpose of each of these operations was to contribute to efforts to peacefully resolve antagonism between the government and ethnic Albanian insurgents.

In June 2001 President Boris Trajkovski wrote to Lord Robertson, then the NATO secretary general, to request the Alliance's assistance in collecting weapons from the ethnic Albanian National Liberation Army (NLA). NATO replied by setting conditions for assistance, including a cease-fire and agreement by the main political parties to a plan brokered by the European Union and the United States to disarm the NLA. The government and ethnic Albanian representatives concluded the Ohrid Framework Agreement on August 13, 2001.

Three NATO-led operations in FYROM followed. Operation Essential Harvest, from August 22 to September 26, 2001, concentrated on the collection and destruction of weapons surrendered voluntarily by the NLA and other ethnic Albanian groups. Operation Amber Fox, from September 27, 2001, to December 15, 2002, contributed to the protection of EU and OSCE monitors overseeing the national peace plan's implementation. Operation Allied Harmony, from December 16, 2002, to March 31, 2003, furnished further support to the international monitors and advice to the government on security arrangements.[58]

These NATO operations were followed by the first EU-led peacekeeping mission, Operation Concordia, in FYROM from March to December 2003. NATO made assets available to the European Union for Operation Concordia, and the operational commander was the Alliance's Deputy Supreme Allied Commander Europe (DSACEUR). NATO, the European Union, and the OSCE cooperated effectively in 2001–2003 in efforts to avert a civil war in FYROM.[59]

NATO first designated FYROM as one of three Balkan countries "under consideration for future membership" at the Prague Summit in November 2002.[60] In April 2008, at the Bucharest Summit, the Allies announced that they had invited two of these three countries, Albania and Croatia, "to begin accession talks to join our Alliance." The Allies added that "an invitation to the former Yugoslav Republic of Macedonia will be extended as soon as a mutually acceptable solution to the name issue has been reached."[61] Albania and Croatia joined the Alliance in April 2009, but action on FYROM's candidacy has remained blocked by the name issue.

Some observers have questioned FYROM's viability as a state, owing to the divisions between ethnic Albanian and Slavic Macedonians and the risk of secessionism in the western part of the country.[62] Membership and participation in major international institutions might, however, enhance the country's prospects for cohesion. In R. Craig Nation's view, "No Balkan state needs the kind of reassurance that the NATO context can provide more than Macedonia."[63]

FYROM joined the Alliance's Membership Action Plan (MAP) in 1999. Since 2003 NATO Headquarters Skopje (renamed NATO Liaison Office Skopje in 2012) and a NATO Advisory Team in the defense ministry have assisted the country in defense and security sector reform and in meeting NATO membership standards.[64] The Alliance has continued to reaffirm its preparedness to invite FYROM to join, once Greece and FYROM have resolved the name issue to their mutual satisfaction.

NATO's Vision for the Western Balkans

The Allies set out their vision for the future of South-East Europe at the Prague Summit in November 2002:

> We will continue to work with our partners in SFOR and KFOR, the United Nations, the European Union, the OSCE and other international organisations, to help build a peaceful, stable and democratic South-East Europe, where all countries assume ownership of the process of reform, and are integrated in Euro-Atlantic structures. We remain determined to see that goal become reality. We expect the countries of the region: to continue to build enduring multi-ethnic democracies, root out organised crime and corruption and firmly establish the rule of law; to cooperate regionally; and to comply fully with international obligations, including by bringing to justice in The Hague all ICTY [International Criminal Tribunal for the former Yugoslavia] indictees. The reform progress that these countries make will determine the pace of their integration into Euro-Atlantic structures.[65]

The Allies used a variation of the phrase "Euro-Atlantic structures," which has become shorthand for NATO and the European Union, in their November 2010 Lisbon Summit Declaration: "In the strategically important Western Balkans region, democratic values, regional cooperation and good neighbourly relations are important for lasting peace and stability. We will continue to actively support Euro-Atlantic aspirations in this region."[66]

The NATO Allies have made clear that this inclusive vision applies to Serbia, albeit with certain conditions—above all, cooperation with the ICTY in the apprehension of people indicted for war crimes and meaningful efforts to support "the consolidation of peace and stability in Kosovo."[67]

The European Union, not NATO, has become "the lead actor in the Western Balkans," to use the phrase of Witold Waszczykowski, a Polish member of parliament. Waszczykowski notes, however, that the EU's effectiveness in this role has been limited by "the combined impact of enlargement fatigue, the global financial and economic crisis and the debate over the Union's absorption capacity. . . . The promise of membership in itself does not guarantee institution-building and democratisation, particularly in relation to those countries confronted with unresolved border and status issues."[68]

In this context, NATO's continuing engagement in the western Balkans—in KFOR and via liaison missions and partnership activities—makes an important contribution to political stability. The Alliance serves as a key element in a framework designed to promote positive political change, with all the states in the western Balkans expected to eventually gain membership in Euro-Atlantic institutions.

NATO's Engagement in Afghanistan

Specific NATO Allies, although not the Alliance as a whole, were engaged from the outset in 2001 in the U.S.-led coalition conducting Operation Enduring Freedom in Afghanistan.[69] In view of the terrorist attacks against the United States in September 2001 that led to the engagement in Afghanistan, nations participating in the coalition have had to take the risk of terrorist retaliation into account. Antonio Martino, then the Italian defense minister, said in November 2001, "We cannot underestimate the risk that this mission brings. . . . The possible risks . . . include terrorist actions, both in the areas where the military is deployed as well as on respective national territories."[70]

The Alliance's engagement in Afghanistan has been a response to terrorist attacks and threats. It is intended to prevent the emergence of future terrorist challenges, although NATO and the other organizations active in Afghanistan clearly have additional purposes. After the U.S.-led Operation Enduring Freedom coalition deposed the Taliban government, the UN Security Council in December 2001 authorized the establishment of ISAF to provide a secure environment for postconflict reconstruction. ISAF's declared mission is to provide security and stability to enable the Afghan government and other organizations to do their work.

According to the ISAF website, "In support of the Government of the Islamic Republic of Afghanistan [GIROA], ISAF conducts operations in Afghanistan to reduce the capability and will of the insurgency, support the growth in capacity and capability of the Afghan National Security Forces (ANSF), and facilitate improvements in governance and socio-economic development in order to provide a secure environment for sustainable stability that is observable to the population." The website elaborates on this mission statement under the three headings of security, reconstruction and development, and governance:

Security
In accordance with all the relevant Security Council Resolutions, the main role of ISAF is to assist the Afghan government in the establishment of a secure and stable environment. To this end, ISAF forces conduct security and stability operations throughout the country together with the Afghan National Security Forces and are directly involved in the development of the Afghan National Security Forces through mentoring, training and equipping.

Reconstruction and development
Through its Provincial Reconstruction Teams, ISAF supports reconstruction and development (R&D) in Afghanistan, securing areas in which reconstruction work is conducted by other national and international actors. Where appropriate, and in close cooperation and coordination with GIROA and UNAMA representatives on the ground, ISAF also provides practical support for R&D efforts, as well as support for humanitarian assistance efforts conducted by Afghan government organizations, international organizations, and NGOs.

Governance

ISAF, through its Provincial Reconstruction Teams (PRTs), helps the Afghan Authorities strengthen the institutions required to fully establish good governance and rule of law and to promote human rights. The principal mission of the PRTs in this respect consists of building capacity, supporting the growth of governance structures and promoting an environment within which governance can improve.[71]

This ambitious mission statement helps to explain why the Allies have sought in Afghanistan to pursue a "comprehensive approach" involving coordination and cooperation with other international organizations and with nongovernmental organizations.

ISAF was led by a series of NATO Allies—the United Kingdom, Turkey, and Germany and the Netherlands—from December 2001 to August 2003. The Alliance began to play a direct role in ISAF in October 2002, when the North Atlantic Council approved a request from Germany and the Netherlands for NATO support in force generation, intelligence, communications, and other areas for the German/Dutch command of ISAF beginning in early 2003. ISAF was not yet a NATO-led mission, however. It was in April 2003 that the Allies decided that NATO would take over the ISAF command in August 2003.[72]

As noted previously, since 2001–2003 the United States has increasingly recognized the value of NATO contributions in Afghanistan. The Alliance framework has been helpful in keeping together the broader coalition, gaining contributions from partner and other nations, and giving governments a stake in the operations and a greater sense of responsibility for the outcome. Moreover, the Alliance framework has made it harder for adversaries and critics to portray the campaign as simply an American war, when it is in fact intended to defend international order against terrorists and other extremists. While many international organizations are active in Afghanistan, NATO has made contributions beyond security in areas such as governance and humanitarian relief.

Obstacles to Security in Afghanistan

ISAF has been mandated by a series of UN Security Council resolutions. The first in the series, approved unanimously in December 2001, authorized the establishment of "an International Security Assistance Force to assist the Afghan Interim Authority in the maintenance of security in Kabul and its surrounding areas, so that the Afghan Interim Authority as well as the personnel of the United Nations can operate in a secure environment."[73] Subsequent resolutions have reconfirmed the essential ISAF mission of providing security so that the government of Afghanistan and the United Nations and other international organizations can pursue their work.

The insurgency has been only one of two major internal threats to the ISAF mission of providing security and stability. According to the analysis by General Stanley McChrystal, then the commander of ISAF, in 2009,

The ISAF mission faces two principal threats and is also subject to the influence of external actors. The first threat is the existence of organized and determined insurgent groups working to expel international forces, separate the Afghan people from GIRoA [Government of the Islamic

> Republic of Afghanistan], and gain control of the population. The second threat, of a very differ-
> ent kind, is the crisis of popular confidence that springs from the weakness of GIRoA institutions,
> the unpunished abuse of power by corrupt officials and power-brokers, a widespread sense of
> political disenfranchisement, and a longstanding lack of economic opportunity.[74]

General David Petraeus also highlighted the problems presented by the Afghan government's corruption and abuses of power. In his words, "governance, to be successful, has to be seen as serving the people, as providing a better future for them, not being predatory or corrupt as has been the case in a number of instances in past years, without question."[75]

The shortcomings of the central government include its perceived weakness. As one expert put it, "In the epithets of many Afghans" President Hamid Karzai is "the mayor of Kabul," because of his limited visibility and influence in much of the country.[76] As for corruption, many U.S. and Allied officials have called upon President Karzai to take action, but without any notable success.[77] Perceptions of the central government as weak and corrupt reinforce the tendency of Afghans to fall back on their ethnic or tribal identity. As General McChrystal noted in his assessment, "All ethnicities, particularly the Pashtuns, have traditionally sought a degree of independence from the central government, particularly when it is not seen as acting in the best interests of the population. These and other factors result in elements of the population tolerating the insurgency and calling to push out foreigners."[78]

The Afghan government's continuing weakness and lack of credibility with the country's population constitute profound obstacles to the success of the NATO-led ISAF mission. The central purpose of this mission from the outset has been to provide security and thereby support the establishment of an Afghan government capable of preventing the use of the country's territory as a base for terrorist operations. In October 2011, in its semiannual report to Congress on Afghanistan, the U.S. Department of Defense stated that

> the capacity of the Afghan Government has been limited by a number of issues, including
> the political dispute in the Lower House of the Afghan Parliament, the continued absence
> of an International Monetary Fund program, widespread corruption, and the lack of political
> progress in enacting key reforms announced at the July 2010 Kabul Conference. Setbacks in
> governance and development continue to slow the reinforcement of security gains and threaten
> the legitimacy and long-term viability of the Afghan Government. . . . The Afghan Govern-
> ment must continue to make progress toward key governance and development initiatives in
> order for security gains to become sustainable.[79]

In other words, "for security gains to become sustainable" the Afghan government must win the support of the people. Although the Afghan government must become capable of providing for the country's internal and external security without depending on a large foreign military presence, the governance task involves justice, public health, economic development, and other functions in addition to security. Joseph Collins concluded his recent study of the conflict in Afghanistan as follows: "As we work on building national security and local defense forces, we need to redouble our efforts at building up Afghan human capital and the institutions of governance that one day will enable the state to stand on its own two feet as a decent and effective government. If this does not come to pass, the United States and its allies will ultimately fail in Afghanistan."[80] The success of the NATO-led ISAF mission thus depends ultimately on the establishment of a strong Afghan government that can perform its essential tasks and command the respect and allegiance of the public.

NATO's Interactions with Other Organizations in Afghanistan

While NATO's main mission in Afghanistan is sustaining security, the Allies support a "comprehensive approach" in which other international organizations, notably the United Nations and the European Union, and nongovernmental organizations undertake complementary missions in support of reconstruction.

Indeed, some NATO officials—and officials in Alliance countries—like to underscore the fact that responsibility for Afghanistan rests ultimately with the UN Security Council, not NATO. The titles of documents can be revealing in this regard. In November 2010 the "Declaration by the Heads of State and Government of the Nations contributing to the UN-mandated, NATO-led International Security Assistance Force (ISAF) in Afghanistan" included the phrase "UN-mandated" in its title, even though ISAF has been UN-mandated since the outset in 2001.[81]

Similarly, in the Chicago Summit Declaration in May 2012, the Allies noted, "At the International Conference on Afghanistan held in Bonn in December 2011, the international community made a commitment to support Afghanistan in its Transformation Decade beyond 2014."[82] The conference in question attracted the participation of eighty-five countries and fifteen international organizations, including the European Union and the United Nations.[83] In the same paragraph of the Chicago Summit Declaration, the Allies twice again invoked "the international community," suggesting that many countries and organizations in addition to NATO share responsibility for Afghanistan's future.

Many fundamental objectives in Afghanistan are in fact outside ISAF's and NATO's control, such as addressing the country's reconstruction, development, and governance problems. These problems are supposed to be dealt with by a coalition encompassing many non-NATO as well as NATO nations, the United Nations, the European Union, several other international organizations, and many nongovernmental organizations.

The "comprehensive approach" endorsed by the Alliance at the November 2006 Riga Summit calls for NATO to work in cooperation with other organizations and nations toward a common objective combining security and development, not for NATO to coordinate or direct civilian assistance efforts. As the Allies agreed at Riga,

> There can be no security in Afghanistan without development, and no development without security. The Afghan people have set out their security, governance, and development goals in the Afghanistan Compact, concluded with the international community at the beginning of the year. . . . Guided by the principle of local ownership, our nations will support the Afghan Government's National Development Strategy and its efforts to build civilian capacity and develop its institutions. We encourage other nations and international organisations, notably the UN and the World Bank, to do the same. NATO will play its full role, but cannot assume

the entire burden. We welcome efforts by donor nations, the European Union (EU), and other international organisations to increase their support.[84]

The reference to the "international community" supporting the "security, governance, and development goals in the Afghanistan Compact" invites consideration of the mechanism established to pursue these goals. The Afghanistan Compact, concluded in January 2006, led in April 2006 to the founding of an organization for its implementation: the Joint Coordination and Monitoring Board (JCMB).

The JCMB is composed of seven Afghan government representatives, all members of the Afghanistan National Development Strategy Oversight Committee, and twenty-one representatives of the "international community." The JCMB's quarterly meetings are cochaired by the senior economic adviser of the president of Afghanistan and the special representative of the UN secretary-general (SRSG) for Afghanistan, who also serves as the head of the UN Assistance Mission in Afghanistan (UNAMA). In addition to the SRSG, the representatives of the "international community" include "Afghanistan's six largest development assistance contributors (United States, United Kingdom, Japan, Germany, European Union, and India), three neighboring countries (Pakistan, Iran, and China), three regional countries (Saudi Arabia, Turkey, and Russia), the international military supporters (NATO, CFC-A, Canada, Netherlands, Italy, and France), and two international financial institutions (the World Bank and Asian Development Bank)."[85]

The JCMB's inclusiveness does not appear to have translated into a high level of effectiveness, at least in the view of some U.S. and Allied observers. In 2009 General McChrystal, then commander of ISAF, wrote that "poor unity of effort among ISAF, UNAMA, and the rest of the international community undermines their collective effectiveness, while failure to deliver on promises further alienates the people."[86] Later that year NATO secretary general Rasmussen said, "What we need is a much broader strategy which stabilizes the whole Afghan society.... We have to look closer into how we can improve the organization of and coordination of the efforts in the area of civilian reconstruction and development.... And obviously ISAF and NATO do not have the capacity internally to conduct this civilian process. We have to cooperate with the UN, with the European Union, with other actors on the international scene. And to that end we need an improved coordination."[87]

The deficiencies of the international coordination effort are frustrating for the United States and the other Allies because the fate of Afghanistan is widely viewed as NATO's responsibility. As General Jones noted, "NATO has a minor role with regard to the more difficult problems, such as narcotics and police and judicial reform, but the future of the country and the perception of NATO's success or failure depend on the outcome of these problems."[88]

Problems Internal to the Alliance in Afghanistan

The problems internal to the Alliance have included unrealistic expectations, failures to meet resource commitments, differing motives, divergent strategies, restrictions on the usability of forces, poor comprehension of Afghan society and culture, and an excessive reliance on firepower.

In retrospect it appears that the NATO Allies did not understand the magnitude of the challenges in Afghanistan when they agreed in April 2003 to take over responsibility for ISAF. Owing in part to the swift initial victory of the U.S.-led coalition in late 2001—deposing the Taliban government in weeks—Allies had unrealistic expectations. It seems that experts and officials in some Allied governments thought that the operations in Afghanistan would be relatively easy and that casualty rates might not be much greater than in NATO's peacekeeping operations in Bosnia and Kosovo.

Another factor contributing to unrealistic assumptions in NATO about the gravity of the tasks at hand in Afghanistan at the outset was the fact that the United States accorded the operations in the country secondary status in comparison with the campaign in Iraq.[89] In September 2009 Robert Gates, then the U.S. secretary of defense, said that U.S. and Allied efforts in Afghanistan had not to date achieved conclusive results because the George W. Bush administration had regarded the combat in Afghanistan as "a holding action" while it was "very deeply engaged in Iraq."[90]

The challenges in Afghanistan are immense, but NATO and other international organizations have not committed resources at levels equivalent to their engagement in the Balkans. In 2008 Paddy Ashdown, who served as the high representative for Bosnia and Herzegovina in 2002–2006, compared the levels of military assistance and aid by international organizations in Afghanistan to those provided for Bosnia and Kosovo. "We are putting into Afghanistan one 25th the troops and one 50th of the aid per head of population that we put into Kosovo and Bosnia."[91]

The mismatch persists between the magnitude of the declared objectives and the limited resources contributed by the coalition of states, international organizations, and nongovernmental organizations active in Afghanistan. Even the NATO Allies have fallen short of declared objectives in certain areas—for example, helicopters. In 2008, Jaap de Hoop Scheffer, then the NATO secretary general, said,

> I'm disappointed there to say it in frank terms. There are thousands of helicopters in the NATO fleet. And Allies should definitely not have this kind of trouble getting a few hundred to theatre to support our operations. . . . Why is this so difficult? There are technical reasons. There are financial reasons. A technical reason is that for instance in a theatre like Afghanistan, the climatic conditions are such that you cannot just transport any helicopter to Afghanistan and at that height and in those summer temperatures fly any helicopter. . . . But the bottom-line is that we need political will.[92]

A less anecdotal indication of the Alliance's shortcomings in providing resources for operations in Afghanistan is the fate of the Combined Joint Statement of Requirements (CJSOR). As General John Craddock, then SACEUR, noted in 2007, "The CJSOR is based upon the minimum military requirement to execute the task this Alliance has set for its military."[93] As discussed in chapter 1, in 2009, shortly after he stepped down from serving as SACEUR, General Craddock pointed out that "since mission inception, NATO nations have *never* completely filled the *agreed* requirements for forces needed in Afghanistan."[94] Allies ought to provide resources consistent with the CJSOR for the operations in Afghanistan instead of simply sending what they prefer on a national basis to dispatch. The Allies have reportedly failed consistently to meet the CJSOR in troop numbers, helicopters, and logistics, and in medical, intelligence, and engineering support.[95]

The NATO Training Mission–Afghanistan (NTM-A) offers an important example of the failure of Allies to meet their agreed-upon objectives in staffing. Training Afghan National Security Forces to act on their own remains an essential goal of the ISAF mission, but it was not until April 2009, at the Strasbourg/Kehl Summit, that the Allies decided to establish the NTM-A. The mission was formally activated in November of that year. In March 2010, the NTM-A commander, Lieutenant General William Caldwell, reported that the mission was 1,901 police and military trainers short of the authorized level of 5,200. He had sought 1,200 trainers at a recent force generation conference. "We had pledges and commitments last week of 541. That's going to leave you a delta there of about 660 that we're still looking for. And of course, those pledges and commitments we're still going to look to arrive in Afghanistan."[96]

Allies seem to have had differing motives for engagement in Afghanistan. It appears that some Allies—for instance, Poland and the Baltic states—have committed forces to the operations in Afghanistan with the intention of building solidarity and reciprocity in NATO that will pay off in terms of national security in Europe—that is, strengthening their defensive position in relation to Russia. Since the August 2008 Georgia-Russia conflict, these Allies have faced domestic political pressures to shift their military investments away from Afghanistan to defense of the national territory. A response to such pressures has been to argue that, as Radoslaw Sikorski, the Polish foreign minister, put it in 2009, "our interest in Afghanistan is really our interest in NATO succeeding. We invoked Article 5 in defense of our ally, the United States, and so we want NATO to succeed so as to maintain conviction for future challenges. When NATO goes to war, NATO wins."[97]

Some Allies appear to have sent forces to Afghanistan out of a sense of historical obligation to Washington and a desire to show solidarity with their collective defense guarantor, the United States, not because they deem the intervention prudent and deserving of their full commitment. For Belgium, France, and Germany, a related motive has been to demonstrate that their ties with the United States remain strong, despite the discord in 2003 over the U.S.-led intervention in Iraq. As Jamie Shea, a British expert and NATO International Staff official, has observed, "Too frequently the Europeans imply that they are in Afghanistan first and foremost to prove their loyalty to NATO and America."[98]

General Harald Kujat, who served as the chief of staff of the German Armed Forces in 2000–2002 and as chairman of NATO's Military Committee in 2002–2005 before retiring, said in October 2011, "The mission fulfilled the political aim of showing solidarity with the United States. . . . But if you measure progress against the goal of stabilizing a country and a region, then the mission has failed."[99]

The apparent failure of the mission in relation to the Alliance's declared goals does not profoundly disturb many Allied observers because the main aim of their nations has been to demonstrate good will to the United States. In the words of Alexander Mattelaer, a scholar at the Institute for European Studies in Brussels, "Europeans, at least by their own calculations, have hardly anything at stake in Afghanistan, apart from providing the minimum required to satisfy American expectations."[100] According to Professor Hew Strachan of Oxford University, Britain's principal motive in participating in the Afghan operations has been to maintain its privileged relationship with the United States.[101]

Brigadier General Jo Coelmont, a former permanent Belgian representative to the EU Military Committee, described the motives of European Allies in Afghanistan as follows: "Based on their own logic and priorities, governments set an upper and lower limit for their respective contributions, which differ widely, but are all based on the same premise of doing 'the minimum necessary' to maintain 'good relations' with the US."[102]

Coelmont's generalization is no doubt unfair to some Allies, notably those which have made large contributions and/or suffered a high level of casualties. The generalization may nonetheless apply to certain other Allies. If their motive has been "doing 'the minimum necessary' to maintain 'good relations' with the US," this would help to explain the resource shortfalls, the mounting interest in achieving sufficient stability to justify a transition to Afghan responsibility, and the national restrictions on the usability of forces known as caveats.

With regard to caveats, General James Jones, a former SACEUR, observed,

> Caveats are restrictions that virtually all capitals put on their forces when they provide them to NATO. . . . It is partly an economic issue, because logistics are still a national responsibility and there exists a lack of common funding to pay for force redeployments. More broadly, it is also a national sovereignty issue, owing to the fear of casualties and domestic political consequences. Political fear is real, and therefore governments put "strings" on how their forces can be used. While all nations have imposed caveats at one time or another (yes, even the United States), some are much more damaging to our missions than others. . . . However, caveats are still cancers that weaken efforts to conduct a successful NATO mission. The most insidious caveat is the "undeclared caveat." Caveats go too far if they degrade the operational utility of NATO's forces. They then become an anchor holding NATO back.[103]

Caveats concerning the types of action troops may undertake—and where and under what conditions—create friction among the Allies, owing to perceptions of unfair burden sharing and unequal exposure to combat risks, to say nothing of their impact on operational effectiveness. Discord over caveats has arisen in NATO's Balkan operations since the early 1990s, but the irritations among the Allies have been sharper in Afghanistan, owing to the higher risks and losses.[104] According to some sources, British, Canadian, Dutch, and U.S. forces in Afghanistan have been less subject to caveats than the forces of other nations,[105] and they have been among the forces that have suffered disproportionately higher levels of casualties. In 2009 James Sperling and Mark Webber conducted a statistical analysis and concluded,

> The caveats with operational significance include those which ban night-time operations, restrict the geographical mobility of national forces, require consultations with national capitals when making tactical decisions, exclude specific categories of activity (notably, counterterrorism operations) and prohibit the helicopter transport of ANA [Afghan National Army] forces or fighting after a snowfall. These caveats generally reflect the difficult domestic political contexts that allied leaders must negotiate in order to make any meaningful contribution to the allied effort, an especially difficult balancing act in Berlin and Rome. Nonetheless, they minimize the risk of combat-related deaths and have shifted the burden of high-intensity warfare onto American, Australian, British and Canadian forces along with those from Denmark, the Netherlands and a few of the east European NATO states.[106]

Caveats on how their forces may be employed remain the price exacted by some Allies for participating. Some NATO Allies have stipulated that their forces be deployed and retained in less dangerous regions. In November 2008 Chris Patten, the former EU commissioner for external relations, wrote that "the non-fighting NATO members should be prepared to join Britain, the Netherlands, Poland and Denmark in the trouble spots of the south and east."[107]

However, in a situation in which over 60 percent of the German public has favored the return home of all Bundeswehr forces, the only way to sustain the presence of German forces has been to accept Berlin's terms for participation and keep them engaged in security and stabilization operations in northern Afghanistan. Since 2010, moreover, these operations have increasingly involved combat—the most intensive fighting for German forces since 1945.[108]

One of the reasons why NATO's efforts, in cooperation with ISAF partners, to provide stability and security have been less than entirely successful is that the various NATO allies in Afghanistan have pursued divergent strategies. It was not until the April 2008 Bucharest Summit that the Allies agreed on what they termed a Comprehensive Political-Military Strategic Plan for Afghanistan.[109]

Moreover, the Allies still disagree on questions as fundamental as whether and how to conduct counternarcotics operations. General James Jones underscored the significance of narcotics in 2007:

> The greatest problem in Afghanistan is the pervasive influence of narcotics, which is fueling crime, corruption, and an insurgency—all of which act in opposition to the government. Narcotics are the foundation of an illegal economy. It is consistently estimated that at least 50 percent of the economy is linked to the drug trade. Afghanistan is clearly becoming a "narco-state," If it is not one already.... Why doesn't NATO take an active role against narcotics? The answer is politics. The mandate for the operation was agreed following the rule of consensus. The lowest common denominator in the Alliance was to agree on a mission for providing stability, security, and reconstruction.[110]

It was not until October 2008 that the Allies agreed that the Allies that wish to take action against narcotics production and trafficking may do so, in concert with the Afghan government. Martin de Retorto, a Spanish journalist with *El Pais*, asked, "If everybody can do whatever . . . why do we need this agreement in which everybody has agreed to do whatever it pleases?" Jaap de Hoop Scheffer, then the NATO secretary general, replied: "What is important about the fact that the Allies agreed is that they agreed. That all twenty-six have agreed that this will be done. I, again, underline the last line I read to you: 'Subject to the authorization of specific nations.'"[111] The NATO Allies wishing to take part in counternarcotics operations have subsequently been able to do so with the forbearance of their fellow Allies.[112]

Allied experts have described their national missions in Afghanistan differently. According to Timo Noetzel, for example, Germany has regarded its engagement in Afghanistan "as a stability operation." In his judgment, "It is a view shared by some continental European NATO members such as Spain and Italy, but thoroughly rejected by NATO members such as the United States, Great Britain, the Netherlands, or Canada, where the debate is whether ISAF should concentrate on counterinsurgency or counterterrorism. . . . German doctrinal thinking differs fundamentally from the comprehensive counterinsurgency doctrines of allies such as the US or Britain."[113] Other observers, it should be noted, have identified contrasts in U.S. and British approaches to operations in Afghanistan.[114]

Aside from the divergent strategies pursued by the NATO Allies, their national investments have varied in trying to understand the history, culture, politics, and society of Afghanistan. Some Alliance experts maintain that the NATO Allies have on the whole shown a limited comprehension of Afghan society and have tended to rely excessively on the use of force, with consequences adverse to the ISAF mission. In August 2009, General McChrystal, then the commander of ISAF, summed up these shortcomings as follows:

> Afghan social, political, economic, and cultural affairs are complex and poorly understood. ISAF does not sufficiently appreciate the dynamics in local communities, nor how the insurgency, corruption, incompetent officials, power-brokers, and criminality all combine to affect the Afghan population. A focus by ISAF intelligence on kinetic targeting and a failure to bring together what is known about the political and social realm have hindered ISAF's comprehension of the critical aspects of Afghan society. ISAF's attitudes and actions have reinforced the Afghan people's frustrations with the shortcomings of their government. Civilian casualties and collateral damage to homes and property resulting from an over-reliance on firepower and force protection have severely damaged ISAF's legitimacy in the eyes of the Afghan people.[115]

Another problem internal to the Alliance has been the impression on the part of some Allied observers that the United States has at critical junctures formulated its strategy without consulting their governments. According to Bob Woodward's account, in late 2009 some of President Obama's advisers disagreed as to whether "U.S. allies should be consulted" regarding the president's decision making on Afghanistan. The dispute was resolved when "Clinton and Holbrooke stepped in, saying the U.S. should have a rollout plan to explain the president's eventual decision to everyone— first NATO and the allies, of course, and Congress and the public."[116] In November 2010, a high-level Italian observer said,

> We were used to unilateralism from the Bush administration, but we had a hope that it would be different with the Obama administration. That hope turned out to be without foundation. When General Stanley McChrystal prepared his plan, it was not shared with Europe, but sent to Washington. Was any European state asked to give advice? No. We are considered not as partners, but only as force-providers.[117]

This Italian observer's impression differs from that held by those who highlight General McChrystal's extensive interactions with the NATO Allies. General McChrystal referred to NATO's Comprehensive Strategic Political-Military Plan for Afghanistan in his important August 2009 COMISAF Initial Assessment, and he prepared this assessment in consultation with Allied officials and experts. According to Alexander Mattelaer's account of the decisions in the summer and fall of 2009,

> SHAPE had quietly added McChrystal's request for 40,000 extra troops to its own statement of requirements, causing quite a stir in Brussels. Interestingly, the Allies made up their minds about the COMISAF assessment without waiting for Obama's decision. In October 2009, more than a month before the president rendered his verdict in a speech at West Point, the defence ministers broadly endorsed the assessment and broke the logjam on the use of counterinsurgency language within NATO, which until that point had been a political taboo.[118]

The non-U.S. NATO Allies and other ISAF partners in Afghanistan, such as Australia, supported the U.S. plan for a surge to prepare the way for an eventual transition to Afghan responsibility by providing increased force numbers paralleling those of the United States. In February 2010, Robert Gates, then the U.S. secretary of defense, noted that non-U.S. troops were "scheduled to increase from approximately 30,000 last summer to 50,000. By any measure, that is an extraordinary feat—and a clear indication that the international community has the will and the resolve to see this mission through to a successful end."[119]

In view of these efforts, some Allied observers have been chagrined to read accounts of high-ranking U.S. officials comparing their capabilities unfavorably with those of the United States. According to Bob Woodward,

> Petraeus said he strongly supported an energetic effort to get more from NATO, but he said that 10,000 troops from the allies would not be as useful as 10,000 American troops. "Be careful how you characterize our NATO allies," Obama said sharply. "We need them. They will be useful in this coalition."[120]

Many Americans hold that the European Allies have not contributed enough troops or resources to the operations in Afghanistan and that the usability of European troops has too often been hindered by caveats. From 2003 on, when ISAF became a NATO-led operation, the United States expected the other Allies to do more than they did to "take ownership" of the war, rather than deferring to U.S. judgment and leadership.[121] The disappointment of some influential Americans with the Allied performance has been ironic in that one of the main motives for European Allies has been to impress U.S. politicians and opinion leaders by demonstrating their loyalty and to thereby create a sense of obligation in the United States. The general American view is that the other NATO Allies should be contributing to the operations in Afghanistan for their own national and NATO security interests—not to show loyalty to the United States or to build up the U.S. sense of political obligation.

NATO's Evolving Goals in Afghanistan

NATO's declared "end-state" goal in Afghanistan since 2003, when it took over the ISAF leadership role, has been to establish a democratic government that would prevent any terrorist group from operating on its soil: "A self-sustaining, moderate and democratic Afghan government, in line with the relevant United Nations Security Council resolutions, able to exercise its authority and to operate throughout Afghanistan, without the need for ISAF to help provide security."[122] In 2008 the NATO Allies declared that "Euro-Atlantic and wider international security is closely tied to Afghanistan's future as a peaceful, democratic state, respectful of human rights and free from the threat of terrorism."[123]

Some Allied observers hold that the declared aim of democratizing Afghanistan is excessively grandiose in the medium term and that it goes far beyond the more achievable—yet still ambitious—objective of establishing a stable country that is not run by extremists linked to terrorists. In January 2009 Robert Gates said, "This is going to be a long slog, and frankly, my view is that we need to be very careful about the nature of the goals we set for ourselves in Afghanistan. . . . If we set ourselves the objective of creating some sort of central Asian Valhalla over there, we will lose, because nobody in the world has that kind of time, patience and money."[124]

Some experts have speculated that the scarcity—or absence—of references to democratization as an objective in some recent documents may imply a scaling back of declared ambitions to goals that are more achievable. For example, General McChrystal, in his noteworthy "initial assessment" study in August 2009, made no reference to the democratization of Afghanistan as a goal for ISAF. "ISAF's mission statement is: 'ISAF, in support of GIRoA, conducts operations in Afghanistan to reduce the capability and will of the insurgency, support the growth in capacity and capability of the Afghan National Security Forces (ANSF), and facilitate improvements in governance and socio-economic development, in order to provide a secure environment for sustainable stability that is observable to the population.'"[125] Instead of referring to democracy, General McChrystal alluded to "responsive and accountable governance—that the Afghan people find acceptable."[126]

Similarly, without renouncing "the democratic process," in September 2009 Gordon Brown, then the British prime minister, pointed out that "a peaceful and stable Afghanistan would . . . be a severe propaganda blow and strategic failure for Al Qaeda."[127] In the May 2010 report to the Alliance by the Group of Experts chaired by Madeleine Albright, none of the discussions of NATO's purposes in Afghanistan made any explicit reference to democratization. In this report the goal was simply "the creation of an Afghanistan that is stable and that does not serve as a platform for international terrorist activity."[128]

In November 2010 the NATO Allies reaffirmed their "long-term commitment to a sovereign, independent, democratic, secure and stable Afghanistan that will never again be a safe haven for terrorists and terrorism."[129] The phrase "long-term commitment" may be subject to interpretation, however. In a December 2010 discussion of the U.S. government's review of its strategy for Afghanistan and Pakistan, the *Washington Post* reported, "As he determines the pace and size of initial troop withdrawals this summer [that is, in 2011], Obama will have to decide how good Afghan governance needs to be to allow for a U.S. pullout—an acceptable end state that some administration officials refer to as 'Afghan good enough.'"[130]

The expression "Afghan good enough" has in fact become current among U.S. and Allied officials and experts dealing with Afghan issues. It suggests a recalibration of political objectives in the face of recalcitrant realities on the ground in Afghanistan. Some U.S. and Allied officials find the phrase "Afghan good enough" pejorative and patronizing, however, and favor "Afghan right" or "Afghan sustainable."

Success in Afghanistan might be redefined as establishing a stable and effective national government that commands popular support and that can defend the country from terrorism, subversion, and foreign aggression. The obstacles—internal and external—to achieving this appear so great that some observers in recent years have been speculating about the consequences of failure. These consequences include the prospect that Afghanistan would again serve as a haven and training ground for terrorist movements, with implications for the security and stability of Pakistan—a nuclear-armed state that is already beset with terrorist movements.

General James Jones said in 2007, "Failure in Afghanistan—the victory of the Taliban and Al Qaeda—would mean a major boost for radical jihadists and the recruitment of more terrorists in different parts of the world, and much closer to European capitals."[131] Secretary General Rasmussen said in 2009, "Leaving Afghanistan behind would once again turn the country into a training ground for Al Qaeda. The pressure on nuclear-armed Pakistan would be tremendous. Instability would spread throughout Central Asia. And it would only be a matter of time until we, here in Europe, would feel the consequences of all of this."[132]

U.S. authorities have agreed that failure in Afghanistan could have an impact on NATO's cohesion, credibility, and ability to deal with other potential threats. It could, moreover, undermine the mutual confidence of the Allies. Admiral Michael Mullen, then the chairman of the Joint Chiefs of Staff, reportedly said in 2009, "NATO's commitment and future are in the balance."[133] President Obama said in December 2009 that "what's at stake is not simply a test of NATO's credibility—what's at stake is the security of our allies, and the common security of the world."[134]

Madeleine Albright said in May 2010 that her Group of Experts recommended caution in assessing the long-term impact of Afghanistan on NATO's future. "There were people who said, 'Well, Afghanistan is the ultimate test for NATO and whatever happens in Afghanistan will affect NATO forever.' We didn't want to go down that road. We wanted to look at it as a lesson."[135]

The Alliance's implicit long-term scale-down and exit strategy is sometimes termed "Afghanization." NATO intends to hand over responsibility to the Afghan National Army and other state security institutions as soon as training and mentoring efforts enable them to ensure a reasonable level of stability and security on their own.

President Obama in December 2009 announced an increase in U.S. and Allied forces that was intended to create the conditions for starting a withdrawal and transfer of responsibility to Afghan forces in July 2011. "Just as we have done in Iraq, we will execute this transition responsibly, taking into account conditions on the ground. We'll continue to advise and assist Afghanistan's security forces to ensure that they can succeed over the long haul. But it will be clear to the Afghan government—and, more importantly, to the Afghan people—that they will ultimately be responsible for their own country."[136]

This withdrawal began, as planned, in July 2011, and the transfer of responsibility for security to Afghan authorities is to be completed in 2014. In May 2012, in the Chicago Summit Declaration, the Allies stated, "The irreversible transition of full security responsibility from the International Security Assistance Force (ISAF) to the Afghan National Security Forces (ANSF) is on track for completion by the end of 2014, as agreed at our Lisbon Summit."[137] The word "irreversible" suggests that the Allies are resolved not to be drawn back into combat operations after 2014.[138] In the same declaration the Allies indicated that they intended to "continue to provide strong and long-term political and practical support through our Enduring Partnership with Afghanistan." The Allies also declared themselves willing to undertake "a new post-2014 mission . . . to train, advise and assist the ANSF," but they pointedly added, "This will not be a combat mission."[139]

At the Chicago Summit in May 2012, the Allies noted that in December 2011 the participants in an international conference in Bonn "made a commitment to support Afghanistan in its Transformation Decade beyond 2014."[140] In a separate statement at the Chicago Summit, the government of Afghanistan and the governments of all the NATO Allies and partners contributing to the NATO-led ISAF issued a declaration clarifying the obligations they have assumed regarding the ANSF during the "Transformation Decade" from 2014 to 2024. They envisaged "an estimated annual budget of US $4.1 billion" for the ANSF in the 2014–2024 period, with the bulk of these costs paid by governments contributing to ISAF in the initial years. However, the plan calls for a growing share of the costs and (no later than 2024) the totality to be covered by the Afghan government, which would then no longer require assistance from the NATO Allies or other foreign sources to support the ANSF.[141]

The fulfillment of this plan could be placed into question by a failure of the Afghan and U.S. governments to agree on the terms for a continued U.S. military presence after 2014. According to several reports since July 2013, the Obama administration has been considering a "zero option"—a complete withdrawal of U.S. military forces from Afghanistan — if there is no agreement on the status and roles of U.S. military forces after 2014. As with the case of Iraq in 2011, the absence of an agreement on the status of U.S. and other NATO forces could lead to their departure. The "ripple effects" could include substantial reductions in the aid for Afghanistan envisaged in the 2014–2024 "Transformation Decade." Since foreign aid constitutes a huge proportion of the Afghan government's resources, including for the ANSF, the prospects for the country's security could be grave.[142]

NATO and Afghanistan in the Regional Context

In November 2010 the NATO Allies made clear that they were looking beyond 2014, the agreed-on exit date, which was based on their "support for President Karzai's objective for the Afghan National Security Forces to lead and conduct security operations in all provinces by the end of 2014." To this end, the Allies added, they "strongly welcome the long-term partnership that has been announced today between NATO and Afghanistan, which demonstrates that the Alliance's commitment to Afghanistan will endure beyond ISAF's current mission and is intended to be consistent with broader international efforts under UN leadership."[143]

Moreover, the NATO Allies and Afghanistan agreed that the "measures of cooperation" for the Alliance's "sustained support" of the NATO-Afghan "enduring partnership" could include continued Afghan use of "NATO Trust Funds in support of capacity building" and "continuation of the NATO Training Mission Afghanistan (NTM-A), reconfigured as necessary, subject to a NAC decision, to meet evolving Afghan security needs."[144]

In March 2013 Secretary General Rasmussen confirmed that the "new NATO-led mission, to provide training, advice and assistance after 2014 . . . will be called Resolute Support—because our support for Afghanistan remains steadfast."[145] In June 2013 NATO defense ministers approved the "detailed concept" for the new mission. Rasmussen said that "the new mission will not be ISAF by another name. It will be different, and be significantly smaller. Its aim will be to train, advise and assist the Afghan forces, not substitute for them."[146]

The relevance of such measures will hinge decisively on Afghanistan's regional context. Even if NATO and its many international partners succeeded in fostering "a sovereign, independent, democratic, secure and stable Afghanistan that will never again be a safe haven for terrorists and terrorism,"[147] a larger concentration of terrorist threats would remain on the other side of the border in Pakistan.

NATO's security interests in the region are not confined to Afghanistan, owing in part to the fact that al-Qaeda has made Pakistan an important base for its operations. In September 2009, Gordon Brown said, "The sustained pressure on Al Qaeda in Pakistan combined with military action in Afghanistan is having a suppressive effect on Al Qaeda's ability to operate effectively in the region—but despite these difficulties, the main element of the threat to the UK continues to emanate from Al Qaeda and Pakistan."[148] In November 2009, Bob Ainsworth, then the British defense minister, said, "If Afghanistan is not secure, then Pakistan is not secure, and if Pakistan is not secure then Britain is not secure."[149]

The insurgency in Afghanistan derives substantially from the territory of Pakistan. As General McChrystal put it in 2009, "Senior leaders of the major Afghan insurgent groups are based in Pakistan, are linked with al Qaeda and other violent extremist groups, and are reportedly aided by some elements of Pakistan's ISI [Inter-Services Intelligence]. Al Qaeda and associated movements (AQAM) based in Pakistan channel foreign fighters, suicide bombers, and technical assistance into Afghanistan, and offer ideological motivation, training, and financial support."[150]

An important related factor in the U.S. engagement in Afghanistan has become concern that an extremist faction associated with terrorist movements could gain control over Pakistan's nuclear arsenal. Vice President Biden has reportedly said that "Afghanistan is a means to accomplish our top mission, which is to kill al-Qaeda and secure Pakistan's nukes."[151] Paul Miller, a member of the National Security Council staff under President George W. Bush and President Barack Obama, recently wrote that U.S. interests in Afghanistan "include Pakistan's stability and the security of its nuclear weapons, neither of which stand to benefit from a Taliban takeover or a civil war next door."[152]

NATO's official policy has long called for "increased cooperation and engagement with Afghanistan's neighbours, especially Pakistan," as the Allies put it in 2008.[153] One of the difficulties in pursuing this objective is that Pakistan and the other neighbors of Afghanistan have their own competitive objectives. Some experts argue that Pakistan intends to use the Taliban to keep Afghanistan weak and to convert it into a Pakistani sphere of influence—and thereby prevent it from becoming subject to Indian influence. The Pakistani authorities, however, are probably unable to control the Taliban and other extremists either in Afghanistan or Pakistan. Moreover, Pakistan would gain more in economic and security terms from a stable Afghanistan with positive relations with Islamabad than from an Afghanistan torn by civil war and continuing turmoil.

Pakistan may increasingly regard Iran as another rival for influence in Afghanistan. According to General McChrystal's assessment, "The Iranian Qods Force is reportedly training fighters for certain Taliban groups and providing other forms of military assistance to insurgents. . . . Pakistan may see Iranian economic and political initiatives as threats to their strategic interests, and may continue to address these issues in ways that are counterproductive to the ISAF effort."[154]

The countries contributing to ISAF stated in November 2010, "We recognise that many of Afghanistan's challenges cannot be addressed without the constructive support of Afghanistan's regional partners. Enhanced regional co-operation is essential for lasting stability and is most effective when it is regionally-owned, and pursued in a transparent and constructive manner."[155]

According to a November 2010 declaration by NATO and Afghanistan, "The Government of the Islamic Republic of Afghanistan reaffirms its commitment to . . . recognise the importance and relevance of broader regionally-owned co-operation, coordination and confidence building between Afghanistan and its regional partners, as exemplified in the Istanbul Statement."[156] The Istanbul Statement on Friendship and Cooperation in the "Heart of Asia" was issued in January 2010 by Afghanistan, China, Iran, Pakistan, Tajikistan, and Turkey. Representatives of several other countries and organizations (including NATO) joined as observers with those making the statement.[157]

In testimony in June 2011, U.S. secretary of state Hillary Clinton said, "We are engaging the region around a common vision of an independent, stable Afghanistan and a region free of al-Qaida. We believe we've made progress with all of the neighbors, including India, Russia, and even Iran."[158] Secretary Clinton also said, "The Congress of Vienna is an interesting historical example because there was a pact made among regional powers that in effect left the Benelux countries as a free zone. . . . If we could get to that point with the regional powers in South Asia, that [they] would not recommence with the great game in Afghanistan, that would be a very worthy outcome."[159]

In contrast, Jean d'Amécourt, a French diplomat, has suggested that the Helsinki process, the work of the Conference on Security and Co-operation in Europe in the early 1970s, offers a useful analogy for the future of Afghanistan and its neighbors.

> Any lasting stabilization of Afghanistan requires a solution to the crisis in Pakistan. . . . Only a broadening of the dialogue, bringing together neighboring countries, regional actors and the major powers to deal with all the issues—including regional security, cross-border cooperation, trade, technological cooperation, economic development, and energy issues, including civil nuclear power—can lead to a successful conclusion. Pakistan's military officials should be involved in these negotiations. . . . Talks should also include countries that play an active role in Afghan politics (Iran, India, and Pakistan) and in Pakistan (China, Saudi Arabia, the United Arab Emirates, and Turkey). France and Europe must take the lead, but without harboring any illusions concerning the difficulties involved and the time required in undertaking such a project. After all, the effort is not dissimilar to the Helsinki process of the early 1970s, which eventually led to the thawing of East-West relations.[160]

In an analysis based in part on the enduring success of the Swiss model of neutralization, Audrey Kurth Cronin of George Mason University has proposed that "the seven key militarily-capable states that would be threatened by a destabilized Afghanistan (Pakistan, China, Iran, India, Saudi Arabia, Russia, and the United States) might enter into a common agreement to neutralize the state."[161] The national authorities would, according to this design, commit Afghanistan to perpetual neutrality and the external powers would pledge themselves to nonintervention and thereby guarantee the country's independence.

Whether any of these precedents—the Congress of Vienna, the Helsinki process, or Switzerland's neutrality—is an apt and well-founded model for the future relations among the countries in the region surrounding Afghanistan is open to debate. India, Iran, and Pakistan have continued to back proxies in Afghanistan's internal conflicts. These countries and other neighbors of Afghanistan have historically found motives for conflict, with Afghanistan one of several arenas for competition. While an enduring peace among Afghanistan and its neighbors in the region would obviously be desirable—and would, if obtainable, contribute to civil peace within the country—the successful containment and management of internal and foreign conflicts might be the most that can be achieved for many years to come. Temporary and imperfect settlements might in time furnish a basis for more durable achievements in nation and state building. If such settlements could be reached, they would offer a more positive outcome for Afghanistan and its NATO and ISAF partners than the partition of Afghanistan that Robert Blackwill and some other observers have prescribed.[162]

It was perhaps with a view to reassuring other countries in the region that Afghanistan and NATO stated that their cooperative arrangements following the ISAF mission could include "a continuing NATO liaison in Afghanistan to help the implementation of this declaration with a common understanding that NATO has no ambition to establish a permanent military presence in Afghanistan or to use its presence in Afghanistan against other nations."[163]

The countries contributing to ISAF stated in November 2010 that their objective is "long term security, stability and prosperity in an Afghanistan respectful of human rights, that will never again become a safe haven for terrorists and terrorism."[164] Some Allied experts are concerned that unless significant progress is made in containing the Taliban and other insurgent movements, as well as al-Qaeda and associated terrorist groups, Afghanistan after ISAF may—despite the projected "enduring partnership" with NATO—revert to its previous condition. From this perspective, after the eventual withdrawal of NATO forces and the termination of ISAF, some of the antagonists within the country may be better armed and more sophisticated, and suspicious of foreign powers (including those of the Alliance), and yet susceptible to the influence of their immediate neighbors. Indeed, unless Afghanistan becomes capable of defending its sovereignty and frontiers, the states surrounding it may exploit it in their broader competition even more harshly than in the past.

The countries that endorsed the November 2011 Declaration of the Istanbul Process on Regional Security and Cooperation for a Secure and Stable Afghanistan professed, to be sure, to uphold a "strong commitment to a secure, stable and prosperous Afghanistan in a secure and stable region."[165] At the Chicago Summit in May 2012, the NATO Allies declared,

> The Istanbul Process on regional security and cooperation, which was launched in November 2011, reflects the commitment of Afghanistan and the countries in the region to jointly ensure security, stability and development in a regional context. The countries in the region, particularly Pakistan, have important roles in ensuring enduring peace, stability and security in Afghanistan and in facilitating the completion of the transition process.[166]

Given the antagonisms and rivalries between some of these countries (between, for example, India and Pakistan, China and India, and Iran and Saudi Arabia), to say nothing of the visible competition of India, Iran, and Pakistan for influence in Afghanistan, doubts have arisen about the fulfillment of the declared commitments. According to an Indian commentator, Pakistan and other regional states firmly rejected the objective of the United States and other NATO governments to establish a regional security regime on the model of the OSCE and therefore approved "the latest in a series of platitudes" at Istanbul: "In sum, the regional powers are unwilling to collaborate with the US and its allies to choreograph the post-2014 regional security scenario."[167]

In addition to the probability of competition and conflict among Afghanistan's neighbors, the country's prospects are blighted by evidence of the Afghan government's corruption and incapacity and the Taliban's strength. In December 2012, the U.S. Department of Defense reported, "The Taliban-led insurgency remains adaptive and determined, and retains the capability to emplace substantial numbers of IEDs [improvised explosive devices] and to conduct isolated high-profile attacks. The insurgency also retains a significant regenerative capacity."[168]

NATO's official view, as articulated by Secretary General Rasmussen, is that the transfer of security responsibility from ISAF to the Afghan National Security Forces by the end of 2014 is proceeding on schedule, and that ISAF will be followed by a noncombat NATO mission to perform training, advising, and assistance tasks. In Rasmussen's words, "We have a once-in-a-generation opportunity to break the cycle of violence and extremism in Afghanistan, to build long-term security for the Afghans, the wider region and ourselves."[169]

Whether the Afghan government, the NATO Allies, their ISAF partners, and all the other participants in JCMB dedicated to fulfilling the "security, governance, and development goals in the Afghanistan Compact"[170] can succeed in seizing this opportunity remains to be seen. Olivier Neola, a French expert who served as the political adviser for three successive EU special representatives to Afghanistan, warned in 2012, "If Western military efforts fail to reduce the insurgency to manageable levels and no political solution is found, the situation may well be similar to the one that prevailed after the Soviets departed, leaving a weak government dependent on foreign subsidies and only viable as long as its political opponents were disunited."[171]

Conclusion

The NATO Allies intervened in the Balkan conflicts and Afghanistan under the pressure of events. In the Balkan case, violence among NATO Europe's immediate neighbors and refugee flows ultimately compelled the Allies to take action. In the Afghan case, attacks against the United States by terrorists affiliated with al-Qaeda led to the intervention, because al-Qaeda leaders were based in Afghanistan and hosted by its Taliban rulers.

In each case, large-scale intervention did not begin under NATO's auspices but under those of the United Nations. Discord among the Allies about whether and how to intervene led to the establishment of the United Nations Protection Force in Bosnia, with secondary missions, such as maritime embargo and no-fly zone enforcement, under the Alliance's flag. UNPROFOR's inability to take decisive action and the prospect of being obliged to intervene in order to salvage a failure led to Operation Deliberate Force and the Dayton Peace Agreement. The Bosnia experience placed the NATO Allies in a stronger position to intercede forcefully in the Kosovo conflict, although without benefit of a UN Security Council mandate and at the cost of antagonizing China, Russia, and Serbia.

In partnership with the European Union, NATO remains committed to providing a security framework for the western Balkans for the indefinite future. Slovenia joined NATO in 2004, and Albania and Croatia followed in 2009. The other Yugoslav successor states are expected to follow, but the timetable will depend on the candidates and their relations with their neighbors. In the case of the former Yugoslav Republic of Macedonia, the name dispute with Greece will have to be resolved. The obstacles to Alliance membership facing Kosovo and Serbia are even more intractable, given their antagonistic relationship and Kosovo's economic, political, and diplomatic recognition problems. NATO's long-term vision for the western Balkans—eventual membership in the Alliance and the European Union—nonetheless offers direction and standards for democratic transformation.

The U.S.-led intervention in Afghanistan that began in October 2001, Operation Enduring Freedom, was initiated in the context of unanimous UN Security Council support for effective action against the "perpetrators, organizers and sponsors" of the terrorist attacks against the United States on September 11, 2001.[172] This intervention did not at the outset directly involve the Alliance, but many NATO Allies participated in it and in ISAF, mandated by the UN Security Council in December 2001. NATO's formal support role began the following year, and the Alliance took over command of ISAF in August 2003.

The governments of all the NATO Allies and several of the partners contributing to ISAF have assumed obligations to assist the Afghan National Security Forces during the period from 2014 to 2024, the first decade after the end of the Alliance's combat role in 2014. It is, however, clear that the Alliance's staying power and long-term commitment in Afghanistan will be more difficult to sustain than in the Balkans. In contrast with the states of the western Balkans, there is no long-term prospect of EU or NATO membership for Afghanistan, and promoting democratization, economic development, and respect for human rights will present an even greater challenge in Afghanistan than in the Balkans.

Since the terrorist attacks against the United States in September 2001, the Allies have become conscious of the extent to which derelict or failing states—such as Afghanistan under Taliban rule—can become havens for terrorist movements and organized criminal groups. However, many Allied observers agree, NATO's intervention in Afghanistan cannot be a template for the future. The NATO Allies and their partners cannot afford to intervene massively in Pakistan, Somalia, Yemen, and every other country in which al-Qaeda and other terrorist movements operate. In the wake of Afghanistan, the Allies are likely to be cautious about future interventions on the ground in counterterrorist or counterinsurgency operations, and the United States may prefer to employ drone strikes and other long-range means in attempts to contain threats.

Notes

1. For a valuable analysis of this question during the Cold War period, see Douglas Stuart and William Tow, *The Limits of Alliance: NATO Out-of-Area Problems since 1949* (Baltimore, MD, and London: Johns Hopkins University Press, 1990).

2. Manfred Wörner, "The Security Policy of the Federal Republic of Germany in the 1980s," *AEI Foreign Policy and Defense Review* 4, nos. 3 and 4 (1983): 45.

3. Admiral Jonathan T. Howe, USN, "NATO and the Gulf Crisis," *Survival* 33 (May/June 1991).

4. *NATO's Operations 1949–Present*, 1.

5. NATO's precautionary deployment of capabilities in defense of Turkey in 1990–1991 can be regarded as a precedent for comparable deployments in 2003 and 2012–2013.

6. North Atlantic Council, "Strategic Concept," November 7, 1991, par. 5.

7. NATO, Defense Planning Committee, "Final Communiqué," December 13, 1991, par. 10, www.nato.int/docu/comm/49-95/c911213a.htm.

8. *NATO's Operations 1949–Present*, 1. See also North Atlantic Council, "Final Communiqué," December 19, 1991, par. 5.

9. *NATO's Operations 1949—Present*, 1. NATO's 1992 deployment of AWACS to monitor the air approaches from Libya might be seen as a precedent for elements of Operation Unified Protector in 2011.

10. The Alliance's first operations, conducted in 1990–1991 with a view to protecting Turkey and other Allies against possible Iraqi aggression in response to the UNSC-authorized liberation of Kuwait, were clearly within the territory defined by Article 6 of the North Atlantic Treaty, as amended by Article 2 of the Protocol of October 22, 1951, to encompass the territory of Turkey.

11. Rob de Wijk quoted in Steven Erlanger, "So Far, Europe Breathes Easier over Free Hand Given the U.S.," *New York Times*, September 29, 2001.

12. North Atlantic Council, "Final Communiqué," May 14, 2002, par. 5, www.nato.int/cps/en/SID-3672FD28-4108CD25/natolive/official_texts_19577.htm.

13. Talleyrand cited in Wight, *Power Politics*, 199.

14. Jacques Poos on the ITN News, June 28, 1991, cited in James Gow, *Triumph of the Lack of Will: International Diplomacy and the Yugoslav War* (London: Hurst and Co., 1997), 48, 50.

15. North Atlantic Council, "Strategic Concept," November 7, 1991, par. 36.

16. Ibid., par. 31.

17. Ibid., par. 32.

18. North Atlantic Council, communiqué, December 17, 1992, par. 5.

19. Stephanie Anderson, "EU, NATO, and CSCE Responses to the Yugoslav Crisis: Testing Europe's New Security Architecture," *European Security* 4 (Summer 1995): 349.

20. Nicole Gnesotto, *Lessons of Yugoslavia*, Chaillot Paper no. 14 (Paris: Institute for Security Studies, Western European Union, March 1994), 26–27, 35–36, 41.

21. Rob de Wijk, *NATO on the Brink of the New Millenium: The Battle for Consensus* (London and Washington, DC: Brassey's, 1997), 111.

22. General Sir Michael Rose, *Fighting for Peace: Lessons from Bosnia* (London: Warner Books, 1999), 13; italics in the original.

23. For a discussion of the origins of Operation Deliberate Force, see Yost, *NATO Transformed*, 197–199.

24. It should be noted that sources differ regarding this operation's name and duration. For example, the list of NATO operations published by SHAPE distinguishes between Operation Deadeye strikes against Bosnian Serb air defenses (August 30–31, 1995) and more extensive targeting in Operation Deliberate Force (September 5–14, 1995). Several other sources, however, describe Operation Deliberate Force as having lasted from August 30 to September 20. According to David Dittmer and Stephen Dawkins, the bombing was suspended on September 14 for seventy-two hours, but other air missions (such as reconnaissance and no-fly-zone enforcement) continued, and the NATO Allies were prepared to resume bombing "without warning" if the Bosnian Serbs failed to implement the agreement that they had concluded with U.S. assistant secretary of state Richard Holbrooke. This agreement was construed as including a commitment to comply with three conditions set out in a September 3 letter by General Bernard Janvier, French Army, commander of the UN Protection Force. The seventy-two-hour bombing suspension was extended for another seventy-two hours when it expired on September 17, but the threat of a resumption of bombing continued. On September 19 NATO and UN commanders agreed that Bosnian Serb progress in compliance was "satisfactory." On September 20 General Janvier and Admiral Leighton Smith, Jr., USN, the commander of Allied Forces Southern Europe, concurred that the Bosnian Serbs had respected the terms specified in General Janvier's letter, and the bombing campaign formally ended. For the SHAPE account, see *NATO's Operations 1949–Present*, 2. See also David L. Dittmer and Stephen P. Dawkins, *Deliberate Force: NATO's First Extended Air Operation: The View from AFSOUTH* (Alexandria, VA: Center for Naval Analyses, June 1998), 41–45; and Ryan Hendrickson, "Crossing the Rubicon," *NATO Review*, Autumn 2005, www.nato.int/docu/review/2005/issue3/offprint_autumn_eng.pdf.

25. Richard Holbrooke, *To End a War* (New York: Random House, 1998). The country is usually called Bosnia, but the formal name of the state resulting from the 1995 General Framework Agreement for Peace in Bosnia and Herzegovina (known informally as the Dayton Accord or Dayton Agreement or Dayton-Paris Agreement) is Bosnia and Herzegovina (abbreviated as BiH). The state of Bosnia and Herzegovina is composed of three "constituent peoples"

(Bosniaks, Serbs, and Croats) and includes two semiautonomous entities (Republika Srpska and the Federation of Bosnia and Herzegovina, the latter informally called the Bosniak-Croat Federation) and the locally governed Brcko District.

26. The Peace Implementation Council (PIC), consisting of fifty-five countries and organizations, was established in December 1995 to support the "peace process" in Bosnia envisaged in the Dayton Agreement. For background, see Office of the High Representative (OHR), "The Peace Implementation Council and Its Steering Board," November 29, 2006, www.ohr.int/pic/default.asp?content id=38563.

27. OHR, *Thirty-Third Report of the High Representative for Implementation of the Peace Agreement on Bosnia and Herzegovina to the Secretary-General of the United Nations, 1 October 2007–31 March 2008,* par. 9, www.ohr.int/other-doc/hr-reports/default.asp?content_id=41694.

28. Milorad Dodik statement in Kira Kay report, "Bosnia Prepares for Elections as Ethnic Divisions Remain," *PBS NewsHour,* October 1, 2010, www.pbs.org/newshour/bb/europe/july-dec10/bosnia_10-01.html#transcript.

29. "Bosnia Tension Eases as Serbs Cancel Referendum," BBC, May 13, 2011, www.bbc.co.uk/news/world-europe-13389051.

30. North Atlantic Council, "Strasbourg/Kehl Summit Declaration," par. 26.

31. Vice President Joe Biden, address to the Parliament of Bosnia and Herzegovina, May 19, 2009, http://sarajevo.usembassy.gov/speech_20090519.html.

32. Philip H. Gordon, assistant secretary of state for European and Eurasian affairs, on-the-record briefing on Secretary Clinton's Travel to the Balkans and Brussels, October 8, 2010, www.america.gov/st/texttrans english/2010/October/20101008163138su0.5044217.html?CP.rss=true.

33. North Atlantic Council, "Lisbon Summit Declaration," par. 17.

34. North Atlantic Council, "Chicago Summit Declaration," par. 28.

35. President George Bush cited in John M. Goshko, "Bush Threatens 'Military Force' If Serbs Attack Ethnic Albanians," *Washington Post,* December 29, 1992.

36. "Clinton Warns Serbian Leaders on Military Action in Kosovo," *Washington Post,* March 2, 1993.

37. Secretary of State Madeleine Albright cited in "U.S. Credibility on the Line," *Washington Post National Weekly,* March 23, 1998.

38. Serbia and Montenegro, two former republics of the Socialist Federal Republic of Yugoslavia, formed the Federal Republic of Yugoslavia in 1992. The loose confederation, which was also known as Serbia and Montenegro, came to an end in June 2006, when each republic declared its independence. Slobodan Milošević was president of the Federal Republic of Yugoslavia during NATO's 1999 air campaign, and NATO's attacks were directed primarily against targets in Serbia.

39. Javier Solana, statement in interview on March 30, 1999, quoted in Craig R. Whitney, "For NATO, Doubts Lag," *New York Times,* March 31, 1999.

40. General Wesley K. Clark, quoted in R. Jeffrey Smith and William Drozdiak, "A Blueprint for War," *Washington Post National Weekly Edition,* April 19, 1999. See also the autobiographical account of Operation Allied Force in Clark, *Waging Modern War.*

41. Tony Blair's speech to the House of Commons, March 23, 1999, in the *Guardian,* www.guardian.co.uk/world/1999/mar/23/balkans.tonyblair.

42. These numbers are provided by the NATO website in "The Kosovo Air Campaign: Operation Allied Force," www.nato.int/cps/en/natolive/topics_49602.htm.

43. For example, according to a U.S. Department of Defense report, "reducing the Serb defensive radar-guided surface-to-air missile systems that are effective against aircraft flying at higher altitudes proved more difficult than anticipated as a result of the tactics employed by the Serbs. By conserving their systems and attempting to down NATO aircraft as targets of opportunity, they gave up many of the advantages of a connected and continuously operating system in order to achieve tactical surprise in a few instances." Department of Defense, *Kosovo/Operation Allied Force After-Action Report to Congress* (Washington, DC: Department of Defense, January 31, 2000), 65.

44. Ibid., 11.

45. UN Security Council Resolution 1244, June 10, 1999.

46. Tony Barber, "Brussels Sees Progress on Kosovo Dispute," *Financial Times,* October 7, 2013.

47. Marc Weller, "The Vienna Negotiations on the Final Status for Kosovo," *International Affairs* 84, no. 4 (July 2008): 660.

48. "Kosovo and Serbia: The Fallout from a Surprisingly Pro-Kosovo Legal Decision," *Economist,* July 31, 2010.

49. United Nations Security Council, *Report of the Secretary-General on the United Nations Interim Administration Mission in Kosovo,* November 24, 2008, S/2008/692, Annex I, par. 49–50, cited in David Harland, "Kosovo and the UN," *Survival* 52, no. 5 (October-November 2010), 92.

50. Harland, "Kosovo and the UN," 94.

51. NATO, "NATO's Role in Kosovo," www.nato.int/cps/en/natolive/topics_48818.htm.

52. Gordon, on-the-record briefing, October 8, 2010.

53. R. Craig Nation, "NATO in the Western Balkans: A Force for Stability?," *Southeastern Europe* 35 (2011): 134-135.

54. Jean-Christian Cady, *Establishing the Rule of Law: The U.N. Challenge in Kosovo*, Focus Stratégique no. 34 bis (Paris: Institut Français des Relations Internationales, June 2012), 37.

55. North Atlantic Council, "Lisbon Summit Declaration," par. 5.

56. North Atlantic Council, "Chicago Summit Declaration," par. 34.

57. The dispute between Greece and the former Yugoslav Republic of Macedonia about the name of the latter remains unresolved. In deference to Greece, all European Union countries and most NATO countries refer to it as FYROM. NATO communiqués and other Alliance documents consistently include a note stating that "Turkey recognises the Republic of Macedonia with its constitutional name."

58. NATO, "Peace Support Operations in the former Yugoslav Republic of Macedonia," www.nato.int/cps/en/natolive/topics_52121.htm#Skopje.

59. This cooperation is discussed in chapter 7. For a brief but valuable account, see also Mihai Carp, "Back from the Brink," *NATO Review*, Winter 2002. For a more extensive discussion of this interorganizational cooperation, see Yost, *NATO and International Organizations*, 115–117. Regarding the voluntary disarmament of the NLA and other groups and the difficult conflict resolution process in FYROM, see Suzette R. Grillot, Wolf-Christian Paes, Hans Risser, and Shelly O. Stoneman, *A Fragile Peace: Guns and Security in Post-Conflict Macedonia* (Geneva: United Nations Development Programme and the Small Arms Survey, June 2004).

60. North Atlantic Council, "Prague Summit Declaration," par. 6.

61. North Atlantic Council, "Bucharest Summit Declaration," par. 20.

62. Rafael Biermann, *NATO Enlargement—Approaching a Standstill*, Security Insights no. 4 (Garmisch-Partenkirchen, Germany: College of International and Security Studies, George C. Marshall Center, December 2009), 4, www.marshallcenter.org/mcpublicweb/MCDocs/files/College/F_Publications/secInsights/SecurityInsights_04_fullsize.pdf.

63. Nation, "NATO in the Western Balkans," 128.

64. NATO, "NATO's Relations with the former Yugoslav Republic of Macedonia."

65. North Atlantic Council, "Prague Summit Declaration," par. 13.

66. North Atlantic Council, "Lisbon Summit Declaration," par. 15.

67. Ibid., par. 18-19.

68. Witold Waszczykowski, *The Western Balkans: Securing a Stable Future*, Draft Special Report, Committee on the Civil Dimension of Security (Brussels: NATO Parliamentary Assembly, April 24, 2013), par. 70.

69. Among the many books on the war in Afghanistan since 2001, particularly useful are Joseph J. Collins, *Understanding War in Afghanistan* (Washington, DC: National Defense University Press, 2011); Andrew R. Hoehn and Sarah Harting, *Risking NATO: Testing the Limits of the Alliance in Afghanistan* (Santa Monica, CA: RAND Corp., 2010); Dexter Filkins, *The Forever War* (New York: Knopf, 2008); and Seth G. Jones, *In the Graveyard of Empires: America's War in Afghanistan* (New York: W. W. Norton and Co., 2009).

70. Antonio Martino quoted in Daniel Williams, "Italy Commits Troops for Afghan Conflict," *Washington Post*, November 8, 2001, 19.

71. "About ISAF," www.isaf.nato.int/mission.html.

72. For a lucid account of NATO's initial engagement in Afghanistan, see Diego A. Ruiz Palmer, "The Road to Kabul," *NATO Review*, Summer 2003. See also Lieutenant Colonel Steve Beckman, U.S. Army, *From Assumption to Expansion: Planning and Executing NATO's First Year in Afghanistan at the Strategic Level* (Carlisle Barracks, PA: U.S. Army War College, 2005).

73. UN Security Council Resolution 1386, adopted December 20, 2001.

74. General Stanley A. McChrystal, U.S. Army, *COMISAF's Initial Assessment* (Kabul, Afghanistan: Headquarters, International Security Assistance Force, August 30, 2009), 2–5, redacted PDF version available at washingtonpost.com.

75. General David Petraeus, interview with Fareed Zakaria on CNN, March 7, 2010.

76. Candace Rondeaux, a senior analyst for Afghanistan at the International Crisis Group, in Jackie Northam, "In Afghanistan, U.S. Success Depends On Karzai," National Public Radio, December 21, 2009, www.npr.org/templates/story/story.php?storyId=121509106.

77. Giles Whittell, "NATO Will Fail unless You End Corruption, US Commander Tells Karzai," *Times*, March 30, 2010, www.timesonline.co.uk/tol/news/world/afghanistan/article7080660.ece; and Jon Boone, "WikiLeaks Cables

Portray Hamid Karzai as Corrupt and Erratic," *Guardian*, December 2, 2010, www.guardian.co.uk/world/2010/dec/02/wikileaks-cables-hamid-karzai-erratic.

78. General McChrystal, *COMISAF's Initial Assessment*, 2–4.

79. *Report on Progress toward Security and Stability in Afghanistan* (Washington, DC: U.S. Department of Defense, October 2011), 5–6.

80. Collins, *Understanding War in Afghanistan*, 114.

81. NATO, "Declaration by the Heads of State and Government of the Nations Contributing to the UN-mandated, NATO-led International Security Assistance Force (ISAF) in Afghanistan," November 20, 2010, www.nato.int/cps/en/natolive/news_68722.htm.

82. North Atlantic Council, "Chicago Summit Declaration," par. 7.

83. The list of participants is available on the website of the German Foreign Ministry at www.auswaertiges-amt.de/cae/servlet/contentblob/603574/publicationFile/162321/Teilnehmerliste.pdf .

84. North Atlantic Council, "Riga Summit Declaration," par. 6.

85. "Joint Statement on Outcome of 1st JCBM Meeting," April 30, 2006. The initialism CFC-A stands for the Coalition Forces Combined Forces Command-Afghanistan.

86. General McChrystal, *COMISAF's Initial Assessment*, 2–10.

87. Anders Fogh Rasmussen, in a press conference following the meeting of the North Atlantic Council in defense ministers session in Bratislava, Slovakia, October 23, 2009, www.nato.int/cps/en/natolive/opinions_58469.htm.

88. Yost, *An Interview with General James L. Jones*, 6.

89. This circumstance explains the main title of a prominent article about the development of U.S. and Alliance strategy in the country: Lieutenant General David W. Barno, U.S. Army, "Fighting 'The Other War': Counterinsurgency Strategy in Afghanistan, 2003–2005," *Military Review* 87, no. 5 (September–October 2007): 32–44.

90. Robert Gates, interview with Larry King on CNN, quoted in Martin Schram, "Washington's Honest Man," Scripps Howard News Service, September 30, 2009.

91. Paddy Ashdown, "A Strategy to Save Afghanistan," *Financial Times*, February 13, 2008.

92. Jaap de Hoop Scheffer, press conference at informal meeting of NATO defense ministers, Budapest, Hungary, October 10, 2008, www.nato.int/docu/speech/2008/s081010c.html (accessed 27 July 2011).

93. General John Craddock, statement following the defense ministerial meeting in Seville, Spain, February 9, 2007, www.nato.int/shape/opinions/2007/s070209a.htm.

94. General John Craddock, interview with Arnaud de Borchgrave, "'Caveats' Neuter NATO Allies," *Washington Times*, July 15, 2009, www.washingtontimes.com/news/2009/jul/15/caveats-neuter-nato-allies/; italics in the original.

95. Author interviews with British and Dutch experts in Brussels, December 5, 2008.

96. Lieutenant General William Caldwell, commander of the NATO Training Mission–Afghanistan (NTM-A), press briefing, March 3, 2010, www.nato.int/cps/en/natolive/opinions_61890.htm. General Caldwell described the NTM-A goals regarding literacy and numeracy: "Most of the young recruits that come in, we have about a 14 percent literacy rate . . . which means that 86 percent really can't read or write. So that means everything we do is done on a show-and-tell basis. . . . And what we're going to do is we're going to teach them letters, alphabet, numbers and how to write their name. I mean, that's our goal . . . that everybody will come out of basic training being able to understand all the letters of the alphabet, how to write their name and understand the numbers."

97. Radoslaw Sikorski, interview with *Foreign Policy*, November 2, 2009, www.foreignpolicy.com/articles/2009/11/02/interview_radoslaw_sikorski?print=yes&hidecomments=yes&page=full.

98. Jamie Shea, "NATO at Sixty—and Beyond," in *NATO in Search of a Vision*, ed. Gülner Aybet and Rebecca R. Moore (Washington, DC: Georgetown University Press, 2010), 25.

99. General Harald Kujat, interview with *Mitteldeutsche Zeitung*, quoted in "German General Says NATO Mission Has 'Failed,'" in *Spiegel Online International*, October 7, 2011, www.spiegel.de/international/world/ten-years-in-afghanistan-german-general-says-nato-mission-has-failed-a-790539.html.

100. Alexander Mattelaer, "How Afghanistan Has Strengthened NATO," *Survival* 53, no. 6 (December 2011–January 2012), 137.

101. "The United Kingdom is not primarily in Afghanistan to address the developmental difficulties of the Afghans, nor to tackle terrorist threats to the British homeland at source. Britain is in Afghanistan for the same reason that it took part in the invasion of Iraq: the Anglo-American alliance is the cornerstone of British foreign and defence policy." Hew Strachan, "The Strategic Gap in British Defence Policy," *Survival* 51, no. 4 (August–September 2009), 51.

102. Jo Coelmont, *End-State Afghanistan: A European Perspective*, Security Policy Brief no. 2 (Brussels: Royal Institute for International Relations, November 2009), 3.

103. Yost, *An Interview with General James L. Jones*, 6.

104. David P. Auerswald and Stephen M. Saideman, *NATO at War: Understanding the Challenges of Caveats in Afghanistan* (Montreal, Canada: McGill University, 2009), www.aco.nato.int/resources/1/documents/NATO%20at%20War.pdf.

105. De Borchgrave, "'Caveats' Neuter NATO Allies." The caveats on the usability of the forces of most NATO Allies and partners in Afghanistan have given an edge to the joke among U.S. soldiers that ISAF stands for "I Saw Americans Fight."

106. James Sperling and Mark Webber, "NATO: From Kosovo to Kabul," *International Affairs* 85, no. 3 (May 2009): 509.

107. Chris Patten, "How Europe Can Respond to Obama," *Financial Times*, November 26, 2008.

108. Tom Coghlan, "German Troops Face Pitched Battles in Afghanistan as Insurgency Spreads," *Times*, May 3, 2010, www.timesonline.co.uk/tol/news/world/afghanistan/article7114552.ece.

109. See "ISAF's Strategic Vision," April 3, 2008, www.nato.int/cps/en/natolive/official_texts_8444.htm. The Comprehensive Political-Military Strategic Plan for Afghanistan was not published. "ISAF Nations Affirm Long-Term Commitment to Afghanistan," April 3, 2008, www.nato.int/docu/update/2008/04-april/e0403g.html.

110. Yost, *An Interview with General James L. Jones.*

111. De Hoop Scheffer, press conference, October 10, 2008.

112. As a British expert in Brussels put it, the decision in Budapest in October 2008 meant that the Allies that wish to act against narcotics producers and dealers can "get on with it." In other words, the Allies ready to act are "not being vetoed by the laggards" any more. Author interview on December 5, 2008.

113. Timo Noetzel, "Germany," in *Understanding Counterinsurgency: Doctrine, Operations, and Challenges*, ed. Thomas Rid and Thomas Keaney (Abingdon and New York: Routledge, 2010), 46, 51.

114. David Betz and Anthony Cormack, "Iraq, Afghanistan and British Strategy," *Orbis* 53, no. 2 (Spring 2009): 326.

115. General McChrystal, *COMISAF's Initial Assessment*, 2-10.

116. Bob Woodward, *Obama's Wars* (New York: Simon and Schuster, 2010), 238.

117. This statement was made by a prominent Italian observer at an off-the-record workshop in Rome, November 8, 2010.

118. Alexander Mattelaer, "How Afghanistan Has Strengthened NATO," *Survival* 53, no. 6 (December 2011–January 2012): 130.

119. Robert M. Gates, remarks as delivered, NATO Strategic Concept Seminar, National Defense University, Washington, DC, February 23, 2010, www.defense.gov/speeches/speech.aspx?speechid=1423.

120. Woodward, *Obama's Wars*, 294. See also ibid., 150–151.

121. Some Allied observers have expressed the judgment that deferring to U.S. leadership in Afghanistan and accepting U.S. strategy offer the non-U.S. allies an advantage: political responsibility for the eventual outcome is placed on U.S. shoulders.

122. Longer-term strategy for the North Atlantic Treaty Organization in its International Security Assistance Force role in Afghanistan, approved by the North Atlantic Council on October 1, 2003 and submitted by Lord Robertson, the NATO secretary general, to Kofi Annan, the UN secretary-general, on October 2, 2003, available in UN Security Council document 2/2003/970.

123. North Atlantic Council, "Bucharest Summit Declaration," par. 6.

124. Robert M. Gates, testimony before the Senate Armed Services Committee, January 27, 2009, quoted in Ann Scott Tyson, "Gates Predicts 'Slog' in Afghanistan," *Washington Post*, January 28, 2009.

125. General McChrystal, *COMISAF's Initial Assessment*, 2–2.

126. Ibid., 2-2. The only reference to democratization as a goal in this lengthy study appeared in a quotation from Afghan Defense Minister Abdul Rahim Wardak. See ibid., 1–4.

127. Gordon Brown, speech at the International Institute for Strategic Studies, London, September 4, 2009.

128. *NATO 2020: Assured Security; Dynamic Engagement, Analysis and Recommendations of the Group of Experts on a New Strategic Concept for NATO* (Brussels: NATO Public Diplomacy Division, May 17, 2010), 9, www.nato.int/strategic-concept/expertsreport.pdf. See also pp. 31, 47.

129. "Declaration by the North Atlantic Treaty Organisation (NATO) and the Government of the Islamic Republic of Afghanistan on an Enduring Partnership Signed at the NATO Summit in Lisbon, Portugal," November 20, 2010, par. 3, www.nato.int/cps/en/natolive/official_texts_68724.htm.

130. Karen DeYoung and Scott Wilson, "One-Year Review Is Mixed on Afghanistan-Pakistan Strategy," *Washington Post*, December 17, 2010.

131. Yost, *An Interview with General James L. Jones*, 6, www.ndc.nato.int/download/publications/rp_34.pdf.

132. Anders Fogh Rasmussen, "New Challenges—Better Capabilities" (speech at the Bratislava Security Conference, October 22, 2009), www.nato.int/cps/en/natolive/opinions_58248.htm.

133. Admiral Mullen quoted in Woodward, *Obama's Wars*, 223.

134. Barack Obama, remarks in an address to the nation on the way forward in Afghanistan and Pakistan, U.S. Military Academy, West Point, New York, December 1, 2009, www.whitehouse.gov/the-press-office/remarks-president-address-nation-way-forward-afghanistan-and-pakistan.

135. Madeleine Albright quoted in Nikola Krastev, "Albright Presents Strategic Concept For NATO's Next Decade," May 28, 2010, www.rferl.org/content/Albright_Presents_Strategic_Concept_For_NATOs_Next_Decade/2055739.html.

136. Obama, remarks, U.S. Military Academy, December 1, 2009, www.whitehouse.gov/the-press-office/remarks-president-address-nation-way-forward-afghanistan-and-pakistan.

137. North Atlantic Council, "Chicago Summit Declaration," par. 5.

138. Alexander Mattelaer has suggested that "the word 'irreversible' was . . . inserted into summit language with a view to ensuring that the transition of security responsibility could not be used as a mechanism for working around geographical caveats through the backdoor (i.e. handing over security responsibilities in the quieter northern sector so as to force Allies like Germany to move their forces elsewhere)." Letter to the author, May 25, 2013. The author thanks Alexander Mattelaer for this insight and several others concerning NATO's operations. With regard to the meaning of "irreversible" in this context, see also Alexander Mattelaer, *The Politico-Military Dynamics of European Crisis Response Operations: Planning, Friction, Strategy* (New York: Palgrave Macmillan, 2013), 133.

139. North Atlantic Council, "Chicago Summit Declaration," par. 6.

140. Ibid., par. 7.

141. "As the Afghan economy and the revenues of the Afghan government grow, Afghanistan's yearly share will increase progressively from at least US $500m in 2015, with the aim that it can assume, no later than 2024, full financial responsibility for its own security forces. In the light of this, during the Transformation Decade, we expect international donors will reduce their financial contributions commensurate with the assumption by the Afghan government of increasing financial responsibility." "Chicago Summit Declaration on Afghanistan Issued by the Heads of State and Government of Afghanistan and the Nations Contributing to the NATO-led International Security Assistance Force (ISAF)," May 21, 2012, par. 16–18, www.nato.int/cps/en/natolive/official_texts_87595.htm?.

142. Mark Mazzetti and Matthew Rosenberg, "U.S. Considers Faster Pullout in Afghanistan," *New York Times*, July 9, 2013; Trudy Rubin, "On Afghan Options, Obama Floats a Big Zero," *Philadelphia Inquirer*, July 14, 2013; and Matthew Rosenberg in "Is Withdrawal from Afghanistan Still on Schedule?" *PBS Newshour*, October 6, 2013, www.pbs.org/newshour/bb/military/july-dec13/rosenberg_10-06.html.

143. "Declaration by the Heads of State and Government of the Nations Contributing to the UN-mandated, NATO-led International Security Assistance Force in Afghanistan," November 20, 2010, par. 2, www.nato.int/cps/en/natolive/news_68722.htm.

144. "Declaration by the North Atlantic Treaty Organisation and the Government of the Islamic Republic of Afghanistan on an Enduring Partnership," November 20, 2010, par. 6, www.nato.int/cps/en/natolive/official_texts_68724.htm. For background on the NATO Training Mission Afghanistan (NTM-A), see Mattelaer, *The Politico-Military Dynamics of European Crisis Response Operations*, 122–126.

145. "Joint Press Conference with NATO Secretary General Anders Fogh Rasmussen and the President of Afghanistan, Hamid Karzai," March 4, 2013, www.nato.int/cps/en/SID-9A25BBA1-E8DC1B28/natolive/opinions_98905.htm.

146. Rasmussen quoted in "NATO Defence Ministers Endorse Concept for New post-2014 Mission in Afghanistan," June 5, 2013, www.nato.int/cps/en/natolive/news_101248.htm.

147. "Declaration by the North Atlantic Treaty Organisation and the Government of the Islamic Republic of Afghanistan on an Enduring Partnership,", par. 3.

148. Gordon Brown, speech, September 4, 2009.

149. Bob Ainsworth in a BBC interview during a visit to Saudi Arabia, quoted in Alissa J. Rubin, John F. Burns and Taimoor Shah, "Troop Deaths in Afghanistan Stir Outcry in Britain," *New York Times*, November 5, 2009.

150. General McChrystal, *COMISAF's Initial Assessment*, 2–10.

151. Vice President Biden quoted in Bob Woodward, "Obama's Wars: Locked In," *Washington Post*, September 28, 2010.

152. Paul D. Miller, "The US and Afghanistan After 2014," *Survival* 55, no. 1 (February–March 2013): 87.

153. North Atlantic Council, "Bucharest Summit Declaration," par. 6.

154. General McChrystal, *COMISAF's Initial Assessment*, 2–11.

155. "Declaration by the Heads of State and Government of the Nations contributing to the UN-mandated, NATO-led International Security Assistance Force in Afghanistan," par. 10.

156. "Declaration by the North Atlantic Treaty Organisation (NATO) and the Government of the Islamic Republic of Afghanistan on an Enduring Partnership," par. 4.

157. "The Istanbul Statement on Friendship and Cooperation in the 'Heart of Asia,'" January 26, 2010, www.mfa.gov.tr/istanbul-statement-on-friendship-and-cooperation-in-the-_heart-of-asia_.en.mfa.

158. Hillary Clinton, "The Way Forward in Afghanistan," testimony before the Senate Foreign Relations Committee, Washington, DC, June 23, 2011, www.state.gov/secretary/rm/2011/06/166807.htm.

159. Clinton quoted in Daniel Dombey and Matthew Green, "US Aims to Turn Afghanistan into Neutral Zone," *Financial Times*, June 28, 2011.

160. Jean d'Amécourt, "Europe in Afghanistan," *International Herald Tribune*, July 2, 2011. M. d'Amécourt served as France's ambassador to Afghanistan in 2008–2011.

161. Audrey Kurth Cronin, "Thinking Long on Afghanistan: Could It Be Neutralized?" *Washington Quarterly* 36, no. 1 (Winter 2013): 68.

162. In Robert Blackwill's view, NATO should "let the Taliban control the Pashtun south and east, [because] the American and allied price for preventing that is far too high." Blackwill quoted in Damien McElroy, "NATO Is Urged to Pull Back and Allow Partition of Afghanistan," *Daily Telegraph*, September 13, 2010.

163. "Declaration by the North Atlantic Treaty Organisation and the Government of the Islamic Republic of Afghanistan on an Enduring Partnership," par. 6.

164. "Declaration by the Heads of State and Government of the Nations contributing to the UN-mandated, NATO-led International Security Assistance Force in Afghanistan," par. 1.

165. "Declaration of the Istanbul Process on Regional Security and Cooperation for a Secure and Stable Afghanistan," November 2, 2011, par. 1, www.cfr.org/afghanistan/declaration-istanbul-process-regional-security-cooperation-secure-stable-afghanistan/p26434. The declaration was approved by Afghanistan, China, India, Iran, Kazakhstan, Kyrgyzstan, Pakistan, Russia, Saudi Arabia, the Tajikistan, Turkey, Turkmenistan, and the United Arab Emirates.

166. North Atlantic Council, "Chicago Summit Declaration," par. 10.

167. M. K. Bhadrakumar, "US's post-2014 Afghan Agenda Falters," *Asia Times*, November 4, 2011, http://atimes.com/atimes/south_asia/mk04df03.html.

168. *Report on Progress toward Security and Stability in Afghanistan* (Washington, DC: U.S. Department of Defense, December 2012), 5, www.defense.gov/news/1230_Report_final.pdf.

169. Anders Fogh Rasmussen, "NATO's Plan Is Working in Afghanistan," *Daily Telegraph*, October 23, 2012.

170. North Atlantic Council, "Riga Summit Declaration," par. 6.

171. Olivier Neola, *Building Security Institutions: Lessons Learned in Afghanistan*, Focus Stratégique no. 38 (Paris: Institut Français des Relations Internationales, July-August 2012), 38.

172. UN Security Council Resolution 1368, approved unanimously on September 12, 2001, called "on all States to work together urgently to bring to justice the perpetrators, organizers and sponsors of these terrorist attacks" and stressed that "those responsible for aiding, supporting or harbouring the perpetrators, organizers and sponsors of these acts will be held accountable."

5

Crisis Management Elsewhere

While NATO's longest and most demanding operations have been those in the Balkans and Afghanistan, the Alliance also intervened decisively in the Libyan civil war in 2011. In addition, NATO has furnished training to Iraqi military forces and support for the African Union in Darfur and Somalia. Moreover, NATO has contributed to counterpiracy efforts off the Horn of Africa. Among its other roles, NATO has served as a general "toolbox" for ad hoc operations by the Allies, such as providing security for the Olympic Games in Athens in 2004 and supplying humanitarian relief in the wake of natural disasters in Pakistan and elsewhere.

This chapter's discussion of NATO's evolving crisis management tasks reviews these missions, with particular attention to the 2011 Libya intervention. It then compares the most prominent cases—Afghanistan, the Balkans, and Libya—before considering some of the general issues raised by these operations and other missions. These general issues include the challenge of developing and maintaining capabilities for both crisis management and collective defense, the extent to which crisis management can contribute to (or compete with) collective defense, and the risk of a collective defense contingency arising from a crisis management operation.[1]

NATO and Iraq

The March 2003 invasion of Iraq by a U.S.-led coalition deeply divided the NATO Allies. The issue came before the North Atlantic Council in February 2003, when the United States proposed that the NATO military authorities be tasked to plan for defense and deterrence measures in light of a possible Iraqi threat to Turkey. Allies disagreed as to whether such measures were necessary or opportune. However, Turkey's formal invocation of Article 4 of the North Atlantic Treaty on February 10, 2003, forced the Allies to deliberate on the question. Ankara requested consultations on Alliance measures to defend Turkey, if necessary, in case the Iraqi government of Saddam Hussein attacked Turkey in response to a U.S.-led intervention in Iraq. The

French in particular refused to approve the measures on the grounds that they had not endorsed the intervention in the UN Security Council, so they could not approve it in the North Atlantic Council.

Although Belgium, France, and Germany all regarded the invasion as unwarranted and ill-advised, Paris was exceptionally firm in not accepting a compromise solution. To work around the French opposition in the North Atlantic Council, the other Allies decided to meet about Turkey's situation in the Defense Planning Committee (DPC). France had abstained from deliberations in the Alliance's DPC since 1966 as part of its long-standing policy of not participating in NATO's integrated military structure. The other Allies, meeting in the DPC, decided on February 16, 2003, to ask the NATO military authorities to furnish advice on potential defensive measures. On February 19, 2003, the same other Allies, again meeting without France in the DPC, made the decisions necessary to bolster Turkey's defenses. The measures under Operation Display Deterrence in February–April 2003 included alerting and augmenting NATO's Integrated Air Defense System in Turkey, deploying four NATO Airborne Warning and Control System (AWACS) aircraft to Turkey, and sending Dutch and U.S. Patriot air defense batteries to Turkey.[2]

Nicholas Burns, then the U.S. ambassador to NATO, said that the discord between the Allies was so profound that the Alliance had undergone "a near-death experience."[3] In contrast, Lord Robertson, who was then the NATO secretary general, argued in February 2003 that the confrontation between Allies over Iraq was less severe than previous crises in NATO's history.

> This is damage above, not below, the waterline.... Does the story I have described really equate to Suez, Vietnam, the INF deployments or the early days of Bosnia? ... I don't think so. All Allies, including France, strongly support the need to defend Turkey.... All Allies agree on the aim of disarming Saddam and said so at NATO's Prague Summit in November [2002] in a robust and unambiguous statement.... In the end, this was not, and is not, remotely the kind of issue to break an alliance as strong and enduring as NATO.[4]

As soon as May 2003, the North Atlantic Council (that is, all the Allies, including France) responded positively to Poland's request for NATO assistance in its leadership of one of the sectors in the U.S.-led multinational force in Iraq.[5] After reviewing the advice of NATO military authorities, the North Atlantic Council in June 2003 approved providing Poland with "intelligence, logistics expertise, movement co-ordination, force generation and secure communications support" in its role as leader of a multinational division in Iraq. The NATO and partner contributors to the Polish-led division in Iraq included Bulgaria, Denmark, Hungary, Latvia, Lithuania, Kazakhstan, the Netherlands, Norway, Romania, Slovakia, Spain, Ukraine, and the United States. Lord Robertson said, "Together with other NATO operations in the Balkans and in Afghanistan, the Alliance's support for Poland in Iraq demonstrates the important contribution NATO is making to stability and crisis management and the fight against terrorism."[6]

In June 2004, moreover, the NATO Allies decided to act on a UN Security Council call for support for the multinational force in Iraq by offering "assistance to the government of Iraq with the training of its security forces."[7] The aims of the NATO Training Mission-Iraq (NTM-I), under way from 2004 to 2011, included the education and training of military officers and the donation of equipment. NATO backed the establishment of the Iraqi National Defense College and the development of curricula with "values that are in keeping with democratically-controlled armed forces." From 2007 to 2011, Italy's Carabinieri took the lead in gendarmerie training for Iraq's federal police. In 2008, at the request of the Iraqi government, NATO extended the NTM-I mission to encompass "navy and air force leadership training, defence reform, defence institution building, and small arms and light weapons accountability." The Strategic Security Advisor and Mentoring Division of NTM-I assisted the Iraqi government in establishing operations centers for the prime minister, the defense minister, and the interior minister.[8]

Of NATO's twenty-eight members, twenty-three contributed equipment, funds, staff, or education and training in or outside Iraq. Moreover, the Allies collectively supported education and training facilities attended by some Iraqi officers, including the NATO Defense College in Rome, Italy, the NATO School in Oberammergau, Germany, and the Joint Warfare Center at Stavanger, Norway. Aside from personnel costs, which were covered on a national basis, the Allies spent 22.5 million euros a year on NTM-I, which was conducted in 2004–2011. This amount was modest in comparison with that spent by the United States on the reconstruction of the Iraqi military and in relation to the magnitude of the tasks at hand. According to Florence Gaub's incisive assessment, the NTM-I mission, with 170 personnel in and near Baghdad, was hampered by budget shortfalls, "understaffing," and a "lack of cultural preparation," with little or no linguistic or regional education to enable NATO trainers to surmount their ethnocentric attitudes.[9] The problems of the Iraqi Armed Forces included a "lack of qualified officers, absenteeism, lack of cohesion and under-equipment for missions."[10] As Gaub pointed out in April 2011, another danger that could not be ruled out was that

> the Iraqi Army . . . could feel frustrated with the sectarian political system and resort, for the eighth time in its history, to a coup d'état. In this case, NATO could be accused of having trained a putschist force and ultimately failed at reforming the security sector. It thus remains crucial that the Alliance continues its efforts on the ground, and improves in those areas that show deficiencies.[11]

This prescription was overtaken by events in December 2011, when all U.S. and NATO troops were withdrawn from Iraq. Although some high-level Iraqi officers had warned in 2010 that the Iraqi Armed Forces would not be prepared to defend the country from external adversaries until 2018–2020,[12] the Iraqi government chose not to extend the 2009 agreement on the legal status of U.S. and other NATO forces in Iraq. That agreement expired on December 31, 2011, and all Allied forces were "permanently withdrawn" from Iraq by that date.[13] At the May 2012 NATO summit in Chicago, the Allies emphasized the mission's achievements: "We have successfully concluded the NATO Training Mission in Iraq (NTM-I) which contributed to a more stable Iraq by assisting in the capacity building of Iraq's security institutions."[14]

NATO and the African Union

The Alliance undertook its first action in Africa at the request of the African Union. From July 2005 to December 2007 NATO provided airlift to AU peacekeepers in Darfur, Sudan, as part of the African Union Mission in Sudan (AMIS). NATO furnished this airlift support in cooperation with the European Union. NATO-EU Air Movement Coordinators worked with an AU Air Movement Cell in Addis Ababa, Ethiopia, and NATO and the European Union supplied staff to this AU Air Movement Cell. NATO and the European Union together provided air transport to "some 37,500 troops, civilian police and military observers in and out of the Sudanese region." Moreover, NATO offered training in strategic and operational planning, "lessons learned" analysis, or information management to a total of 265 AU officers. The Alliance's role in support of AMIS ended in December 2007, with the transition of authority from AMIS to UNAMID, the United Nations/African Union Mission in Darfur.[15]

The African Union in May 2007 requested that NATO provide strategic airlift for AU countries willing to deploy forces in Somalia under the African Union Mission in Somalia (AMISOM). The North Atlantic Council agreed to do so in June 2007, and this support has subsequently been extended in a series of six- to twelve-month increments. Since 2009 NATO has also provided strategic sealift in support of the AU's AMISOM operation.[16] NATO furnished its first airlift in support of AMISOM in June 2008, when it transported a battalion of peacekeepers from Burundi to Mogadishu. In March 2010 the United States, acting "under the NATO banner," provided airlift for 1,700 troops from Uganda to Mogadishu and transported 850 Ugandan troops out of Mogadishu.[17]

The Alliance has become a member of the International Contact Group on Somalia (ICGS) and the Contact Group on Piracy off the Coast of Somalia (CGPCS), and NATO has sent three experts to Addis Ababa to help the AU Peace Support Operations Division supporting AMISOM.[18]

The Alliance has supported African Union capacity-building efforts since 2005. Since 2007, at the request of the African Union and with a view to strengthening the African Union's peacekeeping capabilities for the long term, NATO has offered training support to the African Standby Force (ASF). The training support has included courses at the NATO School in Oberammergau and training programs for AU staff organized initially by Joint Force Command Lisbon and more recently by Joint Force Command Naples, the NATO headquarters responsible for implementing the Alliance's cooperation with the African Union. The "full operational capability" of the ASF is planned in 2015, but will probably be delayed.[19]

According to Michel Soula of the NATO International Staff,

> NATO has sought to keep a low profile in providing its support.... NATO's key aim has always been to encourage and assist towards African solutions to African problems, and hence its support to the AU has been driven by the principle of African ownership, with assistance provided exclusively on the basis of the AU requests and needs.... NATO has a comparative advantage

and a distinct and unique experience and expertise in building peacekeeping capabilities, which is of great use to the AU as it seeks to build its own.[20]

NATO and Counterpiracy Operations

The Alliance has to date conducted three counterpiracy operations off the Horn of Africa and in the Gulf of Aden: Operation Allied Provider (October–December 2008), Operation Allied Protector (March–August 2009), and Operation Ocean Shield (since August 2009). These counterpiracy operations have been conducted in support of relevant UN Security Council resolutions and in coordination with the actions of the European Union and other organizations. NATO's engagement in these operations began in 2008, with a request by the UN secretary-general that NATO provide escorts to protect World Food Program ships.[21]

Ocean Shield, the current operation, is distinctive in its "capacity-building" dimension—that is, helping regional states develop their own counterpiracy abilities. The Allies have taken care not to raise excessive expectations in this regard. As noted on the NATO website, the Alliance has "recognised the continued need for regional capacity-building, within means and capabilities, and focused on areas where it provides added value."[22] While Ocean Shield concentrates mainly on counterpiracy operations at sea, with a view to preventing and interrupting hijackings, the Allies have responded positively to the UN request to escort ships supporting the UN Support Office for AMISOM to the Mogadishu harbor. Moreover, the Alliance has recently taken "measures aimed at eroding the pirates' logistics and support base." These measures include "disabling pirate vessels or skiffs, attaching tracking beacons to mother ships and allowing the use of force to disable or destroy suspected pirate or armed robber vessels."[23]

NATO's Ocean Shield has been conducted by three to six ships from the Standing NATO Maritime Groups, plus maritime patrol aircraft.[24] The European Union's Naval Force (EUNAVFOR) Somalia (Operation Atalanta), initiated in December 2008, has usually consisted of five to ten ships, one or two auxiliary ships, and two to four reconnaissance aircraft.[25] A French expert, Hugues Eudeline, has pointed out that Ocean Shield provides a NATO framework for non-EU NATO Allies to participate in these counterpiracy operations.[26] Norway (a non-EU NATO Ally) nonetheless contributed a ship to Operation Atalanta in 2009.[27]

NATO's Ocean Shield and the European Union's Operation Atalanta are two of many counterpiracy operations off the Horn of Africa and in and around the Gulf of Aden.[28] As Andrew Shapiro of the U.S. State Department noted in 2011, "On any given day up to 30 vessels from as many as 20 nations are engaged in counter-piracy operations in the region."[29] In addition to NATO and EU countries, China, India, Iran, Japan, Russia, South Korea, and the Gulf States, among others, have contributed ships to counterpiracy patrols ranging from the Red Sea to the Indian Ocean.[30]

Some countries conduct counterpiracy patrols in the region on a national basis, while others engage in counterpiracy operations under the auspices of Combined

Task Force 151, established in January 2009 under the U.S.-led Combined Maritime Forces (CMF).[31] Since December 2008 the twenty-seven countries of the CMF have convened quarterly Shared Awareness and Deconfliction (SHADE) conferences to coordinate their counterpiracy activities and to agree on how to ensure the safety of ships passing through the Internationally Recommended Transit Corridor.[32] The chairmanship of the SHADE conferences rotates among the CMF, EUNAVFOR, and NATO, despite the fact that India and some other countries would prefer that the United Nations take over leadership of these UN Security Council–authorized operations.[33]

The North Atlantic Council decided in March 2012 to extend the Ocean Shield operation until the end of 2014.[34] The Allies may continue to renew the operation indefinitely, so long as a plausible requirement persists. According to the NATO website, in 2011 there were 129 pirate attacks off the Horn of Africa, but only nineteen attempted attacks in the first eleven months of 2012.[35] In December 2012, Commodore Ben Bekkering of the Netherlands, then the commander of Ocean Shield, said that in the previous six months NATO forces had disrupted four attacks, and that there were no successful hijackings of merchant ships.[36] NATO secretary general Rasmussen characterized this as "significant progress," but added, "We cannot lower our guard."[37]

The recent decline in piracy off the Horn of Africa has been attributed to multiple factors in addition to the efforts by the "coalition of coalitions" at sea, including NATO's Ocean Shield. These factors include political developments ashore in Somalia and measures taken by shippers, such as hiring armed guards and installing barbed wire and water cannons to make their ships more defensible and harder to board.[38]

John Patch, an American expert, has characterized piracy as "high-seas criminal activity" and has rightly added, "As a localized nuisance, it should not serve to shape maritime force structure or strategy."[39] The NATO Allies do not appear to be in any danger of making this mistake. As noted, they have dedicated three to six ships at a time to Ocean Shield. While some NATO Allies have also (or have instead) committed ships under European Union auspices, the counterpiracy mission has been a secondary task, one of the miscellaneous activities that have led commentators to use the word "toolbox."

Ad Hoc "Toolbox" Operations

Despite the widespread distaste for the term "toolbox," the Allies have in fact used their common assets as ad hoc instruments for a variety of purposes. These purposes have included helping to provide security for major public events, such as the Olympics in Athens in 2004, and transporting humanitarian relief to victims of natural disasters or political upheavals. Two of NATO's first missions, Operations Goodwill I and II in February–March 1992, consisted of transporting humanitarian assistance and medical experts to Russia and other CIS countries after the December 1991 disintegration of the Soviet Union and "the collapse of its centrally-controlled economic system."[40]

The Alliance conducted one of its most noteworthy disaster-relief operations in October 2005–February 2006, when it airlifted almost 3,500 tons of supplies to earthquake-stricken Pakistan. This operation involved the deployment to Pakistan of about one thousand engineers and support personnel, plus two hundred medical staff, to help the earthquake victims.[41] In July 2010, the floods along the Indus River in Pakistan led Islamabad to request NATO's assistance again, and the Alliance furnished airlift and sealift for the transport of supplies donated by NATO and partner countries, as well as nongovernmental organizations.[42] Other countries assisted by NATO after natural disasters include Albania, the Czech Republic, the former Yugoslav Republic of Macedonia, Hungary, Moldova, Portugal, Romania, Turkey, Ukraine, and the United States.[43]

As with the training mission for Iraq, the assistance to the African Union, and the counterpiracy operations, all the NATO Allies contribute, directly or indirectly, to "toolbox" operations and more ambitious undertakings. By providing personnel to NATO's command structure, its International Staff, and other organizations, and by making payments to sustain commonly funded activities, all Allies help to support efforts pursued in the Alliance's name. This general principle also applied to the intervention in the Libyan civil war in 2011, despite the high level of national abstentions from NATO military actions in this conflict.

NATO Air Policing

Some observers would categorize NATO's air policing missions under a "toolbox" or "miscellaneous" heading, but the Allies have in some statements rightly characterized them as part of collective defense. In the 2012 Chicago Summit Declaration the Allies commended the NATO Air Policing Mission in the Baltic states: "This peacetime mission and other Alliance air policing arrangements demonstrate the Alliance's continued and visible commitment to collective defence and solidarity."[44]

The Baltic air policing mission began in April 2004 under the authority of SACEUR. It involves the continuous readiness of armed fighter aircraft from NATO nations at Lithuania's Siauliai Air Base. This base has been modernized, thanks in part to NATO's commonly funded Security Investment Program. The standard deployment of each contributing NATO nation in succession has been four fighter aircraft and 50 to 100 personnel for four months. Fourteen Allies have performed this assignment so far. Their role has been to preserve the airspace integrity of the three Baltic state Allies against adverse incidents, violations, and infringements. This contributes to the preparedness for collective defense of Estonia, Latvia, and Lithuania, and of the Alliance as a whole.

Slovenia has benefited from similar air policing under Alliance auspices since 2004, with its airspace covered by Italian air assets, while air policing for Albania has been provided since 2009 by Greek and Italian air defense assets. The Allies regard cooperation in air policing as an example of "smart defense" in that the beneficiaries can dedicate their scarce defense resources to other tasks in support of the Alliance's purposes.[45]

In contrast with the continuous air policing for Albania, Estonia, Latvia, Lithuania, and Slovenia, the Allies have established a different approach for what they term "airborne surveillance and interception capabilities to meet Iceland's peacetime preparedness needs." Since 2008 Allies have cooperated in sustaining "a periodic presence" of NATO fighter aircraft at Keflavik. Allies have conducted air defense training in Iceland three times a year, with each training deployment lasting three to four weeks. The training maintains the skills of the Icelandic staff and enables the contributing Allies to hone their capabilities in a demanding environment. Each deployment includes a demonstration that "involves arming and disarming NATO aircraft before and, usually, after a quick-reaction training 'scramble,' which is conducted to exercise the air surveillance and control system."[46]

NATO and Libya

The Alliance's involvement in Libya began in the context of the so-called Arab Spring: a wave of protests, civil uprisings, and demonstrations in many Arab countries under way since December 2010. In Libya the protests against the Muammar Qadhafi regime, in power since 1969, began peacefully in mid-February 2011. The regime responded with violence, however. Some commentators, officials, and political leaders in Alliance countries raised the question of a possible intervention by NATO. Secretary General Rasmussen said on February 24, 2011, "I would like to stress that NATO as such has no plans to intervene. We have not received any request in that regard and any actions should be based on a UN mandate."[47]

The UN Security Council approved the first of two mandates about Libya on February 26, 2011. UNSCR 1970 referred the situation in Libya after February 15, 2011 (the date of the initial protests in Benghazi) to the Prosecutor of the International Criminal Court (ICC), imposed an arms embargo on Libya, and established travel bans and asset freezes on key figures in the Qadhafi regime.[48]

The Security Council endorsed the second mandate regarding the Libyan situation on March 17, 2011. UNSCR 1973 authorized "Member States that have notified the Secretary-General, acting nationally or through regional organizations or arrangements, and acting in cooperation with the Secretary-General, to take all necessary measures . . . to protect civilians and civilian populated areas under threat of attack in the Libyan Arab Jamahiriya, including Benghazi, while excluding a foreign occupation force of any form on any part of Libyan territory." This resolution also called for enforcement of a no-fly zone, redefined the terms of the arms embargo established in UNSCR 1970, and extended the scope of the asset freeze decided in UNSCR 1970.[49]

The next day, on March 18, 2011, the NATO secretary general announced that "NATO is now completing its planning in order to be ready to take appropriate action in support of the United Nations Security Council Resolution 1973, as part of the broad international effort. There is an urgent need, firm support from the region and a clear UN mandate for necessary international action. Allies stand behind the legitimate aspirations of the Libyan people for freedom, democracy and human rights."[50]

Rasmussen had worded his statement artfully: while all Allies could express support for "the legitimate aspirations of the Libyan people for freedom, democracy and human rights," one prominent member state (Germany) had abstained in the UN Security Council vote on resolution 1973,[51] and half of the Allies did not participate in NATO's military operations concerning the Libyan situation.

Germany's position was distinctive. Angela Merkel, the chancellor, declared, "We unreservedly share the aims of this resolution [UNSCR 1973]. Our abstention should not be confused with neutrality."[52] In March 2011, however, the German government withdrew its personnel serving in NATO AWACS aircraft away from Libya no-fly zone enforcement and "detached German Navy ships in the Mediterranean from NATO command."[53] These steps were apparently intended to avoid a risk—or perception—of German operational involvement in the NATO-led intervention to implement UNSCR 1973. At the same time German personnel continued their work in NATO's military command structure and other NATO institutions, and Germany did not oppose the use of commonly funded NATO assets, including AWACS, by the Allies taking part in Operations Odyssey Dawn and Unified Protector.[54]

Moreover, in March 2011 the German Parliament approved the government's proposal to send up to 300 German military personnel to Afghanistan to conduct NATO AWACS surveillance operations and thereby lessen the burden on Allies taking action in Libya.[55] German defense minister Thomas de Maizière said that the German government's decision in this regard was a "political sign of our solidarity with the alliance."[56] In August 2011 Merkel declared, "We back our allies and I have the deepest respect for NATO's involvement. . . . As for our side, we pursued political and economic sanctions against the regime. . . . Germany will participate in a supporting role when a new Libya will be rebuilt."[57]

The use of force by outside powers began on March 19, 2011, with air strikes by France, the United Kingdom, and the United States. The United States Africa Command exercised strategic command initially and coordinated operations until responsibility could be transferred to NATO. On March 22, 2011, the NATO secretary general announced that NATO had decided to enforce the arms embargo, and on the following day he added that it would also enforce the no-fly zone.[58] NATO command of the enforcement of the arms embargo began on March 23, 2011, followed by the no-fly zone on March 25 and the operations to protect civilians on March 31.[59]

It had appeared for a few days that there might be, as Rasmussen put it, "a coalition operation and a NATO operation."[60] That is, NATO would be responsible for enforcing the arms embargo and the no-fly zone, and a coalition of powers would undertake the more politically contentious task of conducting air strikes designed "to protect civilians and civilian populated areas under threat of attack," as indicated in UNSCR 1973.

France in particular favored retaining the control of air strikes under a coalition distinct from the Alliance and led by Britain, France, and the United States. France invited neither Turkey nor the NATO secretary general to the meeting in Paris on March 19, 2011, at which President Sarkozy announced that France was initiating air strikes against targets in Libya.[61]

Paris reportedly accepted a compromise arrangement, however. Under this arrangement, NATO was to have command responsibility for all the military operations, including the civilian protection mission, but political oversight would be exercised by a committee composed of the states actually taking part in these operations.[62] As noted, by March 31, 2011, the Allies had extended the scope of NATO's Operation Unified Protector, initially limited to the naval arms embargo, to command of all the military operations.[63]

The political oversight committee distinct from NATO envisaged in late March 2011 was in practice displaced by the North Atlantic Council and the Contact Group on Libya. On April 14, 2011, NATO foreign ministers drew a distinction between the role of the Contact Group "in providing wider political guidance" and that of the North Atlantic Council in supplying "political direction of the military mission . . . with the indispensable involvement of its OUP partners."[64]

The Contact Group on Libya first met on April 13, 2011. The participants included delegates from twenty-one countries and representatives from the Arab League, the Cooperation Council for the Arab Gulf States, the European Union, NATO, the Organization of the Islamic Conference,[65] and the United Nations. The Contact Group concluded at its first meeting that "Qadhafi and his regime had lost all legitimacy and he must leave power allowing the Libyan people to determine their own future." To that end, "Participants supported the efforts of the UN to help the Libyan people develop a political transition plan and such constitutional and electoral processes as may be required to establish a democratically elected government which represents their interests."[66]

In April 2011 the foreign ministers of the NATO Allies announced their goals in Libya in relation to the tempo of strike operations:

> A high operational tempo against legitimate targets will be maintained and we will exert this pressure as long as necessary and until the following objectives are achieved:
>
> 1. All attacks and threats of attack against civilians and civilian-populated areas have ended;
>
> 2. The regime has verifiably withdrawn to bases all military forces, including snipers, mercenaries and other para-military forces, including from all populated areas they have forcibly entered, occupied or besieged throughout all of Libya . . . ;

3. The regime must permit immediate, full, safe and unhindered humanitarian access to all the people in Libya in need of assistance.[67]

The defense ministers of the NATO Allies reaffirmed these goals in June 2011. They added that, once these goals had been fulfilled, "NATO stands ready to play a role, if requested and if necessary, in support of post-conflict efforts that should be initiated by the United Nations and the Contact Group on Libya."[68]

In other words, NATO's immediate practical goals were limited to enforcing the arms embargo and no-fly zone and protecting civilians, as per the relevant Security Council resolutions. However, the Allies looked beyond these goals and endorsed the regime-change goals articulated by the Contact Group on Libya. In April 2011 the NATO foreign ministers backed the Contact Group's "call for Qadhafi to leave power."[69] In June 2011 the NATO defense ministers declared, "Time is working against Qadhafi who has clearly lost all legitimacy and therefore needs to step down."[70] In a coauthored article in April 2011, the British prime minister and the presidents of France and the United States also called for Qadhafi to surrender power:

> Our duty and our mandate under U.N. Security Council Resolution 1973 is to protect civilians, and we are doing that. It is not to remove Qaddafi by force. But it is impossible to imagine a future for Libya with Qaddafi in power.... So long as Qaddafi is in power, NATO must maintain its operations so that civilians remain protected and the pressure on the regime builds. Then a genuine transition from dictatorship to an inclusive constitutional process can really begin.... Qaddafi must go and go for good.[71]

The distinction between what UNSCR 1973 mandated and what NATO Allies judged necessary for Libya's constitutional future matters because Russia has continued to maintain that the Alliance set out and pursued goals going beyond what the Security Council authorized—protecting civilians and enforcing the arms embargo and no-fly zone. The Russians have also argued that the French airdrops of weapons and the insertion of expert advisers by various Allies and coalition partners into Libya constituted violations of the arms embargo.[72] The countries making such arms transfers did so on a national basis, not under the auspices of an agreed NATO policy. Indeed, the French reportedly chose to provide arms "without consulting France's NATO allies."[73]

The official NATO position, as articulated by its secretary general, is that "we have fully complied with the historic mandate of the United Nations to protect the people of Libya, [and] to enforce the no-fly zone and the arms embargo."[74] According to Lieutenant General Charles Bouchard, the NATO commander of the operation, "We stayed focused on the [United Nations] mandate, and stayed well within it."[75]

In March 2011 Rasmussen said, "The 28 NATO Allies have now decided to take on the enforcement of the no-fly zone over Libya."[76] In another statement, Rasmussen said, "All NATO Allies are committed to fulfill their obligations under the UN resolution."[77]

In fact, however, only fourteen of the twenty-eight NATO Allies provided air or naval forces in the operations concerning Libya (Belgium, Bulgaria, Canada,

Denmark, France, Greece, Italy, the Netherlands, Norway, Romania, Spain, Turkey, the United Kingdom, and the United States). Of these fourteen Allies, only eight participated in strike operations (Belgium, Canada, Denmark, France, Italy, Norway, the United Kingdom, and the United States). After Norway withdrew from Operation Unified Protector on August 1, 2011, seven of the twenty-eight Allies participated in strike operations.[78] Some Allied observers saw Operation Unified Protector as an ironic aspirational name for the intervention, given the manifest lack of unity in the Alliance.

Five non-NATO countries contributed to the NATO-led intervention in Libya: Jordan, Morocco, Qatar, Sweden, and the United Arab Emirates.[79] Morocco's contribution consisted of intelligence support rather than forces, and Morocco participated in meetings of the North Atlantic Council in Operation Unified Protector format.[80] Jordan reportedly contributed twelve aircraft (transports and fighter escort jets)[81] but did not publicize its role. Swedish aircraft conducted air defense and reconnaissance missions, while Qatar and the United Arab Emirates conducted air strike missions.[82] According to an unnamed British Ministry of Defense official, "The countries that deserve most credit in this conflict are Qatar and the United Arab Emirates. They provided the rebels with the training and weapons they needed, and acted as their leaders."[83] In October 2011, after Qadhafi's death, Qatar revealed that "it had deployed hundreds of soldiers in Libya to help" the anti-Qadhafi forces, as well as providing "air support, water, weapons and hundreds of millions of dollars worth of other aid," with "Qataris . . . 'running the training and communication operations' of the anti-Qaddafi forces."[84]

In June 2011, Robert Gates, in one of his last speeches as secretary of defense, deplored the deficiencies in Allied capabilities revealed by the Libya operations.

> Frankly, many of those allies sitting on the sidelines do so not because they do not want to participate, but simply because they can't. The military capabilities simply aren't there. In particular, intelligence, surveillance, and reconnaissance assets are lacking that would allow more allies to be involved and make an impact. The most advanced fighter aircraft are little use if allies do not have the means to identify, process, and strike targets as part of an integrated campaign. To run the air campaign, the NATO air operations center in Italy required a major augmentation of targeting specialists, mainly from the U.S., to do the job—a "just in time" infusion of personnel that may not always be available in future contingencies. We have the spectacle of an air operations center designed to handle more than 300 sorties a day struggling to launch about 150. Furthermore, the mightiest military alliance in history is only 11 weeks into an operation against a poorly armed regime in a sparsely populated country—yet many allies are beginning to run short of munitions, requiring the U.S., once more, to make up the difference.[85]

In this statement Gates emphasized that many Allies lack capabilities suitable for modern air operations, and this was no doubt a major factor ruling out contributions by most NATO Allies in Central and Eastern Europe.[86]

With some Allies, however, nonparticipation derived from political choices. In a meeting of NATO defense ministers in June 2011 Gates criticized Germany and Poland, two Allies with substantial numbers of modern combat aircraft, for choosing not to participate in Operation Unified Protector. He also argued that the Netherlands, Spain, and Turkey should expand the scope of their participation beyond enforcing the no-fly zone to encompass ground-attack sorties and/or reconnaissance or in-flight refueling.[87]

As with Afghanistan, some Allies expressed recriminations over perceived deficiencies in burden sharing. For example, in July 2011 Liam Fox, then the British defense minister, said, "There are rather too many absentees, which is unfair on our defence forces."[88] Some French observers argued, however, that the British committed "far less" to the Libya operations than the French.[89]

During the intervention both British and French officials deplored the fact that the United States considerably scaled back its operational involvement after taking a strong role in the initial strike operations against Libyan air defenses from March 19 to April 4, 2011.[90] In retrospect, however, as early as February 2012 London and Paris hailed their joint leadership in the intervention: "Our cooperation in Libya has been a defining moment—and one on which we will continue to build in the future. . . . France and the UK successfully answered a UN call for civilians in Libya to be protected and led the NATO mission. The shared experience has validated and accelerated our cooperation."[91]

On March 26, 2011, President Obama said that "responsibility for this operation is being transferred from the United States to our NATO allies and partners."[92] The president elaborated on March 28 as follows:

> Our most effective alliance, NATO, has taken command of the enforcement of the arms embargo and the no-fly zone. Last night, NATO decided to take on the additional responsibility of protecting Libyan civilians. . . . In that effort, the United States will play a supporting role—including intelligence, logistical support, search and rescue assistance, and capabilities to jam regime communications.[93]

Despite reports that the last U.S. strike operations in Libya to protect civilians took place on April 4, 2011,[94] U.S. forces continued to conduct strikes as well as support operations. During the first twelve days of April 2011 the United States flew 35 percent of all sorties in the Libyan effort, with the rest conducted by the other participating NATO Allies and the four non-NATO countries participating in the air operations (Jordan, Qatar, Sweden, and the United Arab Emirates). The U.S. contribution included 77 percent of the aerial refueling sorties and 27 percent of sorties for intelligence, reconnaissance, and surveillance (ISR).[95]

In view of the fact that NATO's air campaign in the Kosovo conflict lasted seventy-eight days, in June 2011 the *Financial Times* compared the Kosovo and Libya air operations over the same duration. At the seventy-eight-day point, the Libya campaign had seen 11,107 sorties, of which 4,212 were strike sorties, while the Kosovo conflict had involved 38,004 sorties, of which 10,484 were strike sorties. The numerical differences stemmed in part from the divergent numbers of aircraft committed. There were 1,100 Allied aircraft operating by the close of the Kosovo campaign, but only 250 Allied aircraft were in action in the Libya conflict at the seventy-eight-day point.[96]

The reduced level of U.S. participation in strike operations also helps to explain the disparities. In the Kosovo conflict, the United States flew 61 percent of all sorties, and the other NATO Allies flew the remaining 39 percent.[97] During the course of the intervention in Libya, the U.S. share of the sorties declined, and by the end of Operation Unified Protector the United States had flown only "a quarter of all sorties over Libya." Moreover, in contrast with NATO's air campaign in the Kosovo conflict, in which the United States employed "90 percent of all precision-guided munitions," non-U.S. "Allies struck 90 percent of the more than 6,000 targets destroyed in Libya."[98]Such a low level of U.S. participation in a major NATO combat operation was unprecedented. It has been attributed in part to an Obama administration policy of "leading from behind"[99] and in part to the controversy that the Libya intervention generated in U.S. politics. U.S. restraint helped to account for the leading roles of France and the United Kingdom, which together "flew one third of all missions" and struck "over 40 percent of all targets."[100]

Despite the comparatively low level of U.S. participation—and the complete lack of participation in air or naval operations by half of the Allies—the countries taking part in the NATO-led operations achieved their declared goals. In June 2011 the NATO defense ministers declared, "By maintaining a high operational tempo and carrying out precision strikes against legitimate military targets, we have seriously degraded the ability of the Qadhafi regime to attack civilians and relieved the pressure on civilian populated areas such as Misratah."[101] In July 2011 Oana Lungescu, the NATO spokesperson, offered the following assessment:

> We are continuing to successfully fulfil the mandate, the arms embargo is effective, the No-Fly Zone is effective, and there are no coordinated attacks by regime forces against civilians. Where we see an attack, or the threat of attack, we take it out, exactly as mandated by UN Security Council Resolution 1973.... So NATO and our partners are doing the job they were mandated to do. That's the military job. We will continue to do it until the three clear military goals have been met. An end to all attacks against civilians, the withdrawal of all regime forces to bases and full and unhindered humanitarian access.[102]

She underscored the Alliance's restrained political role: "NATO is doing its job on the military track. It is for others, in particular the United Nations and the Contact Group to take the lead on the political track."[103]

The effective removal of Qadhafi from power in August 2011 raised the question of the character of the successor regime. In June 2011 a journalist pointed out that opposition groups in Iraq had provided false information about supposed WMD in the country and asked whether the NATO Allies might be misled by opposition groups in Libya as to their intentions. Secretary General Rasmussen replied, "There are many contacts with the opposition and we have got a pretty clear picture of the composition of the opposition."[104] In October 2011, he said, "I take it for granted that the new authorities in Libya will live up to their international responsibility, will live up to the basic principles of democracy, including the respect for the rule of law and human rights."[105]

The Allies concluded Operation Unified Protector on October 31, 2011. Rasmussen said in October 2011, "If requested, we can assist the new Libyan government in the transformation to democracy, for instance with defense and security sector reform. But I wouldn't expect new tasks beyond that."[106] He repeated this offer in September 2012, and said that "it is a matter of concern that individual and independent armed groups operate without superior control in Libya."[107]

In December 2012, Russian president Vladimir Putin described the intervention in Libya by the NATO Allies as "a mistake" and added, "No matter how they explained their position, the state is falling apart. . . . Interethnic, interclan and intertribal conflicts continue. Moreover, it went as far as the murder of the United States ambassador."[108]

Experts associated with NATO have speculated that the Alliance may in future, at the request of the Libyan government, establish a training mission on the model of its training missions in Afghanistan and Iraq. Moreover, Libya may eventually choose to join NATO's Mediterranean Dialogue.[109]

Despite NATO's avoidance so far of a ground role in Libya, its intervention in 2011 has implicated it in Libya's future. As Florence Gaub has observed, "Whether the Alliance likes it or not, its reputation is at stake in Libya's long reconstruction process."[110] At present the prospect of NATO assuming a role in Libya analogous to its missions in the Balkans and Afghanistan—providing security in support of work by other international organizations—appears remote, but it cannot be ruled out completely.

When the Libyan prime minister visited NATO Headquarters in May 2013, Secretary General Rasmussen was careful not to go beyond repeating earlier offers of Alliance assistance "in the reform of security and defence sectors, especially when it comes to institutional education and training," and to add, "let me stress, just to avoid any misunderstanding, this is not about deploying NATO troops to Libya. This is about technical assistance upon request of the Libyan Government."[111] In June 2013 the NATO defense ministers approved a "decision to send an expert delegation to Libya to identify how NATO could best respond to the request by the Libyan Prime Minister for NATO advice on the development of the country's national security forces."[112]

Such assistance, and probably much more from the European Union, the United Nations, and others, will almost certainly be needed if Libya is to address its enormous challenges successfully. As Florence Gaub pointed out in June 2013,

> What began as a popular uprising . . . has now turned into a potentially toxic security vacuum. . . . The National Transitional Council, Libya's interim decision-making body, rejected in-country support (such as a UN observer mission) but failed to propose a sound alternative. Instead, security was managed provisionally in pockets—by emerging neighbourhood watch organisations, revolutionary brigades under no or limited supervision, or simply by armed gangs pursuing criminal goals.[113]

The upheavals within Libya affect not only the Libyan people but also their neighbors. The disorders in Libya since the fall of the Qadhafi regime, notably in the southern part of the country, have become linked to the wider instability in the Sahel, including Mali. NATO, the European Union, the United Nations, and other organizations may conclude that it is in their interest to take more action than has seemed necessary to date.

Libya in Comparison with Afghanistan and the Balkans

NATO's intervention in the Libya conflict was, as a British expert observed, "the anti-Afghanistan." Compared with the operation in Afghanistan, the action in Libya was brief and cheap, and there was no "quagmire" sensation.[114] In contrast with Afghanistan and the Balkans, NATO did not assume any long-term role on the ground in Libya in support of state building or nation building.

As noted in chapter 4, NATO's operational engagement in the Balkans has been under way since 1992 and promises to continue indefinitely, notably via KFOR. NATO has been leading ISAF in Afghanistan since 2003, and training, advising, and assisting functions under Alliance auspices are envisaged well beyond the end of NATO participation in combat operations at the end of 2014. In contrast with the Alliance's lengthy and ongoing involvement in the Balkans and Afghanistan, its intervention in the Libya conflict lasted only about seven months, from late March through late October 2011.

The United States had lost 2,155 service members in the Afghan war and related operations by January 2013,[115] while none of the NATO Allies suffered any fatalities among their forces in the Libya intervention. The absence of combat fatalities for NATO made Operation Unified Protector in Libya similar to Operation Deliberate Force in Bosnia and Operation Allied Force in the Kosovo conflict.

Comparing financial costs is difficult because published information is generally fragmentary and not calculated in terms of constant dollars. Moreover, aggregate cost figures accounting for the participation of all the NATO Allies and partners in specific operations do not appear to be available. It is nonetheless worth recalling that in 1999 the annual cost of the U.S. contribution to peacekeeping in Bosnia was estimated to be $1.8 billion, while that in Kosovo was projected to be $2 billion to $3.5 billion per year.[116] The United States planned to spend $113 billion on military operations in Afghanistan in fiscal year 2011, and the U.S. Department of Defense proposed to spend $12.8 billion in fiscal year 2012 simply "to continue training and equipping Afghan soldiers."[117] In contrast, the intervention in the Libya conflict in 2011 cost the United States "just over $1 billion."[118]

NATO's ambitions in Libya in 2011 were much less extensive than they have been in the Balkans and Afghanistan. In the Libya case NATO acted at a distance to enforce the no-fly zone and arms embargo and to protect civilians. These actions effectively supported the local regime-changers, assisted by Qatar and the United Arab Emirates, who took the lead on the ground.

In contrast with NATO's operations in Afghanistan, Operation Allied Force in 1999 and Operation Unified Protector in 2011 had in common a focus on influencing the decision making of a single individual—Milošević and Gadhafi, respectively. In 1999, however, the Allies were prepared to undertake a peacekeeping operation on the ground in Kosovo of indefinite duration, while in 2011 they made clear their determination to avoid such responsibilities in Libya. This determination remained firm, despite the humanitarian considerations that furnished a motive for intervention in each case. As Adrian Hamilton wrote in a British newspaper, "We went into Libya because politicians (understandably) didn't want to see another Srebrenica in Benghazi on their television screens."[119]

In the Balkans, notably since the initiation of peacekeeping in Bosnia in 1995 and in Kosovo in 1999, the Alliance has worked with the United Nations, the European Union, and other international organizations to promote state building and cooperation. In Afghanistan NATO forces have been engaged in combat on the ground, and their objective has been to provide security for international efforts to strengthen the regime and enable it to resist the local insurgency and become an effective government.

The Allies closed the Libya case in October 2011, though they are open to the idea of assisting the new Libyan government in limited ways, if requested to do so, perhaps via Libyan participation in NATO's Mediterranean Dialogue. In contrast, NATO's combat operations in Afghanistan are expected to continue until 2014, with a new noncombat train, advise, and assist mission, as well as an enduring partnership, envisaged after that date. The duration of the Alliance's peacekeeping engagement in the Balkans is even more open-ended.

Despite its brevity and comparatively small scale, the intervention in the Libya conflict shared various characteristics with NATO's long and extensive engagements in the Balkans and Afghanistan. These characteristics include the Alliance's reliance on UN Security Council mandates,[120] national caveats among the NATO Allies on whether and how to participate in operations, and dependence on the United States to provide key capabilities.

Implications of the Libya Intervention for NATO

Without the initial suppression of Libyan air defenses, accomplished mainly by the United States, and the U.S. provision of critical enabling capabilities (including intelligence, electronic warfare, and aerial refueling), the Alliance and its coalition partners could not have accomplished the mission. The United States furnished 75 percent of the aerial refueling planes and 75 percent of the ISR information.[121] A widely reported confidential NATO report concluded that "NATO remains overly reliant on a single ally to provide I.S.R. collection capabilities that are essential to the commander."[122] The United States also served as the main supplier of precision munitions for Allies running low in their national stockpiles.[123]

The NATO secretary general highlighted the capability shortcomings of certain Allies in November 2011: "The Libya operation . . . made visible that some European allies lack critical capabilities, in particular within intelligence, surveillance, reconnaissance and air-to-air refueling. . . . I urge those allies to focus their defense investments in these areas to acquire the needed capabilities."[124] It is noteworthy in this respect that France and the United Kingdom in February 2012 declared as a fundamental lesson from the Libya intervention the need "to prioritise our joint work in the key areas of: command and control; information systems; intelligence, surveillance, targeting and reconnaissance; and precision munitions."[125]

Allied acquisition of such capabilities is all the more imperative in light of the fact that the United States chose to limit its operational roles to an unprecedented extent in the Libya intervention. As James Blitz of the *Financial Times* has observed, "The Libya conflict of 2011 . . . may . . . come to be seen as the point when the US signalled to the nations of Europe that they must start thinking harder about how to provide security in their own backyard."[126]

Indeed, despite its modest dimensions, the Libya operation may have strengthened the tendency of self-selected Allies and partners to form "coalitions of the willing." The traditional approach—a legacy of the Cold War focus on collective defense as NATO's core mission—called for all Allies to participate in some fashion in all non-Article 5 operations. The Libya intervention was the clearest indication to date that the "in together, out together" principle is beginning to fade. This may be inevitable as the Allies undertake more and more operations. Some NATO experts judge that it would be unrealistic to expect all Allies to participate in all non-Article 5 operations. In their view, coalitions of the willing are increasingly a fact of life. Coalition members may be volunteers from among the NATO Allies and partners. Some Allies may act while others abstain constructively by supporting the operation politically and endorsing the use of commonly funded NATO assets and facilities.[127]

Admiral James G. Stavridis, then SACEUR, said in October 2011 that the Libya intervention demonstrated that the capacity of NATO Allies to undertake such operations has been enhanced by their combined efforts in Afghanistan. "NATO works, and it can work at speed. . . . The difference is that 10 years of integrated operations in Afghanistan have created an alliance that can move quickly, can move with alacrity—not without controversy, not without some nations moving faster and some moving slower and some saying we are not going to participate in this operation."[128]

The open acknowledgment by SACEUR that some Allies may choose not to participate in specific operations shows that expectations have changed. Kurt Volker, a former U.S. ambassador to NATO, has deplored this change as corrosive of Alliance solidarity:

> The concept of an alliance is one of sharing common strategic purposes and being willing to fight together for the common good. . . . This solidarity was already severely damaged by the war in Afghanistan, when despite having agreed to a NATO mission, several allies then put caveats on the use of their forces, such as limiting them to noncombat zones, even when it came to flying medical support missions. . . . Even so, the United States worked hard and successfully made the case that because Afghanistan is a NATO mission, every NATO ally must contribute in some way. And each one did. But if solidarity started fraying in Afghanistan, in the case of

Libya it went out the window...The United States itself became a caveat country, putting limits on the roles it would play and specific capabilities it would contribute in support of the NATO mission in Libya.[129]

In Volker's view, "We can do coalitions of the willing but that's not an alliance."[130]

Other observers take a less restrictive view of what constitutes an alliance. Non-Article 5 interventions are in principle optional, and divergent decisions about whether and how to contribute to them need not necessarily place into question the bedrock foundation of the Alliance, the mutual defense commitment in Article 5 of the North Atlantic Treaty. In support of this commitment the Allies have since 1949 built up a large number of commonly funded assets, including radars, pipelines, headquarters facilities, communications, and command and control networks. If all the Allies agree that a number of their fellow Allies can use these facilities for non-Article 5 purposes, that is obviously their prerogative.

Indeed, some experts maintain that the Alliance's collective assets could serve as an "enabler" or "gap-filler" for Allies undertaking operations with the concurrence of their fellow Allies. Karl-Heinz Kamp, then the head of the research division at the NATO Defense College, has noted that Britain, France, and the United States—the three NATO Allies with the greatest autonomous power-projection capabilities—chose in the end to support conducting the Libya intervention in an Alliance framework. In Kamp's view, "This is a sign, also particularly with regard to lacking money, that in today's times NATO is the enabler. It enables countries to conduct military operations they probably are not able to do alone anymore or willing to do alone."[131]

If some NATO Allies choose to form a coalition for a specific operation, they may find their fellow Allies particularly well-suited to take action in concert with them, owing to the Alliance's efforts over decades to make forces interoperable through exercises and combined action. Political circumstances in particular cases would determine whether nonparticipating Allies would endorse the use of NATO auspices and facilities by the coalition. The coalition members might prefer to take action under NATO auspices to benefit from the Alliance's political capital and legitimacy as well as its assets and facilities, including the command structure. The political constraints of some Allies might prevent them from providing operational support, but they might nonetheless be capable of offering political support through Alliance institutions and commonly funded and staffed facilities. Such an approach has sometimes been termed "constructive abstention."

Some observers have even speculated that the Allies might engage in commonly funded procurement to a greater extent in order to make NATO a more effective "enabler" for coalitions of the willing composed of NATO Allies and partners. According to the long-standing "costs lie where they fall" principle, each member state has been responsible for procuring munitions for its national forces. Given that some of the Allies conducting air strike operations in the Libya intervention ran out of munitions rather quickly and had to turn to the United States for supplies, some observers have asked, should the Allies invest in commonly funded munitions stockpiles? It has been argued that such investments could be a manifestation of solidarity and burden sharing, a hedge against future operational requirements, and a contribution to deterrence.[132]

In 2007, in a widely noted study, retired high-level military officers from Britain, France, Germany, the Netherlands, and the United States called for a common-funding approach to financing Alliance operations:

> New procedures for funding NATO operations are urgently needed. The current cost-sharing system of 'costs lie where they fall' must be abandoned entirely. At present, that means that those who contribute are bearing both the risk of casualties and the financial burden, whereas those who simply talk are rewarded twice. Such a principle can erode NATO's cohesion and it definitely reduces NATO's ability to sustain operations. What is needed is a common cost-sharing formula, to which all allies contribute. We therefore recommend the creation of a commonly financed NATO operations budget.[133]

The NATO-led intervention in the Libya conflict in 2011 has revived proposals for a commonly funded NATO operations budget, but there is no Allied consensus to support such an approach.

A tendency to form NATO-sponsored coalitions of the willing composed of self-selected groups of Allies and partners would not necessarily sap Alliance cohesion. Much would depend on the decisions made in specific cases of crisis management, and on the ability of the Allies to sustain unity in their activities relevant to NATO's other core tasks—collective defense and cooperative security.

Such a tendency would nonetheless present certain risks. If specific Allies consistently abstained from operations, this could lead to a pattern of nonparticipation that could weaken the Alliance. If some Allies avoided investments in expeditionary capabilities suitable for crisis management interventions, this could enhance the likelihood of a "two-tier" Alliance, with certain Allies much more willing and capable of taking action than others.

It is not clear whether an "enabling" model for coalitions drawing on NATO's capacities could be sustained over the long term, given asymmetries in political will and responsibilities sought and assumed. Ellen Hallams and Benjamin Schreer have in this regard discreetly referred to "limited European leadership capacity," as well as well-known divisions within the Alliance.[134]

Moreover, some Allies might question whether Allies that systematically choose not to participate in non-Article 5 crisis management operations would have the political will and capability to meet their obligations in a collective defense contingency. In Afghanistan, in contrast with Libya, all the NATO Allies have made direct practical contributions, and these contributions have in some ways enhanced their capacity to uphold their collective defense commitments.[135]

Another risk in selective à la carte participation in non-Article 5 crisis management operations is that uneven or poor performance by a coalition of Allies and partner countries could undermine the confidence of certain Allies, notably in Central and Eastern Europe, in the reliability of Article 5 collective defense commitments. The political and psychological impact of poor performance by such a coalition might also affect Turkey's confidence in the Alliance's ability to honor Article 5 commitments.

Capabilities for Crisis Management and Collective Defense

To what extent is there a conflict or tension between the Alliance's original and enduring purpose of collective defense and its crisis management functions?[136] This question has been formulated in various ways. For example, some observers have asked, what should be the balance between preparations for Article 5 collective defense missions and conducting non-Article 5 operations, such as crisis response, peacekeeping, humanitarian intervention, and stabilization and reconstruction?

Some Allied observers, notably in Poland and the Baltic states, have suggested that the Alliance's focus of attention has in recent years been too heavily tilted toward non-Article 5 operations and that Russia could in some circumstances become a more fundamental and existential threat than the Taliban or al-Qaeda. Some Allied observers in Italy, Spain, and other nations on the Mediterranean littoral have, however, emphasized the advantages of expeditionary capabilities that could counter potential asymmetric challenges arising in Africa or the Middle East. Canadian, Danish, and Norwegian observers have noted the relevance of expeditionary capabilities for the protection of the national interests of Allies in the "High North."[137] Owing in part to climate change, disputes might arise between Russia and specific Allies over rights of passage and/or ownership of natural resources, such as oil and gas deposits. In 2010, Admiral James Stavridis, then SACEUR, said, "For now, the disputes in the north have been dealt with peacefully, but climate change could alter the equilibrium over the coming years in the race of temptation for exploitation of more readily accessible natural resources."[138]

To what extent is there a contradiction between transforming forces for expeditionary operations and sustaining preparedness for territorial defense? This is to some degree an ill-framed debate. Some capabilities, such as static air defenses, pipelines, and fortified barriers, are indeed expressly designed for territorial defense. Moreover, resources are finite, and forces committed to operations in Afghanistan and other countries distant from NATO national homelands are obviously not on duty for immediate territorial defense. The home base must nonetheless be secure in order to support expeditionary power projection. The authors of a recent report in Washington came up with a concise formula to make this point: "If NATO cannot protect, it cannot project."[139]

Forces capable of conducting expeditionary operations may also be better equipped to undertake collective defense missions. During the Cold War, most of the Allies planned to "fight in place" rather than to project troops or firepower at great distances. Only a few countries, including Canada and the United Kingdom, were prepared to assist the United States with their own dedicated airlift in tasks such as reinforcing Denmark, northern Greece, northern Italy, northern Norway, and eastern Turkey.[140]

The Alliance has expanded from sixteen countries at the end of the Cold War to twenty-eight countries today, and some of these countries can be defended only if their Allies are prepared to project power. In other words, NATO today needs improved expeditionary capabilities not only for crisis response operations distant from Alliance territory but also for collective defense itself. This means investing in airlift and other "strategic mobility" logistical assets, mobile communications networks, combat support, and combat service support.[141] The Allies must be able to project capabilities to every part of the significantly enlarged treaty area. For collective defense and deterrence, they need agile and rapidly deployable forces and high-readiness headquarters.

Lack of agreement on definitions may account for some perceptions of a dichotomy between capabilities suitable for collective or territorial defense, on the one hand, and expeditionary or crisis response operations on the other. Some terminological purists hold that "expeditionary operations" are by definition outside NATO territory and that territorial defense means responding to direct attacks against a member state's territory.

Policymakers do not, however, respect these distinctions in discussing NATO's capability requirements. In October 2009, for example, Ambassador Alexander Vershbow, then the U.S. assistant secretary of defense for international security affairs, said, "We're familiar by now with some of the biggest obstacles the Alliance faces in having deployable expeditionary forces that can do both territorial defense and missions beyond Allied territory."[142] In a speech at the same event, Secretary General Rasmussen said, "We must ... realize that territorial defence very often starts far from our own borders, like in Afghanistan."[143]

The essential point about "expeditionary" operations is that they require movement at "strategic distance."[144] For Canada and the United States, for example, any force deployment to Europe, whether for the territorial defense of a member state or for crisis response beyond allied territory, is an expeditionary operation. NATO's 2006 Comprehensive Political Guidance called for "the ability to conduct and support multinational joint expeditionary operations far from home territory with little or no host nation support and to sustain them for extended periods."[145] Although host nation support might well be available for collective defense, many of the other requirements for the movement of forces from the Atlantic seaboard (from the United Kingdom or France or Portugal or Spain) to the Baltic states or Poland or eastern Turkey or northern Norway would amount to those needed for an expeditionary operation, including strategic mobility and logistical assets, and command, control, and communications. In other words, crisis response and collective defense capability requirements overlap to a considerable extent.

Moreover, expeditionary operations—that is, missions at "strategic distance"—can provide training and experience relevant to possible Article 5 endeavors. The more the Allies demonstrate successfully their ability to conduct demanding non-Article 5 tasks at strategic range—for instance, in the Balkans (which are distant from some

Allies) and Afghanistan—the more they should feel able to rely on each other in an Article 5 contingency.

Expeditionary operations may differ in their demands on forces, however. As Jüri Luik, then the Estonian ambassador to NATO, stated in May 2009, "Training to fight in an Afghan village doesn't necessarily translate into being able to stop a tank in an Article 5 scenario."[146] Similarly, a Lithuanian expert pointed out in June 2012 that "expeditionary forces are trained to deal with poorly armed and trained insurgents, which is not the same as determined conventional armies."[147]

Russia's armed intervention in Georgia in 2008 has led some Allied observers to underscore the distinction between forces designed for high-intensity combat and those prepared for peacekeeping in the Balkans and counterinsurgency operations in Afghanistan. By this logic, the NATO Allies need to renew their investments in fighter aircraft, precision-guided antiarmor munitions, and maritime forces.[148]

Given the need to curtail casualties in military operations, particularly in what are widely seen as "optional" crisis management and peace support operations, the Alliance needs to maintain capabilities to perform such operations with minimal risks. The political sustainability of non-Article 5 operations depends on reducing risks of casualties, and this necessitates an ability to dominate the field in crisis contingencies. In other words, practical factors—including the need to be able to counter asymmetric threats—justify the maintenance of a substantial conventional military posture, even when large-scale collective defense contingencies appear remote.

Certain steps to improve the Alliance's collective defense capabilities—for example, enhanced situational awareness and command structures—could also support more effective action in non-Article 5 operations. Crisis management operations serve the security interests of the Allies, albeit without the immediacy of preparations for collective defense of Alliance territory in response to direct aggression. The Alliance's agreed-on force transformation goal is to sustain reliable capabilities across the full spectrum of missions.[149]

Crisis Management in Support of Collective Defense

Although the traditional meaning of collective defense—action by the Allies to counter "an armed attack" against any member state— remains valid, the distinction between Article 5 and non-Article 5 operations has become less clear-cut and more elusive, at least in some circumstances. On some occasions the Allies have undertaken crisis management operations in support of collective defense, in that one of their objectives has been to prevent the development of conditions that could lead to threats to their security. Moreover, in some cases the Allies have offered security commitments in support of their crisis management efforts.

During the Balkan conflicts of the 1990s, for example, NATO found it advisable at times to extend security assurances to states neighboring the Federal Republic of Yugoslavia—in effect, promises of protection against possible retaliation by Belgrade for cooperation with the Alliance. The Alliance expressed such security assurances most explicitly during the 1999 Kosovo conflict, when the neighboring states—Albania, Bosnia and Herzegovina, Bulgaria, Croatia, the former Yugoslav Republic of Macedonia, Romania, and Slovenia—helped the Allies by aiding refugees, hosting NATO forces, granting access to airspace for operations, and/or imposing economic sanctions.[150] In April 1999, NATO heads of state and government met with representatives of these seven states and "reaffirmed that the security of the neighbouring states was of direct and material concern to Alliance member states and that NATO would respond to any challenges by Belgrade to the neighbouring states resulting from the presence of NATO forces and their activities on their territory during this crisis."[151]

In other words, in order to conduct non-Article 5 crisis management operations, the NATO Allies chose to extend security commitments to third parties. These security commitments were, however, circumscribed and not equivalent to Article 5 pledges.

NATO's role in leading ISAF in Afghanistan has been mandated by UN Security Council resolutions, and the Allies generally regard it as a non-Article 5 operation. It should nonetheless be recalled that the UN Security Council first established ISAF in December 2001 in circumstances deriving from what the NATO Allies had declared an Article 5 contingency. The United States and its coalition partners in Operation Enduring Freedom, including several NATO Allies, intervened in Afghanistan in response to al-Qaeda's attacks in New York and Washington on September 11, 2001. These attacks led the NATO Allies to invoke Article 5 of the North Atlantic Treaty, and they took several steps to facilitate the conduct of Operation Enduring Freedom and to help ensure the defeat of the Taliban regime in Afghanistan, which had served as a base of operations for the al-Qaeda terrorist network.[152]

The UN Security Council authorized the establishment of ISAF because the United States and its coalition partners (many of them NATO Allies) had forcibly ousted the Taliban regime. ISAF's initial mission was "to assist the Afghan Interim Authority in the maintenance of security in Kabul and its surrounding areas, so that the Afghan Interim Authority as well as the personnel of the United Nations can operate in a secure environment."[153] From the outset, NATO member states (including the United States) have contributed most of the forces in ISAF. Moreover, as noted previously, ISAF was led by a series of NATO Allies—the United Kingdom, Turkey, Germany and the Netherlands—from December 2001 to August 2003, when it became a NATO-led operation.

NATO's subsequent contributions to the implementation of the 2006 Afghanistan Compact and other measures intended to promote the establishment of a stable and democratic government in the country may be regarded as moves to prevent the return of the Taliban to power and to block the reconstitution of al-Qaeda terrorist training camps and operational headquarters there. In other words, these measures may be considered actions intended to prevent the reemergence of an Article 5 threat. To quote a UN Security Council resolution in December 2001, the goal is "to help the people of Afghanistan to bring to an end the tragic conflicts in Afghanistan and promote national reconciliation, lasting peace, stability and respect for human rights, as well as to cooperate with the international community to put an end to the use of Afghanistan as a base for terrorism."[154] Thus there may be an element of collective defense in a nominally non-Article 5 crisis management operation. The security of the Allies may depend on events far from their national territories, and the Allies clearly have incentives to deal with emerging threats at their source, whenever possible.

Other factors also tend to obscure the difference between collective defense (Article 5) and crisis management (non-Article 5) operations. While the Alliance's Balkan and Afghanistan operations are all officially regarded as non-Article 5 operations, the NATO Allies have suffered greater casualties in combat in Afghanistan since 2001 than they have incurred in their operations in the Balkans since 1992.

Moreover, the NATO Allies face a genuine threat of terrorist attacks against their homelands, and these attacks may be portrayed by their perpetrators and sympathizers as retaliation for NATO's intervention in Afghanistan—to say nothing of other grievances that might be cited by terrorists. In short, NATO's ostensibly non-Article 5 engagement in Afghanistan differs from its Balkan operations because it originated in what the Allies regarded as an Article 5 contingency—an act of aggression against a NATO member state—and because it involves greater combat and homeland security risks.

Some of NATO's newest Allies have underscored another connection between collective defense and crisis management operations: combined action in support of collective defense in Europe may enable Allies to devote resources to a crisis management operation far from Europe. In 2009, Rasa Jukneviciene, then the Lithuanian defense minister, said that

> Lithuania sees the need for the right balance between the Alliance's core function [of collective defense] and out-of-area operations. These directions of the Alliance activities have to complement and reinforce each other. A good example of such synergy is [the] NATO Regional Air Policing Mission in the Baltic States. It provides us with a quality security reassurance and enables the Baltic States to devote our scarce national resources to contributing to the Alliance's ongoing operations, especially currently in Afghanistan. Thus, in ISAF, Lithuania leads a Provincial Reconstruction Team under Regional Command West and provides a special operations forces contingent in the troublesome Region South.[155]

Finally, it should be noted that the Alliance's "procedural machinery" for combined operations, including collective defense, derives to a large extent from its experiences in crisis management operations since the early 1990s. These experiences inform the NATO Defense Planning Process, the NATO Crisis Response System, the Guidelines for Operational Planning, and the Comprehensive Operations Planning Directive.

Collective Defense Arising from Crisis Management

The danger that a non-Article 5 crisis management mission could turn into a collective defense contingency has been present since 1992, when the Allies first undertook such operations in the Balkans. In both the Bosnia and Kosovo conflicts there were incidents in which the NATO Allies faced a risk of confrontation with Russia.[156] NATO forces operating in Afghanistan or another location distant from their national territories could face attacks by a foreign government (as opposed to attacks by terrorists or insurgents), and these attacks might be conducted with conventional forces and/or nuclear, chemical, or biological weapons.

The core security interests of NATO or of specific Allies could be affected by such attacks. If NATO forces came under attack by a foreign government outside the Article 6 area, how would the Allies respond? Would they regard such an attack as an Article 5 case? If core security interests came under attack, the Allies might choose to treat this as an Article 5 collective defense contingency—even if the attack took place outside the Article 6 area. Given that deterrence may require sending messages about vital interests, the NATO Allies may find it prudent to state that their vital interests include their armed forces when they are engaged in Alliance operations beyond the geographic area of Article 6.

A related question concerns nuclear protection for Allied forces conducting operations outside the geographic area defined in Article 6. If a country used a nuclear weapon to attack NATO forces deployed outside Alliance territory, the Allies would have to consider whether to make a nuclear response. Should nuclear deterrence regarding such a contingency be a matter for possible national policy declarations by Britain, France, and the United States, the Alliance's three nuclear-weapon states? Or should the NATO Allies make a statement about such a contingency? Would it be sufficient to rely on the fact that there is an inherent nuclear dimension in the military operations undertaken by any nuclear-weapon state?

In addressing these questions, it should be recognized that some doctrinal differences among NATO's three nuclear-weapon states persist, and that these three allies long resisted the definition of an Alliance policy on, for example, negative security assurances, on the grounds that such commitments are matters of national policy.[157] The statement by the Allies about negative security assurances in the May 2012 Deterrence and Defense Posture Review underscored the fact that the British, French, and U.S. negative security assurances are "independent and unilateral" commitments by the three NATO nuclear-weapon states.[158]

Moreover, taking up the issue of nuclear protection outside NATO territory might reignite debates such as that which took place in France in the late 1970s concerning the implications of deploying nuclear weapons on aircraft carriers operating far from the national homeland. Some French observers asked whether the nation's nuclear-armed aircraft carriers should be regarded as protected by nuclear deterrence in the same way as the national homeland. Or should France's nuclear deterrence capabilities be reserved for the protection of more narrowly defined vital interests, such as the national territory?[159] Possible nuclear deterrence contingencies involving the conventional military forces of NATO Allies in operations distant from Alliance territory appear to have received little public attention.

NATO's engagement in Afghanistan suggests that the Allies have recognized the need for preventive action—that is, military operations intended to provide a security environment for political, social, and economic reconstruction and thereby to avert the emergence of new terrorist threats. In 2005 Jaap de Hoop Scheffer, then the NATO secretary general, said, "A passive, reactive approach may have been alright during the Cold War. It clearly has become insufficient now. Either we tackle the challenges to our security when and where they emerge, or they will end up on our doorstep."[160] The anticipatory use of force remains controversial, however, and inextricably linked to debates among the Allies about legality and moral legitimacy.[161]

Conclusion

NATO's operations have demonstrated that the Allies can take action and attract military contributions from partner nations, despite the problems of caveats, abstentions, and resource shortfalls. The continuing challenge for the Allies is to work out through experience the right balance between the core function of collective defense and their various non-Article 5 crisis management operations. Some Allied observers have been concerned that the trajectory—sometimes with a boost from Washington—has been toward making NATO a reservoir of defense resources for potentially global applications, with an emphasis on expeditionary capabilities designed for counterinsurgency and stabilization operations such as those in Afghanistan. How, some observers have asked, can the Allies reconcile a global crisis management perspective with their regional collective defense commitments?

It is clear, however, that NATO must remain an effective collective defense organization—that is, it must perform its bedrock function—if it intends to serve as a platform for organizing crisis management operations beyond the territory of the Allies. As Jamie Shea has written, "NATO must prepare for both types of operations—for its internal consensus as well as for its relevance as a multilateral security provider."[162]

Moreover, in the current financial and economic crisis, the Allies must allocate their scarce military resources with even greater care. Since they do not wish to convert the Alliance into a sort of "global policeman"—and cannot afford to do so anyway—the Allies have to define priorities and take a cautious and selective approach to undertaking additional non-Article 5 tasks. The lack of enthusiasm among the Allies about intervening in the Syrian civil war stems from a combination of factors, including their finite resources, competing priorities, the forbidding local circumstances, and difficulties in obtaining a UN Security Council mandate for action.[163]

The Allies have agreed that further capability development and force transformation are imperative to underpin their means to conduct "the full range" of NATO "missions, including collective defence and crisis response operations on and beyond Alliance territory."[164] For example, at the April 2009 Strasbourg/Kehl Summit, the Allies declared, "We will vigorously pursue our work developing and fielding key enablers, such as mission-capable helicopters, strategic lift and the Alliance Ground Surveillance system."[165] The Libya intervention in 2011 reinforced a lesson about capability requirements that the Allies had already learned, at least in terms of their declaratory policy.

The Allies have also recognized that effective capabilities involve not only the "hardware" of equipment and facilities but also the "software" of well-educated and well-trained personnel working together proficiently. NATO's February 2012 internal study on the Libya intervention found that "nations did not effectively and efficiently share national intelligence and targeting information among allies and with partners." The report blamed "classification or procedural reasons," but it also noted important shortages of several types of specialists, including experts in intelligence, logistics, and targeting.[166] If the Allies had significant teamwork problems after about twenty years of crisis management operations, in a case in which they quickly gained complete air superiority, one must wonder how well they would meet the challenges that might arise in a collective defense contingency more demanding than the September 2001 terrorist attacks against the United States.

The reference in NATO's February 2012 report on the Libya intervention to deficiencies in information sharing "among allies and with partners" implicitly acknowledges the political and practical importance of non-NATO partner countries in the Alliance's non-Article 5 crisis management operations. The importance of other international organizations—above all, the United Nations—has been apparent in the diplomacy preceding and during these operations.[167] The contributions of partner nations and organizations have confirmed to a significant degree the complementarity of NATO's crisis management efforts and its pursuit of cooperative security partnerships.

Notes

1. Another important general issue involves the Alliance's "comprehensive approach" to crisis management. The "comprehensive approach" links crisis management to NATO's cooperative security endeavors, owing to its emphasis on partnerships with other nations and organizations. It is accordingly discussed in chapter 7.

2. NATO, "NATO and the 2003 Campaign against Iraq," www.nato.int/cps/en/natolive/topics_51977.htm. See also Philip H. Gordon and Jeremy Shapiro, *Allies at War: America, Europe, and the Crisis Over Iraq* (New York: McGraw-Hill, 2004), 136–141.

3. Nicholas Burns, interview with *BBC News*, "NATO Turns to Terrorism Fight," October 18, 2003, http://news.bbc.co.uk/2/hi/americas/3201578.stm.

4. Lord Robertson, "Building a Transatlantic Consensus" (speech at the European Institute, Washington, DC, February 20, 2003), www.nato.int/docu/speech/2003/s030220b.htm.

5. NATO, "NATO Council Makes Decision on Polish Request," May 21, 2003, www.nato.int/docu/update/2003/05-may/e0521b.htm.

6. Robertson quoted in NATO, "Poland Assumes Command of Multi-national Division in Iraq with NATO Support," September 3, 2003, www.nato.int/cps/en/SID-DF03846D-63474EE6/natolive/news_20176.htm.

7. North Atlantic Council, "Statement on Iraq," June 28, 2004, www.nato.int/docu/pr/2004/p04-098e.htm.

8. NATO, "NATO's Assistance to Iraq," last updated May 5, 2011, www.nato.int/cps/en/natolive/topics_51978.htm.

9. According to some observers, NTM-I created an essentially positive impression overall with the Allies despite its shortcomings, and this facilitated the establishment with little controversy of the much larger NATO Training Mission-Afghanistan in 2009.

10. Florence Gaub, *Building a New Military? The NATO Training Mission-Iraq*, Research Paper no. 67 (Rome: NATO Defense College, April 2011), 5, 7, www.ndc.nato.int/download/publications/rp_67.pdf.

11. Ibid., 7.

12. For example, Lieutenant General Babakir Zebari said in August 2010 that "the US army must stay until the Iraqi army is fully ready in 2020." Matthew Weaver and agencies, "Iraqi Army Not Ready to Take Over until 2020, Says Country's Top General," in the *Guardian*, August 12, 2010, www.guardian.co.uk/world/2010/aug/12/iraqi-army-not-ready-general.

13. NATO, "NATO's Assistance to Iraq," last updated January 17, 2012,

14. North Atlantic Council, "Chicago Summit Declaration," par. 15.

15. NATO, "Assisting the African Union in Darfur, Sudan," last updated March 30, 2012, www.nato.int/cps/en/natolive/topics_49194.htm.

16. NATO, "Assisting the African Union in Somalia," last updated July 30, 2012, www.nato.int/cps/en/natolive/topics_50099.htm.

17. NATO, "NATO Provides Airlift Support to African Union Mission in Somalia (AMISOM)," March 18, 2010, www.aco.nato.int/page27220646.aspx.

18. NATO, "Assisting the African Union in Somalia."

19. NATO, "Contributing to the Establishment of an African Standby Force," last updated May 4, 2012, www.nato.int/cps/en/natolive/topics_54617.htm. See also "NATO Assistance to the African Union."

20. Michel Soula, acting deputy assistant secretary general for NATO's Operations Division, quoted in NATO, "Of Bagpipes and Capacity-building in Africa," March 25, 2011, www.nato.int/cps/en/natolive/news_71790.htm?selectedLocale=en.

21. Since 2001, NATO's support for international shipping safety has included the work of the NATO Shipping Centre in Northwood, England. The NATO Shipping Centre interacts frequently with international shippers. It provides daily and weekly piracy updates and specific support for NATO's Operations Ocean Shield and Active Endeavour. The NATO Shipping Centre cooperates with the Maritime Security Centre Horn of Africa (MSCHOA), founded by the European Union in 2008. In addition to the NATO Shipping Centre, Northwood also hosts the MSCHOA and the operational headquarters for EUNAVFOR.

22. NATO, "Counter-piracy Operations," last updated May 3, 2012, www.nato.int/cps/en/natolive/topics_48815.htm.

23. Ibid.

24. Ibid.

25. EUNAVFOR Somalia, "Mission," www.eunavfor.eu/about-us/mission/#.

26. Hugues Eudeline, *Contenir la piraterie: Des réponses complexes face à une menace persistante*, Focus Stratégique no. 40 (Paris: Institut Français des Relations Internationales, November 2012), 30.

27. European Union External Action, "Common Security and Defence Policy, EU Maritime Operation against Piracy (EUNAVFOR Somalia-Operation ATALANTA)," EUNAVFOR/42, updated October 16, 2012.

28. For background, see Peter Chalk, "Piracy off the Horn of Africa: Scope, Dimensions, Causes and Responses," *Brown Journal of World Affairs* 16, no. 2 (Spring/Summer 2010): 89–108.

29. Andrew J. Shapiro, assistant secretary of state for political-military affairs, "U.S. Approaches to Counter-Piracy" (remarks to the International Institute for Strategic Studies, Washington, DC, March 30, 2011), www.iiss.org/about-us/offices/washington/iiss-us-events/iiss-us-policy-makers-series-the-united-states-approach-to-countering-piracy/.

30. Donna Miles, "Stavridis: Cooperation Key in Tackling Piracy Threat," American Forces Press Service, September 27, 2012, www.defense.gov/news/newsarticle.aspx?id=118024.

31. On the origins of Combined Task Force 151, see Commander, Combined Maritime Forces Public Affairs, "New Counter-Piracy Task Force Established," January 8, 2009, www.navy.mil/search/display.asp?story_id=41687.

32. Combined Maritime Forces, "Combined Maritime Forces Host 25th International Meeting of SHADE," September 23, 2012, http://combinedmaritimeforces.com/2012/09/23/combined-maritime-forces-host-25th-international-meeting-of-shade/. For background on the Combined Maritime Forces, see http://combinedmaritimeforces.com/about/.

33. Eudeline, *Contenir la piraterie*, 32.

34. NATO, "NATO's Counter Piracy Mission Extended," March 19, 2012, www.nato.int/cps/en/natolive/news_85230.htm?selectedLocale=en.

35. NATO, "Secretary General Thanks Prime Minister of Djibouti for Support against Piracy," December 21, 2012, www.nato.int/cps/en/SID-AA62DBAD-B6D77C16/natolive/news_93310.htm.

36. Commodore Ben Bekkering quoted in NATO, "NATO Counter-Piracy Mission Making Real Progress," December 17, 2012, www.nato.int/cps/en/SID-F584BF65-CDAE56EA/natolive/news_93175.htm.

37. Anders Fogh Rasmussen quoted in NATO, "Secretary General Thanks Prime Minister of Djibouti for Support against Piracy."

38. Abdi Guled and Jason Straziuso, "The Heyday Of Somali Pirates Might Be Over," *Miami Herald*, September 26, 2012.

39. John Patch, "The Overstated Threat," *U.S. Naval Institute Proceedings Magazine* 134, no. 12 (December 2008), www.usni.org/magazines/proceedings/2008-12/overstated-threat.

40. *NATO's Operations 1949–Present*, 1.

41. NATO, "Pakistan Earthquake Relief Operation," www.nato.int/cps/en/natolive/topics_50070.htm.

42. NATO, "NATO Cooperation with Pakistan," last updated November 18, 2010, www.nato.int/cps/en/natolive/topics_50071.htm.

43. NATO, "Crisis Management," last updated March 21, 2011, www.nato.int/cps/en/natolive/topics_49192.htm?selectedLocale=en. NATO helped the United States with relief support in September-October 2005, after hurricane Katrina struck the state of Louisiana. For background, see "Support to the US in Response to Hurricane Katrina," www.nato.int/eadrcc/2005/katrina/index.htm.

44. North Atlantic Council, "Chicago Summit Declaration," par. 56.

45. NATO, Allied Command Operations, "Air Policing," www.aco.nato.int/page142085426.aspx.

46. Allied Command Operations, "Iceland's 'Peacetime Preparedness Needs,'" www.aco.nato.int/icelands-peacetime-preparedness-needs.aspx.

47. NATO, "NATO Secretary General's Statement on the Situation in Libya," press release, February 24, 2011, www.nato.int/cps/en/natolive/news_70790.htm?mode=pressrelease.

48. UN Security Council Resolution 1970, February 26, 2011.

49. UN Security Council Resolution 1973, March 17, 2011.

50. NATO, "Statement by NATO Secretary General Following the United Nations Security Council Resolution 1973," press release (2011) 032, March 18, 2011, www.nato.int/cps/en/natolive/news_71640.htm?mode=pressrelease.

51. Of the fifteen members of the UN Security Council at that time, ten voted for UNSCR 1973 and five abstained: Brazil, China, Germany, India, and Russia.

52. Merkel quoted in "Libya Crisis as It Happened," March 18, 2011, http://news.bbc.co.uk/2/mobile/africa/9429682.stm.

53. Deutsche Welle, "NATO Agrees to Enforce No-fly Zone in Libya," March 24, 2011, www.dw-world.de/dw/article/0,,14940498,00.html.

54. Moreover, while abstaining from participation in the NATO-led operations concerning Libya, Germany "assisted alliance operations as a whole by increasing its involvement in aerial surveillance in Afghanistan." Ivo H. Daalder and James G. Stavridis, "NATO's Victory in Libya: The Right Way to Run an Intervention," *Foreign Affairs* 91, no. 2 (March/April 2012).

55. "German Parliament Backs Afghan AWACS Mission," Associated Press, March 25, 2011, http://news.yahoo.com/german-parliament-backs-afghan-awacs-mission-20110325-044805-173.html.

56. Thomas de Maizière quoted in "Germany's Libya Contribution: Merkel Cabinet Approves AWACS for Afghanistan," *Spiegel Online*, March 23, 2011, www.spiegel.de/international/world/germany-s-libya-contribution-merkel-cabinet-approves-awacs-for-afghanistan-a-752709.html.

57. "Merkel Praises NATO for Libya Campaign," August 27, 2011, www.thelocal.de/national/20110827-37221.html.

58. NATO, "Statement by the NATO Secretary General on Libya Arms Embargo," press release (2011) 033, March 22, 2011, www.nato.int/cps/en/natolive/news_71689.htm?mode=pressrelease; and NATO, "NATO Secretary General's Statement on No-fly Zone over Libya," press release (2010) 035, March 23, 2011, www.nato.int/cps/en/natolive/news_71722.htm?mode=pressrelease.

59. During the initial phase of the intervention, from March 19 to 31, the term Operation Odyssey Dawn was employed by the United States and some of the other states participating in operations—Belgium, Denmark, Italy, and Norway. Other states employed different names for their national operations: Canada (Operation Mobile), France (Opération Harmattan), Spain (Operación Odisea al Amanecer), and United Kingdom (Operation Ellamy).

60. NATO, "NATO Secretary General's Statement on Libya No-fly Zone."

61. Turkey was not the only NATO member state not invited to the March 19, 2011, meeting in Paris (in fact, fifteen NATO Allies were not invited), but the omission of Turkey was regarded as particularly significant. For the par-

ticipants invited by France to the March 19, 2011, meeting in Paris, see the "Déclaration adoptée à l'issue du Sommet de Paris pour le soutien au peuple libyen" (March 19, 2011), www.diplomatie.gouv.fr/fr/pays-zones-geo_833/libye_409/france-libye_1176/evenements_4528/declaration-adoptee-issue-du-sommet-paris-pour-soutien-au-peuple-libyen-19-mars-2011_90900.html. This declaration made no reference to NATO, but mentioned the UN Security Council, the Arab League, the African Union, the Organisation of the Islamic Conference, and the European Union.

62. Ian Traynor and Nicholas Watt, "Libya: NATO to Control No-Fly Zone after France Gives Way to Turkey," *Guardian*, March 25, 2011, www.guardian.co.uk/world/2011/mar/24/france-turkey-nato-libya.

63. NATO, "Statement by NATO Secretary General Anders Fogh Rasmussen on Libya," press release (2011) 036, March 27, 2011, www.nato.int/cps/en/natolive/news_71808.htm?mode=pressrelease (accessed 5 August 2011); and NATO, "NATO Takes Command in Libya Air Operations," March 31, 2011, www.nato.int/cps/en/natolive/news_71867.htm?mode=pressrelease.

64. NATO, "Statement on Libya Following the Working Lunch of NATO Ministers of Foreign Affairs with non-NATO Contributors to Operation Unified Protector," April 14, 2011, www.nato.int/cps/en/natolive/official_texts_72544.htm?selectedLocale=en.

65. The Organisation of the Islamic Conference changed its name to the Organisation of Islamic Cooperation on June 28, 2011.

66. Foreign and Commonwealth Office, "Statement by Foreign Secretary William Hague following the Libya Contact Group Meeting in Doha," April 13, 2011, par. 2, 6, www.fco.gov.uk/en/news/latest-news/?view=News&id=583592582.

67. NATO, "Statement on Libya," April 14, 2011.

68. NATO, "Statement on Libya Following the Working Lunch of NATO Ministers of Defense with non-NATO Contributors to Operation Unified Protector," June 8, 2011, www.nato.int/cps/en/natolive/news_75177.htm?selectedLocale=en.

69. NATO, "Statement on Libya," April 14, 2011.

70. NATO, "Statement on Libya," June 8, 2011.

71. Barack Obama, David Cameron, and Nicolas Sarkozy, "Libya's Pathway to Peace," *International Herald Tribune*, April 15, 2011.

72. Sergey Lavrov quoted in Paul Richter, "NATO Feels Libya Mission Fatigue," *Los Angeles Times*, July 5, 2011. See also Andrew E. Kramer, "Russia Meets with NATO in New Push for Libyan Peace," *New York Times*, July 5, 2011.

73. Michael Birnbaum, "France Sent Arms to Libyan Rebels," *Washington Post*, June 29, 2011.

74. Anders Fogh Rasmussen, "NATO Secretary General Statement on End of Libya Mission," October 28, 2011, www.nato.int/cps/en/natolive/news_80052.htm.

75. Chris Pocock, "NATO's Role in Ghaddafi's Downfall: Operation Unified Protector," *Aviation International News*, November 10, 2011, www.ainonline.com/?q=aviation-news/dubai-air-show/2011-11-10/natos-role-ghaddafis-downfall-operation-unified-protector.

76. NATO, "NATO Secretary General's Statement on No-Fly Zone over Libya," press release, March 23, 2011.

77. Ibid.

78. Laurent Thomet, "NATO Fights on though Libya Coalition Shrinks," Agence France-Presse, July 30, 2011, http://newsinfo.inquirer.net/33383/nato-fights-on-though-libya-coalition-shrinks.

79. Ukraine also attended the meeting of the North Atlantic Council "in Libya format" in Berlin in April 2011. Ukraine was then listed by the German foreign minister as one of the non-NATO contributors to Operation Unified Protector. (Ansprache von Bundesaußenminister Guido Westerwelle zur Begrüßung der Teilnehmer des informellen Treffens der Außenminister der NATO im Libyen-Format, April 14, 2011, www.nato.int/cps/en/natolive/opinions_72444.htm.) Ukraine expressed an intention to contribute a frigate to arms embargo enforcement but did not make it available before the end of Operation Unified Protector. Author interviews with British, Greek, and U.S. observers in Brussels, October 24 and 27, 2011.

80. Author interviews with British, Greek, and U.S. observers in Brussels, October 24 and 27, 2011.

81. "NATO Operations in Libya: Data Journalism Breaks Down Which Country Does What," *Guardian*, October 31, 2011, www.guardian.co.uk/news/datablog/2011/may/22/nato-libya-data-journalism-operations-country#data.

82. Chris Pocock, "NATO's Role in Ghaddafi's Downfall: Operation Unified Protector," *Aviation International News*, November 10, 2011, www.ainonline.com/?q=aviation-news/dubai-air-show/2011-11-10/natos-role-ghaddafis-downfall-operation-unified-protector.

83. James Blitz, "Lessons from Libya," *Financial Times*, August 31, 2011.

84. Major General Hamad bin Ali al-Atiya, Qatar's military chief of staff, quoted in David D. Kirkpatrick and Rick Gladstone, "Libya's Interim Leader Asks NATO to Stay through the End of 2011," *New York Times*, October 27, 2011.

85. Robert M. Gates, "The Security and Defense Agenda (Future of NATO)," Brussels, Belgium, June 10, 2011, www. defense.gov/speeches/speech.aspx?speechid=1581.

86. Bulgaria and Romania each sent a ship to help in enforcing the maritime dimension of the arms embargo. Vladimir Socor, "Coalition of the Willing Stands in for NATO in Libya," *Eurasia Daily Monitor* 8, no. 97 (May 19, 2011).

87. Peter Spiegel, "Gates Criticises NATO Laggards over Air War," *Financial Times*, June 9, 2011. It should be noted that Poland is one of the ten NATO nations participating in the Heavy Airlift Wing (HAW) based in Hungary that owns and operates three C-17 aircraft as part of the Alliance's Strategic Airlift Capability (SAC) initiative. The HAW flew three strategic airlift missions in support of Operation Odyssey Dawn (OOD) in March 2011. (Kristopher Hanson, "Aid Comes from the Sky," *Long Beach Press-Telegram*, April 11, 2011.) An official still photograph showing a Polish aircrew member loading support equipment on a HAW C-17 flying OOD-support missions is available on the U.S. Air Force website, www.af.mil/photos/media_search.asp?q=c-17&?id=-1&page=16&count=48. The author thanks Major Daniel Lang, USAF, for drawing to his attention the contribution of the HAW (and thus Poland) to Operation Odyssey Dawn, which preceded Operation Unified Protector.

88. Liam Fox quoted in Daniel Dombey and Kiran Stacey, "Britain Urges US to Step Up Libya Support," *Financial Times*, July 18, 2011.

89. An unnamed "senior French official" quoted in James Blitz and Anna Fifield, "NATO's Internal Strains Worsen over Libya," *Financial Times*, June 16, 2011.

90. "By the eighth day of the campaign, the U.S. had fired 184 BGM-109s Tomahawk cruise missiles from ships and submarines against radars, surface-to-air missile sites and communications nodes. As for Libyan air bases, there was one attack by three American Northrop B-2s, flying a 24-hour round-robin mission from their home base in Missouri. The Stealth Bombers were employed as much for their ability to each drop 15 independently targeted JDAM bombs on hardened aircraft shelters, as for their stealth capability." Chris Pocock, "NATO's Role in Ghaddafi's Downfall: Operation Unified Protector," *Aviation International News*, November 10, 2011, www.ainonline.com/?q=aviation-news/dubai-air-show/2011-11-10/natos-role-ghaddafis-downfall-operation-unified-protector.

91. "UK-France Declaration on Security and Defence," February 17, 2012, par. 6, www.number10.gov.uk/news/uk-france-declaration-security/.

92. The White House, Office of the Press Secretary, weekly address, March 26, 2011, www.whitehouse.gov/the-press-office/2011/03/26/weekly-address-president-obama-says-mission-libya-succeeding.

93. The White House, Office of the Press Secretary, remarks by the president in address to the nation on Libya, March 28, 2011, www.whitehouse.gov/the-press-office/2011/03/28/remarks-president-address-nation-libya.

94. "U.S. Combat Air-strikes End in Libya," Agence France-Presse, April 4, 2011, www.newstimeworld.com/archives/284.

95. Some reports characterized sorties to suppress Libyan air defenses as defensive rather than as "strike" operations. Jim Garamone, "U.S. Continues Missions to Support Libya No-Fly Zone," American Forces Press Service, April 13, 2011, www.defense.gov/news/newsarticle.aspx?id=63545. See also, Dave Majumdar, "AFRICOM: AF, Navy Still Flying Libya Missions," *Navy Times*, June 30, 2011.

96. Blitz and Fifield, "NATO's Internal Strains Worsen over Libya." Various factors qualify the comparison. For example, according to the *Financial Times*, poor weather conditions hampered operations on fifty-four of the seventy-eight days of the Kosovo campaign. Inclement weather was less frequent in the Libyan case. The Libya operations were for the most part at a greater range and required more aerial refueling than did the Kosovo operations.

97. Department of Defense, *Kosovo/Operation Allied Force After-Action Report to Congress* (Washington, DC: Department of Defense, January 31, 2000), 78.

98. Ivo H. Daalder and James G. Stavridis, "NATO's Success in Libya," *International Herald Tribune*, October 31, 2011. Ivo H. Daalder was at that time the U.S. permanent representative to NATO, while Admiral James G. Stavridis was then the Supreme Allied Commander, Europe (SACEUR), and Commander of the United States European Command.

99. "One of his advisers described the President's actions in Libya as 'leading from behind.' . . . It's a different definition of leadership than America is known for, and it comes from two unspoken beliefs: that the relative power of the U.S. is declining, as rivals like China rise, and that the U.S. is reviled in many parts of the world. Pursuing our interests and spreading our ideals thus requires stealth and modesty as well as military strength." Ryan Lizza, "The Consequentialist: How the Arab Spring Remade Obama's Foreign Policy," *New Yorker*, May 2, 2011, www.newyorker.com/reporting/2011/05/02/110502fa_fact_lizza (accessed 4 August 2011). It should be noted that the "White House official" who used this phrase in speaking to Ryan Lizza has not been identified. President Obama in October 2011 rejected the phrase and said, "We lead from the front." (Obama quoted in David Jackson, "Obama Never Said 'Leading From Behind,'" The Oval Blog, USAToday.com, October 27, 2011.) In March 2011, however, when NATO initiated air strikes against Libyan targets, U.S. secretary of state Hillary Clinton said, "We did not lead this." (Clinton quoted in Mary Beth Sheridan and Scott Wilson, "Administration Plays Down Its Role in Assault," *Washington Post*, March 20, 2011.) The Obama administra-

tion sought at the outset to "give the perception that others are leading this intervention." (Ash Jain, a former State Department official, quoted in Bob Drogin, "As Libya War Widens, Obama Stays in Background," *Los Angeles Times*, March 20, 2011.)

100. Daalder and Stavridis, "NATO's Success in Libya." In a subsequent article these authors stated that France and the United Kingdom destroyed "more than a third of the overall targets." Daalder and Stavridis, "NATO's Victory in Libya."

101. NATO, "Statement on Libya," June 8, 2011.

102. Oana Lungescu, NATO Spokesperson, press briefing on Libya, July 7, 2011, www.nato.int/cps/en/natolive/opinions_76163.htm.

103. Oana Lungescu, NATO spokesperson, press briefing on Libya, July 19, 2011, www.nato.int/cps/en/natolive/opinions_76568.htm.

104. Anders Fogh Rasmussen quoted in Kim Sengupta, "NATO Chief Makes Promise 'To Stay Committed' in Libya," *Independent*, June 27, 2011.

105. Rasmussen quoted in Henry Chu, "NATO Sets Date to End Operation in Libya," *Los Angeles Times*, October 22, 2011.

106. Anders Fogh Rasmussen quoted in Rick Gladstone, "U.N. Votes to End Foreign Intervention in Libya," *New York Times*, October 28, 2011.

107. Rasmussen quoted in David Brunnstrom, "NATO Worried by Libya Armed Groups, Offers Security Help," Reuters.com, September 27, 2012.

108. Putin quoted in David M. Herszenhorn and Nick Cumming-Bruce, "Putin Defends Stand on Syria and Chastises U.S. on Libya Outcome," *New York Times*, December 21, 2012. Putin was alluding to the murder of U.S. ambassador Christopher Stevens in Benghazi on September 11, 2012.

109. Florence Gaub, *Libya: Avoiding State Failure*, Research Report (Rome: NATO Defense College, September 13, 2011).

110. Florence Gaub, *Six Strategic Lessons Learned from Libya: NATO's Operation Unified Protector* (Rome: NATO Defense College Research Division, March 2012), 6. See also her more extensive study, *The North Atlantic Treaty Organization and Libya: Reviewing Operation Unified Protector* (Carlisle, PA: U.S. Army War College, June 2013).

111. "Joint Press Point with NATO Secretary General Anders Fogh Rasmussen and the Prime Minister of Libya, Mr. Ali Zeidan," May 27, 2013, www.nato.int/cps/en/SID-CAAEE15F-08B745B8/natolive/opinions_100853.htm?selectedLocale=en.

112. NATO, "Defence Ministers Make Progress on Cyber Protection," last updated June 4, 2013, www.nato.int/cps/en/SID-3C648492-46C41C9C/natolive/news_101143.htm

113. Florence Gaub, *Libya: The Struggle for Security*, Issue Brief (Paris: European Union Institute for Security Studies, June 2013), 1–2.

114. Author interview with a British expert in Brussels, October 27, 2011.

115. "Names of the Dead," *New York Times*, January 8, 2013, www.nytimes.com/2013/01/05/us/us-military-deaths-in-afghanistan.html.

116. *After the War: Kosovo Peacekeeping Costs* (Washington, DC: Center for Strategic and Budgetary Assessments, June 7, 1999), cited in Steven Metz, *The American Army in the Balkans: Strategic Alternatives and Implications* (January 2001), 32.

117. Rajiv Chandrasekaran, "Afghan War Cost to Be Big Factor in Troop Drawdown," *Washington Post*, May 31, 2011.

118. Deputy White House national security adviser Benjamin Rhodes quoted in Julian E. Barnes and Adam Entous, "NATO Air Strategy Gains Renewed Praise," *Wall Street Journal*, October 21, 2011.

119. Adrian Hamilton, "No Wonder Hague Can't Explain Himself," *Independent*, April 28, 2011, hwww.independent.co.uk/voices/commentators/adrian-hamilton/adrian-hamilton-no-wonder-hague-cant-explain-himself-2275576.html.

120. The most important exception to this pattern was the conduct of Operation Allied Force, which was undertaken without an explicit authorization under a UN Security Council resolution. Within days after the initiation of Operation Allied Force, Javier Solana, then the NATO secretary general, sent a letter to the UN secretary-general describing NATO's action and its intention to compel the forces of the Federal Republic of Yugoslavia "to meet the demands of the international community." David S. Yost, *NATO and International Organizations*, Forum Paper no. 3 (Rome: NATO Defense College, September 2007), 54, www.ndc.nato.int/download/publications/fp_03.pdf.

121. Daalder and Stavridis, "NATO's Victory in Libya." Another source attributes 80 percent of "NATO air-to-air refueling" to the United States. Ben Barry, "Libya's Lessons," *Survival* 53, no. 5 (October–November 2011): 5.

122. NATO report of February 2012 quoted in Eric Schmitt, "NATO Sees Flaws in Air Campaign Against Qaddafi," *New York Times*, April 14, 2012.

123. Barry, "Libya's Lessons," 10. Poland did not participate in the strike operations under Operation Unified Protector, but sold precision munitions to fellow Allies. Daalder and Stavridis, "NATO's Victory in Libya."

124. "Rasmussen Discusses NATO Campaign in Libya," *All Things Considered*, National Public Radio (NPR), November 7, 2011, www.npr.org/2011/11/07/142111422/rasmussen-discusses-nato-campaign-in-libya.

125. "UK-France Declaration on Security and Defence," par. 7.

126. Blitz, "Lessons from Libya."

127. Author interviews in Brussels, notably with a British observer on October 27, 2011, and a Dutch observer on October 28, 2011.

128. Stavridis quoted in Thom Shanker and Eric Schmitt, "Seeing Limits of 'New' War," *New York Times*, October 22, 2011.

129. Kurt Volker, "Don't Call It a Comeback: Four Reasons Why Libya Doesn't Equal Success for NATO," August 23, 2011, www.foreignpolicy.com/articles/2011/08/23/dont_call_it_a_comeback.

130. Volker quoted in Blitz, "Lessons from Libya.".

131. Kamp quoted in NATO, "We Answered the Call"—The End of Operation Unified Protector," October 31, 2011, www.nato.int/cps/en/natolive/news_80435.htm.

132. Author interviews in Brussels, notably with a Dutch observer on October 28, 2011.

133. General Klaus Naumann, General John Shalikashvili, Field Marshal The Lord Inge, Admiral Jacques Lanxade, and General Henk van den Breemen, *Towards a Grand Strategy in an Uncertain World: Renewing Transatlantic Partnership* (Lunteren, The Netherlands: Noaber Foundation, 2007), 128.

134. Ellen Hallams and Benjamin Schreer, "Towards a 'Post-American' Alliance? NATO Burden-Sharing after Libya," *International Affairs* 88, no. 2 (2012): 324.

135. For background, see Alexander Mattelaer, "How Afghanistan Has Strengthened NATO," *Survival* 53, no. 6 (December 2011–January 2012).

136. In this discussion and the subsequent sections titled "Crisis Management in Support of Collective Defense" and "Collective Defense Arising from Crisis Management," the author has drawn on his article, "NATO's Evolving Purposes and the Next Strategic Concept," *International Affairs* 86, no. 2 (March 2010): 489–522.

137. See, in particular, Norwegian Ministry of Foreign Affairs, *The Norwegian Government's High North Strategy* (February 21, 2007), www.regjeringen.no/en/dep/ud/Documents/Reports-programmes-of-action-and-plans/Action-plans-and-programmes/2006/strategy-for-the-high-north.html?id=448697, and Sven G. Holtsmark and Brooke A. Smith-Windsor, eds., *Security Prospects in the High North: Geostrategic Thaw or Freeze?*, Forum Paper no. 7 (Rome: NATO Defense College, May 2009), www.ndc.nato.int/download/publications/fp_07.pdf.

138. Stavridis quoted in Terry Macalister, "Climate Change Could Lead to Arctic Conflict, Warns Senior NATO Commander," *Guardian*, October 11, 2010, www.theguardian.com/environment/2010/oct/11/nato-conflict-arctic-resources.

139. Daniel Hamilton, with Charles Barry, Hans Binnendijk, Stephen Flanagan, Julianne Smith, and James Townsend, *Alliance Reborn: An Atlantic Compact for the 21st Century* (Washington, DC: Atlantic Council of the United States; Center for Strategic and International Studies; Center for Technology and National Security Policy, National Defense University; and Center for Transatlantic Relations, Paul H. Nitze School of Advanced International Studies, Johns Hopkins University, February 2009), 22.

140. Sean M. Maloney, "Fire Brigade or Tocsin? NATO's ACE Mobile Force, Flexible Response and the Cold War," *Journal of Strategic Studies* 27, no. 4 (December 2004), 602.

141. Combat support consists of units providing fire support (e.g., artillery and close air support) and other operational assistance to combat forces, while combat service support provides supplies, maintenance, transport, medical care, and other essential services. This distinction is reflected in the *NATO Glossary of Terms and Definitions*, AAP-6 (2009) (Brussels: NATO Standardization Agency, 2009), p. 2-C-9, www.nato.int/docu/stanag/aap006/aap-6-2009.pdf.

142. Alexander R. Vershbow, "Crafting the New Strategic Concept: Ambitions, Resources, and Partnerships for a 21st Century Alliance" (keynote speech at the Bratislava Security Conference, =October 22, 2009, http://nato.usmission.gov/Texts/Vershbow10222009.asp.

143. Rasmussen, "New Challenges—Better Capabilities."

144. As noted in chapter 3, the NATO Allies do not appear to have made public an official definition of "strategic distance," but it has been reported to be 15,000 kilometers from Brussels. From a Canadian or U.S. viewpoint, reckoning the distance from Ottawa or Washington might make more sense in terms of deploying forces and conducting operations.

145. North Atlantic Council, "Comprehensive Political Guidance," November 29, 2006, par. 16a.

146. Jüri Luik quoted in indirect discourse in Arnadottir, *Protecting to Project*, par. 26.

147. Lithuanian expert quoted in David S. Yost, *NATO's Deterrence and Defense Posture*, 4, www.ndc.nato.int/download/downloads.php?icode=356.

148. Tim Ripley, "Georgian Crisis Sparks NATO Strategic Debate," *Jane's Defence Weekly*, August 22, 2008.

149. According to the Comprehensive Political Guidance, "NATO must retain the ability to conduct the full range of its missions, from high to low intensity, placing special focus on the most likely operations, being responsive to current and future operational requirements, and still able to conduct the most demanding operations." North Atlantic Council, "Comprehensive Political Guidance," November 29, 2006, par. 7.

150. See the comments by Jamie Shea, then the NATO spokesman, at the press conference of Jamie Shea and Colonel Konrad Freytag, SHAPE, in Washington, April 25, 1999, www.nato.int/Kosovo/press/p990425b.htm.

151. North Atlantic Council, "Chairman's Summary of the Meeting of the North Atlantic Council at the Level of Heads of State and Government with Countries in the Region of the Federal Republic of Yugoslavia," April 25, 1999, par. 5, www.nato.int/cps/en/natolive/official_texts_27439.htm.

152. Until September 2001 the reference in Article 5 of the North Atlantic Treaty to the contingency of "an armed attack" was assumed to concern state aggression, not terrorist attacks.

153. UN Security Council Resolution 1386, adopted December 20, 2001.

154. UN Security Council Resolution 1383, adopted December 6, 2001.

155. Rasa Jukneviciene, *Latest Developments in European Security: A Baltic Perspective* (London: Chatham House, October 20, 2009), 6.

156. For background on the Bosnia case, see Laura Silber and Allan Little, *The Death of Yugoslavia*, rev. ed. (London: Penguin Books and BBC Books, 1996), 311–318, 328–334. For the Kosovo case and the Pristina airfield incident in particular, see Clark, *Waging Modern War*, 375–403. The accidental bombing of the Belgrade embassy of the People's Republic of China on May 7, 1999, during the course of Operation Allied Force damaged U.S.-Chinese relations, but did not create as great a risk of confrontation for the alliance as the incidents involving Russia.

157. See chapter 3 for background on the negative security assurances articulated by London, Paris, and Washington. See also David S. Yost, "New Approaches to Deterrence in Britain, France, and the United States," *International Affairs* 81 (January 2005), esp. pp. 111–114.

158. North Atlantic Council, "Deterrence and Defence Posture Review," May 20, 2012, par. 10.

159. For background, see David S. Yost, *France's Deterrent Posture and Security in Europe, Part I: Capabilities and Doctrine*, Adelphi Paper 194 (London: International Institute for Strategic Studies, Winter 1984–1985), 55.

160. Jaap de Hoop Scheffer, "Addressing Global Insecurity" (speech in Vienna, Austria, November 3, 2005, www.nato.int/docu/speech/2005/s051103b.htm.

161. These issues are discussed in greater detail in David S. Yost, "NATO and the Anticipatory Use of Force," *International Affairs* (January 2007), 39-68.

162. Shea, "NATO at Sixty—and Beyond," 22.

163. Michael Birnbaum, "European Leaders Cautious on Syria," *Washington Post*, June 1, 2012.

164. North Atlantic Council, "Strasbourg/Kehl Summit Declaration," par. 42.

165. Ibid., par. 45.

166. NATO report of February 2012 quoted in Eric Schmitt, "NATO Sees Flaws in Air Campaign against Qaddafi," *New York Times*, April 14, 2012.

167. As noted previously, with the key exception of Operation Allied Force in the Kosovo conflict in 1999, the Alliance has usually relied on the UN Security Council for an authorizing resolution for these operations.

6

Cooperative Security and Partnerships

In the 2010 Strategic Concept the Allies declared that one of NATO's "three essential core tasks" is "cooperative security." The Allies defined "cooperative security" as encompassing efforts "to enhance international security, through partnership with relevant countries and other international organisations; by contributing actively to arms control, non-proliferation and disarmament; and by keeping the door to membership in the Alliance open to all European democracies that meet NATO's standards."[1]

It should be understood from the outset that the Allies have always supported in principle what they have recently termed "cooperative security," and that in doing so they have emphasized their commitment to democratic values. The preamble of the North Atlantic Treaty states, "The Parties to this Treaty reaffirm their faith in the purposes and principles of the Charter of the United Nations and their desire to live in peace with all peoples and all governments. They are determined to safeguard the freedom, common heritage and civilisation of their peoples, founded on the principles of democracy, individual liberty and the rule of law."[2]

Throughout the Cold War the Allies repeatedly declared their interest in promoting constructive change peacefully and in upholding their political values. The reference in the 2010 Strategic Concept to "common values of individual liberty, democracy, human rights and the rule of law" confirmed continuity with the North Atlantic Treaty and long-standing Alliance ideals.[3]

At the end of the Cold War, in 1991, the Allies declared, "The peoples of North America and the whole of Europe can now join in a community of shared values based on freedom, democracy, human rights and the rule of law. As an agent of change, a source of stability and the indispensable guarantor of its members' security, our Alliance will continue to play a key role in building a new, lasting order of peace in Europe: a Europe of cooperation and prosperity."[4]

The geographic scope of the Alliance's field of action and interest has broadened since the end of the Cold War, however. In the 2010 Strategic Concept the Allies declared, "The promotion of Euro-Atlantic security is best assured through a wide network of partner relationships with countries and organisations around the globe."[5] In their May 2012 Deterrence and Defense Posture Review, the Allies stated that their cooperative security activities such as "cooperation and contacts with the armed forces of partner countries . . . can have broader stabilising effects by helping to shape and improve the Alliance's security environment, project stability, and prevent conflicts."[6]

This attractive (albeit vague) vision has proven at times hard to pursue in the face of intractable realities, including countries and organizations that have their own agendas at variance with NATO's cooperative security vision.

NATO's Partnerships

The Alliance has made many efforts to employ organizational mechanisms to shape the international security environment. At present NATO's most important multilateral organizational frameworks are the Partnership for Peace, the Euro-Atlantic Partnership Council, the Mediterranean Dialogue, and the Istanbul Cooperation Initiative.

The key bilateral initiatives include the NATO-Russia Council, the NATO-Ukraine Commission, and the NATO-Georgia Commission. In addition, NATO has pursued cooperation and dialogue with non-NATO nations outside the Euro-Atlantic area, including Afghanistan, Australia, Iraq, Japan, Mongolia, New Zealand, Pakistan, and South Korea.

NATO's "comprehensive approach" to security has also involved outreach to international organizations (including the United Nations, the European Union, and the OSCE) as well as nongovernmental organizations (see chapter 7).

Partnership for Peace and the Euro-Atlantic Partnership Council

Both Partnership for Peace (PfP) and the Euro-Atlantic Partnership Council (EAPC) have their origins in NATO's first partnership framework, the North Atlantic Cooperation Council (NACC). The NACC in turn derived from the Alliance's political vision of peace in Europe.

At NATO's July 1990 London Summit, the first after the collapse of the Communist governments in Eastern Europe in the fall of 1989, the Allies affirmed their determination to maintain the peace and asserted an unprecedented confidence in the Alliance's ability to serve as an "agent of change," an instrument useful in constructing "a Europe whole and free." In the words of NATO's London Declaration, "We need to keep standing together, to extend the long peace we have enjoyed these past four decades. Yet our alliance must be even more an agent of change. It can help build the structures of a more united continent, supporting security and stability with the strength of our shared faith in democracy, the rights of the individual, and the peaceful resolution of disputes."[7]

NATO added in its London Declaration that it would "reach out to the countries of the East which were our adversaries in the Cold War, and extend to them the hand of friendship." In terms of concrete proposals, NATO suggested "military contacts" between NATO and Warsaw Pact commanders, "regular diplomatic liaison" between NATO and the states of the Warsaw Pact, and a joint declaration by the nations of NATO and the Warsaw Pact affirming that they were "no longer adversaries."[8] Such a declaration by the members of the opposing alliances was made in Paris in November 1990, less than a year before the Warsaw Pact was formally disbanded in July 1991.

In November 1991, NATO proposed "a more institutional relationship of consultation and cooperation on political and security issues" with Bulgaria, Czechoslovakia, Estonia, Hungary, Latvia, Lithuania, Poland, Romania, and the Soviet Union.[9] (The Baltic republics regained their independence from the Soviet Union and were admitted to the United Nations in September 1991, before the collapse of the Soviet Union in December 1991.) The mechanism for the "more institutional relationship" was called the North Atlantic Cooperation Council, and it consisted of meetings of representatives of the invited states with representatives of the NATO Allies and Alliance officials.[10]

In their November 1991 Strategic Concept, the Allies stated that "with the radical changes in the security situation, the opportunities for achieving Alliance objectives through political means are greater than ever before." As a result, "Allied security policy" would henceforth be based on "three mutually reinforcing elements. . . dialogue, co-operation, and the maintenance of a collective defense capability."[11]

In January 1994, NATO went well beyond declaring the addition of "cooperation" as a basic purpose. The Alliance announced its intention "to launch an immediate and practical program that will transform the relationship between NATO and participating states. This new program goes beyond dialogue and cooperation to forge a real partnership—a Partnership for Peace. We invite the other states participating in the NACC, and other CSCE countries able and willing to contribute to this program, to join with us in this Partnership."[12]

What would the PfP accomplish? According to the North Atlantic Council, "The Partnership will expand and intensify political and military cooperation throughout Europe, increase stability, diminish threats to peace, and build strengthened relationships by promoting the spirit of practical cooperation and commitment to democratic principles that underpin our Alliance."[13]

NATO has been the sponsor or "senior partner" in PfP in that the Alliance has determined the scope and purposes of PfP, including the menu of activities available for partners. Since 2011 these activities have been specified in two-year Individual Partnership and Cooperation Programs (IPCPs). Until 2011 these were known as Individual Partnership Programs in PfP, Individual Cooperation Programs in Mediterranean Dialogue and Istanbul Cooperation Initiative, and Tailored Cooperation Programs for Partners across the Globe. The significance of introducing IPCPs in 2011 was to provide a harmonized format for all partnership frameworks.

As NATO officials have pointed out, one could say that there are twenty-two "Partnerships for Peace," because each Partner has concluded an IPCP with NATO.

In other words, the PfP has allowed for "self-differentiation." The twenty-eight NATO Allies and the twenty-two PfP partners together constitute the EAPC, a multinational forum for consultation on security-related issues. These issues include a broad field of topics, including civil emergency planning, air traffic management, arms control, scientific cooperation, nuclear safety, international terrorism, and defense planning and budgeting.[14]

The NATO Allies in 1997 founded the EAPC to replace the NACC. While the theme of reconciliation between former adversaries had limited NACC membership to NATO nations, former Warsaw Pact states, and former Soviet republics, the EAPC has included all the Allies and all the PfP partners.

What security obligations has NATO accepted regarding PfP partners? In language that appeared to have been copied from Article 4 of the North Atlantic Treaty, the North Atlantic Council declared in January 1994 that "NATO will consult with any active participant in the Partnership if that partner perceives a direct threat to its territorial integrity, political independence, or security."[15]

The significance of NATO's commitment became apparent on March 11, 1998, when Albania became the first partner to exercise its PfP emergency consultation rights. Albania's deputy defense minister, Perikli Teta, addressed the North Atlantic Council and asked whether "the deployment of a NATO peacekeeping contingent on the Albania-Yugoslav border [that is, the border with Kosovo] would contribute to stability in the region." The Allies responded that there was no "urgent requirement" to send such forces and decided to take other measures to demonstrate, in the words of NATO secretary general Javier Solana, that "Albania has the solidarity of NATO."[16] The other measures taken under PfP auspices included civil emergency and humanitarian assistance (to help deal with ethnic Albanian refugees from Kosovo), military training, and aid in securing ammunition stockpiles and other military depots.[17] These measures proved insufficient to counter Milošević's policies, and NATO's deepening engagement in the Kosovo conflict followed.

The accomplishments of PfP include a vast array of exercises and associated exchanges, including education and training activities, and the practical application of PfP "lessons learned" in NATO-led operations in the Balkans, Afghanistan, and Libya. In March 2012 the Partnership and Cooperation Menu offered by NATO Allies, partners, and institutions encompassed around 1,600 activities available to partners in PfP and other NATO-sponsored cooperative frameworks.[18]

These activities have promoted the acquisition and improvement of capabilities, defense and security sector reform, training and education, professional development, and interoperability and transparency among the participating forces of NATO and partner countries.[19] PfP has also encouraged regional military cooperation, and this has contributed to the attenuation and resolution of some long-standing political differences.

PfP has made possible permanent partner representation at NATO's political headquarters in Brussels and at Supreme Headquarters Allied Powers Europe

(SHAPE) at Casteau, near Mons, Belgium. The Allies have over the years trans-formed the Partnership Coordination Cell (PCC) established in 1994 at SHAPE for PfP partners into an institution for practical security-related cooperation for all partners (including PfP, Mediterranean Dialogue, Istanbul Cooperation Initiative, and others) that choose to send representation or liaison personnel. In 2008 the North Atlantic Council replaced the PCC with the Military Cooperation Division (MCD) at SHAPE, and in 2012 the MCD was renamed the Military Partnerships Directorate (MPD). The MPD's mission includes planning, implementing, and eval-uating military partnership activities under both Allied Command Operations (also known as SHAPE) and Allied Command Transformation in Norfolk, Virginia.[20]

Since PfP was launched in 1994, twelve PfP partners have become Allies (Alba-nia, Bulgaria, Croatia, the Czech Republic, Estonia, Hungary, Latvia, Lithuania, Po-land, Romania, Slovakia, and Slovenia). The twenty-two current PfP partners include twelve former Soviet republics (Armenia, Azerbaijan, Belarus, Georgia, Kazakhstan, Kyrgyzstan, Moldova, Russia, Tajikistan, Turkmenistan, Ukraine, and Uzbekistan), four former Yugoslav states (Bosnia and Herzegovina, Montenegro, Serbia, and the former Yugoslav Republic of Macedonia), and six European countries with traditions of neutrality (Austria, Finland, Ireland, Malta, Sweden, and Switzerland). The PfP was designed to allow for flexibility and self-differentiation, because some partners, such as Switzerland and Uzbekistan, had goals other than membership in NATO.

The effectiveness of PfP has been clear with regard to what became a function for several partners—paving the road toward membership in the Alliance. In French scholar Vivien Pertusot's view, "That success was not so much the result of a good strategy NATO implemented as it was a shared determination to achieve that objec-tive."[21] That is, the countries seeking membership and the NATO Allies had a com-mon goal, and the aspirants were highly motivated. This was an initially unintended function for PfP, because the Allies did not agree on an enlargement policy until 1995.[22]

The EAPC, bringing together the twenty-eight NATO Allies and the twenty-two PfP partners, has increasingly lost momentum as twelve aspirants have moved from partner to member status. In 2006 Karl-Heinz Kamp, a German expert, wrote that the monthly EAPC meetings had become "a mere routine" of "diminished rel-evance" in which "NATO members complained about partner countries whose con-tributions were limited to the recitation of previously prepared statements of little import. Conversely, partner countries were perturbed by the lack of information about developments relevant to NATO, which they claimed they were only able to glean from the press."[23] In 2012 Heidi Reisinger, another German expert, observed, "Experienced participants dread these meetings, which they see as having become boring and meaningless."[24]

Allies and partners have agreed in regarding EAPC meetings as increasingly less useful over the years. One of the objectives of the April 2011 reform of the Alliance's partnerships (discussed later in this chapter) is to establish the possibility of flexible formats for meetings involving only the partners interested in specific topics. Some experts hold that EAPC meetings in Political and Partnerships Committee format have been invigorated since 2012 by a new approach based on prior preparation of discussion topics by self-selected groups of Allies and partners.[25] NATO favors revitalizing the EAPC by encouraging more bottom-up initiatives from groups of Allies and partners. For example, experts in Brussels have noted, "Switzerland has taken on a leading role in bringing to EAPC/PfP the topic of international standards for the regulation of private security companies."[26]

Many PfP partners (as well as partners from other frameworks) have contributed to NATO-led crisis management operations, and some PfP partners have participated in NATO's Operation Active Endeavour in the Mediterranean, which the Allies have defined as a continuing Article 5 operation. These contributions could be regarded as PfP achievements, owing in part to the emphasis on force interoperability and capability building in PfP activities.

In contrast with the Mediterranean Dialogue and the Istanbul Cooperation Initiative, the Allies set out explicit democracy-promotion goals for PfP. According to the PfP Framework Document, "Protection and promotion of fundamental freedoms and human rights, and safeguarding of freedom, justice, and peace through democracy are shared values fundamental to the Partnership."[27]

PfP cannot claim a high level of effectiveness in terms of the declared goal of fostering democracy, particularly in Russia and several other partner countries in Eastern Europe, the South Caucasus, and Central Asia. With regard to these PfP members, Vivien Pertusot has observed, "The Allies do not expect much from them in terms of reforms, because of the very static and authoritarian nature of the regimes, although under the various PfP agreements, they are required to implement reforms."[28]

Aside from local historical factors and specific conditions in each country, Russian policies have been a major obstacle to PfP cooperation in the former Soviet space, including democracy promotion under PfP auspices. Russia's substantial financial and military assets, as well as Russian control over critical energy resources, ensure that most of these countries exercise caution in their relations with NATO. As a result, "The Alliance can only move forward prudently, in order not to alienate Moscow and avoid putting those partners in an awkward position vis-à-vis Russia."[29] While some experts have seen in Kazakh policies an interest in PfP cooperation as a means of attenuating Astana's dependence on Russia and China,[30] Central Asian officials generally appear to have decided several years ago that "bilateral agreements with the US and Turkey offer more political and operational benefits than do PfP programmes. . . . Downgrading involvement with NATO is a low-cost way of pleasing Moscow."[31]

Mediterranean Dialogue

NATO's Mediterranean Dialogue (MD) originated in the judgment of some Allies, notably Italy and Spain, that the Alliance's eastward orientation with PfP should be complemented with greater attention southward. Northern European and North

American Allies were less enthusiastic about the idea but approved it on a preliminary low-cost basis. According to Pertusot, the NATO Allies were also concerned about upholding the nuclear nonproliferation regime and being prepared to counter "the worsening of the situation in Algeria and the danger of a spillover effect in the region."[32]

In December 1994, the North Atlantic Council declared that NATO was prepared "to establish contacts, on a case-by-case basis, between the Alliance and Mediterranean non-member countries with a view to contributing to the strengthening of regional stability."[33] The MD began with five countries: Egypt, Israel, Mauritania, Morocco, and Tunisia. Jordan joined in November 1995 and Algeria followed in March 2000. Each dialogue has been bilateral between NATO and the specific country, although the participants have also convened multilateral (NATO+7) meetings on a regular basis. As with PfP, the principle of self-differentiation has allowed individual MD countries to determine their own programs of activities in agreement with the Alliance.

At the June 2004 Istanbul Summit, the Allies offered to "elevate the MD to a genuine partnership whose overall aim will be to contribute towards regional security and stability and complement other international efforts through enhanced practical cooperation, and whose objectives would include: enhancing the existing political dialogue; achieving interoperability; developing defence reform; [and] contributing to the fight against terrorism."[34]

The work programs with individual MD countries have included seminars and workshops on these topics and many others related to international security. In addition, the Allies have invited MD countries to observe or participate in NATO and PfP exercises; to send civilians and military officers to courses at the NATO School in Oberammergau, Germany, and the NATO Defense College in Rome, Italy; and to host on-site educational and training programs and port visits by NATO's Standing Naval Forces. The Allies have over the years made available to MD partners a large number of "cooperation tools" originally developed under PfP/EAPC auspices, including the Trust Fund mechanism, the Euro-Atlantic Disaster Response Coordination Center, and the Partnership Action Plan Against Terrorism.[35]

At the May 2012 Chicago Summit, the Allies welcomed "the Moroccan-led initiative to develop a new, political framework document for the MD," and stated that they "look forward to developing it together soon with our MD partners." The Allies added that they regard the MD as "a natural framework" for partnership with Libya. If Libya wanted assistance from the Alliance, the Allies would focus on "areas where NATO can add value." The Allies stipulated that "NATO's activities would focus primarily on security and defence sector reform, while taking into account other international efforts."[36]

Despite some statements by the NATO Allies and specific NATO and national officials, particularly in relation to hopes for the "Arab Spring," the Alliance has not pressed its MD partners to pursue democratization. Paradoxically, in the eyes of some political leaders in certain MD countries, the MD may have served as an attractive means of countering pressures to undertake democratic reforms. As Belkacem Iratni, an Algerian scholar, has noted, the several motives of Maghreb states in participating in the MD have included "legitimization of their own struggle against terrorism and easing of Western pressure (mainly from NGOs) to speed up and increase democratic reforms and practices."[37]

The vagueness of the MD's goals makes any assessment of its effectiveness elusive. Some observers have described the MD as little more than a "diplomatic talking shop."[38] It should be recalled, however, that Egypt, Jordan, and Morocco contributed forces to the NATO-led Stabilization Force in Bosnia and Herzegovina,[39] and that Morocco has contributed troops to the NATO-led Kosovo Force. Jordan conducted air transport and fighter escort missions in support of the NATO-led Operation Unified Protector in Libya, while Morocco furnished intelligence support. Participation in MD activities, notably those that address force interoperability, may well have facilitated these contributions to Alliance-led operations.

Istanbul Cooperation Initiative

The NATO Allies launched the Istanbul Cooperation Initiative (ICI) at the June 2004 Istanbul Summit, a little over a year after a U.S.-led coalition intervened in Iraq. The ICI's origins reside in the resolve of the United States and certain other Allies to promote greater Alliance cooperation with the Gulf Cooperation Council (GCC) states and others in the Middle East regarding energy security and other issues.[40] These Allies evidently convinced the skeptical Allies, which had overlapping reservations. First, some of the new NATO Allies feared that "such a partnership would detract from the priority that NATO should, in their view, be giving to Russia on the one hand, and on the other to the Eastern European states that have not yet joined the Alliance." Second, some Allies "are afraid that if the Alliance plays too strong a role in the Middle East, including through the ICI, they will be drawn insidiously into a stabilization mission on the ground, which could turn out to be very risky, very costly," demanding in personnel numbers, and hard to conduct.[41]

The Allies stated in June 2004 that the ICI was designed to "be complementary to the Alliance's Mediterranean Dialogue and could use instruments developed in this framework, while respecting its specificity."[42] According to the NATO Policy Document on the ICI,

> The aim of the initiative would be to enhance security and regional stability through a new transatlantic engagement with the region. This could be achieved by actively promoting NATO's cooperation with interested countries in the field of security, particularly through practical activities where NATO can add value to develop the ability of countries' forces to operate with those of the Alliance including by contributing to NATO-led operations, fight against terrorism, stem the flow of WMD materials and illegal trafficking in arms, and improve countries' capabilities to address common challenges and threats with NATO.[43]

In the same document, however, the NATO Allies noted "the need to avoid misunderstandings about the scope of the initiative, which is not meant to either lead to

NATO/EAPC/PfP membership, provide security guarantees, or be used to create a political debate over issues more appropriately handled in other fora."[44] Despite the Alliance's explicit exclusion of security guarantees, the ICI countries "see NATO as an additional insurance policy to protect them against Iran."[45] This motivation probably outweighs their interest in gaining other benefits from more systematic interactions with the NATO Allies.

Some observers hold that NATO's ICI engagement provides a degree of protection, despite the Alliance's having explicitly ruled out security commitments and despite the continuing concerns of some Allies that "outreach" partnerships in distant regions may distract attention from collective defense preparedness in Europe. They recall the 1990–1991 Gulf War, when NATO nations led a coalition including Arab units to expel Iraqi forces from Kuwait, without benefit of any defense treaties between Kuwait and the coalition powers. Since it remains in the overall security interests of the Alliance to protect the ICI states, it is argued, these states should recognize that "their technical partnership with NATO will inevitably enhance their armed forces' effectiveness and interoperability with any forces deployed to assist them."[46]

In June 2004, NATO announced, "Based on the principle of inclusiveness, the initiative could be opened to all interested countries in the region who subscribe to the aim and content of this initiative, including the fight against terrorism and the proliferation of weapons of mass destruction."[47] The Alliance intended to start with the member states of the GCC, but it did not exclude the Palestinian Authority from cooperation under ICI auspices.[48]

Of the six members of the GCC, four have chosen to become ICI partners: Bahrain, Kuwait, Qatar, and the United Arab Emirates. Oman and Saudi Arabia have expressed interest but have not joined. As with the PfP/EAPC and the MD, ICI meetings take place on a bilateral basis (NATO and the individual ICI partner) and on a multilateral basis (NATO and all four ICI partners).

NATO announcements of such meetings sometimes note the attendance of Oman and Saudi Arabia as observers.[49] Saudi Arabia has attributed its decision not to join the ICI to its determination to maintain its sovereignty and autonomy, but the country's leaders may also have little interest in a partnership framework putting Riyadh on the same level as the other GCC capitals. Oman's position is "extremely circumspect," owing to concerns about possibly annoying Tehran or Washington and London—or weakening the support of the country's armed forces for the regime.[50]

The menu of ICI activities with NATO has been similar to that pursued with the MD partners. It has included intelligence sharing related to terrorism and "military-to-military cooperation to contribute to interoperability through participation in selected military exercises and related education and training activities that could improve the ability of participating countries' forces to operate with those of the Alliance; and through participation in selected NATO and PfP exercises and in NATO-led operations on a case-by-case basis."[51] At the May 2012 Chicago Summit, the Allies declared, "We warmly welcome the generous offer by the State of Kuwait to host an ICI Regional Centre, which will help us to better understand common security challenges, and discuss how to address them together."[52]

Several factors have hampered the development of the ICI. First, as the NATO Allies have discovered, the GCC countries lack a common strategic outlook, and there has been "scarcely any cooperation within the GCC" on security matters.[53] Second, as a result of the "mistrust" among the GCC countries, each of the four ICI partners has favored a bilateral relationship with NATO and eschewed simultaneously pursuing a multilateral regional framework on the model of the Mediterranean Dialogue.[54] Third, the four GCC states participating in the ICI have all preferred to cultivate bilateral relations with specific NATO Allies—above all, France, the United Kingdom, and the United States—over relations with the Alliance as a whole.[55] Fourth, Saudi Arabia, the most powerful of the GCC states, has been "apprehensive of any Western interference in Gulf security affairs." Riyadh remains reluctant to establish formal relations with NATO, unless perhaps "in a tailored one-on-one framework," which the Alliance has not pursued.[56]

It is difficult to assess the effectiveness of the ICI. In 2008, the Alliance proposed 470 partnership activities to the four ICI countries, and they selected 88 and actually conducted only 57 of them. Pierre Razoux, a French scholar, has attributed this disparity to the "lack of qualified personnel available to take part in partnership activities" in the ICI countries.[57] Some observers have noted that the contributions by the United Arab Emirates and Bahrain to the ISAF in Afghanistan and by the United Arab Emirates and Qatar to Operation Unified Protector in Libya had "nothing to do with the ICI *per se* and could well have taken place without it."[58]

Mindful of the unwillingness of MD and ICI members to accept consolidation in a single framework, the Allies declared at the Chicago Summit that "the MD and ICI remain two complementary and yet distinct partnership frameworks." Emphasizing the partnership flexibility principles adopted in Berlin in April 2011, the Allies noted their openness to multiple formats for dialogue: "NATO is ready to consult more regularly on security issues of common concern, through the Mediterranean Dialogue (MD) and Istanbul Cooperation Initiative (ICI), as well as bilateral consultations and 28+n formats."[59]

Partners across the Globe

Since 1998 the Alliance has cultivated relationships with what it has called "contact countries," "global partners," or "partners across the globe."[60] According to a dossier on the NATO website, these countries "share similar strategic concerns and key Alliance values. Australia, Japan, the Republic of Korea and New Zealand are all examples." While this dossier also cited Argentina and Chile as examples, in view of their contributions to NATO-led operations in the Balkans,[61] another NATO website dossier stated that the "global partners" of the Alliance "include Australia, Japan, the Republic of Korea, New Zealand, Pakistan, Iraq and Afghanistan."[62] At the May 2012 Chicago Summit the Allies hailed "our newest partner Mongolia."[63]

In October 2012 the NATO website stated that the Alliance intends "to develop dialogue with countries that do not have a formal bilateral programme of cooperation," including China, Colombia, India, Indonesia, Malaysia, and Singapore.[64] The NATO-China relationship began in 2002, and it has included a series of discussion visits by NATO officials in China and by Chinese delegations at NATO headquarters.[65]

Countries in the "partners across the globe" category have contributed in various ways to NATO activities and operations. Australia was, for example, for some time "the largest non-NATO contributor of troops to ISAF."[66] New Zealand has sent forces to lead a Provincial Reconstruction Team in support of ISAF in Afghanistan, and previously contributed troops to SFOR in Bosnia.[67] The Republic of Korea has also led a Provincial Reconstruction Team in Afghanistan and has contributed to the Afghan National Army Trust Fund.[68] Mongolia contributed to KFOR in Kosovo in 2005–2007 and has provided forces to ISAF in Afghanistan since 2010.[69]

Japan has been "NATO's longest-standing global partner," with increasingly extensive dialogue and cooperation since the first Japan-NATO meeting in 1990.[70] Since the 1990s Japan has been "a major donor nation" supporting recovery and reconstruction projects in the Balkans. Japan has subsequently contributed to NATO/PfP Trust Funds for projects in Afghanistan and Tajikistan.[71] Japan has backed ISAF "without being involved militarily by funding various development projects and dispatching liaison officers."[72]

The Allies have made clear their openness to partnerships with countries around the world. "NATO is prepared to develop political dialogue and practical cooperation with any nation across the globe that shares our interest in peaceful international relations."[73] The Allies have nonetheless articulated criteria for the optimal use of their finite resources for partnership activities, including

- whether the partner concerned aspires to join the Alliance;
- whether the partner in question shares the values on which NATO is based and, where appropriate, is engaged in defense and larger reforms based on these values;
- whether the partner concerned supports militarily, politically, financially or otherwise NATO's ongoing operations and missions or NATO's efforts to meet new security challenges;
- whether the partner is of special strategic importance for NATO;
- whether the partner has a special and developed bilateral cooperation framework with the Alliance; and
- the capacity of the partner to finance its cooperative activities with NATO.[74]

In 2006–2008, particularly in the run-up to the NATO summit meetings in Riga (November 2006) and Bucharest (April 2008), the United Kingdom and the United States advocated the establishment of a "Global Partnership Forum" that would bring together democratic countries throughout the world that were ineligible for (or uninterested in) NATO membership but prepared to contribute to NATO-led operations. One of the main rationales for this approach was to provide a vehicle for partners contributing substantially to Alliance-led operations, such as Australia and

Japan, to have greater influence in decision making about these operations. France, Germany, and other Allies rejected this proposal, owing in part to concerns about the misperceptions that the word "global" might foster and the possible implications for the Alliance's other partnership frameworks.[75]

The Allies have over the years taken a different approach to revitalizing their partnership frameworks and addressing in particular the decision-making issue in NATO-led operations.

Efforts to Revitalize NATO's Partnership Policies

The Allies have steadily augmented the scope of their multinational partnership programs, especially PfP. In January 1995 the Allies supplemented PfP with a Planning and Review Process (PARP) that closely parallels NATO's own defense planning system. For partners that choose to participate, PARP enhances transparency and improves the interoperability of partner forces with those of the Allies. PARP also offers a mechanism for identifying, assessing, and developing "Partner forces and capabilities that could be available to the Alliance for multinational training, exercises and operations."[76] Over the years the Allies have developed and improved consultation, education, training, and exercise programs dealing with standardization, operational preparedness, counterterrorism, and defense institution building, among other topics.[77]

At the 2002 Prague Summit, moreover, the Allies launched Individual Partnership Action Plans (IPAPs). Such plans are two-year programs that enable the Alliance to "provide focused, country-specific advice on reform objectives."[78] Seven PfP partners have to date concluded IPAPs with NATO: Armenia, Azerbaijan, Bosnia and Herzegovina, Georgia, Kazakhstan, Moldova, and Montenegro.

In November 2010, at the Lisbon Summit, the Allies decided to streamline NATO's partnership structures and, subject to certain reservations, to open all activities to all partners. In April 2011, the Allies announced a recasting of their partnerships policy: "the Alliance, in consultation with partners, will establish a single Partnership Cooperation Menu and a tailored Individual Partnership and Cooperation Programme (IPCP) as an entry-level programme available to all partners. The Individual Partnership Action Plan (IPAP) and Planning and Review Process (PARP) will also be opened to partners beyond the EAPC/PfP, on a case by case basis and on decision of the NAC [North Atlantic Council]."[79]

The Allies underscored the remarkable breadth of this new policy by spelling out that "partners" would encompass all the countries in the Alliance's multilateral frameworks and bilateral programs: "While respecting the specificity of existing partnership frameworks, all partners will be offered access to the whole spectrum of partnership activities NATO offers. All partners with which NATO has a partnership programme—whether they be Euro-Atlantic partners, or partners in the Mediterranean Dialogue and the Istanbul Cooperation Initiative, or global partners—will have access to the new Partnership and Cooperation Menu, which comprises some 1600 activities."[80]

Furthermore, the Allies announced a new "28+n" partnership meeting formula—that is, all twenty-eight NATO Allies with an indefinite number of partners from multilateral or bilateral frameworks. "The '28+n' formula provides a mechanism for consultations and, as appropriate, cooperation in flexible formats across and beyond existing frameworks. This mechanism can be thematic or event-driven and will develop through practice, as part of a process to enhance NATO's partnerships."[81] For example, in May 2012, at the Chicago Summit, the Allies demonstrated this new flexibility by convening a meeting with thirteen partners that had "recently made particular political, operational and financial contributions to NATO-led operations," plus another meeting with four candidates for NATO membership (Bosnia and Herzegovina, Georgia, Montenegro, and the former Yugoslav Republic of Macedonia).[82] The "28+n" formula is distinct from that of "28+all partners." In January 2012 the chairman of NATO's Military Committee chaired a "big tent" meeting of chiefs of Defense Staff from sixty-seven NATO and partner countries, plus the chairman of the European Union's Military Committee.[83]

Another major element of NATO's new partnership policy, also announced in April 2011, has been a clarification of the enhanced roles of partners in shaping Alliance decisions concerning operations to which partners have contributed forces. It is in the context of the Political Military Framework that Allies meet with their operational partners—such as meetings of the North Atlantic Council at various levels in KFOR format and in ISAF format.[84] The new Political Military Framework for Partner Involvement in NATO-Led Operations addresses the long-standing concerns strongly expressed by Australia and other non-NATO force providers.

As Kevin Rudd, then the Australian foreign minister, noted, Australia and other countries contributing to NATO-led operations will no longer be presented policies "precooked by NATO members." The April 2011 Berlin reforms "formalise a role for partners in shaping decisions in NATO-led operations to which they contribute. . . . NATO's new partnerships policy locks in this principle and ensures its implementation, not just for Afghanistan but for any future missions."[85] According to the new Political Military Framework, "While operational partners are fully involved in the decision-shaping process," the North Atlantic Council "retains the ultimate responsibility for decision-making."[86]

In April 2011 Secretary General Rasmussen said, "The 'Berlin partnership package' approved today will allow us to work on more issues, with more partners, in more ways."[87] As Heidi Reisinger of the NATO Defense College has observed, "In practical cooperation in missions, the distinction between being a member or being a partner thus seems to be fading."[88]

The Allies were nonetheless relatively cautious about security commitments in their new partnership package. Rather than extending the language echoing Article

4 of the North Atlantic Treaty that appears in the PfP Framework Document to all partners, the Allies stated simply that "the Alliance will be open to consultation on issues of particular security interest to partners. These consultations will not duplicate conflict resolution processes in other international fora. The NAC will retain the authority to agree to each of these consultations."[89]

In 2012 the Alliance first employed two new cooperation mechanisms for "global partners." First, in March 2012 the North Atlantic Council endorsed an Individual Partnership and Cooperation Program for Mongolia. This was the first IPCP concluded in accordance with the Alliance's April 2011 redefinition of its partnership policy.[90] Second, in June 2012 Secretary General Rasmussen and Julia Gillard, then the Australian prime minister, signed in Canberra an Australia-NATO Joint Political Declaration. This was the first such agreement between the Alliance and a partner nation, and it complements the IPCP for Australia.[91]

According to the joint declaration, "Australia particularly welcomes the decision to formalise the role of operational partners in shaping strategy and decisions in NATO-led missions to which they contribute."[92] The joint declaration's references to shared values and strategic interests help to explain the motives of Australia and a number of other partners in formalizing partnership relations that look beyond missions such as ISAF in Afghanistan. As Brendan Nelson, then the Australian ambassador to NATO, observed in 2011, "NATO now has a global approach to Euroatlantic security, recognising that threats can emerge from any part of the world and in many different forms. . . . What we need most is one another. That is why NATO will have a long term partner in Australia."[93]

The organizational mechanisms of NATO's partnerships offer considerable latitude to Allies and partners. All NATO Allies and partners can propose partnership activities or events via the ePRIME network.[94] Once these proposed activities and events are approved by the North Atlantic Council, they become part of the Partnership Cooperation Menu (PCM). Even before the partnership reforms were adopted in Berlin in 2011, ePRIME included activities for all partnership frameworks, but in different work plans. Since 2011 the Alliance has maintained a single work plan—the PCM, which is reflected in ePRIME.

The NATO member state or partner sponsoring and conducting the activity (for example, an exercise, seminar, training event, or course of study) serves as the "action authority" and can specify limits on eligibility for participation—for example, that interested partners must have met certain standards concerning information security and/or satisfy language requirements. Partnership activities and events may also be proposed by NATO-sponsored institutions, such as Partnership Training and Education Centres, located in NATO or partner nations, or Centres of Excellence accredited by the Alliance.[95]

NATO has reportedly concluded security agreements with all European Union members that are in the Alliance's PfP (that is, all EU members except Cyprus), and with some other partners, such as (for example) Australia, Jordan, and New

Zealand. The scope and requirements of specific security agreements apparently differ, and they limit the participation of partners and prospective partners in specific activities.[96]

As with most NATO activities, the consensus principle applies to the Alliance's decision making about partnerships.[97] According to many accounts, Turkey has demonstrated the power of a member state to exclude a partner from specific activities.[98] Indeed, Turkey reportedly for a time blocked approval of all updates to the PCM if the choices would be available to Israel. There was apparently a compromise at or after the December 2012 ministerial meeting whereby the Allies agreed that in the 2013 PCM, certain partnership activities such as exercises and counter-improvised explosive device (IED) training would be reserved for "operational partners," defined as contributors to ISAF and KFOR. Since Israel is not such an "operational partner," these activities have gone forward without Israel and with Turkey's approval.

Before the April 2011 meeting in Berlin, partnership activities were organized via the EAPC/PfP, MD, and ICI work plans and the work plans for individual contact countries (currently known as "partners across the globe"). Since Berlin, there has been one PCM for all partners, so Turkey's action in declining to approve all updates to the PCM temporarily arrested the development of the Alliance's entire partnership policy.[99] Moreover, Turkey blocked a projected meeting of MD foreign ministers in conjunction with a meeting of NATO foreign ministers in April 2013, a meeting that would have been the first NATO-MD foreign ministers meeting since 2008. Since the approval of the Berlin reform package in April 2011, the Alliance's general policy has continued to be that all activities offered to partners must be approved by the North Atlantic Council. This principle also applies to the concept approved at Berlin of "28+n" meetings with partners.

Perhaps the most fundamental question raised by the Alliance's April 2011 partnerships reform concerns NATO's continuing commitment to "the principles of democracy, individual liberty and the rule of law" evoked in the North Atlantic Treaty. According to NATO's key April 2011 policy declaration on partnerships,

> NATO's partnerships make a clear and valued contribution to Allied security, to international security more broadly and to defending and advancing the values of individual liberty, democracy, human rights and the rule of law, on which the Alliance is based. Commitment to these values remains fundamental to NATO's partnership policy. Allies and partners remain committed to fulfil in good faith the obligations of the Charter of the United Nations and the principles of the Universal Declaration on Human Rights.[100]

The Allies directed this document to all of the Alliance's partners, including those in the MD, the ICI, and PfP that have historically received little attention from the Allies concerning democratic reform. The somewhat paradoxical result is that, despite the professed enduring commitment to democratization, the Alliance seems to be placing less emphasis on it than it did during the early years of PfP, when candidates for membership sought to demonstrate their democratic credentials. It is noteworthy in this regard that the key April 2011 declaration on partnerships also includes the following paragraph:

The strategic objectives of NATO's partner relations will be, without any indication of priority ranking, to:

- Enhance Euro-Atlantic and international security, peace and stability;
- Promote regional security and cooperation;
- Facilitate mutually beneficial cooperation on issues of common interest, including international efforts to meet emerging security challenges;
- Prepare interested eligible nations for NATO membership;
- Promote democratic values and reforms;
- Enhance support for NATO-led operations and missions;
- Enhance awareness on security developments including through early warning, with a view to preventing crises;
- Build confidence, achieve better mutual understanding, including about NATO's role and activities, in particular through enhanced public diplomacy.[101]

The objective calling for partner relations to "promote democratic values and reforms" appears as fifth in the list of eight. The fact that the Allies have listed their "strategic objectives" for partner relations "without any indication of priority ranking" suggests that they do not know what their true priorities are concerning partnerships—or do not wish to make them publicly known.

As a result, a number of critical observers have formed the impression that the Alliance's approach to partnerships might become increasingly managerial, utilitarian, and pragmatic, with little more than perfunctory lip service paid to the original goals of promoting democracy and human rights. As Heidi Reisinger has written, "Critics of the reform were concerned that the new . . . programme structure . . . would turn out to be a politically neutral option in which priorities such as democratization and human rights would be neglected."[102] In other words, despite the declared importance of democratic ideals,

> sharing the same political values is no longer a prerequisite to becoming a partner of NATO. A willingness to support NATO operations, geographical location or the contribution of needed capabilities can suffice today. This was NATO's approach to MD and ICI partners from the beginning. . . . NATO's former political "mission" to promote democratic values, which was the approach in Eastern Europe, the Caucasus and Central Asia, has been transformed into an offer extended to those interested. In other words, it has moved from compulsory to optional status. . . . The political vision of promoting democratic values through cooperation may move into the background as NATO concentrates on what it can do best: multilateral military action. The "community of values" may make room for the "cooperative approach to security."[103]

The extent to which the Allies sustain the political purposes that helped to inspire the Alliance's founding and its first post–Cold War partnerships will be critical for its legitimacy and staying power.

Comparing NATO's Multilateral Partnership Frameworks

PfP/EAPC, MD, and ICI share certain similarities. In each case, the partnership has provided options for bilateral (NATO+1) as well as multilateral dialogue and cooperation, and the principle of self-differentiation has applied to the definition of individual national programs of cooperative activity. In each case, moreover, NATO has had an interest in preparing partners for possible contributions to NATO-led operations.

In each framework, the heterogeneity of membership has been an obstacle to deeper multilateral cooperation. In the PfP, as noted earlier, the current members fall into three categories: (1) former Yugoslav states that are expected to eventually join the Alliance, if and when they satisfy the membership requirements; (2) relatively prosperous Western European states with traditions of neutrality, a few of which might choose to join NATO at some point; and (3) former Soviet republics whose views (and prospects) regarding possible NATO membership differ substantially. In the MD, the four westernmost members (Algeria, Mauritania, Morocco, and Tunisia) constitute a Maghreb group, with more in common with each other than with the three eastern Mediterranean members (Egypt, Israel, and Jordan). In the ICI, the heterogeneity derives, somewhat paradoxically, from the countries that have been invited from the outset but that have maintained an observer status: Oman and Saudi Arabia.

The PfP differs from the MD and the ICI fundamentally because the PfP Framework Document includes a security consultation commitment and because European PfP partners are eligible for Alliance membership. There is no question of the Alliance offering formal security commitments or the prospect of NATO membership to MD or ICI partners. At the same time, however, Secretary General Rasmussen has pointed out that NATO and ICI partners share general security interests as well as strategic interests specific to the Gulf and the wider region:

> NATO and ICI countries face common security challenges and threats . . . such as failed states, terrorism, the proliferation of weapons of mass destruction, piracy and energy security. . . . Therefore it is clear that the security of Bahrain, and of all our ICI partner countries, is of strategic interest to NATO. We have a shared interest in helping countries like Afghanistan, Kosovo and Iraq to stand on their own feet again, and in preventing countries like Somalia, Yemen and Sudan from slipping deeper into chaos. And we all are seriously concerned about Iran's nuclear ambition—and about the instability this could cause in a region that is pivotal for global stability and security.[104]

The lack of a formal security commitment would not rule out combined action to meet common threats. Several NATO countries participated, for example, in the coalition to liberate Kuwait in 1990–1991, despite the absence of any mutual defense treaty or explicit guarantee.

Because there is no question of joining the Alliance for MD and ICI partners, NATO has no "membership carrot" with which to motivate these partners to pursue democratization. There is no question of NATO helping with security sector reform oriented toward civilian and democratic control of the armed forces unless MD and ICI partners want such reform. In June 2011 Secretary General Rasmussen called for democratization throughout the Middle East and North Africa:

> For too long, many thought that you could not have both stability and democracy in that region. The men and women on the Arab streets have shown they want both. They sent their

governments, and the world, a very clear message: stability at the expense of our aspirations is not true stability. This is because freedom is not just a western value—it is a universal value. It is not a commodity for the few—it should be shared by the many. And it is not to be feared—it is the best guarantee of long-term peace. . . . We want to see the Arab Spring blossom. And a region that is free, democratic, modern and stable. . . . It won't happen overnight. But it can happen. And NATO wants to help make it happen.[105]

Despite Rasmussen's assurance that democratization is "not to be feared," leaders and elites that would lose their positions with democratic reforms dread and actively oppose such reforms.[106] The governing elites in certain MD and ICI countries may therefore have had misgivings about the North Atlantic Council's May 2012 declaration that "NATO supports the aspirations of the people of the [Mediterranean and broader Middle East] region for democracy, individual liberty and the rule of law—values which underpin the Alliance."[107]

NATO has offered to provide its ICI partners "tailored advice on defence reform, defence budgeting, defence planning and civil-military relations."[108] However, as Pierre Razoux has observed, the reigning families in the Gulf "do not always welcome the reform process advocated by NATO, as they are afraid that the military could turn against them."[109] NATO cannot carry partnerships further than the partners are prepared to go.

PfP generally enjoys broader support among the NATO Allies than the MD and the ICI, and the sentiment is reciprocal in some cases. That is, NATO has a higher political standing in several PfP countries than in most MD and ICI countries, and the NATO Allies have historically invested greater resources in PfP than in the MD and the ICI. NATO's objectives for PfP have been more ambitious and precise than for the MD and the ICI.

The Alliance's standing throughout the Middle East and North Africa has been another constraint on the MD and the ICI. NATO has a "negative image," deriving in part from the colonialist past of several NATO European countries, the interventionism of the United States and certain other Allies, and U.S. and Allied support for Israel.[110] As an example of the derogatory initial perceptions of NATO's ICI in the Gulf, one might note that in 2006 Abdulaziz Sager, the Saudi chairman and founder of the Gulf Research Center, wrote that "the initiative being put forward within the framework of NATO has been perceived in negative terms as being no more than a mechanism by which the West can continue to control the region. With the reputation of the United States in the Gulf deteriorating rapidly, NATO was perceived as a wolf in sheep's clothing or as a new package for Western policies of the past."[111]

Vivien Pertusot has described the Arab-Israeli conflict as "poisonous" for the development of the MD and the ICI. Some Arab officials have expressed reluctance to be seen meeting with Israeli representatives because of the Palestinian question, popular perceptions of Israel in their countries, and an impression that Western governments maintain double standards regarding Iranian and Israeli nuclear capabilities. Exceptional 28+7 meetings of NATO and MD representatives have nonetheless taken place at the ministerial level on an "informal" basis, ruling out any debate on the Arab-Israeli conflict.[112]

At the May 2012 Chicago Summit the Allies welcomed the participation of "thirteen partners who have recently made particular political, operational, and financial contributions to NATO-led operations."[113] These thirteen partners—Australia, Austria, Finland, Georgia, Japan, Jordan, the Republic of Korea, Morocco, New Zealand, Qatar, Sweden, Switzerland, and the United Arab Emirates—included PfP, ICI, and MD members, as well as countries outside those frameworks. The Allies described this meeting as "an example of the enhanced flexibility with which we are addressing partnership issues in a demand- and substance-driven way." The Allies indicated that they intend to pursue exercises and joint training as a means to cultivate operationally relevant partnerships beyond current missions, such as ISAF in Afghanistan.[114]

The Alliance's intervention in Libya in 2011 showed the value of such activities in familiarizing partners with the Alliance and preparing the partners willing to take action to participate with confidence in NATO-led operations. For example, Sweden's airpower role in the Libya conflict in 2011 drew attention to its role as a PfP partner.[115] Ann-Sofie Dahl, a Swedish expert, wrote that "Sweden is in many ways closer to NATO, and a more reliable contributor, than several of the allied countries."[116] In March 2012 Secretary General Rasmussen described his meeting with Swedish legislators regarding the Swedish Parliament's deliberations on participation in the Libya operation: "The argument I met, why a broad majority in the Swedish Parliament decided to join the operation was that NATO took on the responsibility for that operation; that it took place within a NATO framework, a tested and tried framework, with all the institutions necessary to also exercise political control."[117]

The importance of partnerships for NATO promises to grow, at least in some domains. As Michael Rühle has pointed out, "The nature of today's security challenges makes NATO's success increasingly dependent on how well it cooperates with others, whether the issue is peacekeeping, cyberdefense, non-proliferation, counterterrorism, or energy security. Hence, enhancing NATO's 'connectivity' . . . is a precondition for its future as a viable security provider."[118] How far effective partnership activities can be carried will be determined by political factors in specific cases.

Prospects for Further Reforms

The prospects for changes in NATO's partnership policies beyond those announced in April 2011 appear limited in the foreseeable future. The critical reactions to the imaginative proposals advanced by Karl-Heinz Kamp and Heidi Reisinger in May 2013 demonstrated at least that there is at present little enthusiasm for a far-reaching new design along the lines they suggested. Kamp and Reisinger incisively analyzed shortcomings in the existing partnership arrangements, and deplored "NATO's failure to establish a 'hierarchy' with regard to the importance of partners." Even within PfP, they noted, democracies such as Finland and Sweden that make significant contributions to NATO-led operations are obliged to make "strange bedfellows with authoritarian regimes."[119]

As a solution, Kamp and Reisinger proposed that the Allies "pension off the old frameworks" of the PfP, ICI, and MD and establish "three concentric circles around NATO." The first circle, that closest to the Alliance, would consist of Advanced Partners from around the world, with Austria and Australia "equally eligible"—"countries which want to engage in partnership with NATO, are politically like-minded (i.e., fully developed Western-style democracies), and are willing and able to contribute to operations." The second circle would be composed of Cooperation Partners—"countries actively interested in partnership and in cooperating with NATO, to the mutual benefit of both sides, in certain areas of common concern," but not necessarily politically like-minded or disposed to contribute to NATO-led operations. The third circle—Dialogue Countries—would contain all other countries interested in exchanges with NATO.[120]

The principal obstacles to implementing the Kamp-Reisinger proposals appear to be twofold. First, on the whole, the Allies and their partners see merits in the existing frameworks and wish to keep them. Second, many observers have argued that to divide partners into categories of "valuable" and "less valuable" would be "insulting," "derogatory," "politically unworkable," and "counterproductive" when NATO needs practical help in operations—for instance, troops, money, and ground and air transit rights. NATO has accepted substantial assistance from nondemocratic partners in operations, notably in Afghanistan and Libya. Placing nondemocratic partners in a second- or third-rank status might be "impolitic" and "unwise," because it might make them less willing to contribute to NATO-led operations or to work with NATO in other ways. The critical reactions from the partner nations not among the thirteen accorded special recognition at the May 2012 Chicago Summit demonstrated that nations are sensitive even to relatively secondary matters of status and protocol.[121]

Conversely, some observers have opined, Kamp and Reisinger have done well to highlight the fact that the Allies have yet to develop a long-term political and strategic design for partnerships. This omission reflects continuing differences about priorities among the Allies, as well as resource constraints.

Moreover, just as the Allies will have to rely on the exercises, training, and education envisaged in the Connected Forces Initiative to maintain readiness and interoperability after the end of the ISAF mission in Afghanistan, the Alliance's partnership activities (notably with "operational partners" currently participating in ISAF and other missions) will require refurbishment after the end of ISAF in 2014 in order to sustain connections with partners and to remain relevant, useful, and inviting. Such refurbishment will also present costs. The end of ISAF will also mean the end of perhaps the most valuable form of "28+n" interactions with partners.[122] While the KFOR format will remain, the Allies have to date not made much use of the "28+n" format outside operations.

It appears that, aside from operations, it is difficult for the Allies to agree on which countries to work with in a "28+n" format—and on which issues . According to an expert observer, aside from operations-oriented sessions, "The '28+n' meetings since the reforms were announced in Berlin in April 2011 have often been informational briefings of a one-off character—that is, without a mandate for a follow-up."[123]

The most fundamental issue remains that of the Alliance's essential political objectives. From the utilitarian viewpoint favored by many experts, the question is simply whether the Allies and partners need to pursue a shared political aim to achieve useful results. Allied experts acknowledge that there is a debate about how to interact with nondemocratic partners. As an expert observer put it, "this is perhaps also an indication of how advanced our partnerships have become; the more partners are integrated into NATO business, the more technical and 'utilitarian' the nature of the relationship becomes; not all engagement can be about values and human rights. It also raises a wider point about the nature of partnerships. . . . [Some people] seem to think that partnerships are fundamentally about values and principles (an 'idealist' vision), but there is a 'realist' case for partnerships as well."[124] Some Allied observers are nonetheless concerned that the Allies are emptying the partnership programs of their democratic political content with the emphasis on contributions to operations and the availability in principle of all activities to all partners.

NATO-Russia Relations

Russia has been one of the Alliance's PfP partners since 1994, but Russia has always been an exceptionally passive participant in PfP,[125] except for programs dealing with civil emergency planning. Various explanations for Russia's passivity have been suggested, including its continuing distrust of NATO and its reluctance to lend support and legitimacy to a NATO-centered network of relationships.[126] Russia participated, however, in the NATO-led peacekeeping forces in Bosnia, beginning in January 1996,[127] and in Kosovo, beginning in June 1999. The Russians withdrew from these engagements in 2003, as discussed below.

Partly with a view to reassuring Russia about the Alliance's prospective decisions to admit new members, the NATO Allies proposed to Moscow the conclusion of a NATO-Russia Founding Act. In this political declaration, signed in Paris in May 1997, the NATO Allies offered assurances about potential force deployments on the territory of new NATO members.[128] The Founding Act was also noteworthy for its "cooperative security" vision.

> NATO and Russia, based on an enduring political commitment undertaken at the highest political level, will build together *a lasting and inclusive peace in the Euro-Atlantic area on the principles of democracy and cooperative security.* . . . Proceeding from the principle that *the security of all states in the Euro-Atlantic community is indivisible,* NATO and Russia will work together to contribute to the establishment in Europe of common and comprehensive security based on the allegiance to shared values, commitments and norms of behaviour in the interests of all states. . . . NATO and Russia will seek the widest possible cooperation among participat-

ing States of the OSCE with the aim of creating in Europe a common space of security and stability, without dividing lines or spheres of influence limiting the sovereignty of any state.[129]

The Russian government condemned the Alliance's use of force in the 1999 Kosovo conflict as inconsistent with Founding Act commitments. Russia responded to NATO's Operation Allied Force by withdrawing some of the Russian personnel from positions at SHAPE and at NATO headquarters; suspending dialogue and cooperation in the PfP framework; suspending dialogue in the NATO-Russia Permanent Joint Council established by the Founding Act; suspending dialogue between the Russian Ministry of Defense and the U.S. Department of Defense (and with other NATO counterparts); closing the NATO documentation center in Moscow; and withdrawing most Russian officers from military schools in NATO countries such as France and the United States. Russia considered halting U.S. assistance with nuclear and chemical weapons security under the Cooperative Threat Reduction (CTR) program, but did not do so.[130] The fact that Russia did not suspend the CTR program in 1999 made its 2012 decision to terminate this program of cooperation with the United States all the more significant.[131] In June 2013, however, Russia and the United States announced the signing of a new cooperative agreement in this domain.[132]

Despite Russia's opposition to NATO's intervention in the Kosovo conflict (and the confrontation between Russian and NATO forces at the Pristina airport),[133] Moscow agreed to contribute forces to the NATO-led KFOR for postconflict peacekeeping. At the same time, Moscow resisted the resumption of NATO-Russia relations without clarification of the consultation obligations in the Founding Act. In September 1999 a Russian spokesman said that "restoration and further development of relations between Russia and NATO can be possible only on a qualitatively new basis. . . . It means that no decisions, projects or plans concerning European security can be adopted, considered or implemented without Russia's participation. If this is formalized in documents and made legally binding, Russia will find it possible to resume relations with NATO. This is our fundamental position and it is an obligatory condition for restoring our relations with the Alliance."[134]

At the beginning of 2000, Lord Robertson, then the NATO secretary general, proposed to visit Moscow with a view to restoring normal NATO-Russian dialogue and cooperation. Some Russian officials reportedly tried to make Lord Robertson's visit and the resumption of dialogue with NATO conditional on the Alliance (a) agreeing to Russia's interpretation of the Founding Act (with Russian rights of codecision with NATO allies regarding non-Article 5 NATO actions), (b) accepting Russian views on the future status of Kosovo, and (c) recognizing the role of the UN Security Council in authorizing military interventions such as the Alliance's action in the Kosovo crisis in 1999.[135] In the event, Robertson went to Moscow, and Russia-NATO relations returned to normal without the satisfaction of these conditions. Many Russians nonetheless continue to regard NATO's use of force in the Kosovo conflict as lawless and unjustified,[136] and some have cited it as an example of what Russia could face from NATO if Moscow did not have a reliable nuclear deterrence posture.[137]

In September 2001 the NATO-Russia Permanent Joint Council condemned the terrorist attacks against the United States: "NATO and Russia will intensify their cooperation under the Founding Act to defeat this scourge."[138]

Subsequent improvements in cooperation concerning terrorism and other challenges led the Allies and Moscow to make a new political declaration, titled "NATO-Russia Relations: A New Quality," in May 2002.[139] The bedrock declaration of political intent defining the relationship was to remain the May 1997 Founding Act.[140] The major innovation in the "new quality" declaration was to replace the Permanent Joint Council with a NATO-Russia Council based on new decision-making principles. In the new decision-making mechanism, the NATO secretary general chairs the NATO-Russia Council, and members act in their national capacities, with no pre-coordination of NATO positions.[141]

Even though Russia and the NATO Allies had agreed on a "new quality" approach to cooperation in 2002, Moscow decided the next year to terminate what many regarded as the most practically significant form of cooperation—Russian participation in NATO-led peacekeeping operations in the Balkans. Russia had taken part in IFOR and its successor, SFOR, in Bosnia and Herzegovina since 1996, and in KFOR in Kosovo since 1999. Alexander Nikitin, a Russian expert, has noted that, in withdrawing its troops from both Bosnia and Herzegovina and Kosovo in mid-2003, "Moscow argued that the objectives of the deployment had essentially been achieved, while expressing reservations about the impartiality of the NATO-led operation in Kosovo." According to Nikitin, in Russian eyes "NATO's actions were generally viewed as being biased against the Serbs."[142]

Other factors that may help to explain why Russia withdrew its forces from SFOR and KFOR in 2003 include the financial costs of maintaining the forces abroad and the political costs of upholding NATO policy, especially at a time when a U.S.-led coalition was undertaking an intervention in Iraq. A Russian impression that Moscow's military presence had little influence on NATO or European Union policy in the western Balkans may have also contributed to the decision to withdraw.

No crisis of the magnitude of the 1999 Kosovo conflict tested the NATO-Russia Council until the Russia-Georgia conflict in August 2008. The NATO Allies criticized Russia's use of force in Georgia: "Russian military action has been disproportionate and inconsistent with its peacekeeping role, as well as incompatible with the principles of peaceful conflict resolution set out in the Helsinki Final Act, the NATO-Russia Founding Act and the Rome Declaration."[143]

Furthermore, the Allies announced conditions for a return to "business as usual" in NATO-Russia relations: "We have determined that we cannot continue with business as usual. We call on Moscow to demonstrate—both in word and deed—its continued commitment to the principles upon which we agreed to base our relationship."[144]

In both "word and deed" (notably with regard to Georgia), Russia has not demonstrated "its continued commitment to the principles upon which we agreed to base our relationship." The Allies declared, for example, that Russia's recognition of the Abkhazia and South Ossetia regions of Georgia as independent states "is inconsistent with the fundamental OSCE principles on which stability in Europe is based."[145] Russia's recognition of Abkhazia and South Ossetia has continued, but the NATO Allies decided in 2009 to overlook this and to resume "business as usual."

The U.S. administration that took office in January 2009 called for a "reset" in relations with Russia. For example, Vice President Biden said in February 2009 that "it's time to press the reset button and to revisit the many areas where we can and should be working together with Russia."[146] Some Allied critics of the term "reset" noted that the United States did not require any "reset" of Georgia's territorial integrity as a condition for improving relations with Russia. Indeed, some Allied observers added, the Russian government seemed to regard the U.S. "reset" policy as a commitment by Washington to correct American mistakes, with no change in Russian policy required.[147]

The Allies suspended formal meetings of the NATO-Russia Council from August 2008 to March 2009. While the Allies shelved cooperation in some areas, they continued to work with Russia in "key areas of common interest, such as counter-narcotics and the fight against terrorism."[148] In December 2009 the Allies marked their "formal resumption, at Ministerial level, of dialogue and cooperation with Russia."[149] The Allies thus formally ended the "no business as usual" interruption caused by the August 2008 Russia-Georgia war.[150] The Allies in December 2009 nonetheless added,

> NATO-Russia relations depend on trust and fulfilment of commitments. In contributing to building that trust we will continue to be transparent about our military training and exercises and look to Russia to reciprocate. We reaffirm the OSCE principles on which the security of Europe is based, and reiterate our continued support for the territorial integrity and sovereignty of Georgia within its internationally recognised borders. We continue to call on Russia to reverse its recognition of the South Ossetia and Abkhazia regions of Georgia as "independent states". We encourage all participants in the Geneva talks to play a constructive role as well as to continue working closely with the OSCE, the United Nations and the European Union to pursue peaceful conflict resolution on Georgia's territory.[151]

The Allies made clear their interest in constructive cooperation with Russia in the 2010 Strategic Concept:

> NATO-Russia cooperation is of strategic importance as it contributes to creating a common space of peace, stability and security. NATO poses no threat to Russia. On the contrary: we want to see a true strategic partnership between NATO and Russia, and we will act accordingly, with the expectation of reciprocity from Russia.[152]

In the November 2010 Lisbon Summit Declaration the Allies reiterated their "call on Russia to reverse its recognition of the South Ossetia and Abkhazia regions of Georgia as independent states" and "to meet its commitments with respect to Georgia, as mediated by the European Union on 12 August and 8 September 2008."[153] The Allies repeated this call in the May 2012 Chicago Summit Declaration.[154]

However, the Allies do not wish to antagonize Moscow, partly because they could benefit from cooperation with Russia regarding terrorism, nuclear nonproliferation, and Afghanistan, among other issues. Indeed, the Allies have repeatedly agreed with Russia on extensive agendas of topics for cooperation, notably in the 1997 NATO-Russia Founding Act, in the 2002 "new quality" statement, and at the meeting of the NATO-Russia Council in December 2009—at which the NATO-Russia Council launched "a Joint Review of 21st Century Common Security Challenges," a review proposed by Secretary General Rasmussen in September 2009.[155] The NATO-Russia Council endorsed the findings of the review in November 2010 and "identified concrete practical cooperation activities" concerning missile defense, Afghanistan, counterterrorism, and piracy.[156] The Allies highlighted their "practical cooperation" with Russia, notably with respect to Afghanistan, at the May 2012 Chicago Summit.[157]

As noted in chapter 2, since the end of the Cold War the official Alliance position has been that Russia is a partner. The Allies wish to find a modus vivendi with Russia and to return to constructive dialogue and cooperation, even though Moscow has become more assertive since early 2007. Critics of Russia's behavior cite various actions, including its suspension of compliance with the 1990 Conventional Armed Forces in Europe Treaty, its exploitation of energy supplies as an instrument of coercion, and (of gravest concern) its use of force against Georgia in August 2008.

The NATO Allies disagree strongly, however, about the extent to which their own decisions and actions may have contributed to Russia's more confrontational approach.

As Jaap de Hoop Scheffer, then the NATO secretary general, observed in July 2009, "Russia's recent assertiveness . . . has exposed a lack of Allied unity vis-à-vis Russia."[158] Some Allied observers interpret Russian behavior and statements as to some extent reactions to U.S. or NATO policies, including the Alliance's enlargement process, the U.S. withdrawal from the 1972 Anti-Ballistic Missile Treaty, the U.S. proposal to deploy missile defense system elements in countries of Central and Eastern Europe, the recognition of Kosovo by most NATO Allies in 2008, and the decision by the NATO Allies not to ratify the 1999 Adapted Treaty on Conventional Armed Forces in Europe until Russia satisfies its treaty obligation to withdraw all its military forces from Georgia and Moldova.

The activities under the auspices of the NATO-Russia Council, particularly since 2002, include counterpiracy cooperation off the Horn of Africa, search-and-rescue exercises at sea, Theater Missile Defense exercises, STANDEX (Stand-off Detection of Explosives) technology development cooperation, Russian naval participation in Operation Active Endeavour in the Mediterranean,[159] dialogues on arms control and nuclear issues, exercises on nuclear weapons incidents and accidents, the Cooperative Airspace Initiative for counterterrorism, and Afghanistan-related cooperation.

Russia and NATO launched the Cooperative Airspace Initiative (CAI) in May 2002 at the first NATO-Russia Council Summit. Russia and the participating NATO countries intend to cooperate in airspace surveillance against terrorists employing civilian aircraft. Aiming for shared airspace awareness, agreed-on procedures, direct communication, rapid coordination, and combined action, Russia and participating NATO Allies conducted the "Vigilant Skies 2011" live exercise in June 2011 with Polish, Turkish, and Russian aircraft. Russia and its NATO partners in this endeavor declared the CAI Information Exchange System (IES) operational in December 2011, and they followed up with a "Vigilant Skies 2012" IES simulation exercise in November 2012.[160]

The Afghanistan-related NATO-Russia cooperation has included training for counternarcotics agents from Afghanistan and adjacent countries in cooperation with the UN Office on Drugs and Crime, maintenance of Russian-built helicopters in Afghan armed forces, and ground and air transit of nonlethal supplies to ISAF via Russian territory and airspace as part of the Northern Distribution Network. Despite objections from communists and nationalists about NATO using the Ulyanovsk transit hub since August 2012, Putin has defended this Alliance activity on Russian soil as consistent with the nation's interests:

> If there is no order in Afghanistan, it will not be calm on our southern borders. The current [Afghan] leadership will have difficulties keeping the situation under control. NATO member states are present there, and are performing this function.... We need to help them [the NATO Allies]. We should not be fighting there again. Let them sit there and fight.... It corresponds to our national interests. On many other issues we have disagreements.[161]

Putin's reference to "disagreements" on "many other issues" with the NATO Allies corresponds with the judgment of Hannes Adomeit, a leading German expert on Russian foreign policy. In Adomeit's view, one of the fundamental contradictions in NATO-Russia relations remains that between "the congenial atmosphere at the NRC, the constructive attitude, and professional engagement of Russian officers and officials in the numerous working groups and expert committees of the NATO-Russia Council, on the one hand, and significant *disagreements* between NATO and the Russian government on major international issues, first and foremost, concerning ordering principles in the post-Soviet geopolitical space, on the other."[162]

Indeed, the word "disagreements" is too weak to capture the intensity of the competition the Russians discern between Moscow and the main Western organizations, NATO and the European Union, concerning the future political orientation of the post-Soviet space. It is this competition that largely explains Putin's 2011 proposal to establish a Eurasian Union,[163] the failure of NATO-Russian cooperation to advance beyond the "technical" or "low politics" level,[164] and Moscow's interest in keeping the "frozen conflicts" (Abkhazia, Nagorno-Karabakh, South Ossetia, and Transnistria) unresolved.[165]

Despite its endorsement of "cooperative security" in the NATO-Russia Founding Act, Russia's responses to the Alliance's cooperative security activities in the Euro-Atlantic area have included suspicion of the PfP as a form of political and ideological imperialism and consistent opposition to NATO enlargement as directed against Russia's interests.

One of Russia's responses has been to try to build up the stature and influence of the Collective Security Treaty Organization (CSTO), which consists of Armenia, Belarus, Kazakhstan, Kyrgyzstan, Russia, Tajikistan, and Uzbekistan.[166] In 2006, it appeared that, in the words of Dmitri Trenin, Russia was "working to create its own solar system."[167]

Trenin and other analysts have subsequently highlighted the CSTO's shortcomings in cohesion and collective action.[168] Despite Russia's lobbying exertions in this regard, no other CSTO member state has recognized the Georgian regions of Abkhazia and South Ossetia as independent states.[169]

Russia's efforts to conclude a formal relationship between NATO and the CSTO have to date been unsuccessful. When Jaap de Hoop Scheffer, then the NATO secretary general, was asked in December 2005 whether the Alliance was "ready to cooperate with this [Collective Security Treaty] organization as a whole entity," he replied, "The Allies prefer the cooperation in the framework as we have it now, that is that the [Russian Foreign] Minister [Sergey] Lavrov, in his capacity as president in office of the CSTO, briefs." Lavrov had briefed both the NATO-Russia Council and the Euro-Atlantic Partnership Council and, as Jaap de Hoop Scheffer pointed out, "all the relevant parties are in the EAPC."[170] CSTO spokesmen have formed the impression that NATO has been reluctant to lend legitimacy and standing to the CSTO by meeting with it as an equal, as proposed by Moscow.[171]

In August 2012, however, Alexander Vershbow, NATO's deputy secretary general, said that "NATO doesn't rule out the possibility of collaboration on some concrete projects with the members of the CSTO and maybe even with the CSTO as an institution. . . . I think that we would be interested in hearing some more specific proposals maybe starting with something modest like counter-narcotics or border security to see whether the potential for an institutional partnership exists."[172] Russian authorities cautiously welcomed Vershbow's statement.[173] In March 2013, CSTO secretary general Nikolai Bordyuzha said that the Alliance had, at Washington's behest, rejected an official CSTO proposal for cooperation. In his view, NATO-CSTO cooperation "is not vital" and the NATO Allies "are not yet ready for it."[174] It is paradoxical that Russia has sought formal NATO-CSTO dialogue and cooperation while arguing that NATO is obsolete and should have long ago been dissolved.

Moscow has in recent years suggested the conclusion of two treaties, one for the entire Euro-Atlantic region and one between Russia and the NATO Allies. Since June 2008 Russia has proposed the conclusion of a legally binding European Security Treaty.[175] According to the November 2009 draft text of the EST, it would be "open for signature by all States of the Euro-Atlantic and Eurasian space from Vancouver to Vladivostok as well as by the following international organizations: the European Union, Organization for Security and Co-operation in Europe, Collective Security Treaty Organization, North Atlantic Treaty Organization and Community of Independent States."[176]

The proposal to make the European Union, the OSCE, the CSTO, NATO, and the CIS parties to a European Security Treaty implies that these organizations would be subordinate to it. NATO officials and governments have to date shown little interest in adopting Russia's European Security Treaty proposal. Jaap de Hoop Scheffer, then the NATO secretary general, said in February 2009, "I cannot see how we can have a serious discussion of such a new architecture, in which President Medvedev himself says 'territorial integrity' is a primary element, when Russia is building bases inside Georgia, which doesn't want them. That cannot be ignored, and it cannot be the foundation of a new European Security Architecture."[177]

A German commentator explained the lack of interest in NATO countries in Moscow's proposed European Security Treaty more bluntly: "After all, in recent years Russia again and again grossly violated the principles which it wants to include in the security treaty."[178] As Rasa Juknevicicne, then the Lithuanian minister of defense, asked, "What reason do we have to believe that Russia will be a trustworthy partner in a new security architecture if it fails to fulfil promises in the existing one?"[179]

The origins of the European Security Treaty proposal appear to reside in Russia's dissatisfaction with the current institutional architecture of European security.[180] As Andrew Monaghan of Chatham House has pointed out, Russian conceptions of the indivisibility of security differ from those current in NATO and EU nations. For NATO and EU nations, in the CSCE/OSCE context the indivisibility of security refers to the interdependence of the three dimensions of security (political-military, economic, and human rights) specified in the Helsinki Final Act.[181] From a Russian perspective, the indivisibility of security in Europe can only be achieved through a pan-European security regime such as Moscow has outlined in its European Security Treaty proposal. In other words, in the Russian view, NATO and the European Union have divided the continent with treaties that exclude European states that are not members of either the European Union or the Alliance. Russians note that more inclusive bodies such as the OSCE and the NATO-Russia Council are based on political declarations, not treaties.[182]

Russia's European Security Treaty proposal accordingly prescribes a regime that would subordinate NATO and the European Union in a new, legally binding framework, along with the OSCE, the CSTO, and the CIS. As Alexander Grushko, then Russia's deputy foreign minister, said in September 2012,

> The point of the Russian proposals regarding the European security treaty is to create the same level of security for all the states of the Euro-Atlantic region, regardless of whether they are members of a military-political pact or not. . . . And then the Euro-Atlantic region will truly turn into a region of stability and peace and the military instruments, including those organizations that were set up back in the era of confrontation, will play a lesser role in determining the key criteria of such a new security order.[183]

Grushko presumably had NATO in mind when he referred to the objective of establishing "a lesser role in determining the key criteria of such a new security order" for "those organizations that were set up back in the era of confrontation."[184]

In December 2009 Russian foreign minister Sergey Lavrov proposed that Russia and the NATO Allies conclude a treaty that would define the phrase "permanent stationing of substantial combat forces" in the NATO-Russia Founding Act.[185] Lavrov indicated that "permanent" would mean more than forty-two days in a calendar year. As for "substantial," as Patrick Nopens, a Belgian analyst, noted, "The limits proposed by Russia are very low, namely at the level of one brigade, wing or attack helicopter battalion."[186]

According to the treaty proposed by Russia, these deployment constraints would apply to Russia and all countries that were members of NATO on May 27, 1997 (the date on which the NATO-Russia Founding Act was signed), and these constraints would concern their deployments on the territory of all other states in Europe. Any exceptions from these deployment constraints would require the consent of all parties to the treaty, including Russia. In other words, Russia's approval would be required for any of the countries that were NATO Allies in 1997 to deploy forces beyond a certain level anywhere in Europe beyond their national territories. As Patrick Nopens has observed, such constraints would be "unacceptable, not only for NATO but also for the EU," because they would mean that "the EU could not deploy forces of its NATO-members wherever it deemed necessary on the whole territory of the [European] Union, of course taking into account existing agreements on arms control, and security and confidence-building measures."[187]

For NATO, one of the most significant effects would be on the security of the Allies that have joined the Alliance since 1997, because Russian approval would be required for any derogation of these deployment constraints. As Kurt Volker noted, such a treaty would mean "an acceptance of a Russian sphere of influence."[188] U.S. secretary of state Hillary Clinton said in February 2010 that "some of Russia's proposals contain constructive ideas and we welcome the opportunity to engage seriously with Russia on this important subject. But . . . the United States does not see the need for new treaties and we believe discussions of European security should take place within existing forums for European security such as the OSCE and the NATO-Russia Council."[189]

It is not clear whether the Russian government expected either of these treaty proposals to win support from NATO. Published sources have reported that at a meeting in Moscow in December 2009 Vladimir Putin, then the Russian prime minister, told Secretary General Rasmussen that "NATO no longer has a purpose and it was in Russia's interest that NATO no longer exist."[190] Similarly, in October 2012, President Putin said, "I cannot understand why it still exists today. This is a Cold War atavism to a large extent."[191]

NATO-Ukraine Relations

Formal relations between NATO and Ukraine began with the breakup of the Soviet Union in 1991, when the Alliance invited the former Soviet republics to participate in the North Atlantic Cooperation Council. In 1994 Ukraine joined NATO's PfP, the first member of the CIS to do so. In 1995, moreover, Ukraine became one of the first former Soviet republics to participate in a NATO-led peacekeeping operation when it joined IFOR in Bosnia. Ukraine also contributed to the follow-on SFOR in 1996–1999.[192]

In July 1997, not long after the signing of the NATO-Russia Founding Act in May 1997, Ukraine and the Alliance concluded a Charter on a Distinctive Partnership. In this document the Allies expressed a commitment to Ukraine's autonomy and security. "NATO Allies will continue to support Ukrainian sovereignty and independence, territorial integrity, democratic development, economic prosperity and its status as a non-nuclear weapon state, and the principle of inviolability of frontiers, as key factors of stability and security in Central and Eastern Europe and in the continent as a whole."[193]

Kyiv articulated a commitment as well: "Ukraine reaffirms its determination to carry forward its defence reforms, to strengthen democratic and civilian control of the armed forces, and to increase their interoperability with the forces of NATO and Partner countries."[194]

The final noteworthy element of the charter was the institutionalization of the security consultation commitment that the Alliance has extended to every country participating in PfP: "NATO and Ukraine will develop a crisis consultative mechanism to consult together whenever Ukraine perceives a direct threat to its territorial integrity, political independence, or security."[195]

The institutionalization of the relationship has gone well beyond the establishment of a NATO-Ukraine Commission, which meets regularly at various levels, from ambassadors and military leaders to ministers of defense and foreign affairs. The Alliance has established two offices in Kyiv to promote cooperation. Since 1997 the NATO Information and Documentation Centre has sought to tell the public about NATO and its activities. Since 1999 the NATO Liaison Office has supported Ukraine's participation in PfP and associated reform programs in cooperation with Ukrainian government agencies.[196]

Moreover, since 1998 the core group of the NATO-Ukraine Joint Working Group on Defense Reform has met eight to ten times a year with the participation of the NATO International Staff and the national delegations of Alliance members.[197] According to the Alliance, its cooperation with Ukraine "in the area of defence and security sector reform is more extensive than with any other Partner country."[198]

Two other signs of the closeness of the Ukraine-NATO relationship stand out. First, Ukraine was the first partner country to contribute to the NATO Response Force. In 2010 this included a unit specialized in countering biological, chemical, and nuclear threats, and in 2011 strategic airlift via Antonov aircraft.[199]

Second, Ukraine has participated more extensively in NATO-led operations than any other partner country. According to the NATO website, in August 2011 Ukraine was "the only Partner country contributing actively to the four main ongoing NATO-led operations and missions"—that is, KFOR in Kosovo, ISAF in Afghanistan, Operation Active Endeavour in the Mediterranean, and the NATO Training Mission in Iraq. Indeed, Ukraine was from March 2005 on "the only partner country providing personnel" to the last of these missions, which ended in December 2011.[200] From the viewpoint of the NATO Allies, "Through such contributions, Ukraine is demonstrating its commitment to help shoulder shared security responsibilities."[201] It should nonetheless be noted that, while Ukraine announced an intention to contribute to NATO's Operation Unified Protector in Libya in 2011, it did not do so. In October 2013, however, Ukraine contributed a frigate to NATO's Operation Ocean Shield and thus became the first partner nation to join the Alliance in this counter-piracy endeavor.[202]

Movement toward Ukraine's membership in the Alliance has not been straightforward, in Ukraine or NATO, owing in part to Russian policies. In May 2002, Leonid Kuchma, then the president of Ukraine, announced that the country would pursue the goal of NATO membership. In accordance with this objective, the Allies and Kyiv in November 2002 approved a NATO-Ukraine Action Plan to support Ukrainian reforms. The Ukrainian government's interest in NATO membership deepened after the "Orange Revolution" brought Viktor Yushchenko to office as president of Ukraine in January 2005. In April 2005, at a meeting of the NATO-Ukraine Commission at the level of foreign ministers, Ukraine and the NATO Allies initiated an Intensified Dialogue on Kyiv's interest in membership.[203] Under President Yushchenko, Ukraine's official policy remained oriented toward membership. In December 2009 Ukraine's foreign minister said, "We are making pragmatic and realistic steps toward our goal: membership in the Alliance."[204]

The Ukrainian government's policy changed when Viktor Yanukovich became president in February 2010. In March 2010 Yanukovich and Russian president Dmitry Medvedev concluded an agreement to extend Russia's lease on Sebastopol, the headquarters of Russia's Black Sea Fleet, for twenty-five years, from 2017 to 2042, in return for discounted prices for Ukrainian imports of Russian natural gas.[205] In May 2010 Yanukovich said, "Entry into NATO is not realistic for our country today," and told Moscow that Kyiv would not join any military alliance, including the Collective Security Treaty Organization led by Russia.[206] In June 2010 the Ukrainian Parliament approved a law proposed by Yanukovich that rules out Ukrainian membership in any "military bloc" but that permits cooperation with alliances, including NATO, as well as the pursuit of integration with the European Union.[207]

In September 2010 Yanukovich said that Ukraine must "maintain the balance in relations with Europe, the US and Russia."[208] Since NATO membership has been ruled out for the foreseeable future, in practical terms Yanukovich's government has been trying to maintain the balance in its relations with Russia and the European Union. Russia has been offering Ukraine further discounts on natural gas prices in return for joining the trade and customs union established by Belarus, Kazakhstan, and Russia.

Membership in that customs union would, however, be incompatible with the closer economic ties with the European Union that Kyiv has been striving to negotiate. The choice involves political values as well as economic considerations. As Neil Buckley of the *Financial Times* has noted, "Closer EU integration means embracing European values on democracy and freedom of speech—not the Russian-style 'managed' democracy Mr Yanukovich is veering towards."[209]

NATO's attitude on Alliance membership for Ukraine has gone from a contested high point of support at the April 2008 Bucharest Summit to relief that Kyiv is no longer actively seeking membership and is satisfied with partnership and cooperation activities.

The high point of support in April 2008 reflected a compromise between the champions of NATO membership for Ukraine and Georgia (which included most of the Central and Eastern European Allies, plus Canada and the United States) and the skeptics (led by France and Germany). According to the April 2008 Bucharest Summit Declaration,

> NATO welcomes Ukraine's and Georgia's Euro-Atlantic aspirations for membership in NATO. We agreed today that these countries will become members of NATO. . . . MAP [Membership Action Plan] is the next step for Ukraine and Georgia on their direct way to membership. Today we make clear that we support these countries' applications for MAP. Therefore we will now begin a period of intensive engagement with both at a high political level to address the questions still outstanding pertaining to their MAP applications. We have asked Foreign Ministers to make a first assessment of progress at their December 2008 meeting. Foreign Ministers have the authority to decide on the MAP applications of Ukraine and Georgia.[210]

The assertion that "these countries will become members of NATO" struck a strangely prophetic or peremptory tone, given the fact that the membership process has always been conditional in multiple ways. The formulation of supporting the applications for MAP status but referring to "questions still outstanding" that would be given "a first assessment" in December 2008 represented a compromise that professed support in principle but postponed indefinitely any actual decision on MAP status.

The skeptics about NATO membership for Ukraine emphasized the lack of popular support in the country for such a step, but they were also concerned that bestowing MAP status on Ukraine and Georgia could dangerously antagonize Russia. Indeed, some observers held that the language qualifying the prospects for MAP status was insufficient to counter the imperative statement that "these countries will become members of NATO." In their view, this statement was a factor contributing to Russian decision making about Georgia in the months before the August 2008 Georgia-Russia conflict.

In December 2008 the NATO foreign ministers announced that the Allies would support a process of indefinite duration that could ultimately lead to membership for Ukraine and Georgia.

> Both countries have made progress, yet both have significant work left to do. Therefore, we have decided to provide further assistance to both countries in implementing needed reforms as they progress towards NATO membership. Through a performance based process NATO will maximise its advice, assistance, and support for their reform efforts in the framework of the NATO-Ukraine Commission and NATO-Georgia Commission, which have a central role to play in supervising the process set in hand at the Bucharest Summit. . . . We have also decided to reinforce the NATO information and liaison offices in Kyiv and Tbilisi. Finally, without

prejudice to further decisions which must be taken about MAP, we have agreed that ... Annual National Programmes will be developed to help Georgia and Ukraine advance their reforms, which will be annually reviewed by the Allies.[211]

In August 2009 Ukraine and the NATO Allies issued a declaration complementing the 1997 NATO-Ukraine Charter. The declaration confirmed that the NATO-Ukraine Commission would have "a central role" in the process initiated at the Bucharest Summit as well as in NATO-Ukraine dialogue and cooperation and in Ukraine's reforms pertaining to membership aspirations.[212]

The change in Ukrainian policy regarding the pursuit of NATO membership since February 2010 has been convenient for the Allies, owing to their divisions and concerns on this question. According to the November 2010 Lisbon Summit Declaration,

> Recognising the sovereign right of each nation to freely choose its security arrangements, we respect Ukraine's policy of "non-bloc" status. . . . We welcome the Ukrainian Government's commitment to continue to pursue fully Ukraine's Distinctive Partnership with NATO, including through high-level political dialogue in the NATO-Ukraine Commission, and reform and practical cooperation through the Annual National Programme, and in this context, we recall that NATO's door remains open, as stated in the Bucharest Summit decision. We remain convinced that mutually beneficial cooperation between NATO and Ukraine will continue to be of key importance for peace and security in the Euro-Atlantic area and beyond, and appreciate the constructive role Ukraine plays in this respect, including through its participation in NATO-led operations.[213]

It may be significant that in August 2011 the NATO website did not use the Bucharest Summit Declaration's "will become" language and employed the word "may" instead of "will" with respect to Ukraine's prospects for Alliance membership: "NATO's door remains open to Ukraine, in line with the decision taken at the Bucharest Summit in April 2008, when Allied leaders agreed that Ukraine may become a NATO member in the future."[214]

At the Chicago Summit in May 2012 the Allies avoided the "will become a member" issue by simply recalling their references to Ukraine at the 2008 Bucharest and 2010 Lisbon Summits and their readiness to continue cooperative activities with Ukraine. The Allies declared, however, that they were "concerned by the selective application of justice and what appear to be politically motivated prosecutions, including of leading members of the opposition, and the conditions of their detention." This referred above all to Yulia Tymoshenko, Ukraine's prime minister in 2007–2010, imprisoned since October 2011. The NATO Allies called for "full compliance with the rule of law" and "free, fair and inclusive Parliamentary elections."[215]

NATO-Georgia Relations

As with Russia and Ukraine, formal relations between NATO and Georgia began with the breakup of the Soviet Union, when the Alliance invited all the former Soviet republics to participate in the North Atlantic Cooperation Council.

Georgia joined the Alliance's PfP in 1994. It has participated actively in various programs within the PfP framework, including the Planning and Review Process since 1999, and this Alliance assistance has "helped Georgia build deployable units according to NATO standards and interoperable with Allied forces."[216]

Georgia has used its forces to contribute extensively to NATO-led operations. Georgian troops participated in peacekeeping in Kosovo in 1999–2008, and Georgia continues to support Operation Active Endeavour, "primarily through intelligence exchange."[217] In 2011 Georgia became "the second largest non-NATO troop contributor" to the NATO-led operation in Afghanistan,[218] and in June 2013 it became the largest.[219] It is noteworthy that Georgia has committed troops to Afghanistan "without national caveats." As Secretary General Rasmussen pointed out in December 2009, "NATO Ministers welcomed these contributions as a demonstration of Georgia's commitment to our shared security."[220]

The commitment implied by the phrase "shared security" remains sensitive, however. It raises the question whether the Allies are prepared to go beyond the security consultations commitment they have made to every participant in PfP and offer Georgia membership in NATO.

Georgia first expressed interest in NATO membership in 2002, under President Eduard Shevardnadze. His successor, Mikheil Saakashvili, continued the pursuit of membership, and the Allies decided in 2006 to establish an Intensified Dialogue with Georgia regarding possible NATO membership.[221]

As noted earlier, at the Bucharest Summit in April 2008 the Allies agreed, in an unusual formulation, that Georgia and Ukraine "will become members of NATO," but postponed a decision on Membership Action Plan status for these countries.[222]

Within days of the Russia-Georgia conflict in August 2008 the Allies decided to establish the NATO-Georgia Commission to "supervise the process set in hand at Bucharest" and declared that "Georgia's recovery, security and stability are important to the Alliance."[223]

The framework document for the NATO-Georgia Commission, established in September 2008, indicated that it would, among other goals, "underpin Georgia's efforts to take forward its political, economic, and defence-related reforms pertaining to its Euro-Atlantic aspirations for membership in NATO, with a focus on key democratic and institutional goals."[224] The Allies also repeated the PfP security consultation commitment, promising the Georgians that "the NGC will be convened following a request from Georgia if Georgia perceives a direct threat to its territorial integrity, political independence, or security."[225]

The Allies decided in December 2008, as already noted with respect to Ukraine, to "maximise . . . advice, assistance, and support" to Georgia and Ukraine, to "reinforce the NATO information and liaison offices in Kyiv and Tbilisi," and "to help Georgia and Ukraine advance their reforms" via Annual National Programs.[226]

As with Ukraine, since 2008 the Allies have repeatedly called on Georgia to pursue democratic reforms. In November 2010, for example, they declared, "We strongly encourage and actively support Georgia's continued implementation of all necessary reforms, particularly democratic, electoral and judicial reforms, as well as security and defence sector reforms, in order to advance its Euro-Atlantic aspirations."[227]

In contrast with the situation in Ukraine, where popular support for NATO membership has never commanded a majority, in Georgia public opinion has stood strongly behind pursuit of membership.[228] As with Ukraine, however, some NATO Allies have not been willing (and indeed remain unwilling) to accord MAP status to Georgia—or to endorse the pursuit of Alliance membership via another procedure—for fear of irritating Moscow. Owing to disagreements among the Allies, chiefly because of concerns about Russia, it appears that it was with some relief that NATO foreign ministers in 2009 "noted that much work remains to be done to implement reforms, and that the Georgian Government, as well as opposition forces, must demonstrate political will in implementing democratic reforms."[229]

At the Chicago Summit in May 2012, the Allies expressed support for "Georgia's ongoing implementation of all necessary reforms, including democratic, electoral, and judicial reforms, as well as security and defence reforms." The Allies stressed "the importance of conducting free, fair, and inclusive elections in 2012 and 2013." The Allies repeated the 2008 Bucharest statement that "Georgia will become a member of NATO" and added, "In that context, we have agreed to enhance Georgia's connectivity with the Alliance, including by further strengthening our political dialogue, practical cooperation, and interoperability with Georgia."[230] The substantive content of this enhanced "connectivity with the Alliance" and prospects for Georgia's membership will no doubt depend in large part on Allied preparedness to assume responsibility for Georgia's security, despite the country's troubled relationship with Russia.

In November 2012 the NATO Allies commended Georgia for augmenting its forces in the ISAF in Afghanistan, thereby becoming "the biggest per capita non-NATO troop contributor to the NATO-led mission in Afghanistan."[231] The following month the Allies "reconfirmed their strong support for Georgia's Euro-Atlantic aspirations and their commitment to continue assisting Georgia in conducting necessary reforms."[232]

Conclusion

The Allies have had multiple objectives in pursuing partnerships. These have included promoting the Alliance's political values, dispelling misinformation and mistaken impressions about the Alliance, preparing candidates for membership, gaining force contributors to NATO-led operations, and extending the Alliance's influence. The participation of multiple partners in NATO-led operations has contributed to the political legitimacy of the missions. Although the Alliance has devised and offered a huge number of partnership activity options, the learning has not by any means been a one-way street. The Allies have learned a great deal from their partners, which have sometimes put sensitive issues on the agenda—for instance, the nuclear programs of Iran and North Korea—more readily than the Allies.[233]

The participation of partner nations in NATO's internal decision making stands out as one of the main questions for the future of the Alliance. The Allies have reached accords about "decision-shaping" participation for partners contributing to the conduct of specific operations, and some partners have already sought a role in planning for future tasks, including assistance to the government of Afghanistan after 2014. Given the magnitude of the contributions by some non-NATO partners (such as those by Australia in Afghanistan), certain partners may become more like Allies in their influence in decision making, and this might include defining the types of tasks undertaken by the Alliance and selected partners—and whether to take action in specific circumstances. Several of these partners appear likely to emphasize crisis prevention and management, stabilization and reconstruction, and humanitarian assistance.[234]

This prospect raises concern among European Allied observers that value collective defense most highly and fear that the Alliance's burgeoning partnership activities and crisis management operations outside the Euro-Atlantic region could lead NATO away from its original core function. In their view, it is imperative that NATO sustain, adapt, and improve its collective defense capabilities and balance that effort with the Alliance's cooperative security and crisis management ambitions.

Another crucial issue concerns the extent to which the Alliance has a political vision or project behind its partnership activities.[235] To what extent are the NATO Allies prepared to uphold their commitment to what the North Atlantic Treaty describes as "the principles of democracy, individual liberty and the rule of law"? Conversely, to what extent are they prepared to make compromises in order to satisfy strategic objectives, in view of—for example—a specific partner's capabilities or facilities or geographic location? As Heidi Reisinger has rightly observed, "The idea of NATO being a military tool-box might work in a practical sense but, without the traditional, built-in emphasis on the Alliance's stature as a community of values, its political legitimacy will erode."[236] The Allies may nonetheless feel obliged on some occasions to strike a balance between their political ideals and practical requirements.

Balancing issues may also arise in the Alliance's relations with Russia, perhaps its most challenging partner. As Rasa Jukneviciene, then the Lithuanian minister of defense, said in 2009,

> Last but not least, we should continue looking for a better and more pragmatic EU and NATO strategy on Russia. This will continue to be a difficult balancing between the extreme evils of head-on confrontation and tacit approval of Russia's breaches of political trust and international law. We must be realistic that Russia will not easily or overnight accept our paradigm of social and political values. But this is no reason for us to abandon them or to betray those young democracies which do accept them. I believe the right strategy for dealing with Russia is a two-track approach: pragmatic cooperation where interests coincide; and where they do not—constant progress toward reconciling them through honest dialogue.[237]

Striking the right balance in relations with Moscow has been a perennial challenge for the Alliance. It is urgent at the current juncture because the resolution—or at least the management—of many important issues depends to a significant degree on Russia. Moscow, however, appears to prefer the status quo to a resolution in cooperation with NATO of several of these issues. These issues include arms control, missile defense, nuclear nonproliferation, and energy security. Other NATO partners, including Georgia and Ukraine, share an interest in constructive relations between Russia and the Alliance.

NATO's partnerships can be regarded as an overall success. Since 1991 NATO has gone from having no partners to having forty-one recognized partners and relations with a number of other countries that contribute to NATO-led operations or pursue a dialogue with the Alliance. The balancing challenges of the future will include promoting the reform agenda, endowing the many partnership activities with substance, and keeping the more difficult partners more interested in cooperation than confrontation.

Notes

1. North Atlantic Council, "Strategic Concept," November 19, 2010, par. 4c.

2. Moreover, according to Article 2 of the North Atlantic Treaty, "The Parties will contribute toward the further development of peaceful and friendly international relations by strengthening their free institutions, by bringing about a better understanding of the principles upon which these institutions are founded, and by promoting conditions of stability and well-being." North Atlantic Treaty, Washington, DC, April 4, 1949, www.nato.int/cps/en/natolive/official_texts_17120.htm?.

3. North Atlantic Council, "Strategic Concept," November 19, 2010, par. 38.

4. North Atlantic Council, "Rome Declaration," par. 2.

5. North Atlantic Council, "Strategic Concept," November 19, 2010, par. 28.

6. North Atlantic Council, "Deterrence and Defense Posture Review," May 20, 2012, par. 17.

7. North Atlantic Council, "London Declaration," July 6, 1990, par. 1-2.

8. Ibid., par. 6–8.

9. North Atlantic Council, "Rome Declaration," par. 11.

10. For a fuller discussion of the NACC, see Yost, *NATO Transformed*, 94–97.

11. North Atlantic Council, "Strategic Concept," November 7, 1991, par. 24. Michael Legge, then NATO's assistant secretary general for defense planning and policy and the chairman of the Strategy Review Group that drafted the 1991 Strategic Concept, wrote that "the former Harmel dual approach of dialogue and defense" was expanded into "a triad of cooperation, dialogue and defense." Michael Legge, "The Making of NATO's New Strategy," *NATO Review*, December 1991, 12.

12. North Atlantic Council, "Declaration," January 11, 1994, par. 13.

13. Ibid., par. 14.

14. NATO, "The Euro-Atlantic Partnership Council," www.nato.int/cps/en/natolive/topics_49276.htm.

15. North Atlantic Council, "Brussels Summit Declaration," par. 14. According to Article 4 of the North Atlantic Treaty, "The Parties will consult together whenever, in the opinion of any of them, the territorial integrity, political independence or security of any of the Parties is threatened."

16. Perikli Teta and Javier Solana cited in Paul Ames, "NATO to Give Albania Extra Aid," *Associated Press Online*, March 12, 1998.

17. William Drozdiak, "NATO to Send More Aid to Albania, but No Troops," *International Herald Tribune*, March 12, 1998; Brooks Tigner, "Kosovo Fray Forces NATO's Hand," *Defense News*, March 16, 1998.

18. NATO, "The Partnership for Peace Programme," last updated March 5, 2012, www.nato.int/cps/en/natolive/topics_50349.htm. The number of partnership activities has ranged from 1,000 to 1,500 in recent years. Letter to the author from an expert in Brussels, June 13, 2013.

19. For an extensive description, see NATO, "Partnership Tools," last updated May 10, 2012, www.nato.int/cps/en/natolive/topics_80925.htm.

20. NATO, Allied Command Operations, "What Does the Military Cooperation/Outreach Mean in Practice?," www.aco.nato.int/page14207304.aspx (accessed February 15, 2013).

21. Vivien Pertusot, *Cooperative Security and NATO Partnerships: What Means for What Ends?*, Diplôme privé d'études supérieures (Paris: Institut de Relations Internationales et Stratégiques, October 2, 2009), 50.

22. Partnership for Peace was belittled at the outset by critics who replaced the word "Peace" with "Postponement" or "Procrastination" or even "Prevarication," owing to an impression that PfP was simply a mechanism for stalling on the question of NATO enlargement. Yost, *NATO Transformed*, 98.

23. Karl-Heinz Kamp, *"Global Partnership": A New Conflict Within NATO?*, Analysen und Argumente aus der Konrad-Adenauer-Stiftung no. 29 (Berlin: Konrad-Adenauer-Stiftung, May 2006), 2.

24. Heidi Reisinger, *Rearranging Family Life and a Large Circle of Friends: Reforming NATO's Partnership Programmes*, Research Paper no. 72 (Rome: NATO Defense College, January 2012), 3.

25. Letter to the author from an expert in Brussels, June 13, 2013.

26. "NATO's Relations with Switzerland," last updated November 21, 2012, www.nato.int/cps/en/natolive/topics_52129.htm.

27. North Atlantic Council, "Partnership for Peace: Framework Document," par. 2.

28. Pertusot, *Cooperative Security and NATO Partnerships*, 50.

29. Vivien Pertusot, *NATO Partnerships: Shaking Hands or Shaking the System?*, Focus Stratégique no. 31 (Paris: Security Studies Center, Institut Français des Relations Internationales, May 2011), 27.

30. Pertusot, *Cooperative Security and NATO Partnerships*, 79.

31. Robin Bhatty and Rachel Bronson, "NATO's Mixed Signals in the Caucasus and Central Asia," *Survival* 42, no. 3 (Autumn 2000): 133.

32. Pertusot, *Cooperative Security and NATO Partnerships*, 46, 66.

33. North Atlantic Council, "Final Communiqué," December 1, 1994, par. 19.

34. NATO, "A More Ambitious and Expanded Framework for the Mediterranean Dialogue," June 28, 2004, par. 4, www.nato.int/cps/en/natolive/official_texts_59357.htm.

35. NATO, "NATO Mediterranean Dialogue," last updated November 10, 2010, www.nato.int/cps/en/natolive/topics_60021.htm.

36. North Atlantic Council, "Chicago Summit Declaration," par. 42, 43.

37. Belkacem Iratni, *The Strategic Interests of the Maghreb States*, Forum Paper no. 4 (Rome: NATO Defense College, November 2008), 56.

38. Helle Malmvig, *From Diplomatic Talking Shop to Powerful Partnership? NATO's Mediterranean Dialogue and the Democratisation of the Middle East*, DIIS Brief (Copenhagen: Danish Institute for International Studies, May 2004).

39. NATO, "Nations of SFOR," www.nato.int/sfor/nations/sfornations.htm and www.nato.int/sfor/nations/pastnation.htm.

40. Pertusot, *NATO Partnerships*, 21.

41. Pierre Razoux, *What Future for NATO's Istanbul Cooperation Initiative?*, Research Paper no. 55 (Rome: NATO Defense College, January 2010), 7–8.

42. NATO, "Istanbul Cooperation Initiative," policy document, June 28, 2004, par. 3c, www.nato.int/docu/comm/2004/06-istanbul/docu-cooperation.htm.

43. Ibid., par. 5.

44. Ibid., par. 3e.

45. Pertusot, *NATO Partnerships*, 22.

46. Razoux, *What Future for NATO's Istanbul Cooperation Initiative?*, 9–10.

47. NATO, "Istanbul Cooperation Initiative," par. 8.

48. NATO, "NATO Elevates Mediterranean Dialogue to a Genuine Partnership, Launches Istanbul Cooperation Initiative," June 29, 2004, www.nato.int/cps/en/natolive/news_20811.htm?.

49. NATO, "Looking at Security in a Whole New Way, with Partners," February 15, 2011 www.nato.int/cps/en/natolive/news_70656.htm.

50. Razoux, *What Future for NATO's Istanbul Cooperation Initiative?*, 5.

51. NATO, "Istanbul Cooperation Initiative (ICI): Reaching Out to the Broader Middle East," www.nato.int/cps/en/natolive/topics_58787.htm (accessed August 18, 2011).

52. North Atlantic Council, "Chicago Summit Declaration," par. 44.

53. Jean-Loup Samaan, *NATO in the Gulf: Partnership Without a Cause?*, Research Paper no. 83 (Rome: NATO Defense College, October 2012), 4–5.

54. Ibid., 5.

55. Razoux, *What Future for NATO's Istanbul Cooperation Initiative?*, 6; and Pertusot, *NATO Partnerships*, 22, 28–29.

56. Samaan, *NATO in the Gulf*, 5.

57. Razoux, *What Future for NATO's Istanbul Cooperation Initiative?*, 4.

58. Samaan, *NATO in the Gulf*, 7.

59. North Atlantic Council, "Chicago Summit Declaration," par. 41.

60. NATO, "NATO's Relations with Partners across the Globe," www.nato.int/cps/en/natolive/topics_49188.htm (accessed February 14, 2013). As this website dossier noted, this meant "allowing these countries to have access, through the case-by-case approval of the North Atlantic Council, to activities offered under NATO's structured partnerships," including "workshops, exercises and conferences." In the late 1990s the Alliance's Asia-Pacific partners were sometimes called "triple no" countries—involved in dialogue and cooperation, but not Allies, not in the PfP/EAPC, and not in the Mediterranean Dialogue.

61. NATO, "NATO's Relations with Contact Countries," www.nato.int/issues/contact_countries/index.html (accessed August 16, 2011).

62. NATO, "Partnerships: A Cooperative Approach to Security," www.nato.int/cps/en/natolive/topics_51103.htm.

63. North Atlantic Council, "Chicago Summit Declaration," par. 22.

64. NATO, "NATO's Relations with Partners across the Globe."

65. NATO, "NATO Deputy Secretary General Visits China," November 10, 2009, www.nato.int/cps/en/natolive/news_59191.htm?selectedLocale=en; and NATO, "NATO Military Delegation Discusses Cooperation with Chinese Authorities in Beijing," www.nato.int/cps/en/natolive/news_84305.htm?selectedLocale=en. According to the NATO secretary general, "NATO needs to better understand China and define areas where we can work together to guarantee peace and stability. This is why I believe we need to hold a more active dialogue with China." Rasmussen, "NATO—Delivering Security in the 21st Century."

66. NATO, "NATO Cooperation with Australia," last updated November 18, 2010, www.nato.int/cps/en/SID-5DAB1D93-21546F02/natolive/topics_48899.htm.

67. New Zealand has, moreover, supported the European Union's EUFOR, which took over from the NATO-led SFOR in December 2004. "NATO Cooperation with New Zealand," last updated August 30, 2011, www.nato.int/cps/en/natolive/topics_52347.htm.

68. NATO, "NATO-Republic of Korea Cooperation," last updated August 31, 2011, www.nato.int/cps/en/SID-5DAB1D93-21546F02/natolive/topics_50098.htm.

69. NATO, "NATO's Cooperation with Mongolia," last updated March 23, 2012, www.nato.int/cps/en/SID-703B8B07-999D8381/natolive/topics_85297.htm.

70. For valuable overviews of relations between Japan and the Alliance, see Michito Tsuruoka, "NATO and Japan: A View from Tokyo," *RUSI Journal* 156, no. 6 (December 2011): 62-69; and Michito Tsuruoka, *NATO and Japan as Multifaceted Partners*, Research Paper no. 91 (Rome: NATO Defense College, April 2013).

71. NATO, "NATO Cooperation with Japan," last updated November 18, 2010, www.nato.int/cps/en/SID-5DAB1D93-21546F02/natolive/topics_50336.htm.

72. NATO, "NATO's Relations with Contact Countries," last updated March 9, 2009, www.nato.int/issues/contact_countries/index.html.

73. NATO, "Active Engagement in Cooperative Security: A More Efficient and Flexible Partnership Policy," April 15, 2011, par. 10, www.nato.int/cps/en/natolive/events_72278.htm.

74. Ibid., par. 16.

75. Karl-Heinz Kamp, *The NATO Summit in Bucharest: The Alliance at a Crossroads*, Research Paper no. 33 (Rome: NATO Defense College, November 2007), 4-5; and Stephan Frühling and Benjamin Schreer, "Creating the Next Generation of NATO Partnerships," *RUSI Journal* 155, no. 1 (February/March 2010): 53–54.

76. NATO, "Partnership for Peace Planning and Review Process," last updated November 17, 2010, www.nato.int/cps/en/natolive/topics_68277.htm.

77. NATO, "The Partnership for Peace Programme," last updated April 12, 2011.

78. NATO, "Individual Partnership Action Plans," last updated October 27, 2010, www.nato.int/cps/en/natolive/topics_49290.htm.

79. NATO, "Active Engagement in Cooperative Security," par. 13.

80. NATO, "Partnerships: A Cooperative Approach to Security." The phrase "Partnership and Cooperation Menu" is often shortened to "Partnership Cooperation Menu."

81. NATO, "Active Engagement in Cooperative Security," par. 11.

82. NATO, "NATO Leaders Meet with Partners in Chicago," last updated May 21, 2012, www.nato.int/cps/en/SID-25C9BBC0-26EAB3C5/natolive/news_87602.htm.

83. Allied Joint Force Command Naples, "NATO and Partner Chiefs of Defence Conclude Two Days of Meetings at NATO," January 19, 2012, www.arrc.nato.int/page372605555.aspx.

84. The Allies introduced the original Political-Military Framework for NATO-led PfP Operations as part of the Enhanced and More Operational Partnership initiative at the 1999 Washington Summit. "Towards a Partnership for the 21st Century: The Enhanced and More Operational Partnership—Report by the Political Military Steering Committee on Partnership for Peace," April 25, 1999, www.nato.int/cps/en/natolive/official_texts_27434.htm.

85. Kevin Rudd, "NATO Partners Earn Respect," *Australian*, April 23, 2011, www.theaustralian.com.au/national-affairs/opinion/nato-partners-earn-respect/story-e6frgd0x-1226043480613.

86. NATO, "Political Military Framework for Partner Involvement in NATO-Led Operations," April 15, 2011, par. 12, www.nato.int/cps/en/natolive/events_72278.htm.

87. Anders Fogh Rasmussen, in a press conference on the second day of the meeting of NATO foreign affairs ministers, Berlin, April 15, 2011, www.nato.int/cps/en/natolive/opinions_72764.htm.

88. Reisinger, *Rearranging Family Life and a Large Circle of Friends*, 6.

89. NATO, "Active Engagement in Cooperative Security," par. 7(a)i.

90. NATO, "NATO and Mongolia Agree Programme of Cooperation," last updated March 23, 2012, www.nato.int/cps/en/natolive/news_85430.htm.

91. NATO, "NATO, Australia Announce Plans to Deepen Security Ties to Meet Common Threats," last updated June 14, 2012, www.nato.int/cps/en/SID-3EDD3915-B212FD89/natolive/news_88426.htm?selectedLocale=en.

92. "Australia-NATO Joint Political Declaration," June 14, 2012, par. 8, www.nato.int/cps/en/SID-8DE69671-8F977679/natolive/official_texts_94097.htm?selectedLocale=en.

93. Brendan Nelson, Australian ambassador to Belgium, Luxembourg, the European Union, and NATO, "Australia's Strategic Priorities—NATO in Partnership" (address to Dr. Manfred Wörner Circle, June 20, 2011); quoted with permission.

94. ePRIME is the password-protected Internet-based Education Partnership Real-Time Information Management and Exchange System. This cooperative project between NATO and Switzerland is managed by NATO's International Staff and International Military Staff and functions under the authority of the Partnership for Peace Political-Military Steering Committee (PMSC). Although ePRIME was originally founded to support Partnership for Peace, the ePRIME network now also encompasses the Mediterranean Dialogue, the Istanbul Cooperation Initiative, the Military Training and Education Program (MTEP), and partnership activities with Afghanistan, Australia, Iraq, Japan, the Republic of Korea, Mongolia, New Zealand, and Pakistan, countries that NATO terms "partners across the globe."

95. Overviews of Partnership Training and Education Centres may be found at www.natoschool.nato.int/PTC.asp and www.act.nato.int/jft-topics/partnership-training-and-education-centres. See also NATO, "Centres of Excellence," last updated July 30, 2012, www.nato.int/cps/en/natolive/topics_68372.htm.

96. Jordan, the only Mediterranean Dialogue nation in NATO's Operational Capabilities Concept Evaluation and Feedback program, concluded a security agreement with the Alliance to participate in the OCC. Jordan may soon become the first Mediterranean Dialogue nation in the Alliance's Planning and Review Process, and this may also require a security agreement. With regard to Colombia, the NATO website stipulated in June 2013 that "the Security of Information Agreement does not formally recognise Colombia as a NATO partner but constitutes a first step for future cooperation in the security field. It will facilitate the participation of Colombia in a number of NATO activities." NATO, "NATO and Colombia Open Channel for Future Cooperation," last updated June 26, 2013, www.nato.int/cps/en/natolive/news_101634.htm.

97. As discussed in chapter 3, the NATO Defense Planning Process (NDPP), with its "consensus-minus-one" procedure, constitutes a significant exception.

98. In February 2013, for example, journalists reported that a German government analysis had stated that "a key problem is the Turks' refusal 'to constructively support the concept of partnership.' The negative assessment by the [German] diplomats refers to the rigid stance taken by Ankara, which refuses to cooperate with NATO partner Israel and is also blocking cooperation with the European Union because of the Cyprus conflict." Matthias Gebauer, Ralf Neukirch, Gordon Repinski, and Christoph Schult, "European Obstruction: NATO Reforms Moving at 'Snail's Pace,'" *Spiegel Online International*, February 25, 2013, www.spiegel.de/international/europe/german-government-analysis-says-europe-blocking-nato-reform-a-885405.html.

99. According to Karl-Heinz Kamp and Heidi Reisinger, "a dispute among NATO members over management of the Alliance's dialogue with Israel brought partnership activities practically to a halt in 2012: hundreds of ... deployment and NRF-related activities on the partnership menu were blocked." Karl-Heinz Kamp and Heidi Reisinger, *NATO's Partnerships after 2014: Go West!*, Research Paper no. 92 (Rome: NATO Defense College, May 2013), 2.

100. NATO, "Active Engagement in Cooperative Security," par. 1.

101. NATO, "Active Engagement in Cooperative Security," par. 4.

102. Reisinger, *Rearranging Family Life and a Large Circle of Friends*, 5.

103. Ibid., 6–7.

104. Anders Fogh Rasmussen, speech on the occasion of his visit to the Kingdom of Bahrain, Ritz Carlton Hotel, Manama, Bahrain, March 7, 2010, www.nato.int/cps/en/natolive/opinions_62052.htm.

105. Anders Fogh Rasmussen, "NATO and the Arab Spring" (speech at the Forum for New Diplomacy hosted by Carnegie Europe, June 1, 2011), www.nato.int/cps/en/natolive/opinions_74993.htm?selectedLocale=en.

106. Kristian Coates Ulrichsen, "Counterrevolution in the Gulf," *Foreign Policy*, May 6, 2011, www.foreignpolicy.com/articles/2011/05/06/counterrevolution_in_the_gulf.

107. North Atlantic Council, "Chicago Summit Declaration," par. 39.

108. NATO, "Istanbul Cooperation Initiative," par. 7a.

109. Razoux, *What Future for NATO's Istanbul Cooperation Initiative?*, 6.

110. With regard to the Alliance's "negative image" and the sensitivity about visible association with Israel in the Mediterranean Dialogue, see Pertusot, *NATO Partnerships*, 19–20. With respect to the "negative perception" of NATO in the Gulf region, see Razoux, *What Future for NATO's Istanbul Cooperation Initiative?*, 4–5.

111. Abdulaziz O. Sager, "What Do the Gulf Cooperation Council States Want from NATO?," in *NATO and Global Partners: Views from the Outside*, ed. Ronald D. Asmus (Washington, DC: German Marshall Fund of the United States, 2006), 17.

112. Pertusot, *Cooperative Security and NATO Partnerships*, 96, 110–111; and Pertusot, *NATO Partnerships*, 20.

113. North Atlantic Council, "Chicago Summit Declaration," par. 24.

114. "Joint training and exercises will be essential in maintaining our interoperability and interconnectedness with partner forces, including when we are not engaged together in active operations." North Atlantic Council, "Chicago Summit Declaration," par. 24.

115. According to Elizabeth Quintana, "Sweden's longstanding collaboration with NATO as a Partner for Peace made cooperation relatively seamless, and may mean that Sweden will participate more readily in future operations." Elizabeth Quintana, "The War from the Air," in *Short War, Long Shadow: The Political and Military Legacies of the 2011 Libya Campaign*, ed. Adrian Johnson and Saqeb Mueen (London: Royal United Services Institute for Defence and Security Studies, 2012), 32.

116. Ann-Sofie Dahl, *Partner Number One or NATO Ally Twenty-nine? Sweden and NATO post-Libya*, Research Paper no. 82 (Rome: NATO Defense College, September 2012), 1.

117. Rasmussen, "NATO 2020—Shared Leadership for a Shared Future."

118. Rühle, "NATO and Emerging Security Challenges," 281.

119. Kamp and Reisinger, *NATO's Partnerships after 2014*, 2.

120. Ibid., 6–7.

121. The judgments in this paragraph and the next are based on the author's interviews in Rome, Istanbul, Berlin, Paris, Warsaw, Brussels, and London in May–June 2013.

122. The ISAF format has involved all twenty-eight NATO Allies and as many as twenty-two non-NATO contributors, including countries that do not participate in any recognized partnership framework, not even that of "partners across the globe," such as El Salvador, Malaysia, Singapore, and Tonga.

123. Author's interview with an expert observer in Brussels, May 30, 2013.

124. Letter to the author from an expert observer in Brussels, June 13, 2013.

125. Russia signed the PfP Framework Document in June 1994 and approved an Individual Partnership Program in May 1995—about a year later. However, it was not until ten years later—in April 2005—that Russia signed a status of forces agreement with NATO, and then it was not ratified until two years after that, in May 2007. For background, see Hannes Adomeit and Frank Kupferschmidt, *Russia-NATO Relations: Stagnation or Revitalization?*, 2008/RP 02 (Berlin: Stiftung Wissenschaft und Politik, May 2008), 25–26.

126. For a fuller discussion, see Yost, *NATO Transformed*, 135–137.

127. NATO, "History of the NATO-led Stabilisation Force (SFOR) in Bosnia and Herzegovina," www.nato.int/sfor/docu/d981116a.htm.

128. Two of these assurances remain particularly significant, and merit careful consideration in the context of the full text of the Founding Act: "The member States of NATO reiterate that they have no intention, no plan and no reason to deploy nuclear weapons on the territory of new members, nor any need to change any aspect of NATO's nuclear posture or nuclear policy—and do not foresee any future need to do so.... NATO reiterates that in the current and foreseeable security environment, the Alliance will carry out its collective defence and other missions by ensuring the necessary interoperability, integration, and capability for reinforcement rather than by additional permanent stationing of substantial combat forces." "Founding Act on Mutual Relations, Cooperation and Security between the North Atlantic Treaty Organization and the Russian Federation," May 27, 1997.

129. Ibid.; emphasis added.

130. According to Pavel Felgengauer, a prominent Russian journalist, "the Russian authorities later decided that the CTR program meant too much to Russia to be sacrificed out of solidarity with the Serbs.... Over the past eight years, Congress has allocated more than $2 billion to CIS [Commonwealth of Independent States] countries and $1.2 billion to Russia to fund CTR projects. The White House has requested $475 million for next year.... The obvious benefits deriving from the Nunn-Lugar program are a good guarantee that it will be the last program to be shut down if relations continue to deteriorate, and the first to be revived as soon as another warming trend arrives in relations between Moscow and Washington." Pavel Felgengauer, "A Month from Now, Russia May Have to Pay for Safeguarding Its Own Nuclear Arsenal," *Sevodnya*, May 21, 1999, in *The Current Digest of the Post-Soviet Press* 51, no. 20 (June 16, 1999): 19.

131. David M. Herszenhorn, "Russia Won't Renew Pact on Weapons With U.S.," *New York Times*, October 11, 2012.

132. The White House, Office of the Press Secretary, "Fact Sheet: United States and the Russian Federation Sign New Bilateral Framework on Threat Reduction," June 17, 2013, www.whitehouse.gov/the-press-office/2013/06/17/fact-sheet-united-states-and-russian-federation-sign-new-bilateral-frame.

133. For firsthand accounts of this confrontation, see Wesley K. Clark, *Waging Modern War*, chap. 15, "Pristina Airfield," and Mike Jackson, *Soldier: The Autobiography of General Sir Mike Jackson* (London and Toronto: Bantam Press, 2007), chap. 12, "An Airfield Too Far."

134. Colonel-General Valery Manilov, first deputy chief of the General Staff, interview with *Interfax-Vremya*, no. 39, September 23, 1999, 8.

135. "Potholes on the Road to Russian-NATO Reconciliation?" and "Moscow Seeks NATO Concessions in Return for Cooperation," both in *Jamestown Foundation Monitor* 6, no. 28 (February 9, 2000); and "Talks Come Despite Hardline Military Opposition?" and "NATO-Russian Talks Take Place in Moscow," both in *Jamestown Foundation Monitor* 6, no. 34 (February 17, 2000).

136. Derek Averre, "From Pristina to Tskhinvali: The Legacy of Operation Allied Force in Russia's Relations with the West," *International Affairs* 85, no. 3 (May 2009).

137. "The presence and high level of combat readiness of nuclear weapons is the best guarantee that the US and NATO will not try to establish their 'order' in our country as well, like the way it was done in Yugoslavia." Major General Vladimir Grigoryev, Colonel Nikolay Radayev and Lieutenant Colonel Yuri Protasov, "An 'Umbrella' Instead of a 'Shield'—Do Nuclear Weapons Have a Future?," *Armeyskiy Sbornik*, February 1, 2000, in Foreign Broadcast Information Service, CEP 20000503000116.

138. NATO, "Press Statement: Meeting in Extraordinary Session of the NATO-Russia Permanent Joint Council at Ambassadorial Level," September 13, 2001, www.nato.int/cps/en/SID-226DFEB9-6BBA8720/natolive/official_texts_18861.htm.

139. "NATO-Russia Relations: A New Quality; Declaration by Heads of State and Government of NATO Member States and the Russian Federation," May 28, 2002, www.nato.int/cps/en/natolive/official_texts_19572.htm.

140. As noted in the "new quality" document, the NATO-Russia Council "will focus on all areas of mutual interest identified in Section III of the Founding Act, including the provision to add other areas by mutual agreement." The list of areas for consultation and cooperation in the "new quality" declaration is for the most part a selection from the more extensive list in the Founding Act. Indeed, the only areas listed in the "new quality" document that are not in Section III of the Founding Act are "search and rescue at sea" (an acknowledgment of Russia's August 2000 *Kursk* submarine disaster) and the vaguely worded "new threats and challenges" paragraph; and the part of the latter paragraph dealing with "civil and military airspace controls" is covered in Section III of the Founding Act.

141. The Permanent Joint Council was "chaired jointly" by a "troika" consisting of "the Secretary General of NATO, a representative of one of the NATO member States on a rotation basis, and a representative of Russia." "Founding Act on Mutual Relations, Cooperation and Security between NATO and the Russian Federation," May 27, 1997.

142. Alexander Nikitin, "Partners in Peacekeeping," *NATO Review*, Winter 2004, www.nato.int/docu/review/2004/issue4/english/special.html.

143. NATO, "Statement: Meeting of the North Atlantic Council at the level of Foreign Ministers held at NATO Headquarters, Brussels," August 19, 2008.

144. Ibid.

145. NATO, "Statement by the North Atlantic Council on the Russian Recognition of South Ossetia and Abkhazia Regions of Georgia," August 27, 2008, www.nato.int/cps/en/natolive/news_43517.htm?selectedLocale=en.

146. Vice President Biden, remarks at 45th Munich Conference on Security Policy, February 7, 2009, www.whitehouse.gov/the_press_office/RemarksbyVicePresidentBidenat45thMunichConferenceonSecurityPolicy/

147. Author interviews in Brussels, October 2011, and Rome, December 2011.

148. NATO, "NATO's Relations with Russia," last updated July 15, 2011, www.nato.int/cps/en/natolive/topics_50090.htm.

149. NATO, "Final Statement: Meeting of the North Atlantic Council at the Level of Foreign Ministers Held at NATO Headquarters, Brussels," December 4, 2009, par. 12, www.nato.int/cps/en/natolive/news_59699.htm?mode=pressrelease.

150. The foreign ministers of the NATO-Russia Council met for the first time after the August 2008 Russia-Georgia war in Corfu on June 27, 2009. The language employed in the December 2009 statement by the North Atlantic Council suggests, however, that NATO foreign ministers did not regard the June 2009 meeting as constituting the formal return to ministerial dialogue and cooperation in the NATO-Russia Council.

151. NATO, "Final Statement," December 4, 2009, par. 13.

152. North Atlantic Council, "Strategic Concept," November 19, 2010, par. 33.

153. North Atlantic Council, "Lisbon Summit Declaration," par. 21, 23.

154. North Atlantic Council, "Chicago Summit Declaration," par. 30, 37.

155. Anders Fogh Rasmussen, press conference after the NATO-Russia Council, December 4, 2009, www.nato.int/cps/en/natolive/opinions_59971.htm; and "NATO and Russia Agree to Move Partnership Forward," December 4, 2009, www.nato.int/cps/en/natolive/news_59970.htm.

156. "NATO-Russia Council Joint Statement," November 20, 2010, www.nato.int/cps/en/natolive/news_68871.htm.

157. "Our cooperation with Russia on issues related to Afghanistan—notably the two-way transit arrangements offered by Russia in support of ISAF, our joint training of counter narcotics personnel from Afghanistan, Central Asia, and Pakistan, and the NRC [NATO-Russia Council] Helicopter Maintenance Trust Fund in support of a key ANSF [Afghan National Security Forces] need—is a sign of our common determination to build peace and stability in that region." North Atlantic Council, "Chicago Summit Declaration," par. 38.

158. Jaap de Hoop Scheffer, "NATO: Securing Our Future" (speech at The Hague, July 6, 2009), www.ata-sac.org/article-78-326-NATO-securing-our-future.

159. As noted in chapter 3, a Russian ship took part in Operation Active Endeavour from September 9 to 25, 2006, and from September 3 to 25, 2007.

160. Among other sources, see Chuck Paone, "'Vigilant Skies' Brings ESC-Infused NATO, Russian Effort to Fruition," 66th Air Base Group Public Affairs, June 23, 2011, www.hanscom.af.mil/news/story.asp?id=123261289; and "NATO-Russia Council Holds Cooperative Airspace Initiative Exercise," November 14, 2012, www.nato.int/cps/en/SID-9E3E42D7-3924AD3E/natolive/news_91277.htm.

161. Vladimir Putin quoted in Reuters, "Putin Says NATO Should Finish Job in Afghanistan," *Moscow Times*, August 2, 2012.

162. Hannes Adomeit, *Inside or Outside? Russia's Policies towards NATO*, FG 5 2007/01 (Berlin: Stiftung Wissenschaft und Politik, January 2007), 31; italics in the original.

163. Vladimir Putin, "A New Integration Project for Eurasia: The Future in the Making," *Izvestia*, October 4, 2011, http://rusemb.org.uk/press/246.

164. Adomeit's observation in 2007 remains valid: "At NATO, there is disappointment that much of the cooperation has remained at the *technical* and 'low-politics' level, that it has assumed a largely symbolic quality, and that it has failed to change the relationship at the 'high politics' and strategic levels. After the foundation of the NRC in 2002, there were hopes at NATO that cooperation would produce 'spillover' effects to the domestic political realm in Russia, strengthen military reform efforts, enhance transparency of defense decision-making, contribute to the creation of a civil society, and internationally help to solve 'frozen' conflicts. Such hopes were dashed. Current perceptions are that Russia has become a much more difficult partner." Adomeit, *Inside or Outside?*, 3; italics in the original.

165. Regarding the EU-Russia competition, see Stefan Meister, *A New Start for Russian–EU Security Policy? The Weimar Triangle, Russia and the EU's Eastern Neighbourhood*, Genshagener Papiere no. 7 (Genshagen, Germany: Stiftung Genshagen, 2011); and Hannes Adomeit, *Russia and Its Near Neighbourhood: Competition and Conflict with the EU*, Research Paper no. 4/2011 (Warsaw, Poland: College of Europe, April 2011).

166. The original parties to the May 1992 Collective Security Treaty (CST) were Armenia, Kazakhstan, Kyrgyzstan, Russia, Tajikistan, and Uzbekistan. Azerbaijan, Belarus, and Georgia soon adhered to the treaty as well. However, Azerbaijan, Georgia, and Uzbekistan declined to sign a protocol extending the treaty in 1999 and instead withdrew. The remaining parties to the treaty founded the Collective Security Treaty Organization in October 2002. Uzbekistan restored its membership in 2006.

167. Dmitri Trenin, "Russia Leaves the West," *Foreign Affairs* 85, no. 4 (July/August 2006): 92.

168. In Trenin's view, "Moscow's nominal allies in the Collective Security Treaty Organization (CSTO) are either too weak (Kyrgyzstan), too self-centered (Armenia), or not loyal enough (Tajikistan). The remaining bigger CSTO members, Belarus and Kazakhstan, are increasingly independent-minded. Even though security relations with each of the CSTO countries are important in the relevant regional contexts, alliance relationships play a secondary and even tertiary role in Russia's strategic calculations. Basically, Russia is on its own, and alone. Its only true allies, just as 120 years ago, are its own Army and Navy." Dmitri Trenin, "Russia's Threat Perception and Strategic Posture," in

Russian Security Strategy under Putin: U.S. and Russian Perspectives (Carlisle, Pennsylvania: U.S. Army War College, November 2007), 37–38.

169. Dmitri Trenin, "What Russian Empire?," *International Herald Tribune*, August 24, 2011.

170. Jaap de Hoop Scheffer, press conference following the meeting of the NATO-Russia Council at NATO headquarters, December 8, 2005, www.nato.int/docu/speech/2005/s051208j.htm.

171. Yost, *NATO and International Organizations*, 171–175.

172. Alexander Vershbow, interview with Defense Writers Group, August 29, 2012, 13, www.airforce-magazine.com/DWG/Pages/default.aspx.

173. Alexander Grushko, then the deputy foreign minister, said, "We shall see." Grushko quoted in a Voice of Russia interview by Petr Zhuravlev, "There's a Threat of NATO Turning into a Global Police State," September 12, 2012, http://english.ruvr.ru/2012_09_12/There-s-a-threat-of-NATO-turning-into-a-global-police-state-expert/.

174. Nikolai Bordyuzha quoted in "NATO Not Yet Ready for Cooperation with Collective Security Treaty Organization—CSTO Secretary General," Interfax, March 26, 2013, http://rbth.ru/news/2013/03/26/nato_not_yet_ready_for_cooperation_with_csto_-_csto_secretary_general_24249.html.

175. Putin expressed interest in a pan-European security regime as early as 2001, when he called for "the dismantling of Nato and its replacement with a 'single security and defence space in Europe.'" Putin quoted in Amelia Gentleman, "Replace Nato by pan European Pact, Putin Says," *Guardian*, July 18, 2001, www.theguardian.com/world/2001/jul/19/eu.russia.

176. European Security Treaty, November 29, 2009, Article 10, available at President of Russia, Official Web Portal, http://archive.kremlin.ru/eng/text/docs/2009/11/223072.shtml. The usual translation into English of the formal name of the CIS in Russian is the "Commonwealth of Independent States," but in this document it is rendered "Community of Independent States."

177. Jaap de Hoop Scheffer, remarks at the Munich Security Conference, February 7, 2009, www.nato.int/docu/speech/2009/s090207a.html.

178. Reinhard Veser, "Der Korfu-Prozess. Russlands Vorstellungen für eine 'europäische Sicherheitsarchitektur,' stossen auf Skepsis," in *Frankfurter Allgemeine Zeitung*, July 1, 2009, cited in Klaus Wittmann, *Towards a New Strategic Concept for NATO*, Forum Paper no. 10 (Rome: NATO Defense College, September 2009), 37–38.

179. Rasa Jukneviciene, *Latest Developments in European Security: A Baltic Perspective* (London: Chatham House, October 20, 2009), 4.

180. In the words of Dmitry Rogozin, then the permanent representative of the Russian Federation to NATO, "We want to build a security architecture on the principles of equal security and no security at the expense of others. . . . In response, we're told by the West that they like NATO and the EU as it is, they suit us fine. Well, they do not suit us. We don't like it." Dmitry Rogozin, *Russia, NATO, and the Future of European Security* (London: Chatham House, February 20, 2009), 6.

181. In the CSCE/OSCE context the "indivisibility of security" also refers to the "collective security" idea that the security of each participating state is linked to the security of all the others. In NATO, the "indivisibility of security" means that the Allies have agreed, as in Article 5 of the North Atlantic Treaty, that "an armed attack against one or more of them in Europe or North America shall be considered an attack against them all." For a fuller discussion, see Yost, *NATO Transformed*, 5–26.

182. Andrew Monaghan, "Defining the Indivisibility of Security: Russia and the Euro-Atlantic Community," in *The Indivisibility of Security: Russia and Euro-Atlantic Security*, Forum Paper no. 13, ed. Andrew Monaghan (Rome: NATO Defense College, January 2010), 15–20.

183. Alexander Grushko quoted in a Voice of Russia interview by Petr Zhuravlev, "There's a Threat of NATO Turning into a Global Police State," September 12, 2012, http://english.ruvr.ru/2012_09_12/There-s-a-threat-of-NATO-turning-into-a-global-police-state-expert/

184. Russia's current proposal for a European Security Treaty might be compared with the Soviet Union's 1955 proposal for a "General European Treaty on Collective Security in Europe." Despite many differences, the proposals share an intent to neutralize NATO and place Moscow in a stronger power position. Regarding the 1955 proposal, see Vojtech Mastny, "The Warsaw Pact as History," in *Cardboard Castle?: An Inside History of the Warsaw Pact, 1955–1991*, ed. Vojtech Mastny and Malcolm Byrne (Budapest and New York: Central European University Press, 2005), 4.

185. There is no agreed-upon definition of "substantial combat forces" in the NATO-Russia Founding Act. The Allies have made the development of a definition conditional on a resolution of differences with Russia regarding the Conventional Armed Forces in Europe (CFE) Treaty. "Upon agreement by NATO and Russia on the parallel actions package [on CFE issues] . . . NATO and Russia will develop a definition of the term 'substantial combat forces' as it is used in the NATO-Russia Founding Act." NATO, "North Atlantic Council Statement on CFE," Press Release (2008) 047, March 28, 2008, par. 5, www.nato.int/docu/pr/2008/p08-047e.html.

186. Patrick Nopens, *A New Security Architecture for Europe? Russian Proposals and Western Reactions, Part II*, Egmont Security Policy Brief no. 10 (Brussels: Egmont-Royal Institute for International Relations, April 2010), 2.

187. Ibid., 5.

188. Kurt Volker quoted in James G. Neuger, "NATO to Rebuff Russian Bid for Separate Treaty, Officials Say," *Bloomberg*, January 18, 2010, www.bloomberg.com/apps/news?pid=newsarchive&sid=aMDbZTRCWiGQ.

189. Secretary of State Hillary Clinton, remarks at the NATO Strategic Concept Seminar, Ritz-Carlton Hotel, Washington, DC, February 22, 2010, www.state.gov/secretary/rm/2010/02/137118.htm.

190. Tron Strand, Per Anders Johannson, and Per Hinrichs, "Amerikanischer Maulwurf beim Nato-Chef," *Die Welt*, February 11, 2011. See also Tron Strand and Per Anders Johansen, "Secret Sources in NATO Leader's Office," Oslo *Aftenposten.no* (in Norwegian), February 11, 2011, available at Open Source Center, EUP20110211340001.

191. "Putin Calls NATO 'Cold War Atavism,'" Interfax, October 5, 2012, www.interfax.com.ua/eng/main/120374/.

192. Mission of Ukraine to NATO, "Ukraine's Contribution to NATO Peace Support Activities," www.mfa.gov.ua/missionnato/en/10257.htm (accessed August 29, 2011).

193. "Charter on a Distinctive Partnership between the North Atlantic Treaty Organization and Ukraine," July 9, 1997, par. 14, www.nato.int/cps/en/natolive/official_texts_25457.htm (accessed August 27, 2011).

194. Ibid., par. 3.

195. Ibid., par. 15.

196. NATO, "NATO's Relations with Ukraine," last updated August 8, 2011, www.nato.int/cps/en/natolive/topics_37750.htm.

197. Mission of Ukraine to NATO, "Ukraine-NATO Co-operation in Defence and Security Sector Reform," www.mfa.gov.ua/missionnato/en/10255.htm (accessed August 29, 2011).

198. NATO, "NATO-Ukraine Joint Working Group on Defence Reform," last updated October 27, 2010, www.nato.int/cps/en/natolive/topics_50320.htm.

199. NATO, "NATO's Relations with Ukraine."

200. Ibid.

201. "Chairman's Statement: Meeting of the NATO-Ukraine Commission at the Level of Foreign Ministers Held at NATO Headquarters, Brussels," December 3, 2008, www.nato.int/cps/en/natolive/official_texts_46249.htm?selectedLocale=en.

202. NATO, "Ukraine Contributes to NATO's Ocean Shield," last updated October 11, 2013, www.nato.int/cps/en/natolive/news_103997.htm.

203. NATO, "NATO's Relations with Ukraine."

204. Petro Poroshenko, opening remarks by the minister of foreign affairs of Ukraine at the meeting of the NATO-Ukraine Commission at foreign affairs ministers level, Brussels, December 3, 2009, www.nato.int/cps/en/natolive/opinions_59820.htm?selectedLocale=en.

205. This agreement was approved in April 2010 by 236 of the 450 members of the Ukrainian Parliament. Yulia Tymoshenko, a former prime minister, said this decision would "go down as a black page in the history of Ukraine and the Ukrainian parliament." Tymoshenko quoted in "Parliamentary Chaos as Ukraine Ratifies Fleet Deal," BBC, April 27, 2010, http://news.bbc.co.uk/2/hi/europe/8645847.stm.

206. Yanukovich quoted in Richard Norton-Taylor, "Ukraine Drops 'Unrealistic' Plans for NATO Membership," *Guardian*, May 27, 2010, www.guardian.co.uk/world/2010/may/27/ukraine-drops-nato-membership-plan.

207. "Ukraine's Parliament Votes to Abandon NATO Ambitions," *BBC*, June 3, 2010, www.bbc.co.uk/news/10229626#story_continues_2.

208. Yanukovych quoted in Pavel Korduban, "Yanukovych Explains Policy Priorities During US Visit," *Eurasia Daily Monitor* 7, no. 178 (October 4, 2010).

209. Neil Buckley, "Kiev's Choice—EU or Russia?" *Financial Times*, October 26, 2010. See also Roman Olearchyk, "Moscow Lures Ukraine with Cheap Gas," *Financial Times*, April 7, 2011. Russia has also proposed to sell Ukraine gas at lower prices in return for agreeing to a Gazprom takeover of the Ukrainian oil and gas industry. For background, see Pavel Korduban, "Time for Kyiv to Choose between East and West," *Eurasia Daily Monitor* 8, no. 141 (July 22, 2011).

210. North Atlantic Council, "Bucharest Summit Declaration," par. 23.

211. NATO, "Final Communiqué: Meeting of the North Atlantic Council at the Level of Foreign Ministers, NATO Headquarters, Brussels," press release (2008) 153, December 3, 2008, par. 18–19, www.nato.int/cps/en/natolive/official_texts_46247.htm?mode=pressrelease.

212. "Declaration to Complement the Charter on a Distinctive Partnership between the North Atlantic Treaty Organization and Ukraine, as Signed on July 9, 1997," August 21, 2009, www.nato.int/cps/en/natolive/official_texts_57045.htm.

213. North Atlantic Council, "Lisbon Summit Declaration," par. 22.

214. NATO, "NATO's Relations with Ukraine."

215. North Atlantic Council, "Chicago Summit Declaration," par. 35.

216. NATO, "NATO's Relations with Georgia," last updated November 30, 2010, www.nato.int/cps/en/natolive/topics_38988.htm.

217. Ibid.

218. Anders Fogh Rasmussen, opening remarks at the meeting of the NATO-Georgia Commission at foreign ministers level, Berlin, April 15, 2011, www.nato.int/cps/en/natolive/opinions_72652.htm?selectedLocale=en.

219. NATO, "Georgia: Now the Top Non-NATO Troop Contributor in Afghanistan," June 26, 2013, www.nato.int/cps/en/natolive/news_101633.htm.

220. NATO, "Chairman's Statement: Meeting of the NATO-Georgia Commission at the Level of Foreign Ministers Held at NATO Headquarters, Brussels," December 3, 2009, www.nato.int/cps/en/natolive/news_59698.htm?selectedLocale=en.

221. NATO, "NATO's Relations with Georgia."

222. North Atlantic Council, "Bucharest Summit Declaration," par. 23.

223. NATO, "Statement: Meeting of the North Atlantic Council at the Level of Foreign Ministers Held at NATO Headquarters, Brussels," August 19, 2008.

224. "Framework Document on the Establishment of the NATO-Georgia Commission," Tblisi, Georgia, September 15, 2008, par. 3, www.nato.int/cps/en/natolive/news_46406.htm?selectedLocale=en.

225. Ibid., par. 6.

226. North Atlantic Council, "Final Communiqué," December 3, 2008, par. 19.

227. North Atlantic Council, "Lisbon Summit Declaration," par. 21.

228. In a nonbinding referendum in January 2008, 72.5 percent of Georgian voters expressed support for NATO membership. Some polls have found comparable levels of support (for example, 69 percent in September 2008), but backing for Alliance membership appears to have subsequently declined. "Poll Shows Decrease in Support for NATO Membership," *Civil Georgia*, May 7, 2010, www.civil.ge/eng/article.php?id=22275.

229. NATO, "Chairman's Statement: Meeting of the NATO-Georgia Commission," December 3, 2009.

230. North Atlantic Council, "Chicago Summit Declaration," par. 29.

231. NATO, "Allies Discuss the Priorities of the New Georgian Government at NATO-Georgia Commission," www.nato.int/cps/en/natolive/news_91429.htm?selectedLocale=en.

232. NATO, "NATO Foreign Ministers Praise Georgia's Commitment to Euro-Atlantic Integration," www.nato.int/cps/en/natolive/news_92889.htm?selectedLocale=en.

233. Michael Rühle, *The Broader Context of NATO's Nuclear Policy and Posture*, Research Paper no. 89 (Rome: NATO Defense College, January 2013), 6.

234. According to the Australia-NATO Joint Political Declaration, "Australia and NATO will consult on security developments with a view to preventing crises and, when required, contribute to their management. We have experiences to share in managing crises and conflicts, stabilising post-conflict situations, supporting reconstruction, and facilitating humanitarian assistance and disaster relief." Australia-NATO Joint Political Declaration, June 14, 2012, par. 18, www.nato.int/cps/en/SID-8DE69671-8F977679/natolive/official_texts_94097.htm?selectedLocale=en.

235. Vivien Pertusot has hypothesized that NATO has pursued vague "cooperative security" relations with most PfP, MD, and ICI partners because there is no political basis for a more constraining institutional framework with "illiberal democracies" uninterested in democratic reforms. Pertusot, *Cooperative Security and NATO Partnerships*, 108. Pertusot employs the term "illiberal democracies" in the sense set out in Fareed Zakaria, "The Rise of Illiberal Democracy," *Foreign Affairs* 76, no. 6 (November/December 1997), 22–43.

236. Reisinger, *Rearranging Family Life and a Large Circle of Friends*, 8.

237. Jukneviciene, *Latest Developments in European Security*, 7.

7

International Organizations and the "Comprehensive Approach"

This chapter examines NATO's relations with the United Nations, the European Union, and the Organization for Security and Co-operation in Europe (OSCE).[1] With regard to each of these organizations, the chapter discusses key issues in the relationship with NATO since the early 1990s, with due attention to problems as well as achievements. This chapter also considers the Alliance's "comprehensive approach," which is intended to deal with international security challenges by bringing together the civilian and military contributions of multiple states and organizations in a coherent and effective fashion.

The mutual defense pledge in Article 5 of the 1949 North Atlantic Treaty was based on the UN Charter's recognition of the inherent right of states to individual and collective self-defense. However, during the Cold War the Alliance had few interactions with the UN Security Council or UN agencies.[2] The Allies focused on collective defense and deterrence as the basis for diplomacy with their adversaries to the east. Indeed, during the Cold War, the principal international organizations that the Allies dealt with were the Warsaw Pact (1955–1991) and the Conference on Security and Co-operation in Europe (CSCE), founded in 1972–1973.[3]

At the end of the Cold War in 1989–1991, the Allies were far-sighted enough to recognize that in the new circumstances NATO would need to work more closely with other major international security organizations, which might—as indicated in the Alliance's 1991 Rome Declaration—constitute an array of "interlocking institutions."[4] However, the Allies did not anticipate the gravity of the challenges that the Balkan conflicts would present. In June 1992, the Allies declared their willingness "to support, on a case-by-case basis in accordance with our own procedures, peacekeeping activities under the responsibility of the CSCE, including by making available Alliance resources and expertise." This decision was made in light of the outbreaks of "violence and destruction . . . in various areas of the Euro-Atlantic region," notably in the former Yugoslavia.[5] In December 1992, the Allies extended the same principle to "peacekeeping operations under the authority of the UN Security Council."[6]

This decision formalized the various NATO activities under the Security Council's auspices under way since mid-1992. These activities extended beyond lending elements of NATO's Northern Army Group command to the operational headquarters of the UN Protection Force (UNPROFOR). The NATO Allies employed Alliance airborne early warning aircraft to monitor the Security Council–mandated no-fly zone over Bosnia and Herzegovina (Operation Sky Monitor) and worked with the Western European Union to enforce Security Council–mandated economic sanctions against Serbia and Montenegro and the arms embargo against all the successor states of the former Yugoslavia (Operations Maritime Monitor and Sharp Guard). As the Allies noted in a December 1992 communiqué, "For the first time in its history, the Alliance is taking part in UN peacekeeping and sanctions enforcement operations."[7]

The Balkan conflicts since 1991 and NATO's engagement in Afghanistan since 2002–2003 have been the main drivers of the Alliance's increasingly extensive cooperation with other international organizations. Other operations—for instance, the intervention in Libya in 2011—have also involved other international organizations, such as the League of Arab States,[8] partly for political legitimization purposes.

Alex Bellamy and Paul Williams have suggested that the League of Arab States, the Gulf Cooperation Council, and other regional organizations may increasingly function as "gatekeepers" that exert influence "by framing the issues and defining the range of feasible international action."[9]

Practical needs, specific tasks in operations, and partnership activities such as assistance in security sector reform have led NATO to work with many collective groups, including national and nongovernmental organizations as well as intergovernmental organizations.[10] For example, NATO reported to the UN Security Council in October 2004 that the Clearing House/Steering Committee mechanism established to rehabilitate the Kabul Afghanistan International Airport included NATO, the Afghan Transitional Authority (ATA), the UN Assistance Mission in Afghanistan (UNAMA), the World Bank, the International Civil Aviation Organization (ICAO), the International Air Transport Association (IATA), and the U.S. Federal Aviation Administration.[11]

All the Allies recognize NATO's limitations and the fact that the Alliance cannot achieve its political, development, and reconstruction goals in Afghanistan or elsewhere without help from other international organizations and NGOs. International financial institutions such as the World Bank and donor groups such as the G-8 fulfill important roles by supporting long-term stabilization and reconstruction. NATO's efforts to help prevent the proliferation of weapons of mass destruction may lead to information sharing and other forms of cooperation with bodies such as Interpol, the World Customs Organization, the International Maritime Organization, and the World Health Organization.[12] In its counterterrorism efforts NATO has cooperated with, among other organizations, ICAO, IATA, the UN Office on Drugs and Crime (UNODC), the European Organisation for the Safety of Air Navigation (EuroControl), and the UN Counter-Terrorism Committee.

The Allies have come to take it for granted that in non-Article 5 operations—the tasks that have consumed most of NATO's resources and day-to-day attention since the early 1990s—the Alliance will work in cooperation with other international organizations. Other organizations have capabilities and mandates that the Alliance lacks but that are essential for success in the overall mission. The Allies have recognized this practical necessity in the 1999 Strategic Concept, the 2006 Riga Summit Declaration, the Comprehensive Political Guidance, and other policy statements. In their 2010 Strategic Concept the Allies expressed a willingness to work with "relevant" organizations worldwide.[13]

At the 2006 Riga Summit, the Allies agreed, "As in Afghanistan, success in Kosovo will depend on a concerted effort. Accordingly, NATO activity to provide a secure environment will continue to be coordinated with the activities of the UN, the EU and the OSCE to build governance and support reform."[14] In the Comprehensive Political Guidance endorsed at Riga, a document "setting out, for the next 10 to 15 years, the priorities for all Alliance capability issues, planning disciplines and intelligence,"[15] NATO heads of state and government declared that

> Peace, security and development are more interconnected than ever. This places a premium on close cooperation and coordination among international organisations playing their respective, interconnected roles in crisis prevention and management. Of particular importance because of their wide range of means and responsibilities are the United Nations and the European Union. The United Nations Security Council will continue to have the primary responsibility for the maintenance of international peace and security. The European Union, which is able to mobilise a wide range of military and civilian instruments, is assuming a growing role in support of international stability. The Organisation for Security and Cooperation in Europe also continues to have important responsibilities in this field.[16]

The three international organizations that NATO has identified most consistently as key partners—the United Nations, the European Union, and the OSCE—are distinctly different in their origins and purposes. The United Nations was organized by the leading powers fighting the Axis during World War II. The UN Charter, signed in San Francisco in June 1945, was intended to serve as a basis for international order, peace, and security superior to any other treaty arrangement. The United Nations is a global organization with 193 member states.

The European Union can be seen as the current embodiment of an integration movement under way since the early 1950s. European states have been engaged in an unparalleled political project—the transfer of sovereignty in several policy areas to common institutions, with enhanced coordination of foreign and security policy. The European integration movement began in 1951 with six member states in the European Coal and Steel Community, and the European Union currently has twenty-eight member states.[17]

In contrast to the United Nations, the European Union, and NATO, the OSCE, as it has been known since 1995, is based not on treaty arrangements but on political commitments. The OSCE began with the preparatory talks in 1972–1973 for the Conference on Security and Co-operation in Europe, a pan-European conference in 1973–1975 involving all the states in the Euro-Atlantic region except Albania. The first major achievement of the CSCE was the 1975 Helsinki Final Act, which furnished the basis for subsequent meetings and decisions. Until 1990, the CSCE had thirty-five participating states. Owing to various political changes in the Euro-Atlantic region since 1990, particularly the disintegration of the Soviet Union and the former Yugoslavia, the OSCE currently has fifty-seven participating states.

NATO and the United Nations

The North Atlantic Treaty refers repeatedly to the UN Charter, and UN Security Council resolutions have furnished the basis for almost all non-Article 5 NATO operations.[18] Moreover, the Allies have reported to the Security Council about all their operations involving the use of force—including the Operation Allied Force air campaign in the 1999 Kosovo conflict—even though the Allies undertook this operation without benefit of an explicit UN Security Council mandate.[19]

While the UN Security Council's exceptional responsibilities in international security constitute a central aspect of the NATO-UN relationship, the United Nations offers much more than a framework of legitimacy for the actions of the Alliance and other international organizations. Since the early 1990s, United Nations specialized departments and agencies have worked closely with the Alliance in coordination with other international organizations and nongovernmental organizations.

According to Article 24 of the UN Charter, the UN Security Council bears "primary responsibility for the maintenance of international peace and security." However, the authors of the charter recognized that the UN Security Council might be incapable of timely and effective action, and for this reason referred explicitly in Article 51 to "the inherent right of individual or collective self-defense." Article 51 furnished the basis for the collective defense pledge in Article 5 of the North Atlantic Treaty.[20]

While the framers of the North Atlantic Treaty reaffirmed in Article 7 "the primary responsibility of the Security Council for the maintenance of international peace and security," they deliberately excluded any reference to any of the articles in Chapter VIII of the UN Charter. Article 52, part of Chapter VIII, refers to "regional arrangements or agencies for dealing with such matters relating to the maintenance of international peace and security as are appropriate for regional action." Article 53, also part of Chapter VIII, declares that "regional arrangements or agencies" are unable to undertake enforcement actions without the approval of the UN Security Council.

The Allies have generally agreed since 1949 that the Alliance is not a regional arrangement or agency under Chapter VIII of the UN Charter, and that the Alliance is not subordinate to the Security Council, notably with respect to "the inherent right of individual or collective self-defense" under Article 51. Subordinating NATO to the Security Council could in practice mean subordinating it to Russia and China. According to Article 27 of the UN Charter, the Security Council can make decisions on nonprocedural matters only with the concurrence of its five permanent members—also known as the P5—that is, China, France, Russia, the United Kingdom, and the United States. This provision of the UN Charter is popularly known as the veto.[21]

Because the Allies have always rejected the idea of a Chapter VIII–style dependence on the UN Security Council, it was not entirely surprising that they were prepared to use force in the 1999 Kosovo conflict in the absence of an explicit UN Security Council mandate to do so. This was a highly controversial decision. Some Allied observers argued that, in order to persuade other countries to respect the United Nations, NATO governments should set standards of strict conformity with international law as defined in the UN Charter, rather than setting precedents (such as asserting a humanitarian necessity to justify unilateral action) that could be used by other states and coalitions to legitimize interventions. Moreover, some observers maintained that in non-Article 5 (that is, non-collective defense) contingencies such as Kosovo, the Allied security interests at stake were not fundamental. In their view, the Allies could have afforded to wait until a combination of economic, political, and military pressures could be constructed to bring about acquiescence, if not active consent and participation, in support of intervention.

An explicit UN Security Council mandate would have also provided, it was noted, greater legitimacy in the eyes of public opinion. The decisive counterargument was the humanitarian emergency at hand in Kosovo. The German foreign minister at the time, Joschka Fischer, said, "I am not a friend of using force, but sometimes it is a necessary means of last resort. So I am ready to use it if there is no other way. If people are being massacred, you cannot mutter about having no [UN Security Council] mandate. You must act."[22]

While all Allies held that Operation Allied Force (the air campaign in the Kosovo conflict) was justified on grounds of humanitarian necessity, some Allies also based their policy on interpretations of relevant UN Security Council resolutions, including Resolution 1199 of September 23, 1998, and Resolution 1203 of October 24, 1998, although no Security Council resolution explicitly authorized the Alliance's use of force in the Kosovo conflict. The Allies agreed that they had an "appropriate" or "sufficient legal base in international law" for their use of force, but they did not agree on its specific content. Each member state was responsible for formulating its own national justification.[23]

Lord Robertson, then the NATO secretary general, issued the following statement a year after NATO's military intervention in the Kosovo conflict:

> The Allies were sensitive to the legal basis for their action. The Yugoslavs had already failed to comply with numerous demands from the Security Council under Chapter VII of the UN Charter and there was a major discussion in the North Atlantic Council, during which the Council took the following factors into consideration:

- the Yugoslav government's non-compliance with earlier UN Security Council resolutions,
- the warnings from the UN Secretary General about the dangers of a humanitarian disaster in Kosovo,
- the risk of such a catastrophe in the light of Yugoslavia's failure to seek a peaceful resolution of the crisis,
- the unlikelihood that a further UN Security Council resolution would be passed in the near future,
- and the threat to peace and security in the region.

At that point, the Council agreed that a sufficient legal basis existed for the Alliance to threaten and, if necessary, use force against the Federal Republic of Yugoslavia.[24]

Dick Leurdijk, a Dutch expert, has concluded that—aside from the inherent right to collective self-defense recognized by the UN Charter—there are two models for NATO action. The first is a "subcontracting model" under UN Security Council resolutions, as with IFOR and SFOR in Bosnia and Herzegovina and ISAF in Afghanistan. The second is an "autonomy model," as with Operation Allied Force in the Kosovo conflict, because NATO "is not willing to subordinate itself to the UN under all conditions." Leurdijk explains these two models by referring to what he calls "NATO's . . . inherently ambivalent character as a collective defence organization that is also willing and capable of performing as an instrument of the UN system of collective security."[25]

Some observers in NATO nations object to the "subcontracting" metaphor employed by Leurdijk, because in their view this implies a subordination of NATO to the UN Security Council. As long ago as 1993, Manfred Wörner, then the secretary general of NATO, said that "NATO cannot be regarded as an instrument or as a military sub-contractor to the United Nations. Nor do we expect that the United Nations should accept NATO's leadership. Both must retain the possibility to act independently."[26]

The Allies generally agree that NATO's legal bases for action, including the use of force, are not limited to UN Security Council resolutions, and encompass "humanitarian necessity" and related principles in addition to the inherent right to self-defense recognized in Article 51 of the UN Charter.[27]

Thierry Tardy of the Geneva Centre for Security Policy has written, "The old motto 'with the UN whenever possible, without when necessary' encapsulates NATO's view of the conditions under which a UN Security Council resolution is needed before military action is taken. In the field of peace operations, NATO's eagerness to act under a UN mandate (as is the case in Kosovo or Afghanistan) is more obvious, but this cannot be taken for granted." Tardy points out that NATO's operations in the former Yugoslav Republic of Macedonia—Essential Harvest, Amber Fox, and Allied Harmony—were not authorized by UN Security Council resolutions.[28]

The sharp criticisms by Russia and China of NATO's use of force in the Kosovo conflict demonstrated that two of the five permanent members of the Security Council did not accept the view of the Allies that they had a sufficient legal justification in the absence of an explicit Security Council authorization. The Russian government has often argued that, in the words of Vladimir Putin, "The use of force can only be considered legitimate if the decision is sanctioned by the UN. And we do not need to substitute NATO or the EU for the UN."[29]

However, the Russian government has also argued that the Commonwealth of Independent States has the authority to mandate peacekeeping missions.[30] From 1994 to 2008 Russia maintained that its "peacekeeping" military presence in the Georgian region of Abkhazia was authorized by the CIS.[31] Since 2008 Russia has recognized Abkhazia as an independent state and has held that its military presence falls under a bilateral Abkhaz-Russian agreement.[32] Russia's use of force against Georgia in August 2008 was not authorized by the UN Security Council, and in 2009 Russia employed its veto in the UN Security Council to block the renewal of the mandate of the UN Observer Mission in Georgia.

The NATO Allies strongly prefer to rely on UN Security Council resolutions as a legal basis for non-Article 5 operations and a political framework of legitimacy for such operations. This legal basis and political framework help the Alliance by furnishing a context for the contributions of other international organizations and nongovernmental organizations in demanding tasks such as stabilization and reconstruction, state building, and promoting sustainable security. The political legitimacy provided by a UN Security Council resolution creates a "moral atmosphere" in which NATO is more readily perceived as part of the solution. As Peter Viggo Jakobsen, a Danish scholar, has noted, UN Security Council mandates are "important with respect to mobilising international acceptance of a global NATO role, particularly in Africa and the broader Middle East."[33] This has been politically helpful with regard to sensitive missions such as the intervention in Libya in 2011 and the training of Iraqi security forces in 2004–2011.[34]

Aside from its legitimization functions, the United Nations has been significant to NATO in the conduct of operations. Since the dysfunctional "dual key" regime of 1992–1995, when a representative of the UN Secretary General had to approve the use of NATO airpower, the Alliance has learned how to define the terms of reference for NATO-UN interactions concerning command and control in a more productive fashion.[35] The three NATO Allies that are permanent members of the UN Security Council (Britain, France, and the United States) have played an important role in this regard.

Moreover, the NATO Allies regard UN leadership in the coordination of multilateral stabilization and reconstruction efforts as highly desirable, as with the UN Interim Administration Mission in Kosovo (UNMIK) and the UN Assistance Mission in Afghanistan (UNAMA).

The United Nations has learned since the early 1990s that the Alliance has resources, expertise, skills, and capacity. NATO's "capacity" resides not only in its military capabilities but also in its experience in preparing and leading states to work together in complex multinational and multiservice operations. NATO has an unrivaled capacity to offer large-scale support and to sustain a long-term commitment.

NATO has also developed expertise in defense and security sector reform through its partnership and enlargement programs.

Marten Zwanenburg, a Dutch analyst, has concluded that the Alliance's development of the NATO Response Force and other flexible and readily deployable capabilities "are likely to make the UN more dependent on NATO to undertake or support peace-support operations under the aegis of the UN." However, Zwanenburg has added, "In doing so the Alliance will insist on a certain independence from the UN," owing in part to "the scepticism that all partners share over a UN role in military decision-making after the 'dual-key' experience in the former Yugoslavia."[36]

The dysfunctional "dual key" experience has been a factor contributing to close attention by NATO Allies to negotiations within the UN Security Council about the formulation and renewal of Security Council resolutions mandating operations, notably with respect to command and control arrangements. NATO governments have been concerned that Security Council resolutions be practical and consistent with projected NATO operations, such as KFOR and ISAF. The "dual key" experience in Bosnia and Herzegovina in 1992–1995 helps to explain the reference to "unified command and control" for an "international security presence with substantial North Atlantic Treaty Organization participation" in the pivotal resolution concerning Kosovo adopted in June 1999 by the UN Security Council after the NATO air campaign.[37]

NATO's secretary general has submitted reports to the UN Security Council, via the UN secretary-general, about three categories of operations. The first category consists of non-Article 5 operations pursued under UN Security Council resolutions, such as IFOR and SFOR in Bosnia and Herzegovina, KFOR in Kosovo, and ISAF in Afghanistan. The second category consists of non-Article 5 operations undertaken without an explicit authorization under a UN Security Council resolution. To date there is only one prominent example in this category—Operation Allied Force in March–June 1999. The third category consists of operations undertaken under Article 5 of the North Atlantic Treaty since the terrorist attacks against the United States on September 11, 2001.

Experts at NATO headquarters began to take an interest in formalizing the NATO-UN relationship in response to what appeared to be signs of interest at the United Nations in 2004–2005.

In September 2005 the Alliance reportedly proposed a document setting out with greater precision possible elements of a framework for more structured and comprehensive UN-NATO cooperation.[38] Three years later, in September 2008, the UN secretary-general and the NATO secretary general approved a Joint Declaration on UN/NATO Secretariat Cooperation.[39] In November 2010, the NATO Allies declared that

> We welcome the strengthened practical cooperation following the Joint Declaration on UN/ NATO Secretariat Cooperation of September 2008. We aim to deepen this practical cooperation and further develop our political dialogue on issues of common interest, including through

enhanced liaison, more regular political consultation, and enhanced practical cooperation in managing crises where both organisations are engaged.[40]

NATO and the European Union

The European Union has formally been pursuing a European Security and Defence Policy (ESDP) since the European Council meeting at Cologne in June 1999.[41] The key step that made this possible—the abandonment by the United Kingdom of its long-standing opposition to EU involvement in military security and defense matters—took place in late 1998.[42] From the beginning of the European Union's Common Foreign and Security Policy (CFSP) in December 1991, with the framing of the Maastricht version of the Treaty on European Union, until October 1998, the United Kingdom held that the Western European Union (WEU), an organization based on the 1948 Brussels Treaty, as modified in 1954, should be responsible for implementing EU decisions with defense implications.

Since all members of the WEU were members of the Alliance, it was possible to regard the effort to construct what was called a European Security and Defence Identity (ESDI) during most of the 1990s as essentially a project within the Alliance. During the WEU-centered phase of this effort, from 1991 to 1998, the focus was on strengthening the WEU, as the European pillar of the Alliance and the defense instrument of the European Union.

After the shift in British policy in late 1998, EU members decided to pursue an ESDP under EU auspices and turned away from the previous WEU-centered focus. The WEU member governments (which were all EU members) transferred most of the WEU's assets to the European Union, including the WEU's military staff, situation center, satellite data interpretation center, and security studies institute, as well as the WEU-related bodies involved in promoting European armaments cooperation.[43] Since some EU members are not Alliance members,[44] the challenge at hand was no longer constructing a WEU-based ESDI within the Alliance but working out arrangements for the European Union to pursue an ESDP in cooperation with the Alliance.

The Alliance took an important step with a view to effective NATO-EU teamwork at the Washington Summit in 1999. The Allies approved principles for cooperation with the European Union known as "Berlin Plus," to signify that they would build on the 1996 agreements in Berlin regarding NATO-WEU cooperation. The Allies declared that they were "ready to define and adopt the necessary arrangements for ready access by the European Union to the collective assets and capabilities of the Alliance, for operations in which the Alliance as a whole is not engaged militarily as an Alliance," and added that these arrangements would address:

> Assured EU access to NATO planning capabilities able to contribute to military planning for EU-led operations;
>
> The presumption of availability to the EU of pre-identified NATO capabilities and common assets for use in EU-led operations;

Identification of a range of European command options for EU-led operations, further developing the role of DSACEUR in order for him to assume fully and effectively his European responsibilities;

The further adaptation of NATO's defence planning system to incorporate more comprehensively the availability of forces for EU-led operations.[45]

According to the 2002 EU-NATO declaration, the ESDP's "purpose is to add to the range of instruments already at the European Union's disposal for crisis management and conflict prevention in support of the Common Foreign and Security Policy, the capacity to conduct EU-led crisis management operations, including military operations where NATO as a whole is not engaged." The declaration also stated that "a stronger European role will help contribute to the vitality of the Alliance, specifically in the field of crisis management."[46]

On March 17, 2003, NATO and the European Union exchanged official letters establishing a framework for NATO-EU relations—that is, a package of arrangements to allow the Alliance to support EU-led operations in which the Alliance as a whole is not engaged and to support cooperation in capability development. The package consists of fourteen agreements, most of which are classified.[47]

The March 2003 agreement on the Berlin Plus package made possible the first EU-led peacekeeping mission, Operation Concordia in the former Yugoslav Republic of Macedonia, from March to December 2003. Operation Concordia was the successor to a series of three NATO-led operations in the former Yugoslav Republic of Macedonia. As noted in chapter 4, the Alliance provided assets to the European Union for Operation Concordia, and the operational commander was NATO's deputy supreme allied commander Europe (DSACEUR).

In July 2003 the European Union and the Alliance agreed on "a common vision" for the western Balkan region: stability, democracy, prosperity, and closer cooperation with (and possible eventual membership in) European and Euro-Atlantic organizations.[48]

In the framework of this vision the Alliance decided at the June 2004 Istanbul Summit to conclude its SFOR operation in Bosnia and Herzegovina by the end of 2004 and to work with the European Union in the Berlin Plus framework to organize the transition to an EU-led operation in Bosnia and Herzegovina named Althea.[49]

Operation Althea began in December 2004. The commander of the European Force (EUFOR) responsible for Operation Althea is NATO's DSACEUR. This command arrangement helps to ensure NATO-EU coordination and facilitates EU access to NATO collective assets and capabilities. The small NATO headquarters in Sarajevo remains collocated with the headquarters of the EU-led Operation Althea.[50]

As Roy Ginsberg and Susan Penksa have observed, "The irony of Berlin Plus is that it provides for EU action in the absence of NATO action. However, Berlin Plus does not provide for instances where the EU and NATO would act cooperatively or even jointly in the same theater. Neither EU nor NATO anticipated such a scenario at the time the Berlin Plus agreement was put into effect."[51] NATO-EU cooperation has, however, been of significant value for the member states of both organizations, notably in the Balkans.

With the entry into force of the European Union's Lisbon Treaty in December 2009, the ESDP was renamed the CSDP, the Common Security and Defense Policy.[52] The Lisbon Treaty explicitly recognized the importance of collective defense through NATO for the EU members that are members of the Alliance.[53] In their 2010 Strategic Concept, the NATO Allies stated:

> We welcome the entry into force of the Lisbon Treaty, which provides a framework for strengthening the EU's capacities to address common security challenges. Non-EU Allies make a significant contribution to these efforts. For the strategic partnership between NATO and the EU, their fullest involvement in these efforts is essential. NATO and the EU can and should play complementary and mutually reinforcing roles in supporting international peace and security. We are determined to make our contribution to create more favourable circumstances through which we will:
>
> - fully strengthen the strategic partnership with the EU, in the spirit of full mutual openness, transparency, complementarity and respect for the autonomy and institutional integrity of both organisations;
>
> - enhance our practical cooperation in operations throughout the crisis spectrum, from coordinated planning to mutual support in the field;
>
> - broaden our political consultations to include all issues of common concern, in order to share assessments and perspectives;
>
> - cooperate more fully in capability development, to minimise duplication and maximise cost-effectiveness.[54]

The explicit references to "complementarity" and the contributions by "non-EU Allies" hint at the difficulties in NATO-EU relations. Despite the achievements of NATO-EU cooperation and the substantial shared tasks facing these organizations, serious difficulties have hampered their relations: institutional and national rivalries, the participation problem, and disagreements about the proper scope and purpose of NATO-EU cooperation.

As Simon Lunn, then the secretary general of the NATO Parliamentary Assembly, observed in 2006, "Whenever a fresh crisis arises, there is always a strong sense of institutional rivalry and competition."[55] Rivalries were, for example, apparent in the "beauty contest" between NATO and the European Union about assistance to the African Union regarding Darfur in the spring and summer of 2005. In the event, both NATO and the European Union assisted the African Union regarding Darfur (outside the Berlin Plus framework, it should be noted). Countries that are members of both organizations have in several cases made contributions under the auspices of both NATO and the European Union.[56]

The competition over missions derives in part from the fact that NATO's non-Article 5 operations and the European Union's chosen security tasks concern the same types of challenges. As Rafael Biermann, a German scholar, has observed, "The frequent use of alternatives to NATO—be it the ESDP or ad hoc coalitions and unilateral action—stimulates not only sustained inter-, but also intra-institutional conflicts within NATO and the EU, particularly on the division of mandates, tasks and resources." Biermann has noted that "for many Europeans, NATO is a fall-back institution for those tasks where autonomous European action is not feasible."[57]

To some extent, competition between NATO and the European Union has derived from the instrumentalization of these institutions by certain states for their own national objectives. France has, for example, generally regarded sub-Saharan Africa as reserved for the European Union, while the United Kingdom and certain other NATO Allies have seen no convincing a priori basis for excluding the Alliance from particular regions of the world.

NATO secretary general Rasmussen has articulated the Alliance's official policy on NATO-EU relations with conviction:

> This is not a competition. We are complementary. And there is ample scope for cooperation between our two organisations. . . . NATO has shown its capacity to act quickly and in high intensity crises, while the European Union is able to deploy a wide range of civilian and military expertise to help rebuild nations. The most recent example is Kosovo. NATO has ensured a safe and secure environment for over a decade, allowing the European Union to use its diplomatic and economic tools to consolidate institutions and the local economy. . . . So NATO and the European Union have to be more ambitious to complement and reinforce each other.[58]

The "participation problem" is shorthand for the conflict of principles that has since the 2004 enlargement of the European Union limited effective cooperation between the members of the European Union and NATO. EU member states hold that all EU members should attend NATO-EU meetings, while NATO member states maintain that the Alliance must uphold the NATO-EU agreement on security that stipulates that classified information can only be shared with EU members that have joined NATO's Partnership for Peace (PfP) and concluded a security agreement with NATO in that framework. Turkey in particular has adopted a restrictive approach. Ankara has on various occasions blocked consensus within NATO concerning interactions with the European Union, including the distribution of information to EU members. Turkey is not an EU member, while Cyprus is currently the only EU country that is not a PfP member and that has not concluded a security agreement with NATO in that framework.

Operation Althea is the only ongoing EU-led operation under Berlin Plus, and it is the sole operation that can be discussed in a formal NATO-EU format. All the EU countries participating in Operation Althea are in PfP and have a security agreement with NATO. As a result, aside from capability development issues, Operation Althea is the only agreed-upon agenda subject that can be discussed at meetings of the North Atlantic Council with the European Union's Political and Security Committee without the presence of Cyprus.

Turkey has since 1963 refused to recognize the government of the Republic of Cyprus, which joined the European Union in May 2004. Turkey has since 1983 recognized the Turkish Republic of Northern Cyprus and has maintained that the Nicosia government has lacked the legal authority to represent Cyprus as a whole and to join the European Union.[59] Since all NATO Allies must recognize and approve candidates for PfP membership, Ankara's nonrecognition policy vis-à-vis the Nicosia government blocks any move toward PfP membership by Cyprus. This makes it impossible for Cyprus to conclude a security agreement with NATO in the PfP framework. The NATO-EU "participation problem" is thus rooted in part in the absence of a negotiated settlement in Cyprus.[60]

The "participation problem" is one of the main explanations for the suboptimal relations between NATO and the European Union, and it accounts for the jocular assertions that NATO and the European Union are divided by a common city and that the relationship amounts to a "frozen conflict." The principal solution to the "participation problem" to date has been to convene informal meetings at multiple levels, including "transatlantic" lunches and dinners for NATO and EU foreign ministers since 2005.[61] Such "work-arounds" have enabled the European Union and the Alliance to coordinate activities, despite formal constraints. Moreover, the NATO secretary general and the EU high representative for foreign affairs and security policy and other NATO and EU officials have continued to meet regularly at headquarters and in staff talks about NATO-EU cooperation in ongoing missions such as Kosovo and Afghanistan.[62]

The formal diplomatic obstacles to more comprehensive cooperation have persisted, despite efforts to surmount them. In 2010, Secretary General Rasmussen proposed that, in return for Turkey accepting the participation of Cyprus in NATO-EU deliberations, the European Union should offer Turkey an arrangement with the European Defense Agency similar to that which the European Union has established with Norway (like Turkey, a non-EU NATO member state), a Turkish-EU security agreement, and decision-making consultations with Turkey about CSDP operations to which Turkey is contributing forces. This would make possible the full involvement of all EU members in NATO-EU cooperation.[63]

Rasmussen's proposal is still under discussion. There appears to be little flexibility in Ankara or Nicosia. Many Turks familiar with these issues regard the EU measures that Rasmussen has suggested as overdue and not deserving of Turkish compromises concerning Cyprus. Some observers hold that Cyprus and Greece are trying to use the issue to make Turkey recognize the Republic of Cyprus, while at least some Turks are interested in leverage regarding Turkey's pursuit of membership in the European Union. The UN talks on Cyprus appear to be in complete deadlock.

Despite the political stalemate, Turkey made an exception to its policy and approved an Alliance invitation to the EU to participate in NATO's 2012 crisis management exercise (CMX 2012). According to informed observers, the Turkish government stipulated that this was an ad hoc decision for this specific occasion and that it did not establish a precedent. The exercise (and the European Union's participation in it) received little publicity, despite its remarkable content. According to the European Union's European External Action Service (EEAS),

> The exercise scenario portrayed an escalating threat from chemical, biological, and radiological proliferation events, and cyber attacks affecting EU Member States, with major incidents in Italy and Latvia. The EEAS participation consisted of information exchanges with NATO at staff level on the evolving crisis situation and on the actions being fictitiously taken in sup-

port of the stricken countries. The EEAS Managing Director for Crisis Response briefed the North Atlantic Council about the assets that the EU would deploy in the event of such a crisis situation.[64]

Judgments differ as to the achievements of NATO-EU cooperation concerning capabilities. According to Paul Sturm, "The EU-NATO Capability Group is largely a compulsory political exercise to make it appear as if the organisations are sitting at the same table; neither side can afford to suggest that there is no cooperation.... Results of meetings are marginal at best, but non-papers and recommendations can still be churned out, even if useless."[65] In contrast, Leo Michel has highlighted the value of exchanges between the European Union's European Defense Agency (EDA) and NATO's Allied Command Transformation:

> The NATO-EU Capability Group has scored some modest successes by sensitizing their member states to the problems of duplicative and/or conflicting capabilities development efforts and by exploring possibilities for technical cooperation on specific projects.... Within this context, the EDA and NATO's Allied Command Transformation (ACT) have undertaken promising steps to cooperate on capability development.... According to senior NATO officials, ACT and EDA have informally "deconflicted" multilateral projects covered under their respective "Smart Defense" and "Pooling and Sharing" initiatives.[66]

Michel has pointed out, however, that the European Union's efforts to promote "pooling and sharing" in equipment procurement have been limited by the scarcity of bilateral and multilateral endeavors. In Michel's words, "despite EDA efforts to rationalize defense spending, only one-quarter of all procurement spending in the European Union during 2010 went to collaborative projects involving more than one member state."[67]

According to an analysis published by the International Institute for Strategic Studies, defense budget cuts by NATO and EU member states have led to "a haphazard, incoherent series of capability reductions at the European and NATO level, with little attempt at coordination."[68] It remains to be seen whether financial necessity will compel NATO and EU governments to cooperate more effectively in acquiring capabilities and to accept the principle of mutual interdependence in the provision of certain types of military assets.[69] The French permanent representative to NATO, Philippe Errera, said in January 2013, "Despite the constrained political framework of relations between the two organizations, direct contacts between Allied Command Transformation and the European Defense Agency, both under French leadership, enabled us to avoid any duplication with the projects developed in the framework of the European 'pooling and sharing' initiative."[70]

NATO and EU members have disagreed frequently and sometimes heatedly about the proper scope and purpose of NATO-EU cooperation. Many observers have attributed to France a desire to confine NATO's potential and enlarge that of the European Union by limiting the scope of NATO-EU dialogue and cooperation.[71] France's objectives have evidently included containing U.S. influence and creating greater room for the European Union to expand its field of competence. The widespread and long-standing French conviction that the European Union should become an autonomous great power, *une Europe-puissance*, is linked to French conceptions of the EU's *finalité*, or ultimate purpose. The French have not been entirely alone in championing this vision of the European Union's future, and have won support from various other EU members on specific issues. Belgium, Germany, Greece, Luxembourg, and Spain have been among the EU members supporting French views on particular matters. France has, however, been the most consistent and systematic advocate of this vision of the European Union's future political and strategic autonomy.[72]

In 2005 Fraser Cameron observed, "There has long been an underlying tension between those, led by France, with a desire to have a fully autonomous ESDP and those, led by the UK, with a determination to keep ESDP wedded to NATO."[73] This tension appears, however, to have been attenuated since Nicolas Sarkozy returned France to the Alliance's integrated military structure in 2009.

The NATO Allies have supported European Union–led crisis management operations since 2003. In terms of the formal "Berlin Plus" framework, as noted previously, there have been only two examples so far: Operation Concordia in the former Yugoslav Republic of Macedonia in 2003 and Operation Althea in Bosnia and Herzegovina since 2004. However, there has also been coordination between NATO and the European Union outside the Berlin Plus framework, for instance with the support to the African Union in Darfur in 2005–2007, in Afghanistan since NATO took over command of ISAF in 2003, and in the counterpiracy operations off the coast of Somalia since 2008. According to Admiral Édouard Guillaud, the chief of staff of the French Armed Forces, NATO suggested that the European Union take responsibility for managing the maritime embargo part of the NATO-led Libya intervention in 2011, but the European Union "missed the boat in Libya" and played no role in the intervention.[74] The European Union's divisions during the 2011 Libya crisis were rooted in deeper differences among the EU member states about the European Union's CSDP. According to Olivier de France, an expert at the European Council on Foreign Relations, "There is no shared ambition about Europe as a global player or about the allocation of defense resources."[75]

Some NATO European Allies have long seen U.S. policy as a hindrance to the development of the European Union's CSDP because of an American tendency to stipulate boundaries. In December 1998, promptly after the landmark British-French initiative at Saint-Malo that effectively launched what was then called the ESDP, Madeleine Albright, then the U.S. secretary of state, listed three conditions:

> First, we want to avoid decoupling: NATO is the expression of the indispensable transatlantic link. It should remain an organization of sovereign allies, where European decision-making is not unhooked from broader alliance decision-making. Second, we want to avoid duplication: defense resources are too scarce for allies to conduct force planning, operate command structures, and make procurement decisions twice—once at NATO and once more at the EU. And third, we want to avoid any discrimination against NATO members who are not EU members.[76]

U.S. officials were especially concerned about certain ESDP initiatives in 2003, including the proposed EU operational headquarters in Tervuren, Belgium. Nicholas

Burns, then the U.S. ambassador to NATO, called these initiatives "one of the greatest dangers to the transatlantic relationship."[77]

In September 2005, Eric Edelman, then the U.S. under secretary of defense for policy, offered another list of stipulations:

> We want to be sure EU efforts do not undercut NATO's work by becoming a competitor for scarce European defense resources. . . . The US has long supported the European Security and Defense Policy (ESDP) based on the understanding that it would:
>
> - help build new European capabilities
> - for operations "where NATO is not engaged"
> - in a manner that would be cooperative, not competitive, with NATO.[78]

Stipulations that seem moderate, self-evidently reasonable, and consistent with agreed-on Alliance policy to Americans have not always been well received by Europeans committed to seeking greater autonomy through the CSDP. Indeed, some U.S. attempts to influence the CSDP's development have come across as heavy-handed and have had effects contrary to those intended. That is, in some cases they have strengthened the resolve of Europeans to pursue autonomy and increase the capacity of EU member states to take action without support from NATO.

Similarly, some U.S. policy statements have seemed to minimize the options available with EU military capabilities—for instance, Daniel Fried's observation in 2007 that "there are going to be tasks better suited for the European Union, maybe lower-end peacekeeping, humanitarian tasks, [and] other, higher-end, rougher tasks where you need NATO."[79] Such statements have convinced some Europeans that the European Union needs to improve its "high-end" military capabilities and lessen its dependence on NATO.

It is nonetheless worth noting that in February 2007, Michèle Alliot-Marie, then the French minister of defense, drew a comparable contrast in discussing NATO and EU capabilities. She described the Alliance as "particularly adapted to operations requiring a high level of equipment and long-term deployments, because it can call on American means and has command structures accustomed to periodic rotations," whereas the European Union, thanks to its 1,500-person battlegroups, has "a very rapid reaction capability enabling it to intervene effectively in regions it knows well, in the framework of operations conceived from the outset as being of short duration, notably for operations intended to prevent the extension of conflicts."[80] The European Union has maintained battlegroups on standby since 2005, but (as of June 2013) it has never employed them in an operation, owing to a lack of consensus among the EU members.[81]

The U.S. government adopted an increasingly positive policy regarding ESDP in the latter years of the George W. Bush administration. In 2008, Victoria Nuland, then the U.S. ambassador to NATO, said, "I am here today in Paris to say that we agree with France—Europe needs, the United States needs, NATO needs, the democratic world needs—a stronger, more capable European defense capacity. An ESDP with only soft power is not enough. . . . President Sarkozy is right—'NATO cannot be everywhere.'"[82]

The Obama administration has continued the U.S. support for the ESDP and close NATO-EU cooperation articulated during the final years of the George W. Bush administration. In October 2009, Alexander Vershbow, then the U.S. assistant secretary of defense for international security affairs, said,

> The ideological debate over whether NATO and the European Union are complementary or competitive has ended. As we've seen in the Balkans and are seeing today in Afghanistan, each institution has distinct capacities that it brings to crisis management, stabilization operations, and responses to threats to our economic and security interests. We support steps that strengthen the EU's capacity to contribute, and we look forward to expanded continued close, results-oriented NATO-EU cooperation in the years ahead. [83]

The European Union's pursuit of a CSDP seems, however, to have slowed down. The European Union has continued three ongoing military operations—EUFOR Althea in Bosnia and Herzegovina (initiated in 2004), EUNAVFOR Atalanta off the coast of Somalia (initiated in 2008), and EUSEC RD Congo in the Democratic Republic of the Congo (initiated in 2007)—but it did not establish a new military mission until January 2013. According to the Council of the European Union, the new military mission—the EU training mission in Mali (EUTM Mali)— is "intended to help improve the military capacity of the Malian Armed Forces in order to allow, under civilian authority, the restoration of the country's territorial integrity." It is a relatively small mission, with EU "common costs" estimated at €12.3 million for a fifteen-month mandate. Moreover, the Council of the European Union specified that "the mission will not be involved in combat operations."[84]

Most of the European Union's active and new CSDP missions are classified as civilian operations, including police, rule of law, border control, support for humanitarian assistance, and monitoring tasks, with civil-military security sector reform in a special category.[85] The United Kingdom has continued to block the proposal, supported most strongly by France, to establish an EU operational headquarters for CSDP operations. The British hold that it would signify "an unnecessary and costly duplication of NATO structures."[86]

The future of the European Union, including its CSDP, will be shaped to a significant degree by the ongoing financial crisis, notably in the eurozone.[87] Another important factor will be the future participation of one of the European Union's largest military powers, the United Kingdom. Under the coalition government led by Conservative party leader David Cameron since May 2010, the United Kingdom has been cautious about further development of the CSDP. In January 2013 Prime Minister Cameron announced that he would seek reforms in the European Union with a view to a referendum on British membership in the organization.[88]

NATO and the Organization for Security and Co-operation in Europe

The Conference on Security and Co-operation in Europe was an important element in the Cold War's East-West political competition.[89] The CSCE originated in a series of proposals and counterproposals made by NATO, the Soviet Union, and the Warsaw Pact during the 1950s and 1960s for an all-European security conference. These proposals finally led to a conference of thirty-five participants—all the countries of Europe (except Albania), plus Canada and the United States—that took place in Helsinki in 1973–1975.

The concluding document of the conference in 1975, called the Helsinki Final Act, is not a legally binding treaty but a political declaration covering three dimensions of security, known as "baskets." Basket I encompasses political-military matters, including a Declaration on Principles Guiding Relations between Participating States (for instance, refraining from the threat or use of force and respecting the inviolability of frontiers and the territorial integrity of states) and a document on confidence-building measures (for instance, prior notification of major military maneuvers).[90] Basket I has also come to include provisions for arms control, owing to the agreements that have been adopted in the CSCE framework since 1975. Basket II concerns cooperation in economics, science and technology, and the environment. Basket III covers cooperation in humanitarian domains, such as human rights, freedom of information, culture, and education.[91]

These three dimensions define the broad scope of the activities of the Organization for Security and Co-operation in Europe, as the CSCE has been officially known since January 1995. As was the case with the CSCE, the OSCE is not treaty-based but dependent on the political commitments of the participating states. Owing mainly to the emergence of multiple successor states following the disintegration of the Soviet Union and the Federal Republic of Yugoslavia, there are now fifty-seven participating states in the OSCE from Europe, North America, the Caucasus, and Central Asia.[92]

The moral standing and political legitimacy earned by the CSCE during the Cold War became apparent when NATO took its first steps to intervene in an international crisis after the end of the Cold War. In June 1992, in the face of the conflict in the former Yugoslavia, the Allies declared their willingness "to support, on a case-by-case basis in accordance with our own procedures, peacekeeping activities under the responsibility of the CSCE, including by making available Alliance resources and expertise." Although NATO has not yet undertaken any peacekeeping activities "under the responsibility" of the OSCE, it has worked closely with the OSCE in crisis management activities in the Balkans.[93]

The NATO Allies have always supported the human rights dimension of the CSCE and its successor, the OSCE. NATO has not, however, been involved in implementing the economic or human rights dimensions of the OSCE, and has concentrated on the international security dimension. NATO has generally not directly supported OSCE operations except by providing security, logistics, planning, information, and communications support for OSCE activities in territories in which NATO forces have been deployed. The first noteworthy NATO-OSCE cooperation of this nature took place regarding Bosnia and Herzegovina in the mid-1990s.[94]

NATO conducted Operation Eagle Eye, the air reconnaissance mission in support of the verification on the ground accomplished by the OSCE in Kosovo, from October 1998 to March 1999. During the same period the Alliance organized an Extraction Force prepared to evacuate OSCE personnel from Kosovo in an emergency. Following the safe withdrawal of OSCE monitors from Kosovo and the initiation of Operation Allied Force in March 1999, both Operation Eagle Eye and the Extraction Force were terminated.

Ad hoc NATO-OSCE cooperation, in conjunction with EU efforts, has also been effective. For example, in January 2001 the OSCE established a mission to the Federal Republic of Yugoslavia that focused on the problematic area of southern Serbia, where there had been an ethnic Albanian insurgency. This mission coordinated its work with that of international partners, including NATO and specific NATO nations, such as the United Kingdom and the United States, to stabilize the situation and implement confidence-building measures. The peace agreement concluded in 2002 provided for the disarmament of insurgents, the integration of ethnic Albanians into state institutions, and local elections on a proportional basis.

The crisis at the same time in the former Yugoslav Republic of Macedonia also called for NATO-EU-OSCE coordination.[95] As Mihai Carp, a NATO staff officer, has written,

> In managing both crises, the international organisations involved successfully avoided duplication of efforts and engaged in the areas in which they had the most expertise. . . . In the former Yugoslav Republic of Macedonia, . . . frequent joint high-level visits by the NATO Secretary General, the EU High Representative, and the OSCE Chairman-in-Office to Skopje added political weight over the main players and underscored the international community's unity of purpose and vision. Despite heavy conflicting schedules and other pressing responsibilities, near-weekly meetings by the *Troika* of Lord Robertson, Javier Solana and Mircea Geoana to the offices of President Trajkovski and other senior government officials in Skopje became a common feature and, more than symbolically, underscored international commitment.[96]

In addition to this preventive diplomacy, NATO and the OSCE have cooperated in the Ohrid border management process that was initiated in May 2003 and involves what are officially termed the Four Partner Organizations: NATO, the OSCE, the European Union, and the Stability Pact for South Eastern Europe.[97]

Aside from coordination in the field in the Balkans, the specific areas of NATO-OSCE interaction in recent years have included border security and management-related issues;[98] the security and disposal of small arms, light weapons, ammunition, and rocket fuel; antiterrorism work, including an initiative against man-portable air-defense systems (MANPADS); combating human trafficking; and regional cooperation, notably in the south Caucasus, southeastern Europe, and Central Asia. Regional cooperation meetings have involved NATO, the United Nations, the International Organization for Migration (IOM), the UN Development Programme (UNDP), the European Union, and the UN High Commissioner for Refugees (UNHCR). Working-level meetings of OSCE and NATO staff members are complemented by addresses by the NATO secretary general to the OSCE Permanent Council and by the OSCE chairperson-in-office to the North Atlantic Council and the Euro-Atlantic Partnership Council.[99]

NATO as an institution did not formally take part in the negotiation of the OSCE Vienna Document on confidence- and security-building measures, revised most recently in 2011, but the NATO Allies did coordinate their policies regarding this document. Similarly, the NATO Allies coordinated their positions during the negotiation of the Open Skies Treaty, concluded under the auspices of the OSCE. As with the CFE Treaty, states parties have convened relevant meetings in the Hofburg in Vienna and its work is served by the OSCE Secretariat.

The OSCE concentrates on promoting democratization, the rule of law, respect for human rights, reconciliation, conflict prevention, and postconflict rehabilitation and peacebuilding. The Allies emphasized the latter activities as areas for NATO-OSCE cooperation in their Chicago Summit Declaration.[100] In the political-military domain the OSCE has provided a broad framework for arms control.[101]

Moscow has in recent years complained that the prevailing agenda in the OSCE has become tilted against Russian priorities, owing to what Moscow regards as an unbalanced focus on democratization and conflict resolution.[102] The Russians have increasingly seen the OSCE not as a means by which they might influence NATO and EU policies but as a vehicle for NATO and EU interference in what they regard as their sphere of influence. Russian objections and resistance to the OSCE's election monitoring and human rights activities constitute one of the main reasons why some observers hold that the OSCE has been in decline in recent years.

Many Russians have asserted that the OSCE has been fomenting "colored revolutions" in former Soviet republics—above all, the "Orange Revolution" in Ukraine and the "Rose Revolution" in Georgia. The Russian objections have sometimes been formulated in terms of "East and West of Vienna"—that is, OSCE election monitoring and other activities have concentrated on cases east of Vienna. In February 2007, Russian president Vladimir Putin complained about the OSCE "interfering in the internal affairs of other countries" and asserted that "people are trying to transform the OSCE into a vulgar instrument designed to promote the foreign policy interests of one or a group of countries. And this task is also being accomplished by the OSCE's bureaucratic apparatus which is absolutely not connected with the state founders in any way."[103]

Russia has made clear its interest in eliminating the autonomy of the OSCE's Office for Democratic Institutions and Human Rights (ODIHR) and scaling down its activities. Russian foreign minister Sergey Lavrov has reportedly proposed that reports by OSCE election-monitoring teams receive the unanimous approval of all OSCE participating states before being published.[104] Russia has also been trying to bound the latitude of the OSCE chairman-in-office and to institute control mechanisms that would prevent any OSCE institutional action without the approval by consensus of all OSCE participating states.[105] Russia has gained backing from allies in the Collective Security Treaty Organization (CSTO) for proposals designed to diminish the significance of the OSCE's human rights dimension and to gain control over ODIHR and other autonomous OSCE institutions.[106]

In areas in which consensus is required for OSCE action, Russia has blocked action that it regards as inconsistent with its interests—for instance, extending the mandate of the OSCE monitoring mission in Georgia. As with Moscow's decision in the UN Security Council to block the continuation of the UN mission in Georgia, Russia did not join in the consensus in the OSCE Permanent Council regarding the prolongation of the OSCE mission in Georgia. Moscow objected to the geographic scope of the proposed mandate, which included Abkhazia and South Ossetia, which Russia had recognized as independent states.

This step followed Russia's use of force against Georgia, an action regarded by most OSCE participating states as a violation of the Helsinki Final Act. The United States and other NATO governments deplored Russian behavior. In the words of Ambassador Vershbow, "Russia's August 2008 invasion of Georgia represented a violation of Georgia's territorial integrity and Principle Four of the Helsinki Final Act. We regret the end of the OSCE and U.N. missions in Georgia and the lack of access to the separatist regions, which impedes efforts to reduce tensions and prevent incidents from spinning out of control."[107]

Foreign Minister Lavrov declared at the December 2010 OSCE Summit Meeting that "there can be no talk whatsoever of the territorial integrity of Georgia within its former boundaries."[108] As a result, the final declaration of the summit made no reference to Georgia at all. The European Union attached a statement reiterating "its firm and consistent commitment to the sovereignty and territorial integrity of Georgia within its internationally recognized borders, in full respect of international law and the Helsinki Final Act," as well as "its support for the OSCE engagement in Georgia, including for the restoration of a meaningful OSCE presence."[109]

Prospective areas of future NATO-OSCE cooperation or parallel activity include cyber and energy security and the implementation of UN Security Council Resolutions 1540 (on the nonproliferation of weapons of mass destruction) and 1325 (on women and peace and security). Whether such positive steps can be pursued will depend largely on relations among the OSCE participating states. Aside from the disagreements concerning Georgia's territorial integrity, the most serious discord has concerned the OSCE's human rights dimension. The OSCE chairperson-in-office in 2012, the Irish foreign minister, deplored the lack of movement in this regard at the December 2012 ministerial meeting,[110] and Hillary Clinton, then the U.S. secretary of state, said,

> More than 20 years after the end of the Cold War, the work of creating a Europe that is whole, free, and at peace remains unfinished. . . . For example, in Belarus, the Government continues to systematically repress human rights, detain political prisoners, and intimidate journalists. In Ukraine, the elections in October were a step backwards for democracy, and we remain deeply concerned about the selective prosecution of opposition leaders. In Tajikistan, Turkmenistan, Uzbekistan, and Kazakhstan, there are examples of the restrictions of the freedom of expression online and offline as well as the freedom of religion. In the Caucasus, we see constraints on judicial independence, attacks on journalists, and elections that are not always free and fair.

> And we have seen in Russia restrictions on civil society including proposed legislation that would require many NGOs and journalists to register as foreign agents if they receive funding from abroad.[111]

Foreign Minister Lavrov complained in his speech at the same OSCE ministerial meeting about EU visa requirements for Russians, OSCE election observation practices and reports, Latvian citizenship policies affecting ethnic Russian residents, and NATO missile defense, among other matters.[112]

Secretary Clinton identified Russian efforts to gain greater influence in the post-Soviet space as a pivotal issue: "There is a move to re-Sovietize the region.... It's not going to be called that. It's going to be called customs union, it will be called Eurasian Union and all of that.... But let's make no mistake about it. We know what the goal is and we are trying to figure out effective ways to slow down or prevent it."[113]

The OSCE's consensus problems have tended to overshadow achievements such as the border-management training center in Tajikistan and the relatively successful mediation efforts in Kyrgyzstan.

The OSCE's "Corfu process," a dialogue launched in June 2009 in conjunction with a meeting of the NATO-Russia Council, represents to some extent a response by other participating states to Russia's wish to review the European security architecture and to promote its proposed European Security Treaty. As noted in chapter 6, Russia's proposed EST would make the CIS, the CSTO, the EU, NATO, and the OSCE parties to the EST; this suggested arrangement implies that these organizations would be subordinate to the EST.

One of the most noteworthy recent developments in the OSCE, Mongolia's accession in November 2012, might have repercussions for NATO's Partnership for Peace. As Paul Pryce has pointed out, Mongolia's accession represents a break from prior assumptions about the necessary criteria for OSCE membership.[114] Mongolia is not one of the successor states of a country that had participated in the CSCE (like the Central Asian states that were formerly Soviet republics), nor is it a European state that had abstained from participation in the CSCE (like Albania). In welcoming Mongolia as an OSCE participating state, the OSCE Ministerial Council stipulated that the zone of application for Vienna Document confidence- and security-building measures will not extend to Mongolia's territory but only to any Mongolian armed forces that may be deployed in the agreed-on zone as it stands.[115]

As a result, in order to become an OSCE participating state, Mongolia was obliged only to profess support for the 1975 Helsinki Final Act, the Charter of Paris, and other key CSCE and OSCE declarations of principle. The Russian government assented to Mongolia's accession to the OSCE as "an exceptional case," given that it is "a State that does not fall within the geographical zone of responsibility of the CSCE/OSCE defined by the Helsinki Final Act." In Moscow's view, Mongolia's accession "cannot be regarded as setting a precedent for other OSCE Partners for Co-operation and other States that are not participating States of the OSCE."[116] Pryce has speculated that U.S. motives in supporting Mongolia's accession may have included strengthening the case for an OSCE field mission in Afghanistan and/or promoting Afghan accession to the OSCE.[117]

Mongolia's OSCE accession raises the question of whether it could also be eligible to join NATO's Partnership for Peace. The January 1994 invitation to join the PfP was extended to states participating in the North Atlantic Cooperation Council "and other CSCE countries able and willing to contribute to this programme."[118] According to the PfP Framework Document, countries joining the partnership must "reaffirm" their commitments to honor the UN Charter, the Universal Declaration on Human Rights, "the Helsinki Final Act and all subsequent CSCE documents," as well as "the commitments and obligations they have undertaken in the field of disarmament and arms control."[119] Mongolia has now satisfied these requirements. Similarly, the Basic Document of the EAPC states, "The Euro-Atlantic Partnership Council is open to the accession of other OSCE participating states able and willing to accept its basic principles and to contribute to its goals."[120]

The wording of the PfP invitation and the obligation to "reaffirm" CSCE commitments in the PfP Framework Document indicate that the NATO Allies originally intended to limit PfP membership to the non-NATO countries then in the CSCE that they chose to invite.[121] Mongolia's accession to the OSCE might, however, be regarded as making it eligible for PfP membership. Whether the NATO Allies will reach such a conclusion and invite Mongolia to join the PfP and the EAPC remains to be seen.[122] At present the Allies appear disposed to continue with the Individual Partnership and Cooperation Program (IPCP) concluded with Mongolia in March 2012.[123]

NATO's "Comprehensive Approach"

Since the Alliance's first peacekeeping operation, IFOR in Bosnia in 1995–1996, the Allies have devoted increasing attention to interinstitutional cooperation involving military forces, civilian agencies, international organizations, nongovernmental organizations, and local government authorities. While the Allies have employed several concepts to describe the effort to achieve more effective collaboration with these partners in crisis management and cooperative security,[124] since the 2006 Riga Summit the preferred phrase has been the "comprehensive approach."[125]

The comprehensive approach calls for coordinated activity by multiple types of organizations in cooperation with local authorities to promote security and development. In the words of the Riga Summit Declaration, "Experience in Afghanistan and Kosovo demonstrates that today's challenges require a comprehensive approach by the international community involving a wide spectrum of civil and military instruments, while fully respecting mandates and autonomy of decisions of all actors, and provides precedents for this approach."[126]

If the Allies intend to ensure that conflicts among local antagonists do not resume and that no new havens for terrorists or criminals can be established, they must achieve much more than victory in the traditional sense of defeating an enemy's forces in combat. The tasks of state building and democratization cannot be accomplished with purely military means. Sustainable security requires stabilization, reconstruction, economic and social development, and good governance. Constructive intervention therefore requires the contributions of multiple international organizations and nongovernmental organizations.[127]

The fact that international organizations have differing strengths and mandates has often facilitated cooperation in working out a sensible division of labor. NATO's most obvious comparative advantage resides in its military capabilities, including its expertise in the planning, organization, and conduct of operations involving the armed forces of the Allies and security partners. On some occasions the Allies have intervened decisively to separate warring parties and to put an end to atrocities—as with, for example, Operation Deliberate Force in 1995 in Bosnia and Operation Allied Force in 1999 in the Kosovo conflict. The Allies have also played a leading role in providing a secure environment for the activities of other organizations—as with IFOR and SFOR in Bosnia from 1995 to 2004, KFOR since 1999, and ISAF in Afghanistan since 2003.

While the Alliance has some nonmilitary civil capabilities (notably with respect to civil emergency planning, defense aspects of security sector reform, and partnership cooperation programs), NATO is clearly incapable of undertaking the full range of tasks required for state building and social and economic development.

In the 2010 Strategic Concept, however, the Allies underscored an aspiration of growing importance: "The Alliance will engage actively with other international actors *before, during and after crises* to encourage collaborative analysis, planning and conduct of activities on the ground, in order to maximise coherence and effectiveness of the overall international effort."[128] To work with other international organizations and "stakeholders" before crises emerge and during their development could imply unprecedented information-sharing and coordinated assessment and planning efforts.

The Alliance's intervention in the Libya conflict in 2011 furnished a reasonably successful fulfillment of this aspiration. The secretariats of NATO and the United Nations cooperated regarding this intervention to an unprecedented extent. It appears that the two organizations benefited from having developed greater mutual understanding and from the contacts each has cultivated with specific bodies, such as the United Nations' Department of Peacekeeping Operations (DPKO) and Office for the Coordination of Humanitarian Affairs (OCHA) and NATO's Operations Division, Supreme Headquarters Allied Powers Europe (SHAPE), and Joint Forces Command Naples.

Some observers hold that Libya offered the most positive example to date of the "comprehensive approach" envisaged by the Alliance. In addition to working closely with the UN Secretariat, NATO coordinated its actions with the League of Arab States, the African Union, the International Organization for Migration, and the humanitarian agencies of the United Nations, among other organizations. Cooperation and dialogue involving these various organizations enabled NATO to take the movements of humanitarian actors into account in planning military operations.[129]

By keeping the United Nations and other organizations informed as to its intentions and activities, NATO could more readily turn over the lead regarding Libya to the United Nations in the postconflict phase. The Libya case thus confirmed one of the lessons of previous and ongoing non-Article 5 interventions: NATO's role needs to be "nested" in a coherent framework involving other international organizations; and all Allies would prefer the endorsement and involvement of the United Nations in particular, if possible.[130]

In the 2010 Lisbon Summit Declaration, moreover, the Allies announced that "the Alliance must . . . have the ability to plan for, employ, and coordinate civilian as well as military crisis management capabilities that nations provide for agreed Allied missions. To improve NATO's contribution to a comprehensive approach and its ability to contribute, when required, to stabilisation and reconstruction, we have agreed to form an appropriate but modest civilian capability to interface more effectively with other actors and conduct appropriate planning in crisis management."[131] This decision suggests a dampening of the long-standing disputes between some Allies, notably France and the United States, about the proper roles of the Alliance and the expanse of the civilian "turf" reserved for UN and EU agencies.[132]

In September 2011, the Allies approved "political guidance on ways to improve NATO's involvement in stabilization and reconstruction." This document noted the need "to avoid unnecessary duplication with other international organisations, particularly the UN and the EU, which could provide complementary capabilities in the field of stabilisation and reconstruction." It called for NATO to conduct its operations "with due respect for the humanitarian space in accordance with the 2008 'UN Civil-Military Guidelines and Reference for Complex Emergencies.'" It underlined that the "ultimate goal" of stabilization and reconstruction "efforts is to maintain or return to a stable, self-sustaining peace," and added that "it will be important in this context for the Alliance to seek, in accordance with the Comprehensive Approach Action Plan, unity of effort with the other members of the international community, in particular its strategic partners the UN and the EU."[133] The emphasis in this political guidance document on the United Nations and the European Union as the chief international organizations that NATO intends to work with was consistent with the Allies choosing not to refer at all to the OSCE in this document or in the 2010 Strategic Concept. The Allies are far from having written off the OSCE, however. In the 2012 Chicago Summit Declaration they stated that they intend to "work closely" with the OSCE "in areas such as conflict prevention and resolution, postconflict rehabilitation, and in addressing new security threats." Moreover, in the same declaration they noted their intention to work "closely with the OSCE, the UN, and the EU to pursue peaceful conflict resolution in the internationally-recognised territory of Georgia."[134]

Beyond the major international organizations that this discussion has focused on, the Alliance intends to continue to develop means to interact more effectively with the many nongovernmental organizations (NGOs) that constitute essential elements of the "comprehensive approach" envisaged by the Allies. This represents a great challenge for the Allies for two basic reasons. First, NGOs differ substantially in their principles, agendas, and methods. Second, many disapprove of military organizations, and are wary of being closely associated with NATO forces.

In 2010, Secretary General Rasmussen said, "I recently suggested publicly that we needed to work more closely with NGOs, so that their 'soft power' could complement our hard power. Their reaction, I can tell you, was not very receptive. I think they are worried about becoming a party to a conflict. They wish to remain neutral. Therefore, they are often reluctant to work under military protection." Rather than simply deploring the "lack of communication" with NGOs, Rasmussen called for "more discussion and, where appropriate, more coordination between the military and civilian sides, from the planning stages to field operations. In peacetime, we must get to know each other and train together, for the inevitable moment when we are thrown together in a real crisis."[135]

Implementing this recommendation would require much of the Alliance as well as the NGOs, because the Allies themselves have not reached a full consensus on the practical requirements of the comprehensive approach. Preparations in peacetime and learning from past crises (as in Afghanistan and Libya) may, however, provide a basis for improvisations tailored to the unique features of upcoming emergencies.

Conclusion

NATO's relations with the UN Security Council must be distinguished from the Alliance's cooperation with the UN Secretariat and specific UN agencies. Cooperation with the UN Secretariat and UN agencies has developed well since the early 1990s, reaching what some deem an unprecedented level of effectiveness in the 2011 Libya intervention.

In contrast, the NATO Allies have been cautious since the outset regarding certain interpretations of the UN Security Council's authority. In drafting the North Atlantic Treaty in 1948–1949, the Allies took care not to establish a regional arrangement under Chapter VIII of the UN Charter but instead founded the Alliance on Article 51 of the Charter, their inherent right to collective defense. While the NATO Allies recognize the respect accorded to the UN Security Council, and would prefer to benefit from UN Security Council authorizations for any operations involving the use of force, the Alliance's action in the 1999 Kosovo conflict showed that the Allies may in exceptional circumstances take action without UN Security Council approval.

The view that legitimizing authority resides solely with the UN Security Council would present risks for international security because it would make all action dependent on a P5 consensus. From NATO's viewpoint, it would mean that the

Allies could undertake non-Article 5 missions only with the concurrence of Russia and China. As the Kosovo conflict demonstrated vividly, however, the UN Security Council may be politically immobilized and therefore incapable of intervening to address injustice and aggression.[136]

Sometimes, however, the Allies have found it in their interests to insist on a requirement for UN Security Council authorization before contemplating any deployment of military capabilities. This applies to any possible role in peacekeeping in the event of an Israeli-Palestinian settlement. In February 2011 Secretary General Rasmussen repeated a long-standing Alliance policy:

> NATO is not involved in the Middle East peace process and is not seeking a role in it. The three conditions for any possible NATO involvement are well known: if a comprehensive peace agreement between Israel and the Palestinians was reached; if both parties requested that NATO should help them with the implementation of that agreement; and if the United Nations endorsed NATO's possible involvement.[137]

Three key issues have arisen in the Alliance's relations with the European Union since 1998–1999, when the European Union began pursuing its Common Security and Defense Policy. First, despite the fact that twenty-two countries are members of both NATO and the European Union, the "participation problem" rooted in the discord between Cyprus and Turkey has made dialogue and cooperation among the members of these organizations suboptimal. NATO and EU countries have had to devise "work-arounds" to move forward. Second, a "scope problem" persists, in that some countries in NATO and/or the European Union differ as to the extent to which the Alliance should undertake "civilian" measures and as to how to define the appropriate role and "level of ambition" for each organization in specific operations. These differences overlap with the third issue—defining a satisfactory "division of labor" and managing competition between the organizations. Competition arises because non-Article 5 NATO operations could also be regarded as part of the preferred spectrum of CSDP missions.

The NATO and EU countries each have only one set of national capabilities. These are the forces on which they must rely to undertake action, whether under national, NATO, EU, UN, or coalition auspices. Given the current economic context, the turbulent strategic environment, and the high rate of inflation in the cost of advanced military equipment, NATO and EU countries should pursue the potential advantages of what the Alliance currently calls "smart defense" and the European Union terms "pooling and sharing." This would imply a higher level of multinational acquisition and role specialization, among other measures. The shared security interests of NATO and EU countries, to say nothing of their common values, ought to lead them to more effective cooperation and less national and inter-institutional rivalry.

As Robert Gates, then the U.S. secretary of defense, said in 2010, "One of the lessons of Kosovo and Afghanistan is that the missions we are most likely to undertake require a comprehensive approach that leverages both military and civilian capabilities. In recent years, there has been a recognition that the EU will not supplant

NATO or vice versa—but that both organizations have unique skill-sets that can, if used properly, add up to more than the sum of their individual parts."[138]

For the NATO Allies the most important function of the OSCE has been as a vehicle for articulating and upholding political standards. These standards—including democracy, human rights, and principles of international security—have furnished a basis for pursuing positive political change throughout the Euro-Atlantic region, notably in former Warsaw Pact countries, and in successor countries of the former Yugoslavia and the former Soviet Union. Russia and its CSTO allies have increasingly objected to the emphasis placed on human rights and democracy in the OSCE by NATO and EU countries and have sought means to limit the latitude and autonomy of OSCE institutions such as ODIHR. The NATO Allies have, however, every reason—in terms of their political values as well as their security interests—to uphold the established standards of the OSCE and institutions such as ODIHR. These standards and institutions offer a more promising basis for preventing and resolving conflicts on a just and durable basis than the prescriptions proffered by the CSTO.

Disagreements persist among the NATO Allies on what precise meaning to give to a phrase in the 2006 Riga Summit Declaration: "a comprehensive approach by the international community involving a wide spectrum of civil and military instruments."[139] However, despite their differences as to the right mix of tools for particular cases, the Allies recognize that improvements in the coordination of efforts by states, international organizations, NGOs, and local authorities enhance the prospects for success. Ambitious goals such as democratization and sustainable security can only be achieved through economic and political development, and such development requires a comprehensive approach, including the contributions of many organizations in addition to NATO.[140] In short, the Allies are engaged in a complex balancing act in their cooperation with other major international security organizations.

Notes

1. This chapter draws heavily on Yost, *NATO and International Organizations*.
2. Martin A. Smith, "At Arm's Length: NATO and the United Nations in the Cold War Era," *International Peacekeeping* 2, no. 1 (Spring 1995): 56–73.
3. NATO Allies participated in CSCE deliberations on a national rather than collective basis, and the same principle applied to negotiations with Warsaw Pact states on arms control and confidence- and security-building measures (CSBMs).
4. North Atlantic Council, "Rome Summit Declaration," par. 3.
5. North Atlantic Council, communiqué, June 4, 1992, par. 4, 11.
6. North Atlantic Council, communiqué, December 17, 1992, par. 4.
7. North Atlantic Council, communiqué, December 17, 1992, par. 5.
8. "Last year, through the UN-mandated Operation Unified Protector (OUP), and with the support of the League of Arab States, our Alliance played a crucial role in protecting the civilian population in Libya and in helping save thousands of lives." North Atlantic Council, "Chicago Summit Declaration," par. 13.
9. Alex J. Bellamy and Paul D. Williams, "The New Politics of Protection? Côte d'Ivoire, Libya and the Responsibility to Protect," *International Affairs* 87, no. 4 (July 2011): 841.
10. With regard to cooperation with nongovernmental organizations, see Laure Borgomano-Loup, *Improving NATO-NGO Relations in Crisis Response Operations*, Forum Paper no. 2 (Rome: NATO Defense College, March 2007), www.ndc.nato.int/download/publications/fp_02_en.pdf.

11. "Quarterly Report to the United Nations on ISAF Operations," submitted by the NATO secretary general on September 22, 2004, transmitted by the UN secretary general to the president of the Security Council on October 1, 2004, S/2004/785, par. 26.

12. Guy Roberts, deputy assistant secretary general for NATO's policy on weapons of mass destruction, video interview, NATO headquarters, Brussels, September 27, 2005.

13. "We are prepared to develop political dialogue and practical cooperation with any nations and relevant organisations across the globe that share our interest in peaceful international relations." North Atlantic Council, "Strategic Concept," November 19, 2010, par. 30.

14. North Atlantic Council, "Riga Summit Declaration," par. 9.

15. North Atlantic Council, "Comprehensive Political Guidance," November 29, 2006, par. 1.

16. Ibid., par. 3.

17. Croatia became the twenty-eighth member country of the European Union on July 1, 2013.

18. For a thorough and authoritative historical analysis, see Lawrence S. Kaplan, *NATO and the UN: A Peculiar Relationship* (Columbia and London: University of Missouri Press, 2010).

19. For background on NATO–United Nations relations during Operation Allied Force, see Ryan C. Hendrickson, *Diplomacy and War at NATO: The Secretary General and Military Action after the Cold War* (Columbia and London: University of Missouri Press, 2006), 89–116; and Kent J. Kille and Ryan C. Hendrickson, "Secretary-General Leadership Across the United Nations and NATO: Kofi Annan, Javier Solana, and Operation Allied Force," *Global Governance* 16, no. 4 (October–December 2010), 505–523.

20. Article 5 of the North Atlantic Treaty refers explicitly to Article 51 of the UN Charter as well as to the responsibilities of the UN Security Council. Article 5 of the North Atlantic Treaty reads as follows: "The Parties agree that an armed attack against one or more of them in Europe or North America shall be considered an attack against them all and consequently they agree that, if such an armed attack occurs, each of them, in exercise of the right of individual or collective self-defence recognised by Article 51 of the Charter of the United Nations, will assist the Party or Parties so attacked by taking forthwith, individually and in concert with the other Parties, such action as it deems necessary, including the use of armed force, to restore and maintain the security of the North Atlantic area. Any such armed attack and all measures taken as a result thereof shall immediately be reported to the Security Council. Such measures shall be terminated when the Security Council has taken the measures necessary to restore and maintain international peace and security."

21. "When a bewildered non-P5 ambassador once asked the Soviet representative how one could tell the difference between a procedural matter and a substantive matter, he was informed dryly, 'We shall tell you.' And so it remains today." Paul Kennedy, *The Parliament of Man: The Past, Present, and Future of the United Nations* (New York: Random House, 2006), 36. For an analysis of interpretation and practice, see Stefan Brunner, Hans-Peter Kaul, and Bruno Simma, "Article 27," in *The Charter of the United Nations: A Commentary*, 2nd ed., vol. I, ed. Bruno Simma (Oxford and New York: Oxford University Press, 2002), 476–523.

22. Joschka Fischer quoted in Roger Cohen, "'We Will Deal with Our History': Fischer, Germany's Foreign Minister, Looks Ahead to Berlin," *International Herald Tribune*, January 29, 1999. The British government offered a similar rationale for action: "In the exceptional circumstances of Kosovo it was considered that the use of force would be justified on the grounds of overwhelming humanitarian necessity, without [United Nations] Security Council authorization." Baroness Symons of Vernham Dean, the parliamentary under-secretary of state, Foreign and Commonwealth Office, in *House of Lords, Parliamentary Debates*, November 2, 1998, Written Answers, col. 11.

23. For an illuminating discussion, see Dick A. Leurdijk, "NATO as a Subcontractor to the United Nations: The Cases of Bosnia and Kosovo," in *NATO after Kosovo*, ed. Rob de Wijk, Bram Boxhoorn, and Niklaas Hoekstra (The Hague: Netherlands Atlantic Association, Netherlands Institute of International Relations "Clingendael," and the Royal Netherlands Military Academy, 2000), 130–132, 135–137. For an example of an official statement justifying the use of force by reference to both humanitarian necessity and UN Security Council resolutions, and thereby affirming national policy regarding the Security Council's authority, see the speech by Alain Richard, then France's minister of defense, in Munich on February 6, 1999. Jacques Chirac, then France's president, underscored his view that in the Kosovo conflict NATO was acting in support of Security Council resolutions—and could not legitimately use force in such an operation without the approval of the Security Council—in his press conference at the NATO summit in Washington, DC, April 24, 1999.

24. Lord Robertson of Port Ellen, *Kosovo One Year On: Achievement and Challenge* (Brussels: NATO, March 21, 2000), 24.

25. Dick Leurdijk, "NATO and the UN: The Dynamics of an Evolving Relationship," *RUSI Journal* 149 (June 2004): 26–27.

26. Manfred Wörner, speech at the annual conference of the International Institute for Strategic Studies, Brussels, September 10, 1993.

27. As Katariina Saariluoma, a Finnish scholar, has pointed out, in several resolutions since the early 1990s the UN Security Council has held that "lack of respect for human rights and humanitarian law" could "give rise to a threat to international peace and security." Katariina Saariluoma, *Operation Allied Force: A Case of Humanitarian Intervention?* (Garmisch-Partenkirchen, Germany: Partnership for Peace Consortium of Defense Academies and Security Studies Institutes, September 2004), 54. The concepts of "humanitarian necessity" and "humanitarian intervention" nonetheless remain controversial. In 2002, an authoritative analysis held that "there is still no consensus in international legal doctrine on the unlawfulness of forcible humanitarian intervention, that is, the use of armed force for the prevention or discontinuation of massive violations of human rights in a foreign State." Albrecht Randelzhofer, "Article 2(4)," in *The Charter of the United Nations: A Commentary*, 2nd ed., vol. I, ed. Bruno Simma (Oxford and New York: Oxford University Press, 2002), 130. The debate over "humanitarian intervention" has increasingly been pursued in conjunction with that over the "responsibility to protect." For background, see Bellamy and Williams, "The New Politics of Protection?"

28. Thierry Tardy, "The EU and NATO as Peacekeepers: Open Cooperation *versus* Implicit Competition," in *Peacekeeping-Peacebuilding: Preparing for the Future*, ed. Hanna Ojanen (Helsinki: Finnish Institute of International Affairs, 2006), 33.

29. Vladimir Putin, speech at the 43rd Munich Conference on Security Policy, February 10, 2007, www.securityconfer ence.de/archive/konferenzen/rede.php?menu_konferenzen=&sprache=en&id=179&.

30. In 2006 Sergei Ivanov, then Russia's deputy prime minister and minister of defense, wrote that Russia was "ready to run peacekeeping operations mandated by the UN or CIS." Sergei Ivanov, "Russia Must Be Strong," *Wall Street Journal*, January 11, 2006.

31. Boris Yeltsin, then the president of Russia, issued a decree on June 9, 1994, to implement the CIS decision to authorize a peacekeeping operation in Abkhazia. On July 21, 1994, UN Security Council Resolution 937 noted "with satisfaction the readiness of the Russian Federation to continue to inform the members of the Security Council on the activities of the CIS peace-keeping force." As the *New York Times* noted, this UNSCR "in effect lends international legitimacy to Russia's disputed peacekeeping operation without formally authorizing the dispatch of the troops." ("U.N. Endorses Russian Troops For Peacekeeping in Caucasus," *New York Times*, July 22, 1994, www.nytimes. com/1994/07/22/world/un-endorses-russian-troops-for-peacekeeping-in-caucasus.html.) Whatever the legality of the CIS mandate for peacekeeping, it should be noted, "no international or domestic legal act can justify the Russian military invasion of the sovereign territory of the Republic of Georgia, or the recognition of the self-proclaimed independence of Georgian separatist regions by the Russian Federation." Peter Roudik, *Russian Federation: Legal Aspects of War in Georgia* (Washington, DC: Law Library of Congress, September 2008), 13.

32. Vladimir Socor, "Russia Discards Its 'Peacekeeping' Operation in Abkhazia," *Eurasia Daily Monitor* 5, no. 196 (October 14, 2008).

33. Peter Viggo Jakobsen, "Should NATO Support UN Peacekeeping Operations?" *NATO Review*, Summer 2005.

34. "In response to the request of the Iraqi Interim Government, and in accordance with [UN Security Council] Resolution 1546 which requests international and regional organisations to contribute assistance to the Multinational Force, we have decided today to offer NATO's assistance to the government of Iraq with the training of its security forces." Statement on Iraq issued by the heads of state and government participating in the meeting of the North Atlantic Council in Istanbul, June 28, 2004.

35. For background on the "dual key" episode, see Yost, *NATO and International Organizations*, 46–53.

36. Marten Zwanenburg, "NATO, Its Member States, and the Security Council," in *The Security Council and the Use of Force: Theory and Reality—A Need for Change?*, ed. Niels Blokker and Nico Schrijver (Leiden and Boston: Martinus Nijhoff Publishers, 2005), 211.

37. UNSC Resolution 1244 (1999), Annex 2, par. 4.

38. The NATO spokesman, James Appathurai, said that the NATO secretary general intended to "move forward the establishment of . . . a strategic relationship" between NATO and the UN on issues such as terrorism, proliferation, and Afghanistan. (Video background briefing, September 16, 2005.) The NATO secretary general, Jaap de Hoop Scheffer, said that he had met with the UN secretary-general "to establish a more structural relationship" between the two organizations. "NATO: Safeguarding Transatlantic Security" (speech at Columbia University, New York, September 20, 2005).

39. Ban Ki-Moon and Jaap de Hoop Scheffer signed the joint declaration in New York on September 23, 2008. The delay may be partly attributed to perceptions among many non-NATO members of the United Nations. A great deal of anecdotal evidence indicates that NATO's purposes and consensual decision-making processes are poorly understood in the United Nations and many of its member states. At UN headquarters and in many member states of the United Nations, NATO is widely perceived as an expansionist Cold War military bloc and tool of the United States that has at times resorted too readily to the use of force. Some UN experts have indicated that there are intrinsic limits to developing an institutional relationship between a universal organization and an alliance composed of wealthy "northern" countries, several of which are former colonial powers. Another issue is the fact that a number of "southern"

UN members are not committed to the Western democratic standards and principles championed by NATO. Expert observers consider this a secondary element in the suspicions regarding NATO in the United Nations and far less important than the perception of the Alliance as a U.S.-dominated organization.

40. North Atlantic Council, "Lisbon Summit Declaration," par. 10. For background and analysis, see Brooke A. Smith-Windsor, ed., *The UN and NATO: Forward from the Joint Declaration*, Forum Paper no. 17 (Rome: NATO Defense College, May 2011), www.ndc.nato.int/download/downloads.php?icode=276.

41. This section is based on the more extensive discussion in Yost, *NATO and International Organizations*, 72–111. Two book-length studies are especially useful: Jolyon Howorth, *Security and Defence Policy in the European Union* (Basingstoke, UK, and New York: Palgrave Macmillan, 2007), and Roy H. Ginsberg and Susan E. Penksa, *The European Union in Global Security: The Politics of Impact* (New York: Palgrave Macmillan, 2012).

42. Tony Blair, then the British prime minister, indicated that changes in British policy in this regard were at hand in his remarks at a press conference in Pörtschach, Austria, on October 25, 1998. The changes received formal expression in the joint declaration by the heads of state and government of France and the United Kingdom at St-Malo, December 3–4, 1998.

43. These bodies included the Western European Armaments Group (WEAG) and the Western European Armaments Organisation (WEAO), which the nations concerned closed in May 2005. The WEAG and WEAO functions were transferred to the European Union's European Defence Agency. For background, see WEU, "Western European Armaments Group," www.weu.int/weag/index.html. Turkey had been an associate member of the WEU and a member of the WEAG. The transfer of WEU and WEU-related activities to the European Union (and the eventual termination of the Brussels Treaty and the WEU) signified reduced influence and a greater sense of exclusion for Ankara. For background, see Yost, *NATO and International Organizations*, 152–155.

44. The EU members that are not members of NATO are Austria, Cyprus, Finland, Ireland, Malta, and Sweden. The NATO members that are not members of the European Union are Canada, Iceland, Norway, Turkey, and the United States.

45. North Atlantic Council, "Washington Summit Communiqué," April 24, 1999, par. 10. The statements in the 1999 Strategic Concept about NATO-EU cooperation, adopted the same day as the Washington Summit Communiqué, are less precise and not entirely consistent with the political reality of an emerging ESDP, perhaps owing to a residual wish on the part of some NATO Allies to retain the previous concept of an ESDI within the Alliance. For example, the Strategic Concept states that "the European Security and Defence Identity will continue to be developed within NATO" and adds that "This process will require close cooperation between NATO, the WEU and, if and when appropriate, the European Union." The call in the Strategic Concept for "the full participation of all European Allies if they were so to choose" may have reflected the concerns of Turkey and other non-EU European Allies. North Atlantic Council, "Strategic Concept," April 24, 1999, para. 30.

46. NATO, "EU-NATO Declaration on ESDP," December 16, 2002, press release (2002), 142.

47. The fact that most of the "Berlin Plus" agreements are classified may be a factor contributing to continuing disputes about the scope of the arrangements and the specific political obligations assumed by NATO and the European Union, notably with respect to crisis consultations.

48. See NATO, "EU and NATO Agree Concerted Approach for the Western Balkans," press release (2003) 089, July 29, 2003.

49. NATO had agreed to consider this option at the meeting of NATO and EU foreign ministers in December 2003. See the joint press statement by the NATO secretary general and the EU presidency, NATO press release (2003) 153, December 4, 2003.

50. Leo Michel, "NATO, the EU, and the United States: Why Not a Virtuous Ménage à Trois?," in "The Future of US European Command," July 19, 2012, note 20, www.acus.org/files/ISP/michel_eucomib.pdf.

51. Roy H. Ginsberg and Susan E. Penksa, *The European Union in Global Security: The Politics of Impact* (New York: Palgrave Macmillan, 2012), 188–189.

52. In March 2010 the states party to the 1948 Brussels Treaty announced that, in light of the entry into force of the Lisbon Treaty, they were terminating the Brussels Treaty and the Western European Union. "With the entry into force of the Lisbon Treaty, a new phase in European security and defence begins. Article 42.7 of the Treaty on the European Union now sets out that, if a Member State is the victim of armed aggression on its territory, the other Member States shall have towards it an obligation of aid and assistance by all the means in their power, and states that commitments and cooperation in this area shall be consistent with commitments in NATO, which for its members remains the foundation of their collective defence and the forum for its implementation. . . . The WEU has therefore accomplished its historical role. In this light we the States Parties to the Modified Brussels Treaty have collectively decided to terminate the Treaty, thereby effectively closing the organization." "Statement of the Presidency of the Permanent Council of the WEU on behalf of the High Contracting Parties to the Modified Brussels Treaty—Belgium, France, Germany, Greece, Italy, Luxembourg, the Netherlands, Portugal, Spain and the United Kingdom," March 31, 2010.

53. "The policy of the Union in accordance with this Section shall not prejudice the specific character of the security and defence policy of certain Member States and shall respect the obligations of certain Member States, which see their common defence realised in the North Atlantic Treaty Organisation (NATO), under the North Atlantic Treaty and be compatible with the common security and defence policy established within that framework." Article 42, par. 2 of *Consolidated Version of the Treaty on European Union*, published by the Council of the European Union, April 15, 2008.

54. North Atlantic Council, "Strategic Concept," November 19, 2010, par. 32, www.nato.int/cps/en/natolive/official_texts_68580.htm.

55. Simon Lunn, letter in *Europe's World*, Spring 2006, 26.

56. Another approach has been to contribute to EU-led operations to demonstrate support for its security dimension and to contribute to NATO-led operations to cultivate links with the United States. "By sending our soldiers to Chad, we are building Poland's position in Europe, and by taking responsibility for the Ghazni province in Afghanistan, we are strengthening our ties to the Americans." Bogdan Klich, then the defense minister of Poland, interview in *Rzeczpospolita*, June 3, 2008, in *BBC Monitoring Europe*, June 3, 2008.

57. Rafael Biermann, "NATO's Institutional Decline in Post-Cold War Security Governance," in *European Security Governance: The European Union in a Westphalian World*, ed. Charlotte Wagnsson, James A. Sperling and Jan Hallenberg (London and New York: Routledge, 2009), 58.

58. NATO secretary general Anders Fogh Rasmussen, monthly press conference, May 6, 2013, www.nato.int/cps/en/natolive/opinions_100206.htm?selectedLocale=en.

59. According to the Turkish Ministry of Foreign Affairs, "in 1963 . . . the Turkish Cypriots were ousted by force from all organs of the new Republic by their Greek Cypriot partners in clear breach of the founding documents and the Constitution. The claim put forth thereafter by the Greek Cypriots to represent the 'Republic of Cyprus' has been illegal, and has not been recognized by Turkey. . . . Turkey and [the] TRNC [Turkish Republic of Northern Cyprus] argued that the Greek Cypriot side had no authority to negotiate on behalf of the whole Island and that this accession [to the European Union] would be in contravention of the relevant provisions of the 1959–1960 Treaties on Cyprus, and thus, constituted a violation of international law. The said Treaties prohibit Cyprus from joining any international organization of which both Turkey and Greece are not members." See "Cyprus Issue (Summary)" on the Web site of the Turkish Ministry of Foreign Affairs, www.mfa.gov.tr/MFA/ForeignPolicy/MainIssues/Cyprus/Cyprus_Issue.htm.

60. Some observers maintain that there are three possible solutions, all improbable in the near term: Turkish membership in the European Union, the reunification of Cyprus, or Cyprus becoming a member of Partnership for Peace and concluding a security agreement with NATO in that framework. The last solution is the most plausible in the near term, if only because Turkish recognition of the Nicosia government would presumably have to precede the reunification of Cyprus or Turkish membership in the European Union. However, in current circumstances Turkey's nonrecognition policy vis-à-vis the Nicosia government would prevent a NATO consensus to approve a hypothetical Cypriot application to join NATO's Partnership for Peace. Turkey might reconsider its position in light of progress on the Cyprus question and/or improvements in its relations with the European Union.

61. Hillary Clinton, then the U.S. secretary of state, hosted the "transatlantic dinner" in New York in September 2012. The guests included the NATO secretary general, the EU high representative, the foreign ministers of the NATO and EU countries, as well as Switzerland and the former Yugoslav Republic of Macedonia. "NATO Secretary General Holds High-level Meetings in New York," September 26, 2012, www.nato.int/cps/en/SID-6DD8D625-4A59298F/natolive/news_90246.htm?selectedLocale=en.

62. Leo Michel, "La défense européenne en 2013: Une perspective américaine," *Revue Défense Nationale* (Summer 2013): 121–124.

63. See the speech by Anders Fogh Rasmussen at the annual conference of the Security and Defence Agenda in Brussels, June 21, 2010, www.nato.int/cps/en/natolive/opinions_64563.htm. Rasmussen also advanced this proposal in his press conferences on May 25, 2010, and September 15, 2010.

64. European External Action Service, "NATO Exercise CMX 12," http://eeas.europa.eu/crisis-response/what-we-do/exercises/index_en.htm.

65. Paul Sturm, "NATO and the EU: Cooperation?" ISIS Europe, *European Security Review*, no. 48, (February 2010): 12.

66. Michel, "NATO, the EU, and the United States."

67. Leo G. Michel, *Cross-Currents in French Defense and U.S. Interests*, Strategic Perspectives no. 10 (Washington, DC: National Defense University Press, April 2012), 14.

68. "NATO Leaders to Consider Smart Defence in Chicago," *Strategic Comments* 18, no. 4 (2012).

69. The IISS publication rightly observed that "the notion of ceding sovereignty to another country in pursuit of specific capabilities is highly sensitive. There are obvious risks: would governments be drawn into missions in which they did not wish to participate? And what if their troops were forced to depend on a capability that was not in fact delivered by the supplier country?" "NATO Leaders to Consider Smart Defence in Chicago."

70. Audition au Sénat de M. Philippe Errera, Ambassadeur, Représentant Permanent de la France à l'OTAN, January 22, 2013. By "French leadership," M. Errera was evidently referring to General Jean-Paul Paloméros, supreme allied commander transformation since 2012, and Madame Claude-France Arnould, chief executive, European Defense Agency, since 2011.

71. See, for example, Nora Bensahel, *The Counterterror Coalitions: Cooperation with Europe, NATO, and the European Union* (Santa Monica, CA: RAND, 2003), 52–53; and Daniel Keohane, "Unblocking EU-NATO Cooperation," *CER Bulletin* 48 (June/July 2006).

72. The French permanent representative to NATO observed in January 2013 that, "notably on the preservation of the industrial and technological base for European defense, it must nonetheless be noted that we are unfortunately receiving little support at present from certain principal European partners, such as Germany and Great Britain." Audition au Sénat de M. Philippe Errera, January 22, 2013.

73. Fraser Cameron, *The EU and International Organisations: Partners in Crisis Management*, EPC Issue Paper no. 41 (Brussels: European Policy Centre, October 24, 2005), 22.

74. Amiral Édouard Guillaud, "Questions de la Commission des Affaires Étrangères et de la Défense au Sénat," October 21, 2011, www.defense.gouv.fr/ema/le-chef-d-etat-major/interventions/discours/audition-de-l-amiral-guillaud-dans-le-cadre-du-plf-2012/questions-senat. Leo Michel has added that "the European Union subsequently agreed to mount a CSDP military mission to facilitate humanitarian assistance to Libyan civilians, but its execution was made contingent upon a request from a UN agency widely believed to oppose any such military involvement. (In fact, the mission never advanced beyond the planning stage.)" Michel, *Cross-Currents in French Defense*, 14. For an incisive analysis of the potential implications for the European Union's CSDP, see Anand Menon, "European Defence Policy from Lisbon to Libya," *Survival* 53, no. 3 (June–July 2011).

75. Olivier de France quoted in Judy Dempsey, "E.U. Refuses to Cooperate on Security," *International Herald Tribune*, June 11, 2013.

76. Madeleine K. Albright, "The Right Balance Will Secure NATO's Future," *Financial Times*, December 7, 1998.

77. Burns quoted in Judy Dempsey, "US Calls NATO Meeting on EU Defence," *Financial Times*, October 17, 2003.

78. Eric Edelman, speech presented to the Center for Strategic and International Studies, September 20, 2005.

79. Daniel Fried, assistant secretary of state for European and Eurasian Affairs, testimony before the House Foreign Affairs Committee, June 22, 2007.

80. Alliot-Marie testimony of February 6, 2007, reproduced in Jean François-Poncet, Jean-Guy Branger, and André Rouvière, *Rapport d'information fait au nom de la commission des Affaires étrangères, de la défense et des forces armées sur l'évolution de l'OTAN*, no. 405 (Paris: Sénat, July 19, 2007), 74.

81. For background, see "Europe's Rapid-Response Forces: Use Them or Lose Them?," *Strategic Comments* 15, no. 7 (September 2009); and Myrto Hatzigeorgopoulos, "EU Battlegroups— Battling Irrelevance?," *ISIS Europe*, July 4, 2012, http://isiseurope.wordpress.com/2012/07/04/eu-battlegroups-battling-irrelevance/.

82. U.S. ambassador to NATO Victoria Nuland's speech in Paris, February 22, 2008, www.america.gov/st/texttrans-english/2008/February/20080222183349eaifas0.5647394.html.

83. Vershbow, "Crafting the New Strategic Concept: Ambitions, Resources, and Partnerships for a 21st Century Alliance."

84. Council of the European Union, "EU Training Mission in Mali Established," Brussels, press release 5428/13, January 17, 2013.

85. Evita Mouawad, *CSDP and EU Mission Update*, CSDP Note 5 (Brussels: International Security Information Service, November 2012).

86. Michel, *Cross-Currents in French Defense*, 14. The British have, however, endorsed the establishment of a civilian/military cell within the EU Military Staff that might in some circumstances plan and lead CSDP operations. For a fuller discussion, see Yost, *NATO and International Organizations*, 87–88, www.ndc.nato.int/download/publications/fp_03.pdf.

87. Aaron L. Friedberg, "The Euro Crisis and US Strategy," *Survival* 54, no. 6 (December 2012–January 2013).

88. David Cameron, "EU Speech at Bloomberg" (speech, January 23, 2013), www.number10.gov.uk/news/eu-speech-at-bloomberg/.

89. This section is based on the more extensive discussion in Yost, *NATO and International Organizations*, 112–130.

90. The first basket's ten principles guiding relations between the participating states are sometimes called the "Helsinki Decalogue" or simply the "Decalogue."

91. For a brief discussion of the CSCE during the Cold War, see Yost, *NATO Transformed*, 37–39. The single best source on the origins of the CSCE and the proceedings that produced the Helsinki Final Act remains John J. Maresca, *To Helsinki: The Conference on Security and Cooperation in Europe 1973–1975* (Durham, NC, and London: Duke University Press, 1985). Regarding the CSCE during the Cold War, see Daniel C. Thomas, *The Helsinki Effect: International Norms, Human Rights, and the Demise of Communism* (Princeton, NJ, and Oxford: Princeton University Press, 2001).

92. Mongolia became the fifty-seventh participating state in the OSCE in November 2012.

93. It is unclear, as a matter of international law and practical politics, whether NATO could in fact undertake operations "under the responsibility" of the OSCE without the involvement of the UN Security Council. In July 1992 the CSCE heads of state or government declared that "the CSCE is a regional arrangement in the sense of Chapter VIII of the Charter of the United Nations" and that "the rights and responsibilities of the United Nations Security Council remain unaffected in their entirety." *CSCE Helsinki Document 1992: The Challenges of Change*, part IV, par. 2. As noted previously, Article 53 of the UN Charter (part of Chapter VIII) states that "regional arrangements or agencies" are unable to undertake enforcement actions without the approval of the UN Security Council: "no enforcement action shall be taken under regional arrangements or by regional agencies without the authorization of the Security Council."

94. Lamberto Zannier, "Relations Between the OSCE and NATO with Particular Regard to Crisis Management and Peacekeeping," in *The OSCE in the Maintenance of Peace and Security: Conflict Prevention, Crisis Management and Peaceful Settlement of Disputes*, ed. Michael Bothe, Natalino Ronzitti, and Allan Rosas (The Hague: Kluwer Law International, 1997), 262–263.

95. For a judicious and detailed account of the origins of the crisis and interinstitutional cooperation in managing its initial phases, see Alice Ackermann, "On the Razor's Edge: Macedonia Ten Years after Independence," in *OSCE Yearbook 2001* (Baden-Baden: Nomos Verlagsgesellschaft, 2002), 117–135.

96. Mihai Carp, "Back from the Brink," *NATO Review*, Winter 2002 (italics in the original).

97. Ohrid (pronounced "okh-rid") is the name of a lake in Macedonia. The name has been applied to the border management process in southeastern Europe. In May 2003 the four partner organizations agreed at a conference near this lake to initiate a process for the reform of border management affecting five countries: Albania, Bosnia and Herzegovina, Croatia, the former Yugoslav Republic of Macedonia, and Serbia and Montenegro. Montenegro gained independence in 2006 and remained part of the process. The Ohrid border management process initiated in May 2003 is distinct from the Ohrid Framework Agreement of 2001, which concerns political reconciliation, reform, and reconstruction within the former Yugoslav Republic of Macedonia.

98. The OSCE is involved in border security and management processes in Eastern Europe (Belarus, Moldova, and Ukraine) and in the Caucasus and Central Asia. However, the Ohrid border management process in southeastern Europe is the only one involving both NATO and the OSCE.

99. OSCE website, "NATO," www.osce.org/ec/43242.

100. "We continue to work closely with the Organisation for Security and Co-operation in Europe, in particular in areas such as conflict prevention and resolution, post-conflict rehabilitation, and in addressing new security threats. We are committed to further enhancing our cooperation, both at the political and operational level, in all areas of common interest." North Atlantic Council, "Chicago Summit Declaration," par. 21.

101. However, the 1990 Conventional Armed Forces in Europe (CFE) Treaty is not an OSCE matter, and its states parties do not include all OSCE participating states. Although the CFE negotiations in 1989–1990 were conducted within the framework of the CSCE, the negotiations were autonomous and resulted in a legally binding treaty. OSCE commitments are politically and not legally binding, and only the states parties have obligations under the CFE Treaty.

102. Moscow has in effect returned to its complaints in the 1970s and 1980s about the human rights dimension of what was then the CSCE. In retrospect, the policies under Mikhail Gorbachev and Boris Yeltsin from the late 1980s through the 1990s appear as variations from Moscow's fundamental position. The Russian government today would not endorse the principles that the Soviet government under Gorbachev approved in 1991: "The participating States emphasize that issues relating to human rights, fundamental freedoms, democracy and the rule of law are of international concern, as respect for these rights and freedoms constitutes one of the foundations of the international order. They categorically and irrevocably declare that the commitments undertaken in the field of the human dimension of the CSCE are matters of direct and legitimate concern to all participating States and do not belong exclusively to the internal affairs of the State concerned." "Document of the Moscow Meeting of the Conference on the Human Dimension of the CSCE," October 3, 1991.

103. Vladimir Putin, speech at the Munich Conference on Security Policy, February 10, 2007, www.securityconference.de/archive/konferenzen/rede.php?menu_konferenzen=&sprache=en&id=179&.

104. Judy Dempsey, "Russia Most Concerned with Itself in the Battle for Human Rights," *International Herald Tribune*, June 29, 2007.

105. See, among other studies, Wolfgang Zellner, "Russia and the OSCE: From High Hopes to Disillusionment," *Cambridge Review of International Relations* 18, no. 3 (October 2005); and Victor-Yves Ghebali, "Growing Pains at the OSCE: The Rise and Fall of Russia's Pan-European Expectations," *Cambridge Review of International Relations* 18, no. 3 (October 2005).

106. Elena Kropatcheva, "Russia and the Role of the OSCE in European Security: A 'Forum' for Dialog or a 'Battlefield' of Interests?," *European Security* 21, no. 3 (September 2012): 382–383.

107. Alexander Vershbow, testimony at hearing of the Commission on Security and Cooperation in Europe, U.S. Helsinki Commission, October 28, 2009, http://csce.gov/index.cfm?FuseAction=ContentRecords.ViewDetail& ContentRecord_id=463&ContentType=H,B&ContentRecordType=H&CFID=18849146&CFTOKEN=53. Principle IV (Territorial Integrity of States) of the Principles Guiding Relations between Participating States in the Helsinki Final Act states, "The participating States will respect the territorial integrity of each of the participating States. Accordingly, they will refrain from any action inconsistent with the purposes and principles of the Charter of the United Nations against the territorial integrity, political independence or the unity of any participating State, and in particular from any such action constituting a threat or use of force. The participating States will likewise refrain from making each other's territory the object of military occupation or other direct or indirect measures of force in contravention of international law, or the object of acquisition by means of such measures or the threat of them. No such occupation or acquisition will be recognized as legal."

108. Sergey Lavrov quoted in Farkhad Sharip, "Astana OSCE Summit Ends in Division," *Eurasia Daily Monitor* 7, no. 223 (December 14, 2010).

109. The delegation of Belgium, on behalf of the European Union, "Interpretative Statement under Paragraph IV.1(A)6 of the Rules of Procedure of the Organization for Security and Co-operation in Europe, Attachment 1, Astana Commemorative Declaration towards a Security Community, Organization for Security and Co-operation in Europe Summit Meeting, Astana 2010," SUM.DOC/1/10, December 3, 2010.

110. "The lack of a consensus to agree any decisions in the human dimension is a matter of regret. . . . It is unfortunate that this worrying trend of recent ministerial councils has continued. Of even greater concern, is the sad reality that respect for basic human rights and fundamental freedoms is currently under great threat in many parts of the OSCE region." Eamon Gilmore, quoted in Mary Fitzgerald, "OSCE Summit Ends with Few Strides in 'human dimension,'" Irish Times, December 8, 2012, www.irishtimes.com/newspaper/ireland/2012/1208/1224327654537.html.

111. Hillary Clinton, intervention at the OSCE Ministerial Council First Plenary Session, Dublin, December 6, 2012, www.state.gov/secretary/rm/2012/12/201606.htm.

112. Sergey Lavrov, speech at the plenary meeting of the Council of the Ministers of Foreign Affairs of the OSCE, Dublin, December 6, 2012, http://en.interaffairs.ru/lavrov/307-speech-of-the-minister-of-foreign-affairs-of-russias-v-lavrov-at-the-plenary-meeting-of-the-council-of-the-ministers-of-foreign-affairs-of-the-osce-dublin-december-6-2012.html.

113. Hillary Clinton quoted in Bradley Klapper, "Clinton Fears Efforts to 'Re-Sovietize' in Europe," *Associated Press*, December 6, 2012, http://news.yahoo.com/clinton-fears-efforts-sovietize-europe-111645250--politics.html. It is worth noting that other prominent observers have discerned a trend to "re-Sovietize" in Russia's social and political order. According to Sabine Leutheusser-Schnarrenberger, the German justice minister, "The conviction of the dead Magnitsky is further evidence of the Sovietisation of Russia." Sabine Leutheusser-Schnarrenberger quoted in Courtney Weaver and Charles Clover, "Russia Convicts Magnitsky of Tax Evasion in Posthumous Trial," *Financial Times*, July 11, 2013.

114. Paul Pryce, "The OSCE's 'Asia Pivot'? Implications of the Mongolian Accession," www.academia.edu/2325678/The_OSCEs_Asia_Pivot_Implications_of_the_Mongolian_Accession.

115. Ministerial Council, Organization for Security and Co-operation in Europe, "Decision no. 2/12, Accession of Mongolia to the OSCE," MC.DEC/2/12, November 21, 2012.

116. Russian Federation, "Interpretive Statement under Paragraph IV.1(A)6 of the Rules of Procedure of the Organization for Security and Cooperation in Europe, Attachment to MC.DEC/2/12," November 21, 2012.

117. Pryce, "The OSCE's 'Asia Pivot'?"

118. North Atlantic Council, "Partnership for Peace: Invitation," press communiqué M-1(94)2, January 10–11, 1994, www.nato.int/docu/comm/49-95/c940110a.htm.

119. North Atlantic Council, "Partnership for Peace: Framework Document."

120. NATO, "Basic Document of the Euro-Atlantic Partnership Council," Sintra, Portugal, May 30, 1997, www.nato.int/docu/basictxt/b970530a.htm.

121. The PfP Framework Document makes three references to the CSCE and two to "the Euro-Atlantic area."

122. If Mongolia became a PfP partner, it would benefit from the security consultation pledge in the PfP Framework Document patterned after Article 4 of the North Atlantic Treaty. Mongolia's entry into the OSCE might also affect NATO's long-standing tacit definition of the Euro-Atlantic area as limited to the territory of the states participating in the CSCE/OSCE.

123. "NATO and Mongolia Agree Programme of Cooperation," last updated March 23, 2012, www.nato.int/cps/en/natolive/news_85430.htm.

124. The concepts have included enhanced civil-military cooperation, concerted planning and action, and the effects-based approach to operations. For background, see Yost, *NATO and International Organizations*, 23–26.

125. The Allies assigned the term "comprehensive approach" a different meaning in the 1991 Strategic Concept: "The Alliance has always sought to achieve its objectives of safeguarding the security and territorial integrity of its members, and establishing a just and lasting peaceful order in Europe, through both political and military means. This comprehensive approach remains the basis of the Alliance's security policy." North Atlantic Council, "Strategic Concept," November 7, 1991, par. 23.

126. North Atlantic Council, "Riga Summit Declaration," par. 10.

127. As an expert in London put it in August 2006, "NATO doesn't build prisons or provide alternative livelihoods, but those activities are part of the exit strategy."

128. North Atlantic Council, "Strategic Concept," November 19, 2010, par. 21, www.nato.int/cps/en/natolive/official_texts_68580.htm; emphasis added.

129. Under the heading of "humanitarian assistance," the Alliance noted in November 2011 that "over 2,500 air, ground and maritime movements into Libya" were "de-conflicted by NATO." NATO, "Operation Unified Protector Final Mission Stats," November 2, 2011, www.nato.int/nato_static/assets/pdf/pdf_2011_11/20111108_111107-factsheet_up_factsfigures_en.pdf.

130. The "nested" metaphor was suggested by a German observer in Brussels, October 28, 2011.

131. North Atlantic Council, "Lisbon Summit Declaration," par. 9.

132. Michèle Alliot-Marie, then the French minister of defense, wrote in October 2006 that "reconstruction missions must imperatively be a matter for the competent organizations—particularly the UN and the European Union. . . . Let us be careful not to dilute the Alliance with vague missions in which it would lose its soul and its effectiveness." Michèle Alliot-Marie, "L'Otan doit rester une organisation euro-atlantique," Le Figaro, October 30, 2006. This question of appropriate missions for specific international organizations has been related to the "scope problem" in NATO-EU cooperation. See Yost, NATO and International Organizations, 98–103.

133. NATO, "Political Guidance on Ways to Improve NATO's Involvement in Stabilisation and Reconstruction," September 23, 2011, par. 2, 11, and 4, www.nato.int/cps/en/SID-56926A04-32533258/natolive/official_texts_78314.htm.

134. North Atlantic Council, "Chicago Summit Declaration," par. 21, 30.

135. Secretary General Anders Fogh Rasmussen, "Afghanistan and the Future of Peace Operations," speech at the University of Chicago, April 8, 2010, www.nato.int/cps/en/natolive/opinions_62510.htm.

136. For an extensive discussion, see Yost, NATO Transformed, 248–259.

137. Anders Fogh Rasmussen, speech at the 11th Herzliya Conference in Herzliya, Israel, February 9, 2011, www.nato.int/cps/en/natolive/opinions_70537.htm.

138. Secretary of Defense Robert M. Gates, remarks as delivered, NATO Strategic Concept Seminar, National Defense University, Washington, DC, February 23, 2010, www.defense.gov/speeches/speech.aspx?speechid=1423.

139. North Atlantic Council, "Riga Summit Declaration," par. 10.

140. For a fuller development of this theme, see Yost, NATO and International Organizations, 176–183.

8

NATO Enlargement

The Alliance began with twelve members: Belgium, Canada, Denmark, France, Iceland, Italy, Luxembourg, the Netherlands, Norway, Portugal, the United Kingdom, and the United States. During the Cold War, four additional countries acceded to the North Atlantic Treaty: Greece and Turkey in 1952, the Federal Republic of Germany in 1955, and Spain in 1982. The post–Cold War NATO enlargement process has increased the Alliance's membership from sixteen countries at the end of the Cold War in 1989–1991 to twenty-eight today.

To be more precise, the Alliance has to date conducted three post–Cold War rounds of enlargement. The Allies invited three countries—the Czech Republic, Hungary, and Poland—to join in July 1997, and they concluded the accession process in March 1999. The Allies extended invitations to seven countries—Bulgaria, Estonia, Latvia, Lithuania, Romania, Slovakia, and Slovenia—in November 2002, and their accession process was completed in May 2004. Finally, the Allies asked Albania and Croatia to join in April 2008, and these countries concluded the accession formalities in April 2009.

Multiple Rationales for Enlargement

The Allies have had multiple motives in pursuing the Alliance's enlargement. Fundamentally, the Allies have sought to balance their preferred political values with their perceived security interests. Despite the ultimate primacy of security considerations, the Allies have in their statements of policy emphasized the rationale of advancing their political values.

The preamble of the North Atlantic Treaty refers to "principles of democracy, individual liberty and the rule of law." The Allies have over the decades described NATO as a coalition of nations determined to promote certain values or standards—what some would call an ideology—of principles of government (democracy) and international relations (peaceful settlement of disputes). In April 1997, U.S. secretary of state Madeleine Albright said, referring to NATO, "It brought the former fascist nations, first Italy, then Germany, then Spain, back into the family of European democracies."[1] This formulation, however, probably overstates NATO's role while giving inadequate attention to other factors that promoted the advance of democracy in these countries.[2]

John Duffield has suggested that "the existence of NATO may provide at least as much support for the theory that ideological affinity determines alliances as it does for balance-of-power theory."[3] The difficulty with this proposition is that, while NATO has generally consisted of a coalition of democracies, there have been exceptions. When the Alliance was formed, Portugal was governed by a dictatorship little different from that in Spain, but the Azores were too important to the security of the Allies in the event of war to let Portugal's form of government pose an obstacle to membership. In other words, military necessity overcame ideological preferences. Similarly, when Greece was ruled by a military junta in 1967–1974 and when Turkey was governed by the military on various occasions (1960–1961, 1971–1973, and 1980–1983), there was never any question of refusing to conduct Alliance business with the nondemocratic regimes or of expelling these countries from the Alliance. Moreover, several European democracies (for instance, neutral states such as Ireland, Sweden, and Switzerland) chose—despite obvious ideological affinity—to refrain from seeking membership in the Alliance during the Cold War.

One can say, however, that democratic ideals were generally constructive for Alliance cohesion—and for the legitimization of the Alliance within specific member nations—during the Cold War, and that these ideals have helped to give direction for Alliance policies in the post–Cold War world. In Duffield's view, "NATO's continued existence even after the collapse of the Soviet Union implies ... that liberal states based on democracy, political pluralism, and the rule of law may be inclined to maintain (if not to form in the first place) alliances even in the absence of a compelling external threat, since they are much less likely to perceive one another as dangerous."[4]

Since the end of the Cold War the Allies have emphasized successful democratization as a criterion for NATO membership, to give would-be allies an incentive for good behavior. According to the Alliance's July 1997 Madrid Declaration, "NATO remains open to new members under Article 10 of the North Atlantic Treaty. . . . No European democratic country whose admission would fulfil the objectives of the Treaty will be excluded from consideration."[5] Article 10 of the Treaty does not, however, refer to democratic rule as a criterion for admission—only to being "in a position to further the principles of this Treaty and to contribute to the security of the North Atlantic area." Paradoxically, during the Cold War—an ideological confrontation between a political system based on liberal democracy and one based on communism—democratization was not as vital a criterion for membership as military strength or geostrategic location. Threat perceptions have, however, been drastically reduced since the collapse of the Soviet empire.

Since the mid-1990s, when the post–Cold War enlargement process began, the Allies have felt freer to make democratization a requirement for membership. The

1995 *Study on NATO Enlargement* stated, "New members must . . . be prepared to contribute to collective defence under Article 5, to the Alliance's new evolving missions and to Alliance budgets."[6] The same document, however, repeatedly called upon new member states to "conform to basic principles embodied in the Washington Treaty: democracy, individual liberty and the rule of law."[7]

According to the Alliance's 2010 Strategic Concept,

> NATO's enlargement has contributed substantially to the security of Allies; the prospect of further enlargement and the spirit of cooperative security have advanced stability in Europe more broadly. Our goal of a Europe whole and free, and sharing common values, would be best served by the eventual integration of all European countries that so desire into Euro-Atlantic structures. The door to NATO membership remains fully open to all European democracies which share the values of our Alliance, which are willing and able to assume the responsibilities and obligations of membership, and whose inclusion can contribute to common security and stability.[8]

It is at first glance surprising that the Allies listed NATO enlargement under "cooperative security" in the 2010 Strategic Concept when each new member state has involved an increase in collective defense responsibilities. This is, however, consistent with the official rationales emphasized by the Alliance since the post–Cold War enlargement process began in 1994–1995. Just as the 2010 Strategic Concept highlighted the importance of "sharing common values" and promoting "common security and stability" through enlargement without any explicit reference to collective defense, the Alliance's official *Study on NATO Enlargement* in 1995 advanced seven rationales for NATO enlargement without mentioning collective defense:

> Therefore, enlargement will contribute to enhanced stability and security for all countries in the Euro-Atlantic area by:
>
> - Encouraging and supporting democratic reforms, including civilian and democratic control over the military;
>
> - Fostering in new members of the Alliance the patterns and habits of cooperation, consultation and consensus building which characterize relations among current Allies;
>
> - Promoting good-neighbourly relations, which would benefit all countries in the Euro-Atlantic area, both members and non-members of NATO;
>
> - Emphasizing common defence and extending its benefits and increasing transparency in defence planning and military budgets, thereby reducing the likelihood of instability that might be engendered by an exclusively national approach to defence policies;
>
> - Reinforcing the tendency toward integration and cooperation in Europe based on shared democratic values and thereby curbing the countervailing tendency towards disintegration along ethnic and territorial lines;
>
> - Strengthening the Alliance's ability to contribute to European and international security, including through peacekeeping activities under the responsibility of the OSCE and peacekeeping operations under the authority of the UN Security Council as well as other new missions; [and]
>
> - Strengthening and broadening the Trans-Atlantic partnership.[9]

Of these rationales, only the reference to "common defence" might be construed as referring to collective defense, but any hint that it might concern combined action in resisting aggression by an external adversary is obscured by the emphasis on the intra-Alliance purpose of promoting mutual confidence and trust: "increasing transparency in defence planning and military budgets, thereby reducing the likelihood of instability that might be engendered by an exclusively national approach to defence policies."

Similarly, during the first post–Cold War round of NATO enlargement in 1997–1999, Secretary Albright and other U.S. officials avoided reference to collective defense for the most part. In 1997, for example, one of Secretary Albright's most widely distributed discussions of the purposes of NATO enlargement conspicuously omitted collective defense against state adversaries: "At the same time, we will gain new allies who are eager and increasingly able to contribute to our common agenda for security, from fighting terrorism and weapons proliferation to ensuring stability in trouble spots like the former Yugoslavia."[10]

The absence of any reference to collective defense—or Russia—in Secretary Albright's statement was probably not accidental. NATO's balancing act concerning enlargement has involved the differing priorities, interests, and perceptions of the Allies, notably with respect to the extent that they regard Russia as a partner and/or still a potential threat. With respect to some candidates for membership in the western Balkans, however, the main concern of the Allies has not been about generating further irritations in NATO's troubled relations with Russia but about whether all the Yugoslav successor states can meet NATO and EU democratic standards, resolve their internal cohesion and governance problems, and establish peaceful relations with their neighbors in the western Balkans.

The first post–Cold War round of NATO enlargement attracted the highest level of political attention, with considerable debate in 1995–1997 about the implications for the Alliance's cohesion and its relations with Russia.[11] One of the main arguments for this first post–Cold War round of enlargement—and indeed for launching the enlargement process—was that the alternative of refusing to accept new Allies would oblige the excluded countries to define other security arrangements. Rather than undercutting prospects for stability in Europe by obliging these states to fend for themselves in security terms, the Allies saw it as more prudent to promote their political and economic confidence by offering them a pathway to membership. In 1997 Javier Solana, then the NATO secretary general, said "If we refused to accept the challenge of enlargement, confidence in Central and Eastern Europe would be undermined. The countries in this region would look for security by other means, possibly resorting to arms build-ups and fearing intentions of their neighbours."[12]

The second round—the so-called big bang involving invitations to seven new allies in 2002, with the accession process concluded in 2004—caused much less controversy than anticipated. Despite the fact that it involved three former Soviet republics (Estonia, Latvia, and Lithuania) and hence a "red line" for Russia, Moscow's complaints regarding this round of enlargement had less resonance with the NATO Allies. After the September 2001 terrorist attacks against the United States, the threat of terrorism dominated security planning to an unprecedented extent, and Washington sought new Allies in the campaign against terrorist organizations.[13] Another factor in the second post–Cold War round of enlargement was the "dual enlargement" approach adopted by the European Union members of NATO—that is, welcoming several states into NATO and the European Union more or less concurrently.[14] In the second round of enlargement, the Alliance's democratization agenda complemented "geopolitical" collective defense motives.

In the third post–Cold War round of enlargement—that involving Albania and Croatia—the democratization or values-based agenda took precedence and defined the course forward, much more than considerations of collective defense. The democratization agenda featured prominently in the 1995 *Study on NATO Enlargement*, but it has received its purest application to date in decision making about the western Balkans, notably Albania and the former Yugoslav republics.

The Western Balkans and NATO Enlargement

As noted above, two states of the western Balkans, Albania and Croatia, joined the Alliance in 2009. Two additional western Balkan states are currently participating in NATO's Membership Action Plan (MAP): the former Yugoslav Republic of Macedonia, since 1999, and Montenegro, since 2009. The Allies in April 2010 invited Bosnia and Herzegovina to participate in the MAP, subject to the still-pending registration of immovable defense properties as state possessions. It should nonetheless be recalled, as the Allies have repeatedly noted, "Participation in the MAP does not prejudge any decision by the Alliance on future membership."[15]

As suggested in chapter 4, the future of Bosnia and Herzegovina depends on whether the ethnic Serbs and Croats can develop allegiance to the state they share with the Bosniaks. The failure to uphold the national institutions established by the Dayton settlement could place the country's future into question. The NATO Allies have to date shown themselves unwilling to disregard the conditionality standards for Alliance membership set out in the *Study on NATO Enlargement* and other policy documents. The failure of the country's authorities to register immovable defense properties as possessions of the state has caused, as a Polish observer put it, "disappointment" in the Alliance. "The problem of immovable property is seen by NATO not only as a practical issue for the armed forces, but also as a test for the country's politicians—failure to agree on this relatively minor problem raises questions on Bosnia's ability to make decisions on more important issues of Euro-Atlantic security."[16]

There is no near-term prospect of NATO membership for Serbia or Kosovo. Many Serbs remember with bitterness NATO's air campaign in 1999 and the recognition in 2008 of Kosovo's independence by most NATO member states (all except Greece, Romania, Slovakia, and Spain). Public enthusiasm in Serbia for NATO membership remains correspondingly limited. Serbia's refusal to recognize Kosovo and the fact that Kosovo's territory remains in dispute, as does the status of its ethnic Serb minority, rule out NATO membership for both states in the foreseeable future. As noted in chapter 4, Kosovo remains dependent on KFOR and EULEX.

Montenegro's candidacy for membership illustrates NATO's political stabilization role. Although every new member state signifies an additional collective defense responsibility for all the other Allies, in this case some Allied observers regard membership candidacy as falling under the heading of cooperative security as well as that of collective defense. Membership would be expected to promote Montenegro's participation in an Alliance-guaranteed area of peace, security, and stability. In the judgment of Dessie Zagorcheva, "NATO conditionality in this case has motivated and helped Podgorica to establish rule of law, fight corruption more vigorously, and enhance the effectiveness of its newly-formed democratic institutions."[17]

The most contentious case within the Alliance concerning the western Balkan states has been that of Macedonia, formally known as the former Yugoslav Republic of Macedonia (FYROM) to many states in NATO, the European Union, and other international organizations owing to Greece's insistence on this appellation.[18]

NATO awarded MAP status to FYROM in April 1999, but the Allies have still not offered this country an invitation to join the Alliance. In April 2008 the Allies stated that "an invitation to the former Yugoslav Republic of Macedonia will be extended as soon as a mutually acceptable solution to the name issue has been reached."[19] The Allies have repeated this promise at subsequent summit meetings, including the May 2012 Chicago Summit.[20]

The "name issue" arises from the fact that Macedonia is the name of a northern region of Greece. The Greek government is concerned that allowing FYROM to call itself "Macedonia" could lead to political and security problems.[21] Dimitris Droutsas, then the Greek foreign minister, said in September 2010,

> This is not a bilateral, pedantic dispute about historical symbols, as some may try to portray it, but a regional question, with deep historical roots, related to good neighborliness. . . . A fair and lasting solution can only be based on a name with a geographic qualifier, to be used for all purposes, erga omnes. Macedonia is a large geographic region, most of which lies in Greece. . . . The part cannot represent the whole and the Former Yugoslav Republic of Macedonia's exclusive claims to the name "Macedonia" cannot be allowed to fuel nationalism.[22]

This dispute between Greece and FYROM has been under way since 1991, when the latter gained its independence from the former Yugoslavia and sought to call itself the "Republic of Macedonia." Owing to concerns about historical accuracy and possible territorial claims, Greece objects to FYROM using the name "Macedonia" without a qualifying adjective. Related Greek-FYROM controversies have included the use in FYROM of the ancient "Vergina Sun" design as a national symbol and the naming of major public facilities in FYROM after Alexander the Great and Philip of Macedon.

In the months leading up to the May 2012 Chicago Summit, prominent Americans (including fifty-four members of Congress and former high-level officials, including former secretaries of defense) wrote to President Obama to urge him to support Macedonia's candidacy for membership. They pointed out that Macedonia had given shelter to over 360,000 ethnic Albanian Kosovar refugees fleeing Milo-sevic's forces in 1999, that Macedonia has been one of the largest contributors of troops to ISAF on a per capita basis, and that the country had long ago satisfied the requirements for NATO membership. General James Jones, a retired SACEUR and a former national security adviser to President Obama, noted that in December 2011 the International Court of Justice (ICJ) had ruled by a 15-1 margin that Greece had violated a 1995 agreement with Macedonia by blocking its entry into NATO.[23]

The purpose of these messages to President Obama appears to have been to place the views of the authors on the record, since there was no need to lobby the president to support Macedonia's membership. President Obama had said at the Strasbourg/Kehl Summit in 2009, "I look forward to the day when we can welcome Macedonia to the Alliance."[24] All the Allies except Greece have repeatedly reaffirmed their support for Macedonia's membership in NATO since 2008. Indeed, the Greek position is that Athens supports FYROM's membership in NATO, subject to a mutually agreeable solution to the name issue.

The ICJ ruling did not order Greece, as FYROM had requested, "to cease and desist from objecting in any way, whether directly or indirectly, to the Applicant's membership of the North Atlantic Treaty Organization."[25] As the NATO secretary general noted, the ICJ ruling had no effect on the NATO decision concerning FYROM at the 2008 Bucharest Summit.[26] The ruling left Greece free to maintain its policy, pending a mutually satisfactory agreement concerning Macedonia's name, and Greece repeated its policy at the May 2012 Chicago Summit.

The fact that the other NATO Allies have not taken any noteworthy steps to pressure Greece and FYROM to reach an agreement is significant. They appear to regard it as a second-order issue that does not deserve the expenditure of political capital—a dispute that can be left to the protagonists indefinitely. In terms of NATO's three core tasks, despite the fact that membership means an Article 5 commitment to collective defense, some Allied observers regard FYROM's membership candidacy as falling under the heading of cooperative security, with the decision as to when to cooperate up to Greece and FYROM. In practice, the distinction between collective defense and cooperative security may not do justice to the complexity of the overlapping considerations involved in working with a state as a partner, then as a candidate for membership, and finally as an Ally.

The prolonged stalemate on FYROM's name has not been to the new country's political advantage, internally or externally. Internally, as Witold Waszczykowski, a Polish member of parliament, has noted, "The unresolved issue feeds into state-sponsored nationalist and divisive rhetoric and progressively marginalises compromising views within society. The ethnic Albanian minority is deemed to have a more flexible position on the 'name issue' which further exacerbates mutual mistrust."[27] Externally, Bulgaria recently decided to oppose Skopje's application for membership in the European Union, "alleging discrimination and hate speech towards Bulgarians inside and outside Macedonia."[28] As a result, FYROM must now overcome both Greek and Bulgarian opposition to join the European Union. According to Georgi Spasov, a former FYROM ambassador to Bulgaria, Sofia is likely to oppose FYROM's membership in NATO as well.[29] If Bulgaria opposes FYROM's membership, this would contradict a principle in the Alliance's 1995 *Study on NATO Enlargement*: "The Alliance expects new members not to *'close the door'* to the accession of one or more later candidate members."[30]

NATO's future enlargement discussions appear likely to concern Yugoslav successor states, former Soviet republics, and other European states, including some that asserted their neutrality during the Cold War.

In 2006 Ivo Daalder and James Goldgeier proposed that the NATO Allies amend Article 10 of the North Atlantic Treaty so that further Alliance enlargement would no longer be limited to Europe. According to Article 10, "The Parties may, by unanimous agreement, invite any other European State in a position to further the principles of this Treaty and to contribute to the security of the North Atlantic area to accede to this Treaty." Daalder and Goldgeier recommended that the Alliance "open its membership to any democratic state in the world that is willing and able to contribute to the fulfillment of NATO's new responsibilities."[31] Their proposal for a "global NATO" has to date won little support, and it appears unlikely to command a consensus among the Allies in the foreseeable future.

Further enlargement of the Alliance will therefore probably be confined to Europe, and Russia will almost certainly remain its sharpest critic. It should be recalled, moreover, that Russia's objections to NATO enlargement are not confined to former Soviet republics and former members of the Warsaw Pact. Russia has retained its deep-seated interest in the Balkans. As Witold Waszczykowski has noted, "The establishment of the joint Serbian-Russian crisis management centre in the Serbian town of Nis is a manifestation of that. Russia continues to oppose further enlargement of the Alliance to include Bosnia and the former Yugoslav Republic of Macedonia. Russia also actively advances its economic presence in the region, in particular in Serbia and Bosnia's Republic of Srpska. Russia's energy giant Gazprom, for instance, acquired Naftna Industrija Srbije, one of the largest oil and gas companies in Southeast Europe."[32] The eventual integration of the western Balkan states in the "Euro-Atlantic structures" of NATO and the European Union should not be regarded as automatic, not least from Moscow's viewpoint.

Russia and NATO Enlargement

The Alliance and specific Allies have often shown caution in discussing the collective defense implications of NATO enlargement in an attempt to avoid antagonizing Russia. Furthermore, the NATO Allies have tried to address Russian reservations about enlargement by taking steps to deepen NATO-Russian cooperation and entente before making major enlargement decisions. The NATO Allies and Russia concluded the Founding Act in May 1997, prior to the July 1997 invitations to the Czech Republic, Hungary, and Poland, and they issued the "New Quality" declaration in May 2002, prior to the November 2002 invitations to Bulgaria, Estonia, Latvia, Lithuania, Romania, Slovakia, and Slovenia.

However, Russian officials and experts have consistently expressed concern about the Alliance's enlargement process since President Boris Yeltsin's December 1994 speech warning that it could lead to a "cold peace" in NATO-Russian relations.[33]

Since the mid-1990s competition and discord have become obvious in relations between Russia and some other former Soviet republics, on the one hand, and NATO and the European Union on the other, regarding the future political orientation of the post-Soviet space. This has been most evident with respect to Georgia and Ukraine, but the political rivalry concerns the entire region. As Hannes Adomeit, a German scholar, has observed,

> American and NATO ideas of a "Europe whole and free," the EU's concept of Wider Europe and the European Neighborhood Policy (ENP), and the Common Vision of the countries loosely allied in the Community of Democratic Choice are in conflict with notions of a Wider Russia. Western, including NATO, and Russian perceptions and policies are at odds with each other in the whole area stretching from the Baltic States via Belarus, Ukraine, and Moldova to the northern and southern Caucasus.[34]

Assessments differ concerning this apparent rivalry between Russia on the one hand and NATO and the EU on the other. With the exception of Georgia, Vladimir Socor argued in May 2012, "Europe's East—a 'gray zone' of six countries [Armenia, Azerbaijan, Belarus, Georgia, Moldova, and Ukraine] bordering on NATO and the EU—faces a deepening security vacuum and Russian re-expansion. . . . NATO/US disengagement and Russian sphere-of-influence rebuilding are concurrent processes, mutually reinforcing in this region."[35]

From a Russian perspective taking into account developments since the mid-1990s, however, the NATO and EU enlargement processes since the end of the Cold War form part of a larger pattern of Western expansion into a formerly Soviet- and Russian-dominated sphere of influence.

The three post–Cold War rounds of EU enlargement have, for example, been seen by Russians as setbacks for Moscow, even if distinct in their implications from NATO enlargement. In 1995 the first post–Cold War round of EU enlargement involved three neutral states that would not have joined during the Cold War—Austria, Finland, and Sweden. The eastward expansion of the European Union to embrace these countries was made possible by the Soviet Union's disintegration.

During the Cold War, Finland's relations with Moscow were governed by the 1948 Finnish-Soviet treaty that gave rise to the concept of "Finlandization," often interpreted by outside observers (to the regret of many Finns) to signify a quasi-subservient neutrality deferential to the Soviet Union. Sweden was preoccupied with maintaining its armed neutrality secure within the framework of the "Nordic balance," a political equilibrium shaped in part by the conditions on foreign force deployments in peacetime that Denmark and Norway attached to their membership in NATO and by Finland's neutrality, combined with Helsinki's treaty relationship with the USSR. Vienna's neutrality reflected the constraints of the Austrian State Treaty, concluded in 1955 at the behest of the Soviet Union, apparently in part because Nikita Khrushchev thought that it might provide a model for the neutralization of Germany.

The expansion of the European Union in 1995 to include these three Cold War "neutrals" reflected the contraction of Russian power as surely as the unification of Germany in 1989–1990 and the withdrawal of the former USSR's military forces and political influence from Central and Eastern Europe in 1989–1994. In 2004 the European Union welcomed ten additional countries, including four former Warsaw Pact countries (the Czech Republic, Hungary, Poland, and Slovakia)[36] and three former Soviet republics (Estonia, Latvia, and Lithuania). In 2007 two additional former Warsaw Pact countries (Bulgaria and Romania) joined the European Union.

The EU enlargement process has been accompanied by the NATO enlargement process, and the Russians have strongly opposed the idea of other former Soviet republics, notably Georgia and Ukraine, following the Baltic states into NATO. Alexei Ostrovsky, chairman of the Commonwealth of Independent States Committee in the Duma, said in 2009, "These countries must make their decisions independently but the leaders . . . are clever enough to understand that they are closely related to Russia and entering NATO would bring a certain reaction."[37] Dmitry Medvedev, then the Russian president, had declared the previous year, shortly after the Georgia-Russia conflict, that "there are regions in which Russia has privileged interests. These regions are home to countries with which we share special historical relations and are bound together as friends and good neighbours."[38] In 2013 Alexei Kudrin, a former Russian finance minister, said, "There is a widespread attitude that I call 'imperial syndrome.' A sizeable number of Russians place their country above other nations and see neighboring countries as part of our zone of influence."[39]

NATO Allies and Alliance spokesmen have long argued that NATO enlargement actually serves Russia's security interests. In 1997, Secretary Albright wrote, "Russia, no less than the rest of us, needs stability and prosperity in the centre of Europe."[40] In the same year, Javier Solana, then the NATO secretary general, said, "Like the enlargement process itself, the development of our relationship with Russia is part of a wider transformation of NATO that will be good for Russia, good for NATO, and good for the whole of Europe."[41]

In 2009 Secretary General Rasmussen said, "I do not believe that the enlargement of NATO and the European Union has created any security problems for Russia. On the contrary: A more stable and prosperous Europe is indeed contributing to the security of Russia."[42] Similarly, U.S. ambassador Alexander Vershbow, currently serving as NATO's deputy secretary general, stated in 2009, "Complaints from the Russian leadership about Ukraine and Georgia's pursuit of NATO membership and Russian claims of privileged spheres of influence are troubling, and ones to which we are unequivocally opposed. Russia's leaders must accept that an enlarged NATO is not a threat to Russia—on the contrary, by bringing Central and Eastern European countries into the Alliance, NATO has helped consolidate democracy, security, and stability in the region—a process that has left Russia more, not less, secure."[43]

These arguments have not to date persuaded the Russians. Moscow's policy has remained unchanged since 1997: "The prospect of NATO expansion to the East is unacceptable to Russia since it represents a threat to its national security."[44] The first of the "main external military dangers" listed in the February 2010 Russian military doctrine is "the desire to endow the force potential of the North Atlantic Treaty Organization (NATO) with global functions carried out in violation of the norms of international law and to move the military infrastructure of NATO member countries closer to the borders of the Russian Federation, including by expanding the bloc."[45]

From a Russian perspective, the enlargement of NATO and the European Union has been at the expense of Moscow's influence, and these aggrandizement policies have been successfully pursued owing to Russia's weakness. This outlook informed Vladimir Putin's 2005 statement that "the collapse of the Soviet Union was the greatest geopolitical catastrophe of the century."[46] In March 2007, Putin, then the president of Russia, said,

> I think it is obvious that NATO expansion does not have any relation with the modernisation of the Alliance itself or with ensuring security in Europe. On the contrary, it represents a serious provocation that reduces the level of mutual trust. And we have the right to ask: against whom is this expansion intended? And what happened to the assurances our western partners made after the dissolution of the Warsaw Pact? Where are those declarations today? No one even remembers them. But I will allow myself to remind this audience what was said. I would like to quote the speech of NATO General Secretary Mr Woerner in Brussels on 17 May 1990. He said at the time that: "the fact that we are ready not to place a NATO army outside of German territory gives the Soviet Union a firm security guarantee." Where are these guarantees?[47]

Setting aside slight differences in wording arising from the translation process, Putin accurately reported Manfred Wörner's statement.[48] Wörner appears, however, to have been describing the position taken by the three Western powers (Britain, France, and the United States) and the Federal Republic of Germany in the "two plus four" negotiations with the German Democratic Republic (GDR) and the Soviet Union regarding the future political-military status of the territory in the future united Germany that was in May 1990 still the GDR. The Treaty on the Final Settlement with Respect to Germany did in fact create a zone within Germany (the territory of Berlin and the former GDR) with a special security status—that is, without any stationing or deployment of non-German armed forces or of any nuclear weapons or nuclear delivery systems.[49]

Putin's view that Moscow was given an assurance that NATO would not expand eastward remains highly significant because it reflects a widespread impression in Russia. This impression has, moreover, been shared by some Western observers. For example, Jack Matlock, a former U.S. ambassador to the Soviet Union, said in 1996 that "Gorbachev did get an informal, but clear, commitment that if Germany united and stayed in NATO, the borders of NATO would not move eastward."[50] When asked about Matlock's statement in 1997, Secretary Albright said,

The treaty on the Final Settlement with respect to Germany that was signed in 1990 had to do only with German unification and how NATO would act within Germany, and the treaty restrictions do not apply with respect to other states to the west or east of Germany and therefore have no bearing on NATO enlargement. I think that it is important to put all this into context. Every state has a sovereign right to choose its own security arrangements, including alliances. This is a basic principle of the Helsinki Final Act, the 2 Plus 4 Treaty (the one that was in fact the determination of Germany), the CFE Treaty, and the 1994 OSCE Budapest summit declaration, all of which the Russians have endorsed, and we believe that that is the appropriate interpretation of what happened in 1990.[51]

Indeed, the first principle of the Helsinki Final Act holds that states "have the right to belong or not to belong to international organizations, to be or not to be a party to bilateral or multilateral treaties including the right to be or not to be a party to treaties of alliance; they also have the right to neutrality."[52] If the United States or the Federal Republic of Germany or other NATO Allies had made a commitment to Russia that other states could not join NATO, such a commitment would have been inconsistent with the Helsinki Final Act.

Mark Kramer undertook a thorough analysis of the archives in Germany, Russia, and the United States in order "to determine whether Russian and Western observers and officials are justified in arguing that the U.S. government, and perhaps some of the other NATO governments, made a 'pledge' to Gorbachev in 1990 that if the USSR consented to Germany's full membership in NATO after unification, the alliance would not expand to include any other East European countries." Kramer concluded that "declassified materials show unmistakably that no such pledge was made."[53] Mary Elise Sarotte reached a comparable conclusion in her subsequent archival study.[54]

Despite the archival record, the "broken promise" charge has been widely repeated in Russia and has won extensive support. Russians convinced that such a pledge was made consider NATO enlargement a betrayal and an exploitation of Russia's current weakness. Some speculate that Russian convictions as to a grave injustice could someday assume a mythic status comparable to how many in Weimar Germany viewed the Treaty of Versailles.[55] The assurances that the NATO Allies extended to Moscow in the 1997 NATO-Russia Founding Act regarding the Alliance's nuclear policies and its conventional military forces on the territory of new member states have not satisfied the Russians.[56]

Although some Russian experts have questioned whether NATO enlargement threatens their country's security, they appear to be very much in the minority.[57] Indeed, few Russians would accept the NATO secretary general's assessment in 2011 of the benign achievements of the NATO and EU enlargement processes:

After the end of the Cold War, alongside the European Union, NATO was instrumental in consolidating Europe as an undivided, democratic security space. We opened our door for 12 new member nations in less than a decade—raising our membership from 16 to 28 Allies and spreading freedom, democracy, peace and prosperity across the continent. Our door remains firmly open to European democracies that wish to join us, and that meet our standards.[58]

In the foreseeable future, despite NATO's door being open in principle, there is little likelihood of fully overcoming the continuing factors of distrust in Russia-NATO relations, much less of Russia meeting NATO standards or actively pursuing or obtaining membership in the Alliance.[59] Russia's pursuit of its own vision and agenda constitutes a significant barrier to the fulfillment of NATO's cooperative security vision. Russia continues to regard the Alliance's enlargement policies with opposition and anxiety. As a result, many Russians would not endorse the view expressed by the NATO Allies at the May 2012 Chicago Summit: "the prospect of further enlargement and the spirit of cooperative security continue to advance stability in Europe more broadly."[60]

Georgia's Candidacy for NATO Membership

The NATO Allies differed fundamentally at the 2008 Bucharest Summit regarding two candidates for membership, as noted in chapter 6. The U.S. administration under George W. Bush argued for steps toward membership for Georgia and Ukraine. France, Germany, and several other Allies expressed strong reservations. With regard to Ukraine, skeptical Allied observers noted the low level of support for NATO membership in the country (indeed, the hostility toward NATO and loyalty to Moscow of many ethnic Russians and Russian speakers, notably in the east and in the Crimean peninsula) and the profound historical importance of Ukraine for Russia.

With regard to Georgia, Allied critics of any near-term steps toward NATO membership drew attention not only to democratization shortfalls but also to Tbilisi's unresolved territorial disputes with Moscow. Russia had been maintaining "peacekeeper" troops on Georgian soil since the early 1990s in the territories of Abkhazia and South Ossetia. Allied critics of near-term measures in support of NATO membership for Georgia highlighted the stipulation regarding ethnic or territorial disputes in the Alliance's 1995 *Study on NATO Enlargement*:

> States which have ethnic disputes or external territorial disputes, including irredentist claims, or internal jurisdictional disputes must settle those disputes by peaceful means in accordance with OSCE principles. Resolution of such disputes would be a factor in determining whether to invite a state to join the Alliance.[61]

The solution that won consensus at the April 2008 Bucharest Summit was to postpone any decision on MAP status for Georgia and Ukraine and to make a declaration with a curiously predictive tone: "We agreed today that these countries will become members of NATO."[62]

Four months after the Bucharest Summit,[63] in August 2008, Russian military units intervened forcefully in Georgia and went beyond the separatist territories of Abkhazia and South Ossetia. The Russians have presented their action as justified to protect Russian citizens (residents of Abkhazia and South Ossetia to whom Moscow supplied Russian passports) and South Ossetians under attack by Georgian forces. The Russian military was clearly poised for action. Russian tank columns began moving into Georgia within half an hour of the first Georgian offensive on Tskhinvali in response to South Ossetian militia attacks against Georgian villages. As the International Crisis Group put it, "Apparently, the Russians had anticipated, if they did not actually entice, the Georgian move."[64] David Miliband, the British foreign secretary at the time, pointed out that

> force was being used against Georgia by the South Ossetians, and that's where it's important that the Russian narrative cannot start with Georgian actions, it has to start with the attacks on the Georgians from the South Ossetians—and that is the tit for tat that got out of control. . . . What I've said all along is that the rights and the wrongs both, of each side's actions need to be investigated, but they mustn't occlude the fact that a neighbour with 800,000 people in uniform then invaded a sovereign country that is recognised as part of the United Nations.[65]

In November 2011, Dmitry Medvedev, then the Russian president, said that Russia's use of force in Georgia in 2008 stopped the NATO enlargement process, at least with regard to certain countries formerly under Soviet rule. Without Russia's action, Medvedev told Russian troops at Vladikavkaz, just north of Russia's border with Georgia, "a number of countries which [NATO] tried to deliberately drag into the alliance, would have most likely already been part of it now."[66]

In August 2012, President Putin confirmed that Russia's August 2008 intervention in Georgia was planned well in advance and that the Russian military had trained and armed South Ossetians to participate in the preplanned clash with Georgian forces.

According to Pavel Felgenhauer, a Russian journalist,

> Putin's admission of the prewar integration of the Ossetian separatist militias into the Russian General Staff war plan puts into question the integrity of the independent European Union war report, written by Swiss diplomat Heidi Tagliavini that accused the Georgians of starting the war and attacking Russian "peacekeepers," which, according to Tagliavini, warranted a Russian military response.[67]

American scholar Scott Monje has endorsed this interpretation. In his view, Putin's "assertions that the planning involved South Ossetian militias and that the war began on August 6, when the militias attacked Georgian villages, suggest that these attacks were part of the plan as a provocation."[68] The precise chronology of events nonetheless remains in dispute.[69]

In August 2013 Prime Minister Dmitry Medvedev drew attention to Russia's nuclear weapons when he warned Georgia not to seek NATO membership: "I remind you that Russia is a very big country with a huge nuclear arsenal, which we cannot ignore—there is a country that is a member of another military-political alliance whose nuclear missiles are targeted at sites on Russian Federation territory."[70] According to a Georgian commentary on Medvedev's speech, "Mentioning Russia's nuclear power was meant more for NATO's attention rather than Georgia's. Russia is powerful enough to quickly conquer Georgia with conventional arms. To quote from an old Russian proverb: beat your own people, so that others get scared. Russia is threatening to beat Georgia in order to scare NATO."[71]

Russia's action against Georgia—including its recognition of the Georgian territories of Abkhazia and South Ossetia as independent states under Moscow's protection—appears to have been designed to postpone Tbilisi's candidacy for NATO membership to the indefinite future. This objective was accomplished by demonstrating Russia's seriousness about enforcing its "red lines" on NATO enlargement and by deepening Georgia's unresolved ethnic and territorial disputes with its neighbors.[72]

As noted earlier, NATO Allies reluctant to consider Georgia's candidacy favorably have pointed to the stipulation in the *Study on NATO Enlargement* concerning unresolved territorial and ethnic disputes. In 2012, Karl-Heinz Kamp, a German scholar then serving as head of the research division at the NATO Defense College, analyzed a historical precedent in this regard:

> Some supporters of rapid Georgian admission argue that NATO broke the principle of not importing territorial disputes even in its earliest history: in 1955 Germany was invited to join the Alliance, notwithstanding the fact that more than a third of its territory was occupied by the Soviet Union and that the communist "German Democratic Republic" was internationally recognized only by a few states in the Eastern hemisphere. However, the overall situation at the beginning of the Cold War was fundamentally different and cannot be compared to the Georgian-Russian disputes over Abkhazia and South Ossetia.[73]

Kamp's description of how a number of NATO Allied observers gauge the risks and benefits of Georgia's prospective membership in the Alliance is accurate. This view defers to elements of the Russian interpretation of events, and implicitly awards Russia a veto right over NATO's enlargement decisions.

That is, despite the precedent of a prospective ally being enmeshed in a territorial dispute with a great power, many Allied observers reject the comparison with the invitation to the Federal Republic of Germany in 1955 on the grounds that the circumstances and stakes were fundamentally different. In 1955 the NATO Allies, then fourteen countries, saw the Federal Republic's membership as an imperative political-military necessity to bolster NATO's strategic position in relation to the Soviet Union. Britain, France, and the United States had Four Power responsibilities regarding the ultimate disposition of Berlin and Germany as a whole. The Federal Republic's membership in NATO was the culmination of an intense process of intra-Alliance bargaining that began in 1950 and that involved the detour of the French-proposed, ultimately unsuccessful, European Defense Community as an alternative mechanism to establish West German military forces. In the end, the Allies concluded that the Federal Republic's membership in NATO was essential for their strategic interests.

In contrast, a number of Allied observers do not see Georgia's prospective membership as a net benefit in security terms, but as a summons to confrontation with Russia over Georgia's national integrity and sovereignty. They note that Article 10 of the North Atlantic Treaty concerns possible invitations to membership for European states that would "contribute to the security of the North Atlantic area." From their perspective, Georgia's membership would entail Article 5 responsibilities that would diminish their security, and they regard it as fortunate that Georgia has not yet satisfied all the criteria for democratic development and reform spelled out in the 1995 *Study on NATO Enlargement.* As Kamp has pointed out,

> There are even concerns that a future Georgian leadership could feel tempted to behave more offensively vis-à-vis Moscow, knowing that in a conflict it would be backed by the North

Atlantic Alliance. Admittedly, this "mourir pour . . .?" question was always present during the entire enlargement process: would 28 NATO members be prepared to go to war with Russia to protect, say, Tallinn or Riga?[74]

The argument implies that the capitals of small Allies are somehow less worthy of defense than Berlin or Paris or Rome. This is, however, a matter of essential principle. If NATO's deterrence efforts broke down and the Allies failed to honor their collective defense commitments in the face of aggression against any member state, it would mean the end of the Alliance. It would also degrade the credibility of U.S. and allied commitments throughout the world. This might in turn provoke a global political realignment to the disadvantage of the United States and its allies and security partners.

The interest of the Georgian people in NATO membership has remained strong, despite the casualties suffered by Georgian troops serving in the NATO-led ISAF mission in Afghanistan. The casualties in May–June 2013 nonetheless prompted unprecedented demonstrations against NATO and/or sending Georgian forces to serve in the NATO-led ISAF mission in Afghanistan.[75] In June 2013, Secretary General Rasmussen declared in a speech in Tbilisi:

> I know that many Georgians are asking how many more of their brave soldiers will be lost in order to gain NATO membership. Let me stress. Your soldiers are not in Afghanistan as a means of buying entry into NATO. They are there, first and foremost, because it is in Georgia's security interests for them to be there. Your soldiers are playing a vital part in the international community's efforts to stop extremism and terrorism spreading from Afghanistan to other parts of the world—including this region. Their deployment abroad is helping to make Georgia safer at home.[76]

Rasmussen's argument paralleled the criticisms, discussed in chapter 4, of Allies that profess to be serving in Afghanistan not out of commitment to the mission but in order to demonstrate loyalty to the United States or to build up a sense of political obligation in Washington.

Rasmussen has, however, repeatedly assured the Georgians of their positive prospects for membership: "If you continue your efforts, and with our help, Georgia's Euro-Atlantic integration will only be a matter of time."[77] Only on an exceptional basis has Rasmussen acknowledged that Georgia might not satisfy the requirements, which include a consensus of the NATO Allies: "If and when Georgia meets the necessary requirements, it will find a home in NATO."[78] The Allies are divided, with some wary of Russia and the responsibility of making an Article 5 commitment to Georgia, and the outcome of their deliberations is unclear.

The official U.S. position remains supportive of Georgian membership, with no timetable publicly specified. At the Chicago Summit in May 2012, U.S. secretary of state Hillary Clinton said,

> Georgia will become the largest non-NATO contributor to the ISAF mission in Afghanistan this fall, and we are very grateful for its contributions. Georgia has made democratic reforms, and the upcoming parliamentary and presidential elections are additional opportunities for Georgia to show the world that it is committed to NATO's democratic values. We stand firm in our support for Georgia's sovereignty and territorial integrity. We welcome Georgia's non-

use of force pledge, and we call on Russia to reciprocate with its own pledge. We stand by the Bucharest decision and all subsequent decisions on Georgia.[79]

For some Allied observers, the repetition of the Bucharest Summit pledge has become a routine with little practical meaning. They find the inconclusive causes-of-the-war debate convenient as a mechanism to underscore the fact that Georgia's political and territorial disputes with Russia are far from being resolved. In their view, even if all the democratization issues were settled, these disputes would rule out an invitation to Georgia to join NATO. In the view of Nick Witney, the British expert who formerly served as the chief executive of the European Defense Agency, "The Georgia conflict, which marked the end of the eastwards expansion of NATO, has in practice induced a new sense of stability in the European security order."[80]

In this context, few NATO Allies have stepped forward to remind their fellow Allies that the Alliance's "open door" policy for European democracies could eventually extend to former Soviet republics in addition to Georgia. In 2009 Rasa Jukneviciene, then the Lithuanian minister of defense, said, "Belarus is trying, somewhat clumsily, to break out from the self-inflicted isolation of its authoritarian regime. Our goal is to help those countries integrate into Euro-Atlantic security institutions once they are willing and ready—as it would offer their societies a better chance to prosper in freedom and democracy and at the same time provide more stability and security in our region."[81] Her logic is impeccable in terms of NATO's declared enlargement policy. There is, however, no consensus in the Alliance to pursue this vision vigorously, at least in the near-to-medium term, and not only because of concerns about possible Russian reactions.

Finland and Sweden as Possible Membership Candidates

The strong interest of Finland and Sweden in cooperating more closely with NATO was one of the factors that led the Alliance to establish the Partnership for Peace. Their cooperation with NATO, including participation in NATO-led operations, has been so extensive that some Allied observers regard them as "virtual Allies."[82]

Several Russian observers have warned Finland and Sweden not to take steps toward becoming actual NATO Allies. In 2009, for example, Yuli Kvitsinsky, vice chairman of the Duma's Committee for International Affairs, warned that "Russia could mount a whole range of military, political and economic countermeasures if Finland chose to join NATO. . . . A full NATO membership by Finland may lead to a deterioration of bilateral relations. . . . Finland should not place this relationship at risk by joining a military alliance."[83]

In June 2012 Russian General Nikolai Makarov, then the chief of the General Staff, said on a visit to Helsinki that Finland and Sweden should cultivate deeper military relations with Russia. With regard to Finland, Makarov said, "cooperation between Finland and NATO threatens Russia's security. Finland should not desire

NATO membership, rather it should preferably have closer military cooperation with Russia." Finnish foreign minister Erkki Tuomioja said that "this kind of time-machine speech should no longer come from responsible Russian leaders." Swedish defense minister Karin Enström said, "In Sweden's view, every country has the right to independently make its own security policy choices."[84]

In a subsequent statement in June 2012, Russian president Vladimir Putin told Finnish president Sauli Niinisto that membership in NATO would entail a loss of sovereignty: "The involvement of any country in a military bloc deprives it of a certain degree of sovereignty, and some decisions are made at a different level." Putin warned that Russia might take "retaliatory measures" in response to the deployment of missiles in Finland under NATO auspices.[85]

In May 2013 Sergey Shoygu, Russia's defense minister, advised Finland and Sweden not to seek NATO membership. "NATO's expansion would naturally introduce the need to carry out countermeasures," Shoygu said. "Naturally, we must continue the reforms that are currently going on in our Defence Forces, and implement new arrangements, including nuclear weapons."[86] The Russian prime minister, Dmitry Medvedev, proffered similar advice the following month: "New participants [in NATO] emerging close to our border will change the parity and we'll have to take this into account and respond to that."[87]

Russian warnings along these lines may have contributed to the rise in public support for NATO membership in Sweden. "According to an opinion poll conducted in January 2013, 29 per cent of Swedes were in favour of, and 32 per cent against, joining NATO. More than a third were undecided. Only two years earlier, a full 50 per cent opposed NATO membership."[88] In contrast, while one source in 2012 reported increased support for NATO membership in Finland,[89] another indicated that 18 percent agree that Finland should "strive to become a member of NATO," while 71 percent hold the opposite view. "The support for membership has declined significantly since 2005–2008, when 26 to 28 per cent supported Finnish NATO membership."[90] According to an expert observer in Helsinki, "In Finland Russia's behavior is used as both a reason to join and to abstain from membership, so Russian behavior tends to simply reinforce opinion on both sides."[91]

Factors in addition to Russian statements may have contributed to the increased interest in Sweden in cooperation with NATO and possible membership. In December 2012 the supreme commander of the Swedish Armed Forces, General Sverker Göransson, said that Sweden's military could defend against an attack with a limited objective for "roughly one week" before its resources and resistance capability would run down. In the same interview General Göransson said that Russia under Putin has undertaken "ever larger, ever more complex exercises" in the Baltic and Norwegian Seas. Asked if Sweden could "count on" NATO's assistance, Göransson said, "The West would likely also be engaged in what happens to us. I cannot see a scenario with a limited attack against Sweden, and that nothing is happening in the surrounding world."[92]

When Secretary General Rasmussen was asked about this contingency the following month, he said, "I don't want to go into that because it is a hypothetical scenario. . . . But collective defence only applies to Nato members. . . . If a Nato partner brings a security issue to our table we will of course look at it but there is no guarantee. . . . You cannot be outside Nato but want everything that Nato can give. Sweden knows this and we will not meddle in whether it becomes a member."[93]

Given NATO's position, leading Swedish politicians inferred that, to quote Allan Widman, "we have no plan B. We are largely on our own."[94] Some championed, in the words of Staffan Danielsson, "a significant increase in the defense budget."[95]

In April 2013 it became known that the previous month two Russian bombers (Tupolev-22M3 Backfires) and four Russian fighters (Sukhoi-27 Flankers) had flown close to Sweden, apparently to simulate a bombing raid. No Swedish fighters were available to intercept and shadow the Russian aircraft, partly because it was a holiday weekend. Two Danish F-16s, in Lithuania for NATO's Baltic air policing, scrambled to shadow the Russian aircraft.[96] It is not clear how often Russia has conducted such exercises in relation to Sweden, because the Swedish government normally keeps such incidents secret.[97]

The Russian "fly-by" incident led some Swedish politicians to call for, as Allan Widman put it, "intensifying our cooperation with other countries when it comes to our safety, and in that vein I'm primarily thinking of how we become closer to Nato."[98]

The Swedish defense minister, Karin Enström, rejected such advice and asserted that, in light of the Lisbon Treaty, Sweden could rely on the protection of its European Union partners. She acknowledged that Article 42.7 of the Lisbon Treaty is not equivalent to Article 5 of the North Atlantic Treaty but said, "If you really read it, the Lisbon Treaty says you must support your EU neighbours with all the necessary means."[99]

It should be noted in this regard that the Lisbon Treaty refers to NATO as "the foundation" of collective defense for its members.[100] Shortly before Enström's statement, Charly Salonius-Pasternak, a Finnish expert, wrote, "Sweden has also woken up to the fact that the mutual assistance clause included in the Treaty of Lisbon is meaningless without concrete acts of preparation—which are not to be expected."[101] In 2005 a Finnish diplomat observed, "A separate European defense would be possible only if we could be completely certain that it will not be put to the test in a real situation."[102]

Rather than relying on the Lisbon Treaty, the Swedes might in practice count on what Nick Witney has called "solidarity of fact." In his view, "Nato countries and EU countries are so dependent on one another, their interests run into each other so much . . . no one is going to attack Stockholm and think that British forces or other Nato forces will stand aside and watch."[103]

It is noteworthy that Sweden has since 2009 repeatedly reaffirmed its solidarity with its EU, Nordic, and Baltic neighbors. In July 2009, for example, the minister of defense, Sten Tolgfors, said,

> Sweden shares values and interests with the EU and the Nordic and Baltic countries. One expression of this is our declaration of solidarity. Sweden would not stand passive if a neighbour is threatened or attacked. We expect others not to stand passive if Sweden is threatened. We must be able both to provide and receive support, with relevant capabilities, also of a military nature.[104]

Sweden's EU, Nordic, and Baltic neighbors include NATO nations, and Sweden has supported the membership of the Baltic states in NATO. In view of these facts, there was a certain logic to Sweden's behavior as a "consulting partner" in NATO's October 2011 crisis management exercise (CMX). The 2011 CMX considered a collective defense contingency, including the invocation of Article 5 to protect Norway. As Ann-Sofie Dahl, a Swedish scholar, has reported regarding the 2011 CMX,

> Sweden took the exceptional step for a partner country of offering direct support to NATO, including maritime assets with ships and air capabilities. The clear intention was that they be placed under NATO command and control, though this was an Article 5 crisis.... The Swedish offer of Article 5 assistance to neighbouring Norway astounded everyone around the table.[105]

Dahl wrote that Sweden's behavior involved "a partner country stepping into the role of contributing assistance to the Alliance in a potential Article 5 situation, thereby blurring the distinction between operational partner and Ally."[106] General Göransson noted in his December 2012 interview that Sweden had committed "a large part" of its fleet of Gripen aircraft to the defense of Norway in a NATO-led staff exercise in 2011 and said that he "anticipates the same solidarity" if Sweden is attacked.[107]

Finland and Sweden also participated in NATO's 2012 CMX, noteworthy as the first in which the Allies considered the possible invocation of Article 5 in the framework of a cyber attack. According to a NATO press release, Sweden and Finland acted "as Partners alongside Allies in the exercise, as some elements of the scenario" involved "their geographical proximity."[108]

Finnish deliberations about possible membership in NATO and possible reliance on NATO in a crisis appear to have been much more muted and less public than those in Sweden. Finnish policy on the possibility of NATO membership seems not to have changed since it was first articulated in the late 1990s. According to a standard formula,

> Finnish policy on the question of NATO membership is a clear "No," though it should not be read as "Never." Rather, it should be understood as "Not now," as Finland would like to retain the option of future membership. The Finnish foreign policy leadership has, for that reason, steadfastly underlined every country's right to make its own security choices, including whether or not it wants to join military alliances.[109]

Finland and Sweden have nonetheless coordinated many of their activities in cooperation with NATO, and some observers speculate that Helsinki and Stockholm would act together if they decided to seek NATO membership. Their coordination was apparent in October 2012, when the prime ministers of Finland and Sweden announced that their countries intend to participate in a NATO air training mission in 2014 over Iceland, a NATO member nation that has requested their help.[110] In November 2012, as noted above, Finland and Sweden participated in another

NATO CMX, held concurrently with a cyber-defense exercise, in which the possible invocation of Article 5 was discussed in the framework of a cyber attack.[111]

At present the internal politics of Finland and Sweden seem to favor cultivating and deepening partnership activities with NATO and selected NATO Allies rather than seeking membership.[112] However, Russian behavior may in the long term lead these countries to take greater interest in pursuing membership, which would offer them Article 5 protection and seats on the North Atlantic Council. The current members of the Alliance would probably welcome their applications for membership.[113]

Conclusion

Enlargement has represented many things to the NATO Allies: a means of strengthening the Alliance's collective defense posture while adding new collective defense responsibilities, a vehicle for attracting contributors to crisis management operations, and an incentive for promoting democratization as a fundamental part of the Alliance's cooperative security vision. The prospect of gaining Alliance membership has been the most powerful means of motivating candidates to conform to the standards set out in the 1995 *Study on NATO Enlargement*.

Proponents of NATO enlargement have seen it as a means "to expand the zone of peace and stability in Europe," to quote Jamie Shea, a high-level NATO official.[114] Bruce Jackson, the president of the Project on Transitional Democracies in Washington, has even said that "the defining purpose of NATO since the early 1990s has been the expansion of NATO."[115]

Some analysts have, however, expressed disappointment with the results of the post–Cold War enlargement process. In the words of Karl-Heinz Kamp, "Some of the 12 countries which have become members since 1999 swiftly neglected the promises they made prior to accession (like keeping their level of defense spending at 2% of Gross Domestic Product), and contribute appallingly little to NATO's overall capabilities."[116] The newer Allies have, it should be noted, hardly been alone in not meeting the goal of spending 2 percent of GDP on defense. In June 2013, only four Allies (Estonia, Greece, the United Kingdom, and the United States) met that objective, and nineteen Allies spent less than 1.5 percent.[117] Moreover, for the most part the newer Allies have a creditable record in contributing forces to operations without caveats restricting their usability, in contrast with certain older Allies.

Andrew Bacevich argued in 2008 that "enlargement diluted NATO's actual ability to defend itself." In his view, "the alliance became something more akin to a political club, far more adept at convening conferences than at organizing itself for war."[118]

It is, of course, intrinsically much easier to convene conferences than to prepare for military operations, but if NATO's capacity for organizing for war has declined since the 1990s, this would seem to be despite rather than because of enlargement. For the most part, the newer Allies in Central and Eastern Europe (notably Poland) have been keeping up their defense spending effort, even since the recession began in 2008, with greater determination than Western European Allies. Financial austerity and widespread complacency about external security threats have been the main causes of defense spending cutbacks in NATO nations, not enlargement.

Secretary Clinton said at the May 2012 Chicago Summit, "I believe this summit should be the last summit that is not an enlargement summit."[119] She was evidently referring to the absence at Chicago of NATO decisions to invite additional nations to join the Alliance. As discussed in this chapter, however, substantial hurdles have slowed down the post–Cold War enlargement process.

With regard to the candidates in the western Balkans, progress on enlargement is mainly conditional on their own performance in meeting the standards set out in the 1995 *Study on NATO Enlargement.* The main exception in this regard is the former Yugoslav Republic of Macedonia, whose membership candidacy remains blocked by the stalemate with Greece over the name issue. Some Allied observers regard the Greek position as excessive and obstructionist rather than principled and well-founded, and have raised concerns about the risk of counterproductive political consequences in the candidate country.

With regard to Georgia and other former Soviet republics, no practical prospect of enlargement is at hand in the immediately foreseeable future. Although all the Allies routinely repeat the Bucharest Summit formulas, notably with respect to Georgia, there seems to be a tacit consensus that the Allies are not prepared, at least at present, to go beyond reiterating the "open door" policy. The United States and several of the new Allies in Central and Eastern Europe are regarded as the leading proponents of further enlargement in the post-Soviet space, but some Allied observers suspect that certain Allies are not entirely discontent with the current impasse regarding Georgia's membership prospects.

The result may be a compromise decision such as offering Georgia the MAP status that it did not receive at the 2008 Bucharest Summit. At present, Georgia's prospects for membership are at best unpredictable, if not doubtful, owing in large part to the Russian factor.

Another element in a package of compromises might be for the Allies to commission an update of their 1995 *Study on NATO Enlargement*, as suggested by Patrick Keller of the Konrad-Adenauer-Stiftung in Berlin. As Keller has observed, the study could assess the rounds of enlargement since 1999, and the preparation of such a document might, on the model of the 2012 Deterrence and Defense Posture Review, lead to a new commitment by the Allies to an agreed-upon policy.[120]

With regard to Finland and Sweden and the other remaining potential candidates—European states that are neither former Yugoslav republics nor former Soviet republics—there has been essentially no debate within the Alliance. The self-differentiation principle of the Partnership for Peace allows partners to deepen their cooperation with the Alliance to the mutual satisfaction of NATO and the partners. If Finland and Sweden eventually sought membership, their prospects of admission would be excellent; they are mature democracies that have already demonstrated that they have a great deal to offer the Alliance.

NATO's post–Cold War enlargement process has provided another illustration of the Alliance's balancing act concerning its three core tasks. Enlargement has clearly increased NATO's collective defense responsibilities, but it has also diminished significantly the need to be ready for major crisis management operations in Central and Eastern Europe that would have probably arisen otherwise. In other words, the NATO Allies have helped to stabilize Central and Eastern European countries by welcoming these new Allies as contributors to the Alliance's protective structure. Moreover, as members of the Alliance, these countries are less vulnerable to the continuing Russian efforts to rebuild Moscow's sphere of influence.

In short, acting in cooperation with the European Union, the NATO Allies helped to prevent the emergence of a strategic vacuum in Central and Eastern Europe. Without PfP and NATO enlargement, the states in this region would have been vulnerable to Russian pressures, and they would have probably renationalized their defense policies and engaged in local rivalries and power competitions.

Whether enlargement has enhanced the Alliance's military capabilities to a degree commensurate with its new responsibilities has remained open to debate, particularly in a context of financial crisis and drastic defense budget cuts. Enlargement has provided the Alliance with contributors of personnel, equipment, and funds for crisis management operations. As the 2011 Libya operation and the restrictions on force usability in Afghanistan suggest, however, Allies have become increasingly selective about participating in operations, a trend that may persist in the future. Finally, for many Allied observers the democratization agenda pursued through NATO enlargement has been the central element of the Alliance's cooperative security vision. Pursuing this agenda has been more successful in some new member states than others, but it remains an important element of NATO's identity, despite the compromises made throughout the Alliance's history.

Notes

1. Madeleine Albright, prepared statement before the Senate Armed Services Committee, April 23, 1997, 1.
2. This paragraph and the following three paragraphs are borrowed from Yost, *NATO Transformed*, 70–72.
3. John Duffield, "The North Atlantic Treaty Organization: Alliance Theory," in *Explaining International Relations Since 1945*, ed. Ngaire Woods (London: Oxford University Press, 1996), 344.
4. Duffield, "The North Atlantic Treaty Organization," 345.
5. North Atlantic Council, "Madrid Declaration on Euro-Atlantic Security and Cooperation," July 8, 1997, par. 8.
6. NATO, *Study on NATO Enlargement*, September 3, 1995, par. 43, www.nato.int/cps/en/natolive/official_texts_24733.htm
7. Ibid., par. 70.
8. North Atlantic Council, "Strategic Concept," November 19, 2010, par. 27.
9. NATO, *Study on NATO Enlargement*, par. 3.
10. Madeleine Albright, "Enlarging NATO," *Economist*, February 15, 1997, 22.
11. For an overview of this debate, see Yost, *NATO Transformed*, 100–131. Among the book-length studies of the first post–Cold War round of NATO enlargement, two stand out: James M. Goldgeier, *Not Whether but When: The U.S.*

Decision to Enlarge NATO (Washington, DC: Brookings Institution Press, 1999); and Ronald D. Asmus, *Opening NATO's Door: How the Alliance Remade Itself for a New Era* (New York: Columbia University Press, 2002). For a judicious theoretical analysis, see Frank Schimmelfennig, "NATO Enlargement: A Constructivist Explanation," *Security Studies* 8, no. 2–3 (1998).

12. Javier Solana, "NATO's Role in Building Cooperative Security in Europe and Beyond" (remarks by the Secretary General of NATO at the Yomiuri Symposium on International Economy, Tokyo, Japan, October 15, 1997), www.nato.int/docu/speech/1997/s971015a.htm.

13. Rafael Biermann, *NATO Enlargement—Approaching a Standstill*, Security Insights no. 4 (Garmisch-Partenkirchen, Germany: George C. Marshall Center, December 2009), 2, www.marshallcenter.org/mcpublicweb/MCDocs/files/College/F_Publications/secInsights/SecurityInsights_04_fullsize.pdf.

14. Seven countries joined NATO on March 29, 2004: Bulgaria, Estonia, Latvia, Lithuania, Romania, Slovakia, and Slovenia. Ten countries joined the European Union on May 1, 2004: Cyprus, the Czech Republic, Estonia, Hungary, Latvia, Lithuania, Malta, Poland, Slovakia, and Slovenia. Bulgaria and Romania joined the European Union on January 1, 2007.

15. NATO, "Membership Action Plan (MAP)," last updated June 11, 2012, www.nato.int/cps/en/natolive/topics_37356.htm.

16. Waszczykowski, *The Western Balkans*, par. 21.

17. Dessie Zagorcheva, "NATO Enlargement and Security in the Balkans," *Journal of Regional Security* 7, no. 1 (2012): 19.

18. Since 1999 NATO communiqués have systematically included a note stating that "Turkey recognises the Republic of Macedonia with its constitutional name." This statement first appeared in NATO communiqués in 1996, but consistent use began in 1999. The author is indebted to Diana Wueger for investigating this question.

19. North Atlantic Council, "Bucharest Summit Declaration," par. 20, www.nato.int/docu/pr/2008/p08-049e.html. The Allies made similar statements at their April 2009 and November 2010 summit meetings. North Atlantic Council, "Strasbourg/Kehl Summit Declaration," par. 22; and North Atlantic Council, "Lisbon Summit Declaration," par. 14.

20. North Atlantic Council, "Chicago Summit Declaration," par. 26.

21. For background, see Zoran Kosanic, *Obstacles to FYROM's Membership of NATO: A Tougher Agenda than Expected*, Research Paper no. 44 (Rome: NATO Defense College, February 2009).

22. "Greek Foreign Minister Dimitris Droutsas Addresses UN General Assembly Meeting in New York," *ANA-MPA* (in English), September 28, 2010, available at OpenSource.gov, EUP20100929430001.

23. Pete Kasperowicz, "House Members Urge Obama to Invite Macedonia into NATO," *Hill*, April 3, 2012, http://thehill.com/blogs/floor-action/house/219743-house-members-urge-obama-to-invite-macedonia-into-nato; Sandy Berger, William Cohen, and Donald H. Rumsfeld, letter to President Obama, May 21, 2012, www.foreignpolicy.com/files/fp_uploaded_documents/120521_Letter.pdf; James Jones, "NATO Inaction on Enlargement Risks Balkan Stability," *Roll Call*, May 18, 2012, www.rollcall.com/news/Jones-NATO-Inaction-on-Enlargement-Risks-Balkan-Stability-214633-1.html.

24. President Obama, remarks at meeting of North Atlantic Council, Strasbourg, France, April 4, 2009, www.whitehouse.gov/the_press_office/Remarks-By-President-Obama-At-Meeting-Of-North-Atlantic-Council.

25. International Court of Justice, *Application of the Interim Accord of 13 September 1995 (The Former Yugoslav Republic of Macedonia v. Greece), Judgment*, December 5, 2011, 10, 48.

26. NATO, "Statement by the NATO Secretary General on ICJ ruling," December 5, 2011, www.nato.int/cps/en/SID-969A34D0-C56DB9B7/natolive/news_81678.htm.

27. Waszczykowski, *The Western Balkans*, par. 63.

28. Sinisa Jakov Marusic, "Howitt Alarmed by Macedonia's EU Prospects," May 23, 2013, www.balkaninsight.com/en/article/howitt-macedonian-eu-progress-jeopardized. See also the interview with *Dimitar Tzantchev, Bulgaria's ambassador to the European Union, May 1, 2013, at* http://reuniting-europe.blogactiv.eu/2013/05/01/top-bulgarian-envoy-skopjes-stance-on-neighbours-is-alarming/#.UhAJqrzwaHk.

29. Georgi Spasov quoted in Miki Trajkovski, "Macedonia, Bulgaria Attempt to Improve Relations," *Southeast European Times*, February 6, 2013, www.setimes.com/cocoon/setimes/xhtml/en_GB/features/setimes/features/2013/02/06/feature-00.

30. NATO, *Study on NATO Enlargement*, par. 71; emphasis in the original.

31. Ivo Daalder and James Goldgeier, "Global NATO," *Foreign Affairs* 85, no. 5 (September/October 2006): 106.

32. Waszczykowski, *The Western Balkans*, par. 71.

33. Boris Yeltsin's December 1994 speech at the CSCE summit in Budapest, quoted by Andrei Kozyrev in his article, "Partnership or Cold Peace?" *Foreign Policy* 99 (Summer 1995): 4.

34. Hannes Adomeit, "Inside or Outside? Russia's Policies towards NATO" (paper delivered at the Annual Conference of the Centre for Russian Studies at the Norwegian Institute of International Affairs, Oslo, October 12–13, 2006), 22, quoted with the author's permission.

35. Vladimir Socor, "Chicago Summit: NATO Remains AWOL from Europe's East," *Eurasia Daily Monitor* 9, no. 99 (May 24, 2012).

36. Czechoslovakia was, it should be recalled, a single state from its founding in 1918 to its peaceful dissolution into two successor states (the Czech Republic and Slovakia) in 1993. Czechoslovakia was therefore one state during the Warsaw Pact period (1955–1991).

37. Alexei Ostrovsky quoted in Stefan Wagstyl and Isabel Gorst, "A Harder Power," *Financial Times*, August 3, 2009.

38. Dmitry Medvedev, interview on Television Channels Channel One, Rossia, NTV, in Sochi, August 31, 2008, http://archive.kremlin.ru/eng/speeches/2008/08/31/1850_type82912type82916_206003.shtml

39. Interview with former Russian finance minister Alexei Kudrin, "We Have to Take a Chance with More Democracy," January 23, 2013, www.spiegel.de/international/world/interview-with-putin-ally-alexei-kudrin-on-democracy-in-russia-a-878873.html.

40. Albright, "Enlarging NATO," 23.

41. Javier Solana, speech at the Royal Institute of International Affairs, Chatham House, London, March 4, 1997, www.nato.int/docu/speech/1997/s970304a.htm.

42. Anders Fogh Rasmussen, "NATO and Russia: A New Beginning" (speech at the Carnegie Endowment, Brussels, September 18, 2009), www.nato.int/cps/en/natolive/opinions_57640.htm?selectedLocale=en.

43. Vershbow, "Crafting the New Strategic Concept: Ambitions, Resources, and Partnerships for a 21st Century Alliance."

44. "Russian Federation National Security Blueprint," approved by Russian Federation Presidential Edict no. 1300, December 17, 1997, in *Rossiyskaya Gazeta*, December 26, 1997, in Foreign Broadcast Information Service, FBIS-SOV-97-364, December 30, 1997, 2.

45. "The Military Doctrine of the Russian Federation," approved by Russian Federation presidential edict on February 5, 2010, http://kremlin.ru/, English translation at OpenSource.gov, CEP20100208042001.

46. Putin quoted in Andrew Osborn, "Putin: Collapse of the Soviet Union Was 'Catastrophe of the Century,'" *Independent*, April 26, 2005, www.independent.co.uk/news/world/europe/putin-collapse-of-the-soviet-union-was-catastrophe-of-the-century-521064.html.

47. Vladimir Putin, speech at the 43rd Munich Conference on Security Policy.

48. "Our strategy and our Alliance are exclusively defensive.... This will also be true of a united Germany in NATO. The very fact that we are ready not to deploy NATO troops beyond the territory of the Federal Republic gives the Soviet Union firm security guarantees." Manfred Wörner, "The Atlantic Alliance and European Security in the 1990s" (address, May 17, 1990), www.nato.int/docu/speech/1990/s900517a_e.htm.

49. "Following the completion of the withdrawal of the Soviet armed forces from the territory of the present German Democratic Republic and of Berlin, units of German armed forces assigned to military alliance structures in the same way as those in the rest of German territory may also be stationed in that part of Germany, but without nuclear weapon carriers. This does not apply to conventional weapon systems which may have other capabilities in addition to conventional ones but which in that part of Germany are equipped for a conventional role and designated only for such. Foreign armed forces and nuclear weapons or their carriers will not be stationed in that part of Germany or deployed there." "Treaty on the Final Settlement with Respect to Germany," September 12, 1990, Article 5, par. 3, http://usa.usembassy.de/etexts/2plusfour8994e.htm.

50. Jack Matlock, *Testimony in hearing before the Committee on International Relations, United States House of Representatives*, 104th Congress, 2nd Session, June 20, 1996 (Washington, DC: U.S. Government Printing Office, 1996), 31.

51. Secretary of State Madeleine Albright, *Testimony in the Administration's Proposal on NATO's Enlargement: Hearing before the Committee on Armed Services, United States Senate*, 105th Congress, 1st Session, April 23, 1997 (Washington, DC: U.S. Government Printing Office, 1997), 60.

52. Principle I ("Sovereign equality, respect for the rights inherent in sovereignty") in Conference on Security and Cooperation in Europe, "Final Act," Helsinki, August 1, 1975.

53. Mark Kramer, "The Myth of a No-NATO-Enlargement Pledge to Russia," *Washington Quarterly* 32, no. 2 (April 2009): 55.

54. "For a moment in February 1990, the Soviet Union could have struck a deal with the United States, but it did not. Obviously any agreement among the Americans, West Germans, and Russians would have needed alliance approval, but in the political climate of 1990 it would have been possible to secure it. Even a written press release would have helped the Soviet cause. But Gorbachev did not secure one, and the window closed." Mary Elise Sarotte, "Not One Inch Eastward? Bush, Baker, Kohl, Genscher, Gorbachev, and the Origin of Russian Resentment toward NATO Enlargement in February 1990," *Diplomatic History* 34, no. 1 (January 2010): 140.

55. Yost, *NATO Transformed*, 133–134.

56. These assurances are discussed in chapters 2 and 6. It should be noted that these assurances were not welcomed by all the prospective new Allies. Some Poles, for example, have argued that the Alliance's assurances to Moscow gave the new Allies a "secondary" and "unequal" security status and subjected them to constraints not affecting the older Allies. David S. Yost, *The Future of NATO's Nuclear Deterrent: The New Strategic Concept and the 2010 NPT Review Conference, A Workshop Report* (Rome: NATO Defense College, April 2010), 4-5, www.ndc.nato.int/download/downloads.php?icode=193.

57. See the statements by retired Major General Vladimir Dvorkin, Sergei Karaganov, Andrei Zagorsky, and retired General Pavel Zolotarev cited in Lilia Shevtsova, *Lonely Power: Why Russia Has Failed to Become the West and the West Is Weary of Russia* (Washington, DC: Carnegie Endowment for International Peace, 2010), 144–145.

58. Anders Fogh Rasmussen, "Ukraine and NATO: Partners in Security" (speech at the Kyiv University, Ukraine, February 24, 2011), www.nato.int/cps/en/natolive/opinions_70795.htm?selectedLocale=en.

59. From the perspective of some NATO governments the arguments against Russian membership in the Alliance formulated in the 1990s have remained potent. These arguments include the risk that it could lead to abandoning NATO's role as an instrument of collective defense and turning the Alliance into an ineffective collective security regime for the Euro-Atlantic region; the possibility that it might upset existing patterns of influence in the Alliance, and subordinate the Europeans to a U.S.-Russian tandem; and the prospect that, if NATO remained a collective defense organization, Russian membership would make the Alliance responsible for protecting Russia against China and other powers. For a more extensive discussion, see Yost, *NATO Transformed*, 145–151.

60. North Atlantic Council, "Chicago Summit Declaration," par. 25.

61. NATO, *Study on NATO Enlargement*, par. 6.

62. North Atlantic Council, "Bucharest Summit Declaration," par. 23.

63. The debate on how the Bucharest Summit Declaration may have influenced the Russian government's decision making remains inconclusive. Was the affirmation that "these countries will become members of NATO" a challenge that Russian leaders felt compelled to meet by sending a forceful message and creating new geopolitical facts on the ground? Or was the decision not to award a MAP or invitation to membership a "green light" for the Russian use of force? For a Georgian interpretation taking the latter view, see Messenger Staff, "Medvedev Threatens Georgia If It Joins NATO," *Messenger Online*, August 9, 2013, www.messenger.com.ge/issues/2922_august_9_2013/2922_edit.html.

64. International Crisis Group, *Russia vs. Georgia: The Fallout*, Europe Report no. 195 (Brussels: International Crisis Group, August 22, 2008), 1.

65. Foreign Secretary David Miliband, BBC broadcast transcript of 28 October 2008, http://news.bbc.co.uk/2/shared/bsp/hi/pdfs/21_10_08_fo4_georgia.pdf.

66. Medvedev quoted in Denis Dyomkin, "Russia Says Georgia War Stopped NATO Expansion," Reuters, November 21, 2011, available at http://in.reuters.com/article/2011/11/21/idINIndia-60645720111121.

67. Pavel Felgenhauer, "Putin Confirms the Invasion of Georgia Was Preplanned," *Eurasia Daily Monitor* 9, no. 152 (August 9, 2012). The September 2009 report by the Independent International Fact-Finding Mission on the Conflict in Georgia is available at www.ceiig.ch/pdf/IIFFMCG_Volume_I.pdf.

68. Scott Monje, "The Return of the Russian-Georgian War," August 20, 2012, http://foreignpolicyblogs.com/2012/08/20/the-return-of-the-russian-georgian-war/.

69. For an informative review of the competing narratives, see Rick Fawn and Robert Nalbandov, "The Difficulties of Knowing the Start of War in the Information Age: Russia, Georgia, and the War over South Ossetia, August 2008," *European Security* 21, no. 1 (March 2012): 57–89.

70. Russian prime minister Dmitriy Medvedev's interview with Georgian journalist Nino Shubladze, broadcast on Georgian TV channel Rustavi-2 on August 6, 2013, *Novosti-Gruziya* (in Russian), August 7, 2013, available at OpenSource.gov, CEL2013080747941820.

71. Messenger Staff, "Medvedev Threatens Georgia If It Joins NATO."

72. Russian behavior vindicated the Georgian view that "Russia ... was interested in 'piece keeping, not peacekeeping' in the Caucasus." Uwe Halbach, "The Regional Dimension: Georgia and the Southern Caucasus after the War," in *The Caucasus Crisis: International Perceptions and Policy Implications for Germany and Europe*, ed. Hans-Henning Schröder (Berlin: Stiftung Wissenschaft und Politik, November 2008), 21.

73. Karl-Heinz Kamp, *NATO Enlargement Reloaded*, Research Paper no. 81 (Rome: NATO Defense College, September 2012), 7.

74. Ibid., 6. The phrase "*mourir pour ...?*"— that is, "die for ...?"— alludes to Marcel Déat's notorious article titled "Mourir pour Dantzig?" in *L'Oeuvre*, May 4, 1939. The phrase implied doubt about the wisdom of honoring the commitment to defend Poland by alluding to one of Nazi Germany's demands—an end to the Danzig corridor that linked that city (Gdansk) to the rest of Poland and thereby separated East Prussia from the rest of Germany. A French journalist and politician, Déat argued against the idea that France and the United Kingdom should be prepared to go to war

against Nazi Germany to honor their guarantees to Poland. He supported the armistice with Nazi Germany on June 22, 1940, and was a political ally of Pierre Laval and others in the Vichy regime that collaborated with Nazi Germany.

75. Vasili Rukhadze, "Latest Georgian Casualties in Afghanistan Spark Unprecedented Public Debate and Doubts about Georgia's NATO Perspectives," *Eurasia Daily Monitor* 10, no. 116 (June 19, 2013).

76. NATO secretary general Anders Fogh Rasmussen, "NATO and Georgia—On the Right Path" (keynote speech at the National Library of Georgia, Tbilisi, Georgia, June 27, 2013), www.nato.int/cps/en/natolive/opinions_101755.htm.

77. Secretary General Rasmussen, "NATO and Georgia."

78. Secretary General Rasmussen quoted in NATO, "NATO-Georgia Commission Meets in Tbilisi," June 26, 2013, www.nato.int/cps/en/natolive/news_101668.htm.

79. Hillary Clinton, remarks at the North Atlantic Council Meeting, May 21, 2012, www.state.gov/secretary/rm/2012/05/190466.htm. Secretary Clinton's forecast was vindicated in November 2012 when Georgia announced that it had increased its troop commitment in Afghanistan to 1,570, making it the largest non-NATO contributor to the NATO-led ISAF mission. "Georgia Doubles Afghanistan Troop Deployment," Agence France-Presse, November 27, 2012.

80. Nick Witney, *How to Stop the Demilitarisation of Europe* (London: European Council on Foreign Relations, November 2011), 3.

81. Rasa Jukneviciene, *Latest Developments in European Security: A Baltic Perspective* (London: Chatham House, October 20, 2009), 6–7. The expression "Euro-Atlantic security institutions" is widely used as shorthand to refer to NATO and the European Union.

82. Leo G. Michel, *Finland, Sweden, and NATO: From "Virtual" to Formal Allies?*, Strategic Forum no. 265 (Washington, DC: National Defense University, February 2011), 2.

83. Yuli Kvitsinsky, interview on Finnish public broadcaster YLE, March 28, 2009, quoted in David Pugliese and Gerard O'Dwyer, "Canada, Russia Build Arctic Forces: As Ice Recedes, Nations Maneuver for Control," *Defense News*, April 6, 2009, www.defensenews.com/story.php?i=4025065.

84. Makarov, Tuomioja, and Enström quoted in Gerard O'Dwyer, "Russian Military Chief Stirs Anti-NATO Pot," *Defense News*, June 13, 2012, www.defensenews.com/article/20120613/DEFREG01/306130005/Russian-Military-Chief-Stirs-Anti-NATO-Pot.

85. Putin quoted in "Finland Will Lose 'Sovereignty' If Joins NATO—Putin," rt.com, June 22, 2012, http://rt.com/politics/putin-finland-nato-missiles-509/.

86. Shoygu quoted in Pekka Hakala, "Russian Minister: Stay Away From NATO," *Helsingin Sanomat* website, May 29, 2013, http://search.proquest.com/docview/1357388525/13E6FD1089B6706E06A/1?accountid=.

87. Dmitry Medvedev quoted in Balazs Koranyi, "NATO Expansion In Nordics Would Force Russian Response: Medvedev," Reuters.com, June 4, 2013.

88. Charly Salonius-Pasternak, *Swedish Defence Illusions Are Crumbling*, FIIA Comment no. 6/2013 (Helskinki: Finnish Institute of International Affairs, March 2013).

89. Stephen Blank, "General Makarov Makes Incendiary Remarks in Finland," *Eurasia Daily Monitor* 9, no. 136 (July 18, 2012).

90. Charly Salonius-Pasternak, "Report: Everyone Talks about NATO, but Nothing Happens," February 13, 2013, www.frivarld.se/ny-rapport-alla-talar-om-nato-men-inget-hander/.

91. Author's correspondence with a Finnish observer, June 30, 2013.

92. General Sverker Göransson, interview with Mikael Holmström, "Försvar med tidsgräns" ("Defense with Time Limit"), *Svenska Dagbladet*, December 30, 2012, www.svd.se/nyheter/inrikes/forsvar-med-tidsgrans_7789308.svd, translation by OpenSource.gov, EUP20130103340009.

93. Secretary General Rasmussen quoted in "Sweden Can't Count on Help from Nato," *Local*, January 14, 2013, www.thelocal.se/45608/20130114/.

94. Swedish Liberal Party spokesman Allan Widman quoted in Gerard O'Dwyer, "Sweden's Military Spending to Rise?" *Defense News*, February 1, 2013, www.defensenews.com/article/20130201/DEFREG01/302010015/Sweden-8217-s-Military-Spending-Rise-.

95. Staffan Danielsson, the Center Party's defense spokesman, quoted in O'Dwyer, "Sweden's Military Spending to Rise?"

96. Although the incident took place on March 29, 2013 (Good Friday), it was not reported until the following month: "Ryskt flyg övade anfall mot Sverige," *Svenska Dagbladet*, April 22, 2013, http://www.svd.se/nyheter/inrikes/ryskt-flyg-ovade-anfall-mot-sverige_8108894.svd. See also Richard Milne, "Swedish Angst as Russia Mocks Its Supertroopers," *Financial Times*, May 9, 2013; and "Swedish Lawmakers Irked by Military Non-response to Russian Fly-by," United Press International, April 23, 2013.

97. Mikael Holmström quoted in "Sweden Won't Demand Russia Fly-by Explanation," *Local*, April 22, 2013, www.thelocal.se/47488/20130422/.

98. Allan Widman quoted in "Sweden Won't Demand Russia Fly-by Explanation."

99. Enström quoted in Andrew Rettman, "Sweden: Who Needs Nato, When You Have the Lisbon Treaty?," euobserver. com, April 22, 2013, http://euobserver.com/defence/119894.

100. The full text of the relevant passage of the Lisbon Treaty follows: "If a Member State is the victim of armed aggression on its territory, the other Member States shall have towards it an obligation of aid and assistance by all the means in their power, in accordance with Article 51 of the United Nations Charter. This shall not prejudice the specific character of the security and defence policy of certain Member States. Commitments and cooperation in this area shall be consistent with commitments under the North Atlantic Treaty Organisation, which, for those States which are members of it, remains the foundation of their collective defence and the forum for its implementation." Article 42, par. 7 of the Consolidated Version of the Treaty on European Union (Luxembourg: Publications Office of the European Union, 2010), 39.

101. Salonius-Pasternak, *Swedish Defence Illusions Are Crumbling.*

102. Comment by former Finnish ambassador Leif Blomqvist in "A Dual Pillar NATO Alliance Is Not in Europe's Interest," *Helsingin Sanomat,* January 8, 2005, quoted in Leo G. Michel, *Finland, Sweden, and NATO: From "Virtual" to Formal Allies?,* Strategic Forum no. 265 (Washington, DC: National Defense University, February 2011), 4.

103. Witney quoted in Rettman, "Sweden: Who Needs Nato?"

104. Sten Tolgfors, speech on Baltic Sea cooperation, Almedalen, July 3, 2009, www.government.se/sb/d/12091/a/129883. For an important collection of essays on this theme, see Bo Hugemark, ed., *Friends in Need: Towards a Swedish Strategy of Solidarity with Her Neighbours* (Stockholm: Royal Swedish Academy of War Sciences, 2012).

105. Ann-Sofie Dahl, *Partner Number One or NATO Ally Twenty-nine? Sweden and NATO Post-Libya,* Research Paper no. 82 (Rome: NATO Defense College, September 2012), 7–8.

106. Ibid., 8.

107. Göransson, interview with Holmström, "Försvar med tidsgräns."

108. NATO, "NATO Conducts Annual Crisis Management Exercise (CMX) and Cyber Coalition Exercise," press release (2012) 131, October 31, 2012, www.nato.int/cps/en/natolive/news_91115.htm?mode=pressrelease

109. Pauli Järvenp, "What Comes after Madrid? A View from Helsinki," *NATO Review* 45, no. 5 (September–October 1997): 30–33, www.nato.int/docu/review/1997/9705-10.htm. The author was then the deputy director general, Department of Defence Policy, Ministry of Defence of Finland.

110. Terhi Kinnunen, "Finland, Sweden to Help NATO in Iceland Air Policing," Reuters.com, October 30, 2012. NATO has specified that the Finnish and Swedish assets will be under Norway's "operational control" and that they "will not be placed under NATO's direct authority at any time." NATO, "NATO and Partners to Conduct Air-defence Flying Training over Iceland," last updated July 3, 2013, www.nato.int/cps/en/SID-AC424F4B-C704D6B7/natolive/news_102136.htm.

111. NATO, "NATO Conducts Annual Crisis Management Exercise (CMX) and Cyber Coalition Exercise," press release (2012) 131, www.nato.int/cps/en/natolive/news_91115.htm?mode=pressrelease; and "Hungary Has Performed Excellently on Two NATO Exercises," November 21, 2012, www.kormany.hu/en/ministry-of-defence/news/hungary-has-performed-excellently-on-two-nato-exercises.

112. In another cooperative step involving NATO Allies, Sweden in July 2013 proposed the establishment of a Nordic Battalion Force to be composed of troops from Denmark, Finland, Norway, and Sweden. Gerard O'Dwyer, "Sweden Proposes Nordic Battalion Force Plan," *Defense News,* July 25, 2013.

113. Most Allies have not publicly commented on possible applications for membership by Finland and Sweden. However, in October 2009, Rasa Jukneviciene, then the Lithuanian minister of defense, said, "We would welcome any further deepening of Sweden's and Finland's partnership and interaction with NATO; and Norway's and Iceland's (and EU member Denmark's)—with the European Security and Defence Policy. We would also full-heartedly support membership of those countries in the respective organizations if they chose to pursue it." Rasa Jukneviciene, *Latest Developments in European Security: A Baltic Perspective* (London: Chatham House, October 20, 2009), 5–6.

114. Jamie Shea quoted in Brian Whitmore, "NATO at 60: Has Expansion Reached Its End?" Radio Free Europe/Radio Liberty, March 31, 2009, www.rferl.org/content/Has_NATO_Expansion_Reached_Its_End/1565285.html.

115. Bruce Jackson quoted in Whitmore, "NATO at 60."

116. Karl-Heinz Kamp, *NATO Enlargement Reloaded,* 4.

117. Ambassador Ivo Daalder, U.S. permanent representative to the North Atlantic Council, remarks at Carnegie Europe, Brussels, June 17, 2013, http://nato.usmission.gov/sp-06172013.html.

118. Andrew J. Bacevich, "NATO at Twilight," *Los Angeles Times,* February 11, 2008, http://articles.latimes.com/2008/feb/11/opinion/oe-bacevich11.

119. Hillary Clinton, remarks at the North Atlantic Council Meeting, May 21, 2012.

120. Patrick Keller, *Spaltpilz im Bündnis: Neue Mitglieder für die NATO?,* Analysen und Argumente no. 119 (Berlin: Konrad-Adenauer-Stiftung, April 2013), 6.

9

Arms Control, Nonproliferation, and Disarmament

Arms control, disarmament, and nonproliferation issues have implications for the Alliance's defense and deterrence posture, including its conventional and nuclear capabilities. The Allies have an interest in defining deterrence and defense policies that complement and reinforce their objectives regarding arms control, disarmament, and nonproliferation.

Although NATO itself has never been a party to an arms control agreement, negotiations and proposals concerning constraints on military forces and activities have been elements of the security and defense strategies of NATO Allies since the 1950s. The most prominent arms control agreements in the history of the Alliance have been bilateral (between Moscow and Washington) or multilateral. The multilateral accords of consequence for the NATO Allies have been both universal (open for signature by all countries, such as the 1968 Treaty on the Non-Proliferation of Nuclear Weapons) and regional (open for signature by countries in a specific geographic zone, such as the 1990 Conventional Armed Forces in Europe Treaty).

Despite disagreements on specific issues, the Allies have a long history of taking common positions on arms control and disarmament measures, both bilateral and multilateral. These common positions have often reflected compromises on national policies, even during the Cold War.

While the Alliance itself has never been a party to an arms control negotiation, the NATO Allies have on some issues engaged in systematic consultations and policy coordination. As noted in chapter 1, the Allies defined "contributing actively to arms control, non-proliferation and disarmament" as an element of "cooperative security" in the 2010 Strategic Concept.[1]

The Alliance's role as a mechanism for consultations concerning such policies has grown more significant over the decades. During the initial Cold War years, this role was comparatively marginal, but it gained greater importance during the 1970s and 1980s with the negotiations on Mutual and Balanced Force Reductions (MBFR) and Intermediate-range Nuclear Forces (INF). Since the end of the Cold War, the Allies have sought to raise the public "profile" of NATO's contribution to arms control, disarmament, and nonproliferation.

NATO and Cold War Arms Control

The Alliance's involvement in diplomatic measures intended to advance its security goals has developed in tandem with their pursuit by NATO governments. At NATO's first summit meeting, convened in Paris in 1957, the Allies recalled that

> in the course of this year, the Western countries taking part in the London Disarmament talks put forward to the Soviet Union, with the unanimous agreement of NATO, a series of concrete proposals providing, subject to effective controls:
>
> - for reduction of all armaments and military forces;
> - for the cessation of the production of fissionable material for weapons purposes;
> - for the reduction of existing stocks of nuclear weapons;
> - for the suspension of nuclear weapons tests; [and]
> - for measures to guard against the risk of surprise attack.[2]

Although the Soviet Union rejected these specific proposals, Allied interest in negotiated constraints on military capabilities persisted.

As noted in chapter 1, beginning in the late 1950s and especially after the construction of the Berlin Wall in 1961 and the Cuban Missile Crisis in 1962, the Allies began to subordinate their previous preoccupation with political order in Europe to arms control and the quest for East-West détente. In the 1967 Harmel Report the Allies backed arms control and disarmament measures as an expression of their "will . . . to work for an effective détente with the East."[3]

In the 1960s two NATO governments—Britain and the United States—took the lead in negotiating two key multilateral arms control and nonproliferation measures in cooperation with the Soviet Union, the 1963 Partial Test Ban Treaty (PTBT) and the 1968 Treaty on the Non-Proliferation of Nuclear Weapons (NPT). Except for France, all NATO governments acceded to these treaties during the Cold War period,[4] and all endorsed the U.S.-Soviet negotiations concerning limits on intercontinental nuclear delivery systems.

Italy and the Federal Republic of Germany stipulated in acceding to the NPT that they expected continuing protection from U.S. extended nuclear deterrence in the NATO framework. The Bonn government stated in 1969 when signing the NPT that "the Federal Government [of Germany] understands that . . . the security of the Federal Republic of Germany and its allies shall continue to be ensured by NATO or an equivalent security system."[5] The Italian government noted "the full compatibility of the Treaty with the existing security agreements."[6]

It should be noted in this regard that the NATO Allies have consistently upheld the view that NATO's nuclear-sharing arrangements are compatible with the NPT. In July 1968, Dean Rusk, then the U.S. secretary of state, wrote to President Lyndon Johnson about the NPT as follows:

> It does not deal with allied consultations and planning on nuclear defense so long as no transfer of nuclear weapons or control over them results. . . . It does not deal with arrangements for deployment of nuclear weapons within allied territory as these do not involve any transfer of

nuclear weapons or control over them unless and until a decision were made to go to war, at which time the treaty would no longer be controlling.[7]

Although some nuclear disarmament advocates have argued that the Alliance's nuclear-sharing arrangements violate Articles I and II of the NPT, these articles resulted from intense U.S.-Soviet negotiations in the mid- to late 1960s. The United States made clear to the Soviet Union, the NATO Allies, and other governments its view that the NATO nuclear-sharing arrangements were consistent with Articles I and II of the NPT. In 1969 Spurgeon Keeny of the National Security Council Staff wrote to Henry Kissinger, then the president's assistant for national security affairs, as follows with regard to these two articles:

> These articles, which were the product of a long negotiation with the Soviet Union and our NATO allies, were designed as a compromise that protects existing NATO arrangements but precludes arrangements such as the MLF/ANF.[8] The precise implication of these articles on present and future arrangements was originally a matter of serious concern to our NATO allies, particularly the FRG [Federal Republic of Germany]. To resolve these questions, our interpretations of these articles were given to the Soviet Union and our NATO allies during the course of the negotiations.... While we did not ask the Soviet Union to agree with our interpretations, it was made clear that they would be made part of the legislative record of the treaty and that formal Soviet objections would present serious problems.[9]

Despite Moscow's previously expressed disapproval of NATO nuclear-sharing arrangements,[10] the Soviet Union accepted the U.S. position on NATO nuclear sharing. Moscow may have done so owing in part to the fact that Soviet policy regarding the NPT was "directed primarily at preventing West German acquisition of nuclear weapons."[11] Moscow and Washington compromised on language in Articles I and II of the NPT that would permit the continuation of NATO's nuclear-sharing arrangements, and Moscow seems to have accepted this interpretation because of U.S. assurances that these arrangements would not enable the Federal Republic of Germany to become a nuclear power.[12] It appears that the Soviet Union wished to establish a treaty constraining Bonn's nuclear options before engaging in the U.S.-Soviet negotiations that became known as the Strategic Arms Limitation Talks (SALT).[13] According to Raymond Garthoff, "It was, as the Russians like to say, not by accident that West Germany signed the NPT and the SALT talks began within the same 24-hour period."[14]

The 1972 U.S.-Soviet SALT agreements consisted of an interim agreement on strategic offensive arms and the Anti-Ballistic Missile (ABM) Treaty. The latter was especially significant, owing to its unlimited duration and the restrictions it imposed on U.S. and Soviet defenses against "strategic ballistic missiles." After the 1974 amendment to the ABM Treaty, the USSR and the United States could each maintain only a single ABM deployment area. The ABM Treaty ruled out any U.S. construction of strategic missile defenses in NATO Europe, as well as any transfers of U.S. technology for such defenses to third parties, including the NATO Allies. The U.S. decision in 2001 to withdraw from the ABM Treaty, effective in June 2002, nonetheless provoked some concerns among Allied observers. Their anxieties included the prospect that U.S. withdrawal from the treaty might lead to U.S.-Russian confrontation, provoke an "arms race," undermine strategic stability, and terminate nuclear arms control. These fears seemed to be proved groundless when (1) the Russians expressed only muted regrets about the end of the ABM Treaty and (2) Russia and the United States signed the Moscow Treaty, providing for further strategic nuclear force reductions, in May 2002.[15]

While the NATO Allies of the United States generally endorsed the U.S.-Soviet negotiations concerning limits on strategic nuclear delivery systems, and deferred to U.S. judgments about strategic nuclear force requirements in support of NATO's security, experts in NATO Europe raised questions about the security implications of some U.S.-Soviet agreements, including the 1973 Agreement on the Prevention of Nuclear War and the 1979 SALT II Treaty.

The Soviet Union proposed the Agreement on the Prevention of Nuclear War in 1972. Henry Kissinger, who was then the national security adviser, described the original Soviet draft as follows: "The proposed agreement did not preclude the use of nuclear weapons in a war involving NATO and the Warsaw Pact; however, their use would have to be confined to the territory of allies; employment against the territory of the United States and the Soviet Union was proscribed. . . . It would have been difficult to draw up a more bald or cynical definition of condominium."[16]

In negotiating the final text of the Agreement on the Prevention of Nuclear War the United States did its best to limit the damage it entailed to U.S. relations with other governments.[17] However, according to a leading French diplomatic historian, Georges-Henri Soutou, "This agreement was understood in Paris as tantamount to a Soviet-American condominium over Europe."[18] Kissinger summed up his judgment as to its impact on U.S. alliance relations in Europe as follows: "We gained a marginally useful text. But the result was too subtle; the negotiation too secret; the effort too protracted; the necessary explanations to allies and China too complex to have the desired impact. The Europeans were especially sensitive . . . allied unity eluded us despite the intensive consultation."[19]

The 1973 U.S.-Soviet Agreement on the Prevention of Nuclear War was not as significant in the history of arms control as major Washington-Moscow accords such as SALT I and SALT II, but it illustrated recurring concerns among the European Allies during the Cold War. Their dependence on U.S. nuclear protection made them susceptible to anxieties about (1) a possible superpower agreement at their expense and (2) well-meaning U.S. decisions that might unwittingly result in an erosion of deterrence and strategic stability.

A number of expert observers in NATO Europe criticized the SALT II Treaty, signed by U.S. president Jimmy Carter and Soviet general secretary Leonid Brezhnev in 1979, owing to their judgment that the United States had neglected European security interests. Their specific criticisms included the judgments that the treaty provisions (1) would assist the Soviet Union in gaining ICBM-based counterforce superiority; (2) would constrain NATO's theater nuclear force modernization, notably with regard to cruise missiles; and (3) would not address the growing Soviet advantage in intermediate-range missiles (such as the SS-20) and bombers (such as the Backfire).[20] For example, Laurence Martin, a prominent British scholar in strategic studies, wrote, "Tolerating the Soviet Backfire bomber so long as it is not deployed in an anti-United States mode—that is, so long as it is deployed against areas bordering the Warsaw Pact—is only the most explicit instance of going beyond merely neglecting threats to allies to actually diverting them in that direction, behavior of which Stalin suspected Chamberlain in 1939."[21]

European Allied dissatisfaction with the perceived implications of the U.S.-Soviet SALT negotiations was one of the factors leading to the Alliance's December 1979 double-track decision. In October 1977 Helmut Schmidt, then the West German chancellor, called attention to the apparent impact of the stalemate in U.S. and Soviet intercontinental forces: "SALT neutralizes their strategic nuclear capabilities. In Europe this magnifies the significance of the disparities between East and West in nuclear tactical and conventional weapons."[22]

Schmidt's speech is often cited as the point of departure for NATO's policy debate regarding intermediate-range nuclear missiles. The NATO Allies formulated the 1979 double-track plan mainly in reaction to the Soviet deployment of nuclear-armed intermediate-range SS-20 missiles in the context of the U.S.-Soviet strategic stalemate. The NATO Allies proposed to deploy 108 Pershing II ballistic missiles and 464 ground-launched cruise missiles, but made clear that success in arms control negotiations would enable them to modify the scale of the proposed intermediate-range missile deployments.[23]

In the event, the 1987 U.S.-Soviet INF Treaty called for the elimination of all ground-launched U.S. and Soviet intermediate-range missiles, both ballistic and cruise, with ranges between 500 and 5,500 km.[24] At the end of the Cold War, all the Allies supported the conclusion of the INF Treaty and the 1990 Conventional Armed Forces in Europe (CFE) Treaty with the states of the moribund Warsaw Pact, as well as the 1991 U.S.-Soviet Strategic Arms Reduction Treaty (START) and the 1991–1992 Presidential Nuclear Initiatives undertaken by Moscow and Washington.

During the Cold War the MBFR negotiations constituted the main conventional arms control forum in Europe. Conducted in Vienna by a group of NATO and Warsaw Pact member states from 1973 to 1989,[25] the MBFR negotiations were inconclusive. Lessons learned from the MBFR negotiating effort nonetheless contributed to the formulation of the 1990 CFE Treaty.[26]

NATO and Post–Cold War Arms Control

Since the end of the Cold War in 1989–1991 the NATO Allies have supported Russian-U.S. arms control negotiations and agreements, as well as the establishment and improvement of multilateral arms control regimes, notably with regard to non-proliferation of chemical, biological, and nuclear weapons, often termed weapons of mass destruction (WMD).[27]

At the April 2008 Bucharest Summit the Allies declared that "arms control, disarmament and non-proliferation will continue to make an important contribution to peace, security, and stability and, in this regard, to preventing the spread and use of Weapons of Mass Destruction and their means of delivery. We took note of the report prepared for us on raising NATO's profile in this field."[28] The report "on raising NATO's profile in this field" is known within the Alliance as the German-Norwegian initiative.[29]

The references to the objective of "raising NATO's profile" in both the April 2008 and April 2009 summit declarations demonstrate that it has gained acceptance throughout the Alliance, despite the initial reservations of some allies and the fact that NATO, per se, is not a party to any arms control treaty. The Allies highlighted the importance of "public awareness" in the April 2009 Strasbourg/Kehl Summit Declaration: "NATO and Allies should continue contributing to international efforts in the area of arms control, disarmament and non-proliferation. We aim at achieving a higher level of public awareness of NATO's contribution in these fields."[30]

At the same time, it should be noted that, as with other areas of policy, the NATO Allies have differed regarding arms control, disarmament, and nonproliferation priorities. In June 2012, a Polish expert said that "most of the new member states have been wary of the calls to use the DDPR [Deterrence and Defense Posture Review] process to expand NATO's role in arms control and disarmament. While being generally supportive of the international non-proliferation and arms control efforts, as well as being active in the new NPT Review process, the countries of the Central and Eastern European region wanted the DDPR to concentrate on the NATO defense potential, not the disarmament aspect. They value the conservative, defense-oriented Alliance, which 'does' non-proliferation and arms control as a by-product of its primary mission." From the viewpoint of these Allies, the Polish expert concluded, NATO's proper role with regard to arms control and disarmament is as "a coordinator rather than a leader," and the DDPR rightly rejected "lead by example" proposals to make further unilateral reductions in U.S. nonstrategic nuclear weapons in Europe.[31]

A Lithuanian scholar said in June 2012 that "NATO is already a global leader in disarmament" but dreadful at communicating its steps in support of disarmament, such as the drastic reductions in U.S. nuclear weapons in Europe since the early 1970s.[32] From this perspective, the Allies have only themselves to blame for their lack of a positive arms control "profile" in public perceptions.

A related disagreement among the Allies has been whether to institute a dedicated committee on arms control in addition to their long-established High Level Task Force (HLTF) for conventional arms control. At the November 2010 Lisbon Summit the Allies agreed "to establish a Committee to provide advice on WMD control and disarmament" in support of the DDPR that they commissioned at the same time.[33] The WMD Control and Disarmament Committee provided input to the DDPR, but some Allies—particularly France and some of the new Allies in Central and Eastern Europe—took a cautious and skeptical approach to its deliberations. In their view, the Alliance's traditional methods of dealing with arms control, disarmament, and nonproliferation were sufficient, and it would distort the Alliance's priorities to elevate this field of effort with an additional permanent committee. In contrast, Germany, Norway, and some other Allies favored the establishment of a permanent WMD Control and Disarmament Committee, partly in order to raise the Alliance's public "profile" in such matters.

The Allies reached the following compromise at the Chicago Summit in May 2012: "Allies believe that the Weapons of Mass Destruction Control and Disarmament Committee has played a useful role in the [Deterrence and Defense Posture] review and agree to establish a committee as a consultative and advisory forum, with its mandate to be agreed by the NAC following the Summit."[34] This wording suggested that a behind-the-scenes struggle among the Allies would continue, with the name and mandate of the new committee yet to be negotiated.

In February 2013, after eight months of negotiations, the Allies agreed on terms of reference for a new Special Advisory and Consultative Arms Control, Disarmament and Non-Proliferation Committee. These terms of reference remain classified. It has been reported, however, that they state that the committee will be disbanded when the North Atlantic Council agrees that it has completed its work. This implies that the new committee, sometimes called simply the ACDC (Arms Control and Disarmament Committee), is likely to be de facto a permanent body, as preferred by Germany, despite France's arguments for a committee with a specified life span.[35]

The new committee will reportedly meet in two formats. In the advisory format, chaired by the assistant secretary general for political affairs and security policy, the committee will examine possible confidence-building measures for U.S. and Russian nonstrategic nuclear weapons in Europe. In the consultative format, chaired by the United States, Washington will meet with the other Allies about U.S.-Russian interactions on strategic stability, strategic nuclear arms control, and related matters. The committee's terms of reference reportedly affirm that it will not affect the proceedings of the HLTF regarding conventional arms control, but the Allies have not yet determined its relationship with the High Level Group, the key advisory panel for the Nuclear Planning Group.[36]

Although NATO is not itself a party to any arms control agreement, all the Allies are parties to fundamental multilateral accords such as the NPT. NATO has historically served as a forum for information exchanges related to arms control, disarmament, and nonproliferation issues. Moreover, in conventional arms control negotiations and treaty implementation matters NATO has had "a direct coordinating role."[37] Since 1986 the Allies have determined their conventional arms control policies in an HLTF presided by the deputy secretary general.[38]

In the November 2010 Lisbon Summit Declaration, the Allies confirmed that they "will continue to support arms control, disarmament and non-proliferation efforts."[39] The Allies summed up their current policies on arms control, disarmament, and nonproliferation in a single long paragraph in the 2010 Strategic Concept:

> NATO seeks its security at the lowest possible level of forces. Arms control, disarmament and non-proliferation contribute to peace, security and stability, and should ensure undiminished security for all Alliance members. We will continue to play our part in reinforcing arms control and in promoting disarmament of both conventional weapons and weapons of mass destruction, as well as non-proliferation efforts:
>
> - We are resolved to seek a safer world for all and to create the conditions for a world without nuclear weapons in accordance with the goals of the Nuclear Non-Proliferation Treaty, in a way that promotes international stability, and is based on the principle of undiminished security for all.
>
> - With the changes in the security environment since the end of the Cold War, we have dramatically reduced the number of nuclear weapons stationed in Europe and our reliance on nuclear weapons in NATO strategy. We will seek to create the conditions for further reductions in the future.
>
> - In any future reductions, our aim should be to seek Russian agreement to increase transparency on its nuclear weapons in Europe and relocate these weapons away from the territory of NATO members. Any further steps must take into account the disparity with the greater Russian stockpiles of short-range nuclear weapons.
>
> - We are committed to conventional arms control, which provides predictability, transparency and a means to keep armaments at the lowest possible level for stability. We will work to strengthen the conventional arms control regime in Europe on the basis of reciprocity, transparency and host-nation consent.
>
> - We will explore ways for our political means and military capabilities to contribute to international efforts to fight proliferation.[40]

Of the positions taken above, four stand out—the two global issues of WMD nonproliferation and nuclear disarmament, and the two regional issues of conventional arms control in Europe and reducing the numbers of nuclear weapons in Europe as well as reliance on nuclear weapons in NATO policy.

WMD Nonproliferation

Despite the political and strategic importance that the Allies attribute to WMD nonproliferation, they have not attempted to coordinate their positions on nuclear nonproliferation and deterrence matters in the United Nations or in the review conferences of the NPT.[41] As Roberto Zadra, then the deputy head of NATO's WMD Centre, wrote in 2007,

> the Allies have agreed to limit themselves to the monitoring of developments, to informal information exchanges, and to non-binding consultations.... NATO's role in terms of non-proliferation efforts, i.e. political and diplomatic efforts, remains relatively small. Declarations from NATO Summits and Communiqués from Foreign and Defense Ministers' meetings usually emphasize the Alliance's support for the NPT and its goals, but there is little measurable follow-up in terms of concrete action. These Communiqués are nonetheless important as they demonstrate the Alliance's overall commitment to the principles and objectives of the NPT.[42]

In 2009 the Allies adopted what they termed NATO's Strategic-Level Policy for Preventing the Proliferation of WMD and Defending Against Chemical, Biological, Radiological and Nuclear Threats. Among the many measures set forth in this document,

> Allies emphasise the importance of the implementation of and compliance with the Nuclear Non-Proliferation Treaty (NPT), Chemical Weapons Convention (CWC) and Biological and Toxin Weapons Convention (BWC), as well as relevant United Nations Security Council Resolutions such as UNSCR 1540. . . . Regular consultations, and information and intelligence sharing among Alliance members, partners, international organisations and national authorities, where appropriate, will help foster a common understanding of potential WMD proliferation threats by States and non-State actors, encourage its members, partners and other nations to fully comply with their arms control, disarmament and non-proliferation obligations and enhance the global response to WMD.[43]

Since arms control and disarmament treaties are concluded by states, not international organizations, NATO's main roles concerning conventions to ban or limit WMD consist of consultations, information sharing, and the coordination of national policies. It was not until 2010 that NATO was first invited to participate in an NPT Review Conference as an observer.[44]

The Allies have also issued declarations about specific developments in WMD proliferation. They condemned the nuclear weapons tests conducted by India and Pakistan in 1998,[45] and they deplored North Korea's ballistic missile and nuclear weapons tests in 2006, 2009, and 2013.[46] At their summit meetings in 2009, 2010, and 2012 the Allies called upon Iran and North Korea to comply with UN Security Council resolutions regarding their nuclear and other proliferation activities.[47] In May 2013 the NATO secretary general said with reference to the conflict in Syria that "any use of chemical weapons, whoever might have used chemical weapons . . . is a breach of international law and of course a matter of grave concern."[48]

As with the efforts against other global challenges, such as terrorism, the struggle against WMD proliferation involves many international organizations in addition to NATO. There is in fact some overlap between these efforts, as with the Proliferation Security Initiative and the Global Initiative to Combat Nuclear Terrorism. The Allies strive to avoid duplication and to make NATO's efforts complementary to those of the European Union, the United Nations, and the Organization for Security and Co-operation in Europe, among others.

NATO's May 2012 DDPR stated, "Arms control, disarmament and non-proliferation play *an important role* in the achievement of the Alliance's security objectives. Both the success and failure of these efforts can have a direct impact on the threat environment of NATO and therefore affect NATO's deterrence and defence posture."[49] The reference to the possible impact of failure is entirely pertinent to the Alliance's "threat environment." Nonproliferation regimes are at risk in the Middle East, owing in large part to Iran and its competitors, and the peril of new WMD capabilities adjacent to the Euro-Atlantic region is growing.

Nuclear Disarmament

Interest in nuclear disarmament has been constant since the introduction of nuclear weapons in world politics in 1945. Current efforts to analyze and pursue this objective often pay homage to the 2007 article by George Shultz, William Perry, Henry Kissinger, and Sam Nunn titled "A World Free of Nuclear Weapons."[50]

As noted earlier, in the 2010 Strategic Concept the Allies stated, "We are resolved to seek a safer world for all and to create the conditions for a world without nuclear weapons in accordance with the goals of the Nuclear Non-Proliferation Treaty, in a way that promotes international stability, and is based on the principle of undiminished security for all."

The Allies did not specify what conditions would have to be satisfied to achieve this objective, but the reference to the goals of the NPT suggests that some Allies may have Article VI of this treaty in mind, notably its call for "a treaty on general and complete disarmament under strict and effective international control."[51] In some statements the governments of France and the United Kingdom have indicated that they see general and complete disarmament as the appropriate context for total nuclear disarmament.[52]

Among other arguments for postponing their participation in nuclear arms control negotiations, London and Paris have historically highlighted the numerical disparity between their nuclear forces and those maintained by Moscow and Washington. In 1995, for example, Douglas Hurd, then the British foreign secretary, said, "even when START II is implemented, British nuclear forces will be considerably less than 10% of the total nuclear forces available to the US or Russia. But there is no doubt that a world in which US and Russian nuclear forces were counted in hundreds, rather than thousands, would be one in which Britain would respond to the challenge of multilateral talks on the global reduction of nuclear arms."[53] In 2009, the Foreign and Commonwealth Office declared, "We have made clear that when it will be useful to include in any negotiations the small proportion of the world's nuclear weapons that belong to the UK, we will willingly do so."[54]

In 1983 French president François Mitterrand announced three conditions to be satisfied before France could consider participating in nuclear arms control negotiations: (1) the reduction of the superpower nuclear arsenals to levels much closer to those of the other nuclear-weapon states; (2) limitations on defensive systems capable of neutralizing offensive deterrent forces (such as antimissile, antisubmarine, and antisatellite weaponry); and (3) significant progress in the reduction of the conventional force imbalances in Europe and the global elimination of chemical and biological weapons.[55]

The condition listed first has remained most prominent in subsequent French policy statements. François Rivasseau, a French diplomat, stated in 2005 that if the "considerable imbalance" between U.S. and Russian strategic nuclear forces and those of France were modified through a process of reductions, France "might envisage drawing the consequences from this."[56]

In 2010, Michel Miraillet, the director of the Délégation aux Affaires Stratégiques in the Ministry of Defense (a post equivalent to the U.S. under secretary of defense for policy), wrote, "We can understand that in a 'second nuclear age' certain powers will be in a position to further curb the role of nuclear capabilities in their defense policy and to reduce their arsenals. But as for the role of nuclear capabilities in its defense, France cannot follow the same path, and it will maintain the foundations of its nuclear doctrine as it has publicly articulated them for years."[57]

In its April 2010 Nuclear Posture Review report, the U.S. government indicated that "very demanding" conditions would have to be fulfilled to safely dispose of nuclear weapons:

> The conditions that would ultimately permit the United States and others to give up their nuclear weapons without risking greater international instability and insecurity are very demanding. Among those are the resolution of regional disputes that can motivate rival states to acquire and maintain nuclear weapons, success in halting the proliferation of nuclear weapons, much greater transparency into the programs and capabilities of key countries of concern, verification methods and technologies capable of detecting violations of disarmament obligations, and enforcement measures strong and credible enough to deter such violations. Clearly, such conditions do not exist today. But we can—and must— work actively to create those conditions.[58]

One of the most intriguing aspects of this U.S. policy statement is the reference to "enforcement measures strong and credible enough to deter such violations." The report suggested that this would require a U.S. capability to reconstitute nuclear forces as a hedge against another state's noncompliance and misbehavior: "In a world where nuclear weapons had been eliminated but nuclear knowledge remains, having a strong infrastructure and base of human capital would be essential to deterring cheating or breakout, or, if deterrence failed, responding in a timely fashion."[59]

While the NATO Allies collectively have expressed interest in establishing "the conditions for a world without nuclear weapons," it appears that they have not reached any consensus on how to define these conditions and that only the three nuclear-weapon states in the Alliance have published policy statements about the conditions under which they might undertake nuclear force reductions with a view toward nuclear disarmament.

Scholars have suggested that a range of conditions would have to be satisfied to make a world without nuclear weapons feasible, including the resolution of flashpoints such as Kashmir, Palestine, and Taiwan; the development of a substitute for nuclear-weapons as the basis for U.S. central and extended deterrence; decisions by Britain, China, France, India, Israel, Pakistan, Russia, and the United States that they have no further need for nuclear weapons; the termination of the Iranian and North Korean nuclear weapons programs; the establishment of a world government capable of acting against possible violators of a prospective Nuclear Weapons Convention; and the provision of means to manage the potential instabilities resident in national hedges against a nuclear rearmament race.[60]

It is noteworthy that the Allies seek "to create the conditions for a world without nuclear weapons ... in a way that promotes international stability." Some analysts argue that reductions to low numbers of nuclear weapons or efforts to abolish them entirely could in some circumstances create new instabilities in international politics. Thomas Schelling, for example, has drawn attention to the risk of a competition in capabilities for rapid nuclear rearmament. In his view,

> a "world without nuclear weapons" would be a world in which the United States, Russia, Israel, China, and half a dozen or a dozen other countries would have hair-trigger mobilization plans to rebuild nuclear weapons and mobilize or commandeer delivery systems, and would have prepared targets to preempt other nations' nuclear facilities, all in a high-alert status, with practice drills and secure emergency communications. Every crisis would be a nuclear crisis, any war could become a nuclear war. The urge to preempt would dominate; whoever gets the first few weapons will coerce or preempt. It would be a nervous world.[61]

Schelling's vision might be overly optimistic in that it does not take into account the possibility of asymmetries based on national objectives and idiosyncratic politi cal and strategic cultures. Some countries might be more rigorous and ambitious than others in maintaining reconstitution and mobilization capabilities, and/or more assiduous and effective in concealing them. Moreover, the strategic assessments of some countries might lead them to maintain such capabilities with greater determination. For example, as long as Moscow and Beijing view the United States as having substantial conventional military superiority, they might well be more convinced than Washington of the need to maintain and improve their nuclear reconstitution and mobilization capabilities, even in a context of budgetary stringency and competing national priorities.

The U.S. government has argued that future negotiated reductions must include nonstrategic and nondeployed nuclear weapons.[62] However, Russia currently manifests little interest in further negotiations, especially negotiations limited to devising constraints on nuclear arms, including the "aggregate ceiling" with "freedom-to-mix" approach advocated by the U.S. government. Russian leaders have responded to the U.S. proposals by setting out demands for an even more comprehensive negotiations agenda that seem deliberately framed to be impractical. Russian foreign minister Sergey Lavrov has, for example, urged consideration of "the totality of factors that could erode strategic stability," including "the prospect of weapons in outer space, plans for the creation of non-nuclear strategic missile systems, the unilateral strategic missile defense buildup, and the growing imbalance in conventional weapons."[63]

In February 2012 Vladimir Putin, then Russia's prime minister, said that Russia would not discard nuclear weapons unless it could acquire conventional weapons of comparable potency: "We will only abandon nuclear weapons when we have such systems, and not a day earlier. . . . No one should have any illusions about that." Putin added that foreign states "are ahead of us in some respects, especially precision-guided weapons" that are "comparable in their effects to weapons of mass destruction."[64]

Despite the acclaim accorded President Obama's April 2009 Prague speech, including his commitment to pursue "the peace and security of a world without nuclear weapons,"[65] some Allied observers have questioned the merits of the Alliance's agreed-upon goal of nuclear disarmament. At a June 2012 workshop, a French observer said that eliminating nuclear weapons "would not automatically" create "a safer world for all," to use the phrase in the 2010 Strategic Concept and the 2012 DDPR,[66] and that it is not clear how to achieve that objective. At the same event, a German participant asked, with reference to the goal of a world without nuclear weapons, "How could we prevent conventional wars in such a world?"[67] In July 2012 another French observer said, "It would be wiser to emphasize strategic stability instead of pushing for deep reductions in nuclear weapons and nuclear disarmament."[68]

With regard to the pursuit of radical reductions in U.S. and Russian nuclear weapons, NATO Allies would probably welcome assurances that the U.S. approach would be cautious, deliberate, incremental, and closely coordinated with U.S. allies.

The March 2010 speech by the president of Italy, Giorgio Napolitano, is noteworthy in this regard. Napolitano said, "While deterrence still plays a fundamental role in preventing nuclear wars, NATO should consider how to contribute to the nuclear-free world goal of President Obama's Prague speech. Small, well-thought, concrete and concerted steps can go a long way in creating momentum toward the final goal."[69] According to an Italian observer, President Napolitano's speech was prepared by the Italian Ministry of Foreign Affairs and the Ministry of Defense, and it expressed "the Italian preference for small and carefully considered steps in the direction of nuclear disarmament."[70]

The international political context does not appear favorable to nuclear disarmament, despite NATO and U.S. support for the concept and its reiteration in President Obama's June 2013 speech in Berlin. The U.S. president said, "After a comprehensive review, I've determined that we can ensure the security of America and our allies, and maintain a strong and credible strategic deterrent, while reducing our deployed strategic nuclear weapons by up to one-third. And I intend to seek negotiated cuts with Russia to move beyond Cold War nuclear postures."[71] In view of the ceiling in the 2010 New START Treaty of 1,550 in 2018 for U.S. and Russian deployed strategic nuclear warheads, this statement was a call for reductions to approximately 1,000 deployed strategic nuclear weapons for each side.

If New START counting rules were retained, however, the actual number of deployed strategic nuclear warheads on each side might be much higher. According to the New START Treaty, "One nuclear warhead shall be counted for each deployed heavy bomber."[72] Moscow insisted on this counting rule in conjunction with its rejection of the transparency and verification measures for bombers sought by the United States. In Pavel Podvig's words, "The United States said that it was ready to count bombers with their actual weapons load, but Russia objected to the transparency provisions that this arrangement would entail."[73] As a result, to cite Rose Gottemoeller of the State Department, "the parties agreed to an attribution rule of one warhead per nuclear-capable heavy bomber rather than count them as zero."[74] Hans Kristensen estimated in 2010 that, under this counting rule, approximately 450 U.S. warheads and 860 Russian warheads would not be counted.[75] Moreover, it should be recalled that the New START Treaty does not cover nondeployed or nonstrategic weapons. The nominal limit of 1,550 warheads in New START must be kept in perspective as applying only to certain categories of deployed weapons in accordance with specific counting rules.

Despite this qualification, Foreign Minister Sergey Lavrov and other high-level Russian officials responded to President Obama's initiative by repeating a list of preconditions for further negotiations on nuclear arms reductions, including a treaty limiting U.S. missile defenses, the full implementation of the New START Treaty objectives, the removal of all U.S. nonstrategic nuclear weapons from Europe, and the participation of other nuclear-weapon states in the reductions negotiations and process.[76] Alexander Yakovenko, the Russian ambassador to the United Kingdom and a former deputy foreign minister (2005–2011), said that the negotiations should include not only the five NPT-recognized nuclear-weapon states (Britain, China, France, Russia, and the United States) but "all states which in fact possess nuclear weapons." Yakovenko reiterated the Russian position that the negotiations should encompass "the entire complex of factors that influence . . . strategic stability," such as missile defense, "non-nuclear strategic weapons," "the issue of placing weapons in space," and "a serious imbalance in the sphere of conventional weapons in Europe."[77]

It is noteworthy in this regard that President Putin spoke in Saint Petersburg on the same day that President Obama called for U.S. and Russian nuclear arms reductions in Berlin. Putin said that the 1987 Soviet decision to conclude the INF Treaty with the United States was "debatable to say the least," given the restrictions it imposed on ground-based missiles and the fact that "nearly all of our neighbours are developing these kinds of weapons systems." In addition to hinting that Russia might withdraw from the INF Treaty,[78] Putin drew attention to the U.S. strategic missile defense program, and "increasing talk among military analysts about the theoretical possibility of a first disarming, disabling strike, even against nuclear powers." Putin referred to foreign powers developing "high-precision conventional weapons systems that in their strike capabilities come close to strategic nuclear weapons," and concluded that Russia must invest in "air and space defense" in order to "ensure our strategic deterrent forces remain effective."[79]

The contrasting statements by President Obama and President Putin reflect their divergent points of departure. Russia and the United States disagree on acceptable terms for nuclear arms reductions because their policies differ on the utility of nuclear weapons. In December 2012, the U.S. National Intelligence Council summed up this difference as follows: "Nuclear ambitions in the US and Russia over the last 20 years have evolved in opposite directions. Reducing the role of nuclear weapons in US security strategy is a US objective, while Russia is pursuing new concepts and capabilities for expanding the role of nuclear weapons in its security strategy."[80]

Alexander Golts and other Russian experts hold that Moscow opposes further reductions in its nuclear arsenal for status as well as security reasons.[81] The prospects for a U.S.-Russian agreement on nuclear disarmament objectives appear remote in this context. Even the reductions envisaged by the United States in a follow-on to the

New START Treaty seem distant. At present their complex potential implications for strategic stability appear theoretical and improbable.[82]

Conventional Arms Control in Europe

As with the objective of reducing the number of nuclear weapons in Europe, the prospects for conventional arms control in Europe depend mainly on Russia.[83] Moscow suspended its compliance with the 1990 CFE Treaty in 2007. This treaty, it will be recalled, established limits on the numbers of battle tanks, combat aircraft, heavy artillery pieces, armored combat vehicles, and attack helicopters that the treaty parties could deploy in Europe.

The NATO Allies alluded obliquely to one of the reasons for the current stalemate regarding CFE when they stated in the 2010 Strategic Concept, "We will work to strengthen the conventional arms control regime in Europe on the basis of reciprocity, transparency and host-nation consent."[84] Russia has maintained military forces in Georgia and Moldova since the 1990s without the consent of these countries, despite having pledged at Istanbul in 1999 to remove them.

The NATO Allies have consistently cited Russia's failure to honor its 1999 Istanbul commitments concerning its forces in Georgia and Moldova as the principal reason why none of the Allies has ratified the 1999 Adapted CFE Treaty. As noted in a NATO report, "Both of these states have made clear that they will not ratify the Adapted CFE as long as Russian military forces remain on their territory without their consent, which is a violation of Article IV of the CFE Treaty and also would be a violation of Article IV of the Adapted CFE Treaty."[85] The long-standing position of the NATO allies, as noted in the Riga Summit Declaration, has been that "fulfilment of the remaining Istanbul commitments on the Republic of Georgia and the Republic of Moldova will create the conditions for Allies and other States Parties to move forward on ratification of the Adapted CFE Treaty."[86] The Allies have maintained this position but have devised a "parallel actions package" designed to address certain Russian concerns, bring Russia back into compliance with the CFE Treaty, and move forward with ratification of the Adapted CFE Treaty.[87] The Russians maintain that NATO's conditionality on ratifying the Adapted CFE Treaty is an illegitimate "political" interference in their bilateral relations with Georgia and Moldova.

Other Russian concerns include the fact that NATO enlargement was not envisaged when the CFE Treaty was concluded in 1990 and that all non-Soviet former members of the Warsaw Pact have become NATO Allies, and three former Soviet republics (the Baltic states) have also become NATO Allies. The Russians agreed that in the 1999 Adapted CFE Treaty the "group limits" originally established for the NATO state parties and the Warsaw Pact state parties would be replaced by national ceilings. Owing to the fact that the non-Soviet former Warsaw Pact members have now all become NATO Allies, the legal ceilings for NATO treaty-limited equipment in the aggregate have been raised. This fact is qualified by the shrinking of defense spending and military capabilities in most NATO countries; the actual holdings of treaty-limited equipment are well below the treaty-authorized ceilings. From a Russian perspective, however, the treaty limits on national holdings seem unbalanced and "completely arbitrary."[88]

The Russians have complained that the Baltic states are not parties to the CFE Treaty, despite the fact that these states (and Slovenia) have expressed an intention to accede to the Adapted CFE Treaty, once it is ratified and enters into force.[89] Some Russian commentators have argued that, in addition to the NATO nations, "neutral" European states such as Austria, Finland, Ireland, Sweden, and Switzerland, and former Yugoslav republics not yet in NATO should be parties to "an all-European conventional arms control regime," on the grounds that "practically all of them maintain partnership with NATO, and many participated in NATO-led peacekeeping operations."[90]

The Russians have also found the CFE Treaty's flank limits an irksome constraint on their flexibility, notably in the Caucasus, even though the CFE parties agreed to adjust the flank limits in 1996. Some analysts have noted that Russia's suspension of compliance with the CFE Treaty in 2007 enabled it to disregard the treaty's restrictions on equipment concentrations in the Caucasus in the period prior to the August 2008 Russian intervention in Georgia.[91]

The NATO Allies declared at the 2010 Lisbon Summit,

> We are committed to conventional arms control, which provides predictability, transparency, and a means to keep armaments at the lowest possible level for security. ... Building on the CFE Treaty of 1990, the Agreement on Adaptation of 1999, and existing political commitments, our goal would be to take a significant step toward ensuring the continued viability of conventional arms control in Europe and strengthening our common security.[92]

In the same statement, however, the Allies noted that there were limits to their patience in waiting for Russia to honor its 1999 Istanbul commitments and to terminate its suspension of compliance with the CFE Treaty. "The results of our work in the coming weeks and months will guide our future decisions on continued implementation of CFE obligations, given that, as we said at the Strasbourg/Kehl Summit, the current situation, where NATO CFE Allies implement the Treaty while Russia does not, cannot continue indefinitely."[93]

The prospects for Russia's return to compliance with the CFE Treaty appear poor in the foreseeable future, notably in light of Russia's continuing military presence in two regions of Georgia (Abkhazia and South Ossetia) and its recognition of these territories as independent states. In November 2012, Alexander Grushko, Russia's envoy to NATO, said, "If the focus is on arms control, not some political problems, there are chances that a substantive discussion could begin on what kind of arms control is needed today."[94] Given the probability that Moscow will continue to regard its military deployments in Georgia and Moldova as "political" issues distinct from arms control, the prospects for a revival of conventional arms control in Europe are not encouraging. As Jeffrey McCausland has noted, the Russians insist that they "cannot accept any language . . . that recognizes host nation consent for stationed forces as an essential principle."[95]

The NATO Allies nonetheless remain reluctant to abandon the CFE regime and continue to hope for a change in Russian policy. In November 2011, four years after Russia suspended its compliance with the CFE Treaty, the United States and the other NATO Allies party to the CFE Treaty announced that they "would cease carrying out certain obligations" under the CFE Treaty with respect to Russia.[96] These include annual data exchanges, notifications of military activities, and on-site inspections, if requested by Russia. The NATO Allies party to the CFE Treaty are continuing on an indefinite basis to implement their treaty obligations with all parties to the treaty other than Russia.[97] At the May 2012 Chicago Summit the NATO Allies party to the CFE Treaty recalled that "the decisions taken in November 2011 to cease implementing certain CFE obligations with regard to the Russian Federation are reversible, should the Russian Federation return to full implementation."[98]

In the current context, actual holdings of CFE treaty-limited equipment are well below the authorized ceilings, and from a political-military perspective the CFE regime's most valuable elements are the transparency and verification measures, including information exchanges and inspections.

Even if the CFE Treaty parties all returned to full implementation of the treaty's verification and transparency regime, however, it is not clear that this would result in their ratification of the 1999 Adapted CFE Treaty. Aside from the problems of Russian noncompliance, particularly with regard to Moscow's disregard for the host-nation consent principle in Georgia and Moldova, conventional arms control in Europe faces problems more fundamental than Russia's suspension of compliance with the CFE Treaty. As a British expert pointed out in June 2012, "Doctrines and force structures have changed. Holdings of heavy equipment are no longer the right metric, and there is no agreement on what the right metric should be." In his view, "Given the continuing flux in force structure and dominant technologies, parties will resist obligations or constraints that may turn out to be inconsistent with military requirements. Building confidence and reducing uncertainty will have to be the dominant aims of arms control if there are no realistically acceptable formal balances to be calculated and agreed to."[99]

By this logic, the parties to the CFE Treaty and other interested nations—notably the new NATO Allies not party to the treaty—may find it in their interest to return to the humbler but critical goals of defining meaningful and durable confidence-building measures. Such measures, designed to provide transparency and assurance of "the absence of feared threats,"[100] could help to build the trust necessary for more ambitious treaty constraints.[101]

It should be recognized, however, that the Russians might reject a more modest approach to conventional arms control starting with information exchanges and other confidence-building measures. The Russians have argued for a sharply different approach to conventional arms control.

In May 2013, at a conference in Moscow, Russian defense minister Sergey Shoygu referred to the "death" of the CFE Treaty, while Russian foreign minister Sergey Lavrov alluded to its "collapse."[102] Despite this categorical language, Russia's official position remains that it has not withdrawn from the CFE regime but has only "suspended" its observance of the treaty obligations. Russian officials have argued that the NATO Allies should ratify the 1999 Adapted CFE Treaty and make it the basis for negotiating a revised conventional arms control agreement or simply negotiate a new treaty, consigning the CFE regime to history. The Russians have argued that a new regime should abolish the flank limits, revise national ceilings of treaty-limited equipment, and take new military technologies into account.[103]

In May 2013 Deputy Defense Minister Anatoly Antonov described the CFE Treaty as "dead," notably in light of technological advances. In Antonov's view, future arms control accords should encompass "all weapons types, defensive and offensive . . . ranging from unmanned aerial vehicles to military robotics."[104] Russian experts have pointed out that the CFE regime places no restrictions on precision guidance weapons or naval forces, despite the "huge role in recent military conflicts" of naval aircraft and sea-launched cruise missiles.[105] As with the Russian approach to further strategic nuclear arms reductions, Moscow may argue for such a comprehensive concept for conventional arms control that workable agreements may be difficult to define and negotiate.

Reducing Numbers of Nuclear Weapons in Europe

The NATO Allies made clear their policy of reduced reliance on nuclear weapons in the 2010 Lisbon Summit Declaration: "With the changes in the security environment since the end of the Cold War, we have dramatically reduced the number of nuclear weapons stationed in Europe and our reliance on nuclear weapons in NATO strategy. We will seek to create the conditions for further reductions in the future."[106] This statement referred principally to the remaining U.S. nuclear-weapons in Europe. It should be noted, however, that NATO's three nuclear-weapon states have all substantially reduced their numbers of nuclear weapons since the end of the Cold War.[107]

Despite the absence of any explicit reference to Russia as a potential nuclear threat in the 2010 Strategic Concept, the Allies stated that, with reference to possible further reductions in the U.S. nuclear weapons presence in Europe, "In any future reductions, our aim should be to seek Russian agreement to increase transparency on its nuclear weapons in Europe and relocate these weapons away from the territory of NATO members. Any further steps must take into account the disparity with the greater Russian stockpiles of short-range nuclear weapons."[108] The Allies also expressed an interest in discussing in the NATO-Russia Council "military deployments, including any that could be perceived as threatening; information sharing and transparency on military doctrine and posture, as well as the overall disparity in short-range nuclear weapons."[109]

The Congressional Commission on the Strategic Posture of the United States noted in 2009 that "Russia enjoys a sizeable numerical advantage" over the United States in nonstrategic nuclear forces (NSNF) and "stores thousands of these weapons in apparent support of possible military operations west of the Urals. The United States deploys a small fraction of that number in support of nuclear sharing agreements in NATO.... Strict U.S.-Russian equivalence in NSNF numbers is unnecessary. But the current imbalance is stark and worrisome to some U.S. allies in Central Europe. If and as reductions continue in the number of operationally deployed strategic nuclear weapons, this imbalance will become more apparent and allies less assured."[110]

Some European Allied observers have expressed concern in view of Russian declarations that certain new Allies have made themselves potential targets for nuclear attack by supporting U.S. missile defense plans.[111] While the U.S. government revised its missile defense plans regarding NATO and Europe in September 2009, the Russian government has not modified its nuclear doctrine.[112] Recent Russian exercises have simulated nuclear attacks on Poland and other NATO Allies.[113]

Indeed, the Russians have held exercises with the simulated use of nuclear weapons against NATO Allies since 1999.[114] As the U.S. congressional commission noted, "Some allies located near Russia believe that U.S. non-strategic forces in Europe are essential to prevent nuclear coercion by Moscow and indeed that modernized U.S./ NATO forces are essential for restoring a sense of balance in the face of Russia's nuclear renewal."[115]

New NATO Allies generally feel a stronger need for reassurance about the reality of U.S. security commitments, including extended deterrence via nuclear forces, than do most of the older Allies. In most of Central and Eastern Europe, there is a continuing distrust of Russia. This is evident in statements by officials and experts in many of these Allied nations, though they are relatively cautious in their public remarks.

In April 2010, Jiri Schneider, the program director of the Prague Security Studies Institute and a former political director at the Czech Ministry of Foreign Affairs, wrote:

> If these [U.S. nuclear] weapons are withdrawn, it is necessary to answer the question how the United States intends to secure a nuclear umbrella for its European allies.... Is it actually even possible to imagine nuclear deterrence without the physical presence of American weapons in Europe? Although there are two nuclear powers in Europe, it is unfathomable that they could provide nuclear guarantees for their European allies, not to mention for the European Union.

In August 2011, Mart Laar, then the Estonian minister of defense, drew the link to U.S. extended deterrence more emphatically:

> Today, the nuclear burden sharing arrangement in NATO embodies the ultimate level of commitment and coordination between allies and serves as an unmistakable sign of resolve to

any potential adversary. When we are weak in this, when we underestimate the importance of this, we can make an enormously costly mistake. . . . Missile defense does not replace conventional and nuclear deterrence, which forge a clear link with overall US superiority and reaffirm NATO's willingness to engage in collective defense. For health of NATO and transatlantic relations it is of utmost importance that NATO remains a nuclear alliance and that US nuclear weapons remain in Europe.[117]

If the U.S. nuclear weapons presence were withdrawn from Europe unilaterally, without any negotiated Russian reciprocity, the Russians would have fewer incentives to accept any NSNF arms control measures, including any verification and transparency regime. Since the 1950s it has been argued in various quarters that Moscow would be more cooperative in dealings with the West if it were granted its wish that U.S. nuclear weapons in Europe be entirely removed. It is far more likely, however, that the Russians would simply "pocket" a unilateral withdrawal of the U.S. nuclear weapons as something they had always demanded.[118]

From a Russian perspective, a unilateral withdrawal of the remaining U.S. nuclear weapons in Europe would be rectifying what Moscow has long regarded as an imposition, rather than offering a signal for Russian NSNF disarmament. For NATO, even if Russian NSNF could thereby be numerically reduced, there would be little or no strategic gain. Russia would hold a monopoly on NSNF in Europe. Moscow's NSNF holdings would be unverifiable, but would probably remain in the thousands. If drastic reductions in U.S. nuclear weapons in Europe since 1991 have not led Moscow to resolve the massive uncertainties in the West about Russia's NSNF,[119] why should it be expected that complete withdrawal (entirely removing the Alliance's negotiating leverage) would bring about a response that NATO could regard as satisfactory?

According to the U.S. congressional commission, "Senior Russian experts have reported that Russia has 3,800 operational tactical nuclear warheads with a large additional number in reserve. Some Russian military experts have written about use of very low yield nuclear 'scalpels' to defeat NATO forces. The combination of new warhead designs, the estimated production capability for new nuclear warheads, and precision delivery systems such as the Iskander short-range tactical ballistic missile (known as the SS-26 in the West), open up new possibilities for Russian efforts to threaten to use nuclear weapons to influence regional conflicts."[120]

It should be noted that multiple estimates of the number of Russian NSNF are in circulation. As Amy Woolf of the Congressional Research Service has observed, "experts believe Russia still has between 2,000 and 6,000 warheads for nonstrategic nuclear weapons in its arsenal."[121] As this numerical range suggests, significant uncertainties persist about the Russian nonstrategic nuclear arsenal.

The assumption of some disarmament advocates that withdrawing the remaining U.S. weapons from Europe would encourage the Russians to eliminate or substantially reduce their immense holdings of NSNF appears to be based on an excessively sanguine view of Moscow's readiness to undertake action in this respect. As the U.S. congressional commission noted, Moscow has not complied with the

1991–1992 pledges by Soviet president Mikhail Gorbachev and Russian president Boris Yeltsin to eliminate and reduce certain types of NSNF.[122] Both Gorbachev and Yeltsin promised to eliminate all nuclear warheads for artillery and land-based tactical missiles, for example, but the Russian Defense Ministry website affirmed the continuing importance of these nuclear capabilities in May 2011.[123] In 2004 a Russian Defense Ministry representative said that "we are not going to report back to anybody with figures in our hands about how many and what kind of specific tactical nuclear arms we have reduced."[124] The Russian lack of transparency in this regard helps to account for the uncertainties about the number of Russian nuclear weapons, notably in the nonstrategic category.[125]

The U.S. Senate, in its December 2010 resolution of advice and consent to the ratification of the Russian-U.S. New START treaty, stated that "the United States will seek to initiate, following consultation with NATO allies but not later than one year after the entry into force of the New START Treaty, negotiations with the Russian Federation on an agreement to address the disparity between the non-strategic (tactical) nuclear weapons stockpiles of the Russian Federation and of the United States and to secure and reduce tactical nuclear weapons in a verifiable manner." The resolution also stated,

> Recognizing the difficulty the United States has faced in ascertaining with confidence the number of tactical nuclear weapons maintained by the Russian Federation and the security of those weapons, the Senate urges the President to engage the Russian Federation with the objectives of —
>
> (i) establishing cooperative measures to give each Party to the New START Treaty improved confidence regarding the accurate accounting and security of tactical nuclear weapons maintained by the other Party; and
>
> (ii) providing United States or other international assistance to help the Russian Federation ensure the accurate accounting and security of its tactical nuclear weapons.[126]

While the New START Treaty entered into force in February 2011, the Russians have to date not shown any interest in negotiations with the United States concerning nonstrategic nuclear weapons.

Thomas Donilon, then President Obama's national security adviser, indicated in March 2011 that the United States intends to work with its "NATO allies to shape an approach to reduce the role and number of U.S. tactical nuclear weapons, as Russia takes reciprocal measures to reduce its nonstrategic forces and relocates its nonstrategic forces away from NATO's borders." Donilon added, "In advance of a new treaty limiting tactical nuclear weapons, we also plan to consult with our allies on reciprocal actions that could be taken on the basis of parallel steps by each side. As a first step, we would like to increase transparency on a reciprocal basis concerning the numbers, locations, and types of nonstrategic forces in Europe."[127]

The current consensus in the Alliance holds that the near-term way forward resides in pursuing transparency and confidence-building measures with Russia. The Russians have to date, however, resisted the pursuit of such transparency measures. At present the Russians seem unlikely to abandon their long-standing refusal to consider negotiations affecting their NSNF in Europe so long as any U.S. nuclear weapons remain in Europe.

Aside from the apparent Russian lack of interest in participating in NSNF arms control negotiations, defining an arms control regime for NSNF would face several intrinsic problems, including verification, geographic scope, agreement on the participants, the availability of dual-use delivery systems, and the baseline (or initialization) challenge of determining the numbers and locations of Russian NSNF.

The question of geographic scope is raised, for example, by the Alliance objective to "relocate these [Russian] weapons away from the territory of NATO members." Japanese experts have pointed out that this policy statement suggests that the United States and its NATO Allies have forgotten the lessons of the 1980s. Just as the INF Treaty had to involve global constraints on U.S. and Soviet ground-launched cruise and ballistic missiles with ranges between 500 and 5,500 km, effective limitations on NSNF would have to be global. A British expert pointed out at an international conference in June 2012 that negotiating a relocation of Russian nonstrategic nuclear weapons further from NATO territory would not represent a strategically meaningful achievement: "Remember that they are mobile (within a few hours by air, or a couple of days by train) and that their westward return (even if partial or suspected) might itself be a means of intimidation in a crisis."[128]

The political and strategic basis for an NSNF arms control regime would not be self-evident, in view of the fact that the number of U.S. weapons in Europe is not a function of hypothetical targets in Russia. Moreover, the Russians attribute utility to their NSNF for reasons other than the U.S. nuclear weapons presence in Europe—for example, to deter powers other than NATO (such as China), to substitute for advanced nonnuclear precision-strike systems, and to compensate for their perceived conventional military weakness in relation to NATO.[129]

As with previous nuclear arms control treaties affecting European (and global) security, NATO would not be a direct party to the negotiations between Russia, the United States, and perhaps other governments, but its security interests would be affected, and the United States would in all likelihood formulate its positions in close consultation with its NATO Allies.[130]

The U.S. administration supports the general consensus in the Alliance that there should be no further reductions in the U.S. nuclear weapons presence in Europe without Russian reciprocity, although the specific requirements of that reciprocity have yet to be agreed upon among the Allies. It should be noted that this Alliance consensus includes Germany, despite the October 2009 coalition agreement of the Christian Democratic Union/Christian Social Union in Bavaria–Free Democratic Party (CDU/CSU-FDP) government to "engage within the Alliance, as well as across the table with the American Allies, such that the remaining nuclear weapons in Germany are removed."[131] As noted in chapter 3, in April 2011 Germany's ambassador to NATO cosigned the "Letter of 10" (released at the NATO foreign ministerial meeting in Berlin) that made clear in its cover note that any reductions in

NATO nonstrategic nuclear weapons would have to come on the basis of reciprocity with Russia and that the focus for now should be on transparency and confidence-building measures.[132]

The Alliance's established policy implies that the U.S. and NATO negotiating position would be undermined if the Allies undertook further unilateral reductions in the U.S. nuclear weapons presence in Europe (that is, without any Russian reciprocity) or chose not to replace or extend the service lives of their dual-capable aircraft prior to the entry into force of a binding agreement with Russia concerning NSNF.

Some U.S. officials and experts have examined the possibility of a U.S.-Russian agreement on an arms control regime with an aggregate warhead ceiling and "freedom to mix" for all remaining types of U.S. and Russian nuclear weapons, including nondeployed weapons as well as deployed strategic and nonstrategic weapons. This could lead to reductions or restructuring in the U.S. nuclear weapons presence in Europe. Both sides might find appealing elements in such an agreement. Russia, for example, might thereby establish constraints on U.S. strategic nuclear upload potential, while the United States might achieve reductions in Russian nonstrategic nuclear warheads if Moscow decided to diminish the number of these warheads in order to maintain a certain level of strategic nuclear warheads. However, while both sides may wish to explore the parameters and implications of such an aggregate agreement, a new negotiation along these lines appears unlikely in the near term for several reasons: the lack of interest in Russia at present in further negotiations affecting nuclear forces, the continuing Russian-U.S. impasse over missile defense, the substantial importance of nonstrategic nuclear weapons in Russia's defense concept, and Russian uncertainties about limits on warheads that would require new forms of verification.[133]

The Allies have not yet agreed on a definition of satisfactory Russian reciprocity concerning possible reductions in NSNF. In May 2012, however, the Allies announced a decision to analyze this question: "Allies agree that the NAC [North Atlantic Council] will task the appropriate committees to further consider, in the context of the broader security environment, what NATO would expect to see in the way of reciprocal Russian actions to allow for significant reductions in forward-based non-strategic nuclear weapons assigned to NATO."[134]

The reference to taking into account "the context of the broader security environment" when assessing prospects for reducing the number of U.S. NSNF in Europe is significant. According to a French expert, the phrase "broader security environment" is "a code word for all the other things that are out there in NATO's neighborhood—sometimes, quite literally, neighboring states to some of the Allies—that should affect the future of the nuclear element of NATO's force posture."[135]

In other words, the allusion to "the broader security environment" confirms that the Allies recognize that Russia is not the only collective defense issue that they could face, and that U.S. nuclear weapons in Europe might therefore be relevant in contingencies involving countries other than Russia. Moscow is thus not the only factor to be taken into account when considering possible reductions or other adjustments in the U.S. nuclear weapons presence in Europe. In seeking the conditions for further reductions in the U.S. nuclear weapons presence in Europe, the Alliance will have to keep in mind potential non-Russian adversaries that might present nuclear deterrence requirements for NATO.

At the present stage of discussion, it should be noted, U.S. analysts do not agree on what might be reasonable terms of reference for a negotiation involving the remaining U.S. nuclear weapons in Europe, including units of account, participants, geographic scope, and verification measures. Terminology has long been problematic and contentious in this domain. For instance, commentators and NATO governments have long used terms such as "tactical," "substrategic," and "nonstrategic" to describe the remaining U.S. nuclear weapons in Europe. Elaine Bunn has written, "The term 'tactical' or 'non-strategic' nuclear weapons is oxymoronic: all nuclear weapons would be strategic in their effect; 'tactical' or 'non-strategic' nuclear weapons are really just differently-deployed. This is leftover terminology, meaning nuclear weapons not covered by START, SORT or other arms control agreements."[136]

On the other hand, an American expert noted at a recent workshop that using the term "strategic" to describe all U.S. nuclear weapons "could have adverse effects by supporting the traditional Soviet and Russian position that U.S. nuclear weapons in Europe are forward-based strategic systems. The Russians, he said, would almost certainly not agree to call their non-strategic nuclear forces 'strategic.'"[137] If U.S. nonstrategic nuclear weapons were officially described as "strategic" by the U.S. government, this would reinforce Moscow's position that these U.S. weapons are strategic and should be included in strategic arms negotiations while corresponding Russian weapons should be excluded because they are based on Russian territory. As Rose Gottemoeller, the assistant secretary of state for arms control, verification and compliance, observed in August 2011, "Our conversation with Russia must include defining what exactly constitutes a non-strategic nuclear weapon and whether or not a single overall limit on all nuclear weapons would be possible."[138]

Some commentators committed to nuclear disarmament seem to assume that the U.S. nuclear weapons in Europe have no residual security value and that the main task at hand is to move forward promptly with the elimination of all U.S. and Russian nonstrategic nuclear weapons, starting with the removal of U.S. nuclear weapons in Europe on a unilateral basis—that is, without Russian reciprocity.[139]

Official U.S. and Alliance policy is open to reductions in—and the eventual elimination of—U.S. and Russian NSNF, subject to negotiations. It is nonetheless noteworthy that some proponents of negotiated reductions in U.S. and Russian NSNF hold that the reductions process should not lead to the elimination of U.S. nuclear weapons in Europe in "the foreseeable future."[140] In their view, "If parity is unachievable, NATO could envision cutting both sides' forces by a common percentage; deep cuts along these lines could be acceptable as long as European allies retain some credible force on their soil."[141] To quote Frank Miller, a former U.S. Department of Defense official, there should be "a non-zero solution. A residual deployment of some size is needed."[142]

From this perspective, the Alliance's nuclear force negotiating posture must be designed with the risk of non-Russian contingencies in mind, lest its future become dependent on Moscow's arms control policy. As discussed in chapter 2, the Alliance has increasingly acknowledged that collective defense involves much more than preparedness for hypothetical Russian contingencies. The references in NATO's May 2012 DDPR to the "broader security environment" acknowledge that the Allies might in some circumstances face potential adversaries outside the Euro-Atlantic area—for example, non-Russian threats that might arise in the Middle East or Asia.[143]

Conclusion

The difficulties associated with defining a framework to negotiate constraints on U.S. and Russian NSNF—as well as with finding a means to relaunch conventional arms control in Europe—demonstrate some of the limits of arms control, disarmament, and nonproliferation efforts. From a political standpoint, all the NATO Allies agree that these efforts have been and remain essential and indispensable, but their practical achievements have been modest—a mixed complement to the Alliance's other security activities.

It may therefore be hard for the Allies to achieve their agreed-upon objectives of "raising NATO's profile" and "achieving a higher level of public awareness of NATO's contribution" in arms control, disarmament, and nonproliferation. NATO's role has remained essentially to serve as a forum for information sharing and policy coordination.

In bilateral Moscow-Washington negotiations, NATO has offered a privileged venue for the United States to consult with its European Allies about the implications for the Alliance of accords on strategic nuclear arms control such as the 2010 New START Treaty. The NATO Allies support the U.S. proposals for negotiations with Russia about more comprehensive nuclear arms control measures encompassing nondeployed and nonstrategic nuclear weapons. However, Russia has to date refused even to discuss transparency measures concerning its nonstrategic nuclear weapons unless all U.S. nuclear weapons are first removed from Europe.[144] The NATO Allies have agreed not to make further reductions in the remaining U.S. nuclear weapons in Europe without Russian reciprocity, but they have not yet defined the specific requirements of that reciprocity.

Some Allied observers have warned that it would be unwise for the Allies to accept a definition of "reciprocity" that did not involve reductions and constraints on Russian nonstrategic nuclear weapons in return for further reductions in U.S. nonstrategic nuclear weapons in Europe. According to a French observer, for example, to regard Russian transparency measures as acceptable compensation for further reductions in U.S. nonstrategic nuclear weapons in Europe would amount to "an invented and non-pertinent reciprocity," and this "would be dangerous for the credibility of the Alliance in relation to Russia." In her view, "The Allies are in danger of negotiating among themselves and weakening their position in relation to Russia."[145]

The NATO Allies have not coordinated their positions in most multilateral arms control matters, for example, the Conference on Disarmament and NPT review conferences.[146] The principal exception in multilateral matters has been the NATO policy coordination effort in conventional arms control.

In this regard, however, the Allies face an ongoing stalemate. As discussed previously, Russia has continued to maintain military forces in Georgia and Moldova without the consent of the governments of these countries, despite Article IV of the 1990 CFE Treaty and Moscow's commitment to remedy this situation at the 1999 OSCE Istanbul Summit. This is the main reason why the NATO Allies party to the 1990 CFE Treaty have not ratified the 1999 Adapted CFE Treaty. In 2007 Russia suspended its compliance with the 1990 CFE Treaty, including the verification and transparency regime, and in 2011 the NATO Allies party to the treaty announced that they would stop implementing certain obligations under this regime with regard to Russia. As noted previously, the NATO Allies party to the treaty are prepared to resume their performance of these obligations in return for Russian reciprocity. Such reciprocity from Moscow concerning these obligations would, however, not necessarily be accompanied by Russian compliance with Article IV of the treaty—a necessary step for the NATO Allies to ratify the Adapted CFE Treaty.

Some experts in NATO nations have posed questions similar to those raised by prominent Russians as to whether the limits set out in the Adapted CFE Treaty are fully relevant to evolving military technologies, including the increased importance of precision-guided missiles and information, surveillance, and reconnaissance systems. From this perspective, the most promising way forward in conventional arms control in Europe might be to return to the formulation and implementation of confidence-building measures. This might build the trust necessary for the definition of new conventional arms control measures in Europe with greater prospects for success than the troubled CFE Treaty regime. The NATO Allies are nonetheless likely to continue to uphold the host nation consent principle.

As in a number of other policy domains, with respect to arms control, nonproliferation, and disarmament the NATO Allies must strike a balance between their ambitious political objectives and the concrete realities at hand. As in other "cooperative security" endeavors, the Allies themselves may, as in past, differ regarding the right way forward. Even in the presence of an Alliance consensus, the cooperation of parties other than the Allies cannot be guaranteed. Efforts to negotiate constraints on military capabilities and activities reach practical limits when states do not regard such constraints as consistent with their security interests.

Notes

1. North Atlantic Council, "Strategic Concept," November 19, 2010, par. 4.

2. North Atlantic Council, "Final Communiqué," December 16–19, 1957, par. 8, www.nato.int/docu/comm/49-95/c571219a.htm.

3. North Atlantic Council, "The Future Tasks of the Alliance," December 13–14, 1967, par. 13, www.nato.int/cps/en/natolive/official_texts_26700.htm.

4. France maintained a distinctive position regarding the NPT throughout the Cold War and did not accede to this treaty until 1992. France has never acceded to the PTBT, though it ratified the Comprehensive Test Ban Treaty (CTBT) in 1998. For background on French arms control policies during the Cold War, see David S. Yost, "France," in *The Allies and Arms Control*, ed. Fen Hampson, Harald von Riekhoff, and John Roper (Baltimore, MD: Johns Hopkins University Press, 1992), 162–188.

5. In the same signing statement, the West German government stipulated that "the Treaty shall not hamper the unification of the European States." Federal Republic of Germany, "Statement on Signing the Treaty on the Non-Proliferation of Nuclear Weapons," November 28, 1969, http://disarmament.un.org/treaties/a/npt/germany/sig/london.

6. The Italian government also stated that it signed the treaty "in the firm belief that nothing in it is an obstacle to the unification of the Countries of Western Europe and to the justified expectations that the peoples of this area have in the developments and progress towards unity with a view to the creation of a European entity." Italian Government, "Statement on Signing the Treaty on the Non-Proliferation of Nuclear Weapons," January 28, 1969, http://disarmament.un.org/treaties/a/npt/italy/sig/london.

7. "Report by Secretary of State [Dean] Rusk to President [Lyndon] Johnson on the Nonproliferation Treaty, July 2, 1968," in U.S. Arms Control and Disarmament Agency, *Documents on Disarmament, 1968* (Washington, DC: Government Printing Office, 1969), 478.

8. The reference to "the MLF/ANF" concerns two other hypothetical nuclear-sharing arrangements discussed in the Alliance in the 1960s—the U.S. proposal for a Multilateral Force (MLF) and the competing British proposal for an Atlantic Nuclear Force (ANF). Neither proposal won general acceptance in the Alliance.

9. Memorandum from Spurgeon Keeny of the National Security Council Staff to the president's assistant for national security affairs (Kissinger), Washington, January 24, 1969, available in *Foreign Relations of the United States, 1969–1976*, volume E-2, *Documents on Arms Control and Nonproliferation, 1969–1972*, Document 2, at http://history.state.gov/historicaldocuments/frus1969-76ve02/d2. FRUS also offers an image of the original document at http://static.history.state.gov/frus/frus1969-76ve02/pdf/d2.pdf.

10. The Soviet government objected to any arrangements that would give the West German government a role in NATO nuclear deterrence policy, notably the Multilateral Force (MLF) proposal, which was never actually implemented. Thomas W. Wolfe, *Soviet Power and Europe, 1945–1970* (Baltimore, MD, and London: Johns Hopkins University Press, 1970), 281–282.

11. William C. Potter, "The Soviet Union and Nuclear Proliferation," *Slavic Review* 44, no. 3 (Autumn 1985): 471.

12. Robert M. Lawrence and Joel Larus, "A Historical Review of Nuclear Weapons Proliferation and the Development of the NPT," in *Nuclear Proliferation: Phase II*, ed. Robert M. Lawrence and Joel Larus (Lawrence, KS: University Press of Kansas, 1974), 14–20. See also George Bunn, *Arms Control by Committee: Managing Negotiations with the Russians* (Stanford, CA: Stanford University Press, 1992), 81–82. The Soviet Union evidently was not satisfied with the commitment made by the Federal Republic of Germany in 1954 in conjunction with its accession to the modified Brussels Treaty "not to manufacture in its territory any atomic weapons, chemical weapons or biological weapons."

13. NATO's Nuclear Planning Group, founded in 1966–1967, and associated consultation and nuclear sharing arrangements contributed to West Germany's decisions to accept the abandonment of the Multilateral Force (MLF) proposal and to accede to the 1968 Treaty on the Non-Proliferation of Nuclear Weapons (NPT) as a non-nuclear-weapon state. For a lucid account, see Hal Brands, "Non-Proliferation and the Dynamics of the Middle Cold War: The Superpowers, the MLF, and the NPT," *Cold War History* 7, no. 3 (August 2007), esp. 404–409.

14. Raymond L. Garthoff, "BMD and East-West Relations," in *Ballistic Missile Defense*, ed. Ashton B. Carter and David N. Schwartz (Washington, DC: Brookings Institution, 1984), 301.

15. David S. Yost, "The U.S. Nuclear Posture Review and the NATO Allies," *International Affairs* 80 (July 2004): 718–721.

16. Henry A. Kissinger, *Years of Upheaval* (London: Weidenfeld and Nicolson and Michael Joseph, 1982), 277.

17. "The Agreement between the United States of America and the Union of Soviet Socialist Republics on the Prevention of Nuclear War," June 22, 1973, www.state.gov/t/ac/trt/5186.htm.

18. Georges-Henri Soutou, "Three Rifts, Two Reconciliations: Franco-American Relations during the Fifth Republic," in *The Atlantic Alliance Under Stress: US-European Relations after Iraq*, ed. David M. Andrews (Cambridge, UK: Cambridge University Press, 2005), 105.

19. Kissinger, *Years of Upheaval*, 286.

20. For details and references, see David S. Yost, *European Security and the SALT Process*, Washington Paper no. 85 (Beverly Hills, CA, and London: Sage Publications for the Center for Strategic and International Studies, Georgetown University, 1981), 16–25.

21. Laurence Martin, "A Strategic Symposium: SALT and U.S. Defense Policy," *Washington Quarterly* 2 (Winter 1979): 33–34.

22. Helmut Schmidt, "The 1977 Alastair Buchan Memorial Lecture," *Survival* 20, no. 1 (January–February 1978): 3–4.

23. North Atlantic Council, "Special Meeting of Foreign and Defence Ministers," December 12, 1979, www.nato.int/cps/en/natolive/official_texts_27040.htm.

24. The term INF, often used as shorthand for intermediate-range and shorter-range nuclear forces, implies that the INF Treaty limits nuclear weapons. It is in fact a treaty about delivery systems, and its prohibitions apply whether the missile payload is nuclear or nonnuclear. The formal name of the agreement is the Treaty Between the United States of America and the Union of Soviet Socialist Republics on the Elimination of Their Intermediate-Range and Shorter-Range Missiles. The active parties to the treaty today are the United States and four Soviet successor states: Belarus, Kazakhstan, Russia, and Ukraine. For a concise overview, see Daryl Kimball and Tom Collina, "The Intermediate-Range Nuclear Forces (INF) Treaty at a Glance," February 2008, www.armscontrol.org/factsheets/INFtreaty.

25. France consistently refused to participate in the MBFR negotiations. The French held that the terms of reference were ill-conceived and had dangerous long-term implications, including the risk of creating a zone of special security status in central Europe that could be prejudicial to future Western European defense cooperation. For background, see David S. Yost, "France," in *The Allies and Arms Control*, ed. Fen Hampson, Harald von Riekhoff, and John Roper (Baltimore, MD: Johns Hopkins University Press, 1992), 168–169.

26. Among other sources, see Richard A. Falkenrath, *Shaping Europe's Military Order: The Origins and Consequences of the CFE Treaty* (Cambridge, MA: MIT Press, 1995); and P. Terrence Hopmann, "From MBFR to CFE: Negotiating Conventional Arms Control in Europe," in *Encyclopedia of Arms Control and Disarmament*, vol. II, ed. Richard Dean Burns (New York: Charles Scribner's Sons, 1993), 967–989.

27. Developments worldwide in arms control, nonproliferation, and disarmament have a bearing on the Alliance's security interests. The Allies made this long-standing Alliance position clear in, for example, their "Report on Options for Confidence and Security Building Measures (CSBMs), Verification, Non-Proliferation, Arms Control and Disarmament," press communiqué M-NAC-2(2000)121, December 14, 2000, www.nato.int/docu/pr/2000/p00-121e/home.htm.

28. North Atlantic Council, "Bucharest Summit Declaration," par. 39, www.nato.int/docu/pr/2008/p08-049e.html.

29. The German and Norwegian foreign ministers at that time—Frank-Walter Steinmeier and Jonas Gahr Støre—launched this initiative in May 2007.

30. North Atlantic Council, "Strasbourg/Kehl Summit Declaration," par. 55.

31. Polish expert quoted in Yost, *NATO's Deterrence and Defense Posture*, 14.

32. Lithuanian scholar quoted in Yost, *NATO's Deterrence and Defense Posture*, 14.

33. North Atlantic Council, "Lisbon Summit Declaration," par. 31.

34. North Atlantic Council, "Deterrence and Defence Posture Review," par. 30.

35. Oliver Meier, "NATO Agrees on New Arms Control Body," *Arms Control Now*, February 26, 2013, http://armscontrolnow.org/2013/02/26/nato-agrees-on-new-arms-control-body/.

36. Ibid.

37. North Atlantic Council, "Deterrence and Defence Posture Review," par. 23.

38. NATO, "High-Level Task Force on Conventional Arms Control," updated April 20, 2011, www.nato.int/cps/en/natolive/topics_67991.htm. With regard to OSCE-related consultations in Vienna by NATO Allies on conventional arms control, see Yost, *NATO and International Organizations*, 120–121, www.ndc.nato.int/download/publications/fp_03.pdf.

39. North Atlantic Council, "Lisbon Summit Declaration," par. 31.

40. North Atlantic Council, "Strategic Concept," November 19, 2010, par. 26.

41. The twenty-two NATO Allies that are members of the European Union have generally preferred to define joint positions on NPT issues and other WMD nonproliferation matters under EU auspices instead of those of the Alliance. Some non-EU NATO Allies (including Canada, Norway, and Turkey) have been exceptionally active in promoting arms control, disarmament, and nonproliferation under Alliance auspices, and some observers hypothesize that this may be partly attributed to their nonmembership in the European Union.

42. Roberto Zadra, "Nuclear Proliferation and NATO Policy and Posture," in *NATO and the Future of the Nuclear Non-Proliferation Treaty*, Occasional Paper no. 21, ed. Joseph F. Pilat and David S. Yost (Rome: NATO Defense College, May 2007), 107, www.ndc.nato.int/download/publications/op_21.pdf.

43. NATO, "NATO's Comprehensive, Strategic-Level Policy for Preventing the Proliferation of Weapons of Mass Destruction (WMD) and Defending against Chemical, Biological, Radiological and Nuclear (CBRN) Threats," September 1, 2009, par. 6 and 7, www.nato.int/cps/en/natolive/official_texts_57218.htm.

44. Michael Rühle, *The Broader Context of NATO's Nuclear Policy and Posture*, Research Paper no. 89 (Rome: NATO Defense College, January 2013), 8.

45. NATO, "NATO-Ukraine Commission Meeting at Ministerial Level, Luxembourg, 29 May 1998," press release (98) 62, www.nato.int/docu/pr/1998/p98-062e.htm.

46. NATO, "NATO North Atlantic Council Statement on North Korea," press release (2006) 081, July 5, 2006, www.nato.int/docu/pr/2006/p06-081e.htm (accessed 21 January 2010); NATO, "North Atlantic Council Statement on North Korea Nuclear Test," press release (2006) 119, October 10, 2006, www.nato.int/docu/pr/2006/p06-119e.htm; NATO, "North Atlantic Council Statement on North Korea," press release (2009) 077, May 25, 2009, www.nato.int/cps/en/SID-A1BC720E-77E98810/natolive/news_55112.htm?mode=pressrelease; and "North Atlantic Council Strongly Condemns North Korean Nuclear Test," February 12, 2013, www.nato.int/cps/en/natolive/news_98353.htm.

47. North Atlantic Council, "Strasbourg/Kehl Summit Declaration," par. 56; North Atlantic Council, "Lisbon Summit Declaration," par. 33; and North Atlantic Council, "Chicago Summit Declaration," par. 50.

48. Secretary General Rasmussen, monthly press conference, May 6, 2013, www.nato.int/cps/en/natolive/opinions_100206.htm?selectedLocale=en.

49. North Atlantic Council, "Deterrence and Defence Posture Review," May 20, 2012, par. 22; italics in the original.

50. George P. Shultz, William J. Perry, Henry A. Kissinger, and Sam Nunn, "A World Free of Nuclear Weapons," *Wall Street Journal*, January 4, 2007.

51. The full text of Article VI of the NPT reads as follows: "Each of the Parties to the Treaty undertakes to pursue negotiations in good faith on effective measures relating to cessation of the nuclear arms race at an early date and to nuclear disarmament, and on a Treaty on general and complete disarmament under strict and effective international control."

52. "France supports the objective of the final elimination of nuclear weapons in the framework of general and complete disarmament. From now until the realization of this objective.... France intends to maintain in all circumstances the credibility and the effectiveness of its nuclear deterrent force." Hervé de Charette, foreign minister, answer to a written question, *Journal officiel de la République Française, Débats Parlementaires, Assemblée Nationale*, February 24, 1997, 935. "Article VI of the NPT does not establish any timetable for nuclear disarmament, nor for the general and complete disarmament which provides the context for total nuclear disarmament. Nor does it prohibit maintenance or updating of existing capabilities." *The Future of the United Kingdom's Nuclear Deterrent*, Cm 6994 (London: Her Majesty's Stationery Office, December 2006), 14, par. 2–10.

53. Douglas Hurd, statement at the 1995 NPT Review and Extension Conference, April 18, 1995.

54. *Lifting the Nuclear Shadow: Creating the Conditions for Abolishing Nuclear Weapons* (London: Foreign and Commonwealth Office, February 2009), 12.

55. François Mitterrand, "Allocution prononcée par le Président de la République devant la XXXVIIIème session de l'Assemblée Générale des Nations Unies," New York, September 28, 1983, in Ministère des Affaires Étrangères, *La politique étrangère de la France, textes et documents* (Paris: La Documentation Française, September–October 1983), 41. See also the article by Charles Hernu, then the defense minister, "Équilibre, dissuasion, volonté: La voie étroite de la paix et de la liberté," *Défense Nationale* (December 1983): 15; and Yost, "France," 175.

56. François Rivasseau, statement at the 2005 Review Conference of the States Parties to the Treaty on the Non-Proliferation of Nuclear Weapons Main Committee I, New York, May 19, 2005.

57. Michel Miraillet, "La dissuasion et le second âge nucléaire," *Politique étrangère* 75, no. 2 (Summer 2010): 379.

58. U.S. Department of Defense, *Nuclear Posture Review Report* (Washington, DC: U.S. Department of Defense, April 2010), 48–49.

59. Ibid., 48.

60. See, among other sources, Michael Quinlan, "Abolishing Nuclear Armouries: Policy or Pipedream?," *Survival* 49, no. 4 (Winter 2007–2008); and George Perkovich and James M. Acton, *Abolishing Nuclear Weapons*, Adelphi Paper no. 396 (Abingdon, Oxfordshire, UK: Routledge for the International Institute for Strategic Studies, August 2008).

61. Thomas C. Schelling, "A World Without Nuclear Weapons?," *Daedalus* 138, no. 4 (Fall 2009): 127.

62. In August 2011, Rose Gottemoeller, assistant secretary of state for arms control, verification and compliance, said, "The United States has made it clear that we are committed to continuing a step-by-step process to reduce the overall number of nuclear weapons, including the pursuit of a future agreement with Russia for broad reductions in all categories of nuclear weapons—strategic, non-strategic, deployed and non-deployed." Rose Gottemoeller, "21st Century

Deterrence Challenges" (remarks, U.S. Strategic Command 2011 Deterrence Symposium, Omaha, Nebraska, 4 August 2011), www.state.gov/t/avc/rls/169545.htm.

63. Sergey Lavrov, "The New START Treaty in the Global Security Matrix: The Political Dimension," *Mezhdunarodnaya Zhizn*, no. 7 (July 2010), www.mid.ru/brp_4.nsf/e78a48070f128a7b43256999005bcbb3/25909cfe1bbd1c6ec3 25777500339245?OpenDocument.

64. Putin quoted in "Russia Stands by Nuclear Weapons," *RIA Novosti*, February 24, 2012, www.en.rian.ru/world/20120224/171515372.html.

65. President Barack Obama, remarks at Hradcany Square, Prague, Czech Republic, April 5, 2009, www.whitehouse.gov/the_press_office/Remarks-By-President-Barack-Obama-In-Prague-As-Delivered/.

66. North Atlantic Council, "Strategic Concept," November 19, 2010, par. 26, www.nato.int/cps/en/natolive/official_texts_68580.htm; and North Atlantic Council, "Deterrence and Defence Posture Review," par. 24.

67. French and German observers quoted in Yost, *NATO's Deterrence and Defense Posture*, 16.

68. Author interview with a French observer in Paris, July 9, 2012.

69. Giorgio Napolitano, address to the North Atlantic Council, Brussels, March 2, 2010, text in English www.quirinale.it/elementi/Continua.aspx?tipo=Discorso&key=1794.

70. Author interview with an Italian observer in Rome, June 21, 2012.

71. President Obama, remarks at the Brandenburg Gate, Berlin, Germany, June 19, 2013, www.whitehouse.gov/the-press-office/2013/06/19/remarks-president-obama-brandenburg-gate-berlin-germany.

72. "Treaty between the United States of America and the Russian Federation on Measures for the Further Reduction and Limitation of Strategic Offensive Arms," Prague, April 8, 2010, Article III, para. 2.

73. Pavel Podvig, "The New START Bomber Count and Upload Potential," March 31, 2010, http://russianforces.org/blog/2010/03/the_new_start_bomber_count_and.shtml.

74. Statement of Hon. Rose Gottemoeller, *The New START Treaty (Treaty Doc 111-5)*, Hearings Before the Committee on Foreign Relations, United States Senate, 111th Congress, Second Session, April 29, May 18, 19, 25, June 10, 15, 16, 24, and July 15, 2010 (Washington, DC: U.S. Government Printing Office, 2010), p. 218.

75. Kristensen quoted in Peter Baker, "Arms Control May Be Different on Paper and on the Ground," *New York Times*, March 30, 2010.

76. Pavel Felgenhauer, "Obama's Nuclear Cuts Initiative Meets Frosty Response in Moscow," *Eurasia Daily Monitor* 10, no. 117 (June 20, 2013).

77. Alexander Yakovenko, "Is It Possible to Make a Nuclear-free World?," June 28, 2013, http://rt.com/op-edge/nuclear-free-obama-berlin-399/.

78. It should be noted that Russian commentators have suggested since 1999 that Russia might find it advantageous to withdraw from the INF Treaty or seek its renegotiation. In January 2005, Sergei Ivanov, then the Russian defense minister, reportedly raised the question with Donald Rumsfeld, then the U.S. Secretary of Defense. For background, see David S. Yost, "Russia's Non-Strategic Nuclear Forces," *International Affairs* 77, no. 3 (July 2001): 545; and Hubert Wetzel, Demetri Sevastopulo, and Guy Dinmore, "Russia Confronted Rumsfeld with Threat to Quit Key Nuclear Treaty," *Financial Times*, March 9, 2005.

79. Vladimir Putin, "Meeting on Implementing the 2011–2020 State Arms Procurement Programme," St. Petersburg, June 19, 2013, http://eng.kremlin.ru/transcripts/5615.

80. U.S. National Intelligence Council, *Global Trends 2030: Alternative Worlds* (Washington, DC: National Intelligence Council, December 2012), 69, www.dni.gov/index.php/about/organization/global-trends-2030.

81. "The problem is that Russian leaders see nuclear weapons as more than just a security guarantee. ... The Kremlin and military brass realize that Russia's huge nuclear arsenal is the only remaining symbol of its superpower status, a trump card that they will protect at all costs. This is the main reason Moscow is opposed to cutting any further than the New START limits. Trying to convince Russia to reduce its nonstrategic nuclear weapons will be an even harder sell." Alexander Golts, "Does Moscow's New Foreign Policy Come from Pyongyang?," *Russia Beyond the Headlines*, February 19, 2013, http://rbth.asia/opinion/2013/02/19/does_moscows_new_foreign_policy_come_from_pyongyang_44549.html.

82. The potential risks posed by further U.S. and Russian reductions cited by European experts in discussions in 2012 included the following: U.S. anti-cities strategies harmful to the credibility of extended deterrence; renewed European anxiety about a U.S.-Russian condominium; greater vulnerability to Russian cheating, noncompliance, and breakout; incentives to adopt destabilizing "first strike," "preemption," or "launch on warning" strategies; a potential stimulus to nuclear proliferation; an incentive to competition by nuclear-weapon states outside Europe; perceptions of a U.S. disengagement from extended deterrence; possible fragmentation in Alliance defense efforts; political hedging vis-à-vis Russia and perhaps other powers; an increased likelihood of nonnuclear arms competitions and conflicts; and controversial pressures on the British and French nuclear forces. For an overview of these concerns, see David S. Yost,

"Strategic Stability in Europe: Risks with Low Numbers of U.S. and Russian Nuclear Weapons," *Nonproliferation Review* 20, no. 2 (July 2013): 205–245.

83. This discussion focuses on the CFE regime. Owing to space constraints, it does not examine other aspects of the Alliance's involvement in conventional arms control, such as the Vienna Document, the Open Skies Treaty, NATO/Partnership for Peace Trust Fund Projects, the Arms Trade Treaty, and the UN Program of Action to Prevent, Combat and Eradicate the Illicit Trade in Small Arms and Light Weapons (SALW). For background, see NATO, "NATO's Role in Conventional Arms Control," last updated May 8, 2012, www.nato.int/cps/en/natolive/topics_48896.htm; and William Alberque, "NATO's Role in Arms Control, Disarmament and Non-Proliferation" (presentation at the Ninth Annual NATO Conference on WMD Arms Control, Disarmament and Non-Proliferation, Split, Croatia, May 6–7, 2013).

84. North Atlantic Council, "Strategic Concept," November 19, 2010, par. 26.

85. NATO, "NATO's Role in Conventional Arms Control," March 30, 2009, www.nato.int/issues/arms_control/index.html.

86. North Atlantic Council, "Riga Summit Declaration," par. 42.

87. See the North Atlantic Council statement on CFE, March 28, 2008, press release (2008) 047, www.nato.int/docu/pr/2008/p08-047e.html.

88. Sergey Rogov, "European Security and Arms Control," in *Arms Control and European Security*, ed. Stephen J. Blank and Louis H. Jordan, Jr. (Carlisle, PA: Strategic Studies Institute, U.S. Army War College, August 2012), 56–58.

89. Jeffrey D. McCausland, "European/Eurasian Security and the Treaty on Conventional Armed Forces in Europe," in *Arms Control and European Security*, ed. Stephen J. Blank and Louis H. Jordan, Jr. (Carlisle, PA: Strategic Studies Institute, U.S. Army War College, August 2012), 38. It should be recalled that NATO is not a party to the CFE Treaty. The twenty-two NATO Allies party to the treaty are Belgium, Bulgaria, Canada, the Czech Republic, Denmark, France, Germany, Greece, Hungary, Iceland, Italy, Luxembourg, the Netherlands, Norway, Poland, Portugal, Romania, Slovakia, Spain, Turkey, the United Kingdom, and the United States. The eight non-NATO parties to the treaty are Armenia, Azerbaijan, Belarus, Georgia, Kazakhstan, Moldova, Russia, and Ukraine.

90. Rogov, "European Security and Arms Control," 60.

91. Scott Monje, "The Return of the Russian-Georgian War," August 20, 2012, http://foreignpolicyblogs.com/2012/08/20/the-return-of-the-russian-georgian-war/.

92. North Atlantic Council, "Lisbon Summit Declaration," par. 31 and 32.

93. Ibid., par. 32.

94. Grushko quoted in *RIA Novosti*, "Russia Ready to Discuss New CFE Treaty—Envoy," November 15, 2012, http://en.rian.ru/military_news/20121115/177484833.html

95. McCausland, "European/Eurasian Security and the Treaty on Conventional Armed Forces in Europe," 39.

96. Victoria Nuland, spokesperson, U.S. Department of State, statement on implementation of the Treaty on Conventional Armed Forces in Europe, November 22, 2011.

97. Vladimir Socor, "US, NATO Acknowledge Russian Kill of CFE Treaty," *Eurasia Daily Monitor* 8, no. 219 (December 2, 2011).

98. North Atlantic Council, "Chicago Summit Declaration," par. 63.

99. British expert quoted in Yost, *NATO's Deterrence and Defense Posture*, 13, www.ndc.nato.int/download/downloads.php?icode=356.

100. In an often-cited study Johan Jorgen Holst and Karen Alette Melander argued that "confidence building involves the communication of credible evidence of the absence of feared threats." See their article, "European Security and Confidence-building Measures," *Survival* 19, no. 4 (July/August 1977): 147. See also Johan Jorgen Holst, "Confidence-building Measures: A Conceptual Framework," *Survival* 25, no. 1 (January/February 1983): 2–15.

101. Among recent analyses of the CFE Treaty stalemate, two of the most incisive and thoughtful studies are Anne Witkowsky, Sherman Garnett, and Jeff McCausland, *Salvaging the Conventional Armed Forces in Europe Treaty Regime: Options for Washington* (Washington, DC: Brookings Institution, March 2010); and Paul Schulte, "The Precarious State of Flux of the Conventional Armed Forces in Europe Treaty (CFE)" (conference paper, U.S. Global Engagement Program, Carnegie Council, June 2, 2011).

102. Shoygu and Lavrov quoted in Roger McDermott, "Moscow Security Conference Declares Death of CFE Treaty," *Eurasia Daily Monitor* 10, no. 105 (June 4, 2013).

103. Richard Weitz, "Global Insights: As NATO and Russia Argue, CFE Treaty Gathers Dust," *World Politics Review*, July 30, 2013, www.worldpoliticsreview.com/articles/13126/global-insights-as-nato-and-russia-argue-cfe-treaty-gathers-dust.

104. Antonov quoted in McDermott, "Moscow Security Conference Declares Death of CFE Treaty."

105. Rogov, "European Security and Arms Control," 59.

106. North Atlantic Council, "Lisbon Summit Declaration," par. 31.

107. "France has reduced the types of its nuclear systems to two, the number of its nuclear delivery vehicles by over half, and has announced it will reduce the number of its nuclear warheads to fewer than 300, with no other weapons beside those in its operational stockpile. The United Kingdom has reduced to one nuclear system, and has reduced the explosive power of its nuclear stockpile by 75%, and its number of operationally available nuclear warheads to fewer than 160. The United States has reduced its nuclear weapon stockpile to less than 25% of its size at the height of the Cold War, and decreased tactical nuclear weapons assigned to NATO by nearly 90%." North Atlantic Council, "Bucharest Summit Declaration," par. 40.

108. North Atlantic Council, "Strategic Concept," November 19, 2010, par. 26.

109. North Atlantic Council, "Lisbon Summit Declaration," par. 23.

110. Congressional Commission, *America's Strategic Posture*, 21.

111. See, among other examples, the statement by Colonel General Anatoly Nogovitsyn, the deputy chief of the Russian General Staff, quoted in Damien McElroy, "Russian General Says Poland a Nuclear 'Target,'" *Daily Telegraph*, August 15, 2008, www.telegraph.co.uk/news/worldnews/europe/georgia/2564639/Russian-general-says-Poland-a-nuclear-target-as-Condoleezza-Rice-arrives-in-Georgia.html. Russian statements regarding possible deployment of the dual capable Iskander missile in Kaliningrad are also significant in this regard.

112. According to the most recent doctrinal statement, "The Russian Federation reserves the right to utilize nuclear weapons in response to the utilization of nuclear and other types of weapons of mass destruction against it and (or) its allies, and also in the event of aggression against the Russian Federation involving the use of conventional weapons when the very existence of the state is under threat." "The Military Doctrine of the Russian Federation," approved by Russian Federation presidential edict on February 5, 2010, par. 22, http://kremlin.ru/, English translation at OpenSource.gov, CEP20100208042001. In October 2009, Nikolai Patrushev, the head of the Russian Security Council, said, "In situations critical for national security, a nuclear strike, including a pre-emptive one, against an aggressor is not ruled out." Patrushev interview in *Izvestia*, reported by RIA Novosti, October 14, 2009, http://en.rian.ru/russia/20091014/156461160.html.

113. Matthew Day, "Russia 'Simulates' Nuclear Attack on Poland," *Daily Telegraph*, November 1, 2009, www.telegraph.co.uk/news/worldnews/europe/poland/6480227/Russia-simulates-nuclear-attack-on-Poland.html.

114. Jacob Kipp, "Ten Years of Anti-NATO Exercises by Russian and Belarusian Armed Forces," *Eurasia Daily Monitor* 6, no. 178 (September 29, 2009), www.jamestown.org/single/?no_cache=1&tx_ttnews[tt_news]=35552.

115. Congressional Commission, *America's Strategic Posture*, 20.

116. Jiri Schneider, "Road to World Without Nuclear Weapons?," in *Lidovky.cz*, website of *Lidove Noviny* in Czech, 3–4 April 2010, https://www.opensource.gov, EUP20100407249003.

117. Mart Laar, speech at the US Strategic Command deterrence symposium, August 3, 2011, www.youtube.com/watch?v=hr1GtxbMSUQ.

118. This section of this chapter draws on David S. Yost, "The US Debate on NATO Nuclear Deterrence," *International Affairs* 87, no. 6 (November 2011): 1401–1438, and other works by the author.

119. "The total reduction in the current NATO stockpile of sub-strategic weapons in Europe will be roughly 80%." NATO Nuclear Planning Group, "Final Communiqué," October 17–18, 1991, par. 5. "Deployed [U.S.] weapons in Europe have been reduced by more than 97 per cent since their peak in the 1970s." *Report of the Secretary of Defense Task Force on DoD Nuclear Weapons Management, Phase II: Review of the DoD Nuclear Mission* (Arlington, VA: Secretary of Defense Task Force on DoD Nuclear Weapons Management, December 2008), 59.

120. Congressional Commission, *America's Strategic Posture*, 13.

121. Amy F. Woolf, *Nonstrategic Nuclear Weapons*, RL32572 (Washington, DC: Congressional Research Service, February 14, 2012), summary.

122. In the words of the Congressional Commission, Russia "is no longer in compliance with its PNI [Presidential Nuclear Initiative] commitments." *America's Strategic Posture: The Final Report of the Congressional Commission on the Strategic Posture of the United States*, 13.

123. Roger N. McDermott, *Russia's Conventional Military Weakness and Substrategic Nuclear Policy* (Fort Leavenworth, KS: U.S. Army, Foreign Military Studies Office, July 2011), 6–7.

124. ITAR-TASS in Russian, October 7, 2004, available at OpenSource.gov, CEP20041007000187.

125. In 2011, James N. Miller, then principal deputy under secretary of defense for policy, testified that "unclassified estimates suggest that Russia has 4,000 to 6,500 total nuclear weapons, of which 2,000 to 4,000 are non-strategic tactical nuclear weapons. We have a good understanding of the numbers of deployed Russian strategic nuclear warheads.... We have significantly less confidence in estimates of Russian tactical nuclear weapons." James N. Miller, statement before the House Committee on Armed Services, November 2, 2011, 1.

126. Resolution of advice and consent to ratification agreed to as amended in Senate, December 22, 2010, "Treaty between the United States of America and the Russian Federation on Measures for the Further Reduction and Limita-

tion of Strategic Offensive Arms, signed in Prague on April 8, 2010, with Protocol," http://thomas.loc.gov/cgi-bin/ntquery/z?trtys:111TD00005:.

127. Thomas E. Donilon, remarks at the Carnegie International Nuclear Policy Conference, March 29, 2011.

128. British expert quoted in Yost, *NATO's Deterrence and Defense Posture*, 13.

129. Yost, "Russia's Non-Strategic Nuclear Forces," 531–551.

130. The United States and its NATO Allies included the following commitment in the 2010 Strategic Concept: "National decisions regarding arms control and disarmament may have an impact on the security of all Alliance members. We are committed to maintain, and develop as necessary, appropriate consultations among Allies on these issues." North Atlantic Council," Strategic Concept," November 19, 2010, par. 26.

131. "In diesem Zusammenhang sowie im Zuge der Ausarbeitung eines strategischen Konzeptes der NATO werden wir uns im Bündnis sowie gegenüber den amerikanischen Verbündeten dafür einsetzen, dass die in Deutschland verbliebenen Atomwaffen abgezogen werden." *Wachstum. Bildung. Zusammenhalt: Koalitionsvertrag zwischen CDU, CSU und FDP*, 17 Legislaturperiode, October 26, 2009, 120.

132. Nonpaper submitted by Poland, Norway, Germany, and the Netherlands on increasing transparency and confidence with regard to tactical nuclear weapons in Europe, April 14, 2011. The ambassadors to NATO of Belgium, the Czech Republic, Germany, Hungary, Iceland, Luxembourg, the Netherlands, Norway, Poland, and Slovenia signed the April 15, 2011 cover letter to Anders Fogh Rasmussen, www.fas.org/blog/ssp/2011/04/natoproposal.php.

133. From a U.S. perspective, the verification issues associated with limiting warheads (particularly nonstrategic and nondeployed warheads) have yet to be fully resolved, but they would clearly be important to U.S. senators considering whether to give their approval to the ratification of a treaty calling for warhead limitations.

134. North Atlantic Council, "Deterrence and Defence Posture Review," May 20, 2012, par. 27.

135. French expert quoted in Yost, *NATO's Deterrence and Defense Posture*, 12.

136. Elaine Bunn, "The Future of US Extended Deterrence," in *Perspectives on Extended Deterrence*, Recherches et Documents no. 3/2010, ed. Bruno Tertrais (Paris: Fondation pour la Recherche Stratégique, May 2010), 41, www.frstrategie.org/barreFRS/publications/rd/2010/RD_201003.pdf. The acronym SORT refers to the 2002 Strategic Offensive Reductions Treaty, also known as the Moscow Treaty, which was superseded by the New START Treaty in February 2011.

137. American expert quoted in Yost, *Adapting NATO's Deterrence Posture*, 6.

138. Rose Gottemoeller, "21st Century Deterrence Challenges" (remarks at the U.S. Strategic Command 2011 Deterrence Symposium, Omaha, Nebraska, August 4, 2011), www.state.gov/t/avc/rls/169545.htm.

139. See, for example, Miles Pomper, William Potter, and Nikolai Sokov," Reducing Tactical Nuclear Weapons in Europe," *Survival* 52, no. 1 (February–March 2010), 80–81.

140. Joe Ralston, George Robertson, Frank Miller, and Kori Schake, "The Next Arms-Control Agreement," *Washington Times*, April 22, 2010.

141. Franklin Miller, George Robertson, and Kori Schake, *Germany Opens Pandora's Box* (London: Centre for European Reform, February 2010), 4, www.cer.org.uk/pdf/bn_pandora_final_8feb10.pdf.

142. Franklin Miller, "NATO's Nuclear Future: Self-Centered Policies Threaten Collective Security" (remarks at the Brookings Institution, July 19, 2011), www.acus.org/natosource/nato's-nuclear-future-self-centered-policies-threaten-collective-security.

143. North Atlantic Council, "Deterrence and Defence Posture Review," May 20, 2012, par. 26 and 27.

144. For a useful analysis of the challenges involved in devising such transparency measures, see Paul Schulte et al., *The Warsaw Workshop: Prospects for Information Sharing and Confidence Building on Non-Strategic Nuclear Weapons in Europe* (Warsaw: Polish Institute of International Affairs, April 2013).

145. Author interview with a French observer in Paris, May 23, 2013.

146. In April 2013, at the Second Session of the Preparatory Committee for the 2015 NPT Review Conference, four NATO Allies (Denmark, Iceland, Luxembourg, and Norway) endorsed a joint statement on the humanitarian consequences of nuclear weapons. Ambassador Abdul Samad Minty, "The Humanitarian Impact of Nuclear Weapons" (joint statement delivered at the Second Session of the Preparatory Committee for the 2015 Review Conference of the Parties to the Treaty On the Non-Proliferation of Nuclear Weapons, Geneva, April 24, 2013), http://allafrica.com/stories/201304250948.html?viewall=1.

10

Constraints and Prospects

NATO has worked surprisingly well, despite its internal constraints. The Alliance has managed to accomplish its basic tasks with remarkable effectiveness despite the inherent challenges of collective action by twenty-eight sovereign Allies and uneven performance in certain areas.

The Alliance's balancing act regarding its three core tasks has involved a continuing challenge of equilibrium: maintaining a minimum level of cohesion while engaged in the collective management of differing views among the Allies about which threats to counter (and how to deal with them) and about their vaguely worded but important positive political values (and how to define, protect, and advance them in specific circumstances). Threats clearly dominate NATO's collective defense agenda, while the objective of protecting and advancing liberal democratic values outside the Alliance plays a larger role in its crisis management and cooperative security efforts.

Some discord is inherent in the activities of any organization. Additional friction in operations involving sovereign states with their own internal political dynamics must be expected. As noted in chapter 4, the Alliance's operations in Afghanistan—by far the most demanding ever undertaken by the Allies—have revealed their divergent strategies and priorities and their collective failure to meet agreed resource commitments.

Other constraints derive from the magnitude and multiplicity of the new tasks that the Allies have assigned themselves. The Cold War posture of preparedness for deterrence and defense as the foundation for dialogue and arms control was inherently simpler than sustaining collective defense in conjunction with conducting crisis management operations and pursuing a vision of cooperative security. As discussed in chapter 2, collective defense since the 1990s has encompassed not only the long-standing mission of hedging against state aggression or coercion but also preparedness to deal with terrorism and WMD proliferation, and nontraditional security challenges such as cyber and energy security.

Challenges within the Alliance

Within the Alliance, the Allies face two continuing challenges: finding a balance among the three core tasks spelled out in the 2010 Strategic Concept and defining a more balanced responsibility-sharing equilibrium with the United States.

Finding a Balance among the Three Core Tasks

In principle, the three core tasks articulated in the 2010 Strategic Concept—collective defense, crisis management, and cooperative security—mutually support each other with synergy and interdependence. A solid collective defense posture is expected to enable the Allies to undertake crisis management operations and to pursue cooperative security partnerships with other nations and organizations. These partners may contribute to crisis management operations and thereby diminish the risk of a collective defense contingency arising. Crisis management operations may lead to the forging of new cooperative security partnerships, and these partners may—as with Albania and Croatia and other western Balkan states—become Allies or candidates for Alliance membership and collective defense protection.

Other dynamic interactions among the Alliance's three core tasks have stood out. For example, capacity building, security sector reform, and training and mentoring may involve both cooperative security and crisis management operations. Moreover, the Allies have recognized the risk that a crisis management operation could become a collective defense contingency. Indeed, the distinction between crisis management and collective defense has become indistinct in some circumstances. In other words, there are overlaps among the three core tasks, and some issues straddle categories.

Moreover, even with regard to collective defense, which has been NATO's central function from the outset, nontraditional threats and risks have complicated the preservation of Alliance cohesion. While the Cold War threat of Soviet coercion or aggression could have affected specific Allies differently in a crisis or conflict, the prospect of sharply distinct effects on specific Allies is even greater with some of the new threats. In other words, some of the new threats would probably not affect all Allies in the same way, or to the same degree. Cyber attacks, energy supply cutoffs, and terrorist attacks could be focused on specific Allies without necessarily generating a case for a collective Alliance response involving military forces. When security is defined in more complex ways and military power is only one dimension of the security challenges at hand, NATO's power to evoke loyalty and generate a unified agenda may be compromised. The Allies have nonetheless tried to deal with these new threats on a collective basis. The Allies have often limited their collective effort under Alliance auspices to "where NATO may add value." At the same time, the Allies have pursued their crisis management and cooperative security objectives.

Some critics have compared the multifunction post–Cold War, post–September 2001 Alliance to a Swiss Army knife—usable for multiple functions but not optimally designed and equipped for any specific task. An even less flattering metaphor has been to suggest that the Alliance has developed "strategic schizophrenia,"[1] a multiple personality disorder, owing to a lack of unity of purpose. This metaphor rejects the official view that the three core tasks are mutually reinforcing and form a coherent whole. Another critical formula has been to contend that the consensus of the Allies on the three core tasks is "skin deep" and does not command "the heart, the gut, and the brain" of each member state. As pointed out repeatedly in this study, the priorities of Allies regarding these tasks differ.

Proponents of the balancing image suggest that the NATO Allies might be likened to a team of trapeze artists and jugglers. Some performers engage in various trapeze stunts and juggling acts while others are simultaneously tightrope walking. The show never stops, and it is successful as long as the net proceeds show a profit. In NATO's case, success would be measured by criteria such as the prevention of aggression or coercion, the conduct of constructive interventions, and the pursuit of meaningful and productive partnerships with other organizations and countries.

The challenge of striking the right balance among the three core tasks, with a view to maximizing synergy and effectiveness, is complicated by tensions among these tasks. For example, Russia is formally NATO's partner but remains the main source of security concern for some Allies. The Allies are, in other words, engaged in managing a tension—and seeking a balance—between NATO's collective defense mission and its cooperative security vision. President Obama stated in September 2009 that "we want to improve generally not only U.S.-Russian relations, but also NATO-Russian relations, while making absolutely clear that our commitment to all of our allies in NATO is sacrosanct and that our commitment to Article 5 continues."[2]

Moreover, while Russia has contributed support to some NATO crisis management operations (notably IFOR and SFOR in Bosnia and KFOR in Kosovo), Moscow has sharply criticized others (including Operation Allied Force in the Kosovo conflict in 1999 and Operation Unified Protector in Libya in 2011). Russian leaders have also expressed profound reservations about the Alliance's self-assigned role as an international crisis manager, including its refusal to exclude using force without a UN Security Council mandate if necessary.

With regard to Georgia and Ukraine, several Allied observers do not endorse the idea of moving beyond partnership and the promotion of cooperative security and effective crisis management to making collective defense commitments. These observers argue that irritating Moscow by admitting Georgia and/or Ukraine to the Alliance would enlarge NATO's collective defense responsibilities and requirements, complicate the conduct of certain crisis management operations (Afghanistan in particular), and undermine the pursuit of cooperative security with Russia.

Some Allied observers, notably in Central and Eastern Europe, regarded NATO's intervention in the Libya crisis in 2011 as a distraction from the resolve expressed at the November 2010 Lisbon Summit to refocus on collective defense. From their perspective, the Libya operation represented a diversion of resources and an extension of NATO's crisis management ambitions, to the detriment of attention to core collective defense responsibilities.[3]

Certain critics hold that the Allies have concentrated on crisis management operations at the expense of the Alliance's other functions. In their view, such operations demand excessive amounts of resources and political capital and may distort the Alliance's focus. With regard to cooperative security, for example, these observers contend, the Allies are inclined to emphasize current operations in pursuing partnerships with other nations and organizations instead of taking a long-term perspective oriented toward broader political and security objectives. This inclination derives directly from the urgency of addressing immediate operational challenges, especially when Alliance and partner personnel are in harm's way.[4]

To what extent have the Allies succeeded in sustaining NATO's relevance to their security interests in light of the three core tasks? In practice, the Allies have tried to perform all three core tasks, with some success but mixed results on each, owing to inadequate investments and internal dissension, plus the inherent recalcitrance of the international environment that they are trying to shape in the image of their cooperative security vision. The Allies collectively cannot and do not wish to withhold reassurance about collective defense for the Baltic states and other Allies in Central and Eastern Europe, but their efforts in this regard have been deliberately restrained to assure the Russians as to the absence of any hostile intent on NATO's part. The results have failed to fully satisfy the Allies concerned but have nonetheless irritated the Russians.

Jamie Shea has characterized the threefold challenge as one of (1) providing assurances about collective defense, (2) sustaining constructive cooperative security relations with Russia, and (3) keeping focused on NATO's main crisis management operation: "Article 5 assurance must not be done in a way that upsets the strategic balance in Europe. Nor must it be to the detriment of NATO's capacity to generate and equip forces for its Afghan mission, given that the greatest current threat to Allied security is on the Afghan-Pakistan border."[5]

Some Allies have pursued efforts in one core task area for the sake of another. It is, for example, a commonplace observation that some Central and Eastern European Allies have contributed forces to crisis management operations in the Balkans and Afghanistan in order to demonstrate their reliability as Allies and to build up a sense of political obligation regarding collective defense with their fellow Allies, particularly the United States. According to a French observer's analysis in May 2011,

> Allies generally value U.S. protection most highly, so Washington has been successful in persuading them to send forces to Afghanistan, where the United States has the lead. France and the United Kingdom are the leaders in the Libya case, and most Allies have been less forthcoming with force contributions in Libya than in Afghanistan. This is because the Allies count on the United States as their collective defense protector more than on France and the United Kingdom.[6]

This intriguing judgment might be qualified by taking into account other factors that probably played a part in limiting contributions to the NATO intervention in Libya from Central and Eastern European Allies—above all, their limited military resources, ongoing force commitments in Afghanistan, deficiencies in equipment suitable for long-range air strike operations, and judgments as to the intrinsic relevance of the Libyan situation to their security interests.

There has also been competition among the three core tasks, because the Allies differ in their priorities regarding these tasks. Various analysts have discerned "fragmentation" or "multitier" tendencies among the Allies based on their priorities. Some Allies (such as Canada, Denmark, the Netherlands, and the United Kingdom) are regarded as being more focused than others on NATO crisis management and "comprehensive approach" operations in partnership with the European Union and the United Nations, while others (such as the Baltic states, the Czech Republic, Norway, Poland, and Turkey) are viewed as being more preoccupied than others with collective defense.[7]

One of the effects of NATO's enlargement appears to have been to deepen and multiply disagreements among the Allies about threat assessments and priorities. Many policymakers in the new Allies from Central and Eastern Europe regard Russia as a potential security threat and hence emphasize the importance of collective defense, whereas some experts and officials in the "old" Allies in Western Europe do not share this view and even mock those who retain continuing concern about Russia's capabilities, activities, and intentions.[8] Some Western Europeans have belittled the professed security concerns of Central and Eastern Europeans regarding Russia by suggesting that their professions of anxiety are instrumental and designed to gain a more central role in Alliance decision making. Conversely, some Central and Eastern Europeans have questioned the willingness of Western Europeans to honor their Article 5 commitments.[9]

Judgments in this regard are impressionistic, but it is generally agreed that the Western European Allies have in recent years perceived no significant collective defense threat, in contrast with Norway, Turkey, and the Central and Eastern European Allies. The Western European Allies have attached comparatively greater importance to crisis management and cooperative security endeavors (particularly the NATO-Russia Council) than to collective defense. In their view, collective defense has become a remote contingency, at least with regard to state aggression (as opposed to terrorism by nonstate actors), for which NATO serves as the ultimate guarantee; and the main everyday operational activity of the Alliance has become crisis management, supported to some extent by cooperative security endeavors. Indeed, some Allied experts and officials maintain that cooperative security and crisis management activities have become the principal means of ensuring the safety of the Alliance. For many observers in Western Europe, to focus on preparedness for collective defense against aggression in the form of "an armed attack" in the traditional sense of Article 5 of the North Atlantic Treaty seems an old-fashioned hangover from the Cold War.[10]

Among the Western European Allies, Germany is commonly regarded as the most committed to pursuing cooperative security with Russia. Some observers, within and outside Germany, have interpreted the country's continuing reductions in defense spending as evidence of a declining interest in crisis management and collective defense.[11] In May 2011, however, the German Ministry of Defense published a statement that could be construed as offering support for deterrence, crisis management, and cooperative security: "Ensuring security for our nation today means above all keeping the consequences of crises and conflicts at bay and taking an active part in their prevention and containment."[12]

Some French observers maintain that France, despite its extensive crisis management activities, continues to regard collective defense as the Alliance's top mission, and hold that France does so "to prevent movement toward a more politically led set of priorities," inspired by either Germany or the United States. As in the past, some French experts hold that NATO is a temporary insurance policy pending the construction of a self-reliant European Union, an EU capable of providing for its own defense and security without relying on the United States. However, most EU members of the Alliance regard collective defense through NATO as the continuing and long-term foundation of their national security.[13] Observers have attributed to Italy a leading role in crisis management and cooperative security, notably with regard to the Mediterranean Dialogue and the Istanbul Cooperation Initiative.

To what extent can NATO be all things to all Allies? For example, can NATO serve simultaneously as a credible bedrock of collective defense and assurance for the Baltic states, a vehicle for improving political relations with Russia for Germany, and a framework for developing and leading expeditionary forces in distant crisis management operations for the United States?

The balancing challenges have been especially acute with regard to Russia. The Allies appear, for example, to have failed to anticipate the Georgia-Russia crisis before it came to a head in August 2008. As James Sherr, a British scholar, has observed,

> NATO was proud of the fact that we had all these mechanisms of cooperation with Georgia, but [the Allies had] no position at all about what should happen. And that is one reason all of this has happened, because we refused to deal with the fundamental political issues.... Russian Ambassador [Dmitry] Rogozin said: "We called for a meeting of the NATO-Russia Council on 8 August and you did not hold one." I asked him: "You have sat there all this time between April and August: can you identify one occasion where the NATO Allies themselves met to discuss what was happening in Georgia?" He could not.[14]

Part of the explanation for NATO's failure to take crisis-prevention action in this case, despite its commitment to crisis management and its structures for dialogue with Georgia and Russia, resides in the discord among the Allies about the right way to deal with Russia.

In the wake of the August 2008 Georgia-Russia conflict, Radoslaw Sikorski, the Polish foreign minister, proposed the declaration of what some commentators called a "Sikorski Doctrine"—that is, "Any further attempt to redraw borders in Europe by force or by subversion should be regarded by Europe as a threat to its security and should entail a proportional response by the whole Atlantic community."[15] This proposal won support among Central and Eastern European Allies but little interest among other Allies, which were generally disposed to minimize confrontation with

Russia rather than to make such a démarche. Indeed, some blamed the Georgian leader, Mikheil Saakashvili, for poor judgment in taking the bait in the trap that Moscow had set.

Similarly, the 2009 proposal by several Central and Eastern European experts and officials that the Allies "re-think the working of the NATO-Russia Council and return to the practice where NATO member countries enter into dialogue with Moscow with a coordinated position" gained little notice from the Western European and North American Allies. These Central and Eastern European experts and officials argued, "When it comes to Russia, our experience has been that a more determined and principled policy toward Moscow will not only strengthen the West's security but will ultimately lead Moscow to follow a more cooperative policy as well."[16]

The fate of this proposal demonstrated the difficulty of modifying an established consensus among the Allies about how to conduct cooperative security relations with Russia. There has been no consensus to abandon the practice that the Allies agreed upon with Russia in May 2002 (no pre-coordination of NATO positions) and to return to the previous procedure. In other words, the consensus "balance" among the Allies has been to maintain continuity in Alliance policy in this regard.

The Alliance's post–Cold War high-level political-military crisis management exercises from 1992 to 2012 also illustrate the various pressures placed on the Allies as they have attempted to define an appropriate balance among their priorities. These exercises do not involve the deployment of forces but engage senior military and civilian personnel in the capitals of NATO nations, the North Atlantic Council and the International Staff and the International Military Staff at NATO headquarters, and command and staff at Allied Command Operations and Allied Command Transformation.[17]

In the 1992–2012 period the Allies scheduled twenty-one crisis management exercises. Three were cancelled because of the demands of operations in the Balkans (1994, 1996, and 1999), and two (2007 and 2010) were postponed indefinitely because of the impasse in NATO-EU relations since 2004. The Allies conducted four exercises with other international organizations (the member states of the Western European Union in 2000 and the European Union in 2003, before the European Union's enlargement the following year; and the expert staffs of the United Nations in 2009 and the European Union's European External Action Service in 2012). Between 1998 and 2010, six exercises focused on crisis response or peace support operations (non-Article 5 scenarios), three exercises emphasized potential Article 5 situations, and one exercise focused on a non-Article 5 situation that included the risk of becoming an Article 5 crisis (2006). The exercise in 2011 was the first in ten years to focus solely on Article 5. Moreover, at the request of the newer Allies, its scenario was specifically designed to lead to the first exercise invocation of Article 5. It also featured "Counter Surprise and Counter Aggression, and . . . the involvement of Partners in an Article 5 environment."[18]

To be precise, because the 2011 exercise was focused on Norway, described as "the Northern Euro-Atlantic area" on the NATO website, the NATO Allies invited Finland and Sweden to participate in the exercise. NATO informed all Euro-Atlantic Partnership Council (EAPC) partners (including Russia) about plans for the exercise and invited staff members from the United Nations, the European Union External Action Service, the OSCE, and the International Committee of the Red Cross "to observe relevant aspects of the exercise."[19]

The 2012 exercise (discussed in chapter 2) was the first in which the Allies considered the possible invocation of Article 5 in the framework of a cyber attack. As noted in chapter 8, Finland and Sweden participated in the exercise. NATO invited the International Committee of the Red Cross and the Organization for the Prohibition of Chemical Weapons to observe, and the EU's European External Action Service (EEAS) to contribute.[20]

In short, the crisis management exercises in the 1992–2012 period focused to a significant extent on crisis management in the sense that the Allies have given this term since the early 1990s—that is, non-Article 5 operations. The Allies cancelled three planned exercises in the series owing to the pressing requirements of actual non-Article 5 operations in the Balkans. NATO demonstrated an interest in the core task of cooperative security in some of these exercises by seeking the involvement of other international organizations, but apart from 2012, when Allies invited the EEAS to contribute, EU attendance has been blocked by the "participation problem" in NATO-EU relations since 2004—that is, the stalemate arising from the troubled relations between Turkey and Cyprus. Although the 2011 exercise concentrated on a collective defense contingency, with the invocation of Article 5, NATO showed its commitment to cooperative security and transparency by informing all EAPC partners about the exercise, inviting two partner nations to contribute, and inviting other international organizations to send observers.

The Preeminent Role of the United States

The preponderant leadership role of the United States in the Alliance has generally been positive for Washington and the other NATO Allies, but it could be carried to a dysfunctional excess. If the comparative military resource contributions of the other Allies continue to decline in relation to those of the United States, this will be damaging for Alliance cohesion and effectiveness. The other Allies need to increase their defense investments, improve their military capabilities, and work with Washington to define a more balanced responsibility-sharing equilibrium with the United States.

From a U.S. perspective, as noted in the 2010 National Security Strategy, "Our relationship with our European allies remains the cornerstone for U.S. engagement with the world."[21] Secretary of State Hillary Clinton said in 2010, "Our nation faces threats elsewhere in the world, but we view peace and stability in Europe as a prerequisite for addressing all of the other challenges."[22] According to the January 2012 U.S. defense guidance,

Europe is home to some of America's most stalwart allies and partners, many of whom have sacrificed alongside U.S. forces in Afghanistan, Iraq, and elsewhere. Europe is our principal partner in seeking global and economic security, and will remain so for the foreseeable future. At the same time, security challenges and unresolved conflicts persist in parts of Europe and Eurasia, where the United States must continue to promote regional security and Euro-Atlantic integration. The United States has enduring interests in supporting peace and prosperity in Europe as well as bolstering the strength and vitality of NATO, which is critical to the security of Europe and beyond.[23]

The European Allies have often underscored the need, from their perspective, for the United States to serve as the leader of the Alliance, and as the ultimate security guarantor and pacifier of Europe.[24] In 1992 Manfred Wörner, then the NATO secretary general, said, "If the United States disengages, I foresee a certain temptation for Western European nations to revert to past patterns of power politics."[25] The following year Wörner added, "We need United States' leadership. Without the leadership of the US there will be no leadership at all, and most likely no meaningful action in crisis situations."[26] Rob de Wijk, a Dutch scholar, wrote in 2000, "Both NATO's internal pacifying function and heavy crisis response operations require leadership. At present there is no alternative to US leadership. The major European powers are too divided to play the role of lead nation and too weak to play the role of pacifier."[27] In 2010, the current NATO secretary general, Anders Fogh Rasmussen, also expressed support for the "pacifier" role of the United States: "The history of the last century makes it clear that Europe is most stable and at peace when the United States is present here, politically and militarily. . . . NATO is the framework for that presence today."[28]

To function effectively, the Alliance needs U.S. leadership, which flows naturally from U.S. military strength. However, the imbalance in military capabilities between the United States and its NATO Allies, notably with regard to certain advanced technologies, could become excessive and damaging to the Alliance's cohesion and effectiveness. U.S. leaders have been concerned about this risk of European dependence since the 1950s. As Marc Trachtenberg has pointed out with regard to U.S. policy during the Eisenhower administration (1953–1961),

Eisenhower wanted the Europeans to be real allies, the sort who felt responsible for their own defense. He complained increasingly that the Europeans had lost this sense of responsibility. They should be "ashamed" of that fact, and America had to do more to "wean our allies from overdependence upon us and to encourage them to make better efforts of their own." The Europeans had to be made to see that their "security cannot always and completely depend on the U.S."[29]

Beyond the risk of fostering a pattern of dependence, the high level of reliance on the United States and its military capabilities could also aggravate a divide within the Alliance between the "old" Western European Allies and the "new" Central and Eastern European Allies. Most of the latter were under Soviet influence during the Cold War as members of the Warsaw Pact or (in the case of the Baltic states) as Soviet republics. These Allies tend to place greater reliance on U.S. security assurances than on Article 5 of the North Atlantic Treaty, owing to doubts about the reliability of their Western European allies. As Aleksander Smolar, the president of the Stefan Batory Foundation in Warsaw, said in 2003, "The U.S. is more credible for us as a guarantor of security than western Europe, which is still looking for an idea of security and cannot assure its reality."[30]

Doubts in this region about the reliability of the Western European Allies in collective defense contingencies derive not only from the asymmetry in military capabilities between the United States and the other NATO Allies but also from historical factors. While some resentments accumulated in Central and Eastern Europe during the centuries in which this region functioned as a buffer sheltering Western Europe,[31] contemporary observers in Central and Eastern Europe highlight events during the interwar period and the Cold War.

In the interwar period, the 1938 Munich conference stands out as the occasion when Britain, France, Italy, and Germany decided the future of Czechoslovakia. Many Czechs and Slovaks—and other Central and Eastern Europeans—remember that Édouard Daladier, the French prime minister, was at Munich with Neville Chamberlain, the British prime minister, in September 1938. Although London and Paris honored their commitment to declare war on Germany when Poland was invaded in 1939, this action seems less vivid than the Munich betrayal (and certain events during World War II) in the historical memories of some Central and Eastern Europeans. Moreover, some Central and Eastern Europeans recall Western passivity and restraint in response to events such as the 1948 communist coup d'état in Prague, the 1956 Hungarian uprising, the 1968 Warsaw Pact invasion of Czechoslovakia, and the 1981 imposition of martial law in Poland. Another historical factor is persistent resentment in some quarters in Central and Eastern Europe derived from the judgment that the policies of détente pursued by West Germany and other Western European states during the Cold War stabilized and prolonged Soviet rule. From the perspective of some Central and Eastern European observers, Western European governments gave priority to their dialogue with the Soviet Union rather than to solidarity with Central and Eastern European nations.

Some Central and Eastern European observers have also perceived a recurrent tendency on the part of some of their Western European allies to adopt a superior and condescending "we know best" attitude. They cite as an example of this tendency French president Jacques Chirac's February 2003 statement that the nations that had endorsed the Vilnius Group declaration supporting U.S. policy on Iraq were "infantile" and "poorly brought up," had "missed a good chance to shut up," and had placed in danger their prospects of joining the European Union.[32] In contrast, despite the reservations of some Western European allies, the United States championed the post–Cold War NATO enlargement process and provided substantial advice and assistance to Central and Eastern European countries to prepare them for Alliance membership.[33]

Some Allied observers have raised questions about the future of U.S. leadership in NATO in light of the January 2012 U.S. defense guidance. According to this guidance,

> U.S. economic and security interests are inextricably linked to developments in the arc extend-
> ing from the Western Pacific and East Asia into the Indian Ocean region and South Asia, cre-
> ating a mix of evolving challenges and opportunities. Accordingly, while the U.S. military will
> continue to contribute to security globally, *we will of necessity rebalance toward the Asia-Pacific*
> *region.* . . . Most European countries are now producers of security rather than consumers of it.
> Combined with the drawdown in Iraq and Afghanistan, this has created a strategic opportunity
> to rebalance the U.S. military investment in Europe, moving from a focus on current conflicts
> toward a focus on future capabilities. *In keeping with this evolving strategic landscape, our posture*
> *in Europe must also evolve.* As this occurs, the United States will maintain our Article 5 com-
> mitments to allied security and promote enhanced capacity and interoperability for coalition
> operations.[34]

The Obama administration announced in January 2012 that it would remove two of the four army brigades in Europe, leaving one in Germany and one in Italy. The United States intends to compensate for these troop withdrawals and others by sending forces to Europe in a "rotational presence" mode for joint training and exercises with European allies and partners.[35] In May 2013 a French critic of the U.S. "rotational presence" plan compared it to *le jeu de bonneteau*—that is, a shell game or confidence trick like three-card monte.[36] Some European experts regarded the removal of the last U.S. main battle tanks based in Germany in March 2013 as a highly significant step.[37]

The *Economist*, a British weekly newsmagazine, titled its editorial on the new U.S. defense guidance "Rebalancing America's Forces: The Downgrading of Europe."[38] General Mieczyslaw Cieniuch, chief of the General Staff of the Polish Armed Forces, said, "We are not very happy that the U.S. military involvement in Europe will be smaller than today's, especially from the Polish point of view, because we are a border country of the [NATO] alliance."[39] Gideon Rachman of London's *Financial Times* wrote a column titled "A Disarmed Europe Will Face the World on Its Own."[40] Former German foreign minister Joschka Fischer wrote, "This new, more focused and limited American role thus raises the following question for America's European partners: Can they afford the luxury of being unable to defend themselves without US help?"[41]

Despite the anxieties expressed by some European commentators, U.S. leadership in NATO is expected to persist, owing to the predominance of U.S. military capabilities and the absence of any plausible alternative leadership. Moreover, some Allies have endorsed the new U.S. approach to maintaining a visible and credible military presence in Europe. The Norwegian minister of defense, Espen Barth Eide, said that, given the increased U.S. attention to the Asia-Pacific region,

> reduction of US static, military presence in Europe is quite logical. . . . However, this does not
> have to entail a weakening of the transatlantic ties. Current plans suggest that [the] previously
> static presence (permanent bases) is substituted by [a] more dynamic presence, like frequent
> and large-scale exercises, prepositioning of equipment, for instance in Norway, and increased
> intelligence sharing and situational awareness.[42]

The preeminent role of the United States in NATO may, moreover, be subject to adjustment in specific contingencies. As noted in chapter 5, the Alliance's intervention in Libya in 2011 demonstrated that the United States need not provide a preponderance of resources in every major operation and that for some missions NATO Allies can form an effective coalition of the willing supported by commonly funded and staffed capabilities. Secretary General Rasmussen said in March 2012 that "the positive story from the Libya operation is that for the first time in the history of our Alliance European Allies and Canada provided the majority of assets for an operation." Rasmussen nonetheless acknowledged that "that very successful operation couldn't have been carried out that successfully without a significant input of critical military capabilities from our American Ally."[43]

Recalcitrant Realities outside the Alliance

The constraints facing the Alliance have been most apparent in relation to its vision of cooperative security, but they have also applied to its crisis management operations. With each of these core tasks the Allies have looked beyond collective defense to transformative goals. The limits to what the Alliance has been able to achieve in pursuing these goals stand out with regard to cooperation with Russia, the general goal of democratization in the Euro-Atlantic region, and crisis management and postconflict reconstruction.

Cooperation with Russia

Russia has been less than fully compliant regarding the Alliance's cooperative security vision. As discussed in chapter 9, Russia has declined to honor its obligation in the 1990 CFE Treaty to withdraw its forces from Georgia and Moldova, despite its promise at the 1999 OSCE Istanbul Summit to do so. This stalemate may last indefinitely, in view of Russia's occupation of the Abkhazia and South Ossetia regions of Georgia in 2008 and its recognition of these territories as independent states that have chosen to make agreements for a long-term Russian military presence. In August 2008, in the face of the violent Georgia-Russia conflict, the NATO Allies declared, "We remind all parties that peaceful conflict resolution is a key principle of the Partnership for Peace Framework Document."[44] This rather abject statement was clearly decoupled from reality. Belligerents engaged in combat or poised to resume fighting generally do not see peaceful conflict resolution as an option. The Georgia-Russia conflict demonstrated the limits of NATO's cooperative security vision.

Since August 2008 the NATO Allies have regularly repeated certain principles, as in the November 2010 Lisbon Summit Declaration: "We continue to call on Russia to reverse its recognition of the South Ossetia and Abkhazia regions of Georgia as independent states…[and] we urge Russia to meet its commitments with respect to Georgia, as mediated by the European Union on 12 August and 8 September 2008."[45] As noted in chapter 7, Russia has not responded favorably to these urgings and has continued to block the return of UN and OSCE missions to Georgia. According to Rose Gottemoeller, some Russian commentators anticipate that the Georgia-Russia conflict may last as long as the Cyprus dispute,[46] which has remained unresolved since 1963.[47] It appears that one of the reasons why the Georgia problems and other "frozen conflicts" in the post-Soviet space (including the Moldova-Transnistria and the Armenia-Azerbaijan Nagorno-Karabakh cases) have remained unresolved has been their utility for Russia as mechanisms for the exertion of influence.

Russian reactions to the NATO enlargement process illustrate most acutely the divergence between the Alliance's "cooperative security" view and Moscow's assessment of its implications for Russia.

In April 1997, some months before NATO extended invitations to the Czech Republic, Hungary, and Poland for the first post–Cold War round of enlargement, Madeleine Albright, then the U.S. secretary of state, argued that the Russians should learn to move beyond an adversarial and competition-oriented worldview: "The truth is, the quest for freedom and security in Europe is not a zero-sum game, in which Russia must lose if central Europe gains, and central Europe must lose if Russia gains. Such thinking has brought untold tragedy to Europe and America, and we have a responsibility as well as an opportunity to transcend it."[48] Similarly, in the George W. Bush administration, Condoleezza Rice, then the U.S. secretary of state, said in 2008, "We don't see any of this as a zero-sum game . . . [and] we don't see and don't accept any notion of a special sphere of influence."[49] Speaking for the Obama administration, Vice President Joseph Biden said in 2009, "We will not recognize any nation having a sphere of influence. It will remain our view that sovereign states have the right to make their own decisions and choose their own alliances."[50]

In March 1997, Javier Solana, then the NATO secretary general, said that "NATO's enlargement is . . . one part of a wider package that is designed to develop closer relationships with all countries in the Euro-Atlantic area. The whole package is about uniting the whole of the Euro-Atlantic community around a common security culture. It is about consigning concepts like dividing lines, buffer zones and spheres of influence where they belong: in the dustbin of history."[51] One of Solana's successors as secretary general, Jaap de Hoop Scheffer, repeated the argument in 2009: "We . . . need to move beyond a 19th century 'Great Game' idea of spheres of influence."[52]

NATO and Russia agreed in the 1997 Founding Act that they would "build together a lasting and inclusive peace in the Euro-Atlantic area on the principles of democracy and cooperative security."[53] Moscow's acceptance of this language does not, however, mean that the Russians have attached the same significance as the NATO Allies to the Alliance's "cooperative security" vision. NATO's objective, as articulated by Solana, of "uniting the whole of the Euro-Atlantic community around a common security culture" will not be achieved if the Russians choose not to accept the principles of that culture.[54]

NATO's transformative effort appears to have come up against the same obstacle faced by the European Union in dealing with Russia—that is, a persistent conviction that certain ideas championed by the European Union and NATO could threaten Russia's autonomy, security interests, and political status. As Katinka Barysch wrote in 2004, "Large parts of Russia's policy establishment remain wedded to old-fashioned concepts such as spheres of influence, zero-sum games and strict reciprocity. Many EU policy-makers and most Brussels bureaucrats believe in 'post-modern' ideas of statecraft, such as mutual interests, shared sovereignty and win-win solutions."[55] Given predominant Russian views, it is not surprising that in August 2008, in the wake of the Georgia-Russia war, Russian president Dmitry Medvedev announced that, "as is the case of other countries, there are regions in which Russia has privileged interests."[56]

Rather than seeing NATO enlargement as a benign process of "exporting stability" and promoting democratic values that is in the general interest of all nations in the Euro-Atlantic area, including Russia, many Russian officials and experts profess to view the NATO enlargement process as an expansion of the Alliance's sphere of influence. From the perspective of these Russians, NATO's rhetoric is contradictory: if NATO wants to build a relationship of partnership and cooperation with Russia, why have NATO governments enlarged the Alliance and extended collective defense commitments to nations that have expressed distrust and antipathy toward Russia? From a Russian perspective, NATO and the European Union have encroached on Russia's sphere of influence and have cynically and disingenuously denied doing so.[57] Secretary General Rasmussen identified a key factor in Russian distrust of the Alliance's intentions: "Russia expected NATO to be dissolved when the Warsaw Pact collapsed. Because it didn't, many in Russia can only find one explanation—that the Alliance still sees Russia as a threat. And every thing we do is seen through that prism: enlargement, missile defence, even our partnerships."[58]

Russia's consistent rejection of the NATO enlargement process since it began in the mid-1990s and the 2008 Georgia-Russia conflict in particular have raised questions about the attainability of the Alliance's "cooperative security" vision. In July 2009 Jaap de Hoop Scheffer, then the NATO secretary general, said that some Allied observers "question the future of NATO enlargement as a benign means of consolidating Europe."[59]

This raises the question of alternatives. James Sherr has argued that the alternative to NATO enlargement was the renationalization of the security and defense policies of the non-Soviet former Warsaw Pact states and the Soviet successor states seeking autonomy from Russia. "The whole purpose of the first round of NATO enlargement was to ensure that neither Europe nor Russia was surrounded by half a dozen Georgias: apprehensive, proud, impulsive, incompetent states. Does someone care to make the argument that it would be less dangerous if the countries now surrounding Russia had their defences re-nationalized?"[60] In 1997 Javier Solana predicted that "Russia will ultimately come to the conclusion that a privileged relationship with an enlarged NATO is far preferable to any other alternative."[61]

As discussed in chapter 6, owing in part to differences among the NATO Allies regarding policy toward Russia, the Allies have chosen to emphasize the areas in which they have been able to work constructively with Moscow, such as logistical transit support for the NATO-led forces in Afghanistan. This has become the de facto balance of feasibility in the Alliance's Russia policy: regular restatements of principle regarding the territorial integrity of Georgia, CFE Treaty obligations, and so forth, plus concerted efforts to pursue practical cooperation and dispel Russian myths about the Alliance and its purposes. In the words of the NATO secretary general, "Russian misperceptions about NATO's Open Door policy persist. As do many other myths about the Alliance. We must work to overcome this. To help Russia understand that it can build security together with us, not against us. NATO's security and Russia's security are intertwined. That is why our stated goal is to forge a true strategic partnership."[62]

Democratization in the Euro-Atlantic region

In 1990 all the member states of what was then the Conference on Security and Cooperation in Europe signed the Charter of Paris for a New Europe. This document included a commitment "to build, consolidate and strengthen democracy as the only system of government of our nations."[63]

Promoting democracy is, to be sure, consistent with NATO's "cooperative security" vision. The Alliance as a whole and individual NATO nations have strived to encourage democracy, notably via Partnership for Peace (PfP) and the enlargement process. PfP activities and the reforms required in the enlargement process have contributed to what some observers have called the "socialization" of new Allies and partners with democratic practices, including civilian control and parliamentary oversight of the armed forces.[64] The concurrent outreach and enlargement processes of the European Union have fostered similar values.

It has proved difficult, however, to promote democracy in states with few traditions supportive of democratic rule or with political elites that see democracy as a threat to their power and status. The French scholar Pierre Hassner highlighted the challenge of building democracy by citing Bergson:

> The French philosopher Henri Bergson put forward a thesis that seems to me as true as it is shocking: Liberal democracy is the least natural regime on earth. What is natural is the rule of the strongest. Democracy can come into being only through an uphill struggle that requires courage and perseverance and that aims at a profound change in attitudes and institutions.[65]

Within the OSCE, as the Hungarian scholar Pál Dunay pointed out in 2006, "Growing dissension is emerging between states which actively advocate the spread of liberal democracy and those which are opposed to spreading it to their countries and their neighbourhood."[66] The champions of extending liberal democracy have been mainly the member states of NATO and the European Union. The governing elites in several states, including Belarus, Kazakhstan, Kyrgyzstan, Russia, Tajikistan, Turkmenistan, and Uzbekistan, have resisted the advance of liberal democracy. Russian foreign minister Sergey Lavrov in 2005 voiced a complaint that Moscow has subsequently repeated many times: "NATO deals with security issues, the EU with economic issues, while the OSCE will only monitor the adoption of these organizations' values by countries that have remained outside the EU and NATO."[67]

As Alexander Warkotsch has pointed out, with regard to the Soviet successor states in Central Asia, the prospects for democratization under OSCE auspices via "strategic calculation" are "bleak" because the OSCE has little to offer in terms of "large-scale welfare and security benefits," because it has no membership conditionality lever to obtain "norm-compliance," and because its financial and personnel resources are limited.[68] The prospects for democratization via "normative suasion" are also poor because the "ingrained beliefs" and "culture" of the societies are "not democratic, but authoritarian, patrimonial, and personal."[69]

NATO and the European Union have greater institutional resources to bring to bear than does the OSCE. In practice, however, both organizations have demonstrated in their behavior that they have priorities in addition to promoting democracy. As Marc de Brichambaut, then the secretary general of the OSCE, observed in 2010, in their democracy-promotion activities EU member states have shown "a reluctance to antagonize major trading and geopolitical partners, such as Russia, China or key Middle Eastern countries."[70] This "reluctance to antagonize" regarding noncompliance with democratic practices has also characterized the NATO member nations in their dealings with Russia and certain other post-Soviet states, especially the states of Central Asia with significant energy resources or airfields, rail lines, and other logistical assets valuable for NATO's operations in Afghanistan. A comparable "reluctance to antagonize" has extended to NATO partners in the Mediterranean Dialogue and the Istanbul Cooperation Initiative, and to certain "partners across the globe" such as Afghanistan and Pakistan.

NATO's relations with Uzbekistan illustrate the compromises reached in efforts to satisfy competing imperatives: the Allies have generally regarded the democratization called for by the Alliance's cooperative security vision as less urgent than the logistical requirements of NATO's crisis management operations. In May 2005, when the government of Uzbek president Islam Karimov reportedly killed hundreds of demonstrators in Andijan, Jaap de Hoop Scheffer, then the NATO secretary general, issued a statement: "The Alliance expects Uzbekistan, a member of Partnership for Peace, to honour the principles of PfP, including the peaceful resolution of conflicts."[71]

The Allies differed, however, as to whether to support calls for an independent investigation, owing to concern that the Uzbek government might deny access to the airfield at Karshi-Khanabad. The value of this airfield for supplying NATO forces in Afghanistan prevented consensus in the Alliance on endorsing such an investigation. In the words of "a senior defense official" in Washington, "If there was tension . . . it was between supporting 'democracy in Uzbekistan' and 'democracy in Afghanistan.'"[72]

According to the NATO website, Uzbek-NATO "relations declined to some extent following the events in Andijan in 2005," and "there was a pause" from 2005 to 2010 in Uzbek participation in the Partnership for Peace Planning and Review Process (PARP).

In 2009, however, "Uzbekistan, along with Russia, Ukraine, Kazakhstan and Belarus, completed an agreement with NATO allowing the transportation of non-lethal ISAF cargo to Afghanistan by rail. The first trial shipment was successfully completed in June 2010."[73]

Secretary General Rasmussen defended his decision in January 2011 to meet with Islam Karimov, the president of Uzbekistan since 1991, by referring to the need "to strike the right balance" among the Alliance's priorities:

> I keep in mind the interest of our soldiers in Afghanistan. We owe it to them that we do our utmost to ensure that we can provide necessary equipment for their daily operations in Afghanistan. So I think, based on experience, that it . . . will be possible for me to strike the right balance, to discuss human rights and democracy and at the same time, practical cooperation on transit facilities and other elements in practical cooperation that can be to the benefit of our operations in Afghanistan.[74]

After the meeting, Rasmussen said that he "spoke with President Karimov about our common commitment to democratic principles and NATO's ongoing efforts to assist partners towards democratic reforms through various Partnership tools." Rasmussen added, "The transit through Uzbekistan in support of our ISAF operation is valuable. . . . We are grateful for the support of Uzbekistan and of all our other Central Asian Partners to our mission in Afghanistan."[75]

Crisis Management and Postconflict Reconstruction

The NATO Allies have learned that there are limits to what can be achieved in crisis management interventions and postconflict state building, even when the efforts are inspired by a cooperative security vision.

In the operations in the Balkans, Afghanistan, and Libya, the Allies seem to have underestimated the duration and magnitude of the effort required, and in each case some Allies did not participate in the operations or attached caveats to the usability of their forces. In each case, the political justification for NATO's action has included the promotion of democracy and other elements of cooperative security, such as the peaceful settlement of disputes. With the exception of the 2011 Libya intervention, each case has involved continuing NATO engagement. (The Allies deliberately limited their action in Libya to an air and maritime intervention, with no follow-on NATO contribution to state building.) As discussed in chapter 4, the Alliance has remained engaged in Bosnia, not only because of continuing defense reform, PfP, and membership-candidacy activities but also because the European Union's EUFOR could turn to NATO in extremis if internal antagonisms in the country exceeded EUFOR's capacity to deal with them.

In the November 2010 Lisbon Summit Declaration, the Allies stated,

> Our operational experience has taught us that military means, although essential, are not enough on their own to meet the many complex challenges to our security. Both within and outside the Euro-Atlantic area, NATO must work with other actors to contribute to a comprehensive approach that effectively combines political, civilian and military crisis management instruments. Its effective implementation requires all actors to contribute in a concerted effort,

based on a shared sense of responsibility, openness and determination, and taking into account their respective strengths, mandates and roles, as well as their decision-making autonomy.[76]

The comprehensive approach's effective implementation requires, in other words, a degree of harmony that cannot be realistically obtained, given the fact that other nations and organizations have their own agendas and idiosyncrasies.

There are political obstacles—within and outside the Alliance—to deepening NATO's cooperation with other states and international organizations beyond certain boundaries. Competition is endemic in international politics, even when states and international organizations have shared interests and are ostensibly committed to cooperation to achieve common goals.

Despite the fact that they have twenty-two member states in common, a certain rivalry between NATO and the European Union has persisted: they have in some cases competed for missions and for leadership in the conduct of missions, owing in part to national ambitions for one organization or the other. Furthermore, their cooperation has remained suboptimal and to a significant extent channeled into "workaround" mechanisms owing to the intractable Turkey-Cyprus dispute.

Pakistan offers one of the clearest illustrations of how difficult it can be to achieve constructive cooperation in crisis management, despite the harmonious ideals of the "comprehensive approach." Pakistan is in principle a partner of the Alliance and Afghanistan in the Tripartite Commission, a joint forum on security matters affecting the NATO-led International Security Assistance Force (ISAF) operation in Afghanistan. Pakistan stands out as a country of immense importance to the ISAF operation in Afghanistan for multiple reasons, including its role as a supply route for NATO logistics and the fact that various insurgent and terrorist organizations (such as the Taliban and al-Qaeda) are active on both sides of the Afghanistan-Pakistan border.

According to the NATO website, "Allied nations and Pakistan share a common interest in stability in the region and in defeating extremism."[77] In fact, however, Pakistan would not support "stability in the region" if that meant a regime in Kabul aligned with India, to say nothing of Pakistan's unwillingness to accept a solution to the Kashmir question on Indian terms. As General McChrystal noted in his assessment as the ISAF Commander in 2009, "The current Afghan government is perceived by Islamabad to be pro-Indian.... Increasing Indian influence in Afghanistan is likely to exacerbate regional tensions and encourage Pakistani countermeasures in Afghanistan or India."[78]

Moreover, agencies of the Pakistani government have long made use of "extremism" to pursue Pakistani interests. As Vali Nasr of the Johns Hopkins School of Advanced International Studies has noted, "Pakistan's strategic calculus has long been shaped by its rivalry with neighboring India. Because it had never done well against India on the battlefield, Pakistan's military turned to jihadi fighters and terrorists to further its interests against India and in Afghanistan."[79] Since 2008 many sources have reported that Pakistan's Inter-Services Intelligence (ISI) agency has assisted Afghan insurgents.[80] In September 2011, Admiral Michael Mullen, then the chairman of the U.S. Joint Chiefs of Staff, said that the ISI had helped insurgents attack the U.S. embassy in Kabul.[81]

In other words, one of the many challenges facing the Alliance's "comprehensive approach" to crisis management in Afghanistan is that one of the country's key neighbors has its own agenda regarding the future of the country. Indeed, certain agencies of the Pakistani government reportedly have their own priorities at variance with the declared priorities of Islamabad. What the NATO Allies can do collectively regarding insurgents and terrorists based in Pakistan is limited by their mandate from the UN Security Council. As Secretary General Rasmussen observed in September 2010, "Let me stress once again that we operate within the mandate provided by the United Nations so we operate within Afghan borders. So I have no comments whatsoever on the alleged drone strikes [by the United States]. But in general I can assure you that it has, of course, an impact on our operations in Afghanistan whether terrorists and extremists in the border region are . . . addressed or not. And this is also the reason why we have encouraged the Pakistani military and the Pakistan government to step up their fight against terrorists in the border region."[82]

The example of Pakistan shows how the bureaucratic and national policies of a critically important Alliance partner can affect the prospects for success of a crisis management operation involving many states and organizations in addition to the NATO Allies.

Pakistan is, however, only a particularly striking example of broader coordination problems in multilateral interventions involving many states and organizations. Richard Holbrooke described the "Afghan aid effort" as "the most wasteful, duplicated, and uncoordinated effort he . . . witnessed in a lifetime of dealing with internal conflicts."[83]

Even if one imagined that multistate, multi-organizational collaboration in crisis management could be as smooth and melodious as envisaged by NATO's "comprehensive approach," there would clearly be boundaries to what could be accomplished absent changes in the social order in the territories in which NATO and other outside organizations intervene. Robert Cooper has wisely underscored the fact that there are limits to what can be achieved by interventions by external agencies, because effective state building ultimately depends on genuine nation building.

> If we want to . . . prevent Afghanistan from being a base for international terrorists, there is no substitute for a functioning state. In the post-imperial age the question is how much can foreigners do to rebuild other people's states. The state is an organisation: it has a constitution, an army, a civil service; it makes laws, protects its citizens and collects taxes from them. The nation, in Benedict Anderson's phrase, is an 'imagined community.' . . . Foreigners can help rebuild the functions of a state—but you can't build a state without a nation. And no foreigner can rebuild a nation; that can only be done from within. . . . Foreign powers can rebuild infrastructure and train soldiers or civil servants. What is the use of an army if the soldiers are disloyal? Or a police force if it is corrupt? If family ties count more than loyalty to the state, it doesn't matter how much money or good advice foreigners give; the state will not function well. You need commitment to the nation; and nations are not built by foreigners.[84]

The Alliance's ambitious objectives include harmonious collaboration in a "comprehensive approach" to crisis management, plus a broader cooperative security consensus for international order. In practice, however, the Allies have been forced to make choices and strike a balance between their ideals and what can be practically achieved, given their own limitations and those of their partners in crisis management interventions.

Vision and Political Will

Do the Allies have the vision and political will to sustain their pursuit of the three core tasks? Only the Allies themselves can answer this question. The picture is mixed, but there are solid grounds for hope.

The picture is mixed because there are several rather negative indicators, notably inadequate defense spending by many Allies; national caveats by several Allies on where, when, and how their forces may be used in operations; minimal contributions of forces and equipment to specific operations by some Allies (or nonparticipation, as was the case for several Allies in the Libya intervention); and continuing disagreements among the Allies as to how to rank their priorities and pursue their objectives.

Moreover, some Allies have failed to meet their capabilities commitments in rotations of the NATO Response Force (NRF), and the Allies have yet to develop more comprehensive common funding arrangements to support various activities, including contingency deployments by the NRF.[85] General James Jones, a former SACEUR, has argued that common funding for the NRF is an especially crucial reform:

> The NRF cannot function effectively without common funding for its operations, yet some nations resist and, by doing so, are holding NATO back from progress that must be made. The "costs fall where they lie" principle is obsolete. The Allies need a more agile system, and common funding whenever possible, which could make a positive difference in this regard. Above all, we need common funding for NATO Response Force missions. Some Allies are reluctant to pursue these ideas; and some in the NATO bureaucracy are highly resistant to innovation. Opponents of the NRF claim that implementation of common funding would increase SACEUR's ability to act "independently." This claim is absurd, because SACEUR can never, and will never, act without instructions from the North Atlantic Council. The system has been that NRF "bills" are borne by the nation providing forces in a specific operation. This is no longer the best way to proceed as it slows things down and places excessive burdens on certain individual nations, and none on others.[86]

The Alliance's renewal depends on the exertion of political will by Allied governments to follow through on their commitments with investment and action. Without sufficient consensus on their collective purposes the Allies may face increasing political fragmentation, continued inadequate defense spending, more shortfalls in meeting commitments to operations and NRF rotations, and uncertainties among geographically exposed Allies about the reliability of NATO collective defense commitments.

There are nonetheless solid grounds for hope because the Allies have experienced and surmounted—or managed to work around—similar problems in the past. Disagreements among the Allies about how to rank their priorities and pursue their objectives have been characteristic of the Alliance throughout its history.

The Allies face five major challenges in pursuing their core tasks. The first and most fundamental is the permanent challenge of balancing actions taken in response to threat assessments with the pursuit of positive political purposes. A second fundamental challenge will be to overcome long-standing patterns of reactiveness and to take more steps to actively shape the security environment. While meeting these basic challenges, the Allies will increasingly have to take developments in the Middle East and the Asia-Pacific into account, owing to their growing significance for Euro-Atlantic security. Since Afghanistan has been by far NATO's largest and most demanding crisis management operation, it will be imperative to draw the right lessons from this engagement. Finally, the Allies will have to grapple with the enduring challenge of achieving more balanced and effective burden sharing.

Balancing Threat Assessments and Positive Political Purposes

In July 2009, Jaap de Hoop Scheffer, then the outgoing NATO secretary general, pointed out that, at least in relation to some security challenges, the post–Cold War security environment "does not present the kind of visible, tangible threat to all NATO Allies that we were used to in the Cold War."

> And this is perhaps the greatest challenge to our Alliance. Why? Because it leads to a tendency to multiply the number of threats that NATO is called upon to deal with, with many Allies having different perceptions according to their geographical location, their history or simply the last problem they faced—whether a terrorist attack or the breakdown of their computer systems or an instance of mass migration. The degree of solidarity that a nation wants to render today is very much at its own discretion. The test of our Alliance, therefore, is in its ability to convince Allies to show the necessary solidarity and to increase their willingness to share burdens equitably.[87]

De Hoop Scheffer's statement that "the degree of solidarity that a nation wants to render today is very much at its own discretion" serves as a commentary on the changed international context. It underscores the challenge for the Allies in defining their common purposes. Article 5 has always provided for national discretion, in that the mutual defense pledge is qualified: "The Parties . . . agree that, if such an armed attack occurs, each of them, . . . will assist the Party or Parties so attacked by taking forthwith, individually and in concert with the other Parties, *such action as it deems necessary*, including the use of armed force, to restore and maintain the security of the North Atlantic area" (emphasis added).

In contrast with the Cold War situation, when an "opt out" from replying forcefully to direct Soviet aggression was generally deemed implausible, the NATO Allies now face threats and discern security imperatives in addition to (and more complex than) the classic collective defense contingency of responding to "an armed attack" by the military forces of foreign states. They may therefore have greater latitude in relation to some contingencies—and indeed must exercise judgment—in allocating limited resources to multiple security tasks.

Compared with the situation during the Cold War, in which the Soviet Union posed a clear threat to the security interests of all the Allies, today's threats are diffuse, complex, heterogeneous, and perceived differently by the Allies.[88] Without a shared perception of the security challenges, it is difficult for the Allies to develop a common vision of future purposes. The tendencies to fragmentation in the Alliance are, moreover, sharpened by differing priorities and capabilities.

To what extent can shared values and purposes compensate for uneven consensus on a multiplicity of diffuse threats? Some analysts have argued that shared values do not have a sufficiently centripetal effect to hold an alliance together, and that threats are more centripetal than common political objectives. Martin Wight maintained, for example, that "alignments are formed under external pressure rather than from common sentiment, and their cohesion varies with the pressure."[89] In his view, "The establishment of the North Atlantic Treaty Organization in 1949 was entirely due to the external pressure of Soviet Russia."[90]

It should be recalled, however, that the founding Allies had political objectives in addition to collective defense, deterrence, and containment. They made clear in the North Atlantic Treaty that they intended to uphold and advance positive political purposes. Many of the founding political leaders and diplomats, such as Harry Truman and Ernest Bevin, had experienced one or both of the world wars. They were interested in pursuing a constructive approach to international politics and preventing a recurrence of the conditions that had produced the world wars. From their perspective, the Alliance had to be based on a common commitment to positive and enduring purposes.[91] As Diego Ruiz Palmer has pointed out, the overriding political ideals of the Alliance have from the outset made it more than simply a transactional bargain struck for "transient purposes."[92]

Despite lingering historical grievances in some intra-Alliance relationships, the conviction among the NATO Allies as to their shared interests, values, and purposes—a common "narrative," as it is sometimes called—is the most fundamental factor in Alliance cohesion and yet the most difficult to spell out. It encompasses the political foundations of the Alliance, including the shared commitment to freedom, democracy, human rights, and the rule of law. It implies that Allies are prepared to defend each other's security interests for fundamental political reasons in addition to military security considerations. In other words, the political foundations of the Alliance contribute to trust in the reliability of the mutual defense pledges of the Allies.[93]

From this perspective, without a sense of shared political ideals, the Alliance would be empty and hollow, whatever the external threats. Historically, the Allies have resolved the latent tension between threat-based incentives for cooperation and shared positive political objectives by asserting a coincidence of values and security interests. The May 2010 U.S. National Security Strategy stated, for example, that "we are committed to partnering with a stronger European Union to advance our shared goals, especially in promoting democracy and prosperity in Eastern European countries that are still completing their democratic transition and in responding to pressing issues of mutual concern."[94]

In other words, the promotion of democratic values implicitly supports U.S. and Alliance security interests. The Allies highlighted their shared values in the 2010 Strategic Concept: "Our Alliance thrives as a source of hope because it is based on common values of individual liberty, democracy, human rights and the rule of law, and because our common essential and enduring purpose is to safeguard the freedom and security of its members."[95]

For the sake of the Alliance's long-term legitimacy, cohesion, and staying power, the Allies must strive to uphold its political ideals, even if practical requirements lead them to make compromises—as with certain decisions about Russia and Uzbekistan discussed earlier.

Other compromises have concerned choices regarding the behavior of fellow Allies. In a revealing statement, Secretary General Rasmussen said in June 2013 that "NATO is . . . a community of values . . . based on freedom, individual liberty, democracy, the rule of law, respect for human rights, including rights of minorities. And for aspirant countries it is absolutely crucial to fully live up to and respect these principles."[96]

As noted previously, the NATO Allies were not during the Cold War so exigent in upholding requirements for membership, nor have they over the decades seen it as their responsibility to deal with nondemocratic conduct or "backsliding" by fellow Allies. Since the end of the Cold War, as discussed in chapter 6, the Allies have chosen to make compromises about democratic values by accepting Russia and several other states as partners, despite their nondemocratic practices, and welcoming their contributions to NATO-led operations. Similarly, the Allies have at times shown restraint and a certain "reluctance to antagonize" concerning values in partnership activities. Such compromises seem inconsistent with the statement in the 2010 Strategic Concept that "these values and objectives are universal and perpetual, and we are determined to defend them through unity, solidarity, strength and resolve."[97] However, as Helene Sjursen has pointed out, "the fact that a norm is not always respected does not mean that it is not considered legitimate."[98] As she observes, "NATO's fundamental goal . . . ranks security above the principles of democratic governance."[99]

This formula implies that the Allies prize their military security more highly than their political values. It would be hard, however, for the Alliance to be more consistent in promoting its values than its member nations. The United States, for example, has long worked closely with nondemocratic states such as Bahrain, Qatar, Saudi Arabia, and the United Arab Emirates; and France and other Allies have also cultivated cooperative relations with nondemocratic states.

The Allies implicitly recognize that there is no guarantee that upholding what they deem the right values will deliver security, and they have over the decades made a number of compromises placing security first in relation to their democratic values—to say nothing of decisions motivated by economic, political, or other factors. In other words, in the recurring tension between the preferred political values of the Allies and their perceived security imperatives, the latter have proven to be decisive on various occasions. Without its values, however, the Alliance would stand for little more than the military security of its member states. Moreover, as Azar Gat has observed, "For all the criticism leveled against it, the United States—and its alliance with Europe—stands as the single most important hope for the future of liberal democracy."[100]

Since the early 1990s a basic values question has arisen for the Allies: deciding which non-Article 5 operations to undertake, because (as discussed in chapters 4 and 5) the Allies cannot afford to intervene in every crisis abroad. As Norwegian scholar Janne Haaland Matlary has remarked, "Hard questions remain about willingness and ability to contribute with risk and money to non-existential operations, for NATO as well as for the EU."[101] In the wake of the Afghanistan experience, the Allies are likely to be more selective about undertaking crisis management operations, with multiple factors to consider, including their security interests. Their commitment to uphold democracy, human rights, and the rule of law will nonetheless probably be an important element in decisions to act in specific cases.

The recurrent return of the Allies to their values is not simply a routine "default position" or mindless repetition of "agreed language" in their enormous accumulation of communiqués. The values do matter to their Alliance's political legitimacy and identity and to their long-term purposes, for their own sake, and for that of other nations. What Hannes Adomeit wrote about the European Union and Russia also applies to NATO and Russia: "To delete values from Europe's approach to Russia and the post-Soviet states would be detrimental not only to the interests of the EU and its member states but also to Russia."[102]

As noted in the introduction to this study, NATO's declared policies have often been aspirational. The positive political aims set out in the preamble of the North Atlantic Treaty—such as safeguarding and promoting "the principles of democracy, individual liberty and the rule of law"—have provided guidance for the way forward. If the Allies are to keep their balance in grappling with demanding and intractable challenges, they must recognize their compromises and shortcomings in relation to their political ideals.

Acknowledging pragmatic compromises for what they are will help the Alliance preserve its values. As Steven Smith wrote, "Lincoln reminds us that statecraft requires an attention to both principle and compromise. Principle without compromise is empty; compromise without principle is blind."[103] The challenge for the Allies, once again, is striking the right balance: deciding which compromises are prudent and necessary to serve a larger purpose, and determining when no compromises should be made.

Actively Shaping the Security Environment

Martin Wight wrote in the early 1970s that "the ramshackle Atlantic alliance falls short of that creativeness which might control and shape circumstances instead of following them."[104]

Throughout the Alliance's history, the Allies have usually reacted to events rather than shaping them. This pattern began in the 1950s. In 1950, in response to the outbreak of the Korean War, the North Atlantic Council appointed General Dwight

Eisenhower to serve as the first SACEUR, with the authority to set up the Supreme Headquarters Allied Powers Europe (SHAPE). In 1957, in response to the Soviet Union's rejection of arms control proposals and development of ICBMs and other capabilities, they established the Alliance's nuclear risk- and responsibility-sharing arrangements and other measures intended to reinforce deterrence and assurance. In 1959, in response to the 1958 Soviet ultimatum on Berlin, Britain, France, and the United States established the "Live Oak" planning staff colocated at SHAPE as a preparedness measure for deterrence and conflict prevention.

One of the Alliance's most remarkable reactive choices during the Cold War was the farsighted 1979 double-track decision, which set out a plan for the deployment of intermediate-range nuclear-armed missiles if arms control negotiations with the Soviet Union to constrain such missiles failed. The success of this plan appears to have exceeded the expectations of its authors. As noted in chapter 9, it resulted in the 1987 INF Treaty, which eliminated and prohibited all U.S. and Soviet ground-based missiles with ranges between 500 and 5,500 km.

The main exception to the reactive pattern during the Cold War was the 1967 Harmel Report, which set out a visionary concept of "defense and détente." This concept furnished the basis for Alliance cohesion and policy formulation during the Cold War.[105]

In the post–Cold War period NATO established a WMD Non-Proliferation Centre in response to the mounting evidence of WMD proliferation, including discoveries by the UN Special Commission in Iraq in 1991, and the Allies devised a Military Concept for Defence against Terrorism in the wake of the terrorist attacks against the United States in 2001.

NATO's interventions in the Bosnia, Kosovo, Afghanistan, and Libya conflicts were essentially reactive as well. The main exception to this pattern of reactiveness in crisis management was the Alliance's contribution to the joint effort with the European Union and the OSCE in the former Yugoslav Republic of Macedonia in 2001–2003.

The Alliance's "cooperative security" efforts—particularly its partnerships and NATO enlargement activities—offer an example of foresight and striving to shape the international environment. The "socialization" efforts have helped, among other achievements, to develop reliable Allies and security partners that have contributed to the Alliance's crisis management operations.

Unfortunately, however, what Gerhard Schröder, then the German chancellor, said in 2005 remains true: "NATO . . . is no longer the primary venue where transatlantic partners discuss and coordinate strategies."[106] The tendency of the Allies to focus on an institutional agenda emphasizing military instruments has narrowed its vision and hobbled its capacity to deal with the full spectrum of security challenges. As Michael Rühle has written,

> NATO must develop a culture of political discussion which is not confined to issues that may involve NATO militarily, but which also includes issues of broader political relevance. As long

as every debate in NATO is suspected to serve only the preparation of military operations, an enlightened, forward-looking debate about emerging 21st century challenges will remain elusive.[107]

Jamie Shea of the new Emerging Security Challenges Division at NATO headquarters has also made a case for a more anticipatory approach to policymaking:

> The security challenges of the twenty-first century are so multiple, interconnected, and potentially destructive that a strategy of reacting only after the event will not work. Anticipation, preventive diplomacy, and a prioritization of efforts according to where the threats are most pressing will become increasingly crucial to a viable security strategy.... A situation like that whereby NATO deployed forces in Afghanistan in August 2003 but only produced a comprehensive political-military strategy for that nation at its 2008 Bucharest Summit should not occur again.[108]

Some signs of positive change in this direction have emerged, notably the establishment of a Strategic Analysis Capability office dedicated to long-range forecasting in the Emerging Security Challenges Division. The new office's mission is "to monitor and anticipate international developments that could affect Allied security."[109]

Taking the Middle East and the Asia-Pacific into Account

The Alliance's mainly Euro-Atlantic focus during the Cold War reflected its origins. When the Allies concluded the North Atlantic Treaty in 1949, they wished to focus on security in Europe and to avoid assuming security obligations beyond their territories, populations, and forces in Europe and North America, notably with respect to overseas colonies. The geographic limits in Article 6 of the treaty therefore concern the area of application of the mutual defense pledge in Article 5.

NATO's engagement in Afghanistan since 2003 and its intervention in Libya in 2011 are only two of several indicators of how the long-standing Eurocentric concentration has been qualified since the end of the Cold War and may be subject to further adjustment. As discussed in chapter 6, the Allies have since 1994 sought cooperative relationships with North African and Middle Eastern partners in the Mediterranean Dialogue, and since 2004 with Gulf Cooperation Council states in the Istanbul Cooperation Initiative. Moreover, since 1990, when the Japan-NATO relationship began, NATO has cultivated links with several "partners across the globe," including Australia, New Zealand, and the Republic of Korea. As noted in chapter 9, the Allies deplored the nuclear tests by India and Pakistan in 1998, and the ballistic missile and nuclear tests by North Korea in 2006, 2009, and 2013. In 2009, 2010, and 2012 the Allies urged Iran and North Korea to respect the UN Security Council resolutions about nuclear and other proliferation activities.[110]

The importance of the Middle East and the Asia-Pacific for Euro-Atlantic security appears likely to mount. Conflicts among Middle Eastern and Asia-Pacific powers could have grave strategic and economic implications for the security and well-being of the NATO allies and many partner nations, especially if they involved risks of nuclear escalation. Indeed, the NATO Allies have increasingly been obliged to take into account political dynamics in the Middle East and the Asia-Pacific region, because events in these regions affect the context for the Alliance's three core tasks of collective defense, crisis management, and cooperative security.

As Julian Lindley-French, a British expert, recently observed, "All the ingredients exist for state competition, particularly over resources and life fundamentals, and particularly in East and South Asia." Political-military competition in Asia could, Lindley-French noted, raise burden-sharing questions in transatlantic relations, particularly if the United States is obliged to dedicate more resources to the Asia-Pacific region. In these circumstances Europeans may need to "at least start to perform more credibly in keeping the famous 'in and around Europe' reasonably stable so that NATO can help keep the U.S. strong in East and South Asia."[111] Secretary General Rasmussen has rightly noted in this regard that "it is in Europe's interest that the United States, with whom we share our most fundamental values, contributes to upholding global peace and stability by engaging in the Asia-Pacific region."[112]

It appears that the Alliance will have to adjust to what President Obama has called America's "pivot to the Asia Pacific region."[113] The president told the Australian Parliament in November 2011, "As we end today's wars, I have directed my national security team to make our presence and mission in the Asia Pacific a top priority. As a result, reductions in US defense spending will not—I repeat, will not—come at the expense of the Asia Pacific."[114] U.S. Air Force General Philip Breedlove, who recently took command as SACEUR, said, "The reason that our nation can consider a rebalance to Asia is because of the long-standing partnerships and the capacity and the ability of our European allies."[115]

Stephan Frühling of the Australian National University and Benjamin Schreer of the Aspen Institute Germany recently argued cogently that

> NATO as a whole must pay greater attention to power shifts in the Asia-Pacific and the implications for the Alliance. . . . Any additional demands on US defence efforts in the Pacific would thus reinforce . . . US demands for better transatlantic burden-sharing. Finally, major conflict in the Asia-Pacific . . . would immediately raise the question of possible European participation—in much the same way as events in Afghanistan did so in 2001, in a previously unthinkable manner. . . . The rise of China reinforces the need for transatlantic allies to discuss the geographic scope of NATO operations, the geographic priorities of European military engagement and the respective global security roles of NATO and the EU. This debate has to occur *before* urgent crises demand immediate and improvised responses.[116]

Whether the Alliance will devote more attention to potential security challenges beyond the Euro-Atlantic region remains to be seen. Aside from resource limitations, differences persist among the Allies regarding the prudence of expanding the Alliance's remit beyond the geographical area so far encompassed by its three core tasks. In January 2010, Secretary of State Clinton said that "there is an awareness of the global nature of a lot of these problems, but a great reluctance to go beyond the geographic reach of NATO." As she observed, in the face of "rogue regimes" such as North Korea, "there are some who say this is too complicated, it is out of area, it is not our responsibility."[117]

Events may, however, oblige the allies to grapple with the consequences of security challenges originating in the Middle East and the Asia-Pacific. Espen Barth Eide, the Norwegian minister of defense, said in February 2012 that "we Europeans need to look beyond our own borders in order to take a co-responsibility for global security in a changing landscape. The rise of Asia isn't just happening in America's world. It is our world, too."[118]

In January 2013, Leon Panetta, then the U.S. secretary of defense, said that "the United States and Europe should work together and ensure our efforts are coordinated through regular consultations between European and U.S. defense officials focused on Asia-Pacific security issues. The bottom line is that Europe should not fear our rebalance to Asia; Europe should join it."[119]

How the European Allies might contribute in this respect remains to be determined. At a NATO workshop in June 2012 a Hungarian participant asked whether the European Allies should help the United States dedicate greater resources to the Asia-Pacific by undertaking more extensive responsibilities in the Mediterranean and the Middle East. A British participant said that for "political legitimacy" purposes, at least two European NATO Allies should accompany the United States in some Asia-Pacific activities.[120] Tomas Valasek has argued that "an expanded European military role on the Continent would free the United States to shift more of its troops and money to the Pacific."[121]

French analyst Corentin Brustlein has pointed out that, while there are uncertainties about the extent to which the United States will be able to afford its "rebalancing" to the Asia-Pacific, given its financial constraints and the high risk of competing demands for U.S. military capabilities in the Middle East or elsewhere, the bottom line for the European Allies is likely to be increased responsibilities not only on the European continent but also in the broader neighborhood, particularly Africa, as suggested by recent operations in Libya and Mali. It may be difficult for the European Allies to compensate for their long-standing dependence on certain U.S. capabilities, such as intelligence, surveillance, and reconnaissance, and long-range precision strike assets for the suppression of enemy air defenses and other purposes. More fundamentally, Brustlein has expressed concern that the reduction in the U.S. military posture in Europe in conjunction with the U.S. Asia-Pacific "pivot" may imply a lasting "weariness" with the transatlantic relationship in Washington and a "structural weakening" of this relationship.[122]

It is important to note that in his remarks in Tokyo in April 2013, Secretary General Rasmussen "was careful not to send any signal that could be interpreted as a sign of support for Japan in a possible conflict with China."[123] Rasmussen said,

> NATO and Japan are like-minded. We share the same values. We share the same security challenges. And we share the same desire to work together. So we can help the United Nations and the international community to reinforce the rules-based international system. . . . But let me make one thing clear. The Alliance's global perspective does not mean that NATO seeks a presence in the Asia-Pacific region. What it does mean, is that NATO seeks to work with the Asia-Pacific region. . . . we do not consider China a direct threat to NATO Allies. We hope that China will use its increasing influence on the international scene in a peaceful way and in a constructive way to maintain international peace, security and stability.[124]

Drawing the Right Lessons from Afghanistan

NATO's responsibility in leading the ISAF in Afghanistan is currently projected to last until the end of 2014, when Afghan national security forces are expected to take the lead in providing security throughout the country. Allied officials and experts have for years been speculating as to what conclusions should and will be drawn from the Afghanistan experience.

One of the key questions has been how to more effectively conduct such operations. Aside from the mixed results in the Alliance's efforts to make the "comprehensive approach" work in interactions with other nations and organizations, coordination among the Allies themselves has sometimes been unsatisfactory. As discussed in chapter 4, the Allies have disagreed on questions as fundamental as whether to conduct counternarcotics operations. The suboptimal strategic coordination was noted in 2009 by Bernard Kouchner, then the French foreign minister: "Asked if the NATO alliance was not working very well in Afghanistan, he said: 'It's not working at all.' 'What is the goal? What is the road? And in the name of what?' Mr. Kouchner asked."[125]

Allied officials and experts disagree as to the prospective lessons of Afghanistan for the future balance of the Alliance's three core tasks. According to Henning Riecke of the German Council on Foreign Relations in Berlin, "Afghanistan has led NATO countries to rethink their attitude about crisis management, to be less willing to have really complex operations that might spiral into civil wars, where you find yourself with a problem that's so complex you cannot solve it."[126]

A "never again" conclusion might lead the Allies to engage in fewer and less demanding crisis management operations in the future and to be more selective about undertaking them, and they might place more emphasis on collective defense and cooperative security. Another possible consequence of "intervention fatigue" might be increased reliance on drones and other long-range means to disrupt the activities of terrorist organizations based in failed and failing states.

Some observers argue that the Allies made a mistake in 2003, when they took command of ISAF, in trying to make all of the NATO Allies capable of contributing to the long-range expeditionary operations in Afghanistan. In their view, the Allies post-Afghanistan should focus on Article 5 purposes and capabilities. By this logic, most Allies would need some expeditionary capabilities, mainly to make their collective defense commitments to the Baltic states and other geopolitically exposed Allies credible.

This proposal implies, however, that only a few European Allies would have expeditionary capabilities for crisis management operations. It is not clear if this would be politically sustainable and acceptable to the other Allies. Some experts maintain that the Alliance would have more balance and cohesion if most Allies developed such capabilities and accepted the risks and responsibilities of such operations. In other words, it could be politically unhealthy to deliberately foster a "multitier" Alliance in which some Allies have capabilities and responsibilities not shared by others. It could encourage the formation of ad hoc coalitions of the willing and provoke political disunity in the Alliance, with damaging consequences for the Alliance's ability to pursue its core tasks.

While a post-2014 continuation in some form of the NATO Training Mission Afghanistan (NTM-A) appears probable, Allied governments are considering additional means to maintain the readiness of their military capabilities after the end of their involvement in combat roles in Afghanistan. These means may include an intensified program of exercises, training activities, and simulation events oriented toward both Article 5 and non-Article 5 contingencies. As noted, the Allies intend through the Connected Forces Initiative to sustain the readiness and interoperability of their forces and those of partner nations.

One of the positive lessons of the Alliance's engagement in Afghanistan is that it has demonstrated NATO's expeditionary potential. Despite its shortcomings, NATO has led a large number of intervening troops (as many as 140,000 in ISAF) in an elaborate and demanding operation far from Europe. This has included attracting and coordinating contributions from more than twenty partner nations from around the globe. Moreover, as discussed in chapter 6, partner nations have contributed to "decision shaping" regarding Afghanistan through the Alliance's consultation mechanisms, including meetings in ISAF format at various levels.

Achieving More Balanced and Effective Burden Sharing

Agreement on the Alliance's constructive purposes is irrelevant without the political will to act on them, and this leads inevitably to the question of burden sharing. The Allies have disagreed since the founding of the Alliance about how to define and measure equitable burden sharing. All measures have shortcomings, and no measures—including quantitative measures—are regarded universally as objective and thorough.

As measured by defense spending as a percentage of GDP, for example, burden sharing within the Alliance has always been uneven and unbalanced. In June 2011, Robert Gates, then the U.S. secretary of defense, said, "Today, just five of 28 allies—the U.S., U.K., France, Greece, along with Albania—exceed the agreed 2% of GDP spending on defense."[127] However, this seemingly impartial gauge of burden sharing does not, as many experts have pointed out, indicate anything about the efficiency with which funds are spent, nor does it spell out the specific purposes of the spending (for instance, personnel, equipment modernization, force transformation, or current operations and maintenance) or whether a member state employs its forces to support its own national priorities or NATO objectives or directs them to serve under other auspices (such as the United Nations, the European Union, or an ad hoc coalition). With regard to personnel, for example, twenty of the twenty-eight Allies dedicate over half of their defense budgets to personnel—in some cases, 70 to 80 percent. In contrast, the United States devotes around 40 percent of its defense budget to personnel costs.[128]

Funds invested in force transformation—for instance, developing forces capable of expeditionary operations in addition to forces designed for static territorial defense—may be regarded as contributions to burden sharing just as valid as funds supporting current NATO operations. Some Allies maintain, despite the doubts of critical Allied observers, that development aid, technical assistance, and humanitarian relief can also be considered contributions to Alliance burden sharing because they are intended to promote a more benign international security environment.

In other words, some Allies argue that there is more to burden sharing than current force levels in Afghanistan and the degree of engagement of these forces in combat operations. Moreover, with respect to the forces committed to missions in Afghanistan, some allowance must be made for differing national capabilities. It is, furthermore, difficult to make meaningful comparisons between, for example, contributions of light infantry, helicopters, Special Forces, and medical personnel and equipment.

The Allies have not agreed how to identify, measure, and compare contributions to NATO. Critics have accused some Allies of abstaining from participation in certain NATO commonly funded equipment procurement budgets in order to protect their national military industries. Some of these same accused Allies spend substantially more than others on military capabilities, however, and make large contributions to current operations. This circumstance reflects the long-standing capability gaps in the Alliance—notably, the gap between the United States and the rest of the NATO Allies, and the gap between France and the United Kingdom, considered together, and the other European Allies.[129]

These gaps continue to widen, raising questions about the future of the Alliance's cohesion and its ability to perform its three core tasks. The imbalances in military capabilities are most significant for collective defense. In crisis management, some of the smaller Allies—for instance, Denmark, the Netherlands, and Norway—have made distinctive contributions.[130]

The capability gaps reflect the size of national economies to a considerable extent, but other factors—including the priority attached to military investments and capabilities for operations—are also involved. As Yves Boyer, a French scholar, noted in 2008, "Of the 27 EU countries, only six—France, Germany, UK, Italy, Spain and the Netherlands—accommodated for 82% of all EU defence spending. Put another way, 21 of the Union's member states contribute between them a mere 18% of EU defence expenditure."[131] According to Charles Grant, a British expert, "Only about a third of the [EU] member states take defence seriously and believe in intervening to solve security problems."[132] These observations about defense investments and attitudes in the European Union are pertinent to the Alliance because twenty-two EU members are NATO Allies.[133]

Some European experts have warned that the consequences of decreased military funding in Europe could include, in the words of Christian Mölling, "bonsai armies"—that is, miniature defense establishments.[134] Camille Grand has suggested that the downward trends in defense procurement could lead European nations to form a "coalition of the unable and the unwilling."[135] Bastian Giegerich and Alexander Nicoll have argued, however, that "there is still much room for increased efficiency" in European defense efforts. "If European countries are to build future capabilities that match the still significant amounts that they spend on defence, there is no escaping the fact that more effective cooperation on investments, force structures and equipment requirements will be necessary."[136]

In February 2010, Robert Gates, then the U.S. secretary of defense, expressed concern about the defense funding and capabilities of European allies.

> Since the end of the Cold War, NATO and national defense budgets have fallen consistently—even with unprecedented operations outside NATO's territory over the past five years. . . . These budget limitations relate to a larger cultural and political trend affecting the alliance. . . . The demilitarization of Europe—where large swaths of the general public and political class are averse to military force and the risks that go with it—has gone from a blessing in the 20th century to an impediment to achieving real security and lasting peace in the 21st. Not only can real or perceived weakness be a temptation to miscalculation and aggression, but, on a more basic level, the resulting funding and capability shortfalls make it difficult to operate and fight together to confront shared threats. For many years, for example, we have been aware that NATO needs more cargo aircraft and more helicopters of all types—and yet we still don't have these capabilities. And their absence is directly impacting operations in Afghanistan.[137]

Secretary General Rasmussen pointed out in October 2010 that "there are many Americans who think it is unfair that the US is taking on an increasing share of the responsibility to defend international security, even though they face the same financial pressures as the rest of us. To speak frankly about it, they are right. The more that imbalance grows, the harder it will be to explain to the United States why it should see Europe as a serious partner, or why it should invest in NATO."[138]

The causes of declining NATO European spending on military capabilities and operations encompass more than a lack of political will in the current economic context. As the U.S. Department of Defense noted in 2006, "In many European allied states . . . aging and shrinking populations are curbing defense spending on capabilities they need for conducting operations effectively alongside U.S. forces."[139]

Political leadership will nonetheless remain indispensable if Allies are to increase their efforts. This will require more than greater reliance on common funding mechanisms for specific capabilities or purposes. However, such mechanisms could contribute to more equitable burden sharing, especially if the funding shares were based on each member state's GDP.

Costs establish limits to what NATO can achieve, especially in the continuing financial austerity crisis. Indeed, costs make clear the competition among core tasks. In 2010, for example, a study regarding measures to reassure new Allies about collective defense highlighted the rivalry with crisis management: "The missions in Afghanistan, Kosovo and elsewhere have consumed so much money and attention that NATO rarely holds military exercises rehearsing the defence of its borders."[140] On some occasions Central and Eastern European Allies have urged their fellow Allies to conduct reinforcement exercises to reassure public opinion about the Alliance's commitment to collective defense, only to be told that "real world crisis management operations" limit funding for such purposes and take priority.[141]

If the Allies had plenty of money, they could afford to undertake multiple expeditionary crisis management operations while investing in collective defense, including new collective defense challenges such as cyber security. Finances are certain to influence decisions about what can be done to implement the decisions reached in the Alliance's May 2012 Deterrence and Defense Posture Review. Additional funding for missile defenses and conventional military capabilities is likely to be scarce.

With severely diminished defense spending in most European Allied nations, the need to choose among tasks will become more imperative. As a French expert has pointed out, NATO's activities are constrained by an *effet d'éviction*.[142] In this context this phrase might be translated as a "crowding-out effect" or a "displacement effect." The idea seems to be similar to that of an opportunity cost. That is, money or time invested in one purpose is not available for another. In NATO, for example, money spent on cyber security cannot be dedicated to missile defense. The imperative of choice becomes more acute in the presence of shrinking budgets. Some Western European Allies skeptical about collective defense requirements vis-à-vis Russia appear to have found the financial crisis since 2008 a persuasive context in which to justify cuts in defense spending. Governments have cut back defense spending not only because of financial austerity but in response to complacency about the international security situation, especially in Western Europe.

Some Allies have argued that increased reliance on common funding would be a solution, but no consensus has been reached on specific new themes. For example, in the domain of collective defense some of the smaller Allies, owing to their budgetary limitations, reportedly want the Alliance to pay for cyber protection collectively. Larger Allies, including France and the United States, agree that NATO's institutional communications and command and control networks should be collectively protected, but hold that cyber defense is primarily a national task.[143] At the Chicago Summit in May 2012, the Allies endorsed "centralised cyber protection" for their "collective investment in NATO" but subtly underscored the importance of "national cyber defence capabilities."[144] As in many areas, the Allies appear to have found a provisional solution through compromise that may endure indefinitely.

Several Allies have reservations about increasing common funding for crisis management operations, partly for fear that it might facilitate the initiation of further interventions and/or the acceptance of a surge of costs in specific operations. Some Allies are also concerned that greater reliance on common funding for operations would mean that they would "pay twice"—that is, by paying for their national force deployments and by helping to defray the costs of deployments by other Allies. The main providers of funds for the NATO Security Investment Program, a key mechanism for common funding of defense facilities and capabilities, also furnish the largest numbers of troops in NATO-led operations. Yet without common funding, many of the smaller Allies will not be able to make substantial contributions to NATO operations. At the same time, some of the same Allies that wish to reduce the scale of NATO's operational engagements resist funding NATO-led capacity-building activities that could help partners and other non-NATO countries undertake greater responsibilities and thereby lessen reliance on NATO forces in the long term.[145]

The Allies have for many years endorsed the principle of pooling resources and seeking greater investment in shared military capabilities, and this approach has produced some noteworthy achievements, including the NATO AWACS aircraft and the initiatives to lease or jointly procure and maintain strategic airlift capabilities.[146]

Such multinational initiatives, sometimes called "smart defense" measures, are constructive but can offer no more than partial solutions. In one of his last major speeches as secretary of defense, Robert Gates, in Brussels in June 2011, called upon European leaders to recognize the limitations of such praiseworthy cooperative solutions and muster greater resources and commitment:

> While it is clear NATO members should do more to pool military assets, such "Smart Defense" initiatives are not a panacea. In the final analysis, there is no substitute for nations providing the resources necessary to have the military capability the Alliance needs when faced with a security challenge. . . . The blunt reality is that there will be dwindling appetite and patience in the U.S. Congress—and in the American body politic writ large—to expend increasingly precious funds on behalf of nations that are apparently unwilling to devote the necessary resources or make the necessary changes to be serious and capable partners in their own defense. . . . . The good news is that the members of NATO—individually, and collectively—have it well within their means to halt and reverse these trends, and instead produce a very different future. . . . But it will take leadership from political leaders and policy makers on this continent.[147]

For the Alliance to be formed in 1948–1949, the Europeans had to convince the Americans of their seriousness by organizing the Brussels Treaty. One might argue that for NATO to continue, the European Allies will have to demonstrate their seriousness by keeping up their military capabilities. As a corollary, European inaction may doom the Alliance, as Robert Gates suggested in his speeches in 2010–2011.

Envoi

During the Cold War NATO's balancing act was comparatively simple: as articulated in the 1967 Harmel Report, the Allies intended to keep the peace through deterrence and defense capabilities, and NATO's steadfastness in this respect made possible the successful pursuit of dialogue and positive political change without war. Since the end of the Cold War the Alliance's balancing act has become much more complicated. In addition to meeting new collective defense and deterrence requirements, the Allies have conducted multiple crisis management interventions while pursuing an ambitious vision of positive political change via cooperative security endeavors.

The risk of the Alliance's overextension has become obvious. The fatigue with Afghanistan has become palpable, the budget crunch has constrained resources for operations and force modernization, and the consensus on how to address long-standing challenges (such as relations with Russia) and emerging issues (such as energy security) has become fragile.

Continuing divergence among the strategic interests and priorities of an ever greater number of Allies could place into question NATO's ability to pursue its missions effectively. As noted in the introduction to this study, the Alliance remains an intergovernmental organization. The Allies know that compromises regarding national interests and priorities are essential to reach a workable consensus, and they have usually succeeded in reaching at least a minimal level of mutual understanding.

Since the end of the Cold War, the Allies have lacked a single unifying threat to bring them together, but they have stayed together—and they have even enlarged their Alliance and undertaken crisis management operations and cooperative security activities—on the basis of their shared values and security interests. They have demonstrated and cultivated an unparalleled ability to organize and conduct combined operations involving a large number of Allies and partners. Despite the caveats by many force contributors, the Allies have gained experience that should reinforce their confidence about their ability to handle potential crisis management and collective defense contingencies in the future.

A constructive path forward requires consensus on the complementarity of pursuing dialogue and cooperation with Russia, conducting missions beyond Europe, if necessary, and reassuring the new allies in Central and Eastern Europe regarding the Alliance's commitment to their collective defense. The successful pursuit of this new consensus promises to be a daunting leadership challenge, but it is essential to the future relevance of the Alliance.

Despite the difficulty of mustering determination to meet diffuse new security challenges that affect NATO countries to different degrees, the Allies need to find the political will and funding necessary to meet these challenges and thereby uphold their values and positive political purposes. While the results achieved may be mixed, the continuing effort must meet the fundamental security needs of the Allies if they are to preserve this instrument of collective defense, crisis management, and cooperative security. NATO remains indispensable to the defense of the values and security of all the Allies, including the United States.

Notes

1. Jens Ringsmose, "NATO's Response Force: Finally Getting It Right?," *European Security* 18, no. 3 (September 2009): 302.

2. President Obama and Secretary General Anders Fogh Rasmussen, remarks after meeting. Office of the Press Secretary, The White House, September 29, 2009, www.whitehouse.gov/the_press_office/Remarks-by-President-Obama-and-NATO-Secretary-General-Anders-Fogh-Rasmussen-after-Meeting/.

3. For an example of this viewpoint, see Vladimir Socor, "Coalition of the Willing Stands in for NATO in Libya," *Eurasia Daily Monitor* 8, no. 97 (May 19, 2011).

4. Author interviews in Brussels, October 2011.

5. Shea, "NATO at Sixty—and Beyond," 30.

6. Author interview in Paris, May 27, 2011.

7. See, among other sources, Timo Noetzel and Benjamin Schreer, "Does a Multi-Tier NATO Matter? The Atlantic Alliance and the Process of Strategic Change," *International Affairs* 85, no. 2 (March 2009): 211–226. The Allies that were formerly Soviet republics or members of the Warsaw Pact are sometimes characterized as "new allies who joined for the old reasons"—that is, security through collective defense, guaranteed by Article 5 of the North Atlantic Treaty.

8. An Italian observer compared the Central and Eastern Europeans to the protagonists of Samuel Beckett's play *Waiting for Godot* and Valerio Zurlini's 1976 film *The Desert of the Tartars*. In this Italian's view, the Central and Eastern Europeans are wasting their time and NATO's resources in defense investments hedging against the contingency of aggression from Moscow because the Russians—like the Tartars in the movie—"will never come." Author's interview in Brussels, October 28, 2011.

9. In the words of a Polish observer, "Article 5 is not automatic. Germany has a lot of trade with Russia. Would the Germans endanger that? We wonder. As for Spain or Portugal, they may send us an SMS: 'We pray for you!' This would be their implementation of Article 5." Author's interview with a Polish observer in Warsaw, May 22, 2013.

10. As discussed in chapter 2, Swedish scholar Pal Jonson has suggested that the Allies are divided by their priorities into three categories: "collective defenders," "expeditionaries," and "Russia Firsters."

11. Some U.S. and Allied observers have criticized the October 2009 decision of the CDU/CSU-FDP coalition government to seek the removal of the remaining U.S. nuclear weapons in Germany on the grounds that this could lead to the end of the Alliance's nuclear risk- and responsibility-sharing arrangements and thereby weaken NATO's deterrence and defense posture. See, for example, Miller, "NATO's Nuclear Future."

12. *Defence Policy Guidelines* (Berlin: German Ministry of Defence, May 27, 2011), 4.

13. Author interviews in Paris, May 2011.

14. James Sherr in the discussion following Przemyslaw Zurawski vel Grajewski, "Why Kiev and Tbilisi Matter: The Reasons for Poland's Support of NATO Enlargement to Ukraine and Georgia," in *NATO's New Strategic Concept: Moving Beyond the Status Quo?*, ed. Bram Boxhoorn and David den Dunnen (The Hague: Netherlands Atlantic Association, 2009), 121.

15. "Transcript: Polish Foreign Minister Radoslaw Sikorski Talks to Council," *Federal News Service*, November 19, 2008, www.acus.org/event_blog/polish-foreign-minister-radoslaw-sikorski-talks-council/transcript.

16. "An Open Letter to the Obama Administration from Central and Eastern Europe," July 16, 2009, www.wyborcza.pl.

17. NATO, "NATO Conducts Annual Crisis Management Exercise (CMX)," last updated October 12, 2011, www.nato.int/cps/en/natolive/news_79269.htm.

18. This paragraph updates and paraphrases the summary in an unpublished paper by Ilay Ferrier, "Overview of Crisis Management Exercises (CMX)," February 2012, 6. It is also based on information provided by Ilay Ferrier and Jean-Dominique Dulière at NATO headquarters. The author thanks these gentlemen warmly for their assistance.

19. NATO, "NATO Conducts Annual Crisis Management Exercise (CMX)."

20. For further details, see chapter 2 and the sources therein cited as well as European External Action Service, "EEAS to contribute to NATO's Crisis Management Exercise CMX12," November 2012, www.eeas.europa.eu/csdp/documents/pdf/announcement_to_press_en.pdf; and European External Action Service, "NATO Exercise CMX 12," http://eeas.europa.eu/crisis-response/what-we-do/exercises/index_en.htm.

21. *National Security Strategy* (Washington, DC: The White House, May 2010), 41, www.whitehouse.gov/sites/default/files/rss_viewer/national_security_strategy.pdf.

22. Hillary Clinton, remarks at the NATO Strategic Concept Seminar, Washington, DC, February 22, 2010, www.state.gov/secretary/rm/2010/02/137118.htm.

23. *Sustaining U.S. Global Leadership: Priorities for 21st Century Defense* (Washington, DC: U.S. Department of Defense, January 2012), 2-3.

24. According to an Italian expert on Alliance security affairs, "NATO was created to dominate power politics in Europe. We want the United States as a guarantor against external threats and internal competitions. We need U.S. leadership. We need constant concrete signs of the U.S. presence." Author interview with an Italian expert in The Hague, May 28, 2009. For discussions of the hypothesis that the United States has served as the pacifier of Europe since the late 1940s, see Josef Joffe, "Europe's American Pacifier," *Foreign Policy* 54 (Spring 1984); and David S. Yost, "Transatlantic Relations and Peace in Europe," *International Affairs* 78, no. 2 (April 2002).

25. Manfred Wörner cited in Alan Riding, "At East-West Crossroads, Western Europe Hesitates," *New York Times*, March 25, 1992.

26. Manfred Wörner, speech on October 6, 1993, www.nato.int/docu/speech/1993/s931006a.htm.

27. Rob de Wijk, "What Is NATO?," in *NATO after Kosovo*, ed. Rob de Wijk, Bram Boxhoorn, and Niklaas Hoekstra (The Hague: Netherlands Atlantic Association, Netherlands Institute of International Relations "Clingendael," and the Royal Netherlands Military Academy, 2000), 3-4.

28. Anders Fogh Rasmussen, speech at the Institut Français des Relations Internationales, October 15, 2010, www.nato.int/cps/en/natolive/opinions_67051.htm.

29. Marc Trachtenberg, *A Constructed Peace: The Making of the European Settlement, 1945–1963* (Princeton, NJ: Princeton University Press, 1999), 154. These statements by President Eisenhower were made in 1956, 1958, and 1959.

30. Aleksander Smolar quoted in Duncan Shiels, "East Europe Engaged to EU, Flirts with Old Flame US," Reuters, May 14, 2003.

31. "Western Europe, in the farthest extremities of the European peninsula, was sheltered and insulated by Eastern Europe, whose history was punctuated by the flow of invasions from the east and their reflux from the west." Martin Wight, "Eastern Europe," in *The World in March 1939*, ed. Arnold Toynbee and Frank T. Ashton-Gwatkin (London: Oxford University Press for the Royal Institute of International Affairs, 1952), 213. See ibid., 220, 223, and 236.

32. The foreign ministers of Albania, Bulgaria, Croatia, Estonia, Latvia, Lithuania, the former Yugoslav Republic of Macedonia, Romania, Slovakia, and Slovenia published a statement concerning U.S. policy on Iraq on February 5, 2003. Chirac replied on February 17, 2003. "Conférence de presse de M. Jacques Chirac (17 février 2003), Président de la République, à l'issue de la réunion informelle extraordinaire du Conseil Européen, Bruxelles, Belgique," *Le Monde diplomatique*, February 12, 2004, www.monde-diplomatique.fr/cahier/europe/conf-chirac.

33. This discussion of Central and Eastern European historical grievances is drawn from David S. Yost, "Assurance and US Extended Deterrence in NATO," *International Affairs* 85, no. 4 (July 2009): 765–766.

34. *Sustaining U.S. Global Leadership*, 2–3; italics in the original.

35. According to Secretary of Defense Leon Panetta, "In the briefing we've been giving the Europeans, we have made clear that there is going to be this rotational presence there that will be conducting exercises. . . . As a matter of fact, they will probably see more of the Americans under the new strategy because the brigades that were there were actually fighting in Afghanistan and weren't even there. . . . What you are going to have is two [brigades] plus this large rotational presence that is going to be there." Panetta quoted in Greg Jaffe, "2 Army Brigades to Leave Europe," *Washington Post*, January 13, 2012.

36. Author's interview with a French observer in Paris, May 24, 2013. On May 31, 2013, an American observer in Brussels took note of the uncertainties created by the sequester legislation and other downward pressures on U.S. defense spending, and said, "The real issue is, can we even afford the rotational deployments?" Force rotations for exercises and training are funded by "operations and maintenance" accounts, which can be cut more easily than accounts for personnel and procurement.

37. John Vandiver, "US Army's Last Tanks Depart from Germany," *Stars and Stripes*, April 4, 2013, www.stripes.com/news/us-army-s-last-tanks-depart-from-germany-1.214977.

38. "Rebalancing America's forces: The Downgrading Of Europe," *Economist*, January 14, 2012, www.economist.com/node/21542789. This editorial noted that the defense guidance "glibly refers to 'most European countries' now being 'producers of security rather than consumers of it,'" but it did not point out that this argument in the defense guidance is inconsistent with long-standing U.S. pleas to the NATO Allies to increase their defense efforts. In October 2009, Alexander Vershbow, then the U.S. assistant secretary of defense for international security affairs, declared, "Consensus around collective defense cannot take place if there are perceptions that some members are true security providers while others are security consumers. In constant dollars, European defense spending has remained flat since 1998." Vershbow, "Crafting the New Strategic Concept."

39. Cieniuch quoted in Marcus Weisgerber, "In Europe, Mixed Feelings about U.S. Troop Cuts," *Defense News*, January 16, 2012.

40. Gideon Rachman, "A Disarmed Europe Will Face the World on Its Own," *Financial Times*, February 19, 2013.

41. Joschka Fischer, "Missing America," May 30, 2013, www.project-syndicate.org/commentary/the-growing-chaos-of-a-post-american-world-by-joschka-fischer.

42. Eide, "Transatlantic Ties in Times of Financial Austerity."

43. Rasmussen, "NATO 2020—Shared Leadership for a Shared Future."

44. NATO, "Statement: Meeting of the North Atlantic Council at the Level of Foreign Ministers Held at NATO Headquarters, Brussels," August 19, 2008, www.nato.int/cps/en/natolive/official_texts_29950.htm?selectedLocale=en.

45. North Atlantic Council, "Lisbon Summit Declaration," par. 21 and 23.

46. Rose Gottemoeller, *Russian-American Security Relations after Georgia*, Policy Brief (Carnegie Endowment for International Peace, October 2008), 2–3.

47. Although the contemporary Cyprus dispute has deep historical origins, it might be said to have begun in 1963, with the breakdown of the constitution that had provided for power sharing by the Greek Cypriot and Turkish Cypriot communities. The violence led the UN Security Council to recommend the establishment of the peacekeeping force that has remained in place from 1964 to the present.

48. Madeleine Albright, prepared written submission for testimony before the Senate Armed Services Committee on April 23, 1997, 9.

49. Condoleezza Rice, remarks en route to Astana, Kazakhstan, October 5, 2008, http://merln.ndu.edu/archivepdf/SA/State/110626.pdf.

50. Joseph Biden, remarks at the 45th Munich Conference on Security Policy, February 7, 2009, www.whitehouse.gov/the_press_office/RemarksbyVicePresidentBidenat45thMunichConferenceonSecurityPolicy.

51. Secretary General Javier Solana, speech at the Royal Institute of International Affairs, Chatham House, London, March 4, 1997, www.nato.int/docu/speech/1997/s970304a.htm.

52. Secretary General Jaap de Hoop Scheffer, remarks at the Munich Security Conference, February 7, 2009, awww.nato. int/docu/speech/2009/s090207a.html.

53. "Founding Act on Mutual Relations, Cooperation and Security between NATO and the Russian Federation," May 27, 1997.

54. Jamie Shea recently wrote that "Russia in its current nationalistic and assertive mood, and with its opposition to core NATO policies such as enlargement, may not desire a truly cooperative relationship, no matter how sincerely and often Brussels extends the hand of friendship to Moscow." Shea, "NATO at Sixty—and Beyond," 25.

55. Katinka Barysch, *The EU and Russia: Strategic Partners or Squabbling Neighbors?* (London: Centre for European Reform, May 2004), 9, www.cer.org.uk/pdf/p564_russia_strat_squabb.pdf.

56. Medvedev, interview, August 31, 2008.

57. Some Russians have accordingly rejected NATO and EU calls for non-zero-sum "win-win" solutions as sanctimonious and self-serving humbug.

58. Secretary General Rasmussen, "NATO and Russia: A New Beginning" (speech at the Carnegie Endowment, Brussels, September 18, 2009), www.nato.int/cps/en/natolive/opinions_57640.htm?selectedLocale=en.

59. De Hoop Scheffer, "NATO: Securing Our Future."

60. James Sherr in the discussion following Przemyslaw Zurawski vel Grajewski, "Why Kiev and Tbilisi Matter: The Reasons for Poland's Support of NATO Enlargement to Ukraine and Georgia," in *NATO's New Strategic Concept: Moving Beyond the Status Quo?*, ed. Bram Boxhoorn and David den Dunnen (The Hague: Netherlands Atlantic Association, 2009), 120.

61. Solana, speech, March 4, 1997.

62. Anders Fogh Rasmussen, "NATO—Delivering Security in the 21st Century" (speech at Chatham House, London, July 4, 2012), www.nato.int/cps/en/natolive/opinions_88886.htm.

63. CSCE, "Charter of Paris for a New Europe," November 21, 1990.

64. Alexandra Gheciu, *NATO in the "New Europe": The Politics of International Socialization after the Cold War* (Palo Alto, CA: Stanford University Press, 2005).

65. Pierre Hassner, "Russia's Transition to Autocracy," *Journal of Democracy* 19, no. 2 (April 2008), 14-15. The source cited is Henri Bergson, *Les deux sources de la morale et de la religion*, Remarques finales, Société naturelle et démocratie (Paris: Presses Universitaires de France, 1932), 299, in Quadrige Series, 1990.

66. Pál Dunay, *The OSCE in Crisis*, Chaillot Paper no. 88 (Paris: European Union Institute for Security Studies, April 2006), 31.

67. Sergey Lavrov, "Democracy, International Governance, and the Future World Order," *Russia in Global Affairs* 3, no. 1 (January–March 2005), 152.

68. Alexander Warkotsch, "International Socialization in Difficult Environments: The Organisation for Security and Cooperation in Europe in Central Asia," *Democratization* 14, no. 3 (June 2007), 495–497.

69. Alexander Warkotsch, "International Socialization in Difficult Environments," 499–500.

70. Marc Perrin de Brichambaut, "Jump-Starting Democracy," *Survival* 52, no. 2 (April–May 2010), 222.

71. "Statement by the Secretary General on the Situation in Uzbekistan," press release (2005) 062, May 14, 2005, www. nato.int/docu/pr/2005/p05-062e.htm.

72. R. Jeffrey Smith and Glenn Kessler, "U.S. Opposed Calls at NATO for Probe of Uzbek Killings, Officials Feared Losing Air Base Access," *Washington Post*, June 14, 2005.

73. NATO, "NATO's relations with Uzbekistan," last updated December 10, 2010, www.nato.int/cps/en/natolive/topics_22839.htm.

74. NATO, "Secretary General's Monthly Press Conference," January 24, 2011, www.nato.int/cps/en/natolive/opinions_69914.htm (accessed 20 September 2011).

75. NATO, "NATO Secretary General Discusses Partnership and Afghanistan with Uzbek President," January 24, 2011, www.nato.int/cps/en/natolive/news_69950.htm.

76. North Atlantic Council, "Lisbon Summit Declaration," par. 8.

77. NATO, "NATO Cooperation with Pakistan," last updated November 18, 2010, www.nato.int/cps/en/natolive/topics_50071.htm.

78. McChrystal, *COMISAF's Initial Assessment*, 2-11.

79. Vali Nasr, "Our Challenge to Pakistan," *Washington Post*, May 5, 2011.

80. Vincent Morelli and Paul Belkin, *NATO in Afghanistan: A Test of the Transatlantic Alliance*, CRS Report RL33627 (Washington, DC: Congressional Research Service, December 3, 2009), 3.

81. Elisabeth Bumiller and Jane Perlez, "Pakistan's Spy Agency Is Tied to Attack on U.S. Embassy," *New York Times*, September 23, 2011.

82. NATO, "Monthly Press Briefing by NATO Secretary General Anders Fogh Rasmussen," September 15, 2010, www.nato.int/cps/en/natolive/opinions_66220.htm.

83. Richard Holbrooke, remarks at a conference on the Future of NATO, Ditchley, England, October 23-25, 2008, quoted in paraphrase in Shea, "NATO at Sixty—and Beyond," 24.

84. Robert Cooper, "Picking Up the Pieces," *Financial Times*, October 25, 2008.

85. For a valuable discussion of this point, see Diego Ruiz Palmer, "From AMF to NRF: The Roles of NATO's Rapid Reaction Forces in Deterrence, Defence and Crisis-Response, 1960–2009," *NATO Review*, 2009, "NATO at 60" special issue, www.nato.int/docu/review/2009/0902/090204/EN/index.htm.

86. Yost, "An Interview with General James L. Jones."

87. De Hoop Scheffer, "NATO: Securing Our Future."

88. This is a comparative judgment. There were significant disputes among the Allies during the Cold War regarding how to assess the Soviet threat. Moreover, the Soviet Union might have considered attempting to isolate and coerce (or attack) a single member state. The West Germans probably felt more threatened than most of the other Allies, and more subject to "salami tactics." It was partly for this reason that the Allies organized the "layer cake" deployment of Allied forces on West German soil—to send the Kremlin a message that any aggression against the Federal Republic would immediately involve several other NATO Allies. Because the geographic and operational exposure of the Allies differed, they devised mutual reinforcement capabilities, starting in 1960 with the Allied Command Europe (ACE) Mobile Force, to impress upon Moscow the Alliance's determination and readiness to defend all the Allies, including those as geographically remote as Norway and Turkey.

89. Martin Wight, *Power Politics*, 157.

90. Ibid., 103.

91. Compromises began at the outset, of course, even with regard to the commitment to democracy. As noted in chapter 8, when the Alliance was established, the dictatorship in Portugal was comparable to that in Franco's Spain, but the Allies saw the Azores as important to the security of the Alliance. For a fuller discussion, see Yost, *NATO Transformed*, 70–72.

92. Diego Ruiz Palmer, "The Bargain That Wasn't and the 'Compact' That Was," in *The Transatlantic Bargain*, ed. Mark D. Ducasse (Rome: NATO Defense College, January 2012), 47.

93. This paragraph is largely borrowed from the author's article, "Assurance and US Extended Deterrence in NATO," *International Affairs* 85, no. 4 (July 2009): 766.

94. *National Security Strategy*, 42.

95. North Atlantic Council, "Strategic Concept," November 19, 2010, par. 38.

96. President Mikheil Saakashvili of Georgia and NATO Secretary General Anders Fogh Rasmussen, joint press conference, June 27, 2013, www.nato.int/cps/en/natolive/opinions_101792.htm.

97. North Atlantic Council, "Strategic Concept," November 19, 2010, par. 38.

98. Helene Sjursen, "On the Identity of NATO," *International Affairs* 80, no. 4 (2004): 693.

99. Ibid., 702.

100. Azar Gat, "The Return of Authoritarian Great Powers," *Foreign Affairs* 86, no. 4 (July/August 2007): 68.

101. Janne Haaland Matlary, "Much Ado About Little: The EU and Human Security," *International Affairs* 84, no. 1 (2008), 143.

102. Hannes Adomeit, *Putin's 'Eurasian Union': Russia's Integration Project and Policies on Post-Soviet Space*, Neighbourhood Policy Paper (Istanbul: Kadir Has University, 2012), 9.

103. Steven B. Smith, "Lives of the Party," *New York Times*, February 17, 2013, a review of John Burt, *Lincoln's Tragic Pragmatism: Lincoln, Douglas, and Moral Conflict*. Smith's formula brings to mind a complementary observation by Pascal: "Justice without force is impotent: force without justice is tyrannical. Justice without force is impossible, because there are always evil-doers; force without justice stands accused. It is therefore necessary to put together justice and force; and for that to ensure that what is just is strong, or that what is strong is just."

104. Martin Wight, *Power Politics*, 134. This book was prepared for publication by two of the late Professor Wight's associates, and they judged that this passage was written in the early 1970s.

105. See chapter 1 for a discussion of the Harmel Report and related statements of Alliance policy during the Cold War.

106. Gerhard Schröder, speech at the 41st Munich Conference on Security Policy, February 12, 2005, www.securityconference.de/archive/konferenzen/rede.php?menu_2005=&menu_konferenzen=&sprache=en&id=143&.

107. Rühle, "NATO and Energy Security." See also Rühle, "NATO and Emerging Security Challenges" 282.

108. Shea, "NATO at Sixty—and Beyond," 20.

109. NATO, "New NATO Division to Deal with Emerging Security Challenges," www.act.nato.int/component/content/article/91-new-nato-division-to-deal-with-emerging-security-challenges.

110. Specific Allies have in recent years devoted more attention than in the past to economic and political-military developments in the Asia-Pacific region in their defense assessments. See, for example, the French defense white papers in 2008 and 2013: *Défense et sécurité nationale: Le Livre blanc* (Paris: Odile Jacob/La Documentation Française, June 2008), 33–35; and *Livre Blanc: Défense et sécurité nationale 2013* (Paris: Direction de l'Information Légale et Administrative, 2013), 27–46.

111. Julian Lindley-French, "Stratcon 2010: NATO's Strategic Transformation," in *NATO's New Strategic Concept: Moving Beyond the Status Quo?*, ed. Bram Boxhoorn and David den Dunnen (The Hague: Netherlands Atlantic Association, 2009), 69-70.

112. Rasmussen, "NATO 2020— Shared Leadership for a Shared Future."

113. Barack Obama, remarks in the Third Presidential Debate, Lynn University, Boca Raton, Florida, October 23, 2012, www.whitehouse.gov/the-press-office/2012/10/23/remarks-president-and-governor-romney-third-presidential-debate.

114. Barack Obama, "Remarks by President Obama to the Australian Parliament" (speech, Canberra, Australia, 17 November 2011), www.whitehouse.gov/the-press-office/2011/11/17/remarks-president-obama-australian-parliament.

115. Breedlove quoted in Andrew Tilghman, "NATO Bases Critical for U.S., Leader Says," *Army Times*, August 26, 2013.

116. Stephan Frühling and Benjamin Schreer, "NATO's New Strategic Concept and US Commitments in the Asia-Pacific," *RUSI Journal* 154, no. 5 (October 2009): 98, 100, 102; emphasis in the original.

117. Hillary Clinton, "Remarks on the Future of European Security" (remarks, L'École Militaire, Paris, January 29, 2010), www.state.gov/secretary/rm/2010/01/136273.htm.

118. Eide, "Transatlantic Ties in Times of Financial Austerity."

119. Leon E. Panetta, speech at Kings College London, January 18, 2013, www.defense.gov/speeches/speech.aspx?speechid=1744.

120. Yost, *NATO's Deterrence and Defense Posture*, 11.

121. Tomas Valasek, "Europe and the 'Asia Pivot,'" *International Herald Tribune*, October 25, 2012.

122. Corentin Brustlein, "La nouvelle posture militaire américaine en Asie," *Politique Étrangère* 78, no. 2 (2013): 61–65.

123. Theresa Fallon, "NATO and Its Limits in the Asia-Pacific," *China Brief* 13, no. 14 (July 12, 2013).

124. Secretary General Rasmussen, "NATO and Japan—Natural Partners" (speech at the Japan National Press Club, Tokyo, Japan, April 15, 2013), www.nato.int/cps/en/natolive/opinions_99634.htm?selectedLocale=en.

125. Steven Erlanger, "Kouchner Urges Stronger Afghan Role for Europe," *New York Times*, November 5, 2009.

126. Henning Riecke quoted in Isabelle de Pommereau, "France's Afghanistan Pull-Out Signals War Fatigue Driving European Defense Cuts," *Christian Science Monitor* (csmonitor.com), May 25, 2012.

127. Robert M. Gates, "The Security and Defense Agenda (Future of NATO)" (speech, Brussels, Belgium, June 10, 2011), www.defense.gov/speeches/speech.aspx?speechid=1581.

128. *Financial and Economic Data Relating to NATO Defence* (Brussels: NATO, Public Diplomacy Division, April 2012), 8, www.nato.int/nato_static/assets/pdf/pdf_2012_04/20120413_PR_CP_2012_047_rev1.pdf

129. David S. Yost, "The NATO Capabilities Gap and the European Union," *Survival* 42 (Winter 2000–2001); and James Appathurai, "Closing the Capabilities Gap," *NATO Review*, Autumn 2002.

130. As Robert Gates, then the U.S. secretary of defense, pointed out in June 2011, "though some smaller NATO members have modestly sized and funded militaries that do not meet the 2 percent threshold, several of these allies have managed to punch well above their weight because of the way they use the resources they have. In the Libya operation, Norway and Denmark have provided 12 percent of allied strike aircraft yet have struck about one third of the targets. Belgium and Canada are also making major contributions to the strike mission. These countries have, with their constrained resources, found ways to do the training, buy the equipment, and field the platforms necessary to make a credible military contribution." Gates, "The Security and Defense Agenda (Future of NATO)."

131. Yves Boyer, *ESDP Is Badly Damaged but It's Far from Dead*, SDA Discussion Paper (Brussels: Security & Defence Agenda, April 2008), 16.

132. Charles Grant, "How to Make Europe's Military Work," *Financial Times*, August 16, 2009.

133. It should be pointed out that Denmark has formal reservations with regard to the European Union's Common Security and Defense Policy. This should be taken into account in assessing the military capability investments of EU nations. Author's correspondence with a Danish observer, November 2011.

134. Christian Mölling, *Europe without Defence*, SWP Comments no. 38 (Berlin: Stiftung Wissenschaft und Politik, November 2011), 3.

135. Camille Grand quoted in Fabrice Renouard, *Quelle ambition stratégique pour la France?*, Tribune no. 390 (Paris: Revue Défense Nationale, June 5, 2013), 5.

136. Bastian Giegerich and Alexander Nicoll, "The Struggle for Value in European Defence," *Survival* 54, no. 1 (February–March 2012), 79.

137. Robert M. Gates, remarks as delivered, NATO Strategic Concept Seminar, National Defense University, Washington, DC, February 23, 2010, www.defense.gov/speeches/speech.aspx?speechid=1423.

138. Rasmussen, speech, October 15, 2010.

139. *Quadrennial Defense Review Report* (Washington, DC: U.S. Department of Defense, February 6, 2006), 88.

140. Ronald Asmus, Stefan Czmur, Chris Donnelly, Aivis Ronis, Tomas Valasek, and Klaus Wittmann, *NATO, New Allies, and Reassurance* (London: Centre for European Reform, May 2010), 2, www.cer.org.uk/pdf/pb_nato_12may10.pdf.

141. Author interview with a French expert in Paris, May 27, 2011.

142. Ibid.

143. Author interviews in Paris in May 2011 and in Brussels in October 2011.

144. "We have committed to provide the resources and complete the necessary reforms to bring all NATO bodies under centralised cyber protection, to ensure that enhanced cyber defence capabilities protect our collective investment in NATO. We will further integrate cyber defence measures into Alliance structures and procedures and, as individual nations, we remain committed to identifying and delivering national cyber defence capabilities that strengthen Alliance collaboration and interoperability, including through NATO defence planning processes." North Atlantic Council, "Chicago Summit Declaration," par. 49.

145. The author is indebted to Diego Ruiz Palmer for his reflections on common funding challenges and other topics.

146. For background, see NATO, "Strategic Airlift Interim Solution (SALIS)," last updated November 9, 2010, www.nato.int/cps/en/natolive/topics_50106.htm; and NATO, "Strategic Airlift Capability," last updated December 6, 2010, www.nato.int/cps/en/natolive/topics_50105.htm.

147. Gates, "The Security and Defense Agenda (Future of NATO)."

Index

About the Author

David S. Yost is a professor at the U.S. Naval Postgraduate School, Monterey, California. He was a senior fellow at the United States Institute of Peace in Washington, DC, in 1996–1997, and a senior research fellow at the NATO Defense College in Rome in 2004–2007. His publications include *NATO and International Organizations* (NATO Defense College, 2007), *NATO Transformed: The Alliance's New Roles in International Security* (United States Institute of Peace Press, 1998), and *The US and Nuclear Deterrence in Europe* (International Institute for Strategic Studies, 1999).

U.S. Institute of Peace
Jennings Randolph Fellowship Program

This book is a fine example of the work produced by Senior Fellows in the Jennings Randolph fellowship program of the United States Institute of Peace. As part of the statute establishing the Institute, Congress envisioned a program that would appoint "scholars and leaders of peace from the United States and abroad to pursue scholarly inquiry and other appropriate forms of communication on international peace and conflict resolution." The program was named after Senator Jennings-Randolph of West Virginia, whose efforts over four decades helped establish the Institute.

Since 1987, the Jennings Randolph Program has played a key role in the Institute's effort to build a national center of research, dialogue, and education on critical problems of conflict and peace. Fellows come from a wide variety of academic and other professional backgrounds. They conduct research at the Institute and participate in USIP's outreach activities to policymakers, the academic community, and the American public.

Fellowship recipients are selected after a rigorous, multistage review that includes consideration by independent experts and professional staff at the Institute. The final authority for decisions regarding Senior Fellowship awards rests with USIP's board of directors. The Jennings Randolph Program also awards Peace Scholar Dissertation Fellowships to students at U.S. universities who are researching and writing doctoral dissertations on conflict and international peace and security issues.

United States
Institute of Peace Press

Since its inception in 1991, the United States Institute of Peace Press has published more than 175 books on the prevention, management, and peaceful resolution of international conflicts—among them such venerable titles as Raymond Cohen's *Negotiating Across Cultures*; John Paul Lederach's *Building Peace*; *Leashing the Dogs of War* by Chester A. Crocker, Fen Osler Hampson, and Pamela Aall; and *The Iran Primer*, edited by Robin Wright. All our books arise from research and fieldwork sponsored by the Institute's many programs, and the Press is committed to extending the reach of the Institute's work by continuing to publish significant and sustainable works for practitioners, scholars, diplomats, and students. In keeping with the best traditions of scholarly publishing, each volume undergoes thorough internal review and blind peer review by external subject experts to ensure that the research and conclusions are balanced, relevant, and sound.

Valerie Norville
Director

About the United States Institute of Peace

The United States Institute of Peace is an independent, nonpartisan institution established and funded by Congress. The Institute provides analysis, training, and tools to help prevent, manage, and end violent international conflicts, promote stability, and professionalize the field of peacebuilding.

Chairman of the Board: Stephen J. Hadley
Vice Chairman: George E. Moose
Acting President: Kristin Lord
Chief Financial Officer: Michael Graham

Board of Directors

Stephen J. Hadley (Chair), Principal, RiceHadleyGates, LLC

George E. Moose (Vice Chair), Adjunct Professor of Practice, The George Washington University

Judy Ansley, Former Assistant to the President and Deputy Security National Advisor under President George W. Bush

Eric Edelman, Hertog Distinguished Practitioner in Residence, Johns Hopkins University School of Advanced International Studies

Joseph Eldridge, University Chaplain and Senior Adjunct Professorial Lecturer, School of International Service, American University

Kerry Kennedy, President, Robert F. Kennedy Center for Justice and Human Rights

Ikram U. Khan, President, Quality Care Consultants, LLC

Stephen D. Krasner, Graham H. Stuart Professor of International Relations, Stanford University

John A. Lancaster, Former Executive Director, International Council on Independent Living

Jeremy A. Rabkin, Professor, George Mason School of Law

J. Robinson West, Chairman, PFC Energy

Nancy Zirkin, Executive Vice President, Leadership Conference on Civil and Human Rights

Members ex officio

John Kerry, Secretary of State

Chuck Hagel, Secretary of Defense

Gregg F. Martin, Major General, U.S. Army; President, National Defense University

Kristin Lord, Acting President, United States Institute of Peace (nonvoting)